*The Cherokee Struggle to Maintain Identity
in the 17th and 18th Centuries*

"*Long have I wished to see the king my father; this is his resemblance, but I am determined to see himself; I am now near the sea, and never will depart from it till I have obtained my desire.*"—Ostenaco

The Cherokee Struggle to Maintain Identity in the 17th and 18th Centuries

William R. Reynolds, Jr.

McFarland & Company, Inc., Publishers
Jefferson, North Carolina

ALSO BY WILLIAM R. REYNOLDS, JR.
*Andrew Pickens: South Carolina Patriot
in the Revolutionary War* (McFarland, 2012)

Frontispiece: *Chief Ostenaco*, by Sir Joshua Reynolds, 1762.

LIBRARY OF CONGRESS CATALOGUING-IN-PUBLICATION DATA

Reynolds, William R., 1945–
The Cherokee struggle to maintain identity in the
17th and 18th centuries / William R. Reynolds, Jr.
  p.   cm.
Includes bibliographical references and index.

ISBN 978-0-7864-7317-5 (softcover : acid free paper) ∞
ISBN 978-1-4766-1578-3 (ebook)

1. Cherokee Indians—Wars, 1759–1761. 2. Cherokee Indians—History.
3. Cherokee Indians—Government relations. 4. Cherokee Indians—
Ethnic identity. 5. Indians of North America—Wars—1750–1815.
6. United States—History—French and Indian War, 1754–1763.
7. Indians of North America—History—Colonial
period, ca. 1600–1775. I. Title.

E99.C5R47 2015   975.004'97557—dc23   2014046883

BRITISH LIBRARY CATALOGUING DATA ARE AVAILABLE

© 2015 William R. Reynolds, Jr. All rights reserved

*No part of this book may be reproduced or transmitted in any form
or by any means, electronic or mechanical, including photocopying
or recording, or by any information storage and retrieval system,
without permission in writing from the publisher.*

On the cover: *The Cherokee* by Robert Griffing (Paramount Press, Inc.)

Printed in the United States of America

*McFarland & Company, Inc., Publishers
Box 611, Jefferson, North Carolina 28640
www.mcfarlandpub.com*

To:

My wife, Diane.

My mother, Shirley Calton.

My children, Lynne Hathaway, Jonathan, Kelley Gregory,
Melody Thomas, William, Jared, Melissa Mendoza,
Torry Mendoza and Sally Mendoza.

My grandchildren, Christina, Zeniff, Bobby, Aaron,
Kyrra, Tashina, Joshua, Matthew, William Rudy, Hunter,
Amon, Xela, Brigham, Gabriella, Brenden, Nathan,
Emmalee, Joseph, Elizabeth, Grace, Michael and Veronica.

My great-grandchildren, Sylvia, Willow, Thomas, Damon and Ruthie.

Table of Contents

Acknowledgments   ix

Preface   1

1. Pre-European Contact   7
2. Early European Contact   23
3. European Contacts Become Complicated   41
4. Lyttleton, Montgomery and Grant Destroy the Cherokee Community   71
5. Timberlake and the Post-War Cherokee Culture   101
6. Backcountry Discontent, Sycamore Shoals and War   121
7. DeWitt's Corner and Long Island of the Holston   179
8. The Time of the Chickamauga   189
9. The Chickamauga Continue to Defend the Cherokee Nation   217
10. The Final Onslaught   261

Summary   337

Appendices
- A. Author's Cherokee Ancestry   345
- B. Short Biographies of Some Cherokee and Other Indians   351
- C. Short Biographies of Some White Settlers   359
- D. Timberlake's List of Cherokee Villages   369
- E. Published Accounts of the Wallen's Creek Massacre   370
- F. Bartram's List of Cherokee Villages   371
- G. Description of Ball Play at the Conference of Coyatee, May 1792   372
- H. The Black Hole   373

Chapter Notes   381

Bibliography   393

Index   401

Acknowledgments

I owe a debt of gratitude to many people who provided not only material and information but also inspiration and support. One person cannot write a book without participation in many forms by many people. It is hard to find the words that express how thankful I am for the assistance and guidance.

I would first like to thank my wife, Diane Robinson, for her love, encouragement, support, and understanding of the time I needed to spend on this project. Additionally, Diane provided a valuable service. She was the primary editor of the book and is well-qualified for the task. She is a published author, retired editor by profession, retired instructor of English, grammar, and writing at several small colleges, and has judged many writing competitions. Diane unselfishly devoted many hours of editing for this publication.

I would also like to thank my mother, Shirley Calton, who lives in Missouri, for her interest in and support of this endeavor. It is through her line that I trace my ancestry to Chief Doublehead.

I need to express thanks to my children, grandchildren, and great-grandchildren for the inspiration I receive just knowing they are here. Living descendants provide a strong incentive for one to explore ancestry. Genealogy provided a great opportunity for me to learn of my progenitors, and I am convinced that knowing my ancestors helps me to understand who I am. I sincerely hope this book will provide my progeny the desire to learn more of their ancestry. My grown children and grandchildren also provided much moral support during the writing process. It helped me immeasurably, and kept me up to the task, as they asked for periodic updates and expressed their pride in my effort.

My friends at the Monday Writers' Group provided an invaluable service. Each week I read four to six double-spaced pages as the members patiently listened and offered appropriate helpful critique. My thanks to members Ginger Allen, Nancy Altman, George Cetinich, Lou Chandler, Brian Dowell, Terry Frost, Bill Hart, Steve Herndon, Julius Jortner, Jim Kesey, Mary Lou McMillen, Jewell Miller, Virginia Prowell, Diana Sears, and Rhonda Valet.

I am thankful for my Cherokee ancestors, for what they sacrificed, and for what they accomplished in a most historic and troubled era. During research for my previous book, *Andrew Pickens: South Carolina Patriot in the Revolutionary War*, I learned of the inhumanity the Cherokee suffered and their impossible task to try and save the ancestral land as the Over-mountain settlers pushed them out. The Cherokee were continually used by their supposed allies, the British, who offered no reciprocity in their relationship. The Chickamauga factions under chiefs Dragging Canoe, John Watts, Jr., and Doublehead were truly gladiators for their people.

Acknowledgments

There are several people who provided specific material assistance, and proper acknowledgment is given to them throughout the book. I must especially recognize Mr. Charles Baxley, publisher of *Southern Campaigns of the American Revolution (SCAR)*, who provided me with a copy of John Drayton's map of Andrew Williamson's 1776 expedition against the Cherokee and other relevant material. Charles prompted me to seek other alternatives to the location for the Battle of the Black Hole in lieu of the previously-accepted sites north and south of Franklin, North Carolina.

Authors of recently-published material on the Cherokee gave me specific direction to look for the proper Black Hole site to the west of Franklin. Richard D. Blackmon, *Dark and Bloody Ground*, Nadia Dean, *A Demand of Blood*, and Lamar Marshall, *The 1776 Campaign Against the Cherokee*, inspired me to look at the vicinity of present-day Wayah Creek (along Wayah Road) for the likely spot. Period writings, Arthur Fairies' Diary, Francis Ross' Diary, and John Drayton's *Memoirs of the American Revolution, From Its Commencement to the Year 1776, Volumes 1 & 2*, led me to pinpoint the exact site that is likely the Black Hole. The resultant summary of that research, and associated maps, are located in Appendix H.

I must also recognize Mr. D. Ray Smith, who is a valuable authority on Cherokee tribal history, especially the life of War Chief Dragging Canoe. Mr. Smith provided me the drawing of Chief Dragging Canoe (by artist Mike Smith) that is used in this book. He runs an interesting and informative website (see the Bibliography).

Mr. Ricky Butch Walker, author of *Doublehead: Last Chickamauga Cherokee Chief*, deserves special thanks for providing insight about my notorious ancestor.

There is one major group of individuals that provided an invaluable service to this work—the authors listed in the Bibliography. I believe it important to describe the atmosphere that surrounded the Cherokee throughout the era discussed, and some specific authors (living and long passed) deserve special notice for providing much of the required reference material. These individuals are (in alphabetical order): James Adair, Edward Albright, Pat Alderman, William L. Anderson, John Preston Arthur, William Bartram, Robert J. Conley, Lyman C. Draper, John Duffy, E. Raymond Evans, Albert V. Goodpasture, Tom Hatley, Stanley W. Hoig, Washington Irving, Cameron Judd, James C. Kelly, Duane H. King, William L. McDowell, James Mooney, Michael Morris, J. G. M. Ramsey, Anne Frazer Rogers, Vicki Rozema, G. Anne Sheriff, Emmett Starr, John Sugden, H. G. Wells, Samuel Cole Williams, and Grace Steele Woodward. Most of these have written technical historical non-fiction material; however, one novelist, Cameron Judd, is included because his historical novels add great insight to the period. His precise books show he made a diligent effort to research the backcountry and the interaction between the settlers and the Cherokee.

Preface

I wrote my first book, *Andrew Pickens: South Carolina Patriot in the Revolutionary War*, for a purpose. After I delved into my ancestry, I learned that accessible biographical data regarding South Carolina State Militia Brigadier General Pickens (my seventh great-granduncle) was lacking. He was one of a triumvirate of state militia brigade leaders who helped to turn the American Revolution around and deprive British Lieutenant General Charles Lord Cornwallis of continued control in South Carolina. That control would have been necessary for Cornwallis to be successful in his move into North Carolina and Virginia.

The other two brigadiers in the state were Thomas Sumter and Francis Marion, about whom there are plenty of available biographies. Andrew Pickens was just as important to America's success as were Sumter and Marion. He played a huge role in the Battle of Cowpens; subsequently, he harassed Cornwallis, who rested his army in Hillsborough, North Carolina, after he had failed to catch Major General Nathanael Greene in the race to the Dan River. Pickens successfully teamed up with Continental Army Lieutenant Colonel Henry "Light-horse Harry" Lee, whom Greene had assigned to assist Pickens with several actions. Together they ended Thomas "Burn Foot" Browne's hold on backcountry Georgia with their effective Siege of Augusta in 1781.

It was my goal to see that Andrew Pickens received ascribable recognition. The book was published in August 2012.

During years of genealogical research on the Pickens family, I discovered a relationship with the Colonial Cherokee. This relationship was further revealed to me as I wrote the Andrew Pickens book. I soon found that Cherokee (and Chickamauga) chief Doublehead is of the same relationship to me as is Captain Joseph Pickens (Andrew's brother)—that of 7th great-grandfather.

The Cherokee had been British allies since the French and Indian War. They continued the alliance against the Americans because, during an extended period surrounding the revolution, the Cherokee had experienced considerable difficulty with settler incursions onto their lands. However, the British were not much help to the Cherokee with their problem.

My Pickens book had been written totally from the perspective of the patriots in the American Revolution, and especially the southern theater, while centering on Andrew Pickens and the activities around him. I wrote in the preface of that book that I had a desire to write a similar perspective for the Cherokee that covers the same time frame.

As I retain a powerful kinship with my American patriot ancestors, I feel just as strongly about my connection with my Cherokee ancestors (see Appendix A). I plan to sympathetically and efficiently describe the plight of the Colonial Cherokee Nation.

At the outset of this book the early lifestyle of the Cherokee and their initial dealings with the white man is discussed. That relationship throughout the following years is expanded upon to offer an understanding of the one-sidedness of the Cherokee connection to the British during the mid-to-late 18th century.

There are some similarities among the early Cherokee Nation and the Europeans (especially when England was controlled by illiterate tribes from other European countries). There were also some marked differences. A paramount example is that the Cherokee Nation believed in protecting ancestral land from encroachment, while the European practice was to invade and conquer land by sheer strength. The Cherokee lacked experience of such variance, which led to a misinterpretation of how much they could count on the British as allies. The Cherokee learned too late they could not rely on the British for assistance regarding their primary problem of encroaching settlers. The only frame of reference the Cherokee had was that of their reliable relationships with other Indian nations, friend or foe.

The British disappointed the Cherokee Nation several times when it needed assistance. The British used the Cherokee unfairly to satisfy their own needs, not just with their one-sided trading practices, but also by requiring the Cherokee to assist them against the British enemies (the French and the rebellious Americans) without reciprocity.

We cannot ignore the colonial Cherokee mistakes that contributed to the demise of their nation. Their almost total movement away from their heritage (craftsmanship and hunting techniques) to a complete reliance on British trade goods was excessive. The Cherokee became dependent on poorly-made rifles and muskets manufactured specifically for them; yet, the British were reluctant to keep the Cherokee supplied with adequate ammunition for their needs.

Additionally, the Cherokee had altered their proven way of choosing their leaders. In earlier years, debates between competing chiefs were civil (even if they disliked each other intensely). In the end, the people chose a chief they trusted, based on his persuasive ability. The losing chief would relent and await another opportunity. However, in the late 18th century, the older chiefs wanted desperately to hang on to the prestige they had gained over the years by obtaining and retaining British friendship. Any loss of British alliance would have resulted in a forfeiture of that stature. Over time, the older chiefs lost importance among their people. (The local village chiefs were actually called headmen while the overall chief was called headman and first beloved man—later principal chief, after the British became involved. Chief was a term applied by the Europeans.)

The older chiefs, recognized by the British as the Cherokee leaders, ignored the younger chiefs even though the latter seemed to be favored by the people. The nation became severely divided. The older chiefs, located in the mainstream or Upper Town community of present-day eastern Tennessee, had little following and could not adequately defend themselves against the encroaching settlers. Throughout the following years the designated Cherokee principal chief continued to be from the Upper Towns. These headmen constantly gave in to settlers' demands. The younger chiefs, and many young warriors, withdrew from the Upper Towns and established the Chickamauga Cherokee community. They declared themselves to be the true Cherokee Nation based upon their belief in a position of strength and pride. Other young warriors, who remained in the Valley and Middle Towns of present-day North Carolina, and the Upper Towns, also fundamentally declared their allegiance to the Chickamauga chiefs. They believed it necessary to end the relinquishment of their ancestral lands and to defend the Cherokee Nation against encroachers. However it was too late.

The Upper Town chiefs were in an awkward position. They declared themselves still spokesmen for the Cherokee Nation. The settlers, then, would blame them for not controlling the young warriors—which the old chiefs were admittedly not able to do. The division among the Cherokee was deep and contributed to their lack of success in the end. Abraham Lincoln stated, "A house divided against itself cannot stand." This was certainly true for the Colonial Cherokee Nation.

Several actions by the Chickamauga and their allies were ill-timed. They were years too late to effectively withdraw from the Upper Towns because, as time passed, the encroaching settlers had grown stronger and become harder to eliminate. The Cherokee also missed opportunities to attack the Over-mountain settlements at times when the encroachers were weakened by the absence of large numbers of their militiamen. (In 1780, over 1,000 of those militiamen participated in the Battle of Kings Mountain in South Carolina.)

The most damaging decision the Cherokee made was to give in to British political pressure and join the Tories in attacks against the South Carolina, North Carolina, and Georgia backcountry settlements in 1776. Doing so wasted the critical manpower they required to successfully hold back the nearby encroaching settlers.

Additionally, when the warriors moved against the backcountry settlements, they drew the retribution of those three colonies. The Cherokee failed to realize that, had they not attacked the backcountry, those colonists would have retained their militiamen within their own borders. The three rebellious colonies would have preferred to counter the local Tories at home and prepare a defense against possible British invasions than mount a campaign against the Cherokee Nation. The Cherokee Nation would not have become exposed to the colonies' severe reprisal had they simply concentrated on their encroachment problem and let the British worry about the coastal colonies. The Chickamauga, and allied Valley, Lower, and Middle Towns' warriors, suffered the loss of many braves in the resultant 1776 war. Cherokee manpower had been severely weakened, and the warriors often had to retreat from battle due to a shortage of ammunition. Though they continued to fight for many years, their efforts were primarily for naught. They also lost the Lower Towns to South Carolina in the following truce.

The colonial Cherokee Nation might not have been in such an untenable position if the British had dealt with them as honorably as their neighboring Indian nations had in the past. The British consistently defaulted on their responsibilities as Cherokee allies. Though they had battles and traditional enemies, the southeastern tribes had most often settled into boundary agreements and peace treaties that were honored for many years. King George III ordered the Proclamation of 1763 which stated that no settlers could buy, trade for, or otherwise move onto traditional Indian lands. A specific line was delineated that should have protected the Cherokee from the encroachment they had experienced up to 1776; however, the British never did make a move against the violators.

With regard to terminology used in this book, the Cherokee are variously addressed as Cherokee, the Nation, warriors, braves, or Ani-yunwi-ya (originally translated to Real, True, or Principal People). Sometimes the Cherokee had called themselves Ani-Keetoowahgi or People of Keetoowah (also Kituhwa). (Keetoowah was their name for the ancient Cherokee mother town in the vicinity of the Middle Villages of North Carolina. Keetoowah is now used in the name of one of the two primary recognized western bands of Cherokee, the United Keetoowah Band of Cherokee Indians in Oklahoma.) I will use "Cherokee" both for the singular and plural cases. Some dictionaries list both "Cherokee" and "Cherokees" for the plural form. However, during my research I learned that the Colonial, and earlier, Cherokee did not have a plural form for "the people." They took care of plurality by modifiers.[1] In his *History of the American Indians,* historian and trader James Adair (who spent many years living among the Cherokee) simply called the natives "Cheerake" without adding an "s" for plurality.

The term "Indian" is also used, though it was originally misapplied by European explorers. As noted above, one of the western bands includes "Indian" in the name. Additionally, the official museum of the Eastern Cherokee in Cherokee, North Carolina, is called the Museum of the Cherokee Indian. While many will demand the term "Native Americans" be substituted, which is their prerogative, I'm not politically correct enough to be swayed from the term "Indian" which, based on the above, seems to be acceptable among the Cherokee.

"Red man" is occasionally used, but only in the context of quoting Cherokee headmen that used the word. Attakullakulla himself (as did others) often used "red man" to distinguish his people from the Europeans. However, those who did so were not fooled into thinking they actually had a red skin. The Colonial Cherokee, in the time of war and during celebrations, often painted their bodies a brilliant red and used black or white paint on their heads and faces. Their enemies were most intimidated by the red-painted bodies. The Cherokee headmen and warriors knew that, and they were proud of it. Vermilion paint was so important to the colonial Cherokee that it was a primary European trade good along with guns, ammunition, metal knives, and metal hatchets for tomahawks. (Attakullakulla was a principal chief of the Cherokee Nation from 1762 to 1778 and was the primary proponent of alliance and trade with the British. His real name was Ada-Gal'-Kala or Leaning Wood.)

I do not refer to the Cherokee as "savages" except when directly quoting settlement leaders. That is certainly a denigrating term. Though the colonial Cherokee were deemed illiterate by European standards, they were certainly not dumb and no more savage than the white men around them. It is interesting that earlier writers did refer to the Cherokee as being "savage" but did not apply the same term to the French and the British. During the French and Indian War, those Europeans fought viciously. They practiced scalping, mutilating, and even went so far as to offer bounties for scalps. Neither do I generally use "redskins," because it was not used by period Cherokee, but only by the white colonists who meant to disparage them. The term is used only to illustrate that disparagement.

Regarding the white man, I use the terms white men, whites, Europeans, British, rebels, settlers, colonists, militiamen, or Euro-Americans. I do not use the terms "Anglo-Americans" or "Anglo-Saxons" because they are totally incorrect for this treatment. The Angels (often spelled as, and always pronounced as "Angles" with a hard "g") and the Saxons were specific Germanic tribes that invaded Britain in the 5th century shortly after the Romans had left. In fact, the name "England" is taken from the Angels. Though some historians broadly apply the "Anglo-" terminology, I more align with those who refer to the white colonists and European explorers and military as Euro-Americans.

In 1066, the Normans under William the Conqueror invaded England and wrested control away from the Anglo-Saxons. While there was some intermarriage, there was great animosity between the Anglo-Saxons and the Normans, a la Robin Hood and the Sheriff of Nottingham.

My own heritage is mostly Scots-Irish and English, and my English background (the Reynolds family) was Norman and descended from William the Conqueror, who also figures to be my 24th great-grandfather. So, while I do have some Anglo-Saxon blood, it is minimal. It would be an error to refer to me as "Anglo-Saxon," or even just "Anglo," due to my whiteness or even my British heritage. The same is true of many Euro-Americans and British forces that were here in the 18th century.

The research exposed varied accounts of some occurrences. Most are simple variations, such as, an alternative date for the action. Those are noted with an aside at the end of the discussion.

However, others are not that simple. The sources may vary considerably as in the case of noted woodsman and proclaimed "Indian fighter" Josiah Hoskins. The first account of his death dates it in the late summer of 1782 and is found on page 220. The second supposedly occurred in early 1784 and is recorded on pages 231–232. Both versions are included for the reader's pleasure.

My goal for this book is to impart an understanding on the reader of the complications that arose for the colonial Cherokee and how the lack of reciprocal understanding on the part of the British snowballed until the Cherokee lost their ancestral lands. It shows in the end how the Cherokee reacted to great changes over the decades. The present-day Cherokee Bands have exemplified through their tenacity a strong inclination to retain some aspects of their traditions while still successfully functioning in the modern world, albeit because they have been forced to do so. This book takes the reader back to the complicated world of the colonial Cherokee to foster knowledge and understanding of how the Cherokee Bands ended up where they are today.

Chapter 1

Pre-European Contact

The Cherokee lived in a beautiful area that embraced land both east and west of the Appalachians. The land was well-suited for them. It included villages, crop fields, game fields, and hunting grounds. Cherokee had settled the area after the Delaware (an Algonquian tribe) and their Iroquois allies forced them out of the northern country. When the Virginians established the Watauga settlements near present-day Elizabethton around 1769, they found remnants that included graves of those who had died in an ancient Cherokee town. The nearest Cherokee Upper Towns had been established about 50 miles further south by then.

Not yet a nation, the Cherokee generally divided their mostly autonomous settlements by Ayrate (Lower and Middle Settlements) and Ottare (Upper Settlements). These communities were separated by the Appalachian peaks but partially existed in the foothills of the mountains. The Appalachians were more than 100 miles across. The climate was rough. The Lower Villages could be bitterly cold during winter, and the Upper Towns were covered in ice and snow throughout winter and early spring.

Cherokee people often bathed and smeared animal grease or oil on their bodies to protect themselves in the winter. This regimen closed their pores and rendered them resistant to the climate; therefore, they could comfortably continue with outdoor activities such as hunting.

The territory occupied by the Cherokee spanned from what is presently western North Carolina, South Carolina, Virginia, and all of West Virginia southward to northern Georgia and Alabama, westward to include the eastern two-thirds of Tennessee, and northward to include the Cumberland portion of Kentucky that abuts Tennessee. It is said that the Cherokee ancestral land consisted of 40,000 acres, most of which contained vitally fecund hunting grounds. The Cherokee land was irregularly shaped and bounded, and the size was very fluid depending on the relative strength of the Cherokee and their neighbors when at war.

The Powhatan were to the northeast, the Tuscarora, Catawba, and Cheraw to the east and the southeast, the Creek to the south, and the Chickasaw to the west. Each claimed traditional tribal hunting grounds with the rights always in question.

Creek and Shawnee were expulsed from ancestral hunting grounds claimed by the Cherokee.

Cherokee villages were connected to other Indian tribes by groups of well-established trails. They linked with the Shawnee, Mingo, and Iroquois by trails that ran to the Kanawha River in West Virginia, then to the Ohio River. They also began their journeys north on the Tennessee River and eventually to the Ohio.

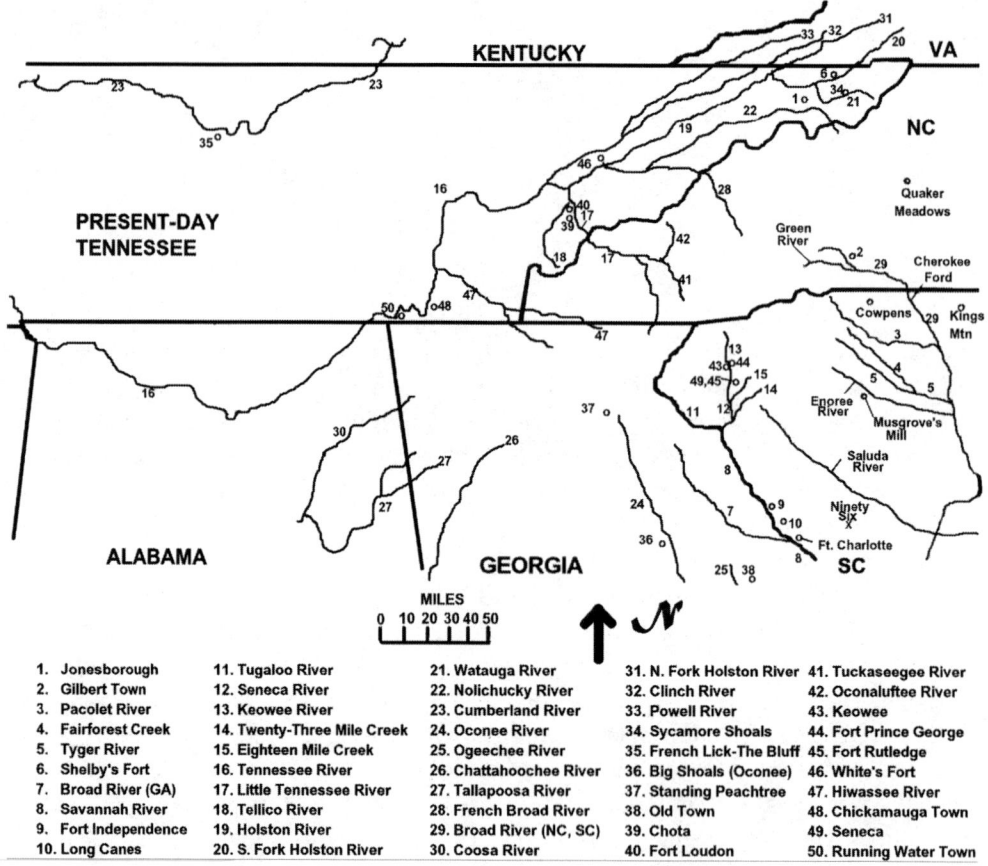

1. Jonesborough
2. Gilbert Town
3. Pacolet River
4. Fairforest Creek
5. Tyger River
6. Shelby's Fort
7. Broad River (GA)
8. Savannah River
9. Fort Independence
10. Long Canes
11. Tugaloo River
12. Seneca River
13. Keowee River
14. Twenty-Three Mile Creek
15. Eighteen Mile Creek
16. Tennessee River
17. Little Tennessee River
18. Tellico River
19. Holston River
20. S. Fork Holston River
21. Watauga River
22. Nolichucky River
23. Cumberland River
24. Oconee River
25. Ogeechee River
26. Chattahoochee River
27. Tallapoosa River
28. French Broad River
29. Broad River (NC, SC)
30. Coosa River
31. N. Fork Holston River
32. Clinch River
33. Powell River
34. Sycamore Shoals
35. French Lick-The Bluff
36. Big Shoals (Oconee)
37. Standing Peachtree
38. Old Town
39. Chota
40. Fort Loudon
41. Tuckaseegee River
42. Oconaluftee River
43. Keowee
44. Fort Prince George
45. Fort Rutledge
46. White's Fort
47. Hiwassee River
48. Chickamauga Town
49. Seneca
50. Running Water Town

They trekked a set of trails to the northeast to meet, trade, or fight with the Mohawk, Seneca, Powhatan, and Delaware.

Travels northeast and east brought the tribal members to the Tuscarora and Catawba near the coasts of present-day North Carolina and Virginia. If they wished to find the Uchee and Cheraw, they followed the Savannah River to the proximity of the coast.

South and east along the Chattahoochee and Coosa Rivers, Cherokee trekkers connected with the Creek. The Chickasaw, Shawnee, Choctaw, and Natchez were located to the west by following the Tennessee River. More Shawnee could be found beyond the Cumberland Gap.

The eastern portion of the Cherokee land was occupied by the Lower Towns in the Piedmont Region of present-day South Carolina, and the Kituhwa (Middle and Valley Towns) of the Blue Ridge slopes of the Unakas (Great Smokies) of today's North Carolina.

The western portion of the Cherokee settlements involved the Upper Towns, which were on the Appalachian Plateau and were separated from the Lower, Middle, and Valley Towns by the peaks of the mountain range.

Rivers in this land flowed in three directions: the Chatooga, Tugaloo, and Keowee rivers emptied into the Savannah River, which opened up to the Atlantic Ocean; the Coosa, Oostanaula, Chattahoochee, and Etowah rivers flowed to the Gulf of Mexico; the Little Tennessee, Tuckaseegee, Nantahala, Hiwassee, and Valley rivers made their way to the Ohio River Drainage and eventually to the Mississippi River.[1]

1. Pre-European Contact

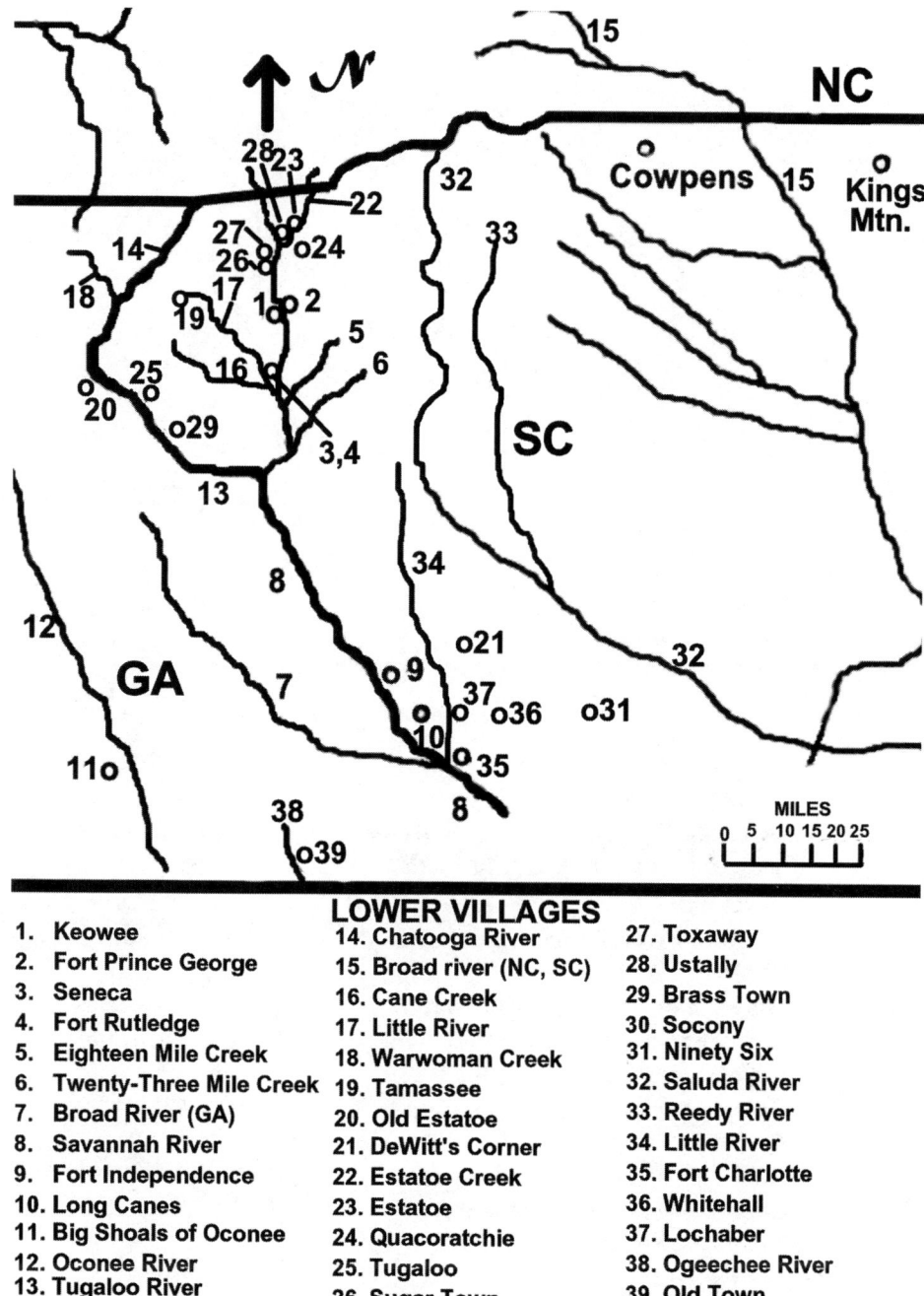

LOWER VILLAGES

1. Keowee
2. Fort Prince George
3. Seneca
4. Fort Rutledge
5. Eighteen Mile Creek
6. Twenty-Three Mile Creek
7. Broad River (GA)
8. Savannah River
9. Fort Independence
10. Long Canes
11. Big Shoals of Oconee
12. Oconee River
13. Tugaloo River
14. Chatooga River
15. Broad river (NC, SC)
16. Cane Creek
17. Little River
18. Warwoman Creek
19. Tamassee
20. Old Estatoe
21. DeWitt's Corner
22. Estatoe Creek
23. Estatoe
24. Quacoratchie
25. Tugaloo
26. Sugar Town
27. Toxaway
28. Ustally
29. Brass Town
30. Socony
31. Ninety Six
32. Saluda River
33. Reedy River
34. Little River
35. Fort Charlotte
36. Whitehall
37. Lochaber
38. Ogeechee River
39. Old Town

The Cherokee established their villages on narrow, flat, fertile land next to rivers. Villages were often not very wide, but were laid out linearly along a stream since flat, irrigable land was limited.

The Lower Settlements of present-day South Carolina were mainly along tributaries of the Savannah River. The Middle Settlements were found in today's northern North Carolina, between the Cowee and Balsam mountains, and established on the eastern or upper

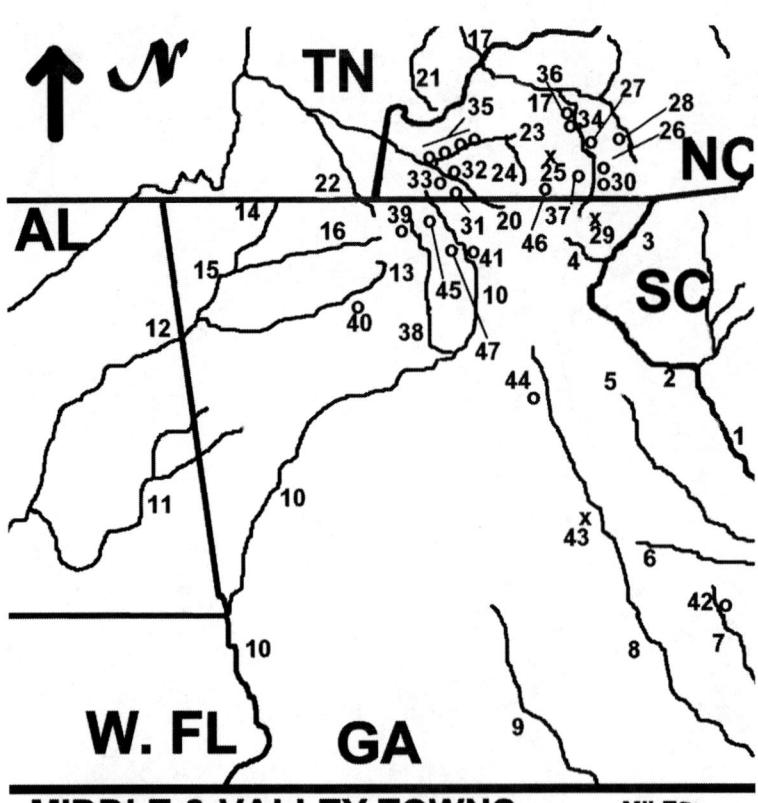

MIDDLE & VALLEY TOWNS

MILES
0 10 20 30 40 50

1. Savannah River
2. Tugaloo River
3. Chatooga River
4. Warwoman Creek
5. Broad River (GA)
6. Little River (GA)
7. Ogeechee River
8. Oconee River
9. Ocmulge River
10. Chattahoochee R.
11. Tallapoosa River
12. Coosa River
13. Etowah River
14. Conasauga R.
15. Oostanaula R.
16. Coosawattee R.
17. Little Tenn. R.
18. Tuckaseegee R.
19. Oconaluftee R.
20. Hiwassee River
21. Tellico River
22. Ocoee River
23. Valley River
24. Nantahala R.
25. Wayah Gap
26. Nikwasi
27. Watauga
28. Tuckaseegee
29. Rabun Gap
30. Echoe
31. Quanassee
32. Hiwassee
33. Brass Town
34. Cowee
35. I-r, Canuce, Little Tellico, Tomassee, Burning Town
36. Alijoy
37. Canucca
38. Chestatoe River
39. Frog Town
40. Long Swamp
41. Little Chota
42. Old Town
43. Big Shoals of the Oconee
44. Standing Peachtree
45. Notally
46. Nowee
47. Nacoochee

ends of the Little Tennessee and Tuckaseegee rivers. The Valley Settlements were in present-day extreme southwestern North Carolina along the Nantahala, Hiwassee, and Valley rivers. The principal towns were located at the headwaters of the Savannah, Hiwassee, and Tuckaseegee rivers and along the full length of the Little Tennessee River. Itsati (Echota) on the south bank of the Little Tennessee River, a few miles above the mouth of the Tellico River, was loosely considered the capital or primary town.[2]

Though later considered a very large nation, the early Cherokee political structure was loose with individual villages stressing self-reliance. This provided a military disadvantage (covered later in this chapter). The British often exploited the structure and played one village against the other. The Cherokee community, being autonomous, was mostly divided over loyalty to the British and trade with the French. The British usually won favor with the headmen (chiefs), so had an advantage.

The Cherokee Nation consisted of 70 to 80 towns or villages. A typical 18th century Cherokee village contained from 12 to 200 houses, though there were rarely over 60.

The villages contained small square cabins usually built with vertical pole walls. These cabins usually surrounded the large Town (or Council) House that was sometimes almost round but most often heptagonal with a domed top. There were large flat fields for ball games and Chunkey (a game described later in this chapter). The villages were usually stockaded like a fort on the three sides away from a river. The people caught fish in weirs constructed on the streams.

> The Cherokees of this period resided in square houses of poles or logs often containing three rooms and built one or two stories high. These dwellings were plastered inside and out with grass-tempered clay and were roofed with chestnut-tree bark or long broad shingles. In the roof a smoke hole was left ... there was little furniture aside from beds consisting of a few boards spread with bear skins.[3]

The Council House was usually seven-sided to accommodate the seven clans. The building contained seating much like a present-day amphitheater. Places were provided around the fire area in the building's center for the headmen. (See later in this chapter for use of the Council House and description of the clans.)

Lieutenant Henry Timberlake, a member of Colonel William Byrd's 2nd Virginia Regiment of State Troops, would specifically describe a Town House in 1776:

> It is raised with wood, and covered over with earth, and has all the appearance of a small mountain at a little distance. It is built in the form of a sugar loaf, and large enough to contain 500 persons, but extremely dark, having, besides the door, which is so narrow that but one at a time can pass, and that after much winding and turning, but one small aperture to let smoak [sic] out, which is so ill contrived, that most of it settles in the roof of the house. Within it has the appearance of an ancient amphitheater, the seats being raised one above another, leaving an area in the center of which stands a fire; the seats of the head warriors are nearest it.[4]

(Lieutenant Timberlake is covered in Chapter 5.)

The principal divisions of the Cherokee settlements (Upper, Middle, Valley, and Lower) were distinguishable by differing dialects of an Iroquois variation. The Iroquois were primarily made up of the Mohawk, Oneida, Seneca, Onondaga, and Cayuga.

The Western (also Upper and Over-mountain) dialect was spoken in the Upper Towns of present-day eastern Tennessee. It was also spoken in villages along the Hiwassee, Cheoah, and portions of the Little Tennessee River of today's North Carolina, as well as in northern Georgia. A variation of the Western dialect is spoken among present-day Oklahoma Cherokee bands.

The Middle (Kituhwa) dialect was spoken on the Tuckaseegee and the headwater tributaries of the Little Tennessee River (the Middle and Valley towns). It was a combination of the Eastern and Western dialects. The Kituhwa dialect is the one mostly preferred by the present-day Eastern Band of Cherokee Indians found in or near the Qualla Boundary (unofficially referred to as the Eastern Cherokee Reservation) in northwest North Carolina.

Those living in the Lower Towns of South Carolina spoke the Lower or Eastern dialect. These towns were found along the Tugaloo, Keowee, and headwaters of the Savannah rivers. Those speaking Eastern dialect used a rolling "r" in the place of the "l" used by the other dialects. For example, the village "Tellico" would be pronounced as "Terrico" in the Lower Towns. The Lower dialect became extinct after the Cherokee were expulsed from the Lower Towns following the war of 1776 (which is covered in Chapters 6 and 7).[5]

The Cherokee called themselves Ani-yunwi-ya which translates nearly to The Real, True, or Principal People. Its similarity to the Iroquois Onwe-Hon-We lends credence to the Cherokee dialects being a derivative of the Iroquois language. The Cherokee more formally called themselves Ani-Keetoowaghi, or the People of Kituhwa. Kituhwa was an ancient village on the western extremity of the present-day Qualla Boundary near today's Bryson City, North Carolina. Kituhwa was considered the center, or Mother Town, of the ancient Cherokee people. (Kituhwa was located aside the Tuckaseegee River. A hillock called the Kituhwa Indian Mound may still be found there. Exit the east end of Bryson City on Main Street and continue on U.S. Highway 19. The mound is about one mile past the bridge over the Tuckaseegee River headwater.)

There were other ancient Cherokee towns said to be in the same vicinity. The ancient village of Nikwasi was at or near present-day Franklin, North Carolina, and Tlanusi-yi (the Leech Place because of a legend about a giant leech named Tlanusi that lived in the nearby river), was along the Hiwassee River at present-day Murphy, North Carolina.

The early Cherokee were numerous. The total population of all villages, regardless of location, was about 32,000 in 1685. This dropped to approximately 12,000 by 1715, which enumeration seems to have been fairly well distributed. There were about 25 percent each of young warriors, young women, children, and aged. The reduction in numbers was caused by wars with neighbors and by such European diseases as tuberculosis and smallpox (which will be discussed in Chapters 2 through 4).[6]

Besides having a similar language, the Cherokee physically resembled the Iroquois of the north. They also were apparently closely related to the Powhatan.

In manner, they were generally described as stately, but guarded. They spoke slowly, honestly, and thoughtfully. Though they were reserved, they were frank and cheerful.

As a rule, the men were medium to tall and slim, but muscular. Their skin's hue was often described as copper or chestnut, and they were of a lighter tone than the neighboring tribesmen. The young ladies were very fair complexioned and described as having a shade similar to the European settlers. Because their coppery skin was usually obscured by red paint, they had been labeled by Europeans as "redskins." After initial contact and trade with the Indians, the Scots-Irish traders were told they must marry into the tribe to live on Cherokee land. This intermarriage altered the physical nature of some of the Cherokee.

Both the Cherokee men and women typically wore their coarse black hair long. It sometimes had an auburn hue. The men usually shaved their heads but left a small scalp lock at the rear of the crown. They would often tie the lock and decorate it with eagle feathers and beads. A few just let the lock hang loose.

Prior to European contact, a few Cherokee wore beards. Their facial hair was usually sparse, rather than abundant. They later plucked their facial hair to avoid similarities to the whites. The Cherokee stretched their earlobes and slit them to accommodate ornaments, such as beadwork, silver rings, and pendants. Nose rings, bracelets, armlets, necklaces, and breastplates of silver and jewels or beads were often worn. Skin was ornamented with paint, usually red, and enhanced with tattoos applied by pricking the skin with a sharp stick coated with gunpowder.

The early warriors took quick but short steps when they walked, and they pointed their toes directly toward the front. They relaxed their backs and were seemingly almost leaning forward. They could often walk 30 miles per a day with that distinctive gait and needed very few rest stops.[7]

Neither the headmen nor the village council established social laws or punishments for breaking them. Old traditions had set the inherent rules for conduct, and any defilement was punished by the violator's clan. (The responsibilities of the headman [white or peace chief] or the Peace Council will be covered later in this chapter. In brief, they were to manage celebrations or rituals and to call the general population together to discuss an important matter, such as turning the leadership over to the red [or war] chief to face an approaching enemy.)

The backbone of early Cherokee life was the clan. There were seven Cherokee clans: Aniwahya (Wolf); Anikawi (Deer); Anitsiskwa (Bird); Aniwodi (Red Paint or just Paint); Anisahoni (Blue Holly, or just Blue); Anigatogewi (Wild Potato); and Anigilohi (Long Hair).

The clan was the ultimate in family organization. Its members were responsible for judging any wrongdoing committed by an associate and for executing an appropriate punishment. They would usually make a retribution payment of trade goods for a member who had wronged somebody outside of the clan. The clansmen could also seek vengeance from one in another circle who had aggrieved a fellow clan member. Sometimes, in the case of a major transgression, the wrongdoer's clan would take his life to avoid being subjected to further retribution from the offended clan.

When the Cherokee traveled they relied heavily on the kinship of clan members. The individual would bide his, or her, time in an unfamiliar village and study the inhabitants to determine which ones were relatives. A Cherokee would always assure the visitor was well provided with food and shelter.

A Cherokee warrior was not allowed to marry a woman from his clan despite the remoteness of their relationship. Once married, the husband usually moved into his wife's house. Cherokee civilly lived in a matrilineal society, and the children were born into the clan of the mother. She had total control over the offspring. Often a member of her clan, such as her brother, would take responsibility for teaching male children how to hunt and how to become warriors. Cherokee youth were trained to endure hunger and pain in preparation for success in wartime. They were also schooled in blood vengeance and other clan responsibilities. The mother's clan was basically an extension of the household. Though they didn't have paper deeds, the woman "owned" the house and the property that held it, along with irrigable land they used.

The average Cherokee family had two children. Cherokee children were rarely punished because the youth were trained to defend themselves at all times. They were raised to respect the old traditions. The father was never allowed to administer punishment because he was of a different clan. However, a woman from the father's family usually selected names for the children. The child would often change names as he matured, based on his accomplishments or abilities. Example: Okoonaka (White Owl) was later known as Adagalkala, which translates to "Leaning Stick." (The whites pronounced it Attakullakulla. He was primarily known to the settlers as the Little Carpenter because of his diplomatic abilities).[8]

There was usually very little ceremony involved in a marriage. The woman might bake a loaf of bread, to symbolize her homemaking skills, from grain that her intended had left at her door step. The warrior, then, might provide her with a leg of venison to demonstrate his hunting competence. Typically they merely began to live together. Either could break the relationship at his or her desire.

One marriage ceremony was witnessed by Anne Matthews, one of two Calhoun sisters who would be captured at the Long Canes Massacre in backcountry South Carolina in 1760. When released many years later, she wrote:

> There were a number of both sexes convened; they arranged themselves in two rows, with a space between them, the males in one row, the females in the other, the groom at the end of one row, the bride at the (far end) of the other. At a signal the two advanced between the rows, till they met in the center. He presented her with a leg of venison, and she gave him an ear of corn, denoting that he would keep her in meat, and she would keep him in bread, ending in loud laughter.[9]

Adultery was usually unacceptable and dealt with by the clan system; however, polygamy was tolerated, and divorces were easily obtained, especially by the woman. The typical Cherokee of the colonial era had many partners, and because the society was matrilineal, the woman had little difficulty disposing of a mate that she did not feel was serving the best interests of her family. She simply found another mate.

Indian trader Alexander Longe later wrote: "Sometimes the young maids come and steal away women's husbands."[10] Another, John Lawson, added, "As for the Indian Women, which now happen in my Way … they are of tawn [sic] complexion; their Eyes very brisk and amorous; their Smiles afford the finest Composure a face can possess … nor are they strangers nor not Proficients [sic] in the soft Passion."[11]

Historian Tom Hatley recently noted, "Cherokee women bolstered by their central place in the kinship system shifted mates with ease and informality."[12] Finally, Indian trader and historian James Adair bluntly penned:

> The Cheerake [sic] are an exception to all civilized or savage nations, in having no laws against adultery; they have been a considerable while under petticoat government, and allow their women full liberty to plant their brows with horns as oft as they please, without fear of punishment. On this account their marriages are ill-observed, and of a short continuance; like the Amazons they divorce their fighting bed-fellows at their pleasure, and fail not to execute their authority, when their fancy directs them to a more agreeable choice.[13]

(Adair's statement about "no laws" is misleading. The overall principal chief of the Cherokee [or first beloved man] had no authority over anything considered a clan responsibility. One clan might have been more strict regarding any topic, such as adultery, than another.)

Some of these statements exaggerate the situation. It is likely that a small percentage of the Cherokee women were sirens, and, as in most cultures, the Cherokee did frown on adultery. Their tradition, however, did allow them (especially the women) to alter their cohabitations when they deemed it appropriate. Marriages and other amorous relationships were often brief.

It has been (and still is) difficult for descendants to track their genealogy through the colonial Cherokee community. Emmet Starr's *History of the Cherokee Indians* is an excellent source of records of many of what are presently referred to as "Old Nation" relationships; yet, even as good as that tome is, it is not, nor could it ever be, complete. There were relationships that simply were not remembered nor passed down and are, therefore, not recorded. The same holds true for the Cherokee rolls pertaining to the post-colonial years. They can only be as complete as the information available which, inherently, is incomplete.

Children of white traders and Cherokee women were often confused and found it difficult to establish an identity. However, most of them who were successful in doing so considered themselves to be Cherokee by their matrilineal heritage. Those children would often grow into the strongest of Cherokee leaders, especially in the 1770s and 1780s when the Cherokee fought for existence in an ever-decreasing ancestral land. (Young Tassel [John Watts, Jr.] and Bench [Bob Benge], who would exemplify their responsibilities as Chickamauga Cherokee chiefs with fervor, will be covered in later chapters.)[14]

Hernando De Soto would identify the Cherokee as "Chalaque," which, being similar to the later British term "Cherokee," he likely picked up in his brief personal dealings with the Cherokee people. He described the Cherokee as peaceful and hospitable. After his visit, the Cherokee continued to lead a balanced and leisurely life. He did not disrupt their existence as he had done to other tribes he encountered. The Cherokee were the dominant tribe of the southeast, self-assured and self-sustained. The vast land that they controlled was necessary to their agrarian lifestyle.

The early Cherokee were egalitarian with matriarchal kinship. Some women were allowed to sit in council with the headmen and warriors. This was especially true of the "honored war-women," one of whom led the council of women to discuss things that needed attention in the Peace Council. (One such woman, Nancy Ward, will be discussed in a later chapter.)

The Cherokee accepted a social responsibility for the indigent. The leading women of the village, or the women's council, would organize a dance, and all of the participants at the event contributed goods. All warriors brought meat, and the women donated household items or crops.

Lieutenant Henry Timberlake, who would volunteer to spend some time with the Cherokee and act as a liaison, would record his witness of just such a dance in 1762:

> The Indians have a particular method of relieving the poor, which I rank among the most laudable of their religious ceremonies…. When any of their people are hungry, as they term it, or in distress, orders are issued out by the headmen for a war-dance, at which all the fighting men and warriors assemble; but here are contrary to all their other dances,

one only dances at a time, who, after hopping and capering for near a minute, with a tomahawk in his hand, gives a small whoop, at which signal the music stops till he relates the manner of taking his first scalp, and concludes his narration by throwing on a large skin, spread for that purpose, a string of wampum, piece of plate, wire, paint, lead, or any thing he can most conveniently spare; after which the music strikes up, and he proceeds in the same manner through all his war-like actions; then another takes his place and the ceremony lasts till all the warriors and fighting men have related their exploits. The stock thus raised, after paying the musicians, is divided among the poor.[15]

In 1783 and 1784, the Reverend Martin Schneider would be in Chota to establish a Moravian mission. He would echo Timberlake with the following statement: "This evening there is to be continued here in Chota a great Dancing of Women, which is to be continued four (4) Evenings. I was told that twice a year or oftener such a Dancing is appointed in every Town, to which no one has Leave to come, except he (or she) brings at least one Skin. And thus they get every time a pretty number of skins together, who are made use of for the poor who suffer want."[16]

Some of the traditions seem strange in today's world, but to the early Cherokee they were extremely important to the success of the community. A pregnant woman was considered hazardous. She was not allowed to enter crop fields nor to prepare food. She had to avoid the vicinity of weirs used as fish traps. She could only eat certain foods, wear particular clothing, and was not allowed to view a corpse. Her husband could not play in the important ball games (detailed later in this chapter) or even help prepare for them. He was also restricted from digging graves.

The immediate kin of a deceased person did not take care of burial arrangements. Usually, a more distant clan member washed the corpse and otherwise prepared it for interment. Warriors who died in battle were brought home by their fellow braves for burial preparation when possible.[17]

The primary occupations of the Cherokee were hunting and war. The men were the hunters, and the women tended to the crop fields and gardens. There was some crossover between the two. Prior to European contact, the Cherokee domesticated dogs which were a part of their diet. The dogs were also used as pack animals.

The boundaries of their hunting grounds were vague and were often the cause for war with other tribes. They considered the land bounded by the Ohio and Tennessee rivers, including parts of Kentucky, to be their primary ancestral hunting grounds.

War was considered more important than hunting for Cherokee men. However, the early Cherokee were dependent upon the forest that provided ample game for meat and furs, so hunting was a close second. Deer were plentiful and were the Cherokee equivalent of cattle. However, since deer were not fenced in, hunting in the old ways was extremely sporting. There were no guns and the warriors had to rely on great skill to hunt or trap animals. Besides deer, their main prey included bear, bison, elk, beaver, turkeys, ducks, and geese. Rivers and creeks provided fish and freshwater clams.[18]

According to Eastern Cherokee legend, man had lived in harmony with his brothers, the animals, for a long time. Natural rules governed man's use of his environment. Man had always been allowed to stalk and kill his animal brother, but only for survival. To honor the spirit of the slain animal, man gave thanks through an offering of tso-la (tobacco). Man's ability to adhere to this tradition assured a natural balance.

However, legend relates that man forgot his responsibilities and misused his animal brothers. Man began to destroy animals wholesale for their skins and furs, not just for needed food. Hunting to excess, he forgot to offer tso-la as a sign of thanks. The smaller animals were ignored and abused at will.

The animals became angry at such treatment. Insulted by man's ingratitude, the animals took action. They resolved to punish mankind. Man's brothers Yo-ny, the bears, were the first to meet in a council called by Old Chief White Bear. Each bear was allowed to express an idea to overcome the problem; however, the council of bears could not reach agreement on any solution.

Next, man's brothers A-wi, the deer, held their own council led by Chief Little Deer. They quickly agreed that if man does not properly get permission from the spirit of a deer before killing it, and then does not give thanks after the killing, he should be cursed with rheumatism. They dispatched their decision to the nearest settlements, those of the Cherokee, to give man a warning.

Little Deer volunteered to be the principal enforcer of this new policy. Little Deer would personally go to the spirit of every deer slain and inquire whether the hunter had followed the natural law: if he sought permission, if he offered thanks. If the spirit of the deer answered that the hunter had indeed followed the rule, Little Deer would leave. If the spirit of the deer indicated that the hunter had not asked permission and had failed to offer thanks, Little Deer would proceed to the hunter's village and strike him with the painful ailment.[19]

Women fashioned breechclouts, buckskin shirts, and moccasins of animal skins. Women were also responsible for the gardens, fields, and orchards. Corn, beans, squash, pumpkin, potatoes, tobacco, and fruit were common commodities. Watermelon, peaches, and yams were obtained through trade with other tribes. Black-eyed peas, also called Appalachian peas, were acquired through trade with the Creek. (Black-eyed peas had been brought from Africa aboard slave ships. They had been grown by the Creek since before the 1700s.)

The Cherokee crafted bows, blow guns, clay pots, and vessels with intricate designs, knives and tomahawks of flint, decorative figurine pipes carved of steatite, and wood carvings, as well as woven baskets and blankets. (Steatite is a crystalline form of magnesium silicate, and is basically a greasy soapstone, sometimes called soap rock. It is a variety of talc.)

The Cherokee were central traders. They traded commodities with coastal Indians and sometimes with northern tribes (except for those with whom they might be at war). Trade became an overreaching activity that ranked in importance next to warfare and hunting. They traded with neighboring and distant tribes and with coastal settlers through neighboring intermediaries, such as the Choctaw and Catawba.

The early Cherokee men went to war most often against the Creek, Choctaw, Chickasaw, Shawnee, and Iroquois Confederacy. Later, of course, they would war with the British settlers. The Cherokee had once fought a 40-year war with the Shawnee over the land around Muscle Shoals on the Tennessee River. That war was settled in 1721 when the Shawnee left for the Ohio River Valley.

The warriors usually painted their bodies with brilliant red paint and added black and white paint for emphasis. They used bows, tomahawks, and knives just as they did when hunting. After the bows were replaced by rifles, the warriors still favored knives and tomahawks for close combat and for removing scalps. A warrior was often referred to as Skyagusta (Wizard Owl), Colonah (Raven), or Outicite (Mankiller). The warriors generally followed a "captain" whom they selected or agreed to follow, not unlike the settlers' militias. Those deemed valiant during a battle were often made a war (or red) chief or were simply honored with the titles already mentioned. (The red and white chiefs are detailed later in this chapter.)[20]

The Cherokee were extremely sociable within their community. The peace chief, or white chief, would officiate at the many holidays. The most important seemed to be the two new moon festivals, marked by dances and a feast. The more important of the two seemed to be the second, the one following the autumnal new moon. (The second New Moon festival is detailed following the descriptions of the interceding festivals.)

The first new moon ritual was in March and celebrated the coming of the sowing season. The seven principal counselors to the white chief determined when the moons would appear, then sent a messenger to announce the upcoming festival to all the Cherokee villages. Designated hunters sought and prepared deer for the feast.

The counselors also selected women to perform the friendship dance, held on the first evening. The second day, all went to the river for a purification ritual. The people fasted on the third day, and on the fourth day everyone participated in the friendship dances which ended the ceremony.

The ripening and the harvesting of corn were celebrated by two green corn festivals. The first was in mid–August when the young corn became fit to eat, and the second was in middle to late September when the corn became fully ripe. The stomp, feather, and buffalo dances were included in the ritual. At certain points of the ceremonies the people played field games and sacrificed green corn in the sacred fire. Following a ceremonial fast, they would feast.

Another festival ritual consisted of bathing in the river and praying. The people's belief held that the cleansing washed away impurities and past bad deeds; thus, the individual could start a new life.

The second green corn festival was the Mature Green Corn Ceremony held about 45 days after the New Green Corn Ceremony. Before the festival, women performed a religious dance and decided when the festival would be held. Hunters were sent out to kill and prepare game as in the first festival.

An arch, built with green branches, made an arbor in the middle of the ceremonial grounds. The evening before the Green Corn Ceremony, members from each clan took a branch for use the next day during a noon ritual. Participants were then cleansed and purified by drinking a special tea called the "Black Drink" (see Chapter 5). The people would then dance, and feasted on game and corn. The entire ceremony lasted four days.

The second new moon festival was the Great New Moon Festival held around October. As the Cherokee believed that the world was created in the fall, this traditionally kicked off the Cherokee new year.

Like the first, this new moon festival involved hunting, feasting, spiritual cleansing, field games, and dancing. Besides fresh game, the food included corn, pumpkin, and beans. About ten days later, a fifth festival was held. It was called the Propitiation and Cementation Festival or Friends Made Ceremony. The purpose of this festival was to renew friendships by forgiving conflicts from the previous year, obtain new friendships, and to become purified. Participants were assigned tasks. Some would help prepare the various ceremonies; others would lead singing, provide instrumentation, cleanse the Council House, hunt, or cook. The celebrants held a dance the night before the festival. Some people fasted, especially during specifically designated days. The New Moon Festival also lasted four days.

The final festival was called the Winter Festival. Those who participated in the feast donated tobacco for a sacrifice to be held on the fourth night. The first dance movement was a march by alternating pairs of males and females—a kind of a grand entrance. During the dance, women wore their turtle shells, formed a circle with the men in a single file, and moved counterclockwise. Each dancer took two twigs of spruce and waved them up and down like pigeon wings. Many present-day Cherokee still observe these festivals on their ceremonial grounds.[21]

The early Cherokee liked diversion as much as does the present-day population. Recreation consisted primarily of two games—the Ball Game and Chunkey.

The Ball Game was similar to today's lacrosse, except it was played much more roughly and without padding. There were often great numbers of men on each team. The matches were frequently played during celebrations like the corn festival. Often one village would challenge another to a game, almost as in the early days of baseball.

Ball play was sacred. It ranked next to war as a major manly occupation. A man had to be of good character to represent a village as a ballplayer. The players watched each other for seven days of preparation to be sure none of them broke a taboo. Taboos were association with women for the seven days, eating meat, salt, or spice (they would usually only eat corn bread and drink corn broth), and further, the food was required to be delivered only by males. Female food preparers could not be pregnant; no woman could come to the location of the ball play on the seventh day of preparation nor walk any paths that the players might walk during the seven days.

A ritual was held the night before the game that consisted of drumming, dancing, and singing. It appeared much as a war dance. The ballplayers would dance around the fire using ball-playing motions in their movements. They would circle the fire four times, then sit for one-half hour. They would then repeat the dance three more times, after which they went to the river for a purification bath. They bathed again the next morning and proceeded to the field.

Spectators gambled, and some warriors were known to have lost all of their possessions from betting on one game.

Chunkey (or Chungke, Chunky, Chenco, or Tchung-kee) had the appearance of modern-day javelin competitions except the Cherokee threw for accuracy rather than distance. Indian trader and historian James Adair referred to this game as "running hard labor."[22] A Chunkey stone was required, as were throwing sticks. The Chunkey stone was a four- to five-inch diameter by one- to two-inch thick disk generally made from hard quartz that had been perfectly smoothed. The stones were considered very valuable because they were difficult to make from this hard material, and they were "owned" by a village, but never by an individual.

The sticks were usually seven- to eight-feet long and sometimes smeared with bear grease. They were marked off throughout their length to measure the distance from where they had landed to where the stone came to rest.

In the most common variation, someone would roll the chunkey stone across the ground or over ice. Two opponents would throw their sticks. When the stone came to rest, the opponent whose stick was closest to it was the winner. Again, the spectators and players, as in the ball games, gambled heavily on the outcome of a Chunkey game. Sometimes a man might risk not only all of his possessions, but even his wife, on the results. Losers were even known to have committed suicide.

In another variation of Chunkey, each contestant took his turn throwing his stick at a stone that had come to rest, while his opponent tried to steal points by catching the stick in the air before it hit the ground.[23]

In the early days, before the existence of an officially designated "Cherokee Nation," a tribal collective of villages prevailed. There was a Mother Town called Chota that served as a capital, and its local headman served, at times, as a collective chief called principal headman (Chief) or first beloved man. In 1761, Lieutenant Henry Timberlake would volunteer to go to Chota to be the liaison with the Cherokee (see Chapter 5). Cherokee principal chief Standing Turkey (Cunne-Shote), who had been selected by the people following the death of Old Hop (Kanagatoga, Conne-Corte), had requested the move. (Old Hop received his name from a youthful leg wound.)

Timberlake would observe an ongoing and severe competition between Chota and Tellico for the honor of Mother Town. Chota would fade from existence after the 1788 killing of the first beloved man, Chief Corn Tassel (Old Tassel, Kahnyatahee).

In 1730, Sir Alexander Cuming, a Scotsman sent by Britain as an envoy to the Cherokee, would find there were seven major towns, each with a headman. Other villages were led by minor chiefs. Cuming would refer to the major chiefs as "kings" and "emperors" and the lesser chiefs as "princes." He also found that each town had not only a civil chief, but also a war chief who was sometimes the same chief.

Another important part of the government was the Chief's Council. Often two leaders would differ on a direction the tribe should take, so they would meet in the Council House where they would politely take turns presenting their reasoning. The consensus would rule, and the result could sometimes mean a change of the village headman or even the principal chief.

Each council member could rise and speak in turn. He expressed his viewpoint without interruption or criticism and in monotone, without emoting. There was a dignified air in council sessions. Anything else would have been deemed contemptible. The Cherokee did have a term that translated to "liar," but it was not considered an insult as it is presently. Rather, in the 18th century Cherokee community, the term indicated disagreement with what was said. Timberlake would record: "They seldom turn their eyes on the person they speak of, or address themselves to, and are always suspicious when people's eyes are fixed on them."[24]

Council sessions were deliberate and solemn events. The leaders were responsible to properly advise regarding the defense of their lands, and the lives of the people were often dependent upon that advice.

Council sessions brought about balance as speakers represented their villages, clans, age, gender, or their politics (hawk versus dove). Once a vote was taken, the leader with the majority was considered the winner. The loser, and his followers, were expected to accept the majority opinion but did not have to participate. No tribal member was forced to follow a decision with which he did not agree, such as going to war.

Timberlake later wrote: "Their government ... is a mixed aristocracy and democracy, the chiefs being chosen according to their merit in war, or policy at home."[25]

All leaders were expected to be fair and not engage in favoritism. If one were to do so, he would likely be replaced.

Cherokee leaders were expected to live amicably among their political rivals. Later exemplars Attakullakulla and Ostenaco would dislike each other intently and would become rivals regarding several political issues, but they would be expected to keep their differences out of the public domain. Timberlake would continue his observations: "Warm in opposing one another, as their interests continually clash, yet these [Attakullakulla and Ostenaco] have no further animosity, no family-quarrels or resentment."[26]

However, they (especially Attakullakulla) would not always comply when talking with the white men. In October 1756, British captain Raymond Demere and a garrison of 90 British regulars and 120 South Carolina militiamen would begin to construct Fort Loudoun near Chota. Demere would complain to Attakullakulla that Old Hop was courting the French. The principal chief would become Attakullakulla's primary opponent of British trade over trade with the French. Attakullakulla, who would see Old Hop as a threat to his prestige, would charge that Conne-Corte was a fool and could do nothing without his (Attakullakulla's) help. (Even Old Hop's captured Creek servant was called French John because of his connections. Details of the division over trade alliances will be covered in Chapters 3 and 4.)

Each village selected its headman by the means of a council session such as noted above. A headman could be replaced if he lost favor with the majority of the village. The headman, called a chief by the white men, was assisted by a council of leaders chosen from each clan. There was a white (peace) chief and a red (war) chief. A headman did not make rules for the community as a European ruler did in those days, but he led by persuasion. In the case of the death of a first beloved man (principal headman of the collective), his replacement would be discussed in a session of every village council, and the villages' headmen would meet in the Chota Council to select the new first beloved man. Again, a live headman could be replaced. (This would later happen with Standing Turkey who was the principal chief following Old Hop. He would be replaced by Attakullakulla at the choice of the people after having been in office for about two years. This is detailed in Chapter 5.)

There were other members of the local councils and the primary one at Chota. These were any women who carried the title of ghighau (beloved woman). The most well-known of these would be Nanyehi (Nancy Ward). She would later earn the distinction of being a war woman when her husband was killed in a major battle with the Creek in 1755. (Her bravery as she would take over his band is described in Chapter 3.)

Timberlake would later note: "These chiefs, or headmen, likewise compose the assemblies of the nation, into which the war-women are admitted ... the story of Amazons not so great a fable ... many of the Indian women being as famous in war, as powerful in council.... This is the only title [ghighau or beloved woman] females can enjoy; but it abundantly recompenses them, by the power they acquire by it, which is so great that they can, by the wave of a swan's wing, deliver a wretch condemned by the council, and already tied to the stake."[27]

The impact of the Women's Councils became pronounced after the example of Nancy Ward. Each village had one as did the Mother Town of Chota where Nancy Ward was honored to be ghighau.

The white (Peace) organization within a village consisted of the headman, seven counselors (clan heads), a council of elders, a woman's council led by a beloved woman, and messengers. White denoted the civil authority. The white chief presided over rituals and celebrations in peaceful times, such as those described earlier in this chapter. He also attended the council at Chota, the center of the Cherokee Nation, where the principal chief (first beloved man) presided.

The white chief, to be a successful leader, needed the support of the seven clans. There were members of each clan in each community. The authority of the white chief did not overshadow the authority of the clan regarding punishment of members or the seeking of vengeance for a member. The authority of the peace chief depended upon the respect he earned. He persuaded, rather than demanded, a following. An important function of the principal chief (white chief of the collective villages) was to call the general population together to discuss an emergency, such as an impending attack (at which time the collective red chief, called Raven of Chota, would take over).

The red (war) chief in each village was responsible to plan and conduct war. He had an organization similar to the one described above for the white chief. Once the war chief made the battle plan, he would (similar to the peace chief) work to persuade the warriors to participate. Individual warriors could choose if they would go to war or not, depending on how well the red chief influenced; however, as war was a major activity for the Cherokee, the warriors would likely follow the red chief into battle. The war chief had sub chiefs (similar to militia captains) who were accomplished in battle, had impeccable reputations, and had their own following of warriors.[28]

The early Shawnee were extremely similar to the Cherokee in their organization and daily life. This lends credence to the suggestion that the Cherokee may once have been of the same origin as the Shawnee.[29]

Chapter 2

Early European Contact

Similarities, but more differences, between the early Cherokee and the early Europeans were exposed as they made contact. At the time of early interaction, the Europeans were considered "civilized"; however, the earlier Europeans had been tribal and illiterate much as the American Indian. There the similarities stopped.

The early tribal Europeans exhibited feral behavior. They were invested in conquest and practiced genocide as they slaughtered entire communities of people they encountered for the want of loot. The American Indians, on the other hand, usually fought with their neighboring tribes only to contest an ancestral land claimed by both sides, and they generally came to a settlement on a common border. (Had the Cherokee known they could not rely on the same types of border agreements with the British, they, in later years, might have allied with the French or the Spanish who seemed less interested in moving in on the tribe—and they would likely have been better off.)

The ancient Britons were not even compatible from community to community. Prior to the Roman invasion in the first century, they had become Celtic in nature when they were invaded by, and dominated by, the Celts about 1,000 years before. They did not live in villages but in temporary camps as they roamed England looking for chances to raid and plunder.

When the Romans began trade with the Britons in about 55 B.C., they thought to bring civilization to the tribes. However, they found the job to be impossible and invaded in A.D. 45. They drove many of the harsher people to the north (present-day Scotland) to join the wild Picts (descendants of early Celts). In 122, Roman emperor Hadrian ordered a wall be built to keep the wild tribes out of southern England. Hadrian's Wall was garrisoned with armed Roman soldiers. The Romans did find many Britons that showed promise for becoming civilized, so they allowed them to remain. Eventually, some intermarried.

The Romans were constantly under attack by the Angles (or Angels pronounced with a hard "g") and the Saxons, groups of Germanic tribes that habitually raided England. The individual tribes of this collection were not much more enlightened than the Britons and constantly fought among themselves. The Romans eventually paid mercenary Saxon tribes to defend England against other Saxon invaders. The Romans finally left about 450; then, the southern part of the island was fully invested by the Saxons, Angles, and also Jutes from Denmark. The Britons and some of the intermarried Romans remained in the western portion of the island.

The combined factions formed a civil government that has been generally referred to as Anglo-Saxon. However, in 1066, Britain was attacked in the north by King Harald III of

Norway (Harald Hardrada). On September 25, 1066, at Stamford Bridge, King Harald was killed and his force was driven off by Anglo-Saxon king Harold II Godwinsson. Then on October 14, 1066, King William I (William the Conqueror of Normandy), after having attacked the southern coast, beat and killed King Harold at Hastings. Hence, the Norman dynasty was established.

One devastating result of European contact for the Cherokee was new illnesses, especially smallpox. Indian trader and historian James Adair would write: "About the year 1738, the Cherake received a most depopulating shock, by the small pox, which reduced them almost one half, in about a years [sic] time: it was conveyed into Charles-town by the Guinea-men [aboard slave ships]."[1]

That deadly transport was most often the source of smallpox outbreaks, not only for the Cherokee, but for the settlers. The 1738 occurrence would be followed in the summer of 1739 when unlicensed traders carried the same disease into the backcountry. Smallpox epidemics in 1697–8, 1738–9, 1759–60, 1780, and 1783 would kill an estimated 7,000 to 10,000 Cherokee (about one-half of the population).

While some Europeans definitely were responsible for passing the contamination to the Cherokee, some possibly by design, it is unlikely that any of the southern colonists, or especially the traders, intentionally subjected the Cherokee to the malady. In the first place, the traders would have been cutting their own throats because they were heavily reliant upon the Cherokee trade for their livelihood. Secondly, the settlers, whose ancestors had been here for generations, had lost their resistance to the disease. It is not likely they risked their own health to accomplish such a dastardly deed.

The danger to the colonials was exhibited by the outbreaks that hit Charles Town several times over many years of slave ships having been received in port. An epidemic hit Charles Town in 1717; other major onslaughts occurred each year from 1730 to 1739. The historian John Duffy wrote: "The population of Charleston was approximately 5,000 in 1738: almost half were infected [By smallpox]."[2]

Duffy continued as he would write of a 1760 epidemic in Charles Town: "In a population estimated at 8,000, there were an estimated 6,000 cases and over 730 deaths, or 9 percent of the population."[3]

The earliest Charles Town outbreak that Duffy acknowledged had been reported on November 11, 1711. He quoted: "Never was there a more sickly or fatall [sic] season than this for the small Pox, Pestilential ffeavers [sic], Pleurisies and fflux's [sic] have destroyed numbers here of all sorts, both Whites Blacks and Indians."[4]

Brigadier General Andrew Pickens' close friend, South Carolina colonel James McCall, would die from smallpox in May 1781. He would contract the disease along with his cohort, Georgia colonel Elijah Clarke, who survived.

The most obvious culprits for intentionally passing smallpox along to the Indians would be the British army officers. Most of them had only recently left Europe and were still somewhat resistant to the disease. The Continental Army soldiers had to be inoculated against smallpox; however, the local colonial militiamen were not afforded that protection.

In June and July of 1763, British colonel Henry Bouquet and Major General Jeffery Amherst (1st Baron Amherst) corresponded. The two damningly discussed providing blankets riddled with smallpox to the Indians. As if that weren't bad enough, Amherst stated in one of the posts: "to try Every other method that can serve to Extirpate this Execrable Race."[5]

Even though the British would fight against the Cherokee (their "allies") in 1760 and 1761, the target of this contemptible plot seems to have been the northern Indians who had been French allies during the French and Indian War. It is doubtful the Cherokee would have sided against the backcountry settlements in 1776 if they had been privy to this bit of history. They likely would have concentrated on the settlers that were encroaching nearer and nearer to the Upper Villages.

Since the British smallpox plot seems to have targeted tribes other than the Cherokee, it is most likely the Cherokee would contract the disease from unlicensed traders as mentioned above. They also probably were exposed when some of their leaders visited Charles Town or accidentally contacted visitors from Charles Town who were carriers. In any case, yes, the Europeans infected the Cherokee. The colonial settlers and traders presumably did not consciously do so.[6]

The Christopher Columbus expedition in 1492 was the first European exploration of America. Reports of Viking discoveries are disregarded for the purpose of this study. The land would not contain any permanent settlements for about another 200 years; however, Columbus and his men opened the floodgates and would initiate an onrush of Europeans the like of which the Cherokee could never imagine. This future influx would forever change the dynamics of Cherokee life, and by 300 years following Columbus' first step, the Cherokee would struggle to maintain their identity and would strive to even exist.

In 1493, Spaniard Juan Ponce de León participated in Columbus' second voyage to the Caribbean in the New World. Then in April 1513, Ponce de León landed a party of men on the southern extremity of the continent. The explorer was so impressed with the abundance of wildflowers in the vicinity that he named the location Florida, which translates in English to "feast of flowers." Ponce de León was supposedly trying to discover a fountain of youth purported to be located within the interior of the continent. However, he hardly had time to penetrate the interior before he left in October.

Ponce de León returned to Florida in 1521; however, he was wounded in the thigh from a poisoned arrow shot by attacking Calusa braves. He sailed to Havana where he died a few days later. (Calusa translates to "fierce people." The men were tall, muscular, and grew long black hair. They were the "Vikings of the Western Hemisphere" and were feared by the several smaller tribes in the area. They did not farm but fished the ocean and rivers of Florida and collected shells which they used for bowls, tools, utensils, jewelry, ornaments, and spearheads. They apparently numbered about 50,000 people.)

Hernando (sometimes Fernando) De Soto was the next to move into Florida. He had arrived in Havana in May 1538. It took him one year to prepare for his expedition to Florida where he landed May 27, 1539. He wasted no time and led over 600 troops into the inner regions a few days after the landing. De Soto had a herd of pigs for meat and 350 pack mules. Primarily soldiers of fortune, the explorers had no thought of a fountain of youth; their only dreams were of riches to be provided by countless cities constructed of gold and silver. Mercenaries might have been a better description of that army considering how cruelly they treated the native hosts they encountered.

Early on their trek as they approached the Savannah River, the Spaniards encountered a beautiful Indian queen, the Lady of Cofitachequi, at today's Silver Bluff, South Carolina, about 10 miles south of present-day Augusta, Georgia. Her father ruled a vast land. When she heard of the Spaniards' approach, and that they had over 200 tamemes (an old Mexican term for porters or serfs) in chains, she decided to take the initiative and make a peace offering. She went to their nearby camp and presented them with shells, blankets, shawls, tools, jewelry, and many other supplies, including food. She gave De Soto her personal string of pearls that she had worn for the occasion, and she invited the Spaniards free access throughout her kingdom. De Soto accepted the invitation and remained at the principal village for one month. When the Spaniards discovered copper hatchets that were unusually light in color, they asked the Indians about them. They were told the metal that was alloyed with the copper came from a 12-days' journey further inland.

The Spaniard decided that the princess would be valuable as a guide through the interior, so De Soto took her captive. They left Cofitachequi on May 13, 1540, and arrived at present-day Highlands, North Carolina, on the 25th. The next day the expedition reached the abandoned ruins of ancient Nikwasi at present-day Franklin, North Carolina, the one-time center of the ancient Cherokee culture. De Soto then headed west into the mountains where, as they camped one night, the Lady of Cofitachequi stole the pearls from the sleeping commander and escaped to her realm. Never again did she trust any Europeans after that experience.

("Tameme" was originally a specific reference to Indians captured by the Aztecs and used as slaves. De Soto's tamemes were Florida Indians whom he obtained by trade from their chiefs or simply captured during his trek inland. De Soto used a pack of trained dogs to attack any Indians who attempted an escape.

(Silver Bluff, South Carolina, was later the location of Fort Galphin which would be captured by Lieutenant Colonel Henry "Light-horse Harry" Lee when he joined Brigadier General Andrew Pickens for the Siege of Augusta on May 19, 1781. Highlands, North Carolina, is located on U.S. Highway 64 at the junction of State Highway 28 about 10 miles south of Thorpe Lake.)

After his guide's escape, De Soto followed an old Indian trail until, on May 30, he arrived at a Cherokee village called Guasili (Guaxule) near present-day Murphy, North Carolina. This apparently was the first discovery of the Cherokee people by any European. The Cherokee were very friendly and gave De Soto hundreds of dogs to use as food as he traveled. He referred to the Cherokee as "Chalaque" and described them as peaceful and hospitable. The Cherokee seemed poor, so De Soto saw no advantage to any further contact. The Spaniards did not harass the Cherokee nor disrupt their balanced and easy existence as they had done with other tribes, except for likely introducing new diseases.

De Soto had told the Indians all along his route that he could never die because he was from the land of the Great Spirit. Thus, the expedition was in a desperate situation when he died in Louisiana on May 21, 1542. Near the mouth of the Red River, a few of his officers wrapped his body in a cloak and, about midnight, rowed to the middle of the Mississippi River. There De Soto received a very quiet, but honorable, burial at river. The expedition was deemed an utter failure and abandoned. The Spanish never did accumulate the riches they were after; they had lost over 300 men to disease and Indian attacks and eventually lost their supreme leader. It took the surviving members over one year to find their way to a Spanish community where most of them lived out the remainder of their lives.[7]

In 1561, the Spanish settled Santa Elena (Saint Helena) near present-day Port Royal,

Burial of de Soto by William A. Crafts, 1876.

South Carolina. (Saint Helena is located at the eastern extremity of U.S. Highway 21.) The first expedition from the new settlements to Cherokee country was led by Juan Pardo. On December 1, 1566, Pardo and 125 men left Santa Elena to trade with nearby Indians for food. He stopped at the village of Yssa near present-day Linville, North Carolina, and again at Jaora near today's Morganton. Pardo likely connected and traded for food with the Catawba during those stopovers. The Spaniards constructed Fort San Juan at Jaora and garrisoned it with 30 men. Pardo then followed the Catawba River and visited the Indian towns of Quinahaqui near present-day Catawba, North Carolina, and Guatari near today's Salisbury. Pardo met with caciques (tribal leaders) and informed the Indians that they were Spanish subjects. He left a chaplain in the area to convert the Catawba to Christianity. Pardo was then ordered to return to Santa Elena and arrived on March 7, 1567.

On September 1, 1567, Pardo, on his second expedition, ventured inland with 100 men. First he returned to the Catawba, who had stored corn for the Spanish. After they were well fed, the Spaniards ventured into the Great Smoky Mountains and met some Cherokee. Pardo returned to Santa Elena on March 2, 1568. He had established rapport with some Catawba and Cherokee headmen and built and garrisoned some forts. He did not lose one man to illness or injury. However, his forts proved to be of little use and were eventually abandoned.

While Pardo was not as aggressive with the Indians as De Soto had been, he unwittingly, as De Soto had done, left a trail of new diseases for them to contend with. They had no riches to exploit, did not impede the expeditions, so were left relatively untouched by Spanish exploration.[8]

The English settled Jamestown in 1607. The Powhatan, a small tribe that led the

Powhatan confederacy, were the colonists' nearest neighbors and helped them to settle. The colonists likely would not have survived their first winter without the Indians' assistance. Their bond grew stronger when colonist John Rolfe married Chief Powhatan's daughter, Matoaka (later called Pocahontas by the whites and then Rebecca Rolfe), in 1614. This was the first known marriage between a European and an Indian.

Jamestown's most valuable crop was tobacco. There was a great demand for it in England, and the colonists exported all they could grow. Rather than clear forest land for more agriculture, they elbowed their way onto already-cleared Powhatan land. Finally, in 1622, the confederation had enough. They attacked several of the expanded settlements and killed about 350 Englishmen. The Indians burned several of the settlements, and the colonists declared war. It was long and bloody. The Powhatan confederation was beaten badly by 1650, and the survivors became subjects of the Jamestown Colony.

Much Powhatan land had been abandoned due to the war, so the Cherokee, in 1654, settled the falls of the James River (present-day Richmond, Virginia) with 650 warriors and their families. The colonists were both afraid and irate. They met in council and declared "that these new come Indians be in no sort suffered to seat themselves there, or anyplace near us, it having cost so much blood to expel and extirpate those perfidious and treacherous Indians which were there formerly."[9]

The colonists armed a 100-man militia to face the Cherokee. They called upon the Pamunkey Indians, members of the old Powhatan Confederacy, to assist. The tribe sent 100 warriors led by Chief Totopotomoy. Greatly outnumbered, the colonists were soundly defeated and quickly retreated, leaving the Pamunkey to fight. The Pamunkey lost nearly all of their 100 warriors. Some have reported that Chief Totopotomoy was among the slain. The colonists approached the Cherokee for peace terms and were required to provide the Indians with a large collection of trade goods that included tools, beads, metal axes (to be used for tomahawks), and metal knives. The Jamestown government was so irked that it removed the militia commander from his post and penalized him to pay the cost of the treaty.[10]

The English began to settle the Carolina coast in 1670. During this time the Virginia settlements grew. The Virginians built Fort Henry (present-day Petersburg, Virginia) in 1645. Abraham Wood was an Indian trader at the fort in the 1670s. He dispatched James Needham and Gabriel Arthur to what he believed was Chota to establish a Cherokee trade agreement. They, accompanied by two English aides and a band of Oconeechee Indians, arrived in Chota on July 15, 1673. The Oconeechee were to act as guides and interpreters. The expedition was well-received by the Cherokee. A small group of Weesock lived at Chota as guests of the Cherokee. The Weesock had been friendly with the Oconeechee.

(Fort Henry was an English frontier stronghold built in 1645 near the Appomattox River Falls. Its exact location has been debated, but the most accepted site is on a bluff four blocks north of the corner of West Washington and North South streets in Petersburg. It is tagged with a historical marker.

(Although Abraham Wood specified that Needham's and Arthur's actions occurred at Chota, they may have happened at Tanase.)[11]

Needham and Arthur explored the area around Chota and, during their visit, greatly impressed the headman of the village. The chief was so touched that he had his warriors build a scaffold in the center of the village upon which he had the two aides placed on exhibition so the Cherokee people could easily view them.

Abraham Wood described Chota in detail (excerpt includes original spelling and grammar):

> The town of Chote is seated on ye river side, having ye clifts on ye river side [meaning across the river] on ye one side being very high for its defence , the other three sides trees of two foot or over [meaning diameter], pitched on end, twelve foot high, and on ye topps scaffolds placed with parapets to defend the walls and offend theire enemies which men stand on to fight, many nations of Indians inhabit downe this river ... which they the Cherokees are at warre with and to that end keepe one hundred and fifty canoes under ye command of theire forts. Ye leaste of them will carry twenty men, and made sharpe at both ends like a wherry for swiftness, this forte is four square; 300: paces over and ye houses sett in streets.[12]

(A wherry is a type of boat that was traditionally used for carrying cargo or passengers on rivers and canals in England; wherries along the tideway in London were water taxis operated by watermen, and in Elizabethan times their use was widespread.)

The Cherokee were reported to have 60 guns, likely muskets, and probably trade guns. An Oconeechee named Hasecoll (Indian John) was the primary interpreter. Indian John accompanied James Needham on a return to Fort Henry to arrange for trade goods. Gabriel Arthur remained at Chota to study the Cherokee lifestyle and become familiar with the language. Abraham Wood was pleased with the progress and was eager to trade guns, ammunition, metal tomahawks, metal knives, and many other items.

(The Indian trade gun was a smoothbore musket—fowling piece—or single barrel shotgun. The Indian trade gun was developed after the introduction of the flintlock in 1620 through 1635. By the mid–18th century, the Indian trade gun was the most traded weapon dealt to the eastern Indian tribes. It had other names, but one of the more common was the Carolina musket. Trade guns were exchanged with the Indians on a large scale and were valued at twenty pelts. English factories were the primary source of the Indian trade guns. The gun makers in Birmingham, England, were often referred to as blood merchants by London manufacturers. The Birmingham trade guns were cheaply made and popular with the American Indian traders because they could profit more from the pelts if they could pay less for the imported guns. There were reportedly numerous cases of gun barrels blowing up when these trade guns were fired. Many Indian warriors likely lost all or parts of their hands shooting a trade gun. The guns also had to be repaired often, and this provided a good income in trade pelts for gunsmiths who made repairs.)[13]

Before he began his return to Chota, Needham quarreled with Indian John. Apparently, Indian John had planned to abscond with the trade, and he killed Needham when they reached the Yadkin River. Several Oconeechee and Cherokee that were in the party witnessed the dispute.

Abraham Wood reported (excerpt includes original spelling and grammar): "[Indian John] catched up a gunn, which he himself had carried to kill meat for them to eate and shot Mr. Needham near ye burr of the eare and killed him ... Indian John drew out his knife, stepped across ye corpse of Mr. Needham, ript open his body, drew out his hart, held it in his hand and looked to ye eastward, toward ye English plantations and said he valued not all ye English."[14]

Indian John sent word via one of his Cherokee traveling companions to Chota to tell the headman he needed to kill Gabriel Arthur. The headman was away visiting, so the messenger delivered the news to a gathering of the people. The Cherokee people liked the visitors and opposed the killing of Arthur; consequently, a rift developed between the Cherokee and the Weesock. The Weesock living in Chota tied Arthur to a stake and piled cane stalks around him to prepare his tortuous burning. Wood described the event (excerpt includes original spelling and grammar):

> Before ye fire was put to ye [Arthur] ye King [Cherokee headman] came into ye towne with a gunn upon his shoulder ... and ye King ran with great speed to the place and said who is that that is going to put fire to the English man. A Weesock borne started up with a fire-brand said that am I. Ye King forthwith cockt his gunn and shot ye Weesock dead, and ran to Gabriel and with his knife cutt the thongs that tide him and had him goe to his house.[15]

Arthur remained with the Cherokee at Chota and donned Cherokee dress. He even applied the bright-red body paint that the Cherokee used. He accompanied them on war parties into Florida and the Ohio River Valley. In 1674, he was wounded and captured by Shawnee. Once the Shawnee realized he was European, they released him. He returned to Chota. On June 18, 1674, the Cherokee escorted Arthur back to Fort Henry where he reported his experiences to Abraham Wood.[16]

In 1674, Henry Woodward made a trip through the Cherokee Lower Towns. He became a pioneer trader with many Indian towns and tribes, and he dealt primarily in deerskins and slaves. However, Woodward had fallen out of favor with Carolina's Lords Proprietors, and in April 1677 they claimed a monopoly on Indian trade. They prohibited any individual trade efforts with the Indians and the Spanish except by official agents of Carolina. In 1682 Woodward had been severely wounded with a ball to the head during some skirmish; however, he determined to go behind the Lords Proprietors' backs and travel to England. There, he applied for and obtained the official position as Indian agent for the Carolina Lords Proprietors. Woodward agreed to receive 20 percent of the profits from the total Carolina Indian trade.

(On March 24, 1663, King Charles II had granted to a group of noblemen called the Lords Proprietors a charter of a piece of North America. The Lords Proprietors were speculators and businessmen seeking to make a profit off of the New World. The colony was to be financed by them, and they were to receive any profit. They were to rule and establish any such local government they might deem necessary. They were responsible only to the king, who hoped that Britain would profit from the imports of goods from America. The Lords Proprietors were named in the charter: the Earl of Clarendon [Edward Hyde], the Duke of Albemarle [George Monck], William Lord Craven, Baron of Stratton [John Berkeley], Earl of Shaftesbury [Anthony Ashley Cooper], Sir George Carteret, Sir William Berkeley, and Sir John Colleton. The most senior of these men was Lord Anthony Ashley Cooper, who designed the street plan for Charles Town, and whose secretary, the philosopher John Locke, penned the Fundamental Constitution of Carolina.)

In 1684, the colony of Carolina made an official trade treaty with the Cherokee that required them to provide deer hides and Indian slaves captured from other tribes when at war. That caused the Cherokee to increase their hunting and warring which, in turn, meant trade for more guns was a necessity. The Cherokee increased their war efforts with the Catawba after the treaty was signed. Up to that time, the Cherokee and the Catawba had been trading partners. The Cherokee, since they were so far inland, had relied on the

Choctaw and the Catawba to be their middlemen, or brokers, for Cherokee trade with colonists. At first, the trade goods were simply popular among the Cherokee who adapted them to their traditional lifestyle; however, the desired merchandise soon became a necessity to their livelihood of increased hunting and warring.

In 1690, James Moore opened an active trade business with the Cherokee. Moore used every opportunity to increase his fortune. He had a huge plantation, but remained active in his mercantile business. He traded furs, but he also dealt with pirates, engaged in the Indian slave trade, and partnered in the ownership of several merchant vessels. Moore had previously been a member of the Carolina Grand Council (an advisory commission) and a deputy for the Lords Proprietors. The Lords dismissed him as a deputy because he had enslaved Indians against new colony regulations. However, those regulations soon changed to align with British colonial economics, and the Lords Proprietors elected Moore governor of Carolina in 1700. He held office until 1702. In 1706, Moore contracted yellow fever and died in Charles Town. His body was burned according to the colonial custom for such deaths. (This governor is not to be confused with Governor James Moore II, December 21, 1719–May 30, 1721.)

Besides Moore, Cornelius Dougherty had opened a thriving trade business with the Cherokee in 1690. He moved into the Cherokee villages, married a Cherokee woman, and lived out his life. This started a trend among traders to actually locate themselves among the Cherokee, whose traditions required that any outsider desiring to settle in their midst must marry into the tribe.

In 1692, the Shawnee, while on a raid to capture slaves for trade with the English, destroyed a major Cherokee village while the town's warriors were on a winter hunt. It would be late in the 18th century before the two Indian nations could establish a mutual trust to work together against encroaching settlers. This exemplified how Britain's demand for slaves, regardless of individual colonial rules, caused all Indian tribes to become dependent upon British trade.

The war between the Cherokee and the Catawba increased until 1693 when the Catawba raided the Cherokee to capture slaves for their own trade efforts with the English. Then the Cherokee headmen traveled to Charles Town to plead for assistance against the Catawba. Carolina, by virtue of a 1684 treaty, agreed to assist.

Slavery had become a big problem for the Cherokee. Carolina, and other colonies, had begun to emphasize trade for captured Indian slaves. Therefore, the best position for the colonies was to align with Britain's colonial slave policy by pitting one Indian tribe against another to create captives. The British were also interested in securing Indian slaves, not only for the coastal southern colonies, but to export for British colonies outside of North America, such as the West Indies.

Some traders in Carolina were outspoken against the Indian slave trade. In 1705, several had complained that former governor James Moore had hired ruffians, and warriors from certain Indian tribes "to set upon, assault, kill, destroy, and take captive as many Indians as they possible [sic] could."

The purpose seemed to be to sell the captives into slavery at a profit. The traders charged that the governor had single-handedly "utterly ruined the trade for skins and furs, whereby we held our chief correspondence with England, and turned it into a trade of Indians or slave making, in blood and confusion."[17]

The traders tried to warn Carolina settlements of probable Indian attacks against the colonists over the matter of slavery. H. G. Wells wrote in *The Outline of History:*

> Slavery began very early in the European history of America ... began with the enslavement of Indians for gang work in mines and upon plantations ... [Marquis de] Las Casas ... urged that negroes should be brought to America to relieve his tormented Indian protégés.... The need for labour upon the plantations of the West Indies and the south was imperative. When the supply of Indian captives proved inadequate, the planters turned not only to the negro, but to the jails and poorhouses of Europe, for a supply of toilers.... The year [1620] ... saw a Dutch sloop disembarking the first cargo of negroes at Jamestown ... Negro slavery was as old as New England; it had been an American institution for over a century and a half before the War of Independence.... But the conscience of thoughtful men in the colonies was never quite easy upon this score ... one of the accusations of Thomas Jefferson against the crown and the lords of Great Britain that every attempt to ameliorate or restrain the slave trade on the part of the colonists had been checked by the great proprietary interests in the mother-country. In 1776 Lord Dartmouth [William Legge, 2nd Earl Dartmouth] wrote that the colonists could not be allowed "... to check or discourage a traffic so beneficial to the nation."[18]

So, even in the early 1700s, although there was considerable dialogue regarding African and Indian slaves, no real progress was made because it was deemed "uneconomical" to intercede. Those who spoke about the lack of ethics in such a trade were in the minority.[19]

In the autumn of 1711, a war with the Tuscarora broke out in present-day North Carolina. The war involved the British, Dutch, and German settlers of Carolina. The Tuscarora had lived in peace with the colony's settlers for over 50 years. During that time, other colonies in America were actively warring with various American Indian tribes.

There were two primary bands of Tuscarora in the early 18th century—the Northern group led by Chief Tom Blunt, and the Southern led by Chief Hancock. The Northern band was located throughout present-day Bertie County on the Roanoke River; the Southern was nearer to today's New Bern, North Carolina, just south of the Pamplico River (present-day Pamlico River). While Chief Blunt became close friends with the Blount family of the Bertie region (likely descendants of Thomas and Mary Blount), Chief Hancock found his villages raided and his people frequently kidnapped and sold into slavery. Not only was each band heavily impacted by the introduction of European diseases, but also each experienced settler encroachment. They decided to attack the settlers and stem the infringement. Chief Tom Blunt had not become involved in the war as yet.

On September 11, 1711, Chief Hancock and his Southern Tuscarora allied with the Pamplico, the Cothechney, the Core, the Mattamuskeet, and the Matchepungo to divide up into several war parties. They attacked settlers in a wide area, and concentrated on planters along the Roanoke, Neuse, and Trent rivers and the settlement of Bath, Carolina. One hundred and thirty-seven settlers were killed and many others were driven away over the next few months.

Carolina deputy governor Edward Hyde (who resided in present-day North Carolina) activated the militia, and asked for assistance from the governor. Carolina governor Robert Gibbs (who lived in today's South Carolina) responded with 600 militiamen and 310 Cherokee commanded by Irish colonel John Barnwell. The combined force attacked the Southern Tuscarora and their allies at the Indians' Fort Narhantes on the banks of the Neuse River on January 29, 1712.

The Southern Tuscarora were defeated and lost more than three hundred warriors killed, and one hundred (mostly women and children) taken prisoners. Some of the militiamen and Cherokee took their respective captives to be sold into slavery. Barnwell marched through the Southern Tuscarora country burning villages, killing warriors, and taking prisoners with a pared force of 25 militiamen and 180 Cherokee warriors.

When Barnwell arrived at the Southern Tuscarora's Bath Town on February 11, he was joined by 70 northern Carolina militiamen. The newly combined force then proceeded to march on the enemy's Fort Hancock (located on the west bank of Contentnea Creek), home of Chief Hancock. Barnwell heard the wailing of the white women and children within the fort and agreed to negotiate with Chief Hancock. The chief agreed to release the white prisoners if Barnwell would withdraw. Barnwell agreed if Chief Hancock would meet him on the 19th of March at New Bern, Carolina, to discuss a general peace.

Hancock did not arrive at New Bern as promised, so on April 12, 1712, Barnwell marched again toward Fort Hancock with 150 militiamen and 130 Northern Tuscarora Indians. Colonel Barnwell had promised Chief Blunt control of the entire Tuscarora tribe, North and South, if he would assist the settlers in defeating Chief Hancock. Chief Blunt was able to capture Chief Hancock, and the Southern Tuscarora surrendered. After Carolina deputy governor Hyde reprimanded Barnwell for not punishing the tribe more severely, Barnwell returned to southern Carolina.

While the two portions of Carolina (north and south) were informally run by the independent Hyde and Gibbs, they each fell under the same Lords Proprietor. On May 9, 1712, Governor Hyde petitioned the Lords to sever the ties between the two regions. They did, and they declared Hyde to be "Governor, Captain General, Admiral, and Commander in Chief of ye Province of North Carolina."[20]

In the summer of 1712, the Southern Tuscarora again attacked the North Carolina settlements. Governor Hyde decided to lead an expedition to punish the Indians. However, the region was hit by yellow fever. Hyde contracted the disease and died on the 8th of September. North Carolina's legislative council, acting in lieu of a governor, asked South Carolina for assistance.

On December 12, 1712, South Carolina colonel Maurice Moore marched with 35 militiamen and 1,000 Yamassee to New Bern, North Carolina. Moore had to bivouac his force through the severe winter of 1712–1713. Finally, on February 4, 1713, Moore's force was strengthened by some North Carolina militiamen, and the combined regiment marched toward the new Southern Tuscarora stronghold of Fort Neoheroka.

After a three-week siege of the fort, Moore captured it, killed 558 Tuscarora, and took 392 prisoners. Later, a number of these prisoners, probably women and children, were sold as slaves. The power of the Southern Tuscarora was broken in North Carolina. Chief Hancock had been executed in South Carolina in 1712. Those who escaped death or capture migrated to New York, and they joined their Iroquois kinsmen, adding a sixth to the original Five Nations.[21]

Most of the few Southern Tuscarora who remained signed a treaty with the settlers in June 1718. It granted them a tract of land on the Roanoke River in present-day Bertie County. Tom Blunt and the Northern Tuscarora were already settled in the area. The tract amounted to 56,000 acres. The North Carolina Legislature renamed Chief Tom Blunt as King Tom Blount (the change in spelling was to more closely align with the Blount family). The last of the Southern Tuscarora were removed from their homes on the Pamplico River and forced to Bertie. Over the next several decades, the Tuscorara lands continually diminished as the tribe sold off land in deals designed by speculators.[22]

The earliest head warrior of the Cherokee, identified in the present-day, is Uskwalena (Big Head or Bull Head). In 1714, he led the Cherokee warriors in a successful battle with the Creek at Pine Island (near present-day Guntersville, Alabama) on the Tennessee River. De Soto had reached the island on July 2, 1540, and visited an old Creek village on the upper end called Coste.

The Yamasee (Yemassee) War of 1715 to 1717 was a conflict between British settlers of colonial South Carolina and the Yamasee and their allies, which at the beginning included the Cherokee, the Creek, and the Shawnee that lived along the Savannah River. Some of the many Indian participants played a minor role, but a few of the larger groups attacked throughout South Carolina.

For years, the Yamasee experienced good relations with their British trading partners. However, by 1715 they found it increasingly difficult to obtain the trade items most coveted by the British. Deerskins were scarce because of the overhunting to fulfill Britain's voracious appetite. Indian slaves had also become very rare following the Tuscarora War. A census taken by the British in 1715 likely promoted a fear of enslavement among the Yamasee. The Yamasee could also see that there were not as many members of other tribes to augment an Indian slave trade necessary for their own survival. The Cherokee, as an example, had dropped in population from 32,000 in 1685 to 12,000 in 1715. Of the 12,000, an estimated 4,000 to 5,000 were warriors. Additionally, the Yamasee debt to the British traders grew rapidly. The traders had given Indians trade goods on credit, but the Yamasee could not obtain skins or captive slaves fast enough to break even.

Rice plantations thrived in South Carolina, and the fields used up much land. The rice growers began to pressure the Yamasee for their land reserve along the South Carolina side of the Savannah River. The trade abuses, the swing in the Indian slave trade, encroachment, depletion of the deer population, and the growing debt of the Yamasee combined to initiate the war.

The Ochese Creek Indians allied themselves with the Yamasee and killed hundreds of colonists and destroyed many settlements. They also killed access to the food supply by murdering active traders. Settlers fled to Charles Town where starvation set in.

South Carolina had been warned by traders of a possible Ochese Creek uprising. The legislature sent a negotiating party to the primary upper Yamasee town of Pocotaligo (near present-day Yemassee, South Carolina). They especially wanted the Yamasee to assist and arrange an emergency meeting with the Ochese Creek leaders.

The delegation sent by the Board of Commissioners consisted of Samuel Warner and William Bray. They were accompanied by Thomas Nairne and John Wright, two important South Carolina Indian trade agents, and also by two aides, Seymour Burroughs and an unidentified South Carolinian. On the evening of April 14, 1715, the men spoke to a gathering of Yamasee headmen and warriors. They promised to make special efforts to correct Yamasee grievances over the trade practices. They also mentioned that South Carolina governor Charles Craven was on his way to the village.

The Yamasee held a council during the night and argued their options. There were some who were not fully convinced that a war with South Carolina was practical, but ultimately the choice was to take aggressive action. The Yamasee applied war paint before dawn; then, they awakened the sleeping delegates with an attack. Two of the men escaped: Seymour Burroughs, who had been shot twice, and the unidentified aide. The wounded Burroughs raised the alarm throughout the Port Royal settlements. The aide watched nervously from the cover of a nearby swamp as the Yamasee tortured and killed Nairne, Wright, Warner, and Bray. The beginning of the Yamasee War occurred early the morning of Good Friday, April 15, 1715.

The Yamasee quickly organized two large war parties. One, unaware that Burroughs had alerted the settlements, attacked at Port Royal. Several hundred settlers took refuge on a captured smuggler's ship that was docked at Port Royal. Many others fled in canoes.

The second war party looted and burned plantations in Saint Bartholomew's Parish. The warriors took captives and killed over a hundred settlers and slaves. Within the week, a large Yamasee army was preparing to engage the South Carolinian militia which had been mustered. The remaining Yamasee went south to find refuge in their ill-made forts.

Governor Craven himself led a force of 240 militiamen against the Yamasee. A tense battle occurred in open terrain near the Indian town of Salkehatchie (Saltcatchers) on the Salkehatchie River. Several hundred Yamasee warriors attacked and tried to outflank the militia. The militia successfully killed several leading warriors, and the Yamasee withdrew to cover in nearby swamps. Reportedly, 24 had been killed from each side. The South Carolina militia split into smaller units and continued to press the Indians. They had many successes.

In May 1715, 240 Catawba warriors attacked several settlements in northern South Carolina. The war party was joined by 70 Cherokee allies. In June, South Carolina responded with a 90-man militia cavalry force commanded by Captain Thomas Barker. The war party ambushed and killed all of Barker's troops. Another band of Catawba and Cherokee attacked a crude fort on Benjamin Schenkingh's plantation; they killed about 20 settlers. South Carolina was struggling to survive the onslaught.

Most of the Cherokee withdrew because they had heard their own towns were threatened with attacks. The Cherokee and their Chickasaw allies drove the Shawnee out of the Cumberland River Valley. The remaining Catawba then faced another militia under the command of Colonel George Chicken. On June 13, 1715, the colonel launched a direct assault upon the Catawba. The warriors could not defend against the attack and withdrew to their village. In July 1715, Catawba representatives arrived in Virginia to inform the British of their willingness to cooperate and to offer military assistance.

The Cherokee were divided. In general those in the Lower Villages, who lived closest to the South Carolina settlements, tended to support the war. Some had participated in Catawba attacks on South Carolina's Santee River settlements. Cherokee in the Upper Towns tended to support an alliance with South Carolina and war against the Creek. One of the Cherokee leaders most in favor of an alliance with South Carolina was Caesar, a chief of a Cherokee Middle Village with great influence over many Lower and Middle villages.

A number of Cherokee chiefs came to Charles Town, in company with a trader, to express their desire for peace. A force of several hundred combined white and black troops under Colonel Maurice Moore went up the Savannah in the winter of 1715–16 and made headquarters among the Lower Cherokee. There they were met by the chiefs of the Middle and some of the Upper Towns. The chiefs reaffirmed their desires for a lasting peace with the English, but refused to fight against the Yamasee, although they were willing to proceed against some other tribes. They laid the blame for most of the trouble upon the traders, who "had been very abuseful to them of late."[23]

A detachment under Colonel Chicken, sent to the Upper Cherokee, penetrated to Guasili (Guaxule) near present-day Murphy, North Carolina, where they found the headmen more defiant. The Cherokee leaders were resolved to continue a war against the Creek and demanded large supplies of guns and ammunition. The English were trying to make peace with the Creek and tried to dissuade the Cherokee who replied that, if they made peace with other tribes, they would have no means to capture slaves with which to trade for ammunition. The Cherokee claimed they had over 2,000 warriors, of whom one-half likely had guns. That estimate probably included only those warriors in the Middle and Upper towns, because they were not aligned with those in the Lower Towns on this matter. After much negotiation, the Cherokee finally agreed to trust the English again, and Chicken arranged to furnish them with 200 more guns and a large supply of ammunition. Chicken also agreed to furnish a detachment of militiamen to assist the Cherokee against tribes that were still fighting the English.

In early 1716, Colonel Moore was told that the Lower Towns had sent a flag of truce to the Creek, and that a delegation of Creek headmen was nearing the Cherokee towns. A Cherokee named Charitey Hagey proposed to broker peace talks between the Creek and South Carolinians.

When the South Carolinians were summoned to Tugaloo, they discovered that the Creek had arrived and held a council with the Cherokee, and that a dozen Creek had been killed by the Cherokee. Chief Hagey explained that the Creek delegation was actually a war party of Creek and Yamasee warriors, and that they had nearly succeeded in ambushing the South Carolinian force as it approached Tugaloo. Colonel Moore had been unsure whether the Cherokee would join the Creek and attack South Carolina or ally with South Carolina and attack the Creek. The massacre of the Creek at Tugaloo resulted in war between the Cherokee and Creek and an alliance between the Cherokee and South Carolina. The Creek and Cherokee continued to launch small-scale raids against each other for generations.

The Creek and the Yamasee were the main concern within the colony's settlements. Ninety percent of British traders in the area had been killed in the first few weeks of the Yamasee War. For over a year South Carolina feared the possibility it might not survive. Approximately 7 percent of South Carolina's white settlers had been killed. The relationships between the Europeans (British, French, and Spanish) and the various Indian tribes were significantly altered.

Anglican missionary Francis Le Jau said: "The Cherokees made peace with us with their wild ceremonies of grave dancing wherein they stripped themselves and put their cloaths [sic] by parcels at the feet of some of our most considerable men who in return must do like for them. Their exchanging of cloaths and smoaking [sic] out of the same pipe is a solemn token of reconciliation and friendship."[24]

This was a turning point for the Cherokee. The colonies increased direct trade with the tribe. More traders settled into Cherokee country and married into the clans. Headman Caesar of Chota was pro–British and sponsored increased trade, and there was an intense competition between Virginia and South Carolina for that trade. South Carolinian traders vastly outnumbered those from Virginia. The Cherokee had become solidly bound to the British (and to South Carolina), which would affect them for the better part of the next century. This was a pivotal point, because one might speculate that, had the Cherokee bonded with the Creek and the French (or the Spanish), they might not have faced some of the trials they would see in the late 18th century. Once the Cherokee made the alliance, they were disappointed right away when the British refused to supply soldiers to help them against the Creek. This was a sure indication of a one-sided commitment, portending of things to come.[25]

The British expected the Cherokee to fight the Creek without assistance from the colonial troops. It appears that the South Carolinians did not understand the importance of the change in clothing ceremony that Le Jau had described. The Cherokee's traditional ceremony was a commitment for each to fight with the other against all enemies of both. The English still had hopes of peace with the Creek and did not want to infuse them with more reasons to war with the colony. The Cherokee were disappointed that South Carolina would not join them against the Creek after the Cherokee had saved the day for the colony in the second part of the Yamasee War. The Cherokee counted the English as disloyal; however, they would forget this lesson in 1776 (see Chapter 6).

The South Carolina agriculturalists were never secure with the free-trade concept. They wanted the Cherokee to trade only at military forts. The Colonial Assembly was controlled by the planters and growers. Although the merchandisers along the coast wanted an open trade agreement to continue, the Assembly, in 1716, voted to disallow private industry direct trade with the Cherokee. The idea was to stop white traders from living in the Indian villages. This put a hardship on not only the traders, but the merchandisers who supplied them. The Virginia traders had no such restrictions and could continue to ship goods to traders living within the villages. The new South Carolina regulations helped the Virginians overcome a problem. Up until that time, they had been greatly outnumbered by the South Carolinians in the Cherokee community.

The Cherokee resisted the idea of traveling many miles to trade at a fort or large town. They were never comfortable with their room and board. There were many restrictions placed upon them while they were in the forts, and they were constantly mistreated by settlers in the communities. Headman Caesar of Chota threatened the colony that the Cherokee would trade with those who appeared ready to come and trade in the villages. Not only was Virginia willing to replace South Carolina as Cherokee trading partners, but likewise were the French. The Cherokee learned they were more ruthlessly cheated on weights and measures when they traveled to Savannah and other towns.

In 1717 the French built Fort Toulouse on the Coosa River ten miles above present-day Montgomery, Alabama. The French had actually traded with the Cherokee before the English did. The French worked to expand their influence among the southern tribes until it was estimated that 3,400 warriors who had traded with South Carolina began to favor French trade. The Cherokee, however, retained England as their primary European trading partner. By 1721, the French earnestly competed with the British for that trade. Many Cherokee preferred French trade alliances. They were the only Indians with whom the British successfully developed trade agreements. There was a real incentive for the British to work at keeping the Cherokee happy with strong trade policies. However, the British were unable to exercise control over the traders, especially those living among the Indians. The traders, at first, found the Cherokee easy to cheat as they thought that illiteracy meant gullibility. The Cherokee were actually very intelligent and quickly figured out how they were being cheated. The only thing in Britain's favor was that the old chiefs were in its corner, and they would exercise their influence among their people to favor the British. In later years, the individual Cherokee was highly disappointed with the British alliance, yet the older headmen continued to ignore the younger chiefs and the best interests of the Cherokee people.

English trader Robert Bunning said: "[The French had] ... brought some Petiaugers [sic] up the River from New Orleans or Mouthkill within 30 or 35 miles of Great Taraqua laden with large Presents of Goods and Ammunition in order to draw the Indians to their Party and to have Leave ... but after Deliberation and Consideration of the head Men and Conjurer, whose name was Jacob, commanded them to be knocked in the head and thrown headlong from his Scaffold on which they were sitting and their bodies to be dragged into the River."[26]

Pettiaugers (Pettiaugers or Periaguers) were large flat-bottom dugout boats. A description recorded in 1709 (contains original spelling and grammar):

> The next day we entered Santee river's mouth.... As we row'd up the river, we found the land towards the mouth, and for about sixteen miles up it, scarce any thing but swamp ... affording vast ciprus-trees, of which the French make canoes, that will carry fifty or sixty barrels. After the tree is moulded and dug, they saw them in two pieces and so put a plank between, and even a small Keel, to preserve them from the Oyster-Banks, which are innumerable in the Creeks and Bays betwixt the French settlement and Charles-Town. They carry two masts and Bermudas sails, which makes them very handy and fit for their purpose.... Of these great trees the pereaugers and canoes are scoop'd and made; which sort of vessels are chiefly to pass over the rivers, creeks, and bays; and to transport goods and lumber from one river to another. Some are so large as to carry thirty barrels, tho' of one entire piece of timber. Others that are split down the bottom, and a piece added thereto, will carry eighty, or an hundred. Several have gone out our inlets on the ocean to Virginia, laden with pork, and other produce of the country. Of these trees curious boats for pleasure may be made, and other necessary craft.... This wood is very lasting, and free from the rot. A canoe of it will outlast four boats, and seldom wants repair.[27]

After the Shawnee were expelled from the Cumberland, the mid–Tennessee region became a Cherokee hunter's paradise. There was an abundance of all game including buffalo, deer, elk, bear, wolves, puma, and foxes. The large number of salt licks in the area helped to support the game. The hunters often traveled to the salt licks to await the animals as they gathered to partake. The Cherokee hunter would trade the pelts from these animals to the English for his goods. He, of course, would always get the worst of the trade. Often a prize pelt would earn him either a steel hatchet or knife, 30 bullets, 12 flints, and a small amount of red paint for him to paint his body in the Cherokee tradition. It took 35 deerskins for him to obtain a cheaply-manufactured musket (trade gun).[28]

In 1721, South Carolina governor Francis Nicholson invited the Cherokee to Charles Town to negotiate a trade agreement. He was concerned about continued trade with the French, and the Cherokee wanted to air their grievances about traders cheating with their weights and measures. Thirty-seven headmen met with Nicholson who promised them he would regulate the trade by selecting a British trade agent to work with all of the Cherokee towns. The governor also recommended that the Cherokee select a trade agent to be the point of contact with the British trade agent. Nicholson suggested the Cherokee select

Wrosetasatow to be the headman of the Cherokee Nation and to work with his selection, Colonel George Chicken. The Cherokee agreed. The British considered Wrosetasatow to be the first principal chief of the Cherokee Nation until 1735. However, the Cherokee considered him as nothing more than a trade commissioner.

Another article of the trade agreement was a cession of land from the Cherokee to South Carolina. The governor explained to the headmen that he only wanted a section of land that the Cherokee no longer used for a hunting ground. The headmen were convinced and ceded 32,000 acres that lay in an area bound on the west by the Edisto River headwaters and following that river to the coast (from 25 miles east of present-day Augusta, Georgia to 20 miles south of Charles Town). The eastern boundary followed the Saluda River and then the Santee River to the coast (from near present-day Columbia, South Carolina, to 10 miles south of today's Georgetown, South Carolina).

In 1725, Colonel Chicken made a tour through the Upper Towns and noted that many were forted up not only with palisades, but also ditches and rough forms of abatis. He was well-received by the Upper Towns, and he was perfectly accommodated by the headmen that promoted English trade. Chicken worked with traders Alexander Wiggan and Joseph Cooper to try and strengthen the Cherokee's confidence in the British confounding trade practices. Chicken was not entirely successful in controlling all English traders. At first, the adjustment seemed to go well. Traders moved into the villages, adapted to the Cherokee way of life, and attempted to trade fairly. Years later, John Stuart, an Indian Agent to the Cherokee, reported:

> An English trader who resided in Tannassee had a Dog which he valued much killed by an Indian. He went to the Town House and complained ... to the Beloved Man, who ordered him a pound of leather in the value of 2 Sterling as a compensation which he (the beloved man) deemed a sufficient price for any dog. The trader was far away from being satisfied and determined to show the injustice of the decision. The next day he loaded his horse with leather, took his gun and as he passed through the town began to kill every dog that was unlucky to fall in his way, saying "a pound of Leather." Amongst others the Beloved Man's dog fell victim to whom when he complained the trader offered a pound of Leather also putting him in mind of the preceding day's sentence. The Indians immediately entered the Trader's hut and altho' they were sorry for their faithful dogs They blamed the Beloved Man more than they did him for the loss of them.[29]

Authority of the headman was challenged by the trader in proper Cherokee fashion.

As the new trade agreement took effect, it caused little change to the tribe's lifestyle, and the Cherokee believed they were getting a fair swap. The demand for skins then skyrocketed in Europe, and put additional pressure on the colonial merchants to demand more skins from the Cherokee. That seemed promising for the Cherokee Nation because there was still a rivalry between South Carolina and Virginia for trade. The increased demand seemed to indicate more trade goods for the Cherokee. However, the traders reverted to cheating by altering the weights and measures used to determine what they owed the Cherokee hunters. The traders also speculated and convinced the Indians it was good to obtain trade goods in excess of their skins' value. They could just owe the traders and pay later when they had more skins. The Cherokee, the Creek, and other tribes ran up huge debts. That would cost them dearly in the future.

Game became scarce as the Cherokee increased the hunting for the many skins to trade to the Europeans. The English trade altered the cycles and the rhythms of Indian life.

The old traditional Cherokee balance of living began to disappear. The English demand for more deerskins helped to drive the point that guns would be more efficient than bows and arrows. The Cherokee style of hunting for food and clothing, and of paying spiritual respects to the slain game, became a merciless profitable endeavor to supply the colonies with skins in exchange for trade goods. English greed had rubbed off on those majestic natives.

Porcelain items acquired in trade were desired only to be broken and the pieces were used to string for necklaces. Iron pots were acquired and eventually replaced Cherokee pottery. English material prints were much brighter and more colorful than traditional Cherokee-dyed clothing. Iron tomahawks and knives acquired in trade held a better edge. The Cherokee gradually became more dependent upon trade goods to the detriment of their native arts. Only the practice of basket weaving was retained unaltered.

Neither side predicted the outcome of their trade arrangement. Europeans totally underestimated the intellect of the Cherokee. The English had no idea that the "savages akin to wild animals" could reason. On the other hand, the Cherokee miscalculated the white man's sense of fairness in diplomacy and trade. The Cherokee would have a rude awakening when they eventually understood the English greed for their land. The Cherokee had given up their position of strength, that of a continued alliance with the Creek and the Yamasee, similar to the Iroquois Confederacy of the north. They could have had a united front to impede English encroachment; the British would have had a second confederation of Indians to worry about which would have benefited the Iroquois, and the Cherokee would have had a strong trade alliance with the French, who were only interested in trade and not colonization of Cherokee land. (The Iroquois Confederacy included the Mohawk, Oneida, Onondaga, Cayuga, Seneca, and more recently the Tuscarora, who had been driven out of Carolina. That confederacy held its own against the British in the North; however, the Indians could have at least impeded the encroachment for a longer period of time had there been a strong Indian confederation in the south.)

Suddenly, the bottom dropped out of the European market for skins. The Cherokee were left holding the bag. They could no longer depend on trade competition between South Carolina and Virginia. Those colonies had turned to their own production for export to Europe, such as rice, tobacco, indigo, and other well-established plantation crops. The Cherokee had lost their traditional talents, but they could no longer rely upon the European trade goods. The only marketable skill the Cherokee retained was war, and that gave the Cherokee a profitable product—Indian slaves. This was not a good situation. The two sides would yet experience many difficulties but would, in the short term, overcome that setback. It would prove to be a mistake for the Cherokee to continue the British trade alliance; however, the headmen would lead them along that road and not look back at the problems they had already experienced—until a younger generation of leaders would come along. It would come too late.[30]

Chapter 3

European Contacts Become Complicated

Before the 1730s, the Cherokee practiced their admittedly-preferred activity of war very well. Most of the eastern tribes were only too happy to accommodate them. The British relied on that innate practice to benefit themselves. The English royal colonial governments actually armed and incited the Cherokee, as well as their neighboring tribes, to war with each other. The English colonists were heavily involved in the slave trade as they needed captive Indians for the West Indies.

In 1715, the Chickasaw united with the Cherokee to evict the Shawnee from Cherokee-claimed ancestral hunting grounds along the Cumberland River. In the same year, during the Yamasee War (see Chapter 2), the Cherokee were at first conjoined with the Yamasee against the South Carolinians. The colony's colonel Maurice Morris could not persuade the Cherokee to help fight the Yamasee, but he did convince them to quit their alliance and attack the Creek who were colluding with the Yamasee.

"[An] example of Europeans pitting Indians against one another occurred in 1715 ... some Cherokees from the lower towns ... [were persuaded to] wage war against the Creeks.... These Cherokees killed sixteen Creek ambassadors in the Tugaloo Townhouse ... Indian practice guaranteed ambassadors safe conduct ... war lasted until the 1750s."[1]

Then in 1718, the Cherokee pushed well into Creek country to attack Coweta, a major Creek village on the lower Chattahoochee River of Georgia. They discovered that traders from France, Spain, and England were in Coweta to develop trade affiliations with the Creek. That provided the Cherokee with a hint that the British were capable of double-dealing. However, trade with the English colonies proceeded to grow and would further strengthen during the 1730s to the 1750s.[2]

A new boon to the relationship occurred when a Scotsman visited the Cherokee country. Sir Alexander Cuming was the son of Alexander Cuming of Coulter who created his barony in 1695. Young Alexander practiced law in Scotland, but that profession did not accommodate his visionary lifestyle. In 1720, Alexander Cuming had suffered in the South Sea Company fiasco which, in today's vernacular, was a Ponzi scheme based on the company's stock. The stock was offered in 1719, absorbed the British National Debt; then, the management marketed the stock as a trading company in South America. Many members of the British hierarchy invested. The company loaned people money to buy the stock which they had to sell to make the payment; thus, the stock rose in demand. It quickly jumped from £100 per share to £1,000 per share. However, operating like a pyramid scheme, the stock dropped back to £100 per share by mid–1720. The company directors were scandalized; several were thrown into prison and their estates confiscated by the British treasury.

The company was reorganized and later passably operated in the slave trade and less well in the whale industry. "A resolution was proposed in parliament that bankers be tied up in sacks filled with snakes and tipped into the murky Thames."[3] By 1725, Cuming dreamed of improved fortunes with an American adventure. However, his vision was far from realistic. He claimed that "with proper management, the Cherokee country would pay the national debt of England in twenty years."[4]

Cuming had detailed his grand scheme by 1727 and is quoted: "The settlement of a college in Bermuda ... the native Indians being instructed and taught a veneration for the customs, manners and laws of our country, they would be the properest instruments to secure their countrymen to our interest against the French."[5]

Interestingly, there is no record of indigenous tribes in Bermuda. Regular shipments of Creek and Cherokee Indians would have been absurdly expensive. It is unlikely that Indians would have been inclined to participate.

When King George II ascended to the throne on June 11, 1727, Cuming appealed for an ambassadorship. Cuming's father apparently had once done the king a great favor; he possibly may have even saved his life. Sir Alexander tactfully reminded the king of his debt. In 1729, the king named Cuming the ambassador to the Cherokee Nation; however, King George II had no illusions and just wanted Cuming out of his way. Cuming's visit to America was likely kept confidential. There was no public discussion of it in Britain until he returned.

Cuming sailed from England for America on September 13, 1729, and arrived in Charles Town on the 5th of December. On March 11, 1730, he set out for Cherokee country as the self-indulgent British ambassador to the tribe—he took the King's assignment to be serious: "On the 13th day of March 1730 Old Stile [sic], Sir Alexander set out from one of the setlements [sic] in South Carolina in order to proceed to the Cherokee Mountains where he was received as their Lawgiver by their Emperor Moytoy of Teliquo, was saluted by his order with 13 Eagles Tails, had the Crown of their Nation & scalps of their Enemies given to him."[6]

Cuming stopped several times during his trek and enlarged his company. He eventually arrived at the vicinity of present-day Long Canes on March 21, 1730. He reached the Lower Cherokee village of Keeakwee (likely Keowee, near present-day Clemson, South Carolina), 300 miles from Charles Town, on the 23rd. He learned that each Cherokee town had a headman and a head warrior. He also found that the Lower Creek were making trade alliances with the French and that the French had asked the Creek to enlist the Cherokee.

Cuming heard that a large gathering of headmen would soon take place in the Council House. When he learned they would consider the Creek overture, he quickly acted. Once the session had begun, Cuming forced his way in. He was fully armed with guns and a saber (weapons were prohibited from the Cherokee Council Houses), and a white Indian trader tried to disarm him. Cuming pushed past and told the 300 gathered of the great British king, and he uttered veiled threats. He had all the chiefs kneel and declare allegiance to King George II. He then demanded that they submit to his authority which, surprisingly, they did without question (the Cherokee, by tradition, jealously guarded their freedoms). Cuming ordered them to send messengers throughout the Cherokee Nation and demand that all headmen attend a council session with him at Nequassee on April 3, 1730.

Sir Alexander's interpreter, William (sometimes said to be Joseph) Cooper, later stated that if he had ... "known beforehand what Sir Alexander would have order'd him to have said, he would not have ventured into the Town House."⁷ Cuming forced all of the traders present to authenticate what had transpired with their signatures. Trader Ludovic Grant later wrote, "This strange speech, which I and the other Traders heard him make did not give … a very favourable impression."⁸

On the 24th, Cuming went to Oconeeon (likely Oconee), 12 miles away. There he observed a solemn event in the Council House that was being repeated in all villages. Wrosetasatow, who had been declared "emperor," a new position, by Governor Francis Nicholson in 1721, had died in 1729. Previously the headman of Chota acted as the headman of the collective villages. Wrosetasatow was really no more than a trade commissioner. Each village was then in a session to determine how to replace Wrosetasatow for the collective.

On the afternoon of March 29, Cuming arrived at Tellico and met Chief Amadohiyi (also Ama-edohi, Trader Tom, or Moytoy II), the Water Conjuror of Tellico. He was the son of a local chief called Ahmahtoya (also the Elder or Moytoy I) and his wife Lokacholakatha (or The Pride of the Shawnee). Moytoy talked long and told Cuming that the talk within the village of Tellico was to make him, Moytoy, the "emperor" (as had been the case with Wrosetasatow, the title would amount to no more than a trade point-of-contact for the British). Moytoy further stated that the will of Cuming should now be done as the Cherokee had accepted the king of England as their sovereign.

(Some historians refer to Amadohiyi, "Emperor" Moytoy as Moytoy I and his son, Savanah [sic] Tom as Moytoy II, omitting Ahmahtoya, Moytoy I, the Elder. In this book I have noted Ahmahtoya, the Elder, as Moytoy I; Amadohiyi, Trader Tom, as Moytoy II; and Savanah Tom, the Raven of Tellico, as Moytoy III. Many historians are in agreement with this identification. Other numerical Moytoy followed who are not significant to the story.)

When Cuming heard of the Crown of Tanasi, which was basically a wig of red-dyed female opossum tails, he expressed a desire for it. He promised Moytoy his support for being named emperor if the chief would present the Crown of Tanasi to him. On the 30th, Moytoy and Jacob the Conjuror did present the Crown.

On April 1, 1730, Cuming and Moytoy traveled to Tassetehee. The Indians of Tassetehee agreed to what Moytoy had done with regard to the Crown of Tanasi when he then declared it a symbol of universal authority over the Cherokee Nation. The people in each village that Cuming visited were greatly impressed with his bearing. That was important because the Cherokee people were ready to depose any of the village headmen that were pro–English and replace them with those who would back trade agreements with the French.

On the morning of April 3, they arrived at Nequassee (near present-day Franklin, North Carolina) with a greatly-increased entourage. Here the people gathered from all villages led by the local headmen as Cuming had ordered. It was a most solemn day in keeping with Cherokee tradition for such important occasions. The headmen met in the Council House with Sir Alexander Cuming where he and several selected village headmen gave speeches to promote Moytoy as the new emperor. After Moytoy was confirmed by a vote of the headmen, the council made a declaration that the gifts they had provided (the Crown of Tanasi, several eagles' tails, scalps of their enemies) were to be tokens to show they accepted King George's sovereignty over their nation. Sir Alexander Cuming repeated the requirement made at Keowee in which all headmen present at Nequassee that day should kneel and profess to recognize Cuming's authority as the king's sole representative. The headmen placed Cuming in Moytoy's seat and performed the Eagle Tail dance for him. The dancers actually stroked his head and body with tail feathers, something which would only have been done as an honorific.

> They repaired to their capital ... a few miles above the mouth of Tellico, on the Little Tennessee River, where a symbol, made of five eagle tails and four scalps of their enemies, which Sir Alexander called the crown of the nation, was brought forth, and he was requested to lay it at the feet of his sovereign on his return.[9]

Cuming, himself, wrote:

> This was a Day of Solemnity the greatest that ever was seen in the Country; there was Singing, Dancing, Feasting, making of Speeches, the Creation of Moytoy Emperor, with the unanimous consent of all the headmen assembled from the different Towns in the Nation, a Declaration of their resigning their Crowns, Eagles, Tails, Scalps of their Enemies, as an Emblem of their all owning his Majesty King George's Sovereignty over them, at the Desire of Sir Alexander Cuming, in whom, an absolute unlimited Power was placed.[10]

Cuming was a model of narcissism and always referred to himself in the third person.[11]

On April 6, Cuming was taken to Ookunny (likely Oconee) where the Cherokee had prepared a house for him. The headman of Ookunny was called Mankiller. The king of Keowee and the prince of Tomassee visited Sir Alexander and presented him with two eagle tails. They knelt and paid homage to King George II.

Then Cuming and six chiefs (or Cherokee headmen) that traveled with him set out for Keowee, the last town of the Lower Villages. These six chiefs were to accompany Cuming to England. He and an aide named Hunter reached a Mr. Kinloch's place with them on April 19, 1730. This was 23 miles from Charles Town. There they were approached by the warrior Ounakannowie, who desired to accompany them. Sir Alexander consented, but he declined to allow Ounakannowie's traveling companions, thus limiting the Cherokee contingent to seven travelers to meet King George II. Those seven Cherokee leaders were Ouka-Ulah (which in itself is a term for headman, so he was likely a local headman in the Upper Villages), Oukaneka (White Owl), later to become Ada-Gal-kala (Attakullakulla or Leaning Stick; also called Little Carpenter by the white men), Kittagusta (or Ketagusta; also called Prince SkaliLosken), Tathtiowie, Clogittah, Collanah, and Ounakannowie. Trader Alexander (sometimes Aleazar) Wiggan went along as interpreter. (Collanah is a Cherokee word for Raven, so this traveler may have been Savannah Tom [Raven of Tellico], or the Raven of Hiwassee, both sons of Trader Tom ["Emperor" Moytoy]. Since the traveler was described as a great warrior, Albert V. Goodpasture and others have suggested he was Oconostota.)

Attakullakulla had this to say about his selection to the team of travelers:

> At night Mr. Wiggan the Interpreter came to the house where I was, and told me that the Warrior [Alexander Cuming] had a particular favour for me, and that if I would consent to go he would be indifferent whither any other Went; ... he assured me ... that I might be back by the end of the Summer or at least some time in the Fall, Upon which assurance I agreed to go; Early next morning One of our people came to me ... He then told me.... That I should not go alone, for that he would accompany me and he knew of Two or three more that he could persuade to go ... making in all Six and we Immediately got ready & soon set off.[12]

(Attakullakulla would gain much prestige from this trip. Then known as Oukaneka, the London press referred to him as Captain Owean Nakan. Mispronunciation of Cherokee

Seven Chiefs in London, 1730, by Isaac Basire—left to right: Ounaconoa, Prince Skaliloskin, Kollanna, Oukah Ulah, Tathtowe, Clogoittah, Ukwaneequa (White Owl or Attakullakulla).

names was common by whites in the 18th century. He had likely been born between 1700 and 1712 on the Big Island of the French Broad River [later called Sevier's Island]. He had a dual relationship of nephew and grandnephew with another future famous headman called Conne-Corte [Old Hop].)

Sir Alexander Cuming and the chiefs arrived at Charles Town on April 13, 1730, and boarded the man-of-war *Fox* on the 4th of May. Moytoy would have accompanied them but declined because his wife was ill. The *Fox,* commanded by Captain Thomas Arnold, sailed in company with the *Garland,* commanded by Captain George Anson (later Lord Anson), and they arrived at Dover June 5 after a quick voyage of one month and a day.

The seven Cherokee were not treated royally in their visitor role. They were first accommodated in rooms above the Mermaid Tavern in downtown London and then moved to the basement of a parlor belonging to an undertaker named Arne who charged a fee for the public to peek in the basement window at the Indians. They were a curiosity and were carefully scrutinized by the English as if in a zoo. They dressed in their native wardrobe of breechclout and colorful body paint as they wandered through London's St. James' Park. They were provided fine British clothing to wear to become more presentable during official visits. They were also taken to visit the Tower of London and to view street plays (of which they were quite bored).

In the meantime, Cuming contacted the Secretary of State who, in turn, arranged an audience with King George II. The king ordered Sir Alexander and the Indians to be present to witness an installation appointed to take place on June 18, 1730. On the 22nd, Sir Alexander and the chiefs were introduced to his majesty. The visitors all knelt, and Cuming in presence of the court avowed the full power he had received from the Cherokee. Cuming laid the Crown of Tanasi before the king along with the five eagles' tails, and four scalps of Cherokee enemies. These were presented as acknowledgments of his majesty's sovereignty, which the king graciously accepted. Cuming wrote of the two visits in his memoirs:

> That upon the 18th day of June 1730 Sir Alexander had the Honour of being introduced to His Majesty King George the Second with Seven Cherokee Warriors by His Majesty's express directions in St. George Chapel at Windsor when the late earl of Burlington was installed, when the present Earl of Chesterfield was installed, and when His Royal Highness the Duke of Cumberland was installed, and when the Heir apparent to the Crown Frederick then Prince of Wales first took his seat as one of the Knights of the Garter, the Savage Chiefs that dwelt in the Wilderness bowed down before His Majesty on that occasion as Subjects to the Crown of Great Britain and as a remarkable Token of the Almighty Favour....
>
> On the 22nd day of June 1730 Sir Alexander Cuming had an Audience of His Majesty in Windsor Castle being attended by the seven Cherokee Warriors which he had brought over to England as witnesses of the Power conferred upon him on the 3rd day of April 1730 O.S. [meaning Old Style or Julian Calendar] at a place called Nequisee in the Cherokee Mountains and in virtue of the unlimited Power given him by the Cherokee Nation as their Lawgiver Sir Alexander laid the Crown of the Cherokee Nation at his Majestys [sic] feet as a token of their Homage and Submission [to] His Majesty as Subjects to the Crown of Great Britain, their Eagles Tails at His Majestys feet as Emblems [of] Glory and Victory, and four Scalps of their Indian Enemies at his Majestys [sic] feet to shew that in their state of savage Liberty they were an over match for any one nation of their Indian Enemies and under the conduct of a proper Leader might probably be an over match for many more.[13]

On September 7, 1730, the British presented Articles of Friendship and Commerce to the Cherokee. The Cherokee names were added to the paper based on an oratory of Oukah-Ulah as translated by Wiggan. Attakullakulla later stated, "Tho I was the first person who had agreed to go ... yet as I was the youngest ... it would not be right that I should be the Speaker, and therefore Oukayuda was appointed." The chiefs answered the British presentation on September 9, orated by Ouka-Ulah and, as before, translated by Alexander Wiggan.

> Articles of Friendship and Commerce, prepared by the Lord Commissioners for Trade and Plantations, to the Deputies of the Cherokee Nation in South Carolina by His Majesty's Order, on Monday the 7th Day of September 1730. Whereas you Scayagusta Oukah, Chief of the town of Tassetsa;—you Scali Cosken, Ketagusta;—you Tethtowe;—you Clogoittah;—you Colannah;—you Oucounacou;—have been deputed by Moytoy of Telliko, with the Consent and approbation of the whole Nation of the Cherokee Indians, at a general meeting at Nikossen 3rd of April, 1730, to attend Sir Alexander Cuming, Bart. [abbreviation for baronet] to Great Britain, where you have seen the Great King George, at whose feet the said Sr. Alexander Cuming, by express Authority for that Purpose from the said Moytoy and all the Cherokee People, has laid the Crown of your Nation, with the Scalps of your Enemies and Feathers of Glory, at His Majesty's feet, in Token of your Obedience.
>
> Now the King of Great Britain, bearing love in his heart to the powerful and Great Nation of the Cherokee Indians, his good Children and Subjects, His Majesty has empowered us to treat with you here and accordingly we now speak to you as if the whole Nation of Cherokees, their Old Men, Young Men, Wives and Children were all present; and you are to understand the words of the Great King our Master whom you have seen; And we shall understand the words which you speak to us as the words of all your People with open and true Hearts to the Great King; And thereupon we give—Four pieces of striped Duffles [a coarse woolen cloth having a thick nap, used for coats, blankets].
>
> Hear then the Words of the Great King whom you have seen, and who has commanded

us to tell you, That the English everywhere on all Sides of the great Mountains and Lakes are His people and His children whom He loves; Their friends are His friends, and Their enemies are His enemies; He takes it kindly that the great Nation of Cherokees have sent you hither a great way, to brighten the chain of friendship between Him and Them; and between Your People and His People; That the Chain of Friendship between Him and the Cherokee Indians is like the Sun, which both shines here and also upon the great mountains where they live & equally warms the hearts of the Indians and of the English; as there are no Spots or Blackness in the Sun, so is there not any Rust or Foulness in this Chain; and as the Great King has fastened one end of it to His own Breast, He desires You will carry the other end of the chain and fasten it well to the Breast of Moytoy of Telliko, and to the Breasts of your old wise Men, your Capts. and all your People, never more to be broken or made loose; and hereupon we give—two pieces of Blue Cloth.

The Great King and the Cherokee Indians being thus fastened together by the Chain of Friendship, He has ordered His people and children the English in Carolina, to trade with the Indians and to furnish Them with all manner of Goods that They want, and to make haste to build Houses, and to plant Corn from Charles Town towards the Town of the Cherokees, behind the great Mountains, for He desires that the Indians and the English may live together as the Children of one Family, whereas the Great King is a kind and loving Father; and as the King has given His Land on both sides of the great Mountains to His own Children the English, so He now gives to the Cherokee Indians the Privilege of living where They please; and hereupon we give—one piece of Red Cloth.

The great Nation of the Cherokees being now the Children of the Great King of Great Britain, and He their Father, the Cherokees must treat the English as Brethren of the same Family, and must be always ready, at the Governor's command, to fight against any Nation, whether they be White Men or Indians, who shall dare to molest or hurt the English; and hereupon we give—Twenty Guns.

The Nation of Cherokees shall on their part take care to keep the Trading Path clean, and that there be no Blood in the Path where the English white men tread, even tho' they should be accompanyd by any other People with whom the Cherokees are at war; Whereupon we give—Four Hundred Pounds Weight of Gunpowder.

That the Cherokees shall not suffer their People to trade with the White Men of any other Nation but the English, nor permit White Men of any other Nation to build any Forts, Cabins, or plant Corn amongst them, or near to any of the Indian Towns, or upon the Lands w'ch belong to the Great King; and if any such Attempt shall be made you must acquaint the English Governor therewith and do whatever he directs, in order to maintain and defend the Great King's Right to the Country of Carolina; Whereupon we give—Five Hundred Pounds Weight of Swan Shott and Five Hundred Pounds Weight of Bullets.

That if any Negroe Slaves shall run away into the Woods from their English Masters, the Cherokee Indians shall endeavor to apprehend them, and either bring them back to the Plantation from whence they run away, or to the Governor, and for every Negroe so apprehended and brought back, the Indian who brings him shall receive a Gun and a Match Coat; Whereupon we give—A Box of Vermillion, Ten Thousand Gun Flints and Six Dozen of Hatchets.

That if by any accidental misfortune it should happen that an English Man should kill an Indian, the King or Great Man of the Cherokees shall first complain to the English Governor, and the Man who did it shall be punished by the English Laws as if he had killed an English Man, and in like manner if an Indian kills an English Man, the Indian who did it, shall be delivered up to the Governor, and be punished by the same English Law, as if he was an English Man; Whereupon we give—Twelve Dozen of Spring Knives, Four Dozen of Brass Kettles and Ten Dozen of Belts.

You are to understand all that we have now said to be the Words of the Great King, whom you have seen, and as a Token that His heart is open and true to His Children and Subjects the Cherokees and to all Their People, He gives His hand in this Belt, which He desires may be kept and shewn to all your People, and to their Children, and Children's Children, to confirm what is now spoken, and to bind this Agreement of Peace and Friendship betwixt the English and the Cherokees, as long as the Mountains and Rivers shall last, or the Sun Shine; Whereupon we give—This Belt of Wampum.[14]

Answer of the Indian Chiefs of the Cherokee Nation, 9th day of September, 1730, to the Propositions made to them in behalf of His Majesty by the Board of Trade, on the 7th of the Same Month. We are come hither from a dark Mountainous Place, where nothing but darkness is to be found; but are now in a place where there is light. There was a person in our Country with us, he gave us a Yellow Token of Warlike Honour, that is left with Moytoy of Telliko; and as Warriors, we received it; He came to us like a Warrior from you, a Man he was, his talk was upright, and the token he left preserves his Memory amongst us.

We look upon you as if the Great King George was present; and we love you, as representing the Great King, and shall Dye in the same way of thinking.

The Crown of Our Nation is different from that which the Great King George wears, and from that which we saw in the Tower; But to us it is all one, and the Chain of Friendship shall be carried to our People.

We look upon the Great King George as the Sun, and as our Father, and upon Ourselves as his Children; For tho' we are red and you white, yet Our Hands and Hearts are join'd together.

When we shall have acquainted our People with what we have seen, our Children from Generation to Generation will always remember it.

In War we shall always be as one with you; the Great King George's Enemies shall be Our Enemies; His People and Ours shall be always one, and dye together.

We came hither naked and poor, as the Worm out of the earth, but you have everything; and We that have nothing must love you, and can never break the Chain of Friendship that is between Us.

Here stands the Governor of Carolina whom We know; this small rope which we shew you, is all we have to bind our slaves with, and may be broken; but you have Iron Chains for yours; However, if we catch your slaves, we shall bind them as well as we can, and deliver them to our friends again, and have no pay for it.

We have looked round for the Person that was in Our Country, he is not here, however We must say, that he talked uprightly to us, and we shall never forget him.

Your white People may very safely build Houses near us, we shall hurt nothing that belongs to them, for we are the Children of one Father the Great King, and shall live and Dye together."

Then laying down his feathers upon the table, he added, "This is our way of Talking, which is the same to us, as your letters in the Book are to you; and to you, beloved Men, we deliver these Feathers, in confirmation of all we have said, and of Our Agreement to your Articles."[15]

Basically, the Cherokee acknowledged the sovereignty of Britain, pledged to have neither trade nor military alliance with any other nation, to not allow white people other than British traders to settle among them, and to return any slaves that might try to seek refuge among them. They also gifted the Crown of Tanasi, the five eagle tails and four scalps of their enemies to the king. In return, the British promised to give them a generous supply of guns, ammunition, and red paint. It amounted to the Cherokee pledging to be an ally against British enemies; however, there was not a reciprocal agreement on the part of the British. The British always seemed to "buy" an alliance or a tract of land without promising any assistance in return for Cherokee support. In this case, the Cherokee alliance was bought for 20 guns, 400 pounds of gunpowder, 10,000 flints, 72 hatchets, vermillion paint, 144 steel knives, 48 brass kettles, 120 belts, and a belt of wampum. The Cherokee agreed to fight for England when needed, keep the trading paths open for the British, and only the British, return any runaway slaves to the colony, deliver up any Cherokee that kills an Englishman, and keep peace with Britain forever. The British tended to think that establishing trade with Indians meant buying loyalty without regard to earning trust. The colonists seemed to think of the Cherokee as having limited political savvy due to their illiteracy (which was misinterpreted as stupidity) when in reality the Cherokee understood the principles of reciprocity very well. The Cherokee could not comprehend that the English did not operate with the same understanding, while the English did not operate that way because they did not realize the Cherokee were their political equals. So, the British decided they could easily "pay" the tribes by "allowing" them to trade with such accomplished and experienced men of the world.

There were some peculiarities with the Cherokee agreement. Supposedly Ouka-Ulah had said "We look upon the Great King George as the Sun, and as our Father, and upon Ourselves as his Children; For tho' we are red and you white, yet Our Hands and Hearts are join'd together."

However, historian Robert J. Conley points out that the Cherokee considered the Sun to be feminine so would not liken it to a father. It is also unlikely that Ouka-Ulah would have described his skin as red. The Cherokee may have been illiterate but were not stupid. They knew their skin was brown, although, the Cherokee had, at times, described themselves as "red men." That was adapted from the white men who were in awe of the red-painted bodies of Cherokee at war. Attakullakulla had many times in later years referred to the Cherokee as "red men."[16]

Regardless, after Ouka-Ulah's oration, and when they were alone, the chiefs demanded that the interpreter, trader Alexander Wiggan, give them an exact translation of the articles and their response. Wiggan truthfully answered that they had agreed to give King George II the rights to all of Carolina. They held a council and some suggested that Wiggan and Ouka-Ulah should be killed at once. However, they considered that since the Cherokee people had not provided the two with authority to sell or trade the land, then no harm had been done.

The chiefs signed the alliance on September 23, 1730, and left London on the *Fox* on the 2nd of October. Cherokee ambassador Sir Alexander Cuming petitioned the king to make him the official overlord to the Cherokee; however, the king refused. Cuming thought he had proven his capabilities, but the king seemed to look upon Cuming's endeavors as an encumbrance and wanted him out of the way. Sir Alexander Cuming was retained in London and faced charges brought against him by the elite colonists of Charles Town. This had nothing to do with his and the chiefs' visit to England. In 1736, Cuming was thrown into debtors' prison in England. He was later commissioned a captain and assigned to Jamaica where he died in 1775.

At Chota, the Cherokee people intently quizzed the seven about the London trip, especially regarding the alliance. That was when Oukaneka (White Owl) became Adagalkala (Attakullakulla or Leaning Stick) and was declared the peace chief (or White Headman) of Tellico. He gained much prestige among the Cherokee from his visit to England, and he extended his influence as he promoted peace and trade treaties with the British for decades. He realized his position was unique and no other Cherokee could deal with the British as he could. He also knew that the strength of his position depended upon the continuations of good British relationships. If they were, his influence was at a high.

Oconostota was not so impressed with the British; in fact, the great warrior leaned toward alliances with the French. Historian Albert V. Goodpasture made interesting comparisons between the two Cherokee leaders: "Attakullakulla perceived with appalling force the defenselessness of his own people as against such an adversary. It became the ruling purpose of his life, chimerical as it was, to keep his nation at peace with the English."[17]

Oconostota was Attakullakulla's father-in-law as well as his first cousin once removed. Politically, the two men were polar opposites. The colonial authorities relied heavily on Attakullakulla's enrapt state regarding the British empire, and continually expanded his authority, in order to undercut Oconostota who was more antagonistic toward the English.

About Attakullakulla, it was written:

> For fifty years he stood out between the contending races, a sublime and, often, a solitary figure, ever pleading, conciliating, pacifying. He was the grandest and most amiable leader developed by his race; and I doubt whether a nobler character, of any race, could have been found on the border ... small, and of slender and delicate frame; but he was endowed with superior abilities. He did little to distinguish himself in war, but his policy and address were such as to win for him the confidence and admiration of his people. He was the leading diplomat of his nation, and conducted some of the most delicate missions with singular tact and sagacity.[18]

Oconostota was more of a warrior: daring, resourceful, and a great general:

> It is said that in all his expeditions his measures were so prudently taken that he never lost a man. Under his leadership the Cherokees reached their highest martial glory. Less diplomatic than Attakullakulla, he was more bold and aggressive, and, at first, hoped by forcible resistance to stay the flood of immigration that was threatening to overwhelm his country.[19]

Regardless, Attakullakulla had an uncanny ability to develop treaty negotiations. While he became a peace chief immediately after the trip to England, he would later become the Cherokee Nation's principal chief (First Beloved Man), from 1762 to 1778. Oconostota would be war (Red) chief while Attakullakulla was Peace Chief and immediately would succeed Attakullakulla as the nation's principal chief, from 1778 to 1785.[20]

In 1736, the French, garrisoned at Fort Toulouse on the Coosa River in Alabama, made serious overtures to the Cherokee regarding a trade alliance. Attakullakulla knew very well he would lose prestige if the Cherokee Nation responded positively to the French. He was worried about his influence; however, he sincerely believed it to be in the best interests of the Cherokee people to continue and promote trade agreements with the English. Attakullakulla became impressed with the British royalty and military when he visited London.

The French continually pointed out that the Choctaw and the Creek were better fed, dressed, and armed than were the Cherokee. This put pressure on Attakullakulla to be convincing. In a council session in 1736, he admonished the other headmen to resist French overtures in favor of Britain. He had competition in this regard from Oconostota who would respond that the French would improve the lot of the Cherokee people.

A man named Christian Gottlieb Priber confused the situation among the Cherokee. He is often described as a Frenchman, but he was really a German with French connections. Priber visited the Cherokee Nation in 1736, described himself as a Jesuit priest, and began to dress and act as a Cherokee. He trimmed his hair to resemble the Cherokee and painted himself accordingly. The Cherokee became quite fond of him, and he won several of them over to the French cause.

Priber solidified his new-found influence over the Cherokee when he married a Cherokee woman named Clogoitah, who was sister to a war chief named Willenawah (Tifftoya, the Great Eagle of Tanasi). Willenawah was a brother to Attakullakulla, each being a son of Savanah Tom (Moytoy III, the Raven of Tellico). Willenawah was the father of a war chief named Doublehead whose prominence will be addressed in later chapters. Christian Priber had a daughter named Creat (with variations) who married Doublehead, her first cousin. He had another daughter, named Susan, who married Doublehead's brother, Red Bird Carpenter (also known as Red Bird I, Aaron Brock, and Tsisquaya). (The author's ancestral relationships with Priber, Willenawah, Doublehead, and Trader Tom are explained in Appendix A.)

Christian Gottlieb Priber had some elaborate plans for liberating the Cherokee Nation from any British alliances or influences. He taught the Cherokee that the British kept encroaching and cheating the nation out of its own land. He explained to the people they would be much better off having trade alliances with France, which would not try to physically take over prime Cherokee land. Priber's philosophy fit right in with that of Oconostota who became an avid Priber ally and active promoter of Priber's ideas. Priber announced to the nation that he was "His Majesty's Principal Secretary of State" to the Cherokee, and he avowed that "Emperor" Amadohiyi, Moytoy II, had given him that title. Moytoy apparently did nothing to discourage the idea, likely because Priber had gained the hearts of many Cherokee making Amadohiyi's support important to his political future.

Priber began to set up the Cherokee Nation in the form of a socialistic government. All Cherokee were to have equal rights (which they believed by tradition, anyway). All Cherokee goods were to be held in common and meted out as needed. Cherokee children would be wards of the state, and each Cherokee was to work for the common good of the nation. Printed matter and writing materials were to be the only privately-held property (which would do the Cherokee no good since they were still illiterate at the time). Christian Priber envisioned a city of refuge in the Cherokee Upper Towns for criminals, debtors, and slaves willing to leave South Carolina.

Interestingly, the Cherokee had lived by similar traditional philosophies for many years, though not as organized and strict. They already had a customary plan to assist the needy with community donations from the as required rather than to maintain a central storehouse (see Chapter 1). In early 1739, South Carolina offered the commissioner, Colonel Joseph Fox, £400 to search the Upper Towns and arrest Priber. However, Priber was protected by the warriors, so Fox was escorted out of the Cherokee villages.

On May 30, 1743, the *South Carolina Gazette* reported that the British commander, Captain Kent, at Fort Augusta, had learned that Priber was not only in the area, but was also about to take a journey to meet with French officers at Fort Toulouse. Kent employed Creek warriors to intercept him at Tallipoose Village in Georgia. Priber was captured and taken, with all his manuscripts and under heavy Indian guard, to Frederica, Georgia, to await General James Edward Oglethorpe's return from his expedition against the Spanish at St. Augustine. Oglethorpe jailed Priber at Fort Frederica (present-day St. Simons Island) where he reportedly died between 1744 and 1753.[21]

The Cherokee blamed the extensive smallpox epidemic of 1738–1739 on the British colonies. They were right to blame the English as the originators of the problem. Trader and historian James Adair wrote: "About the year 1738, the Cheerake received a most depopulating shock, by the small pox, which reduced them almost one half, in about a year's time: it was conveyed into Charles-town by the Guinea-men [slave ships], and soon after among them, by the infected goods."[22]

However, Priber had convinced the Cherokee that English traders were planting smallpox in the trade goods. That was good propaganda but a ridiculous charge. Yet, that some unlicensed traders bore the disease into the backcountry seemed, to the Cherokee, to be corroboration. Conversely, the British traders and colonial commerce managers were under a lot of pressure to obtain huge numbers of deerskins to meet the demand in Europe. They would likely make a lot of money, especially with their abhorrent trading practices of cheating the Indians. It was not logical for the traders to intentionally introduce smallpox to the Cherokee, the only source for obtaining the number of skins they required. However, Priber used that rumor to continue to promote the French as a trading partner for the Cherokee. The outbreak is said to have cost the Cherokee Nation as many as one-half of its inhabitants. Hundreds of once-proud warriors bore frightful scars, became disheartened, and committed suicide.

Oconostota contracted the disease in this outbreak and bore scars from it for the rest of his life. He had never really been a promoter of the British, but his belief that the traders intentionally exposed him to the horrible disease made him downright hostile. Intentional or not, one cannot blame the Cherokee for their ill will regarding the British as the source of contamination. Attakullakulla's own son, Dragging Canoe (Tsiyagunsini), also contracted the disease during that outbreak when he was about eight years old. He would also later become a profound leader of defiant younger chiefs, as would his cousin, Doublehead.

"In the year 1733, when Gen. Oglethorp [sic] brought his colony there [Georgia], he was received by the Lower Creeks, then consisting of eight tribes or clans.... These welcomed the English, and gave them all the land in their country except what they, themselves used. This was the usual custom of the Indians everywhere." However, it goes on to say, "Territory was often, if not generally, acquired by one tribe dispossessing another."[23]

Such expulsion of a tribe mostly occurred when hunting grounds, or other ancestral land, overlapped and infringed upon one another. Usually, Indian tribal boundaries were set by the strongest tribe or by peace treaty between two combatant tribes. Frequently the boundaries were naturally defined: "Rivers, mountains, &c., became boundaries, because they were natural defences."

The Iroquois had frequently raided Cherokee country throughout the 1730s and '40s. Attakullakulla led several war parties to the north. During one of these raids in 1740, he was captured by the Ottawa, who turned him over to the French. When the French found out who he was, they wished to win his favor, so they treated him like a diplomat. They allowed him to return home in 1748. The years Attakullakulla spent with the French were not wasted. While he feigned an interest in learning details of possible trade agreements, he was gaining knowledge for propaganda to use with the Cherokee people.

In 1740, the Cherokee developed a military alliance with Georgia and sent 1,000 warriors, led by the Raven (likely Raven of Tellico, Savanah Tom, Moytoy III), to assist the colony in a war with the Spaniards of Florida. The Cherokee then developed a trail along the Georgia side of the Savannah River that allowed Augusta, Georgia, traders to access the Cherokee villages.

At that time, the Cherokee no longer hunted to provide food and clothing. They only hunted for trade goods. Settlers that hunted on Cherokee land were not the primary cause of the vanishing game. The crucial problem was that each year traders demanded more and more skins for their merchandise. The old Cherokee tradition of "balance of life" had been unalterably disturbed. No longer did the Cherokee hunter ask permission of the deer for his pelt. No longer did he apologize to his quarry after the kill. The trade had demanded 54,000 deer skins per year from 1700 to 1715; 160,000 per annum by 1748, and eventually 1,500,000 by 1760. Regardless of the trade effect, the Cherokee were aware of increase of white hunters in Cherokee land.

"Emperor" Amadohiyi (Moytoy II, Trader Tom) died in 1741. One of his sons, 13-year-old Ammouskossittee (Moytoy V), was the new "emperor," declared by the British. The Cherokee people, however, ignored him. The true first beloved man, or principal chief, in their minds was Ammouskossittee's uncle Conne-Corte (Guhnagadoga, or Old Hop—so called because when he walked he displayed a limp, or hitch, related to an old injury). Old Hop was "Emperor" Amadohiyi's brother and the headman of Chota. That, in itself, carried more weight with the Cherokee people since they had always relied on whomever was the Chota headman to council the entire nation on desperate matters.

Attakullakulla, while still pro–British, realized that South Carolina traders were cheating the Cherokee with mislabeled weights and length measures when trading for Cherokee deer skins and the like. He believed that South Carolina governor James Glen should focus on correcting the illegitimate trade practices. Attakullakulla was also a primary advisor to his granduncle, Old Hop, who was displeased that the British had ignored him when they selected Ammouskossittee for their trade emperor.

Attakullakulla traveled north to visit an old enemy, the Shawnee. He returned with much propaganda and told the headmen that Governor Glen was trying to ally with the Iroquois, Catawba, and the Creek. He was not trying to improve the chances for French trade, but he did think the British traders from Virginia might be an acceptable solution. He worked to advise Old Hop to explore more trade with Virginia and less with South Carolina.

Trader Robert Goudey, who owned and operated a backcountry trading post in Ninety Six, South Carolina, warned Governor Glen of the movement. (Ninety Six was prominent as it was thought to be about halfway between Charles Town and Keowee, the first of the Cherokee Lower Towns.)

Some Cherokee war chiefs were upset that the South Carolina traders treated the Cherokee people poorly, so they launched attacks on backcountry South Carolina settlements. Governor Glen did not realize that his next move would fit right in with Attakullakulla's plan. Glen thought he would punish the Cherokee with a trade embargo. Attakullakulla knew he could use that to press Old Hop and the other headmen to strongly consider trade with Virginia.

It did not go quite as Attakullakulla had envisioned. He had split the Cherokee Nation. He and Old Hop wanted to advance trade agreements with Virginia. Ammouskossittee (who had been reduced in practice to being just the headman of Tellico) led a coalition to negotiate trade with Governor Glen, while Oconostota and others still tried to sway the Cherokee Nation toward the French.

The Cherokee Nation was autonomous, and each town could negotiate whatever agreements it wanted. The principal chief could only speak for the entire nation when the headmen of the villages allowed it. They, in turn, only made such allowances if they were backed by the people of their towns.

Several towns followed Ammouskossittee and joined in peace talks with Governor Glen. One of the requirements the governor placed on the Cherokee was that Attakullakulla be turned over for punishment. Of course, that did not fit in with Cherokee traditions either. Attakullakulla would have been defended by his clan, a clan right. Headmen had no authority to turn any Cherokee over to anybody.

While the negotiations continued in South Carolina, Attakullakulla left Chota in June 1751 and headed for Williamsburg, Virginia. When Attakullakulla arrived at Williamsburg in August, he told the Virginia Council that South Carolina had defaulted on the treaty that he had signed with King George II in 1730. That trip gave Oconostota some propaganda of his own. In 1748, Dr. Thomas Walker had led a group of Virginia hunters and woodsmen over the mountains to the headwaters of the Cumberland River. He ranged to the Kentucky River in his exploration of the Cherokee's ancestral hunting grounds. Oconostota had considered that to be the ultimate intrusion and, as such, it played well into his political position of ousting the British. Governor Glen had heard of Attakullakulla's travel and wrote to the Virginia legislature to convince them, with lies and exaggerations, that Attakullakulla was a troublemaker and advocated alliances with the French. Virginia was, therefore, reluctant to agree to any terms with Attakullakulla that would interfere with South Carolina's dealings with the Cherokee.

Additionally, traders had relocated from the Lower Towns of South Carolina and settled in the Middle Towns of North Carolina and the Upper Towns of present-day Tennessee. That influx magnified the anti–British feelings among Oconostota and his followers. On May 3, 1752, trader Ludovic Grant wrote to Governor James Glen regarding fellow trader Daniel Murphy of the Augusta Company:

> Mr. Brown, one of the Augusta Company, came to this Nation this spring in Pursuit of one Daniel Murphy who had before his Arrival run out of Canutry, a Town where the said Murphy had formerly lived, and designed to settle with his Slaves, Horses and Leather which he had taken at the New Settlement which I mentioned in my former Letter called Aulola, or in the lower Tongue, Aurora, and to supply that Place with Goods from Virginia. Mr. Brown finding he was gone with six Men pursued him to the said Settlements, but being informed he was gone to Virginia for Goods for the Leather he carried with him, endeavoured to get the Slaves, but the Indians said it was like stealing and would not let him have them till Murphy should return Home, and then it was what he would with them.[24]

(Middle Town Cherokee warrior Chiotlohee had killed Daniel Murphy around Aurora in 1752. Some have written 1751; however, the date of this letter indicates that Daniel Murphy was still alive in May 1752. Daniel Murphy is the likely great-grandfather of Mary "Polly" Murphy and 7th great-grandfather of the author. [See Appendix A.] Aulola [Aurora] is historically described as a settlement on the lower Holston River at its junction with North River; however, the present-day North River has a confluence with the Little Tennessee River near the sites of Fort Loudoun and Tuskegee. Aurora had been settled by Cherokee refugees from the Creek war that occurred at that time in Georgia.)

When Attakullakulla returned from Virginia, he reproached Oconostota for promoting the French alliances. This was a break from the Cherokee tradition of polite public debate with unity for the final judgment. Oconostota replied, "What Nation or people am I afraid of? I do not fear the forces which the Great King George can send against me to these mountains."[25]

Oconostota, who carried the title Skiagusta (Warrior of Chota), led several chiefs in support of the French; however, the primary headmen throughout the Cherokee Nation continued to support Attakullakulla in his backing for the British. This remained a primary source of rivalry between Attakullakulla and Oconostota for the rest of their lives, and they did not hide it well. The influence of each upon the people hung in the balance. Oconostota, Old Hop, the people's chosen leader, had aligned with Attakullakulla to not only back British trade, but also to play Virginia against South Carolina.[26]

Shortly after Attakullakulla returned from Virginia, Governor Glen dropped the peace requirement that the chief had to be turned over for punishment. Glen feared that, if the Cherokee negotiated a trade pact with Virginia, South Carolina would no longer be in the trade mix. Glen sent a messenger to ask Attakullakulla to come to Charles Town for negotiations. In reality, the Virginia legislature did not want to harm their agreeable relationship with South Carolina—but they did not apprise Glen of that. Glen had more than trade on his mind. A large slave revolt occurred in 1739 called the Stono Rebellion. Jemmy, a slave who lived on an estate along the Stono River, led 20 other slaves on a march to the south. The group recruited 60 to 65 more slaves, and they killed 25 whites before the South Carolina militia caught up to them at the Edisto River. In the succeeding battle, 20 whites and 44 slaves were killed. The surviving members of the uprising were executed except for the few that were sold to the slave trade in the West Indies. Glen, who feared another revolt of that ilk, decided he needed to keep a South Carolina presence in the Cherokee villages. He did not need French or Creek enemies on his northwestern front.

On July 3, 1753, Attakullakulla arrived in Charles Town at the head of a Cherokee delegation. He was quite confident. The people had tired of Ammouskossittee (Dreadful Water). He was not picked by the people to be anything but the headman of Tellico. Governor Glen had chosen him to be "emperor" of the Cherokee. Ammouskossittee had recently been embarrassed when he was caught trying to sell Cherokee land to Virginians for his own profit. The Cherokee people had been following Old Hop, but in 1753 they made it official and in a council session in Chota, Old Hop was chosen to replace Ammouskossittee as the first beloved man. Attakullakulla was Old Hop's principle advisor, so he had plenty of backing when he met with James Glen.

The first thing that Attakullakulla did was to announce his success as a warrior to Glen. One year earlier, the headman had led a war party to the north and fought against Indian allies of the French. During that time, the warriors had killed eight French; they captured and turned two others over to British officers. Glen then expressed a desire for the Cherokee to talk peace with the Creek. Attakullakulla was surprised and told the governor that, in 1730, the king asked the Cherokee to avenge the deaths of British colonists at the hands of the Creek. Glen stated emphatically that he spoke for the king.

Attakullakulla then announced that he wished to go to England and personally speak with King George II on the matter. The Cherokee headman also wanted to expound to the king that the treaty they had signed in 1730 was not being honored by South Carolina. Governor Glen told Attakullakulla the time was not right, but that maybe he could go in two or three years. Attakullakulla simply shrugged and stated he could sail from another colony that would be willing to assist the Cherokee. Governor Glen responded that the Cherokee leader would not sail from any colony without his (Glen's) approval.

Attakullakulla was embarrassed by the reproach. He considered himself a great politician, as did many in the white community who called him the "Little Carpenter" due to his ability to craft treaties and trade agreements. He certainly felt he was Glen's "equal," if not his "better." He decided to change his strategy. He had complained to Glen before about the traders' cheating the Cherokee, and he hammered on that point again. He told Glen:

> It was not from fear that I came here. I went to Virginia because the Overhill People, being very poor and in straights [sic] for Goods, compelled me to go. There are only two regular Traders in our Nation, Mr. Beamer and Cornelius Dougherty. The others have no goods of their own, except what they get from other Traders with a view to speculating.... Formerly four men resided in our towns. Mr. Elliot [sic] has brought us a great many goods.... Do what we may the White people will cheat us in Weights & Measures. What is it a Trader cannot do? ... Some of the White people borrowed my yardstick and cut it shorter, for which I am blamed.[27]

Attakullakulla again brought up the treaty of 1730. He told Glen, if the trading practices did not improve, the Cherokee would trade with other British colonies. Glen appeased the chief with presents, but was never able to correct the trade inequities.

The Virginians had been trying for quite a while to get Cherokee assistance for the French and Indian War. The South Carolinians prompted the Cherokee to agree. The Virginians welcomed the support. The Cherokee, as a condition, wanted the colonies to build forts on Cherokee land and garrison them to protect the villages while the warriors were away fighting in the north. The Cherokee had really counted on a fort in the Upper Villages, and Governor Glen had plans to accommodate them.

In 1754, Virginia lieutenant colonel George Washington made note that the English needed Indian allies to defeat the French, who already had several Indian allies. Washington suggested that Virginia lieutenant governor Robert Dinwiddie send Nathaniel Gist to the Cherokee to plead for an alliance. Gist had been a trader with the Cherokee. He approached the headmen with the idea to attack the French-allied Shawnee, who were bitter enemies of the Cherokee. Ostenaco (Judd's Friend, Outacite, Mankiller, Skiagusta, Big Head), Oconostota's half-brother and Attakullakulla's first cousin once removed, agreed to send 100 warriors to attack Shawnee villages. Washington was delighted when he heard.

Washington was also prophetic as he cautioned Dinwiddie that the Cherokee needed to be treated with respect when fighting with Virginians: "They will be of particular service—more than twice their number of white men.... It is a critical time. They are very humorsome, and their assistance is very necessary. One false step might not only lose us that, but even turn them against us."[28]

It seems Washington portended dire events that would later occur during the French and Indian War and would lead to the first of the so-called Cherokee Wars.

The mid–1750s was a busy time for the Cherokee. They were still in the midst of their war with the Creek (Muskogee). The number of their warriors had dwindled to 2,500. In 1755 the most important engagement was the Battle of Taliwa. The Cherokee had long wanted to regain northern Georgia, which they considered as their own ancestral hunting grounds. The Battle of Taliwa occurred at present-day Ball Ground, Georgia. Nanyehi (later to become Nancy Ward) was an 18-year-old mother of two, married to a fearless Cherokee war chief named King Fisher. She accompanied her husband as he led his 500-warrior band of followers. The primary war chief of the battle was none other than Principle War Chief Oconostota.

Nanyehi was chewing bullets for Chief King Fisher from behind the safety of a log. The practice roughened the round bullet to create much more damage to an enemy's torso than a smooth ball when it entered an enemy's body. Suddenly, King Fisher was mortally wounded. Young Nanyehi picked up King Fisher's musket, chanted a war song, and rallied the outnumbered Cherokee who had been faltering. The warriors successfully drove the Muskogee out of northeastern Georgia. (The traditional site of the Battle of Taliwa is near the confluence of Long Swamp Creek with the Etowah River. A marker is located in downtown Ball Ground, Georgia, at the railroad crossing.)

When the warriors returned to Chota, they told of Nanyehi's actions in a council session. They sang songs about her as they chanted stories around their campfires. The chiefs and chieftesses proclaimed her Ghighau, or Most Honored Woman (Beloved Woman). That proclamation was a lifetime honor. During tribal council meetings, a ghighau would sit with the peace chief and the war chief in the "Holy Area" of the Council House at Chota. She was also head of the Women's Council and could speak openly and even oppose the chiefs' decisions. Young women often fought alongside warriors, and when older (when they could no longer participate in war) they could be chosen as the ghighau based on their previous heroics. In the coming 1776 Cherokee War, on September 21 (following a skirmish two days after the Battle of the Black Hole), Colonel Andrew Williamson's vanguard would find a wounded female warrior about two miles west of Wayah Gap in the Nantahala Mountains of North Carolina.[29] (The location was on Jarrett Creek which feeds Nantahala Lake from the southeast near where Jarrett Creek Road departs Wayah Road. See Chapter Six.)

(Nanyehi was the daughter of Tame Doe, who was a sister of Attakullakulla and Willenawah. She was born about 1737 in Chota, the Cherokee mother town. After King Fisher's death, Nanyehi married English trader Bryant [or Bryan] Ward and became Nancy Ward. They had a daughter, Elizabeth "Betsy" Ward. Nancy Ward had once been nicknamed Tsistunagiske [Wild Rose] because of her complexion.)

Another event happened in the summer of 1755 that worried the Virginians and made them push for more Cherokee assistance against the French. After George Washington and the Virginia militia had failed in their campaign against the French and subsequently lost Fort Necessity, Virginia lieutenant governor Robert Dinwiddie consistently pushed for the British army to force the French from Fort Duquesne.

Braddock's Defeat occurred shortly afterward. A force of 1,500 British army troops and American militia (from Virginia, Maryland, North and South Carolina) finally answered Dinwiddie's call. They marched from Will's Creek in Maryland under General Edward Braddock in late June 1755. On July 9, they forded the Monongahela River at the forks with the Allegheny and Ohio rivers and began the last leg of seven miles to the fort. An enemy force of 500 Indians (Ottawa, Miami, Huron, Delaware, Shawnee and Mingo) and 30 French colonial troops ambushed and routed them. The losses were staggering: 26 officers killed and 37 wounded, 430 soldiers killed and 385 wounded. This was enough to cause the Virginians around Staunton to construct Fort Defiance, an action typical of several backcountry Virginia communities. (In *The North Carolina Booklet: Great Events In North*

George Washington (on left) at Braddock's Defeat—From *The New World: Embracing American History*—Volume 2, by Henry Howard Brownell / Henry Brownell, 1857.

Carolina History, Vol. 3, it is stated that 20-year-old Daniel Boone was a wagoner under Hugh Waddell in Braddock's campaign as was future American Revolution hero Daniel Morgan. Daniel Boone would become an expansion leader to help the Virginia settlers westward into the Cumberland region, an ancestral hunting ground of the Cherokee.)

On July 9, 1755, 23-year-old Virginia provincial major (provincial ranks were reduced when the officers fought for the British regular army) George Washington, a volunteer aide-de-camp to General Braddock, became very disillusioned with the British troops. He wrote to Lieutenant Governor Dinwiddie:

> We continue our March from Fort Cumberland to Frazier's (which is within 7 miles of Duquesne) without meeting any extraordinary event, having only a straggler or two picked up by the French Indians. When we came to this place, we were attacked (very unexpectedly) by about three hundred French and Indians. Our numbers consisted of about thirteen hundred well armed men, chiefly Regulars, who were immediately struck with such an inconceivable panick, that nothing byt [sic] confusion and disobedience of orders prevailed among them. The officers, in general, behaved with incomparable bravery, for which they greatly suffered, there being near 600 killed and wounded—a large proportion, out of the number we had! The Virginia companies behaved like men and died like soldiers; for I believe out of three companies that were on the ground that day scarce thirty were left alive. Capt. Payroney and all his officers, down to a corporal, were killed; Capt. Polson had almost as hard a fate, for only one of his escaped. In short, the dastardly behaviour of the Regular troops (so-called) exposed those who were inclined to do their duty to almost certain death; and, at length, in spite of every effort to the contrary, broke and ran as sheep before hounds, leaving the artillery, ammunition, provisions, baggage, and in short, everything a prey to the enemy. And when we endeavoured to rally them, in hopes of regaining the ground and what we had left upon it, it was with as little success as if we had attempted to have stopped the wild bears of the mountains, or rivulets

with our feet; for they would break by, in despite of every effort that could be made to prevent it.[30]

Washington's mother had approached him when he was offered the position with Braddock. "Hurrying to Mount Vernon, she entreated him not again to expose himself to the hardships and perils of these frontier campaigns."[31]

On July 2, 1755, Governor Glen met with Old Hop at Saluda (25 miles northwest of present-day Greenville, South Carolina). He wanted to establish peace after a band of Cherokee from Settico attacked several whites along the Yadkin and Catawba Rivers. Glen also wished to negotiate for more land in South Carolina as reciprocity for Fort Prince George that was to be built in the Lower Villages near Keowee. (The fort was 200-foot square with vertical timbered walls 12 to 15 feet high and surrounded by a trench. The site is in modern-day Pickens County, South Carolina, and was excavated one and one-half years before the fort was submerged by Lake Keowee in 1971.)

The land in negotiation was supposedly not being utilized by the Cherokee. It was a 40,000,000-acre tract between the Wateree and Savannah rivers. It was also bounded on the north by Long Canes Creek to leave a buffer between the settlers and the Lower Villages. Old Hop was in favor of the transaction, because he believed the fort would be important. The Cherokee were generally split over the benefits of the fort versus cession of the land.

At the meeting with Glen, Old Hop, who was becoming quite frail, did not wish to speak. The Chota Council chose Attakullakulla to speak for him and Old Hop let Attakullakulla know what he wanted to say. An excerpt from Attakullakulla's oration was printed in the July 31, 1755, issue of the *South Carolina Gazette*:

> I am the only living Cherokee that went to England. What I now speak the great King should hear. We are brothers to the people of Carolina, and one house covers us all.... We, our wives and children, are all children of the great King George. I have brought this child, that when he grows up he may remember our agreement this day and tell it to the next generation that it may be forever known. We freely surrender part of our possessions. The French want our Lands, but we will defend them while one of our Nation is alive. These are the arms we have for our defense [speaking of a bow and arrows]. We hope the Great King will pity his children the Cherokees, and send us guns and ammunition. We fear not the French. Give us arms, and we will go to war against the enemies of the great King. My speech is at an end. It is the voice of the Cherokee Nation. I hope that the Governor will send it to the great King that it may be kept forever.[32]

Attakullakulla then asked the Cherokee that were present if he had spoken the will of the Cherokee people, to which they assented, "Yo-hah." (It was an exaggeration that Attakullakulla was the only living Cherokee that had gone to England in 1730. Prince Skalilosken, who also made the trip, was definitely still alive. See Chapter 4.)

Old Hop and Attakullakulla visited all Cherokee villages and explained the agreement. The Cherokee towns were traditionally autonomous, and the headmen of each needed to be included in the process.

The British government, however, was less than enthusiastic about obtaining the land cessions. The London officials were primarily interested in the Cherokee trade alliance, and they viewed the additional land cessions as an encumbrance. The military was already thinly spread in the lowcountry and could not spare manpower to also enforce laws in the backcountry.

Now that the Cherokee were renewing the trade agreements with South Carolina, they became negligent and did not send warriors to Virginia to aid with the war effort. The Cherokee were somewhat offended that Virginia did not jump at the chance to replace South Carolina as a trade partner. The headmen thought that also meant no armed alliances. The Cherokee were accustomed to reciprocity with agreements and could not understand that the colonists were not always of the same mindset. Old Hop, at Governor Glen's request, reluctantly agreed to send warriors to assist Virginia to protect the northern border.

At the same time the Calhoun family, later to be in-laws of Andrew Pickens, established the Long Canes settlement at the confluence of the Little and Saluda rivers, 60 miles from Keowee. Family leader Patrick Calhoun surveyed property boundaries and established his property on the Cherokee side of the Long Canes Creek. This would later become a source of contention.[33]

The alliance hit a snag early in 1756. Governor Glen could not obtain legislative financial approval for the planned fort in the Upper Villages. Attakullakulla was not happy and was afraid his influence with the Cherokee people would suffer if South Carolina did not produce as promised. He led a delegation of 120 Cherokee headmen and warriors to Charles Town to negotiate. There, he was unsuccessful and regretted he had formed the trade alliance with South Carolina.

Old Hop became frustrated that Glen did not live up to his promises. The other headmen became contentious when South Carolinians did not follow through with the fort in the Upper Villages. Attakullakulla then approached the Virginians. He believed, rightly so that, as each Cherokee village was autonomous and could negotiate treaties on their own, so could each British colony.

In January 1756, Virginia Militia Major Andrew Lewis led an expedition of 250 troops against the Shawnee Indians with War Chief Ostenaco and 130 warriors. Trader Richard Pearis accompanied them as an interpreter. While trying to cross an icy river, about six weeks into the expedition, their boats loaded with provisions overturned, and they nearly starved. Some of the Cherokee were forced to kill their horses for food. Neither Lewis nor Pearis offered them any relief, so the Cherokee left for Chota. As they passed through back-country Virginia, the Cherokee warriors absconded with grazing horses that they thought the whites owed to them for the ones they had lost on the expedition. They also raided root cellars and smokehouses for forage.

Irate Virginia settlers caught and attacked the Cherokee. The settlers killed and scalped 24 and otherwise mutilated the bodies. Lieutenant Governor Dinwiddie had offered bounties for the scalps of Indian allies of the French. The settlers misrepresented the 24 Cherokee scalps as those of France's Indian allies and were paid the bounty.

Meanwhile, in February 1756, Dinwiddie sent commissioners Peter Randolph and William Byrd to visit the Cherokee. They first met with the Tellico chief (likely Ammouskossittee, but possibly Young Hop Moytoy, son of Old Hop) and were joined by Attakullakulla and others at Catawba Town, North Carolina (fifteen miles east of Hickory, North Carolina on U.S. Highway 70). The Cherokee told the Virginians that they required a fort in the Upper Villages to protect their families when their warriors were off fighting the French. Attakullakulla was disappointed that South Carolina governor Glen had not proceeded to build one. The chief said, "I have a Hatchet ready but we hope our Friends will not expect us to take it up, 'til we have a Place of Safety for our Wives and Children."[34]

As they held council, they received a message that the Cherokee who had served with the Virginia troops in the north had been killed and scalped as they were returning home. The Cherokee clansmen of the slain warriors desired retribution against Byrd and Randolph. However, Attakullakulla interceded:

> Never shall the hatchet be buried, until the blood of our countrymen is atoned for, but let us not violate our faith by imbrueing [sic] our hands with the blood of those who are now in our power. They came to us in the confidence of friendship, with belts of wampum to cement a perpetual alliance with us. Let us send them back to their own settlements, then take up the hatchet and endeavor to exterminate the whole race of them.[35]

However, Byrd and Randolph sincerely apologized for the murders and provided the relatives of the killed warriors with £1319 worth of trade goods. The trade council then proceeded, and Attakullakulla iterated that the Cherokee required a fort in the Upper Towns to protect their families when warriors were away fighting the Shawnee. He then reminded the agents that the Virginians had declined Cherokee efforts at trade agreements. He also explained that South Carolina governor Glen had not fulfilled his promises to them. Byrd and Randolph pledged to push for construction of a fort and volunteered to donate some of their own money to that end.

Attakullakulla was elated he could create a trade alliance with the British, other than those in South Carolina, retain a British allegiance among the Cherokee, and finally get the fort in the Upper Villages. Overnight the Cherokee considered proposals made by Randolph and Byrd that the Cherokee supply 400 warriors and open a new trade path to Virginia, in exchange for a new fort in the Upper Villages.

Attakullakulla, Old Hop, and Willenawah tried to appease the governors of both states with letters of apology for misunderstandings, probably adopting the custom they had seen the governors use time and time again.

Dinwiddie tried to beat South Carolina to the punch. Major Andrew Lewis led an expedition of 60 men to the Upper Villages to begin construction of a fort near Chota. Dinwiddie and Glen had planned to create a joint effort to build the fort in the Upper Villages. However, Virginia did not come up with its share of the money for the project, so the race was on. Yet in 1756, Glen rebuilt Fort Prince George which had already fallen into disrepair. He sent commissioners to Chota to assure the headmen that a second fort would be built there in addition to the one at Keowee. He ordered an expedition be ready to go to Chota in June to begin construction; however, Glen would be succeeded by new governor William Henry Lyttleton before that occurred.

Some Cherokee wanted two forts (one each built by Virginia and South Carolina); some wanted no forts, and they could not agree upon where forts should be constructed. The Virginians completed their unnamed fort in August 1756. It was constructed on the north bank of the Little Tennessee River one mile upriver from Chota. The Cherokee did not like the ungarrisoned fort, so they refused to send any warriors to Virginia. Lewis recommended that Dinwiddie send the army and force the Cherokee to acquiesce to the agreement.

South Carolina governor James Glen met Attakullakulla and a delegation at Fort Prince George late in May 1756. They discussed a fort for the Upper Towns. South Carolina captain Raymond Demere, who had been overseeing repairs to Fort Prince George, was also present.

Attakullakulla was exasperated when he arrived at Fort Prince George. He told Governor Glen that the Virginians were already building a fort in the Upper Towns and suggested that South Carolina hurry to do the same. Captain Demere asked the chief why the Cherokee needed two forts. Attakullakulla responded that the Virginia fort had been sited to repel any French or northern Indian attacks from the river, and he said the South Carolina fort could be placed to protect against land invasions from the south. Attakullakulla was not impressed with the construction of the Virginia fort, but he hid that fact quite well.

Actually, Virginia had no plans to garrison the fort. They were preparing to send the entire Virginia militia to their northern border to face the French and their Indian allies. It would be up to the Cherokee to man the fort once it was completed. This was a paradox because the Virginians wanted the Cherokee warriors to assist against the French, but the Cherokee wanted Virginia to garrison the fort so the warriors could be away to fight the French. Attakullakulla was still not happy, but he was not going to tell Governor Glen.

It was agreed that, on July 23, 1756, Captain Demere would lead an expedition of 19 men to the Upper Villages to construct a fort. On June 1, before the meeting ended, James Glen received a message that Governor William Henry Lyttleton had arrived in Charles Town to replace him. Lyttleton had actually been named in 1755; however, his ship had been detained en route by the French. He also indicated that he would not come to Fort Prince George right away. He explained that he needed to take care of South Carolina business, and he invited Attakullakulla to come to Charles Town. However, Lyttleton conceded that Attakullakulla should return to Chota and prepare for the arrival of the fort builders.

Attakullakulla told Governor Glen that it was much too hot in Charles Town in July. He added that he would only return to Chota to gather a war party and join the Virginians against the French. He promised he would meet Lyttleton when he returned in November. Before Attakullakulla left Fort Prince George, he chided Glen and Demere again regarding the trade practices and the shortage of ammunition experienced by the Cherokee. Demere passed this information to Lyttleton in July. The captain added that Attakullakulla had further stated that, if the British traders could not meet Cherokee demands, they would be asked to leave the Cherokee Nation.

When Demere arrived at Chota on October 1, 1756, with 200 troops he began reporting to the new governor, William Henry Lyttleton. Demere learned that Old Hop and Attakullakulla (already back from his foray with the Virginians) were embroiled in conflict. Old Hop had begun to lean toward the French as he had sustained enough broken promises from both South Carolina and Virginia. The chief's servant and adopted son, a Creek named French John, apparently was a French agent and had bent Old Hop's ear. Demere made a comment about Old Hop's leanings to Attakullakulla who replied that his cousin was "a fool who could do nothing without his help."[36] On October 13, 1756, Demere wrote to Lyttleton that Attakullakulla now had more influence among the Cherokee than did Old Hop. The captain expressed there was a subtle difficulty between them. Old Hop told Demere that, should he die, either war chiefs Oconostota or Ostenaco (related to each other as half-brothers) should be his replacement. He further declared that neither Attakullakulla nor Willenawah (related to each other as brothers) was reliable. He and Ostenaco suggested that Attakullakulla would probably align with the French as he had made past overtures to them for an alliance.

Captain Demere's note to Lyttleton stated that he had confronted Attakullakulla with the charge, and that the chief replied: "I am not a Boy ... but the Head Man of this Nation. I give Talks to the Governor of Chota [Old Hop]; not he to me; my mind has always been straight, I always think one Way, and now I take you by the Hand, and you hear what I say and if I perform it not when I come back make me a Lyar [sic]."[37]

The October 28, 1756, memo included that several Tellico leaders had visited Fort Toulouse and signed a tentative alliance with the French and the Creek.[38]

Demere had been accompanied to Chota by Captain John Stuart (who would become a British Indian Agent during the American Revolution) and German engineer William De Brahm. De Brahm and Demere disagreed on the proper location for the fort, so De Brahm obstinately built it where he saw fit. It was located on a crest that overlooked the confluence of the Tellico River with the Little Tennessee River, just downstream from Chota. Named Fort Loudoun, it was 105 feet square, with vertical log construction. Demere garrisoned the fort in January 1757, but he was not impressed. Attakullakulla found that Fort Loudoun was to be much more imposing than he had anticipated and a monstrosity to be so near Chota and Tuskegee. He spoke to the headmen in the Council House at Chota, and they asked the British to stop building the fort; however, the garrison of 200 soldiers was already there.

Old Hop was happy with the fort until Captain Demere explained to him that South Carolina expected him to ignore French trade overtures and help the Virginians fight the French and their Indian allies in the north. Old Hop expected to be able to trade with whomever he wanted. He did not understand the idea of restricting trade to one trading partner. On October 13, 1756, Demere wrote Lyttleton:

> The Emperor (Old Hop) and his Lady came soon after us and brought me some bread, watermelon, &c. The first words he spoke to me was, "What do you think of our having given up one of our towns (as trading partners) to the French?" I said I was very sorry to hear it. Then he says, "have you not got a great many French amongst you at Charles Town? When I was last there I saw a great many myself." I told him that those French People he saw had been there from their Youth and that they came for the sake of their religion and were good subjects to King George [II]. To which he said that it was good to be at Peace with all kings.[39]

Virginia major Andrew Lewis (who commanded the construction of Virginia's fort near Chota) wrote to his South Carolina counterpart, Captain Raymond Demere, that the Cherokee were making overtures toward the French. He explained that Old Hop had a strong relationship with a Creek named French John who resided at Tellico. Old Hop had supposedly convinced many Cherokee that a trade alliance with the French was appropriate. He had also suggested to French John that he should carry a message to the French at Fort Toulouse of the Cherokee interest in a French fort in the Upper Villages.

French John tried to convince the Cherokee that the large quantities of metal received by Demere from Charles Town were for fabricating leg irons. He further charged that the leg irons were to imprison Cherokee women and children for the West Indies slave trade. Demere tried hard to explain to Old Hop that it was a material used in the construction of the fort the Cherokee had requested.

Demere then proceeded to rebuke Attakullakulla and Old Hop for approaching the French for another fort in the Upper Towns. He explained that the two forts in close proximity would lead to warfare between the French and the English, and likely loss of trade goods for the Cherokee. Old Hop replied that the towns were dangerously low on ammunition and the British had better pay attention to supplying such important trade goods to the Cherokee.

The French put even more pressure on the Cherokee for trade alliances. Captain Demere wrote to Governor Lyttleton on November 18, 1756, and stated that if the Tellico Village were to trade with the French, the rest of the Cherokee Nation would follow its lead. He further stipulated if that occurred, the backcountry settlers would be in constant danger. He said, "Indians are a comodity [sic] that are to be bought and sold and the French will bid very high for them. And on this particular occasion if we don't bid as high we shall [absolutely] lose them."[40]

War Chief Ostenaco warned Demere that the French were trying to convince the Cherokee to attack Fort Loudoun, kill the members of the garrison, and bring the scalps to Fort Toulouse to prove their loyalty and to receive a bounty. He also advised that he (Ostenaco) would be patrolling a particular route between Tellico and Chota, and would capture any British settlers, traders, or soldiers and remove their scalps to give to the French. Demere issued warnings for travelers to avoid that specific road. Attakullakulla told Captain Demere that the clansmen of the killed warriors were considering vengeance against the Virginians and that many Cherokee did not wish to assist the Virginians against the French any more.

Attakullakulla received another invitation to go to Charles Town and meet with Governor Lyttleton. Again, he said he was going to ally with the Virginians first. This time he led a war party of 40 men. When he returned, he met with Lyttleton and presented him with French scalps. He complained again of trade conditions (more trader cheating) and especially charged trader John Elliott of misconduct.

Lyttleton asked Attakullakulla to continue and assist the Virginians. Attakullakulla agreed, if the British would arm the warriors and provide additional trade goods to families of warriors killed in action. He also requested that Lyttleton allow him to visit the king.

Lyttleton consented to put Elliott on probation, to warn all traders against unfair trading practices, and to send gifts to Chota so they could be distributed to families as the headmen saw fit. He, however, did not agree to allow Attakullakulla a trip to England.

Earlier, in January 1756, British traders Thomas Leaper and James Kelly had vacated Tellico out of fear and settled with their trade goods into Chatuga; however, there were now reports that Chatuga was ready to follow Tellico toward the French.

Old Hop summoned Demere to Chota and appeared to have a change of heart, likely at the prompting of Attakullakulla. Old Hop explained that all Cherokee towns except Tellico wished to retain trade relations with the British. When Demere returned to the fort, Ostenaco visited and explained that his community, Tellico, was only upset over British trade conditions. Ostenaco then expressed his desire for a permanent British trade representative with a more reliable source of trade goods and lower prices to reside in Tellico.

Demere learned that trader Robert Goudey, who owned the trading post at Ninety Six, South Carolina, had the license for both Tellico and Chatuga. However, Goudey was selling his goods to a disreputable trader who would trade the merchandise at Tellico and Chatuga for very high prices and offer no credit. Goudey had never visited Tellico to inspect his arrangement with the trader. Captain Demere then reckoned that was the primary cause for the British loss of trade alliances in Tellico to the French. The British could ill afford to lose Indian allies.

In January 1757, Demere detached Lieutenant Robert Wall to go to Tellico where Ostenaco explained the trade situation as he had done for Demere. Ostenaco clarified that Chota and those in other towns regularly received gifts from South Carolina, but that Tellico had received none. The Tellico Cherokee believed they had been ignored by the British, so they made overtures to the French.

Old Hop summoned Demere to Chota, and he showed the captain a price list given to him a few years earlier that had been signed by Governor James Glen. The list spelled out what the Cherokee would pay for specific trade goods. He further enlightened Demere that the traders residing with the Cherokee paid no attention to Glen's list. He then stated that the Cherokee impression of Charles Town was that it originates lies and false promises.

Demere then investigated trader John Elliott and found he was charging exorbitant prices. The Cherokee misinterpreted the traders' roles to be agents of the British government and so were sorely disappointed with the outcome. Then Savanah Tom (Moytoy III, the Great Warrior [Raven] of Tellico), came to Demere and complained about Elliott, who had received horses from some Cherokee at Chota. Elliot promised them some rum that he had stored at the village of Keowee. Later Savanah Tom went to Keowee and found the rum. The 1755 Treaty of Saluda, signed by Governor Glen, restricted shipping rum into the backcountry. Demere wrote to Lyttleton who had Elliott's rum confiscated.

Savanah Tom demanded the people of Chota be compensated for their horses; however, Demere could do nothing since it involved an illegal sale. He stated that the Cherokee needed to seek some payment from Elliott, other than rum. This left Savanah Tom unimpressed. He had tried to help, but was left with the belief that the Cherokee had been duped by a complicity between the British government and the traders.

Meanwhile, Richard Pearis, another trader (later a Tory captain during the American Revolution), proposed that Virginia lieutenant governor Robert Dinwiddie open a trading post on the Long Island of the Holston River in Tennessee. He indicated that would be done in partnership with trader Nathaniel Gist, who married Wur-Teh Watts and became the father of Sequoyah (George Gist) who created the first Cherokee syllabary. The only problem was that Nathaniel Gist was unaware of the plan, which eventually fell apart. Dinwiddie had approved of the plan based on Pearis' presentation, and Pearis would eventually open the post in July 1757. (The Virginians had claimed that portion of Tennessee as a part of the colony.) Pearis owed Gist money, and Gist sued for it. (The Long Island of the Holston was a spiritual place for the Cherokee, and they were not enthralled with Pearis' being there.)

Many of the Upper Village Cherokee owed Pearis a lot of money for trade goods. He sent a message to Old Hop along with some trade goods and whiskey. Pearis tried to convince Old Hop that he was an agent for the Virginia colony. Some Cherokee of Gist's acquaintance intercepted the message and took it to Chota where they translated it in a council session. Gist avowed that Pearis lied, so Old Hop had Pearis brought before the council in Chota. Pearis accused Gist of betrayal, so Old Hop had Pearis expelled.

The Cherokee Nation was greatly divided by 1757. The Cherokee did desire increased trade traffic—Old Hop wrote to Demere on October 3, 1756: "I hope when your fort is built that our young Men will always have a place to go for a supply of Necessaries in return for their Deer Skins ... and likeway expect that our Warriors and Headmen will have a Store where they can go and cloath themselves that they may look like Men, and not be ashamed to show themselves for an empty House looks but poorly."[41]

There was an influx of white settlers shortly after Fort Loudoun was garrisoned. South Carolina's Trading Statute of 1752 had allowed many new traders into Cherokee villages. They decided, since there was a new fort, to take advantage of the trade opportunities. Trader and historian James Adair complained: "Such a number of lewd, idle white savages are very hurtful to the honest part of the traders ... by heightening the value of vegetables, especially in the time of light crops, to an exorbitant price."[42]

The traders had many disputes with the villagers. The Cherokee became unhappy with the lack of colonial authority over the white people.

Shortly after he met Governor Lyttleton, Attakullakulla again went to the Ohio River Valley (as promised), accompanied by Oconostota, to fight with the Virginians against the French. While he was away from home, trade goods had become scarce due to the war effort. Many Cherokee headmen blamed Attakullakulla for backing the British. His influence among the Cherokee people had waned. There was strong feeling throughout the Cherokee Nation that Attakullakulla should have at least remained neutral and backed trade alliances with both the French and the English. Trader John Elliott subtly promoted Ostenaco over Attakullakulla among the villagers. Old Hop had expanded his communication with the French and even hosted emissaries in Chota.

When Attakullakulla returned from his foray, he saw what was going on. He immediately confiscated weights and measures and sent them to Captain Raymond Demere who found the tares were two pounds light and the measuring sticks were short. In return Demere complained to the chief that Old Hop had pursued alliances with French agents. Savanah Tom had acted as a guide to bring French agents and their Indian allies into Chota.

In April 1757, Virginia colonel William Byrd came upon Attakullakulla who was leading a Cherokee delegation toward Charles Town. Byrd asked the chief to provide warriors for an attack on Fort Duquesne. Byrd left George Turner in Chota to help organize the war party, but first Attakullakulla went to Charles Town. Lyttleton asked Attakullakulla to support Virginia right away. The war party was selected, and the plan was to leave on June 21, 1757; however, on that day the Cherokee conjurors told the council in Chota that the signs were bad. The Cherokee decided that the war party should be postponed until autumn. The Virginians had already given trade goods and ammunition to the Cherokee for the expedition. Turner begged them to leave without delay, but to no avail.

In July 1757, Attakullakulla announced he would lead 300 warriors to aid Virginia in the fall. He met at Winchester, Virginia, with Lieutenant Governor Dinwiddie, and Dinwiddie complained about horse thievery among the few Cherokee who had already joined the Virginians.

On July 28, 1757, Attakullakulla spoke before the headmen at the Council House and orated: "You say behind my Back that I have given your Lands away, and delivered you up to the English, and that you have no Traders as usual, but I have done all that I can for a Trade that you may be well supplied and want for nothing ... but the reason of its not being done, is your sending for French men to trade with you and believe all you hear from the French."[43]

The headmen were awestruck and Demere wrote to Lyttleton on July 30, when he described the affair, that Attakullakulla was valuable to the British.

Captain Demere had kept Lyttleton apprised of deteriorating conditions in the Upper Towns with regard to the French and the chiefs of Tellico. The Tellico faction of the Cherokee Nation was becoming quite testy against the British. Captain Demere reported to Governor Lyttleton in a letter August 10, 1757, that a white woman, going crazy with fear while traveling with her husband's detachment to reinforce Fort Loudoun, had absent-mindedly strayed away as they neared the fort. She was captured by Savanah Tom , who "executed his inhuman, cruel, and barbarous Will on her body by stabbing her several times with a knife, scalping [her] and opening her belly, and taking out a poor infant Creature that she had in her body."[44] It is believed that Savanah Tom and the pro–French bloc of the Cherokee wanted to contrive a quarrel between the British and the Cherokee Nation.

(Savanah Tom is a son of Trader Tom the emperor and nephew of Old Hop, but never was chosen to lead the Cherokee as beloved man—that fell to his brother Ammouskosittee who was eventually replaced by Old Hop. Savanah Tom is also Willenawah's father and is the 9th great-grandfather of the author.)

Attakullakulla went to confer with Lyttleton in Charles Town where he tried to offset French overtures to Old Hop and Ostenaco. Ostenaco had sent a delegation to Fort Toulouse to try and create a trade alliance. Lyttleton promised to act on the trading abuses of English traders, especially John Elliott. He also promised to deal directly with Attakullakulla rather than Principal Chief Old Hop and Ostenaco.

Attakullakulla convinced Lyttleton that he had the Cherokee Nation under control. Captain Paul Demere replaced his brother, Raymond, as commander of Fort Loudoun in August 1757. Captain Raymond Demere explained to Paul that Old Hop, Oconostota, and the chiefs of Great Tellico were pro–French. He added that the chiefs of Chota and Attakullakulla would stand behind the British alliance.

Attakullakulla, then apparently the real power in the Upper Towns, required all headmen to pledge loyalty to King George II at Fort Loudoun. He required Old Hop to rebuke Savanah Tom for the attack and to also make the pledge at Fort Loudoun.

On September 24, 1757, Attakullakulla led a war party to the west. The warriors killed six French soldiers near Fort Assumption (de l'Assomption, located at present-day Memphis, Tennessee), took their scalps, and captured two others. He returned to Fort Loudoun in January 1758. He waited to make his report until he could go to Charles Town where he hoped he would receive more presents.[45]

On October 10, 1757, Attakullakulla fulfilled his promise and led 30 Cherokee warriors and 30 Catawba warriors to join British brigadier general John Forbes who was planning an attack on Fort Duquesne. Forbes, however, was not impressed with his new Cherokee allies and never did trust them. He believed them to be ignorant and lazy; indeed, he called them savages. He saw no benefit to understanding their methods and beliefs. He complained that he had to supply them with goods at a "relatively high cost."

In reality, the expense of European mercenaries that the British regularly employed, such as the elite Hessian Jäger troops they relied on, were much more exorbitant. Cherokee warriors, of course, were regular soldiers of a nation. That was not their way. Each individual had autonomy and could declare if he would go to war or not, mostly dependent on how persuasive his leaders were. Each warrior could even opt out of a specific battle if he was not convinced it was in his best interest. Thus, a Cherokee warrior was more of a mercenary when fighting for the British.

Forbes wrote of Attakullakulla:

> He is as great a Rascal to the full as any of his companions. In place of going to war with me or persuading those who were with me to stay, he has strengthened them in their extravagant demands, by making his own more unreasonable than the others, and has made four or five stupid speeches all of which I have answered. He gives his final answer tomorrow on which depends whether I shall have one Indian with me or not. If I have any they will cost dear, and yet should any thing fail the cause may be attributed to the want of Indians who's presence I have lost for Saving a few hundred pounds, after foolishly having spent several thousand upon them.[46]

Forbes tried to accommodate the Cherokee warriors, but his heart wasn't in it. Thereafter, he treated Attakullakulla and his warriors with indifference. The general actually believed he must treat the warriors like children. Attakullakulla was unhappy with the treatment his warriors received and desired to leave; however, he believed his leaving would represent to the Cherokee people that he had no real influence among the British. Attakullakulla had heard that the French had abandoned Fort Duquesne just ten days before they were to attack. Actually, Fort Frontenac had fallen, and the Fort Duquesne garrison had begun to withdraw.

Interestingly, Virginia lieutenant governor Dinwiddie sent a letter to Forbes asking him to send Attakullakulla to Virginia to help settle the continuing dispute between the Virginia settlers and the local Cherokee who had even attacked and scalped some Virginians. That allowed Attakullakulla to still claim prestige if he salvaged the agreements with Virginia.

Attakullakulla left with a small delegation of ten warriors on November 18, 1758. Forbes tried to stop him and threatened him with a desertion charge. The group left anyway and headed for Williamsburg. General Forbes had his troops intercept the warriors and confiscate their horses and ammunition which Forbes declared to be British property. (Forbes invested the mostly abandoned fort on the 25th.)

Young Hop Moytoy[47] (a son of Old Hop) and his warriors were infuriated at the British officers as they headed for home. They had lost 20 horses which the British refused to replace. As they passed through Virginia, they took 20 replacements (the first they saw) from a local farmer. The Cherokee, by tradition, believed the whites owed them the horses and figured all was well. The farmers formed a posse and caught the warriors. A skirmish ensued; three Cherokee and one farmer were killed. The local militia then set up an ambush and killed 19 warriors. The Cherokee then raided the Yadkin Valley settlements and scalped 19 German farmers for vengeance.

Virginian vigilantes often attacked small groups of Cherokee who were returning from the war in the north. Ironically, the Cherokee were Virginia allies fighting against the French Indian allies. These vigilantes were actually colonial-sanctioned associations of irregulars that supplemented insufficient numbers of Virginia militias. As an example, a group of these irregulars was stationed at Fort Mayo (Fort Mayo was built on the North Mayo River in present-day Patrick County on land owned by a John Frederick Miller.) The irregulars were paid £10 for each scalp acquired from French-allied Indians. Thirty-five irregular troops marched out to search for enemy tribesmen. They came up on five Cherokee who were catching horses in a place called Draper's Meadow on the Little River. The Indians did not have the certain passes that had been supplied to British allies in the north, and they were carrying white men's scalps. Some of the men accused them of being Shawnee. Captain Robert Wade, the militia officer assigned to the irregulars, decided they must be Shawnee and ordered they be executed. A local hunter named Abraham Dunkleberry interceded and claimed to be familiar with the Cherokee. Although he admitted they were Cherokee, he added that they were hostile. Captain Wade decided to release the Indians. The men declared that they would never assist the militia again if they could not kill the hostile Indians. After Dunkleberry packed his hides to leave, he heard Captain Wade speak an aside to the men. He told them they could track the Indians once the hunter had left. They tracked the Cherokee to a peach orchard and lay in ambush until the Cherokee were ready to leave. Four were killed and one badly wounded who escaped to an island in Little River. The irregulars were sworn to secrecy by Captain Wade that they would deny ever having heard the Indians were Cherokee.

Virginia doubled the bounty on enemy scalps (French and Indian allies). Several traders scalped up to 50 local Cherokee, claiming they were Iroquois, and sought the bounty. Attakullakulla conferred with Dinwiddie at Winchester, Virginia, over the matter. The Cherokee prepared for war with the British colonies.

Historian and trader James Adair wrote of the incident:

> Several companies of the Cheerake, who joined our forces under general Stanwix at the unfortunate Ohio, affirmed their alienation from us, by unjust suspicion of them—were very much condemned,—and half-starved at the main camp: their hearts told them therefore to return home, as freemen and injured allies, though without a supply of provisions.... In their journey, the German inhabitants, without any provocation, killed about forty of their warriors, in different places—though each party was under the command of a British subject. They scalped all, and butchered several, after a most shocking manner ... some who escaped the carnage, returned at night, to see their kindred and war companions, and reported their fate ... those murderers were so audacious as to impose the scalps on the government for those of the French [allied] Indians; and that they actually obtained the premium [bounty for enemy scalps] allowed at that time by law.[48]

On January 1, 1759, Dinwiddie was replaced by Lieutenant Governor Francis Fauquier. Fauquier told his council that Attakullakulla wanted an audience; however, several councilmen did not want to talk with him because of his new reputation as a deserter. Captain Nathaniel Gist of the Virginia Provincial Militia had been a Cherokee trader and was then assigned responsibility for the 200 Cherokee that lived in Virginia. He reminded Fauquier that Attakullakulla had definitive power over the Cherokee Nation and that the council had better hear his words.

The chief conceded that the Virginia Cherokee acted unacceptably; however, he amended that both sides were to blame for the violence. He also recommended that the trouble would be eased if the Virginians would garrison their fort in the Upper Villages. Fauquier would accept no responsibility for the Virginians in the violence, and he declared that Virginia never promised to garrison the fort, just to build it. He said that they would open trade with the Cherokee; however, the Cherokee should not expect promotional gifts.

Fauquier wrote to Colonel William Byrd III: "The Little Carpenter [Attakullakulla] is now here conscious and cast down on account of his bad Behavior, and I believe all Differences are accommodated between us, and he seems glad to get off so. We have engaged to send Goods with which to open Trade in Spring."[49]

Attakullakulla reported to the headmen in the Chota Council House that he had negotiated a trade alliance with the Virginians.

South Carolina governor Lyttleton, upon hearing of the trade agreement between the Cherokee and Virginia, requested a visit with Attakullakulla. When the chief arrived at Charles Town he presented Lyttleton with a Frenchman's scalp. The governor was dumbfounded and accepted it without comment. He then informed the chief that he was displeased with his desertion of Forbes and would be watching his future actions. Attakullakulla returned to Chota.

In March 1759, French John and Great Mortar (Yahatatastenake), a Creek warrior and village chief, again stirred up bitter feelings over the killings of warriors in Virginia. In May 1759, a war party killed another 15 settlers, including women and children, on the Yadkin River. Lyttleton asked Attakullakulla to stay around Chota during the summer to ease tensions among the Cherokee warriors.

Attakullakulla could see the Cherokee clans would avenge the deaths of the warriors no matter what he said. That was Cherokee tradition. He decided that he should gather his remaining followers and go to war with the French. He believed the opposing Cherokee could not ally with the French if the nation was at war with the French. Captain Paul Demere asked Attakullakulla to reconsider and stay to keep things quiet. Attakullakulla told Demere he had no control over the clans.

Attakullakulla was having success in the north. During his departure, however, things were busy. In September 1759, there were increased attacks against backcountry settlers. Governor Lyttleton placed an embargo on trade with the Cherokee, and Oconostota led a delegation to Charles Town to negotiate for peace. Even though Lyttleton's council advised against it, the governor placed the Cherokee delegation under "protective custody."

Governor Lyttleton raised a provincial militia force and headed for the backcountry with the detainees under guard. That would begin a bloody period full of attacks and reprisals that included two major assaults by the British military against the Cherokee Towns. The Cherokee would have only 2,300 able-bodied warriors left by 1760. If the Cherokee Nation had not already picked up on hints of British nonreciprocity in their alliances, they would surely understand it by the end of 1761. However, Attakullakulla was very persuasive.[50]

Chapter 4

Lyttleton, Montgomery and Grant Destroy the Cherokee Community

Atrocities, such as those that occurred in late 1758 (see Chapter 3) when the Cherokee warriors returned through Virginia from the French and Indian War, might have been avoided. Neither side completely understood the other's war practices. A tit-for-tat scenario began that led to a two-year war which decimated the Cherokee Nation.

After the Cherokee had been attacked, killed, and mutilated, the Creek became the main French tool in attempts to convert the Upper Town Cherokee. The French intended to persuade the Cherokee to terminate trade agreements with the English and to partner with the French.

A Waxhaw Presbyterian Church Covenanter, the Reverend William Richardson, embarked upon a missionary effort to the Upper Towns in October 1758. He learned that Attakullakulla, not yet returned from the war, was still with British brigadier general John Forbes. Virginia lieutenant governor Dinwiddie had requested Attakullakulla to come to Virginia and help calm the turmoil between the Virginia settlers and the Cherokee warriors. Attakullakulla had problems with General Forbes over the departure, so he did not go to Virginia until the middle of November.

The Reverend Richardson spent three months in the Upper Towns to try and arrange a meeting with the chiefs in the Council House at Chota. Old Hop received daily reports about the abhorrent treatment of Cherokee warriors in Virginia, so he refused every request that the clergyman made. Old Hop was exasperated and wondered if Richardson "could not be satisfied with one answer as well as a thousand."[1]

The minister began to note a strong shift in Cherokee interest toward the French, who continually offered treaties and applied more pressure through the Creek. The lack of success wore on the Reverend Richardson who noted, "Tho [sic] never much inclined now they shew the greatest indifference."[2] He was behind the curve from the beginning. His predecessor was the Reverend William Martin, also a Presbyterian Covenanter, and Old Hop informed Richardson that William Martin had been invited to leave the Upper Towns. Old Hop said: "[Martin] having preached scripture till both his audience and he were heartily tired, was told ... they [the Cherokee] knew very well, that, if they were good, they should go up; if bad, down; that he could tell no more; that he had longed plagued them with what they no ways understood"[3]

(The Reverend William Richardson never seemed to recover from his discouragement. He was found dead in his study July 20, 1771, kneeling in front of his chair, with his arms extended over his head as if in his normal attitude of prayer. Reliable period reports specify a bridle rein around his neck indicating he committed suicide by tying it off to the chair and then leaning his body weight into the leather until he was strangled. Many reports of the time omit the "rein" supposedly out of respect for the family.)

What Richardson had seen and heard regarding the Cherokee shift toward the French was not new but had grown in intensity for two years. Old Hop had been to Fort Toulouse in 1756 to negotiate with the French. When he returned, he advised that the Cherokee should form treaties and alliances with the French and attack the garrison at Fort Loudoun. That information had been passed along to Captain Paul Demere by Oninaa (Nancy Butler), a mixed-blood Cherokee woman from Tellico who worked at Fort Loudoun for the captain. She had been informed by Old Hop's wife of his pronouncement. Demere then passed the warning along to South Carolina governor William Henry Lyttleton in a letter dated December 20, 1756, which delineated: "The Wench Nancy ... got from her [Old Hop's wife] the news ... which may be depended upon ... these two women are remarkably intimate.... The Wench ... apprehended great concern and cried."[4]

(Nancy Butler is likely the daughter of an early trader to the Cherokee named John Butler.)

Virginia lieutenant governor Robert Dinwiddie, after he learned how the warriors were murdered in Virginia, sent additional gifts to the Upper Towns' headmen to distribute to the families of those killed. He also sent a letter to Attakullakulla in which he criticized the Cherokee for their actions in Virginia but also praised them for their war efforts. This appeared strange to the Cherokee. Attakullakulla told Demere: "I do not know what to make of Governor Dinwiddie's letter, he has sent us a good talk and a bad one together. If he complains of the few men in Virginia, pray what might he expect of the great number he desires?"[5]

The Creek stirred the Cherokee warriors by calling them cowards for not having avenged the deaths. Finally the Cherokee killed two soldiers who were outside of Fort Loudoun and also began to attack the Carolina backcountry settlements. Some Cherokee warriors began to avenge the killings with attacks in the backcountry of Virginia and North Carolina. Lyttleton had already been planning to go to war with the Cherokee. He had approached the legislature in June 1758 for financing and even offered his own salary to help compensate. He had yet to receive a response by the end of the year.

Historian and Indian trader James Adair noted an incident that occurred at Fort Prince George which added fuel to the fire:

> Three light-headed, disorderly young officers of that garrison, forcibly violated some of their [the Cherokee] wives, and in the most shameless manner, at their own houses, while the husbands were making their winter hunt in the woods—and which infamous conduct they madly repeated, but a few months before the commencement of war.... When the Indians find no redress of grievances, they never fail to redress themselves, either sooner or later. But when they begin, they do not know where to end.... The Muskohge [sic] [Creek] also at that time having a friendly intercourse with the Cheerake ... were, at the instance of the watchful French, often ridiculing them for their cowardice in not revenging the crying blood of their kinsmen and warriors. At the same time, they promised to assist them against us ... who they said, were naturally in a bitter state of war against all the red people, and studied only how to steal their lands, on a quite opposite principle to the open steady conduct of the generous French, who assist their poor red brothers, a great way from their own settlements, where they can have no view, but that of doing good.[6]

(Two of the officers involved were likely the commander of the fort, Lieutenant Richard Coytmore and Ensign John Bell. See chapter note 22 regarding sources for Ensign Bell's first name.)

Early in 1759, young Chief Saloue (also called Young Warrior, Raven of Estatoe, Seroweh) of Estatoe formed a war party at Keowee to seek retribution for 24 slain Lower Town warriors in Virginia. The party killed 24 settlers in the South Carolina backcountry, and Saloue thought this would satisfy the required vengeance. It is interesting that he chose to attack settlements in South Carolina rather than Virginia. If one parallels the individual colonies with Cherokee clans, it would seem that any retribution that would fulfill clan vengeance should have been directed at Virginia. When Saloue directed the attack against South Carolina, it was as if someone from the Wolf clan had wronged someone in the Deer clan, and the Deer clan members sought vengeance with an attack on someone from the Long Hair clan. What Saloue accomplished was to give Governor Lyttleton the excuse he needed for his coming Cherokee war.[7]

In May 1759, Governor Lyttleton demanded that Attakullakulla deliver those braves, who had killed the whites, to Charles Town so they might be executed. Captain Paul Demere, likely following Lyttleton's instructions, demanded the specific 24 warriors he suspected of the slayings be turned over to him at Fort Loudoun.

Governor Lyttleton began to prepare for his attack on Keowee as explained in his letter to Captain Demere on June 7, 1759:

> I have instructed Lieut. Coytmore to endeavor to engage a body of Indians in his neighborhood to go and drive away the new Settlers at the forks of the Coosa River ... if the Indians are eager to have any soldiers ... accompany them ... they must be dress'd and painted to look like Indians; for I would wish to conceal the part I take in this business that the Creeks may not consider it as an attack made by me (upon their tribal members) in the new settlement.[8]

Attakullakulla had gone to Illinois as a Virginia ally to fight the French. Captain Paul Demere had asked him to remain in the Upper Towns and moderate the tension among the Cherokee (see Chapter 3). However, Attakullakulla knew he could not control the warriors and he did not want to put himself in the position of looking ineffective. He had only 10 followers left who would accompany him on the warpath, so his best option was to leave and hold on to what power he had remaining.

Old Hop and Savanah Tom led the contingent of Tellico and Settico chiefs that openly did not trust Britain and that favored France for major Cherokee alliances. France had exhibited, by its alliance with the Creek, that it was not trying to settle the Cherokee lands like the British had done, but rather was interested in creating better trade relations with the Cherokee (plus break the military alliance between the Cherokee and Britain in the north as a side benefit). The French were quite concerned with the British and Cherokee relationship. Old Hop, on his visit to Fort Toulouse, had invited a French delegation to Chota for more talks.

Great Mortar (Yahatatastenake), an infamous Creek chief, and 23 Creek warriors came to Chota. Louis de Lantagnac (a Frenchman and representative of the Chevalier de Kerkerec, Governor Louis Belcourt [Billouart]) at New Orleans accompanied the Creek party. These formidable visitors reminded the Cherokee headmen at Chota that Lieutenant Richard Coytmore and an Ensign John Bell had forced their way into a Keowee home and raped two Cherokee women while their husbands were hunting. Continuing to try and humble the Cherokee, Great Mortar reminded them of the Cherokee killed by the Virginians for their scalps.

Lantagnac took a hatchet and struck the Chota Council House war pole and yelled, "Who is there that will take the hatchet for the king of France? Let him come forth."[9]

Chief Saloue, of Estatoe and Wauhatchie, came forward and said, "I will take it."[10]

The Cherokee zeal began to show, and a great war dance ensued. Soon the Cherokee were raiding the South Carolina backcountry settlements. Cherokee warriors expanded their vengeance and killed 15 settlers along the Yadkin and Catawba rivers in North Carolina.[11]

South Carolina backcountry settlers were becoming uneasy. A letter was sent to the *South Carolina Gazette* and was published in the August 4–11, 1759, edition: "It is to be hoped that we may not be incredulous SHEPHERDS ... 'til the wolves in the shape of Indians swarm on the flocks and desolate our back settlements."

The letter's author offered 100 men (similar to those of the Virginia Associations who began the trouble) who would serve for little pay. However, the colony might have trouble taking advantage of that offer since the letter was anonymous. Likely if the author had any authority in the backcountry, he would have signed the letter. Fortified structures began to spring up in the South Carolina backcountry. These were usually stockades often anchored by existing houses or outbuildings. They were usually named for the person upon whose property they existed.

News from the backcountry reached Charles Town. Included were rumors of an impending attack on Fort Loudoun. Governor Lyttleton reacted with a trade embargo against the Cherokee, to include arms and ammunition. He dispatched 70 reinforcements to Fort Loudoun with food and supplies.

Lyttleton began to withdraw the white traders from Settico, and by September tensions between the British and the Cherokee rose nearly to a flash point. Many other traders withdrew from the Cherokee Upper Towns to the Carolinas and Virginia.

Also in September, Chief Ostenaco had tried to rustle the Fort Loudoun cattle herd and failed. Captain Paul Demere moved the cattle to safely within the fort's stockade and prepared for a possible Cherokee siege. The 70 South Carolina provincial forces arrived at Fort Loudoun in October. The fort was crowded with soldiers, their families, and some nearby settlers including peaceful Indians. They were elated to have the delivery of necessities and the additional military assistance; however, sanitation had been sacrificed for the protection of all concerned.[12]

Late in September, Oconostota and Ostenaco led a delegation to Fort Loudoun and explained to Captain Paul Demere that the warriors' discontent was resultant of Lyttleton's embargo on guns and ammunition. Oconostota elucidated that the warriors were reliant upon English firearms to provide meat for their families and that the shortage of ammunition would cause starvation among the people. Demere told the chiefs to present their case at Fort Prince George since most of the trouble had initiated within the Lower Towns.

Oconostota arrived at Fort Prince George. He had gathered what has variously been reported as 55 to 80 Cherokee from the Lower, Middle, and Valley Towns as he traveled. Thirty-two of these were warriors, and included 17 headmen. Meanwhile, Ostenaco returned with the original delegation to Chota to try and calm the younger warriors who had gathered to go on the warpath.

(Among the headmen traveling with Oconostota was Shonguttam [Chief Round-O] of the Valley Towns who, like Attakullakulla, was a noted promoter of English trade alliances. Round-O was from either Tuckaseegee or Stotoree, near present-day Murphy, North Carolina.)

Lieutenant Richard Coytmore listened impatiently, told Oconostota that he had no authority to intervene with Governor Lyttleton's plans, and sent the chiefs to Charles Town. Coytmore sent a messenger ahead to inform the governor of the brewing hostilities and of the coming delegation of Cherokee. When Lyttleton received Coytmore's message, he decided not to wait on legislative action, but on October 5, 1759, declared war on the Cherokee Nation. The House of Commons asked him to relent and await legislative action, but it had already been over one year since he had originally asked for funding. Lyttleton activated the militia under a gubernatorial order and ordered them to gather at Congaree. (Old Fort Congaree was a trading post located at present-day Cayce, South Carolina, a southwestern suburb of Columbia. It was located on the west side of the Congaree River along present-day State Highway 2.)[13]

Oconostota and his party arrived at Charles Town about the 20th and requested a meeting with Governor Lyttleton. The headmen immediately apologized to Lyttleton for attacks in the backcountry settlements and explained that Ostenaco was working diligently to pacify the young warriors. Oconostota orated: "Old Hop, my governor, has always loved the white people, and I am come to make it straight from your Excellency to my governor. There has been blood spilled, but I am come to clean it up. I am a warrior, but want no war with the English."[14]

Oconostota was confident he could negotiate a peace settlement with Lyttleton as soon as the governor understood that the headman was contrite. However, after he'd received gloomy reports from both Captain Demere and Lieutenant Coytmore, Lyttleton was in no mood to take the word of a Cherokee. He was well aware that Old Hop and Ostenaco had visited Fort Toulouse and had also invited French representatives to Chota for discussions of a new trade alliance to supplant the alliances between the British and the Cherokee.

Governor Lyttleton presented the chiefs to the House of Commons where he disparaged the Cherokee much as a prosecutor maligns a murder suspect in closing arguments. Oconostota was sullenly disappointed and remarked: "It is just like a cloudy morning which looks dark but it clears away again. I am endeavoring to clear all that is bad."[15]

The chief then laid deerskins at the governor's feet and made one last attempt at pacification. However, the governor would not let him speak. Lieutenant Governor William Bull, II, tried to intercede on behalf of the Cherokee; however, Lyttleton also tersely cut him off.

Lyttleton declared that the entire congregation of visiting Cherokee would have to accompany him and his army to Fort Prince George. He assured them, however, with: "You, Oconostota, and all with you, shall return safely to your country, and not a hair of your heads should be touched."[16]

However, he told them they must travel with the militia or he would not be responsible for their safety. He then sent a messenger to the Upper Towns that stated the chiefs must turn those warriors who were guilty of slaying whites over to Lieutenant Coytmore at Fort

Prince George to be prepared for execution. He further pronounced that if his demands were not met, he would take the warriors by force.

The warriors and headmen were embarrassed but they had no choice. The Cherokee delegation complied to accompany Lyttleton and his army to Fort Prince George. Lyttleton further denigrated them by placing them under armed guard as if they were prisoners.

Lyttleton set out by early November and, when he reached Monck's Corner, received word that Quebec had fallen to the British on the previous 13th of September. The few militiamen that accompanied the governor from Charles Town fired their rifles and huzzahed in celebration.

The gathering then proceeded to Congaree where they met the agglomeration of activated militiamen. Originally 1,400 men had assembled, and what a variant group it was. Some of the men, mostly from the backcountry, were earnest individuals who simply desired law and order. Their prime desire was to protect their family and property. Most, however, were criminals and vagrants. Some had even been released from local jails to fill out Lyttleton's requirement. It is likely that at least one-fourth of the mob didn't even own a gun. The criminal element lived in the backcountry, only because they realized the British had insufficient manpower to provide proper police action away from the coast. These men wanted it to remain so, thus they could easily continue their illegal enterprises. These are the men who would later become the nucleus of the backcountry Loyalist militia just prior to the American Revolution. They would outnumber the more serious-minded backcountry Patriot militiamen by double.

Additionally, distrust abounded between backcountry militiamen and coastal militiamen who were planters and unaccustomed to the adversities of trudging through the rough backcountry. Letters were published in the November 3–10, 1759, issue of the *South Carolina Gazette* that observed "considerable desertions from the Militia ... the deserters are people of no property and no sense of honor who have fled from other Provinces."

It is an exaggeration that a high percentage of the conscripts were from other provinces, and the desertions should have been expected since Lyttleton, himself, ordered the backcountry justices of peace to conscript vagrants and the like to fulfill his requirements when necessary—it was largely necessary. The total number of militiamen dropped to 1,000 before they left Congaree.[17]

On November 21, 1759, Governor Lyttleton marched his state troops to trader Robert Goudey's Ninety Six Trading Post. They stayed at Ninety Six for one week, and Lyttleton ordered construction of a fort (a 90-foot square stockade) to be erected around Goudey's barn. Though called Fort Ninety Six, it was not at the exact site of the Fort Ninety Six later built at the eponymous village that would later figure prominently in the American Revolution.[18]

Lyttleton arrived at Keowee on December 9, 1759. He and his weary group encamped across the river from the village near Fort Prince George. The Cherokee delegation was kept under guard. This was a conundrum for the Indians. They understood capturing enemies in war to adopt into the tribe or to torture and kill as the situation would dictate; however, the idea of holding hostages for a specific purpose was a new concept to them—one they would make use of in later years.

Historian and trader James Adair stated: "It is well known that the Indians are unacquainted with the custom and meaning of hostages; to them, it conveyed the idea of slaves."[19]

The *South Carolina Gazette* published a comment about the Cherokee in its December 1–7, 1759, edition: "So many headmen of the nation in custody had puzzled the Indians very much and … prevented their doing more mischief."

In the meantime, Attakullakulla returned to the Upper Towns from fighting France's northern Indian allies in Illinois. He had brought eight French scalps with him as he hoped to earn some of the prestige he had lost before his departure. When he became aware that Old Hop had pursued trade and military alliances with France, he became enraged. He confronted him and accused the old principal chief of warmongering. Attakullakulla declared that Old Hop shirked his responsibilities as first beloved man because he did not stand for peace. In reality, this scathing attack was exaggerated. A peace chief civilly led the Cherokee Nation in times of peace; however, he not only had no responsibilities to assure peace but could actually recommend war if he thought it in the best interest of the people. That would be no different than Attakullakulla's fighting the French and the northern Indians. Practically, Attakullakulla was trying to salvage his dwindling reputation in the nation. He even tried to have himself declared first beloved man in his tirade over Old Hop. Attakullakulla had some support but not enough to unseat Old Hop. Attakullakulla was down to his last ten followers, and the younger chiefs and warriors were calling him an "old woman" for trying to salvage peace with the British. He tried another approach and condemned Lyttleton as a scoundrel, but the other headmen called Attakullakulla a deceiver and blamed him for constantly promoting the British.

The people of Keowee were overcome with a smallpox epidemic, so Governor Lyttleton would not allow anyone, including the Cherokee delegation, to cross the river. He sent notorious trader John Elliott to Chota to assure the Cherokee that the prisoners would not be harmed. He also repeated the demand in the message he had sent from Charles Town—that those responsible for murdering white settlers be delivered to Fort Prince George. Lastly, Elliott was to request Attakullakulla to come immediately to Fort Prince George and receive the terms in person.

Elliott happened upon Attakullakulla at Chota and gave him the message. Elliott then presented Lyttleton's demand in the Council House. That angered the younger warriors even more.

Attakullakulla arrived at Fort Prince George on December 14, 1759. He was accompanied by 32 headmen and warriors, many from the Lower Towns, who joined him as he traveled. Included in the party were Ostenaco and Prince Skalilosken (Kittagusta) who was a full brother to Oconostota and half-brother to Ostenaco. He had also traveled with Attakullakulla's party to England in 1730 (see Chapter 3). Another member of the party was Young Warrior (Saloue, Saloweh, Raven of Estatoe) who had earlier struck the war pole when the Creek warriors visited.

When Attakullakulla arrived, he brought a French scalp to Lyttleton as an appeasement; however, the governor ranted, detained his party with the original delegation, and demanded that the 24 Indians who had killed white people should be surrendered for execution. Old Hop called Attakullakulla a traitor to the Cherokee Nation because he had brought difficulty upon the Cherokee by courting the British rather than the French. He then threatened to kill Attakullakulla if he went off to fight the French again.

Old Hop was still the first beloved man of the Cherokee, but he often had asked Attakullakulla to speak for him. However, that closeness had been threatened. Attakullakulla strongly favored alliances with the British while Oconostota favored new alliances with the French. Oconostota took advantage of the time that Attakullakulla was away to persuade Old Hop to join him and court the French. That made Attakullakulla and Oconostota heavy rivals for influence with the Cherokee headmen and the warriors. In the past, the two had been civil to each other as per tribal custom, even as they competed for the ear of the people. That forced cordiality had vanished.

Attakullakulla talked with Lyttleton on December 19, 1759, and the governor again demanded that he hand over those Cherokee warriors who had killed the white settlers. He said: "First of all you are looking toward the French. They can't help you. They themselves are starving and cannot give you blanket or gun. You have to depend on the English for your needs. Your people have killed twenty-four of ours. I expect you to deliver twenty-four warriors of your nation to be put to death for those your people have murdered."[20]

Attakullakulla stated that he would try to talk to the clansmen of the warriors, but that neither he nor Old Hop had any authority to demand that the guilty braves be turned over without clan permission. Oconostota indicated it would be impossible because the clansmen believed their warriors were within the tribal rights of blood vengeance when they had attacked the whites in retaliation for clansmen killed by the Virginians.

Lyttleton, then, asked the Cherokee to burn the shacks of the Keowee residents who had smallpox, and Attakullakulla agreed to talk to the village elders. After they burned the shacks as ordered, the army surgeon, George Milligen-Johnston, stated: "[The wind and smoke] hurried the disease among us, by the smoke driving the infectious particles toward us."[21]

On December 26, 1759, headmen Attakullakulla, Prince Skalilosken, Ostenaco, and Killianca (Killeannakea, Killconnokea), an Upper Town warrior associated with Oconostota and Ostenaco, signed the treaty demanded by Lyttleton. Oconostota sullenly refused to sign the paper and became quite militant. He could not be approached by Attakullakulla or anyone else once the agreement was signed. The Cherokee signatories agreed to deliver the guilty warriors and to kill any French that might enter the Cherokee Nation. Even though the chiefs realized they could not speak for the clans regarding the warriors, they believed the agreement would provide them a stall for time.

Lyttleton originally demanded that all headmen would remain in custody. The rest of the delegation, including those of Attakullakulla's party, was released. However, Attakullakulla advised Lyttleton that he, Attakullakulla, would have a better chance of securing the terms of the treaty if a good faith release of headmen was made. Lyttleton agreed to free Young Warrior (who favored the French), Tiftowe (the headman of Keowee), Oconostota, Ostenaco, and Killianca. Shonguttam (Round-O) had also been included in the negotiation but refused to be released without the remaining headmen. The governor demanded that 24 detainees remain, so some warriors volunteered to stay in the place of some of the released headmen to balance the requirement. The remaining captives were housed in a small cabin designed to accommodate six soldiers.

On December 28, 1759, several of Lyttleton's militiamen began to show smallpox symptoms. Seven hundred men packed their belongings and marched eastward, not only to avoid smallpox infection, but also because the legislature had stopped paying the militia. Lyttleton was irritated because he had not issued any withdrawal order, and the large number of deserters left him short-handed. Upon reflection, he issued orders for the entire force to depart for Charles Town. They left the hostages in the hands of Lieutenant Richard Coytmore at Fort Prince George.

Governor William Henry Lyttleton was hailed as a hero when he returned to Charles Town. The *South Carolina Gazette,* in its January 6–12, 1760, issue printed: "The Cherokee expedition ... of great importance not only to this province but also to North Carolina, Virginia, and Georgia; and in such a very numerous, powerful, treacherous and insolent nation of savages has been compelled to submit to such terms."

The popinjay, Lyttleton, through his insolence, had thrust South Carolina into the center of the Cherokee conflict. The Virginia colony was no longer the primary symbol of British audacity in the minds of the Cherokee warriors and headmen.

Old Hop died on January 28, 1760. Attakullakulla lobbied to be declared first beloved man; however, he was disfavored by the people. His message of tranquility and alliance with the British was unpopular. Standing Turkey (Cunne-Shote), Old Hop's great-grandnephew and brother of Chief Doublehead, agreed with Oconostota's militancy. Standing Turkey was close to Old Hop (who once had also been known as Standing Turkey) and agreed with him regarding a French alliance. The headmen and the warriors believed that a strong warrior with Standing Turkey's belligerent attitude toward Britain was now necessary.

Shortly after Standing Turkey became the principal chief, Attakullakulla tried without avail to influence the warriors. Many Upper Town headmen became incensed with Attakullakulla because he had not secured the release of all headmen, and because the embargo on ammunition had not been lifted. Even the older warriors became inflamed and joined the already irate young ones. They all grabbed their rifles, hatchets, and knives, chanted the Cherokee war song, and attacked the North and South Carolina backcountry settlements. The settlers appealed to Lyttleton, but he could send no help. A smallpox epidemic had affected 4,000 people in Charles Town. Not enough healthy militiamen remained to be assembled.[22]

The Cherokee were not only eager to inflict vengeance for the imprisoned headmen, but they had long awaited an opportunity to correct settler Patrick Calhoun's encroachment on their land at Long Canes. The extended Calhoun family had established the

Chief Standing Turkey, **engraved by James McArdell after a painting by Francis Parsons, 1762.**

settlement of Long Canes in 1758, the first major settlement in the Ninety Six District near present-day Abbeville, South Carolina. Long Canes was located on the border between South Carolina and the Cherokee Nation. When the Calhouns and others settled Long Canes, Patrick Calhoun, the deputy surveyor for the settlement, set his family property up on the Cherokee side of Long Canes Creek in disregard of Governor Glen's agreement.

On January 19, 1760, warriors brutally slaughtered 24 traders near the Long Canes settlement.

The Long Canes settlers, wearied by the Indian threat, decided to vacate their homes and head for Augusta, Georgia. One hundred-fifty settlers, including the Calhouns, took wagons loaded with families and personal effects and crossed Long Canes Creek near present-day Troy, South Carolina. During the crossing, several wagons became mired. One hundred braves suddenly surprised the settlers, and a half-hour battle ensued. That February 1, 1760, battle remains infamous as the Long Canes Massacre. Several settlers were killed before survivors were able to scramble away. A number of children had been lost during the escape; some were severely wounded and left for dead. Eight survived, including several who had been scalped. Fourteen-year-old Rebecca Calhoun, daughter of Ezekial, successfully hid herself in some reeds during the massacre, and later in a calico or kalmia bush. From there, she watched the carnage and saw her grandmother, Catherine Calhoun, murdered and scalped. Aaron Price from Ninety Six, South Carolina, was visiting in Charles Town and reported a story to the *South Carolina Gazette* which was published in its February 3–9, 1760, issue:

> Yesterday se'nnight the whol [sic] of the Long-Cane Settlers, to the Number of 150 souls, moved off with most of their Effects in Waggons; to go towards Augusta in Georgia, and in a few Hours after their setting off, were surprized and attacked by about 100 Cherokees on Horseback, while they were getting their Waggons out of a boggy Place: They had amongst them 40 Gunmen, who might have made a very good Defence, but unfortunately their Guns were in the Waggons; the few that recovered theirs, fought the Indians Half an Hour, and were at last obliged to fly: In the action they lost 7 Waggons, and 40 of their People killed or taken [including women and children] the Rest got safe to Augusta.[23]

A few days later, Patrick Calhoun led a group of settlers to bury the dead. The group managed to rescue the surviving children, including Rebecca. (Young Rebecca Calhoun would later become the wife of South Carolina Militia brigadier general Andrew Pickens.)

The *South Carolina Gazette* reported in its February 17–23, 1760, edition: "Mr. Patrick Calhoun, one of the unfortunate Settlers at Long-Canes, who were attacked by the Cherokees on the 1st Instant ... informs us ... that their Loss in that Affair amounted to about 50 Persons, chiefly Women and Children ... that he had since been at the Place ... in order to Bury the Dead, and found only 20 of their Bodies, most inhumanely butchered."[24]

Patrick Calhoun engraved and set a heavy stone at the site of the massacre which read: "PATK. CALHOUN ESQ.—IN MEMORY OF MRS. CATHRINE CALHOUN AGED 76 YEARS WHO WITH 22 OTHERS WAS HERE MURDERED BY THE INDIANS THE FIRST OF FEB 1760."

Rebecca Calhoun's first cousins, 4-year-old Anne and 2-year-old Mary Calhoun, daughters of Patrick's brother William, had been taken by the Indians. Anne would be returned several years later and would report that she had to run to keep up with the war party. Her sister, Mary, had been killed and scalped; her body was tossed into Long Canes Creek because she could not keep up.[25]

(The original practice of scalping was not done to obtain trophies. It amounted to a spiritual practice that was rarely used. When an enemy's scalp was taken, the Cherokee believed he lost control of his soul and became socially and spiritually dead. The Europeans bastardized the practice in prelude to the French and Indian War as the settlers and soldiers of the two countries began to scalp each other, and each other's Indian allies. They eventually offered bounties for enemy scalps. The promise of bounties caused the practice to grow between whites and Indians alike; among the tribes, scalping then became something different than its original spiritualistic practice, and trophies were collected. Additionally, the killing of prisoners who could not keep up with a war party was a common practice in Indian tribal warfare.)

The Long Canes Massacre, inhumane as it was and certainly a mournful occurrence, cannot be blamed entirely on the Cherokee. The responsibility should mostly lie with South Carolina governor William Henry Lyttleton. He took advantage of a dire situation to satisfy his own ego and began a tragic war that should never have been. That decision cost the lives of not only the 24 traders near Long Canes and the Long Canes settlers during the massacre, but many other backcountry settlers as well. More shameful results were yet to come.

Notorious Creek chief Great Mortar led the war party that accomplished the two ill-reputed attacks, and it has not been determined how many of the band were actually Cherokee warriors. Any Cherokee leaders involved were likely from the Lower Towns.

Principal Chief Standing Turkey agreed with War Chief Oconostota that Fort Prince George should be placed under siege. The offensive occurred early in January after Lyttleton had withdrawn his militia. Then, on February 14, 1760, Attakullakulla joined Oconostota at the fort to negotiate with Lieutenant Richard Coytmore for the remaining prisoners' release. Chief Round-O and four others had died of smallpox during the siege. Coytmore refused to negotiate.

Oconostota delivered missives from Fort Loudoun to Lieutenant Coytmore. Captain Paul Demere had written to request the release of the headmen. Coytmore referred to the signed agreement. Oconostota loudly declared that he signed no such agreement. He further warned Coytmore to release the chiefs or face the warriors of the entire Cherokee Nation, walked off, and Attakullakulla dejectedly followed. Cherokee attacks in the backcountry intensified.

Oconostota and his warriors continued the siege of Fort Prince George. The Cherokee were unaccustomed to the idea of hostages. Their war experience with neighboring tribes dictated that the subjugator of a village usually killed most of the warriors or they captured others (including women and children) to adopt them into the tribe, use them as slaves, or torture them before killing them. Thus, the captives at best, if not killed, lost their original identity. To Oconostota, that's what the future held for the captive headmen. He was determined to free them from such a predicament.

On February 16, 1760, two Cherokee women stood on the bank across the Keowee River from the fort. They were familiar to the garrison, so a soldier came out and spoke to them. Oconostota, on horseback, then joined the two women and told the soldier he wished to speak with Lieutenant Coytmore. Oconostota's demeanor was not as surly as it had been, so Coytmore came out with Lieutenant Thomas Foster (an interpreter), and Ensign John Bell.[26] Oconostota then showed Coytmore a bridle he held and told the lieutenant he was "going to Charles Town to effect the release of the hostages, and desired that a white man might accompany him; and, as the distance was great, he would go and try to catch a horse. Captain [Lieutenant] Coytmore promised him a guard, and hoped he would succeed in catching a horse."[27]

Oconostota had concealed a party of 30 warriors in a heavy thicket also across the river from Fort Prince George. As he rode away, Oconostota "swung his bridle thrice over his head, at which signal a volley of some thirty shots was fired at the officers. All were wounded, Captain [Lieutenant] Coytmore receiving a shot in the left breast from which he died two or three days later."[28]

Foster was wounded in the buttocks, Bell in the calf, and Coytmore had a punctured lung. Foster and Bell were able to drag their commander into the fort.

As Oconostota led his warriors in an attack against the fort, the captive chiefs, who had secreted a few knives and tomahawks, heard the firing and yelled a war-whoop. Then they shouted inspiration for the attackers to "fight like strong-hearted warriors."[29]

Ensign Alexander Milne ordered the hostages to be chained. A soldier seized one of them and was tomahawked to death. The Cherokee headmen fought with their weapons and mortally wounded a second soldier. Other garrison members then fired into the crowd of chiefs and killed them all. Two or three other soldiers had been wounded before the action ceased.

Ensign Milne reported to Lyttleton in a letter on February 28, 1760, that, when the hand-to-hand combat within the fort had ended, he fired the fort's cannons at Keowee and destroyed several structures including the Council House and the conjurer's house.[30]

The garrison was able to repulse the attackers. "Thirty years later, Chief Doublehead mentioned it as one of three occasions on which Cherokee peace envoys had been treacherously murdered."[31]

Garrison surgeon George Milligen-Johnston wrote:

> The soldiers of the Garrison were permitted to kill the innocent and unfortunate Prisoners called Hostages; who were butchered to Death, in a Manner too shocking to Relate ... this Massacre, for I can give it no softer Name.... This Desolation extended upwards of 100 miles; every Hour brought to Charles-town Accounts of ravages, Depredations, Scalpings, and Ruin ... but alas! The Province (distressed by the Expenses of the late Expedition, and at the same time afflicted with Small-pox) ... was unable of itself to manage this War, unwisely brought upon us [by the unwise foray of Governor Lyttleton thrusting South Carolina into the crosshairs of Cherokee vengeance].[32]

The killing of the Cherokee headmen at Fort Prince George gave Lyttleton what he was after—notoriety for "punishing the killers of the white settlers"; however, the Cherokee did not view that as proper vengeance since it did not involve the clans of the original Cherokee instigators. Now the clans of the slain headmen wanted vengeance, but more than that, the Cherokee viewed the massacre of the Cherokee leaders as the wanton slayings of innocent men who had been suing for peace. This, to the Cherokee, meant a day of reckoning would come to the whites—the people who had shown themselves to desire the status of enemies of the Cherokee Nation. Had South Carolina stayed out of it from the beginning, the Cherokee likely would have meted out proper clan vengeance upon the Virginians who had initiated the problem and left backcountry South and North Carolina alone. Now the spiraling cycle of tit-for-tat would continue, thanks to Governor William Henry Lyttleton.

Seemingly, the Cherokee headmen had learned something of the integrity of the British; however, it would not last.[33] In the meantime, they were taking advantage of their newfound aggression against the British colonies. Looked upon as savages by the British, the Cherokee were simply reacting to the mistreatment they had experienced for years. It began with irregular trade practices and culminated with the killing of the headmen at Fort Prince George.

The Cherokee were not done making their point. They continued to launch attacks against traders who had been residing in the Cherokee Nation and had taken advantage of the Cherokee while living among them. Attacks were intensified in the Carolina, Georgia, and Virginia backcountry. However, the Cherokee experienced a shortage of ammunition because of the British embargo, and while the French attempted to make up the difference, they were unable to match the Cherokee needs.

Some of the additional aggressive actions the Cherokee took:
- Two small Upper Town war parties joined to attack trader John Kelly in Chatuga. They killed him, quartered him, and impaled his severed head and hands on stakes.
- One Lower Town war party led by the Cherokee Nation's war chief Oconostota attacked and killed notorious trader John Elliott at Keowee with a hatchet blow to the head. They also slew nine of his associates.
- On February 3, 1760, Young Warrior of Estatoe led 30 Cherokee against Goudey's Fort Ninety Six which was defended by 45 Upper Saluda militiamen commanded by Captain James Francis. After an exchange of gunfire two braves were killed, and the warriors departed. Two wounded warriors were captured. Two militiamen had been slightly wounded. Goudey's home and outbuildings had been burned, but the fort was not harmed. Thirty of the garrison became afflicted with smallpox shortly after the conflict. By this time, approximately 12 additional defensive fortifications had been erected on private property throughout the Ninety Six District.
- On March 3, 1760, two traders who were escaping from the vicinity of Keowee warned Captain Francis at Ninety Six that Young Warrior of Estatoe, and an estimated 300 warriors, were camped nearby. Two hundred braves charged the fort later that day. Francis was only able to muster 25 of his own militiamen healthy enough to fight; however, he had been reinforced by Major John Lloyd with a detachment of 12 men. The battle lasted for nearly 36 hours. On March 6, soldiers explored the grounds and found six dead warriors. Various bloody conflicts with the Cherokee would continue throughout the remainder of 1760.
- On March 4, 1760, while Young Warrior of Estatoe and Creek chief Great Mortar attacked the Carolina backcountry, Oconostota placed Fort Loudoun under siege, and his warriors continually sniped at sentries. According to the *South Carolina Gazette,* February 10–17, 1760, issue, John Stuart had reported on January 12 that the post could hold out for six months during a siege. That is exactly how long the siege would last. The garrison supported and fed 200 men, and their families therein.[34]

Oconostota was assisted during the blockade by chiefs Ostenaco, Standing Turkey, and Willenawah. The garrison fired the cannons periodically to keep the warriors at a distance. Oconostota declared to the headmen that, if peace were declared as many as seven times, he would break it just as often.

That was fair treatment because that is how Cherokee politics had historically worked. If a chief could not convince the other headmen and the warriors that he was right, they would find a new leader. The headmen had to be conscious of the people's consensus.

Several Cherokee women, especially the ones who were married to garrison soldiers, smuggled food into the fort; however, Demere knew it would not be enough. He thought the garrison's only hope would be reinforcements from Charles Town. Chief Willenawah threatened the women with death if they sneaked any more corn to the garrison; however, the women returned the threat—if they were harmed, their clansmen and the families of the garrison would kill him. Willenawah had his warriors hide what corn they could find so the women could not take it to the fort.

The Ghighau, Nanyehi (Nancy Ward) likely helped her husband, Bryant Ward, escape to North Carolina. Even so, Cherokee warriors led by Great Mortar and Young Warrior attacked settlements along the Yadkin River. Attakullakulla warned Moravian settlements near Salem, North Carolina, of impending attacks. Moravian records show:

> The Warrior Band planning to attack the village of Bethbara had surrounded the small settlement. It happened to be on a Church Day. The bell tolled the hour of worship. The Indians thinking their presence had been discovered withdrew for a conference. They decided to make another attempt during the heavy dark of night. Again they surrounded the town. While waiting the signal to attack they heard the bugler tooting the hour of night. Certain their presence had again been discovered and the horn blowing was a warning to those on guard, the Indians left and never bothered the small Moravian settlement.[35]

Finally, Governor Lyttleton was replaced on April 5, 1760, by Acting Royal Governor William Bull II, who was the interim leader until the appointed governor, Thomas Boone, could arrive in December 1761. Bull begged General Jeffery (sometimes Jeffrey or Geoffrey) Amherst (1st Baron Amherst), governor general of British North America, for British troops to relieve the colony and rescue the Fort Loudoun and Fort Prince George garrisons. (Amherst would be promoted to major general on November 29, 1760.) Colonel Archibald Montgomery reached Charles Town with 1,300 troops of the 77th Regiment of Foot (Montgomery's Highlanders) in late April. Once he heard Montgomery was coming, Governor Bull declared the day they would arrive to be "a Day of Fasting, Humiliation, and Prayer to Almighty God for averting the Evil which at present threatens ... a war." His words were published in the *South Carolina Gazette* in the April 6–12, 1760, edition.

In mid May 1760, Captain Paul Demere cut the garrison rations to one quart of corn for each person per day. The troops were starved and had to butcher their horses and dogs for meat.

Colonel Montgomery gathered information and made plans; however, the South Carolina militia was not ready to go until early June 1760. The colonel and his highlanders met 350 militiamen at Congaree as Lyttleton had done in 1759.

Attakullakulla was not trusted by the Upper Village headmen. He was expelled from the Council House on June 2, 1760, and had received some threats, so he concealed his family well within the forest. His prestige had slipped away, as he had long feared would

4. Lyttleton, Montgomery and Grant Destroy the Cherokee Community

happen, because of his strong support for British alliances. He visited Captain Paul Demere at Fort Loudoun as often as he could stealthily do so.

On June 5, Attakullakulla made one last visit to Fort Loudoun. He was grieved by the dire straits of the garrison. Demere, again, pressured him for information. Attakullakulla wanted to blame the Lower Towns for the difficulties, but he had to face the fact that Standing Turkey (his nephew), Oconostota (his first cousin once removed and father-in-law), Ostenaco (his first cousin once removed), and Willenawah (his brother) strongly wanted war with the British.

Attakullakulla responded to Demere essentially: "I am not the man to ask for news. The Indians hide everything from me, and say I am the white man's friend. Only Tomatly town wishes peace; the rest want war."[36]

The women also brought no more food to the garrison beyond that day.

Shortly after the visit with Attakullakulla, a messenger gave Demere news that British colonel Montgomery was coming to the rescue. The spirits of the entire garrison lifted immediately.[37]

When Colonel Montgomery was ordered to South Carolina, General Amherst's specific instructions were to quickly relieve the Carolinas and return soon to Albany, New York, because the reduction of Canada was top priority.

Before he left Congaree, Montgomery imposed a blackout on news from the campaign for security purposes until Major James Grant would post a report at the conclusion of the expedition. When Montgomery arrived at Keowee on June 2 with his 1,650 men, they could all see, atop nearby mountains, the Cherokee who watched the army destroy the abandoned town to the relief of Fort Prince George.

Indian Agent Edmond Atkin, who had so badly mismanaged Indian affairs during the French and Indian War, joined Montgomery at Fort Prince George. Montgomery directed Atkin to dispatch two survivors of Keowee (aged Indian chiefs) to the Middle Towns and to Fort Loudoun. The old chiefs couriered a message that stated the colonel would receive Attakullakulla, who had provided many good services on behalf of the Cherokee, and some headmen at Fort Prince George. Montgomery warned they should answer quickly or the Middle and Upper Towns would be rendered to ashes as had been the Lower Towns. He added that Acting governor William Bull was ready to grant them terms of peace. Bull was a fair-minded man; however, the Cherokee were unfamiliar with him and thought he would be no better than Lyttleton had been. Additionally, they had no confidence in any words uttered by the Indian agent.

The chiefs did not come in, and Attakullakulla was still not held in favor by the other headmen and the younger warriors. Colonel Montgomery determined to continue along the Little Tennessee River into the Cherokee Middle Towns. He was sure that, if he destroyed the Middle Towns, the leading Upper Town headmen would negotiate a peace settlement. On the 24th, the force crossed the Keowee and Oconee Rivers and set out for Estatoe, Toxaway, Qualatchee, and Conasatche which all met the same fate as Keowee.

Each of the Lower Towns, mostly abandoned, were surrounded and destroyed along with the crops. Any warriors found were bayoneted to death. Altogether, Montgomery killed over one hundred Indians in the Lower Towns, captured 40, and drove the remaining population into the mountains. Very few of those slain were warriors able to easily escape into the hills.

As the troops approached the Middle Towns of the Little Tennessee River, they were slowed by steep grades. At 4:00 a.m. on the 27th, they entered Rabun Gap in the Little Tennessee River Valley and moved toward Echoe, the nearest Middle Town to the Lower Towns. George Washington proved to be prophetic when he stated: "What may be Montgomery's fate in the Cherokee country I cannot so readily determine ... he is now advancing his troops in high health and spirits to the relief of Fort Loudoun. But let him be wary. He has a crafty, subtle enemy to deal with that may give him most trouble when he least expects it."[38]

Some of the soldiers had apparently contracted smallpox while at Fort Prince George, and several more soldiers came down with the fever daily as they moved through the mountains. At 10:00 a.m., they had advanced to within five miles of Echoe. They entered Crow's Creek Pass a few miles south of Nikwasi (present-day Franklin, North Carolina) where "there he [Montgomery] found a muddy river with steep clay banks, running through a low valley so thickly covered with bushes that the soldiers could scarcely see three yards before them. A more advantageous position for ambushing and attacking an enemy, after the manner of Indian warfare, could hardly have been chosen."[39]

It was not a favorable environment for the soldiers. Captain Morrison was detached with his company of South Carolina Provincial Rangers to reconnoiter the thicket. Once they advanced to enter it, Cherokee warriors, led by Young Warrior (Seloweh, Raven of Estatoe), raised their war-whoop, emerged from their concealment on elevated ground on both sides of the path, and fired.

"The 77th Foot mounted the ridge to his [Montgomery's] left and the 1st Foot the ridge to the right."[40] They charged the Indians, and a frantic skirmish ensued. Hand-to-hand combat raged throughout the thicket with soldiers and warriors wielding knives and tomahawks.

After four hours of fervent fighting, Young Warrior's braves withdrew and allowed the British to ford the river just north of the battlefield. One British participant recorded: "During the action they endeavored to frighten us with their yelling, but we turned the Cheer upon them, with three Whirra's, and three waves of our Bonnets and hats, which they did not seem to relish."[41]

In truth, the Cherokee withdrew only because of their extreme shortage of ammunition. Had that not been the case, Montgomery's force might have been beaten more severely. As it was, the army is variously reported to have lost 20 killed, including Captain Morrison, and 70–94 wounded.

Montgomery marched into Echoe, but the Battle of Crow's Creek Pass had allowed the warriors time to vacate the town. They took their families and moveable possessions to the nearby mountains. The troops destroyed Echoe and its 200 dwellings much as they had done in the Lower Towns. Montgomery's sentries were sniped at from the surrounding hills; morale was running low, and the South Carolina Provincials had already deserted after the battle. Colonel Montgomery destroyed his remaining supplies and used the packhorses to evacuate the wounded. He abandoned the expedition to relieve Fort Loudoun, which was still under siege, to return to Fort Prince George by July 1, 1760. He was followed and harassed by Cherokee warriors as he traveled.

General Amherst recalled Colonel Montgomery to New York by August 1, which allowed time for the troops to recuperate. Amherst was eager to attack the French in Canada.

However, he was disappointed in Montgomery's efforts. Amherst stated: "I must own I am ashamed, for I believe it is the first instance of His Majesty's troops having yielded to the Indians."[42]

The *South Carolina Gazette* published a report from British lieutenant colonel James Grant to Acting Governor Bull in the July 13–19, 1760, edition that included:

"The Cherokees ... [took] possession of ground that was most advantageous to them ... some of the Indians spoke English and gave us very insulting language, the Raven of Estatouih [See below at Ninety Six] was with them, the Young Warrior seemed to be their commander in chief; his voice was distinctly heard the whole time, calling loudly to his people to fight strong."

Grant added an afterthought, "I could not help pitying them a little ... after killing all we could we marched to Keowee."

(There is a marker along U.S. Highway 23/441 south of Franklin, North Carolina, which reads, "In the French and Indian War, the Cherokees defeated a colonial and British force from N.Y. under Colonel Montgomery near here, June, 1760.")

Historian Albert V. Goodpasture wrote: "The Virginia Assembly at once voted a considerable force for their [the Fort Loudon garrison] relief, but as the troops levied were to rendezvous at [the site of the future] Fort Robinson, on the Holston, two hundred miles distant from Williamsburg, and afterwards to march two hundred miles further, through an unexplored and trackless wilderness, the garrison might as effectually have been succored from the moon."[43]

Virginia Militia colonel William Byrd had marched with 1,000 troops to the Upper Towns to help Montgomery relieve Fort Loudoun. Byrd would have provided a second front for the effort; however, when Montgomery abandoned the campaign, Byrd stopped at the Long Island of the Holston. There he would build Fort Robinson (to be named after his friend, John Robinson) on the North Bank opposite the upper end of the island. Lieutenant Henry Timberlake (who will be covered in Chapter 5) was among the expedition.

Acting Governor William Bull, II, greatly feared for the safety of the Fort Loudoun garrison. It was mid–July before Captain Paul Demere received word that Colonel Montgomery had been attacked, suffered severe losses, and had withdrawn from the campaign. The bottom dropped out of the morale of the entire garrison.

The besieged had eaten the last of the bread and corn on July 7, and Demere reduced the rations to four ounces of horsemeat and one-fourth cup of beans per day. They had eight skinny horses left to butcher for food. Several soldiers had stealthily abandoned the fort by August 4. A few of them found shelters in the forest after a dangerous trek; others successfully made their way east to civilization, but the remainder had either surrendered to, or been captured by, the Cherokee.[44]

On August 6, 1760, five of Captain Paul Demere's junior officers presented him with a written statement that the people at Fort Loudoun were starving and the fort needed to be surrendered. Demere agreed! He knew that Captain John Stuart was respected by some of the Cherokee headmen, so he sent Stuart to discuss surrender terms in the Cherokee Council House with Oconostota, Willenawah, Ostenaco, and Standing Turkey.

The Cherokee dictated terms and told Stuart that the garrison could march to whatever destination they would choose. Further, they would be accompanied partway by Standing Turkey, Oconostota, Ostenaco, and several warriors for their own protection. Each soldier would be allowed to carry one rifle and enough ammunition to secure food for the people during the trek. The Cherokee agreed to supply as many horses as they could spare, and soldiers who were ill or wounded could recuperate in the Upper Cherokee Towns until they could travel. The chiefs demanded that the fort, all cannons, powder, bullets, and other arms be left available for the Cherokee. They specified that such arms were not to be destroyed or hidden, but left in the open within the fort.

Demere was dejected as the negotiations took place. He roamed through the fort expressionless. He felt as if he had failed his assignment. However, Stuart had received excellent terms for the surrender.

Demere signed the pact on August 8, and he sent a messenger to Governor Bull indicating he was comfortable that the Cherokee headmen meant them no harm. He assured the Cherokee that the garrison would evacuate as quickly as possible considering their condition.

At dawn the following morning, the garrison held a solemn ceremony on the parade grounds. Later that morning, 180 men and their families (60 women and children) filed out of the fort behind Captains Demere and Stuart.

The leaders had selected Fort Prince George for their destination. It would be an arduous journey through mountains infested with banditti. They made only 15 miles the first day in their weakened condition. They camped at the confluence of Cane Creek and the Tellico River. Captain Demere expected to reach Fort Prince George before the end of August.

Reportedly, sometime that night Cheulah (Tsula, the Fox, Small Pox Conjuror), the chief of Settico, brought a message to Oconostota regarding Fort Loudoun. The message caused the warriors and chiefs to abandon their escort mission. Apparently, the Cherokee at the fort had discovered ten bags of powder and a large quantity of rifle balls that Captain Demere had ordered buried in the fort before they vacated. Additionally, the warriors found cannons and small arms that had been thrown into the river. Both actions were a total breach of the terms of the surrender. A Cherokee housekeeper had brought the deception to Ostenaco's attention. It is hard to imagine that Demere would have expected the ruse to go undiscovered. He was well aware that the Cherokee were clever and not easily fooled. He likely was not thinking clearly as evidenced by his strange demeanor while Stuart negotiated terms.

Demere and the garrison awakened the morning of the 10th to find no Indians in camp. They were being watched by 700 warriors that had surrounded the camp before dawn. The war party was led by

Chief Ostenaco, by Sir Joshua Reynolds, 1762.

Oconostota and Ostenaco, themselves, and they were irate. The warriors had shucked their clothing and covered their bodies with vermillion paint to prepare for battle.

The Cherokee attacked at dawn as the campers awakened. Shortly, the garrison's 13-man advance began to organize their march. They noticed several Cherokee warriors moving quickly down another trail on the other side of Cane Creek. They were running to create an ambush should any of the garrison escape the coming attack. The remainder of the war party opened fire from concealment, and Captain Demere was wounded. Several of the soldiers had been hit with rifle balls and arrows. Then the Cherokee charged the camp and deftly overcame the starvation-weakened travelers in hand-to-hand combat.

Stuart fought valiantly; however, a warrior named Onatoy wrestled him to the ground, likely for his own protection. Attakullakulla had arranged for Onatoy to claim John Stuart and sell him to Attakullakulla for everything the headman had: arms, ammunition, and even clothing—all except for a breechclout. Stuart became Attakullakulla's "captive" and was housed in Paul Demere's old quarters within Fort Loudoun.

(Onatoy [also Onatowe and Onotony] was from the Valley Towns near Murphy, North Carolina. Some historians have reported him to have been a headman over Little Tellico; however, that is unlikely. He had generally been a British alliance proponent and, therefore, a confederate to Attakullakulla. Thus, it made sense that he would agree for compensation to assist Attakullakulla and save John Stuart. Onatoy was also the brother of Round-O [Shonguttam], who died of smallpox while a hostage at Fort Prince George.)

The housekeeper's statement blamed Demere for the ruse, and Oconostota intended to make him pay. Soon after the battle had wound down, Ostenaco loudly demanded an end to killing of soldiers and civilians. They were primarily after Captain Paul Demere, and the wounded commander was already in captivity.

The warriors surrounded Demere. He had been scalped, and they forced him to dance until he could no longer stand. Once he collapsed, a warrior stuffed his mouth with dirt while shouting words to the effect that white men always want land and here is your share. Then, others severed his arms and legs from his body while he was yet alive. He succumbed to intense pain and loss of blood. Captain John Stuart was the only officer to survive. The warriors reportedly killed Demere and three others: Lieutenant James Adamson, Ensign John Bogges, and another named Wintle.

(It is variously reported by historians that between 23 and 33 were killed during the attack. The most-often reported numbers state that 23 soldiers, three officers, and three women were killed. However, that does not align with the names of the reported slain officers.)

The survivors were taken prisoner by individual Cherokee warriors. Each captor was privileged to treat his prisoner as he was moved to do. Some were to be tortured and killed; yet, others were saved and separated throughout the villages. Most of the whites were treated well. Only a few were badly abused by their Cherokee "owner" depending on who their captor was. The warrior's personality had an important bearing on his prisoner's outcome. Three reportedly had been taken to be tortured. Oconostota, himself, saved a man named Frederick Mouncy and an unidentified boy. The war chief believed the Cherokee had proven their point to the South Carolinians—the nation could, and would, defend itself from British tyranny. However, he was too late to save another, Luke Croft, who had already been burned at the stake.

Oconostota's move was unusual in that the Cherokee valued individual autonomy. It was printed in the October 5–11, 1760, edition of the *South Carolina Gazette* that the Cherokee generally treated their captives humanely. A prisoner would rarely be whipped, tortured, or killed. In such cases where torture and death was selected, it was usually either as a matter of convenience—in the midst of battle, on the way to or from a battle—or a circumstance that caused the warrior some other burden. Sometimes it was because the captive was a brave warrior who deserved to "die well." Mostly, captives became adopted members of the warriors' families. They were well-fed, toiled in the crop fields and gardens, and roamed freely through the village. They were required to adapt to the Cherokee way of life. Historian Albert V. Goodpasture wrote:

> Captain Stuart and those who remained with him, were seized, pinioned, and carried back to Fort Loudoun.... The discovery that the garrison had, in bad faith, concealed a large part of their military stores before evacuating the fort, has been assigned as the cause of this massacre; but the manifest purpose of the Indians was to take satisfaction for the massacre of their peace envoys, at Fort Prince George, which Oconostota and Judge Friend [Ostenaco] had barely escaped.[45]

(The site of the battle is near present-day Tellico Plains, Tennessee. There is a marker located within Tellico Plains at the corner of Tennessee Highway 165 and Hunt Street. It reads, "Four miles N.E., at Junction Cane Creek, Tellico River, Fort Loudoun's Garrison, which had surrendered to Attakullakulla and other Cherokee chiefs, was betrayed Aug. 9, 1760—while returning under safe conduct to Charles Town. Twenty-five were killed; 200 were enslaved, and later ransomed by the Colonial Government."

(Also, in the interest of fairness, the dates variously reported by historians pertaining to the span from the surrender of Fort Loudoun, through its evacuation, and ending with the date of the Cherokee attack upon the garrison differ by as much as two days. The dates shown above for the actions are used by over half of the references researched by the author. Interestingly, the date printed on the roadside marker varies from that.)

In August, Young Warrior of Estatoe (Seroweh) approached Fort Prince George with a peace overture. He must have acted independently, because Oconostota was not yet ready to discuss peace. A war correspondent wrote from the fort and had published in the *South Carolina Gazette* in its August 17–23, 1760, issue: "I confess I don't like the Young Warrior's talk, it looks more like dictation than begging the peace, tho' by an illiterate hand it has too much the language of the conqueror."[46]

Leave it to the British colonial popinjays to decide the force that destroyed a major South Carolina garrison did not deserve to dictate peace terms—regardless of the fact that the colony had forced the issue. The mere fact that a reporter publicized such an idea made it impossible for the colony to treat the Cherokee as even nearly equal to the civilized British.

Oconostota was willing to allow Attakullakulla to set Stuart free if the captain would become the Cherokee's artillery officer. Uplifted by his success against Fort Loudoun, Oconostota wanted to re-establish the siege at Fort Prince George. He expected Stuart to lead other captive soldiers and man the cannons during the blockade. Captain Stuart would also be the Cherokee's stenographer. That is, he would write dictated letters to colonial authorities. The chief informed Stuart of his plan in the Chota Council House. The war chief did not intend another slaughter, unless the garrison forced the issue as the troops at

4. Lyttleton, Montgomery and Grant Destroy the Cherokee Community   91

Fort Loudoun had done. He had just had enough of British colonial troops garrisoned in Cherokee country.

John Stuart decided to escape rather than betray Britain. He informed Attakullakulla of his desires, recognized that they had been like brothers, and asked Attakullakulla to help him escape. Attakullakulla adopted John Stuart and told the captain he was like the exiled chief's own son. They ritualized a ceremony that made them blood brothers.

Not wanting to create suspicion, Attakullakula devised a plan to pretend that he and Stuart were going on a hunting trip. Taking some of Attakullakulla's family along, they left Fort Loudoun on August 31, 1760. On September 8, the group ran into Virginia major Andrew Lewis and 300 men near Long Island of the Holston River (present-day Kingsport, Tennessee). Lewis had been detached by Colonel William Byrd to reconnoiter the vicinity. Lewis took the group to Byrd on the 13th, and Attakullakulla requested the colonel to write a letter to Standing Turkey and Oconostota with terms for peace. Attakullakulla, himself, would carry the letter to Chota. Stuart was able to make his way home from Byrd's camp. Stuart met up with friends at Fort Robinson who helped him travel to his relatives on the coast.

(John Stuart married a Cherokee woman named Susannah Emory. He was called Oo-no-dutu [Bushyhead] because of his thick shock of red-gold hair. Their son, also known as Oo-no-dutu, married Nancy Foreman, a mixed-blood daughter of a Scottish trader and a Cherokee woman. John Stuart's grandson was called Jesse Bushyhead. Beginning with Jesse, the descendants maintained Bushyhead as their surname. Jesse Bushyhead became an ordained Baptist minister. He, and his family were removed during the infamous Trail of Tears in 1838. The Bushyhead surname is found on the Drennen Roll of 1852, a census of "recent" Cherokee arrivals to Oklahoma.

Attakullakulla had also arranged for the safety of an interpreter named William Shorey, who also married a Cherokee woman named Gigui [or GhigGooie]. Their great-grandson was John Ross who, much later, would become principal chief. There will be more information on William Shorey in a later chapter.)

The Cherokee fervor for war had finally cooled, and on September 20, 1760, Attakullakulla met Standing Turkey, Oconostota, Ostenaco, and nearly 2,000 headmen at the Council House in Nequassee. Attakullakulla presented the letter from Colonel Byrd, along with gifts that Byrd had provided, to the chiefs. Attakullakulla was slowly recovering his prestige among the Cherokee. Many headmen had regained a desire for peace with the British. Standing Turkey and Oconostota realized they needed to honor the desires of the Cherokee people and end the war.

In the Council House, both Ostenaco and Oconostota recommended peace with Britain. Oconostota had recently gone to Fort Toulouse, as Old Hop had previously done, to negotiate with the French. However, the French had lowered the Cherokee priority as they needed to divert French ammunition to the north for the defense of Canada. The Cherokee decided, as minimal as it was, the British supply of ammunition was the only reliable source—at least for the time being. Oconostota sent a captive Fort Loudoun soldier to Charles Town to convince Acting Governor William Bull II to arrange a peace conference. The war chief also promised that any Englishman could now pass safely through Cherokee country. However, the desire for peace would transform to disappointment.[47]

On November 1, 1760, Attakullakulla visited Colonel William Byrd at Long Island of the Holston River. The chief had brought ten captives from the original Fort Loudoun garrison as a sign of sincerity. Byrd, again, bestowed presents upon Attakullakulla for his return to Chota. Governor Bull was not impressed with the release of captives. He had not been convinced that the Cherokee truly desired peace. He still promoted that the Cherokee should be punished for the Fort Loudoun incident. If anything, Attakullakulla had simply reminded the governor of the slayings when he brought in released captives. There was still a large schism between the beliefs of the Cherokee and the colonists regarding what was fair; what action really "evened the score." The South Carolina legislature was even debating a new law that would allow the militia to take Cherokee prisoners to be used for slaves in the West Indies.

The more Bull thought about Fort Loudoun, the more irate he became. When Captain Stuart had previously escaped from the Upper Towns, he had immediately warned Governor Bull of the impending siege of Fort Prince George. The fort had only enough provisions to survive for ten weeks. The siege of Fort Prince George never did materialize; however, Governor Bull relied on the report as evidence of Cherokee intent for further militancy.

Governor Bull applied to General Jeffery Amherst for assistance as his predecessor, Governor William Henry Lyttleton, had done. Amherst had completed the conquest of Canada, so he could now spare a force to convince the Cherokee to "repent" of their hostilities. Amherst was still embarrassed by Montgomery's failure, and he desired to teach the Cherokee "savages" a lesson.

Lieutenant Colonel James Grant had succeeded Colonel Montgomery in command of the 77th Regiment of Foot (Highlanders), so Amherst ordered him to South Carolina. Grant arrived at Charles Town in January 1761, and established his winter billets. Lieutenant Governor Bull placed Colonel Thomas Middleton's South Carolina Militia regiment at Colonel Grant's disposal. Included were Lieutenant Colonel Henry Laurens, Major John Moultrie, Captain William Moultrie, Lieutenant Isaac Huger, Lieutenant Francis Marion, and Captain Andrew Pickens. They and a few Catawba and Choctaw warriors would meet Grant's regulars at Ninety Six.

On March 12, 1761, Attakullakulla with 500 of his regained followers visited Fort Prince George and delivered 12 more Fort Loudoun captives. He still tried to dissuade South Carolina from further action. The Cherokee headmen were finally reliant upon him to reestablish his flair for successful negotiations. He feared, that if he failed this time, he might never again recover his prestige.

Grant had made his plans by May. The winter melt had long been over, so he marched his force out of Charles Town. Peter Horry wrote: "On their way they were joined at Ninety-Six, May 14, 1761, by twelve hundred provincials, all men of surest aim with the deadly rifle."[48]

On May 14, 1761, the Grant Expedition arrived at Fort Ninety Six. The fort had been previously reinforced and was defended by some 400 South Carolina rangers. This brought Lieutenant Colonel Grant's complete force to 3,000 men, including British regulars and provincials, South Carolina militiamen and rangers, Indian guides and wagoners. Grant departed Fort Ninety Six for Fort Prince George on the 18th. He left South Carolina Militia captain Daniel to lead a fifty-man defensive garrison at Fort Ninety Six.

Grant's total force then numbered 2,600 troops. It was an interesting agglomeration: British soldiers, militiamen, warriors from two different tribes. There was also reticence between the coastal Carolinians and those of the backcountry (usually considered by the

4. Lyttleton, Montgomery and Grant Destroy the Cherokee Community

coastal elite as no better than Indians themselves). Many backcountry settlers learned from the Cherokee lifestyle and even adapted their own battle tactics from recognized Cherokee strategy. The coastal militiamen, on the other hand, were inclined to imitate the British soldiers in dress and drill. The troops reached Fort Prince George on May 27, 1761.

Attakullakulla went to Fort Prince George to plead with Grant. He said: "I am and have always been a friend to the English, although I have been called an old woman by the warriors. The conduct of my people has filled me with shame, but I would interpose on their behalf and bring about peace."[49]

He asked for 12 days to gather the Cherokee headmen to talk terms. Grant refused with: "No, Attakullakulla. I will not lose half an hour waiting for your people."[50]

With that, Grant continued his expedition on June 7, 1761. The colonel moved out of Fort Prince George with provisions to last one month. Lieutenant Colonel Grant, who had been an officer under Colonel Montgomery in the 1760 campaign, led his men quickly through the Lower Towns. The troops burned the structures and destroyed crops just as Montgomery had done—but faster. Before they headed for Echoe Pass where Montgomery had been ambushed in 1760, Grant ordered his men to prepare for an encounter. At 8:00 a.m. on June 9, when they arrived at Estatoe Old Fields two miles from the pass, Grant's own army was waylaid. Catawba and Choctaw warriors had scouted toward the pass, along with Lieutenant Francis Marion, who was detached with 30 men. They faced a barrage of rifle balls that issued from cover. Twenty-one of Marion's militiamen fell. The lieutenant withdrew the remainder to the main force. The Catawba, then, successfully outflanked the Cherokee until Grant arrived with his army.

Oconostota's force was on a rise. They fired at the troops, who had the river at their backs. The chief also had a detached war party stationed across the river, also firing at the soldiers. One small band of Cherokee heartily attempted to capture the packhorses. Grant was able to send Lieutenant Marion to save the animals and supplies. The battle lasted for three hours and became close-quarter combat until the Cherokee began to run low on ammunition and so withdrew.

Grant moved to Echoe (near present-day Franklin, North Carolina) where he used the Town House for his field hospital. His troops destroyed that town, as well as Tassie. Next to be razed was Nequassee near the Little Tennessee River. From there, they proceeded to Watauga and destroyed it, then burned Ayoree where the troops were rested on the 13th. Grant wrote in his journal at Ayoree:

> We halted. Corn about the town was destroyed, parties sent out to burn the scattered houses, pull up beans, peas and corn, and to demolish everything eatable in the country. Our Indian Scouts, with one of our parties, destroyed the towns of Neowee and Kanuga. A scout of our Indians killed a Cherokee and wounded another at Ayore. A miserable old squaw from Tasso was brought in and put to death in the Indian Camp by the Catawbas.[51]

They next burned the crops at Cowee but left the structures intact. They bivouacked at Ussinah while they destroyed Coweechee and Burning Town.

Next they attacked the Valley Towns, or Out Towns, and destroyed Stecoe, Tuckaseegee, Tessantee, Conutory, and Kituhwa. Then they returned to Cowee and rested. When ready to return to Fort Prince George, they burned Cowee and departed.

After causing desolation in the villages for the better part of a month, Grant returned to Fort Prince George where he reported:

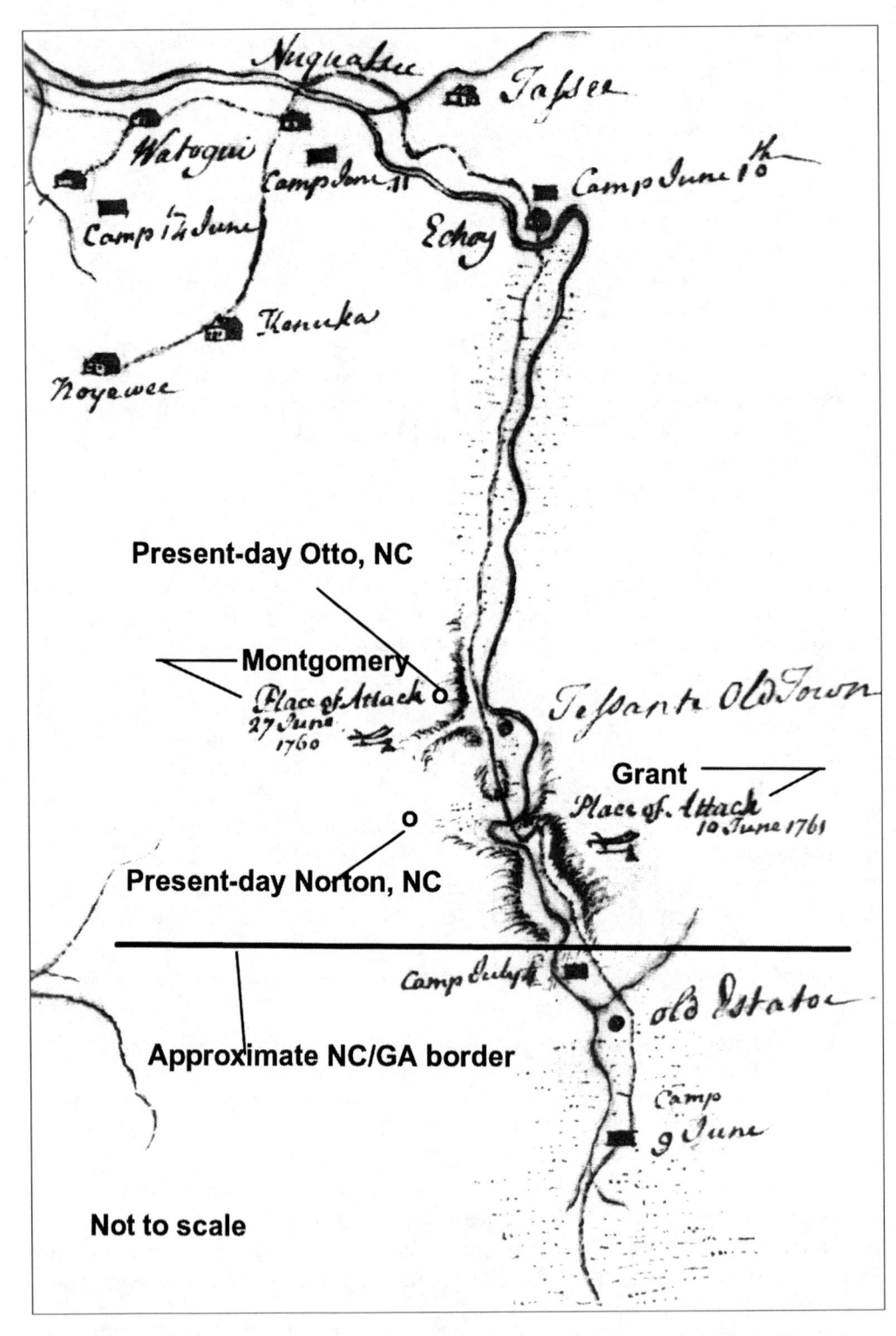

James Grant Expedition, 1761, with notes added by the author—shows the places where Montgomery (1760) and Grant (1761) expeditions were ambushed by the Cherokee.

> Destroying an Indian town ... of no great consequence, where the savages have time to carry off their effects.... All their towns, amounting to fifteen in number, besides many little villages and scattered homes, have been burnt; upwards of fourteen hundred acres of corn, according to moderate computation, entirely destroyed; and near five thousand Cherokees, including men, women, and children, driven to the mountains to starve; their only subsistence for some time past, being horseflesh.[52]

Lieutenant Colonel James Grant had utter contempt for the Cherokee. He didn't think they were smart enough to know they had been soundly defeated.

Indian trader and historian James Adair had a differing viewpoint:

> The year following, Major Grant ... was sent against them with an army of regulars and provincials, and happily for him, the Indians were then in great want of ammunition: they therefore only appeared, and suddenly disappeared. From all probable circumstances, had the Cheerake been sufficiently supplied with ammunition, twice the number of troops could not have defeated them, on account of the declivity of their stupendous mountains.[53]

While Colonel Grant destroyed the Middle Towns, Virginia colonel William Byrd was ordered to attack the Upper Towns wherein the Middle Town Cherokee refugees had withdrawn. Colonel Byrd refused and left his regiment in disgust. Virginia lieutenant colonel Adam Stephen took command and marched his troops to the Long Island of the Holston River. There, he detached Major Andrew Lewis to complete construction of Fort Robinson.

On July 18, 1761, Attakullakulla went to Colonel Stephen's camp and explained that his brothers, war chiefs Oconostota and Ostenaco, were ready for peace. Stephen told Attakullakulla to make his presentation to Colonel Grant and to South Carolina governor Bull.

One might envision the Cherokee people safely retreating from their villages ahead of Grant's army, living off the land, hunting to supply the village with meat, and patiently returning to resume their lives once Grant's campaign was done.

However, realistically the Cherokee people were shocked to see their dwellings burned and their crops destroyed. They could take little with them other than the clothing they wore as they struggled to safety ahead of the approaching force. Often having to leave ammunition and arms, except for what the warriors could carry on horseback, the people had become heavily reliant on trade goods (European) and not easily able to drift back to the old way of life.

Grant had destroyed 15 towns, 1,400 acres of crops, and 5,000 people, including women and children left foraging in the forested mountains. The Cherokee warriors had been greatly reduced from 5,000 before Lyttleton's initial foray to 2,300 after the Grant expedition.

Lieutenant Francis Marion had been touched by the plight of the Cherokee while he was a part of Grant's campaign, and so had Captain Andrew Pickens. Marion later wrote:

> We arrived at the Indian towns in the month of July. As the lands were rich and the season had been favorable, the corn was bending under the double weight of lusty roasting ears and pods of clustering beans. The furrows seemed to rejoice under their precious loads the fields stood thick with bread. We encamped the first night in the woods, near the fields, where the whole army feasted on the young corn, which, with fat venison, made a most delicious treat.
>
> We proceeded by Colonel Grant's orders, to burn the Indian cabins. Some of the men

seemed to enjoy this cruel work, laughing heartily at the cruel flames, but to me it appeared a shocking sight. Poor creatures, thought I, we surely need not grudge you such miserable habitations. But when we came, according to orders, to cut down the fields of corn, I could scarcely refrain from tears. Who, without grief, could see the stately stalks with broad green leaves and tasseled tops, the staff of life sink under our swords with all their precious load, to wither and rot untasted in their mourning field.

I saw everywhere around, the footsteps of little Indian children, where they had lately played under the shade of their rustling corn. When we were gone, thought I, they will return, and peeping through the weeds with tearful eyes, will mark the ghastly ruin where they had so often played. "Who did this?" they will ask their mothers, and the reply will be: "The white people did it—the Christians did it."

Thus for cursed mammon's sake, the followers of Christ have sowed the selfish tares of hate in the bosom of even pagan children.[54]

Fifty years later Andrew Pickens wrote to his friend Henry "Light-horse Harry" Lee of the experience: "I served as a volunteer in Grant's expedition against the Cherokees in the year 1762 [actually 1761]. There I learned someting [sic] of British cruelty which I always abhorred."[55]

On August 21, 1761, Attakullakulla led a delegation to Fort Prince George to confer with Lieutenant Colonel Grant who had returned there. The entourage included chiefs Ostenaco, Savanah Tom, Old Caesar of Hiwassee, and other headmen. They began a council session on the 29th. On September 1, the colonel announced his terms for peace. Attakullakulla agreed to several of the terms: to return the cannons from Fort Loudoun to the British, and to allow the British to erect new forts in Cherokee country, The most difficult of the requirements were that the Cherokee would deliver four warriors to Fort Prince George to be publicly executed; any Cherokee who killed a white man (or killed a brave from the British allied tribes of the Catawba or the Chickasaw) would be executed by his town's chief; and a white man guilty of killing a Cherokee would be turned over to the British for punishment. The Cherokee would also ban French traders and soldiers from the nation; British traders would be unmolested, and the Cherokee would release all captives from the recent war. The clans of the four warriors to be selected had the right to approve or disapprove of any such transaction. A similar problem existed with the return of captives. Each captive belonged to separate and distinct warriors and their families, and would need to be ransomed. A headman, by tradition, could not interfere with that practice. Attakullakulla politely informed Grant he had no authority to intercede with clan responsibilities in such matters and asked permission to talk with Governor Bull. Grant approved the request. Colonel Grant drew up an interim treaty, and Attakullakulla agreed to all terms except: "That four Cherokee Indians be delivered up to Colonel Grant at Fort Prince George, to be put to death in front of his camp; or four green scalps to be brought to him in the space of twelve nights."[56]

Attakullakulla, however, did not go to Charles Town because of a smallpox epidemic there, so Governor Bull agreed to meet him at Ashley's Ferry. Bull was very courteous and treated the chief with distinction.

The conference took place in September. Attakullakulla smoked a pipe with Bull and the governor's council who accompanied him. Bull opened the discourse with:

Attakullakulla, I am glad to see you, and as I have always heard of your good behavior, that you have been a good friend to the English, I take you by the hand, and not only you but all those with you also, as a pledge of their security whilst under my protection. Colonel Grant acquaints me that you have applied for peace; now that you have come, I have met you with my beloved men, to hear what you have to say, and my ears are open for that purpose.[57]

They smoked again, and after a few moments of silence Attakullakulla arose and orated:

When I came to Keowee, Colonel Grant sent me to you. You are on the water side, and are in the light. We are in darkness; but hope all will be clear. I have been constantly going about doing good; and though I am tired, yet I am come to see what can be done for my people, who are in great distress. As to what has happened, I believe it has been order by our Father above. We are of a different color from the white people. They are superior to us. But one God is father to us all, and we hope what is past will be forgotten. God Almighty made all people. There is not a day but that some are coming into, and others going out of the world. The great king told me the path should never be crooked, but open for every one to pass. As we all live in one land, I hope that we shall all live as one people.[58]

Bull responded: "I know your heart is straight … on the advice of my beloved men [his council] I have decided to leave out the clause by which four Cherokees should be put to death."[59]

Attakullakulla closed with: "I am extremely well satisfied."[60]

The two agreed on terms for peace. Once the hostilities seemingly ended, Attakullakulla asked the governor of South Carolina to appoint Captain John Stuart to be the colony's Indian agent and to reside among the Cherokee. He assured the governor such a move would save the colony from further Cherokee molestation.

The Provincial Assembly supported the move as reported by historian Albert V. Goodpasture:

[The assembly] likewise tendered Captain Stuart a vote of thanks, together with a reward of £1,500, for his heroic defense of Fort Loudoun, and recommended him to the governor as a man worthy of preference in the service of the province. When, therefore, the Royal government found it expedient that the southern district should have a superintendent of Indian affairs, with powers similar to those exercised by Sir William Johnson, in the northern district, the appointment was given to Captain John Stuart, who discharged the duties of the office with distinguished ability and fidelity until the beginning of the Revolutionary War.[61]

The September 18–24, 1761, issue of the *South Carolina Gazette* reported: "Attacullaculla … signed the treaty of peace … requested that Captain John Stuart might be made chief white man in their nation…. His request was granted."

Thus, John Stuart became resident Indian agent in the Cherokee Nation and would come to be a formidable enemy to the Patriots in the future American Revolution. He earnestly had the interests of the Cherokee at heart, but was unable to arrange for sufficient British assistance to offset settler encroachment, the major problem for the Cherokee Nation.

On October 13, 1761, Attakullakulla returned to Chota and met with the Cherokee headmen in the Town House where they ratified the treaty.

On November 19, 1761, Principal Chief Standing Turkey, War Chief Oconostota, and four hundred Cherokee (some historians report also Attakullakulla) met with Virginia lieutenant colonel Adam Stephen (Colonel William Byrd's successor) at the Long Island of the

Holston River. They explained that they had reached a peace agreement with South Carolina. After a short negotiation, the parties signed a treaty following which Standing Turkey asked that a Virginia militia officer be sent to the Cherokee Upper Towns to signify sincerity. Colonel Stephen was somewhat bewildered as to whom he might select; however, Lieutenant Henry Timberlake took the pressure off and volunteered for the assignment. (See Chapter 5.)

Attakullakulla delivered the Cherokee-sanctioned treaty to Charles Town on December 16, 1761. He also delivered captives, eight white and one black, who had been held by Cherokee warriors. He had been required to deliver all captives held, but that was an impossible task due to the Cherokee tradition of clan rights. Warriors could possibly agree to ransom their captives; however, South Carolina had no funds for such a transaction.

(Some historians record that the treaty was signed on December 18, and others ascribe it to December 31.)

Some specific terms of the treaty were: a boundary line was established between the colony of South Carolina and the Cherokee Nation at forty miles south of Keowee; Cherokee were barred from crossing the boundary without a white escort, or an order of the South Carolina Assembly; the Cherokee were required to capture and turn over to the British any Frenchmen found in their territories; South Carolina could build forts it deemed necessary, even on Cherokee land; the Cherokee were required to return all captured British citizens and property; trade between the British and the Cherokee would be re-established; and British traders would safely operate within the Cherokee Nation.

On June 20, 1762, the Cherokee partially fulfilled their commitment by taking several white captives to Fort Ninety Six where they were exchanged for Cherokee prisoners who had been held in Charles Town. However, not all captives were located right away, and others were returned over several years. The Cherokee leaders would have had to negotiate the release of any captive with the warrior who claimed rights to the "property."

(Anne Calhoun Matthews, captured during the Long Canes Massacre, is variously reported as having been 17 years old when recovered in 1772, 9 when recovered in 1763 or 1764, or 19 when recovered in 1775. While 1764 or 1765 may align well with the peace treaty agreed to just prior, she seems to have been much older by virtue of her reported maturity. It is also reported that Andrew Pickens had much to do with negotiating the release of his cousin-in-law, and it would have been in the later years mentioned before he would have had the prestige with the Cherokee for such action. However, 1775 would not be likely because new issues arose between the backcountry settlements and the Cherokee Nation. More details are covered in Chapter 7.)

Peace was established throughout the Cherokee Nation; however, Fort Loudoun was totally abandoned, and the rush to settle what is presently eastern Tennessee had slowed significantly. However, settler encroachments onto the Upper Cherokee ancestral land would be in full swing by the 1770s.

The Cherokee had historically fought wars for vastly different reasons than had the Europeans. Cherokee reasoning was for defense of ancestral lands, clan retribution, or alliances. The British had typically fought wars for conquest, power, and control of colonial assets.

Historian Tom Hatley remarked: "The Cherokee war was from the beginning initiated on the Cherokee side by the raiding of specific families who wished to recoup the losses of relatives."[62]

4. Lyttleton, Montgomery and Grant Destroy the Cherokee Community

However, this particular war, while initiated with the Cherokee victims in Virginia and caused by Virginians, was avenged in the backcountry of South Carolina. The Cherokee, it seems by virtue of the rules of clan vengeance, should have treated the Virginians as the "clan" to be dealt with and left South Carolina alone. The Cherokee hurt themselves by dragging another colony into the conflict and taking their vengeance out upon any British settlement.

In the Cherokee frame of reference, everything had reached a balance before Governor William Henry Lyttleton escalated the issue and made hostages of the Cherokee headmen (who were a peace delegation), then marched to Keowee, and left the fate of the hostages to the military establishment. Oconostota, thinking these leaders had been made slaves, tried to free them by first killing Lieutenant Coytmore of Fort Prince George, after which the hostage headmen were slaughtered. Pandora's Box had nothing on what happened next—wave after wave of forays into the Cherokee country for three years that laid waste to the villages. The Cherokee could now see the English in a different light, but they were left with no options for further vengeance. However, some of them would not forget.

In 1872, historian Samuel Gardner Drake wrote:

> Like all aborigines, the Cherokees were cruel in war, and had been in frequent collisions with the Carolinians, but how often would it be found that the Indians were the first transgressors? We know from the history of our own times, that in a majority of cases in which blood has been shed, the white neighbors of the Indians were the aggressors. And yet they [the Indians] have always been ready to fight our battles. No less than five hundred Cherokee warriors fought on the side of independence in the war of the revolution. In the late southern rebellion, the expatriated Cherokees beyond the Mississippi were entirely surrounded by their rebellious neighbors, and it was next to impossible for them to remain neutral, yet a good number of them continued loyal to the end.
>
> I have already alluded to the manner in which the Cherokees were driven from their country, and it is not proposed to expatiate on that painful subject at this time. Yet there will always be associated with their name a reflection, and a feeling in every humane breast, that their expatriation was a crime as nefarious as ever any one people committed against another. It was a crime precisely like one which any state might commit against another, because that state had strength to overpower the other. The Cherokees were advancing in civilization; they had become farmers, mechanics, and proficient in many useful arts as well as their neighbors; but these acquisitions, it would seem, only made those neighbors more avaricious, and more determined on their ruin. They were even becoming, I may say they had become, literary: they prepared and printed school books, published newspapers in their own language, and with an alphabet of the invention of one of their own people; which alphabet was, and still is, an invention challenging the admiration of the learned world.
>
> The wrong to which allusion has been made, was a crime which will never be forgotten or forgiven, and its perpetrators have gone, many of them, and the rest will go, down to their graves in infamy; and the believer in retributive justice may point to the "March To The Sea" as a warning or foreshadowing of one of more terrible desolation, when that colossus, armed with iron hands and leaden feet, shall fully vindicate the law of justice, and the equal rights of man.[63]

Trader and historian James Adair added:

> Before the Indian trade was ruined by our left-handed policy, and the natives were corrupted by the liberality of our dim-sighted politicians, the Cheerake were frank, sincere, and industrious. Their towns then, abounded with hogs, poultry, and every thing

sufficient for the support of a reasonable life, which the traders purchased at an easy rate, to their mutual satisfaction: and as they kept them busily employed, and did not make themselves too cheap, the Indians bore them good-will and respect—and such is the temper of all red natives.... The Cheerake had a prodigious number of excellent horses, at the beginning of their late war with us; but pinching hunger forced them to eat the greatest part of them, in the time of that unfortunate event. But as all are now become very active and sociable, they will soon supply themselves with plenty of the best sort, from our settlements—they are skillful jockies [*sic*].[64]

The Cherokee settled into a period of recovery and rebuilding. They had suffered greatly. In their minds, they had done nothing wrong other than avenge their warriors. They did not understand the concept of hostages (it was different than captives taken for the good of the community) nor did they understand the British penchant for greed, especially land grabbing.

It should have become obvious that in the future they could not rely on the British for a fair alliance—especially regarding reciprocity. All alliances with the British would become one-sided—the Cherokee assisting the British. However, that seems to have been a hard lesson by which to live, and made especially difficult since a primary headman was a strong proponent of British alliances.[65]

Chapter 5

Timberlake and the Post-War Cherokee Culture

Virginia colonel William Byrd had held a peace conference with the Cherokee in 1756 to plead for their assistance against the French and France's Indian allies. Little did the participants realize that the new alliance would lead to war as the Cherokee became humiliated by the Continental Army officers and were contemptibly treated by Virginia settlers.

War was inevitable after several Cherokee headmen were slaughtered at Fort Prince George, South Carolina, in 1759. The Cherokee retaliated as they ambushed and killed Lieutenant Richard Coytmore, the commander of Fort Prince George, and then placed Fort Loudoun (another South Carolina garrisoned fort, but located in present-day Tennessee) under siege. South Carolina state troops commanded by Governor William Henry Lyttleton in 1759 invaded the Cherokee settlements around Keowee. British colonel Archibald Montgomery invaded the Lower and Middle Villages in 1760 as did British lieutenant colonel James Grant in 1761. The Cherokee had attacked the Fort Loudoun garrison after they surrendered the fort following the Montgomery campaign and thereafter withdrew toward Fort Prince George.

Virginia lieutenant colonel Adam Stephen met with Cherokee principal chief Standing Turkey at Fort Robinson in November 1761 to sign a peace agreement. (Stephen had replaced Colonel William Byrd, who chose to resign rather than attack the Cherokee Upper Towns in coordination with Lieutenant Colonel Grant's invasion from the southeast. Byrd had originally been sent to assist Colonel Archibald Montgomery to relieve the Fort Loudoun garrison; however, he remained at Long Island of the Holston and had ordered Fort Robinson to be built there when Montgomery failed to follow through. See Chapter 4).

In December 1761, Attakullakulla signed a peace agreement with South Carolina's acting governor, William Bull II. At that time, Attakullakulla asked Bull to make John Stuart the South Carolina Indian agent to the Cherokee. Bull agreed. The Cherokee population had been greatly reduced and the number of able-bodied warriors had been halved. (See Chapter 4.)

Post-war 1761 led to a revival of trade between the Cherokee and both the South Carolina and Virginia colonies. The trade became equally divided between the two, and the Cherokee found that each colony's traders just as equally cheated them with short weights and measures.

The new peace also brought a resurgence of settlers to backcountry South Carolina. Older settler families, like the Calhouns, returned once imminent danger had disappeared and they had stabilized their affairs in their temporary locations. Some of those settlers had been traders with the Cherokee prior to the war. They settled back into the familiar trade and also became backcountry political leaders.

When Standing Turkey met with Colonel Stephen, the chief asked that an ambassador be sent to Chota to signify peaceful intent on the part of the Virginians. Lieutenant Henry Timberlake recorded of the request:

> We marched ... to the great island on Holston's River, about 140 miles from the enemy's settlements [on the Little Tennessee River] ... we immediately applied ourselves to the construction of a fort, which was nearly completed about the middle of November [1761], when Kanagatuko [Standing Turkey] ... accompanied by about 400 of his people came to our camp ... to sue for peace, which was soon granted by Col. Stephen ... their king [Standing Turkey] ... had one more favor ... to send an officer back with them to their country.... The Colonel was embarrassed at the demand; he saw the necessity ... yet could not command any on so dangerous a duty. I soon relieved him from his dilemma, by offering my services.[1]

Standing Turkey offered to provide a warrior escort for Timberlake to make an overland trek to the Upper Towns; however, Timberlake opted to make the trip by canoe. He was accompanied by a young Sergeant Thomas Sumter and interpreter John McCormack. This group arrived at the Upper Towns on December 20, 1761. War Chief Ostenaco took a liking to Timberlake and offered him residence in the chief's own house at Tomotley. (Timberlake would remain in the Upper Towns for five months and eventually father a child with one of Ostenaco's daughters.)

Timberlake made many interesting observations regarding Cherokee life. He especially observed the relationship between the major chiefs and was enthralled by the politics of which he said:

> Their government, if I may call it government, which has neither laws nor the power to support it, is a mixed aristocracy and democracy, the chiefs being chose according to their merit in war or policy at home; these lead the warriors that chuse to go, for there is no laws or compulsion on those that refuse to follow, or punishment to those that forsake their chief: he strives, therefore, to inspire them with a sort of enthusiasm, by the war-song, as the ancient bards did once in Britain. These chiefs, or headmen, likewise compose the assemblies of the nation, into which the warwomen [sic] are admitted. The reader will ... find the story of Amazons not so great a fable as we imagined, many of the Indian women being as famous in war, as powerful in the council.[2]

Timberlake was stunned by the relationship between Attakullakulla and Ostenaco. Attakullakulla was more of a civil chief than a war chief, although, he did lead raids against the northern tribes that had allied with the French. Ostenaco, however, was a primarily a war chief with decent civil leadership ability, half-brother to Oconostota (who was Attakullakulla's father-in-law), and first cousin once removed from Attakullakulla. Timberlake remarked about the three:

> The over-hill settlement is by these two chiefs divided into two factions, between whom there is often great animosity, and the two leaders are sure to oppose one another in every measure taken. Attakullakulla has done but little in war to recommend him, but has often signaled himself by his policy, and negotiations at home. Ostenaco has a tolerable share of both; but policy and art are the greatest steps to power. Attakullakulla has a larger faction with this alone, while Oconnestoto [Oconostota], sir-named the Great Warrior, famous for having, in all his expeditions, taken such prudent measures as never to have lost a man, has not so much power, and Ostenaco could never have obtained the superiority, if he had not a great reputation in both.[3]

5. Timberlake and the Post-War Cherokee Culture

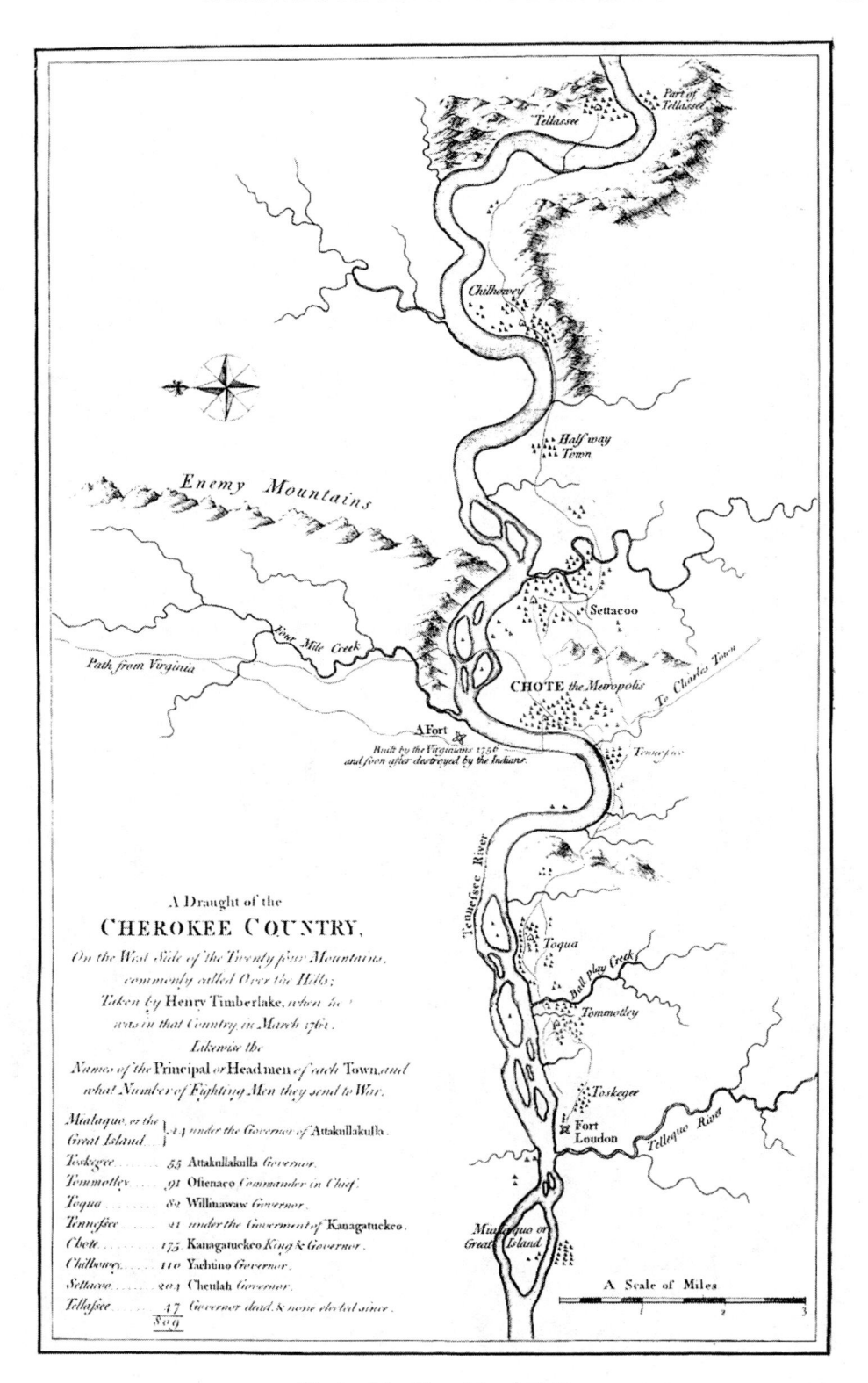

Timberlake Map, March 1762.

(There is some exaggeration in Timberlake's statement leading one to assume that he listened to legends. Oconostota did lose at least one warrior at the Battle of Taliwa when Chief King Fisher was killed. See Chapter 3.)

The lieutenant also witnessed one of the Beloved Women performing her responsibility of creating the "Black Drink." The "Black Drink" was a blend of the leaves and stems of ilex vomitoria, or yaupin holly, or ilex verticillata, a holly shrub often called winterberry. Heavily concentrated with caffeine, it was also called the "fever bush" by the Cherokee. (Backcountry Carolina and Georgia settlers would often substitute it for coffee or especially tea to avoid subsidizing trade with England during the Revolutionary era.)

The Cherokee warriors used the "Black Drink" in purification rituals on the eve of festivals, ball games, or war expeditions. The ingredients were freshly picked shortly before use and slow-roasted in ceramic pots. During the ritual, the drink would be boiled like coffee to distribute the caffeine, then cooled just enough to not blister the mouth. The brew possibly carried two to three times the caffeine strength of strong black coffee. Following consumption, the warriors would intentionally heave. (Some have written that the properties of the drink likely induced the vomiting; however, the retching was purposeful as part of a bodily and spiritually cleansing procedure.)

The drink was originally scooped up in a large community cup made of lightning whelk, horse conch, or emperor helmet shells. However, by the 18th century, the scoop was made of many items, including ceramic or a metal ladle obtained by trade.

Timberlake observed such a ritual prior to a "chunky" game (see Chapter 1) which he described as:

***Typical Black Drink Ceremony*, by Jacques le Moyne, 16th century.**

> Some days after my reception ... the greater part resolved to amuse themselves at a game they call nettecawaw [chunky] ... I was informed there was to be a physic-dance at night, curiosity led me to the townhouse, to see the preparation. A vessel of their own make, that might contain twenty gallons ... was set on the fire, round which stood several goards filled with river-water, which was poured into the pot; this done, there arose one of the beloved women, who, opening a deer-skin bag filled with various roots and herbs, took out a small handful of something like fine salt; part of which she threw on the headman's seat, and part into the fire close to the pot; she then took out the wing of a swan, and after flourishing it over the pot, stood fixed for near a minute, muttering somewhat to herself; then taking a shrub-like laurel (which I supposed was the physic) she threw it into the pot, and returned to her former seat.... At my return I found the house quite full: they danced near an hour round the pot, till one of them, with a small goard that might hold about a gill [one-half cup], took some of the physic [a purgative; also a pick-me-up] and drank it, after which all the rest took in turn.[4]

On January 28, 1762, the Cherokee received a messenger who told them the northern tribes had killed a Cherokee headman near Long Island of the Holston River. Agitation grew among the warriors, and war whoops abounded; however, they cooled until they could receive confirmation. On February 4, a messenger came to Timberlake with news that the northern Indians had turned on the British and were building a breastplate just 400 yards north of Fort Robinson.

Timberlake then recorded:

> The 15th was the day appointed for the return of the Little Carpenter [Attakullakulla]; and his not arriving began to give his friends a great deal of uneasiness. Ostenaco bore likewise his share in it as his brother was of the party. Here is a lesson to Europe; two Indian chiefs, whom we call barbarians, rivals of power, heads of two opposite factions, warm in opposing one another, as their interest continually clash; yet these have no farther animosity, no family quarrels or resentment.[5]

Timberlake immediately sent his servant to Fort Robinson to ascertain what was transpiring there. He returned less than one week later with a letter from Captain McNeil, the Fort Robinson commander. McNeil wrote that 70 northern Indians had visited the fort in November 1761. They told McNeil they were sent to join the Virginians against the Cherokee. (That would have been around the time of the Grant expedition. See Chapter 4.) McNeil then informed the northern Indians of the new treaty with Standing Turkey. The visitors became infuriated. The northern Indians then attacked a Cherokee hunting party. McNeil informed Timberlake that he had been ordered to disband the Fort Robinson garrison and abandon the fort.

Timberlake told Ostenaco that they needed to take any remaining white or black captives to Fort Robinson right away as provided in the treaty. Ostenaco agreed. Attakullakulla arrived on February 23 with corroboration for the messages received by Ostenaco and Timberlake. They left the Upper Towns with 165 warriors and the captives on March 10, 1762.

The expedition arrived at Fort Robinson on the 19th and found it mostly deserted save for interpreter Charles McLamore and another white man.[6]

On March 22, the party split. McLamore went with Standing Turkey and the larger portion of the Cherokee party to Chota while Timberlake and Ostenaco set out for Williamsburg, Virginia, to request an audience with Governor Francis Fauquier. They were also accompanied by the second white man they found at Fort Robinson, Sergeant Thomas

Sumter, a few aides, and enough Cherokee warriors to bring the total number to 72 travelers.

They were late getting away and marched only for ten miles before they camped. Next they made a stop at Fort Attakullakulla. Timberlake recorded: "I was anxious to know what was become of my camp-equipage, cloaths &c. I had left at Fort Attakullakulla.... We called on our way at Fort Attakullakulla, which was likewise evacuated, looked for my cloaths, &c. but they were all stolen and carried off by the soldiers, except a small trunk, with a few trifles, I found afterwards at New River."[7]

(Fort Attakullakulla, a small outpost said to be at "Stalnakres," was constructed by Virginia Militia colonel William Byrd in 1760 when he was en route to Long Island of the Holston where he built Fort Robinson. It was apparently located on the Samuel Stalnaker property on the north side of the Middle Fork Holston River near Chilhowie, Virginia. Virginia Highway marker K-21, located in Chilhowie on U.S. Highway 11, less than one-quarter of a mile south of the intersection with Virginia Highway 107 states, "Near here, in 1750, Dr. Thomas Walker, on his first journey southwest, assisted Samuel Stalnaker in building his cabin. At that time it was the farthest west settlement." In 1755 Samuel Stalnaker was captured by a Shawnee raiding party and his wife and young son were killed. It was recorded "1755, May 3d.—Mary Baker, at Holston's River, wounded. June 18th, Saml. Stalnacker, at Holston's River, prisoner escaped; Saml. Hydon, at Holston's River, escaped; Adam Stalnaker, at Holston's River, killed; Mrs. Stalnaker, at Holston's River, killed; a servant man, at Holston's River, killed; Mathias Counie, at Holston's River, killed.")[8]

Timberlake continued: "We called at Fort Lewis, where we found William Shorey the interpreter, who, by order of Col. Stephen, had awaited our coming, to accompany the Indians to Williamsburg … where we arrived in about eleven days after our departure from Fort Lewis."[9]

(Fort Lewis was constructed just west of today's Salem, Virginia, a western suburb of Roanoke, Virginia. Attakullakulla saved William Shorey, the interpreter, along with Captain John Stuart following the attack on the withdrawing Fort Loudoun garrison. See Chapter 4.)

Timberlake and his party arrived in Williamsburg early in April 1762. Some have written that Standing Turkey and Pouting Pigeon accompanied him to Williamsburg; however, Standing Turkey had gone back to Chota when the party split at Fort Robinson. He must have been sent for and arrived at Williamsburg later than Timberlake, who verified Standing Turkey was not there in the beginning:

> On my arrival, I waited on the Governor, who seemed somewhat displeased with the number of Indians that had forced themselves upon me. Orders however were handed out for their accommodation, and a few days after a council was called, at which Ostenaco, and some of the principal Indians, attended. After the usual ceremonies … the Indians were dismissed, and presents ordered them to the amount of 125£ currency; 12£ 10 s. for Ostenaco, the same sum to be sent back to King Kanagatucko [Principal Chief Standing Turkey].[10]

When the group was preparing to leave Williamsburg, the Reverend James Horrocks (Harrocks by historian Albert V. Goodpasture),[11] a professor at William & Mary, invited the party to dinner. While there, the professor showed Ostenaco a picture of King George III. The chief quietly studied the portrait for several minutes and said: "Long have I wished to see the king my father; this is his resemblance, but I am determined to see himself; I am now near the sea, and never will depart from it till I have obtained my desire."[12]

The next day, Ostenaco pressed Governor Fauquier for permission to visit England until the governor backed off of his tough stance and permitted the voyage. One of the details that caused the governor's change of heart was that Ostenaco told him he wanted to judge whether Attakullakulla had honestly related his experience in England in 1730.

Ostenaco was allowed to take two warriors with him, so he selected Standing Turkey and Pouting Pigeon. He also requested Lieutenant Timberlake and Sergeant Sumter accompany him. Timberlake personally funded the escorts' portion of the voyage. William Shorey was chosen to be the party's interpreter. (Pouting Pigeon was likely Amoya from the Valley Towns. That Pigeon was the son of the Raven of Hiwassee who was the brother of Ammouskossittee [Moytoy V] and Savanah Tom [Moytoy III]. Pigeon was a peer of Saloue [Young Warrior, Raven of Estatoe] and fought often against the British with Ostenaco and Oconostota. See Chapter 4 for Saloue, Chapter 3 for Ammouskossittee, and Chapters 3 and 4 for Savanah Tom.)

Ostenaco sent for Standing Turkey to join him and prepare for the journey across the sea. On May 15, 1762, the expedition embarked on the British frigate *Epreuvre*. William Shorey became ill and died during the voyage. The frigate is variously reported to have docked at Plymouth on either June 5 or June 16, 1762.[13]

Three Chiefs in London, July 1762—Likely left to right represented: Ostenaco, Standing Turkey, Pouting Pigeon—There is much conjecture as to the order of the chiefs; however, the figure on the left definitely contains the head of Ostenaco as drawn by Sir Joshua Reynolds—the figure in the center is likely to represent the principal chief, Standing Turkey, since he holds a peace pipe.

His [Ostenaco's] presence in England created a great furor; thousands of people called to see him, whom he would receive only after going through the elaborate ceremonies of the toilet, which sometimes required as much as four hours. He had his boxes of oil and ochre, his fat and his perfumes, which were quite indispensable to his appearance in public.

Among his callers was the poet [Oliver] Goldsmith, who waited three hours before he could gain admittance. In the course of his visit he presented the chief with a present, who, in the ecstasy of his gratitude, gave him an embrace that left his [Goldsmith's] face well bedaubed with oil and red ochre.

Ostenaco was presented to the king on June 8, 1762, and was received with great cordiality. Due to William Shorey's demise, Sir Alexander Cuming was asked to perform as interpreter. (Cuming had escorted Attakullakulla and seven other Cherokee leaders to England in 1730. See Chapter 3.) However, Ostenaco and Standing Turkey were not able to acquire any major new alliance or treaty, nor obtain more than a few gifts to raise their influence level at home to that regained by Attakullakulla. The Headmen felt somewhat deflated and sailed from England on August 25, 1762. They returned to Charles Town rather than Virginia. That was good for South Carolina because the colony had begun to feel ignored by the Cherokee. Ostenaco addressed the South Carolina General Assembly on October 3, 1762, then the Cherokee left for the Upper Towns to report to the other headmen.[14]

Timberlake drew the Cherokee trade further away from the French and cemented it more firmly with the British, especially with South Carolina and Virginia. Attakullakulla and his followers had ultimately regained all of the influence they had lost during the war years. While Ostenaco and Standing Turkey still had influence, it paled in comparison to that of Attakullakulla. The war chiefs did have some civil sway; however, this had become a time for peace and they could not compete with Attakullakulla. It was about this time that Principal Chief Standing Turkey was deposed by the headmen in favor of Attakullakulla. The old headmen had enough of war with the British and wanted a principal headman who held favor with the colonies.

Timberlake's influence, however, also drew the Cherokee further and further from their traditions. The trade for skins continued to grow, and old beliefs and rituals were ignored. The Cherokee craved trade guns, and they received them. However, the guns continued to be lighter and less well-made than those provided to the colonists. The trade guns were basically all smoothbore, like a musket, and less accurate than settlers' rifles. They were also cheaply made, broke easily, and provided gunsmiths in the backcountry settlements with additional income.

There was an increase in interracial marriage and a change from the Cherokee culture as the Cherokee women began to move to their white husbands' homes and take their husbands' last names. (However, there were still some who kept to the old traditions. The author's 4th great-grandmother, Mary [Polly] Murphy, who was seven-eighths Cherokee by blood, married Cahstahyeestee [Whiplash], who moved to her home and took the white name of Martin Murphy. Whiplash was three-quarters blood Cherokee. See Appendix A.)

The Cherokee dressed more European after Timberlake's visit, and they became extremely reliant upon British trade goods, e.g., guns, metal hatchets, knives, tools, European pottery, and metal cookware. That reliance rendered them highly susceptible to possible British embargos on goods.

The Cherokee dependency on British alliances would hurt them in the future, especially during the American Revolution, after which they would be forced into more land cessions. They were still being cheated by the traders, a problem for which there seemed to be no solution—short of starting another war. Their debts grew incessantly as traders provided them goods "on credit."

The Cherokee headmen seemed to believe resistance to a British monopoly was futile. A group of young chiefs, who were not only aware of the old traditions, but also grieved for their continued loss of ancestral lands, began to watch the older headmen to see what direction they might take in the future. It was not too late to operate from a position of strength to save their lands, but the Cherokee, to be successful, had to act soon to break their reliance on the British or their heritage of skill sets would not be retrieved. After all, they still had to consider the French, and the French had proven, through their alliance with the Creek, that they were not interested in encroachment as in the British "tradition."

The Seven Years War, including the French and Indian War in America, finally came to an end in early 1763. The Treaty of Paris was signed on February 10, 1763, and the primary signatories were Britain, France, and Spain with Portugal being an "interested observer."

Article VII of the Treaty of Paris reads:

> In order to re-establish peace on solid and durable foundations, and to remove for ever all subject of dispute with regard to the limits of the British and French territories on the continent of America; it is agreed, that, for the future, the confines between the dominions of his Britannick Majesty [king of England] and those of his Most Christian Majesty [king of France], in that part of the world, shall be fixed irrevocably by a line drawn along the middle of the River Mississippi, from its source to the river Iberville, and from thence, by a line drawn along the middle of this river, and the lakes Maurepas and Pontchartrain to the sea; and for this purpose, the Most Christian King cedes in full right, and guaranties to his Britannick Majesty the river and port of the Mobile, and every thing which he possesses, or ought to possess, on the left side of the river Mississippi, except the town of New Orleans and the island in which it is situated, which shall remain to France, provided that the navigation of the river Mississippi shall be equally free, as well to the subjects of Great Britain as to those of France, in its whole breadth and length, from its source to the sea, and expressly that part which is between the said island of New Orleans and the right bank of that river, as well as the passage both in and out of its mouth: It is farther stipulated, that the vessels belonging to the subjects of either nation shall not be stopped, visited, or subjected to the payment of any duty whatsoever.

A side agreement was that Spain would cede its rights in Florida to Britain in exchange for Havana, Cuba. Additionally, the treaty meant that all Indian tribes east of the Mississippi River would fall under the dominion of Britain. One portion of the agreement would set off an increase in the already uncontrollable movement of British settlers to the west. The French were diligent to point out to the watchful young Cherokee warriors that encroachment would be on the rise.

The Iroquois were very militant regarding British encroachment and fought desperately to end it. They looked upon the Cherokee as British allies and embroiled the two tribes in what would become a long war.

The French insisted the Creek enlist the Cherokee as allies to fight against Georgia and the Carolinas. The Cherokee, however, were fighting the Iroquois and did not want to split their focus, and also thought they might need British assistance in that war. The Cherokee would learn over the next two decades that the British did not willingly choose to provide military assistance. The Creek were stunned by the Cherokee's reluctance. The Creek thought the Cherokee had good reason to join them and fight encroachment. The *Georgia Gazette* reported in its April 12, 1763, issue that 1,000 families dwelt around Long Canes and 4,000 more were expected in the next few months.

In August 1763, Andrew Pickens and his brother, Joseph Pickens, bought land and would situate their families near Long Canes, South Carolina. The growing settlement of Long Canes consisted of South Carolina land ceded by previous treaties between the colony and the Cherokee; therefore, it was not an immediate threat. Consequently, the Creek tried to convince the Cherokee that the British would use that area as a jumping-off point to reach into Cherokee country. The Creek were right, but, the reach would be primarily from Virginia to the Upper Towns—a move the Cherokee would not foresee in the 1760s.

What the Cherokee did not realize was that the "civilized nations" of Europe had adopted the Doctrine of Discovery. The Papal Bull of 1452 initially allowed Portugal to claim territory that it had explored in West Africa. Over the centuries, it was modified to allow any "Christian" nation to claim discovery and possession of any "non-Christian" land for the enlightenment of the "savages" therein.

In practice, when the British settled the southern coast, they declared that native tribes owned the land and only a "Discovering Country" (Britain in this case) or its representatives could negotiate purchase of, or trade for, said land. It was a simple matter for the royal colonial governments to force an issue to acquire land by treaty, such as was done by South Carolina royal governors James Glen, William Henry Lyttleton, and William Bull II.

On October 7, 1763, King George III issued his famous proclamation which reads in part:

> And whereas it is just and reasonable, and essential to our Interest, and the Security of our Colonies, that the several Nations or Tribes of Indians with whom We are connected, and who live under our Protection, should not be molested or disturbed in the Possession of such Parts of Our Dominions and Territories as, not having been ceded to or purchased by Us, are reserved to them, or any of them, as their Hunting Grounds—We do therefore, with the Advice of our Privy Council, declare it to be our Royal Will and Pleasure, that no Governor or Commander in Chief in any of our Colonies of Quebec, East Florida, or West Florida, do presume, upon any Pretence whatever, to grant Warrants of Survey, or pass any Patents for Lands beyond the Bounds of their respective Governments, as described in their Commissions: as also that no Governor or Commander in Chief in any of our other Colonies or Plantations in America do presume for the present, and until our further Pleasure be known, to grant Warrants of Survey, or pass Patents for any Lands beyond the Heads or Sources of any of the Rivers which fall into the Atlantic Ocean from the West and North West, or upon any Lands whatever, which, not having been ceded to or purchased by Us as aforesaid, are reserved to the said Indians, or any of them.
>
> And We do further declare it to be Our Royal Will and Pleasure, for the present as aforesaid, to reserve under our Sovereignty, Protection, and Dominion, for the use of the said Indians, all the Lands and Territories not included within the Limits of Our said Three new Governments, or within the Limits of the Territory granted to the Hudson's Bay Company, as also all the Lands and Territories lying to the Westward of the Sources of the Rivers which fall into the Sea from the West and North West as aforesaid.
>
> And We do hereby strictly forbid, on Pain of our Displeasure, all our loving Subjects from making any Purchases or Settlements whatever, or taking Possession of any of the Lands above reserved, without our especial leave and Licence for that Purpose first obtained.

And We do further strictly enjoin and require all Persons whatever who have either willfully or inadvertently seated themselves upon any Lands within the Countries above described or upon any other Lands which, not having been ceded to or purchased by Us, are still reserved to the said Indians as aforesaid, forthwith to remove themselves from such Settlements.

And whereas great Frauds and Abuses have been committed in purchasing Lands of the Indians, to the great Prejudice of our Interests, and to the great Dissatisfaction of the said Indians: In order, therefore, to prevent such Irregularities for the future, and to the end that the Indians may be convinced of our Justice and determined Resolution to remove all reasonable Cause of Discontent, We do, with the Advice of our Privy Council strictly enjoin and require, that no private Person do presume to make any purchase from the said Indians of any Lands reserved to the said Indians, within those parts of our Colonies where We have thought proper to allow Settlement: but that, if at any Time any of the Said Indians should be inclined to dispose of the said Lands, the same shall be Purchased only for Us, in our Name, at some public Meeting or Assembly of the said Indians, to be held for that Purpose by the Governor or Commander in Chief of our Colony respectively within which they shall lie.

On the surface, that document appeared to be what Attakullakulla was looking for to cement his position as Principal Headman of the Cherokee Nation. He had put his faith, and his political future, in the hands of the British, and he gained influence as a result.

Often called the Magna Carta of American Indians, the Proclamation of 1763 assigned territorial limits and guaranteed the Indians' rights to their ancestral hunting grounds. It established a "Proclamation Line" that divided British-ruled territory. Settlers were to live only on one side and Indians to live only on the other. The line of demarcation was in essence the crest of the Appalachian Mountains. British settlers were not allowed to settle across the line onto Indian land, and any British settlers already in that territory were ordered to abandon their property and return to the settlers' side of the line.

The government created the Proclamation Line mostly for economic purposes. British settlers had a voracious appetite for land. They needed room to expand. The settlers had driven France out. The war was over; they were ready to claim their reward—the frontier that lay over the mountains.

The British government wanted to reduce conflict between Indians and settlers by physically separating them, forbidding settlers from buying any land from the Indians. The Proclamation of 1763 required that all land deals with Indians be made by royal governors, in the name of the government, and at a meeting held strictly for that purpose. All of this was done to remove mistrust and potential for settlers to abuse the Indians and regain Indian trust of the British. It sounded good in theory.

After the Treaty of Paris, many hunters poured over the mountains into present-day Tennessee, even though King George III had ordered his royal colonial governors to not allow whites to trespass on Indian lands west of the mountains. The governors appointed Indian commissioners to help enforce the proclamation. John Stuart, himself, originally selected as South Carolina's Indian agent to the Cherokee, became appointed British Superintendent of Indian Affairs for the Southern District (*south of the Ohio River*). The Cherokee trusted him and such confidence gave him limitless influence as the Indian Agent; however, the whites persisted. Some were "long hunters" who remained in Cherokee country for a year or more to stalk ancestral Cherokee hunting grounds. Additionally, land warrants had been issued to officers and soldiers who had fought in the French and Indian War. Those veterans, primarily from Virginia and some from North Carolina, wanted to locate near the Cherokee Upper Towns of present-day eastern Tennessee.

Agent Stuart, though charged with stemming the tide of settlers, received no military backing from the royal colonies or the British army. The authorities had their hands full "assuring" that there would be no further slave revolts along the coast to threaten the plantation structure and interfere with commerce. Thus, the Cherokee were out of sight and out of mind. There was no way the British could enforce the Proclamation of 1763. The lack of British support would be a slow lesson for the Cherokee Nation to learn; meanwhile, the British would expect the Cherokee to "honor" the treaties and to ally with the British army and the colonial militias whenever deemed necessary to the royal community. It would not help now that Attakullakulla, the principal proponent of British alliances, was the Principal Headman of the Cherokee Nation.

On November 10, 1763, Attakullakulla and Ostenaco led a Cherokee delegation to Augusta, Georgia, for a large trade conference with four other tribes and four royal colonial governors. It was attended by the Chickasaw, Choctaw, Creek, Cherokee, and Catawba Indians as well as the governors of Georgia, North and South Carolina, and Virginia.

John Stuart presided over the council. A peace treaty was established that ceded land between the Savannah and Ogeechee Rivers to Georgia in payment for Indian trade debts. The Cherokee lost all of their land north of the present-day northern Tennessee border and all east of the Blue Ridge Mountains, also for trade debts.

John Stuart hired two deputy Indian Agents, Alexander Cameron and John McDonald.

Plaque Honoring 1763 Augusta Indian Congress—**Located in Augusta at the corner of Washington (Sixth) and Reynolds Streets.**

Each had married Cherokee women and settled in Cherokee country. Oconostota was especially fond of Cameron and gave him huge tracts of land within the Cherokee Nation. McDonald was married to the late William Shorey's mixed-blood daughter, Anna, and would become the grandfather of future Principal Chief John Ross.[15]

The younger Cherokee warriors began to see the bleak future of their Nation. They were gaining confidence that they held the key to retaining ancestral Cherokee lands. One of those who reversed his trend was Chief Saloue (Seroweh, Young Warrior or Raven of Estatoe). (The warriors themselves had not yet thought of the Cherokee people as the Cherokee Nation; however, the Europeans were beginning to consider them that way. War-

Fort Augusta Marker—**Located in Augusta at the corner of Washington (Sixth) and Reynolds Streets.**

riors like Seroweh acted independently of the Cherokee people as a whole. They would, in a few years, learn the value of unity.)

Young Warrior, with heartfelt hope, told Governor William Bull, II:

> "When we had bad times, in the last unhappy war, I had repeated invitations from the Creeks to come with my whole town and settle amongst them. I answered that I loved my country [The vicinity of Estatoe] ... they were very much vexed...."[16]

However, Young Warrior, and others like him, could see that the Proclamation of 1763 was a swat at the wind—the settlers kept moving into the ancestral lands and could not, or would not, be stopped by the British. Young Warrior began to make raids into backcountry settlements.

It was recorded in the November 13 to 15, 1764, issue of the *London Chronicle,* page 470:

> "By letters from Fort Boone at Long-Canes we are informed, that on the 24th past [October of 1764] Capt. [Patrick] Calhoun, of the Rangers, received information from two Cherokee Indians, that they had discovered some Indians, which they took for Creeks, with two horses, at some distance. Capt. Calhoun immediately dispatched his Lieutenant, with a party, accompanied by one of the Indian Informants as a guide; they soon came up with an Indian camp, round which, as there was nobody in it, they placed themselves in ambush, in order to seize the Indians on their return, which happened soon after, when the Lieutenant took and made prisoner the head of the gang, who, to his great surprise, proved to be a Cherokee from Toogoloo [sic], as were likewise the seven others with him: The Lieutenant took the horses, which he knew to be the property of one of the inhabitants near Long-Canes. We are told a very shameful traffick has been carried on with the Indians for horses, which they are induced to steal in the settlements."[17]

Patrick Calhoun had resumed his role as Deputy Surveyor when he returned to Long Canes following the war. He prospered in the backcountry land-brokerage business as settlers poured into newly-acquired land consequent to the post-war treaty. The South Carolina boundary with the Cherokee had been pushed 40 miles south of Keowee. Although the South Carolina settlers readily settled the new land, they generally respected the boundary lines and did not immediately encroach further into Cherokee land. The fact that South Carolina had been granted so much land near to the Lower Villages severely aggravated Lower Village chiefs like Young Warrior of Estatoe and Skiuka (Skyuka) of Keowee who was the primary chief of the Lower Villages.

There had been some ill will toward Patrick Calhoun since he had settled on the Cherokee side of the previously agreed-upon border with South Carolina (See Chapter 3). Earlier in 1764, Patrick Calhoun had been made Captain over a company of rangers specifically sent to Long Canes by the South Carolina General Assembly to protect the settlers against just such Indian activity. Although experience with the earlier Long Canes Massacre (See Chapter 4) made such a move important in the minds of the Long Canes settlers, it served to further antagonize the Lower Town Cherokee headmen.

Another backcountry settler who prospered very well following the treaty was Andrew Williamson. He had begun his South Carolina upcountry life as a cowboy working for Dr. John Murray (owner of the backcountry land that included the site of the future village of Ninety Six). He made seed money as a cattle contractor to the British government during the French and Indian War, and followed that by entering into land speculation with Murray and Francis Salvador, a Jewish settler in the area.

Interestingly, the older chiefs had no problem with speculator Williamson as the two had often traded over the years. Ostenaco related:

> "My old friend Mr. Williamson has been a great trader. I gave a great deal of land [to Williamson] ... to pay my debts ... the Warriors in the Lower Towns ... cannot take away his land...."

Ostenaco's words were not salve for the feelings of the Lower Village chiefs. The idea that he had accumulated debts was more an indictment of Williamson than a compliment. The younger warriors were irked that Ostenaco had begun to favor British alliances and didn't seem to be cognizant that those alliances were the primary cause for the loss of Cherokee land. Indeed, they viewed Chief Ostenaco as a British pawn as they did Chief Attakullakulla.

Virginia vigilantes in Augusta County tracked down and murdered whom they considered to be five suspicious Cherokee in 1765. Creek War Chief Great Mortar, still active in the Lower Towns, continually tried to stir clansmen of the slain Indians to blood vengeance. While that was a clan right, Attakullakulla and Ostenaco calmed the warriors until Virginia Governor Francis Fauquier could take action. The Governor knew all too well the resultant flame from the spark of such a murderous affair a few years earlier. He wanted no part of another Cherokee war and sent trade goods to Attakullakulla for disbursement to the affected clans. This proved to be enough to offset the need for revenge.

Attakullakulla was still concerned with encroachment, unrestrained by the Proclamation of 1763, as well as with the continual unfair practices of the traders residing within the Cherokee community. He lobbied for an audience with King George III to state his case for more effective assistance from the British military. He was humiliated to find out that the King seemed to not respect him as "head of state" of the Cherokee. The King refused to receive another visit from any Indians. John Stuart was required to tactfully inform Attakullakulla.

The mounting trade debt incurred by Cherokee individuals was particularly distressing. While they had become reliant upon British trade goods, the deer population had drastically decreased. Historians tend to blame the white "long hunters," and they certainly did add to the problem; however, the high European demand for skins initiated a huge hunting foray by the Cherokee, themselves.

Demand began to taper off, and suddenly the bottom dropped. The Cherokee were left with no visible means to pay their trade debts other than capturing enemy warriors and selling them into the West Indies slave trade. What deerskin trade they had was minimal, primarily with Moravians and other Indian Nations. The younger warriors and chiefs realized that their only chance for survival was to revitalize their own self-sufficiency— return to the old ways as much as possible.

They and their Indian allies needed to defend themselves, their homelands, and resist settlers' efforts to encroach and to encumber the Cherokee with mounting trade debt. Ironically, they befriended Tories, who favored a continued effective royal government. That sentiment was driven by the Cherokee and their trust in John Stuart (the British Southern Indian superintendent) and his deputies Alexander Cameron, and John McDonald. However, Stuart and company were never able to fully accommodate the Cherokee with military assistance to resist encroachers. The backcountry Tories were British sympathizers because they realized the British lacked manpower to control the Tories' criminal enterprises. Thus, the Cherokee relationship with the Loyalists was self-defeating. The Tories were willing to fight with the Cherokee but were insufficient in number to be of real value.

Chief Attakullakulla's son, Tsiyagunsini (Dragging Canoe), was now a young chief with an expanded group of followers that grew monthly. Dragging Canoe had become his father's chief political rival. He was in his late twenties or early thirties and had watched the British through the 1750s and 1760s while he was maturing.

Chief Willenawah, Attakullakulla's brother, faced the same challenge as did Attakullakulla, but from his own son, Chief Doublehead. Doublehead, a brother of Standing Turkey, would become one of the most militant of young rebellious Cherokee warriors.

Others who were coming of age followed Dragging Canoe and Doublehead, including Dragging Canoe's brothers Ooskuah (Old Abram), Ocuma (The Badger), Wyuka (Little Owl), Colonah (The Raven of Chota), and Turtle At Home. Doublehead's brothers were Standing Turkey (Cunne Shote), Sequechee (Big Half Breed), Tsisquaya (Red Bird I), Uskwaliguta (Hanging Maw), and Lyahuwagiautsa (Pumpkin Boy). Another brother, Kahnyatahee (Old Tassel or Corn Tassel), continued to follow his Uncle Attakullakulla's leadership and would later become Principal Chief of the Cherokee Nation. (Hanging Maw would later return to the Upper Villages and also become Principal Chief.)

Doublehead's sister, Wurteh, would become the mother of Kunokeski (John Watts, Jr. or Young Tassel) and the grandmother of Bench (Robert or Bob Benge) and Martin Benge (The Tail); each was a half-blood warrior who yet identified totally with his Cherokee heritage and became an extraordinary leader in the likeness of Dragging Canoe and Doublehead. Indeed, though mixed blood, their hearts and desires assured their acceptance as if they were full-blooded Cherokee.

(Short biographical sketches of many Cherokee leaders are included in Appendix B. Chief Doublehead is the present author's seventh great-grandfather.)

The trend toward isolationism was challenged by Attakullakulla, Willenawah, Old Tassel, and Ostenaco. However, women began raising crops as in the old days, but with new methods and equipment that had been acquired through trade. They disparaged hogs; however, they raised them for food to supplement the decline in wild game. They jeeringly referred to pigs as "smiling 'possums." They were slow to raise cattle because the bovine were thought of as "white man's deer."

Agents Alexander Cameron and John Stuart escorted chiefs Attakullakulla and Oconostota to New York in 1767. They boarded the British sloop *Sally* on November 29, and arrived in New York on December 12, 1767. Sir William Johnson, British superintendent of Indian Affairs, hosted them at his home to hammer out a peace accord between the Cherokee and the Iroquois. A tentative agreement was obtained; however, several touchy details needed attention. Primarily, several nations, such as the Cherokee and the Shawnee, had claimed rights to the same ancestral lands. Attakullakulla believed he could settle the issue and further raise his prestige, so he traveled overland and met with Shawnee, Delaware, and others in April of 1768. Oconostota had returned by ship and arrived in Charles Town on April 28, 1768.

Alexander Cameron, John Stuart's chief deputy to the Cherokee, and the Cherokee themselves complicated matters for Stuart when Cameron was given large tracts of land in Cherokee country (see Treaty of Lochaber below for the location). Stuart, fearful that the land was to settle a debt, incurred with Cameron's trading business, protested the gift to Oconostota who declared:

> Mr. Cameron has lived amongst us as a Beloved Man, he has done us justice and always told us the truth ... we all Regard and Love him; and we hope he will not be taken away from us. When a good Man comes among us we are sorry to part with him.... Our beloved Brother, Mr. Cameron, has got a son by Cherokee woman. We are desirous that he may educate the boy like the white people ... that he may resemble both white and red, and live among us when his father is dead. We have given him for this purpose a large piece of land.[18]

On October 17, 1768, John Stuart signed a new treaty with the Cherokee called the Treaty of Hard Labor. (Hard Labor Creek begins just below Greenwood, South Carolina, and runs south by southeast to its confluence with Cuffytown Creek, where its name changes to Stevens Creek. Historian Tom Hatley records in *The Dividing Paths* that the meeting occurred at Lochaber, Alexander Cameron's South Carolina estate. See details of the Treaty of Lochaber below for Lochaber's location.)[19]

The Royal Proclamation of 1763 had prohibited settlements west of the eastern continental divide so to reduce conflict with the Indians. That divide separates the Potomac watershed from the rest of present-day West Virginia. Settlers ignored the proclamation and settled territory claimed by the Cherokee. Tension between British settlers and the Cherokee Nation increased. The settlers demanded access to the land west of the proclamation line. The British government conceded and met the Cherokee leaders at Hard Labor.

Attakullakulla and Oconostota signed the agreement and relinquished all Cherokee land west of the Allegheny Mountains and east of the Ohio River, comprising all of present-day West Virginia except the extreme southwestern part of the state. The new boundary line ran from the confluence of the Ohio and Kanawha Rivers to the headwaters of the Kanawha River. (That line effectively followed present-day U.S. Highway 35 from Point Pleasant, West Virginia, to Charleston, West Virginia, and U.S. Interstate 77 to Wytheville, Virginia.)

On November 2, 1768, Agent John Stuart and Virginia governor Francis Fauquier escorted Attakullakulla, Oconostota, and a Middle Town war chief named Raven of Nequassee to Fort Stanwix, New York. Sir William Johnson had called the council. The fort had been abandoned since 1765 and had fallen into disrepair. A council house, living quarters for colonial officials, and other structures were quickly constructed in preparation for the negotiations.

Some Indians began arriving at Fort Stanwix in August and began early negotiations that lasted into November. The Cherokee were late for these early negotiations but were involved in the final agreement. Aside from those already mentioned, colonial officials attending included Sir William Franklin, the royal governor of New Jersey; Frederick Smyth, the chief justice of New Jersey; Dr. Thomas Walker of Virginia; and Richard Peters and Joseph Tilghman of Pennsylvania. (Dr. Walker was the same Dr. Thomas Walker who, years before, had helped pioneer Samuel Stalnaker build his cabin on the Holston River. See Fort Attakullakulla earlier in this chapter.)

Sir William Johnson estimated that over 3,000 American Indians were present. On November 5, 1768, representatives for the Mohawk, Oneida, Tuscarora, Onondaga, Cayuga and Seneca signed a new Boundary Line Treaty on behalf of the Six Nations: Shawnee,

Delaware, Mingo and other dependent tribes. They also ceded interests in land east and south of the boundary to Great Britain. The new boundary line started at Fort Stanwix and proceeded south and west to the confluence of the Ohio and Kanawha Rivers as outlined in the Board of Trade's instructions. Then, it continued down the Ohio River to its confluence with the Cherokee or Hogohege River (present-day Tennessee River), farther west than the Board of Trade's instructions or what the Treaty of Hard Labor had provided.

The new boundary line was contentious from the start. The goal of the treaty was to resolve issues among American Indians west of the colonies. The Oneida and Sir William Johnson disagreed at the onset about where the boundary line started. The Board of Trade was concerned about renewed conflict between the British and the American Indian nations as well as between the nations themselves.

John Stuart complained that, not only did the new boundary line negatively impact what had been drawn at the Treaty of Hard Labor, but it also negatively affected his relationship with the Cherokee. The Board of Trade and British general Jeffery Amherst chided Johnson and ordered him to renegotiate the line to end at the confluence of the Ohio and Kanawha Rivers. However, Johnson refused.

The relationship between the settlers and the American Indian nations would remain strained for years to come. This new treaty opened lands that would eventually become parts of western Pennsylvania, Maryland, Virginia, and northeast Tennessee, as well as the future states of Kentucky and West Virginia (which would withdraw from Virginia during the future Civil War). The Iroquois ceded the land of Kentucky and western Pennsylvania for £10,000. This disturbed the Shawnee who laid claim to some of this land. On April 3, 1769, when the land made available by the treaty was offered, the Government Land Office in Pittsburgh received 3,000 applications, mostly from land speculators.[20]

Londoner Lord Shelburne was eager to allow the settlers to move westward. His backward thinking was that the move would lessen the possibility of future Indian wars. The Virginia Commissioners assigned to work the issue were Virginia colonel Andrew Lewis and Dr. Thomas Walker. They, not coincidentally, were the respective chief executive officers of the Greenbrier and Loyal land development companies and friends of Shelburne. Lewis and Walker desired to move the boundary as far west as possible in order to validate the then-illegal claims of their companies. Shelburne petitioned the House of Burgesses to request John Stuart, superintendent of Indian Affairs for the Southern Department, to move the boundary to the Ohio River.

Attakullakulla and Oconostota had implored John Stuart to declare that the boundary line should run to the mouth of the Great Kanawha River, in present-day West Virginia, rather than farther west to the Ohio River. Stuart agreed.

On October 18, 1770, Attakullakulla, Oconostota, and 13 other Cherokee headmen attended a conference led by John Stuart at Lochaber, South Carolina. The conference was viewed by over 1,000 Cherokee. Virginia commissioners Lewis and Walker also attended.

Stuart outlined his draft which modified the Treaties of Hard Labor and Fort Stanwix. Considered a compromise, it enlarged the area to be ceded by the Cherokee in Hard Labor but lessened the area that would have been ceded by Fort Stanwix. The Cherokee relinquished all claims to property from the North Carolina and Virginia border to a point near Long Island on the Holston River to the mouth of the Kanawha River at present-day Point Pleasant in Mason County, West Virginia.

Absentee royal governor Sir Jeffery Amherst acted through Council president John Blair, who ordered Walker and Lewis to sign the agreement, because Stuart's position of superintendent of Indian Affairs was the highest British authority at the time for the subject of Indian boundaries in the Southern Department. They reluctantly did so. Stuart signed for the British government; Attakullakulla and Oconostota for the Cherokee.

(Lochaber, Deputy Indian Agent Alexander Cameron's South Carolina estate, was located near present-day South Carolina State Highway 71, halfway between present-day Abbeville and Lowndesville. A marker along the highway reads, "In 1775, William Bartram visited several days at 'Lough-Abber' home of A. Cameron, en route north to the Cherokee country.")

In 1769, the Cherokee made a gift of Cherokee land to Captain Richard Pearis near Captain Evan McLauren's property on Dutch Creek in South Carolina. John Stuart was sure that tract was to satisfy trade debts, as he had suspected was the reason for such a gift to Alexander Cameron; however, trader Pearis also had a Cherokee mate and was the father of mixed-blood children.

In 1771, Colonels John Donelson and Isaac Bledsoe surveyed the Virginia and North Carolina border. As they moved west, they discovered several Virginia settlers that resided in the treaty-designated Cherokee lands between the boundary and the South Fork Holston River in present-day eastern Tennessee. These were likely the Sapling Grove and Keywood Settlements near present-day Bristol, Tennessee. (Additionally, William Bean had been residing in a log cabin where Boone's Creek joins the Watauga River. They formed the Watauga Association in 1772 and elected five commissioners to settle disputes, and to hold judicial powers and perform executive duties. The association functioned as a total democracy. Also, in 1771, two men identified in *Goodspeed's History of Tennessee* as "Messrs. Carter & Parker" set up a store at present-day Rogersville. Soon, people from present-day Abingdon, Virginia—then called Wolf's Hill—joined them in a settlement called Carter's Valley.)

Immediately following the survey, Alexander Cameron, resident Indian agent to the Cherokee, ordered the Holston encroachers to relocate off of Cherokee land. However, Attakullakulla and a few other Cherokee headmen had accompanied the survey party. Attakullakulla had remarked that he "pitied them" for having to relocate and lose their property. He then consented to a new boundary to run along the course of the Holston River to a point six miles east of Long Island of the Holston. Thus the "North of the Holston" settlers were then considered to be outside of Cherokee country. Attakullakulla eventually gave the Watauga Association a ten-year lease for the land that they claimed, a move that even further extended his acceptance of the encroachment which would not yet stop. Shortly thereafter, the Cherokee chiefs were offered £500 by the "Virginia Commissioners" to move the Lochaber line to the Ohio River—and they agreed. Supposedly, the Virginia Commissioners "partied" the older chiefs to gain their agreement. The Cherokee never did receive the payment after they signed away the land. John Stuart could not object since, in his opinion, the chiefs legally signed it away in what became known as The Donelson Purchase.

Dr. Walker moved quickly before there could be any other legal challenges to the newly acquired legal boundary. By December 16, 1773, 201,554 acres of prime once–Cherokee owned land, one-quarter of the original grant, had already been sold.

In 1772, Jacob Brown had opened a store on the Nolichucky River and was joined there by other pioneers to create the Nolichucky Settlement.

The Treaty of Hard Labor, the Treaty of Fort Stanwix, the Treaty of Lochaber, then further cessions by the older Cherokee chiefs together resulted in unlimited encroachment up to a phantom boundary called the Purchase Line. At least John Stuart, at the Lochaber Treaty, made an attempt to stifle the land speculators, but the chiefs chose to override him.

The younger chiefs had enough, treaty after treaty, cession after cession; Attakullakulla and the other older headmen would give them no ear to hear their grievances. It would come to a head in 1775.[21]

CHAPTER 6

Backcountry Discontent, Sycamore Shoals and War

The 1760s and 1770s were paradoxical for the Cherokee. They desired to expand their trade with the British colonists and sought to clearly define a boundary between the two communities. In addition, they invited white traders to marry into their Cherokee clan system and reside in the Cherokee villages. That was counterproductive to a boundary. Britain provided the Cherokee little assistance in quelling the settlers' encroachment onto Cherokee ancestral lands. King George III's Proclamation of 1763 had no teeth when it came to enforcement. The Treaties of Hard Labor and Fort Stanwix in 1768 were inadequate attempts; however, the land speculators had some sway over boundary decisions. Following those two agreements, settlers swarmed into the Holston River Valley in present-day northeastern Tennessee and southwestern Virginia. John Stuart, the superintendent of Indian Affairs in the Southern Department, strongly attempted to protect the Cherokee with the Treaty of Lochaber in 1770, but he was frustrated by the chiefs themselves in 1772 when they moved the boundary to include 10,000 more acres for the speculators for an inadequate amount of money. Chief Attakullakulla had also specifically jogged a boundary line in 1771 that would allow the Holston settlers to remain in place. The younger chiefs were beginning to see problems with the older chiefs' open-arm policy with the British. It seemed to the young warriors that strict isolationism would be better; a Hadrian's Wall in reverse might have accomplished that. (See Chapters 1 and 5.)[1]

In 1772, Jacob Brown settled in the Nolichucky River area. He was a self-supported Indian trader and the Cherokee seemed rather fond of him. He was considered to be more honest than many of the cooperative traders they had dealt with in the past. Brown moved into the area with wagonloads of trade goods that he willingly exchanged with the Indians for skins. He also established a tract of land in the Watauga settlement and became a Watauga commissioner.

Brown's Nolichucky tract provided the Cherokee with a general store. He tended to blacksmithing, gunsmith repair, and traded ammunition for pelts. The Cherokee hunters enjoyed stopping at his place to talk trade and to converse with one another about the hunting grounds. However, his tract was 50 miles beyond the king's proclamation line.

The same year that Brown settled, Alexander Cameron boldly ordered the Watauga area settlers to leave Cherokee land. Brown was one of those warned. He felt there would be safety in numbers, so he gathered his goods and abandoned his store for the Watauga settlement. The Wataugans were not inclined to leave. Chief Oconostota wrote to John Stuart on April 26, 1772, and reported:

> A few days ago Jamie Branham was among them to see how many Plantations they had, which were about Seventy. They asked him if our Brother, Mr. Cameron, was not a mad man or a fool that he did not send them word before they had Planted [sic]; that they had now planted their crops and would not move off till they had got them in.[2]

James Robertson and John Bean led a citizens' committee meeting to discuss the situation. At the meeting, Jacob Brown suggested a 10-year lease idea for the settlers with the Cherokee as their lessors. The other settlers thought that a great idea as they likely realized that in ten years all would be forgotten and the land would be theirs by squatters' rights. They approached Attakullakulla who agreed to take the matter to the Council House in Chota.

Attakullakulla's presentation garnered a majority of votes for the measure (primarily the older chiefs while the younger, more independent and militant younger chiefs opposed it). Interestingly, John Stuart voiced in favor of the petition while Alexander Cameron was vehemently opposed to it.

Chief Attakullakulla eagerly volunteered to negotiate the lease agreement with the Wataugans. He wrote to John Stuart:

> Father, I will eat and drink with my white brothers, and will expect friendship and good useage from them. It is but a little spot of ground they ask, and I am willing that your people should live upon it. I pity the white people, but they do not pity me.... The Great Being above is very good, and provides for everybody.... He gave us this land, but the white people seem to want to drive us from it.[3]

Attakullakulla's propensity for identifying the two cultures in terms of family relationships was never reciprocated by the British. The chief had a strong desire for that bond, and his continued prestige depended upon success.

The Wataugans created the Watauga Association in 1772, and a part of their charter (no longer extant) specified no additional encroachment on Cherokee land. However, they had no power to enforce such an article in their credo. More new settlers came; more land was settled. More white hunters stalked the Cherokee ancestral hunting grounds. The chiefs complained to John Stuart and Alexander Cameron. They received little help since the chiefs had invited the Wataugans and provided the means for them to stay. John Stuart did try when he penned a letter to North Carolina governor Josiah Martin. The governor sent a message to the Watauga Settlement that ordered the encroachers to leave Cherokee land or suffer expulsion. The Wataugans considered themselves to be an independent state, and even so, thought themselves to be more within Virginia's jurisdiction than North Carolina's. They ignored the governor.

Jacob Brown later issued a petition to North Carolina to justify his return to the Nolichucky River tract he had vacated. He reportedly had been sold the land by the Cherokee. His petition of 1776 stated:

> Some time after a line being run and a Proclamation Issued by his Britanic [sic] Majesty's Superintendent of Indian Affairs requiring all persons who had made settlements beyond the said line to relinquish them, Your Petitioner altho' much sollicited [sic] by the Indians of the Cherokee Nation to remain in his settlement yet did remove himself with much trouble and disadvantage to Wattagaw [sic], where he remained until the Chief of said Nation by very pressing Intreaty [sic], and great Incouragement [sic] prevailed upon him your said Petitioner to return to his former settlement whither a Considerable Body of Indians of the aforesaid Nation Escorted your Petitioner and assisted in removing his Effects.[4]

(On Tennessee State Highway 81, near its junction with Taylor Bridge Road north of the Nolichucky River, is a highway marker that reads, "About one mile SW this pioneer from S.C. settled on the Nolichucky River in 1771. Brown's purchase of 2 tracts of land from the Cherokee on March 25, 1775, was made beneath a great oak tree still standing nearby. His sandstone marker reads 'Jacob Brown, d. Jan 25, 1785.' The brick house nearby was built by his grandson, Byrd Brown, about 1800.")[5]

In 1773, John Stuart and Georgia governor James Wright held a conference in Augusta with the Creek and Cherokee that resulted in the signing of the Treaty of Augusta on the 1st of June. Representatives from Virginia and the Carolinas ministered as observers. The Cherokee had by then become enemies with the Creek and with Virginia colony. The Creek derided the old Cherokee chiefs because they would not accede to Creek initiatives to ally with the French and resist settler encroachment. On the other hand, the Virginians chided the Cherokee over the resistance of their young warriors to that same encroachment of Virginia settlers near the Upper Villages. However, individual members of the Creek and the Cherokee communities had accumulated large debts with traders from the colonies, and Georgia was no exception. The debt needed to be settled, and the Georgia governor was interested in opening up more land near the existing Georgia backcountry border. Some of the land was claimed by one tribe or the other, and each tribe maintained rights to some identical territory. Therefore, Stuart and the governor each needed to attend this conference.

On the 1st of June, the Creek ceded 675,000 acres to Georgia while the Cherokee signed off on 2,000,000 acres. Governor Wright quickly acted to issue a proclamation on the 11th that described the newly-opened territory and implored farmers and entrepreneurs to settle the land as quickly as possible.

(A Quaker explorer named William Bartram had attended the conference. Bartram was considered to be a member of the American Enlightenment. The American Enlightenment was an intellectual period from about 1715 to 1789. It was influenced by the scientific revolution of the 17th century and the humanist period of the Renaissance. The Enlightenment applied scientific reasoning and adapted it into the study of human nature, society, and religion. There was an emphasis upon liberty and religious tolerance and an attempt to reconcile science and religion. That resulted in a rejection of possible modern-day prophecy and miracles. More about Bartram will be covered later in this chapter.)

Bartram wrote of the conference:

Early in the morning, we mounted our horses, and in two days arrived in Savanna [sic]; here we learned the Superintendent of Indian affairs ... was on his way to Augusta.... A few days after our arrival ... the chiefs and warriors of the Creeks and Cherokees being arrived, the Congress and the business of the treaty came on, and negociations [sic] continued undetermined many days; the merchants of Georgia demanding at least two million acres of land from the Indians, as a discharge of their debts, due, and of long standing ... and they could not at first be brought to listen to reason and amicable terms; however, at length, the cool and deliberate counsels of the ancient venerable chiefs, enforced by liberal presents of suitable goods, were too powerful inducements for them to any longer resist, and finally prevailed.[6]

As Bartram explained, the older chiefs had, again, settled a treaty with a large cession of land. The younger chiefs were becoming more and more agitated. They knew that the traders had carefully maneuvered the previous generation into huge trade debts to capitalize on them at a later time; however, the older chiefs, in the minds of the incensed younger generation of chiefs, seemed oblivious to the problem. Where the mainstream, or older, Cherokee tried to accommodate the British community, the young warriors would determine to practice resistance. The younger generation had enough, and at first began to attack exposed backcountry settlements in Georgia, but the aggression soon spread into the other colonies. No white traveler encountered on a back road, farmer in his fields, or other susceptible settler was spared the warriors' wrath.[7]

In 1773, an incident that involved William Russell and Daniel Boone not only exemplified the growing aggressiveness of young Cherokee warriors toward encroaching white settlers, but also served as a special warning that the Cherokee warriors involved were partnered with those of the Shawnee and Delaware, traditional Cherokee enemies from the north.

William Russell, a veteran Virginia Militia lieutenant colonel in the French and Indian War, had settled into Castle's Woods settlement on the Clinch River in Virginia (present-day Castlewood, Virginia). He took command of a company of militia and was familiarly known as "Captain" Russell and "Colonel" Russell. Russell was from an aristocratic Virginia family and was eager to advance to the newly-opened Cumberland area of present-day Kentucky. (Though it was not yet a defined state or a colony, it will simply be referred to as Kentucky in the following text.)

Daniel Boone (a first cousin of American revolutionary brigadier general Daniel Morgan who would defeat British lieutenant colonel Banastre Tarleton at the Battle of Cowpens), who resided in the Yadkin Valley of North Carolina, was already associated with Richard Henderson and Nathaniel Hart of the Transylvania Company, a land-speculation enterprise that had notions of settling on, and selling parts of, the Cumberland region. They were keen for Boone to explore the area, blaze trails, and provide recommendations for areas of settlement.

Boone soon entered into an agreement to lead a group of advance settlers into the Cumberland region, including William Russell, his family, and a few friends such as the young David Gass and Michael Stoner. The Russell group would total about 30 people.

Boone and explorer Benjamin Cutbirth returned from a trek into Kentucky (to present-day Jessamine County, just west of today's Richmond, Kentucky) in late summer of 1773. Daniel had carved his initials "D. B." and "1773" into the wall of his cave shelter and on several birch trees nearby (on the bank of Little Hickman Creek). The two were very eager to return.

Boone made plans to relocate his family to the new Cumberland region. Before he left Yadkin Valley with his family, he visited his brother-in-law, William Bryan, who lived 60 miles to the southeast. It was agreed that Bryan and Benjamin Cutbirth would meet the main party at Powell River Valley in Virginia (near present-day Norton, Virginia).

The McAfee party, a group of explorers and surveyors, which had just returned a month prior from an expedition that had gone as far as Big Bone Lick in present-day Kentucky (on the Ohio River 20 miles southwest of present-day Cincinnati, Ohio), was also eager to return. Robert and James McAfee and Captain Thomas Bullitt likewise agreed to meet Boone at Powell Valley.

Boone sold his farm, disposed of any cumbersome household goods and farming equipment, and departed the Yadkin on September 25, 1773. When Daniel Boone, with his main party, arrived in the vicinity of present-day Abingdon, Virginia, he made camp and detached his eldest son, 16-year-old James, along with John and Richard Mendenhall to Castle's Woods. James was to inform Captain Russell that Boone's party was en route to Powell Valley and that Russell's contingent should dispatch for that site immediately.

James Boone and his companions then collected food, seed corn, flour, and other supplies. William Russell was not prepared to leave, but his 17-year-old son, Henry Russell, Isaac Crabtree, Samuel Drake (a son of settler John Drake), and two slaves named Charles and Adam joined the James Boone group and departed with a small herd of cattle. They crossed the Clinch River at Hunter's Ford (present-day Dungannon, Virginia), through Hunter's Valley, east to Rye Cove (on present-day Scott County Virginia Route 619), and across Powell Mountain (likely at Kane's Gap) en route to Wallen's Creek. They encamped near present-day Stickleyville, Virginia, on October 9, 1773. (Stickleyville is located on U.S. Highway 58 about five miles west of present-day Duffield, Virginia. Some reports aver that they camped next to Wallen's Creek at Stickleyville's site, while others claim they camped two and one-half miles west at Fannon Spring, which was a noted drinking water source for travelers of that era.)

Daniel Boone and his party had already arrived at the rendezvous point on the Powell River near present-day Pennington Gap, Virginia. He had also been joined by the Bryan and McAfee parties, whose members had left their families home while the men sought out proper sites for relocation in the new land. Some members of William Russell's community, namely Michael Stoner, William Bush, and Edmund Jennings, had left early and met the Bryan party and were also at the appointed site less than six miles beyond where James Boone and his detachment were camped.

Captain William Russell finally got his contingent organized. He and Captain David Gass embarked to overtake young James Boone. Russell and Gass planned a similar route to that of the Bryan party. They would claim good pieces of property, construct comfortable cabins, plant crops in the spring, and then return for their families. Once the entire expedition was conjoined, it would have amounted to 80 people who would travel to the Cumberland. Russell reached the small group, but their camp was not as he envisioned it to be.

When James Boone and his group camped on the 9th, they did not realize how near they were to the primary assemblage. They had become lost at one point and wandered three miles out of their way—a trek they had to retrace in reverse. Their encampment was forced as night encompassed them in the treacherous terrain. They started a blazing campfire as they were cold, and the skittish Mendenhall brothers were not outdoorsmen. As they sat around the campfire they heard wolves howling in the darkness—a lot of them. Isaac Crabtree was a woodsman and couldn't resist teasing the young brothers about their fears.

Unknown to the little group, the howls they heard were likely Indians trying to keep them awake so they would be tired and sleepy come morning. Reportedly a band of 25 Delaware, Shawnee, and Cherokee warriors had been trailing them since they had gotten lost. The large campfire was an aid to the Indians. Such a diverse group was likely militant and not eager to see a collection of settlers headed for Kentucky.

The campers stirred in the dawn mist, likely awakened by the warriors' rustling as they crept near. The weary travelers could only see shapes of the men who slipped slowly toward the bedrolls. Suddenly, the small detachment was hit by a spate of arrows and rifle balls.

The description of this brutal attack exemplifies just how irate the Indians had become over the loss of their ancestral lands, and how they defended against encroachment the only way they knew how. It was a poignant scene. Young Henry Russell was hobbled by rifle balls through both hips. When rushed by the knife-wielding warriors, he nervously tried to seize the blades with his bare hands which became badly mangled. The Indians pulled his toenails and fingernails out one by one and finally ended his suffering with tomahawk blows.

James Boone was also shot through both hips which were shattered. After he fell, he recognized a Shawnee warrior named Big Jim. Boone was stunned because he remembered Big Jim as a family friend who had shared meals in the Daniel Boone home. Big Jim's unusually high cheek bones and broad face, with a singularly peculiar chin, rendered him recognizable without doubt. The warriors began to torture Boone as they had done Russell. James Boone begged his one-time friend to spare him, but neither former amity nor previously-shared meals altered the outcome. Friendships had existed between individual warriors and white settlers; however, for the Cherokee warriors, war was overriding, and it was required to wage war correctly. Soon, the torture was more than the young man could endure, and he pleaded for Big Jim to end his life.

John and Richard Mendenhall and Samuel Drake were also slain in a similar manner. The warriors had captured Charles, one of William Russell's slaves, but the other, Adam, was able to scamper through the mist and hide himself in some driftwood on the bank of Wallen's Creek. Adam witnessed the brutality through the haze from his cover. Once the Indians left, he wandered carefully through the mountains and arrived back in Castle's Woods on the 21st.

Isaac Crabtree had also been wounded in the initial onslaught and escaped similarly to Adam. Crabtree worked his way deeper into the woods. He was afraid to try and go to the Daniel Boone encampment on Powell River because he believed that would be the next target of the Indians. He made his way back to Castle's Woods, but arrived much more quickly than did Adam. The warriors, however, knew the numbers were not in their favor to attack the main camp, so they opted to take the stolen goods and horses to the Upper Cherokee Villages. After they had traveled 40 miles from the attack site, two warriors argued over possession of Charles. The leader of the party had no time for such trivial matters and, as is the custom, disposed of the problem. He tomahawked Charles to death.

Thomas Sharp, who left William Russell's party early, met up with the Bryan party, and met Daniel Boone and the main contingent at Powell's River. A few months later, Sharp made a deposition regarding the matter:

Deposition of Thomas Sharp, Fur Trader
Fincastle County Virginia

This Day came Thomas Sharp before me and made Oath on the Holy Evangelist of Almighty God, that being on Wattaga River, the fifth Day of October last, a party of Northward Indians, together with two Cherokees one of which he says was called the Elk Warriour, which said Indian had a Spur in his Hand, which your Deponent out of curiosity took from him to look at, upon which Spur there were several Scales, one of which your Deponent broke off. On the Tenth of the same instant, your Deponent set out to Join a Company going with William Russell to Ohio, accordingly your Deponent did Join the said Company, and proceeded on to the head of Powell's River, where the Company had proposed to wait for the said William Russell and some others, who were

expected soon after, having waited two Days, one of the Party gave out the Journey, and on his Return home, about Thirty miles from the said Encampment, found three Persons (as he supposed) killed by the Indians, which caused him to return again to the Company, and after being informed of the accident your Deponent with Twelve men went to bury the Dead, after coming to the Place, among many other Indian War Weapons, your Deponent found a Spurr [sic], which he affirms to be the very same he saw the Elk Warriour have at Wattage:
Sworn before me February the 20th 1774, Thomas Sharp—his [X] mark
Wit: W. Russell[8]

In the main camp the young man referred to in Sharp's deposition had stolen some goods and had been so scorned by the other members that, embarrassed, he decided to return to the settlements. As he left on the 10th, the day of the massacre, he stole some pelts from Daniel Boone. The warriors had not left long before he came upon the massacre sight and immediately returned to the main camp. The burial party set out to look after the slain. James Boone's mother, Rebecca (Bryan) Boone, gave a family member in the sorrowful group a sheet with which to wrap her son's body before his interment. Those who remained quickly erected a palisade wall to help defend against possible attacks.

When the cluster arrived at the massacre site, they found that members of the William Russell party were already there. William Russell was found distraught and seated on a rock, his face buried in his cupped hands. The sheet intended for James Boone was also used for Henry Russell's corpse.

(There are some problems with Thomas Sharp's deposition. There were five bodies rather than three, and the attack was fewer than six miles from the main encampment. Thirty miles would have taken the man days to travel. He would have been well back toward the settlements, would have passed the Russell party twice, and certainly would not have returned to the main encampment in time to initiate the gathering of a burial party that would meet Russell at the site. The timing of the aftermath just does not provide for such travel.

(It is unclear who of the Boone family might have accompanied the burial party. Most reports aver that Daniel Boone returned while others state he remained at the main camp to lead a defense should it be necessary. A few have reported that Daniel's father, Squire Boone, was a member of the party and attended to the burial; however, Squire Boone died in Rowan County, North Carolina, on January 2, 1765. It is possible that Daniel's brother, Squire Boone, Jr., was a member of the party and the family's representative.)

When the group returned to the Powell River, they held a council meeting. Daniel Boone, ever the explorer, was inclined to continue the trek. However, he was expectedly outvoted by the company who, almost to a man, desired to return to the settlements. William Russell, as well as others, had completely lost all spirit for the venture. It was especially mournful for Rebecca Boone, who was one of few family members accompanying the exploration. Most other family members remained in the settlements, awaited word of the group's successful arrival in the Cumberland Valley, and expected to meet up with them the following year.

Daniel Boone and his family did not return to the Yadkin, but rather settled on the Clinch River seven or eight miles southwest of Castle's Woods in a cabin provided by David Gass.

The tale seems cruel. The land was harsh, and the era hard. The only law was vengeance, and each side of any issue defended its rights. Revenge often begat more retribution.[9]

(There was once a roadside marker along U.S. Highway 58 near Eller's Gap on Powell Mountain between Stickleyville and Pattonsville; however, as a result of disagreement as to where the massacre took place, someone stole the sign and moved it near the community of Kaylor. The current highway marker, K-32, is located at the intersection of U.S. Highway 58 and Lee County, Virginia, Route 702 in Stickleyville. It reads: "DEATH OF BOONE'S SON In this valley, on 10 Oct. 1773, Delaware, Shawnee, and Cherokee Indians killed Daniel Boone's eldest son, James, and five others in their group of eight settlers en route to Kentucky. Separated from Daniel Boone's main party, the men had set up camp near Wallen's Creek. At dawn the Indians attacked and killed James Boone, Henry Russell, John and Richard Mendenhall—brothers—a youth whose last name was Drake, and Charles—one of two slaves in the party. Isaac Crabtree and Adam, a slave, escaped. This event prompted Boone and his party to abandon their first attempt to settle Kentucky.")

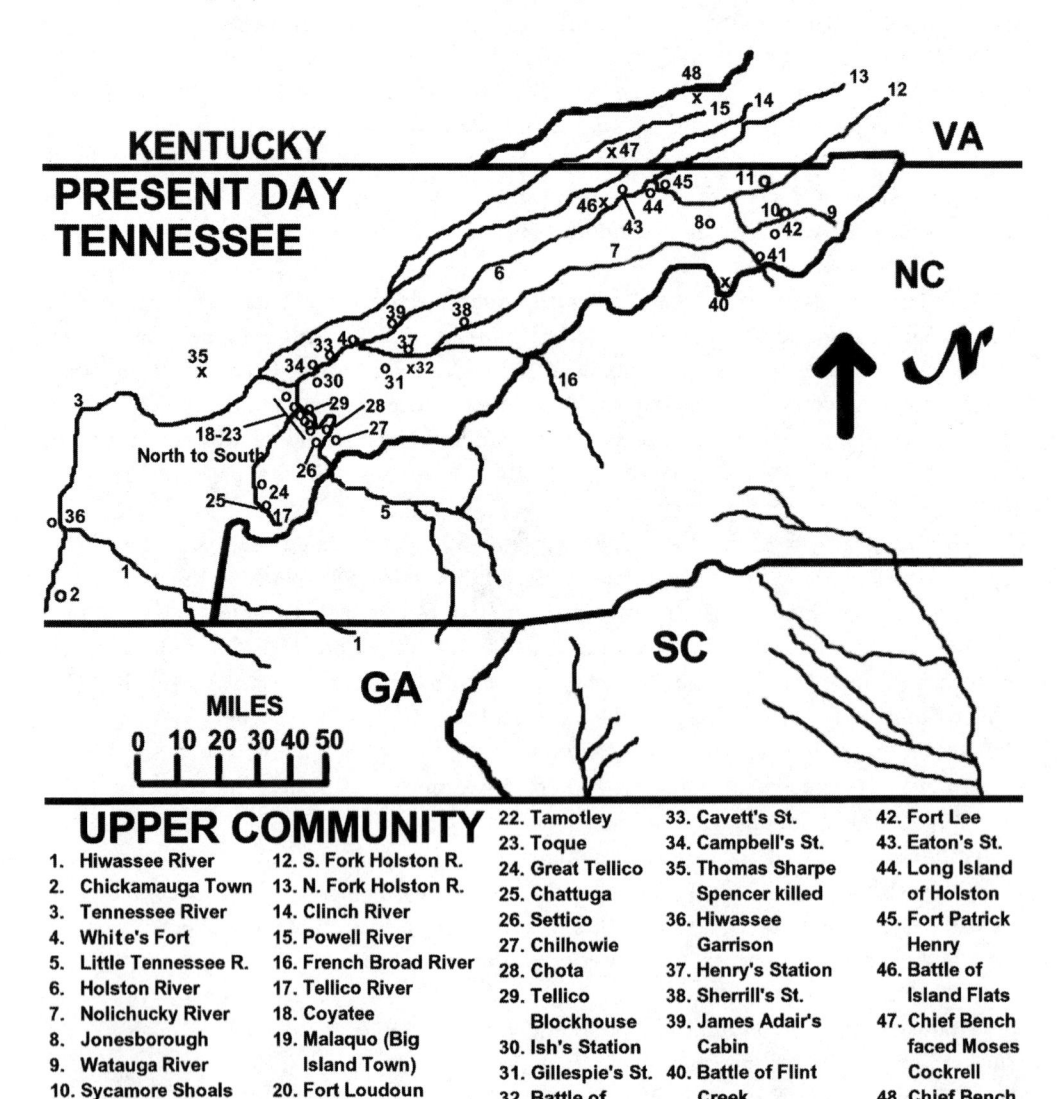

UPPER COMMUNITY

1. Hiwassee River
2. Chickamauga Town
3. Tennessee River
4. White's Fort
5. Little Tennessee R.
6. Holston River
7. Nolichucky River
8. Jonesborough
9. Watauga River
10. Sycamore Shoals
11. Shelby's Fort
12. S. Fork Holston R.
13. N. Fork Holston R.
14. Clinch River
15. Powell River
16. French Broad River
17. Tellico River
18. Coyatee
19. Malaquo (Big Island Town)
20. Fort Loudoun
21. Tuskegee
22. Tamotley
23. Toque
24. Great Tellico
25. Chattuga
26. Settico
27. Chilhowie
28. Chota
29. Tellico Blockhouse
30. Ish's Station
31. Gillespie's St.
32. Battle of Boyd's Creek
33. Cavett's St.
34. Campbell's St.
35. Thomas Sharpe Spencer killed
36. Hiwassee Garrison
37. Henry's Station
38. Sherrill's St.
39. James Adair's Cabin
40. Battle of Flint Creek
41. John Sevier's Home
42. Fort Lee
43. Eaton's St.
44. Long Island of Holston
45. Fort Patrick Henry
46. Battle of Island Flats
47. Chief Bench faced Moses Cockrell
48. Chief Bench killed

Isaac Crabtree, who had witnessed the killing of James Boone and the others, was irate and tried to kill any Indian he saw. He could not bear to be in the presence of a live Indian.

During the time of the Cherokee New Moon Festival in March of 1774, a horse race was arranged at Sycamore Shoals in the Watauga settlement. Horse races between the Wataugans and young Indian warriors were common occurrences there. Associations between the settlers and the Cherokee had been very delicate at that time, especially after the Wallen's Creek incident. The Wataugans had secretly decided to allow the Cherokee racers to win nearly all of the events, a diplomatic move.

During one race, shots rang out from a nearby meadow. A crowd rushed to the scene and found a man named Cherokee Billy lying dead on the ground, a hole in his forehead. Another Cherokee man and a Cherokee woman, each obviously distraught, were bent over him. The woman identified the assailant as having been Isaac Crabtree; however, the killer had left the scene. Several Cherokee warriors removed Cherokee Billy's body. The racing ended for the day, and silence perforated Sycamore Shoals as the Indians left.

The settlers were extremely concerned because Cherokee Billy, then about 50 years of age, was reportedly the son of Small Pox Conjuror and a brother to War Chief Oconostota (who was half-brother to Chief Ostenaco).

Colonel James Robertson, a leader in the Watauga settlement, led a delegation to Chota to appease the chiefs and Cherokee Billy's clansmen. William Falling, a white trader, traveled along to interpret. They spent several hours in the Council House with Attakullakulla, Ostenaco, and Oconostota. Some of the younger chiefs were likely in attendance; however, Raven of Chota, son of Attakullakulla, was in the north conferring with Shawnee chief Cornstalk about an alliance against the whites.

Robertson eventually persuaded Cherokee Billy's clansmen to accept gifts as proper compensation to satisfy the blood vengeance. Robertson promised that Isaac Crabtree would be captured and punished for the killing. He also talked to the chiefs at length to try and convince them that a Shawnee alliance was not in the best interest of the Cherokee. However, the younger chiefs, Dragging Canoe, Raven, Little Owl, Black Fox, and others, would not be convinced. Neither would a few of the elders, including Chief Doublehead.

The Wataugans placed a bounty of £50 sterling for the capture of Crabtree, and Virginia governor John Murray, 4th Earl Dunmore, added £100 more. Crabtree was captured and tried in July. At his trial, he declared that he recognized Cherokee Billy as one of those who attacked his party at Wallen's Creek. He also declared that his brother, John Crabtree, had been a part of the contingent and appeared to have escaped though wounded, but was never heard from again. Crabtree was acquitted.[10]

(Some have recorded that a relative of Isaac Crabtree named William supposedly killed Cherokee Billy in retaliation for the killing of a kinsman at Wallen's Creek. Others have indicated that Isaac Crabtree desired to kill Billy's companions, the Cherokee man and woman who were found with Cherokee Billy's body, as well. However, the others who instantly rushed to the scene of the murder confounded his wish.)

On October 10, 1774, a major battle occurred between the Virginia militia and (primarily) the Shawnee. It was originally called the Battle of Kanawha, later, the Battle of Point Pleasant. This was the only major encounter in what was termed Dunmore's War. Lord Dunmore (Virginia governor John Murray) had petitioned the House of Burgesses to declare war on hostile Indians to the west (present-day West Virginia). The Treaty of Fort

Stanwix in 1768 established the western settlement boundary to be the Ohio River, and that treaty was signed by the Iroquois Confederation. There was some disagreement among other Indians, especially the Shawnee, about whether the Iroquois had the right to sign away that land. Some of the more aggressive young warriors swore not to honor the treaty, which surrendered some of their best hunting land. They aggressively defended the area against encroachers.

Virginia brigadier general Andrew Lewis would lead one part of a two-pronged attack west by northwest from Fort Union (present-day Lewisburg, West Virginia) to the confluence of the Kanawha River at the Ohio (near present-day Point Pleasant, West Virginia). The other contingent, led by Lord Dunmore, would trek northward to Fort Dunmore (once Fort Duquesne and later Fort Pitt), then to Ohio, and then southward toward Point Pleasant to squeeze the Indians between the two groups.

General Lewis led about 1,000 men, mostly Virginians, but some (James Robertson, Valentine Sevier, and Captain Evan Shelby) came from the Holston and Watauga settlements of present-day northeastern Tennessee and extreme southwest Virginia. William Russell of Castle's Woods, Virginia, led a large company of militia.

The Shawnee had been tracking Dunmore's movements and, wanting to avoid entrapment, decided to attack Lewis' troops at Point Pleasant. Shawnee principal chief Cornstalk did not favor the attack; but the majority of Shawnee headmen did, so the chief acquiesced and planned the effort. It is likely that younger Shawnee war chief Blue Jacket was instrumental in convincing the council to make the attack; he led some of the warriors. Another Shawnee war chief, Pukeshenwa (father of six-year-old Tecumseh, and 15-year-old Cheeseekau who would become known as the Shawnee Warrior by the Cherokee), also led a band of the warriors. There were a few Cherokee, Mingo, Huron, Ottawa, and Delaware allied with the Shawnee, but Cornstalk's entire force numbered fewer than 500 warriors.

Lewis was encamped on a bluff overlooking the rivers, and Cornstalk hurried to trap him on the cliff. The fighting lasted for several hours and developed into hand-to-hand combat with knives, tomahawks, and sabers. Lewis was able to have two companies of men slide down the steep terrain and maneuver up the Kanawha to obtain the Indians' rear. Once that was accomplished, Chief Cornstalk withdrew his warriors. Virginia colonel William Christian arrived after the battle's end and surveyed the field. He found 33 dead warriors including Chief Pukeshenwah. Additional dead warriors had been thrown into the Kanawha by their comrades before the withdrawal. The Virginians suffered 75 killed and 140 wounded.

Lewis and Dunmore trailed the Indians into Ohio and, near the Shawnee communities, held a peace conference with Chief Cornstalk. The Virginians hastily erected Camp Charlotte for the purpose. In the Treaty of Camp Charlotte, Chief Cornstalk agreed that Virginia had the land rights to all land south and east of the Ohio River that included present-day West Virginia and Kentucky.

Camp Charlotte was located on present-day Ohio State Route 56, about seven miles southeast of today's Circleville, Ohio, just north of the junction with Ohio State Route 159, at 10104 State Route 56 east. The marker reads:

> In an effort to maintain peace with Native Americans, the British imposed the Proclamation Line of 1763, which prohibited colonial settlement west of the Appalachian Mountains. Some settlers did not recognize British authority and continued to move westward.

6. Backcountry Discontent, Sycamore Shoals and War

Virginia Governor Lord Dunmore, realizing that peace with Native Americans was improbable, amassed troops and headed west, camping at the Hocking River to meet with a unit commanded by Andrew Lewis. En route, Lewis's troops were attacked on October 10, 1774 at present day Point Pleasant, West Virginia, by a force of Delaware and Shawnee led by Cornstalk. After intense battle, the Native Americans retreated north across the Ohio River to villages on the Pickaway Plains. At this point, Dunmore headed to the Shawnee villages to negotiate peace and set up camp at this site. The resulting Treaty of Camp Charlotte ended "Dunmore's War" and stipulated that the Indians give up rights to land south of the Ohio River and allow boats to travel on the river undisturbed. The Treaty of Camp Charlotte established the Ohio River as Virginia's boundary line, aiding in the settlement of Kentucky.

(Young Cheeseekau, who assisted his father, Pukeshenwa, during the battle, is covered in Chapter 9, along with his younger brother, Tecumseh. They assisted the Chickamauga Cherokee leaders in their war with the Overmountain settlers of present-day Tennessee.)[11]

On January 16, 1774, the Creek, and some sympathetic Cherokee who were angered by the recent land cessions, initiated brutal attacks in backcountry Georgia and some neighboring South Carolina settlements. However, the settlers were better protected than they had been in previous incidents. Local stockades and blockhouses had sprung up on private property throughout the area. Settlers around a fortification organized their own militia company for protection. Vigilantes roamed the area along the upper Savannah River to seek out any Indian they determined to look suspicious. On March 24, Creek chief Mad Turkey headed for Savannah, Georgia, to talk peace with the colonial government. As he passed through Augusta, he was killed, without provocation, by Thomas Fee. Fee fled to Ninety Six, South Carolina, where he was captured and imprisoned in the Ninety Six jail. He was rescued by a mob that cheered him for his bravery.

(It is reported that Fee was later captured and convicted in 1785, due to the efforts of then–Georgia governor Samuel Elbert. Elbert, a captain in Savannah's First Regiment of Militia when Mad Turkey was killed, was called upon to escort several Creek chiefs and warriors to Savannah to officially protest the murder before Royal governor James Wright.

(Some have named the slain chief as Head Turkey and some have indicated the murder took place on May 31, 1774; however, the governor's proclamation below clears both matters.)

Georgia governor James Wright was fearful of a full-scale Creek war and did his best to assure Mad Turkey's clansmen that he would do all in his power to apprehend Thomas Fee. He issued the following proclamation on May 28, 1774:

Georgia
BY HIS EXCELLENCY
Sir JAMES WRIGHT, Baronet,
Captain-General, Governor, and Commander in Chief, of His Majesty's Province of GEORGIA,
Chancellor, Vice-Admiral, and Ordinary of the same,
A PROCLAMATION.
Whereas I have received information that a certain Indian, named or usually called the MAD TURKEY, of the Upper Creek Nation, in amity and peace with this Government, was, on the twenty-fourth of that instant March, most cruelly and inhumanely murdered, in the town of Augusta, in this province, and that the said murder was perpetrated and

committed by one THOMAS FEE, heretofore of this province, but who has for some time past resided in the province of South-Carolina, I THEREFORE, taking into my most serious consideration the dangerous tendency such cruel, inconsiderate, and inhuman actions, may have with the Indians in general, and how much they endanger the lives of his Majesty's subjects, and the peace and happiness of these provinces, and, in order to discountenance, as far as in me lies, such illegal and detestable proceedings, and to shew the perpetrator of the murder already committed, and all others who have or may commit any offenses against the Indians contrary to law, that I will not suffer such offences to pass unnoticed, nor be committed with impunity, HAVE THOUGHT FIT, by and with the advice and consent of his Majesty's Honourable Council, to issue this my proclamation, offering, and I do hereby offer A REWARD OF ONE HUNDRED POUNDS STERLING, that is to say, fifty pounds to any person or persons who shall apprehend and deliver the body of said THOMAS FEE into the hands of the Provost Marshal of this province in Savannah, to be then paid unto him or them, and the like sum of fifty pounds sterling, to be paid him of them on the conviction of the said THOMAS FEE of the said murder: AND I do hereby, in his Majesty's name, strictly charge and command all persons whomsoever not to molest, assault, or insult any Indian or Indians whatsoever, who may happen to be down in the settlements, or elsewhere, and behaving themselves quietly and peaceably and all and every person or persons offending in this particular may depend on being prosecuted to the utmost rigour [sic] of the law: AND I do hereby charge and require all Justices, Peace Officers, and all other his Majesty's faithful and liege subjects, to pay due obedience to this proclamation, and to do whatever may lay in their power to bring, or cause to be brought to justice, the said THOMAS FEE, and every other offender or offenders against this proclamation as they will answer the contrary at their peril.

    GIVEN under my hand and the great seal of his Majesty's said province, in the Council-Chamber at Savannah, the twenty eighth day of March, One thousand seven hundred and seventy-four, and in the fourteenth year of the reign of his Majesty King GEORGE the Third.

    By his Excellency's command,
Tho^S. Moodie, Dept. Secr.}   **J.A. WRIGHT.**
                               God Save the King.

A DESCRIPTION of THOMAS FEE:—a slim made man, of about six foot high, ruddy complexion, sandy or reddish hair, and about 26 or 27 years old, and supposed to be born in North-Carolina.[12]

    In the fall of 1774, Daniel Boone prompted Richard Henderson and his partner, Nathaniel Hart (The Transylvania Company), to negotiate with the Cherokee and offer to buy or lease the Cumberland tract of present-day Kentucky and middle Tennessee. Hart traveled to the Otari (Upper Villages) to open the discussion. Indian trader Thomas Price acted as the interpreter. (There is conjecture whether or not Daniel Boone was a partner in the business or a contractor for his services as guide, explorer, and settler. Boone's primary interest was to move his family further west and to gain some capital in the process.)

    The older chiefs were interested in the proposition because they needed supplies and ammunition. The trade industry had slowed to almost nothing. It was agreed that Chief Attakullakulla would set March 1, 1775, as the time for a big treaty to be held at Sycamore Shoals (present-day Elizabethton, Tennessee).

    Attakullakulla believed that the overmountain settlers would leave the Holston, Watauga, and Nolichucky settlements for the Cumberland and that any new settlers from the east would follow, bypass the Cherokee land, and the Cherokee would finally be left alone.

    In the meantime, Raven of Chota had been in the north to meet with the Shawnee

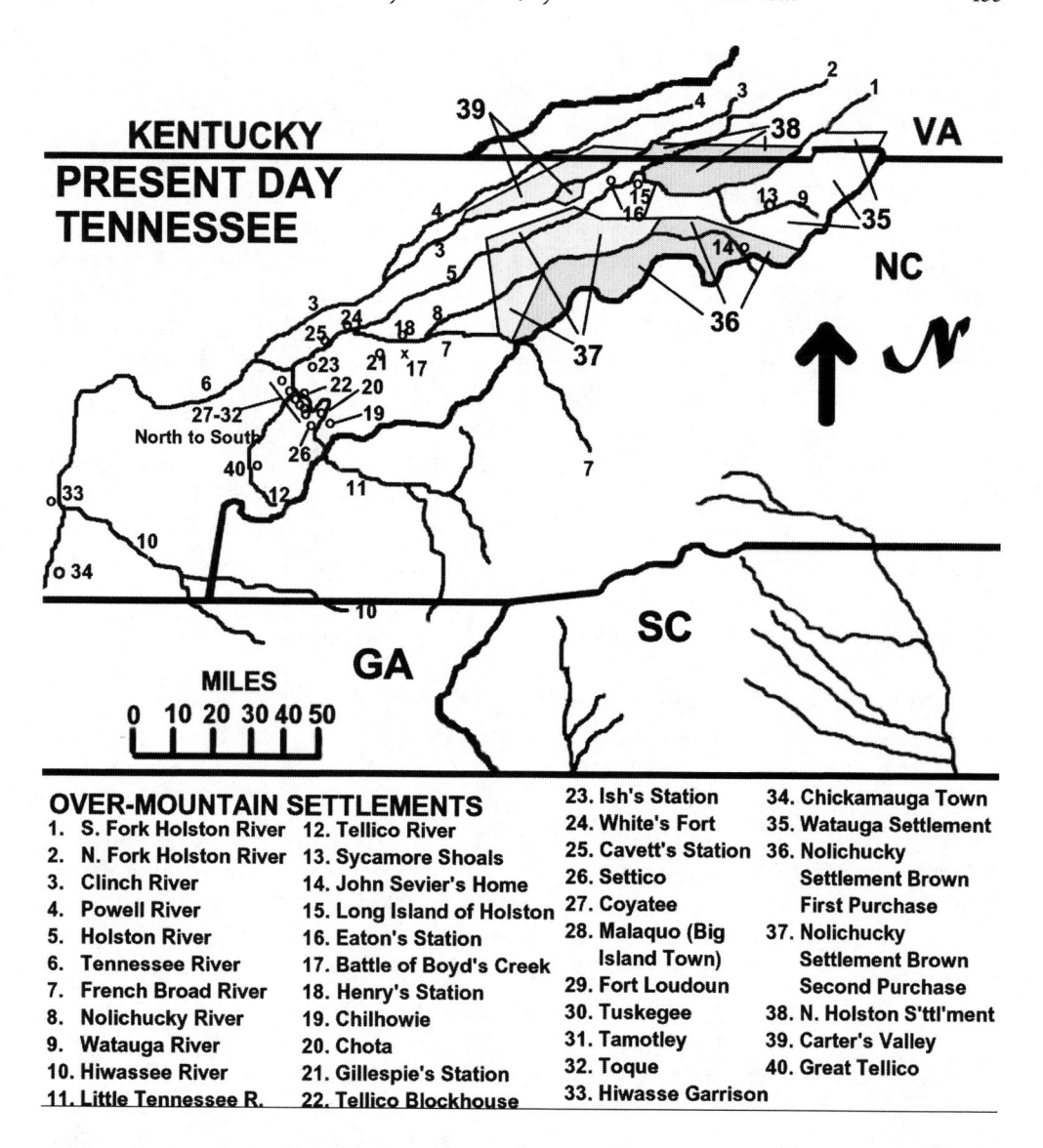

OVER-MOUNTAIN SETTLEMENTS
1. S. Fork Holston River
2. N. Fork Holston River
3. Clinch River
4. Powell River
5. Holston River
6. Tennessee River
7. French Broad River
8. Nolichucky River
9. Watauga River
10. Hiwassee River
11. Little Tennessee R.
12. Tellico River
13. Sycamore Shoals
14. John Sevier's Home
15. Long Island of Holston
16. Eaton's Station
17. Battle of Boyd's Creek
18. Henry's Station
19. Chilhowie
20. Chota
21. Gillespie's Station
22. Tellico Blockhouse
23. Ish's Station
24. White's Fort
25. Cavett's Station
26. Settico
27. Coyatee
28. Malaquo (Big Island Town)
29. Fort Loudoun
30. Tuskegee
31. Tamotley
32. Toque
33. Hiwasse Garrison
34. Chickamauga Town
35. Watauga Settlement
36. Nolichucky Settlement Brown First Purchase
37. Nolichucky Settlement Brown Second Purchase
38. N. Holston S'ttl'ment
39. Carter's Valley
40. Great Tellico

about an alliance against the British; however, he could not interest the older Cherokee chiefs in any such agreement.

On November 23, 1774, Chief Attakullakulla and some warriors left the Upper Towns with Hart and met Henderson at one of Hart's cabins at Wayah Gap (near present-day Franklin, North Carolina). The two speculators showed the chief a sample of such goods that would be available: guns, ammunition, food, clothing, and other supplies. Attakullakulla was satisfied, so he sent some of his men back to the Upper Villages with Hart to begin preparations for the treaty.

Attakullakulla and Henderson proceeded to Cross Creek (present-day Fayetteville, North Carolina) to pick up the merchandise. They left Cross Creek on January 1, 1775, with six loaded wagons. They passed through a Moravian settlement called Bethabara (near present-day Winston-Salem) whereupon some of the church leaders approached the Chief about their sending a minister to the Upper Towns to teach Christianity. Attakullakulla responded that it would be all right with him if they wanted to send a teacher to set up a school for the Cherokee children.

White traders and settlers, as well as Cherokee people, began to travel toward Sycamore Shoals early in 1775. By March 1, there were 600 whites and 1,000 Cherokee gathered to watch the proceedings. The Watauga settlers supplied the visitors with corn and meat.

The Cherokee were represented by chiefs Attakullakulla, Oconostota, Willenawah (father of chiefs Doublehead, Old Tassel, and Standing Turkey. Standing Turkey had been the principal chief prior to Attakullakulla), and Ostenaco. The Indian agent to the Cherokee, Alexander Cameron, and Virginia governor John Murray, Earl of Dunmore, lobbied heavily against such a treaty. Chief Attakullakulla, however, would not listen as he strongly believed that the treaty would empty the Cherokee Upper Village area of white settlers.

The Wataugans had some cabins set aside for storage and display of the trade goods. The Cherokee were welcome to view the merchandise during the preliminaries from March 1 to March 4, 1775, after which Henderson made his proposal. The Transylvania Company would give the Cherokee £12,000 of which £10,000 would be in trade goods. In return, the Cherokee would give the Transylvania Company the rights to 20,000,000 acres of land bounded by the Cumberland River on the south to the Kentucky and Ohio Rivers on the north.

War Chief Oconostota was captivated by the arms that were being made available, while Principal Chief Attakullakulla was willing to satisfy the speculators' demands in exchange for lasting peace. Raven of Chota, like Oconostota, was excited by the arms. (Raven was an honorary title given to a proven warrior. This Raven of Chota was Colonah, the son of Attakullakulla, who had inherited the title Savanooka from his grandfather, Savanah Tom Moytoy III. Savanah Tom's father was the Emperor, Amadohiyi or Trader Tom Moytoy II, who was the previous Raven of Chota.)

Many of the younger chiefs, five of whom included Attakullakulla's sons Dragging Canoe (Tsiyagunsini), Turtle At Home, The Badger (Ocuma), Little Owl (Wyukah), and Old Abram (Ooskiah), were violently opposed as was Doublehead (Taltsuska), Attakullakulla's nephew. Doublehead's father and Attakullakulla's brother, Chief Willenawah (Tifftoya or Great Eagle), was the primary older chief contrary to the treaty. Other young warriors who were opposed to Attakullakulla's actions were his son-in-law Black Fox, Doublehead's brothers Standing Turkey (Gunagadoga or Cunne-Shote), Hanging Maw (Uskwaliguta), Pumpkin Boy Carpenter, Red Bird (Tsisquaya or Aaron Brock), and Big Half Breed (Sequechee), and eventually, Raven of Chota.

(Chief Dragging Canoe, headman at Mialoquo [Malaquo or Big Island Town] and his cousin, Doublehead, would lead separate factions of Chickamauga Cherokee in future intense attacks on the settlers. See Chapter 8.

(Big Island Town's site was on the south bank of the Little Tennessee River's Island Creek confluence, 17 miles above the river's mouth. It was at the site of Rose Island, the largest island on the river, which spanned between 16.8 miles and 18.4 miles above its mouth. It was just south of a bend in the Little Tennessee known as Wears Bend and just north of the river's confluence with the Tellico River. The site is near the end of Wears Bend Road near the point of the isthmus that creates Wears Bend of the Little Tennessee River. It is two miles straight northwest of where U.S. Highway 411 crosses the Little Tennessee River. A portion of Big Island Town may have been on Rose Island itself. Big Island Town and Rose Island were inundated by the creation of present-day Tellico Lake.

(Doublehead, the author's 7th great-grandfather, reportedly had withdrawn from the Upper Villages as early as 1770 and settled in Shoal Town at Muscle Shoals of the Tennessee River west of present-day Chattanooga, Tennessee.)

Chief Attakullakulla stood and spoke following Henderson's presentation. Attakullakulla recalled his experiences with alliances, talked about his visit to the "Great King" in 1730, and how the alliances had been good for the Cherokee. He also spoke about the trade goods that Henderson had provided for the treaty and how much the Cherokee needed the merchandise. He again gave more credit to the whites than deserved and predicted that the treaty would provide peace for the Cherokee.

An excerpt of Attakullakulla's remarks states:

> I am an old man who has presided as chief in councils, and as president of the nation for more than half a century [actually since 1762—he would die 3 years later]; I formerly served as agent to the King of England on business of first importance to our nation; I crossed the big water, arrived at our destination, and was received with great distinction; had the honor of dining with His Majesty and the nobility; had the utmost respect paid to me by the great men of the white people, and accomplished my mission with success; that from long standing in the highest dignities of our nation, I claim the confidence and good faith of all and everyone in defending and supporting the rightful claims of my people to the Bloody Grounds [Kentucky], now in treaty to be sold to the white people.[13]

Following Attakullakulla, Ostenaco spoke for the treaty. Many of the older chiefs nodded for what the two had said.

Dragging Canoe was ready to take charge of the resistance. He eloquently attempted to dissuade the older chiefs from saddling the younger chiefs with the agreement. Dragging Canoe believed the Cherokee had bowed before the white people too often and had given up too much land for the sake of a peace that had become one-sided. Tradition had it that the Cherokee headmen were headmen so long as they listened to the will of the people. The younger chiefs believed they were being disregarded by the older chiefs.

Dragging Canoe's first oration was:

> Whole Indian Nations have melted away like snowballs in the sun before the white man's advance. They leave scarcely a name of our people except those wrongly recorded by their destroyers. Where are the Delawares? They have been reduced to a mere shadow of their former greatness. We had hoped that the white man would not be willing to travel beyond the mountains. Now that hope is gone. They have passed the mountains, and have settled upon Tsalagi [Cherokee] land. They wish to have that usurpation sanctioned by a treaty [an illegal one]. When that is gained, the same encroaching spirit will lead them upon other land of the Tsalagi. New cessions will be asked. Finally the whole country, which the Tsalagi and their fathers have so long occupied, will be demanded, and the remnant of AniYunWiya, the Real [or Principal] People, once so great and formidable, will be compelled to seek refuge in some distant wilderness [Arkansas, Missouri, and Oklahoma years later]. There they will be permitted to stay only a short while, until they again behold the advancing banners of the same greedy hosts. Not being able to point out any further retreat for the miserable Tsalagi, the extinction of the whole race will be proclaimed. Should we not therefore run all risks, and incur all consequences, rather than submit to further loss of our country? Such treaties may be all right for men who are too old to hunt or fight. As for me, I have my young warriors about me. We will hold our land. A-WANINSKI, I have spoken.[14]

Dragging Canoe then stormed out of the session.

Attakullakulla spoke once more to encourage the older chiefs to sign the agreement. Interpreter James Vann quietly spoke to Raven of Chota and War Chief Oconostota and suggested they carefully regard the matter before they sign the treaty. Oconostota's wife had gotten hold of a copy and became worried about the terms. She quietly spoke to several of the chiefs about her qualms. After a few seconds, Oconostota stood and stated that the young warriors had as much right to the ancestral hunting ground as did the older headmen. He had likely been a target for his wife's concerns. Then Attakullakulla ended the session.

On March 10, 1775, the day following the session, Henderson and his cronies prepared a feast for the chiefs that included much rum. Following the meal, he and his partners spoke and again invited the Cherokee to handle the guns. The Cherokee factions were arbitrating the trade. One group complained that the lands Henderson wanted were the Cherokee primary hunting grounds. Debate among the older nonhunters and the younger hunters and warriors continued for some time. Henderson was so sure the treaty would be signed that he sent Boone and 30 men ahead to clear a trail from the Holston settlements to Kentucky—the first regular path to be opened to the Cumberland region.

Each session contained a Henderson presentation and was followed by a private session of the council. The treaty continued to be debated. Chief Attakullakulla explained that he believed, if the Cherokee did not sell the land, the white man would just take it. If the land were to be lost anyway, the treaty would allow the Cherokee to gain something for it. Dragging Canoe and the younger warriors became more irate with Attakullakulla's demeanor. They agreed with his assumption, but avowed the Cherokee people were proud and should aggressively resist such a takeover.

Finally, Raven of Chota convinced Chief Oconostota that he should sign the treaty. It has been suggested that Raven was desirous of Oconostota's position—Red Chief (Principal War Chief) of the entire Cherokee Nation. He may have thought that the people would blame Oconostota as well as Attakullakulla for giving away the land. However, Raven also signed the agreement which belies that reasoning. (Raven would eventually join the Chickamauga Cherokee leaders [Dragging Canoe and Doublehead] in attacks against the settlers. See Chapter 8.)

The signing was set for March 17, 1775. The Treaty of Sycamore Shoals was then in force. The greed for land still not

Tsi'yu-Gunsini "Dragging Canoe" Cherokee War Chief (Artist: Mike Smith, print #48 in possession of author, used by permission of D. Ray Smith, smithdray.tripod.com/draggingcanoe-index-9.html).

satisfied, the Transylvania Company made yet another request to the council. Between the lands already owned by Virginia and the lands covered by the transaction just completed was a strip of land which still belonged to the Cherokees. Richard Henderson told the council: "I have more goods, guns, and ammunition that you have not seen. There is land between where we stand and Kaintuckee. I do not like to walk over the land of my brothers. I want to buy from you the Road to Kaintuckee."[15]

The additional land asked for by Henderson is described by historian John Preston Arthur as:

> It embraced all the land on "the waters of the Watauga, Holston, and Great Canaway [likely the Kanawha] or New river." This tract began "on the south or southwest of the Holston river six miles above Long Island in that river; thence a direct line in nearly a south course to the ridge dividing the waters of Watauga from the waters of Nonachuckeh (Nollechucky or Toe) [the Nolichucky River] and along the ridge in a southeasterly direction to the Blue Ridge or line dividing North Carolina from the Cherokee lands; thence along the Blue Ridge to the Virginia line and west along such line to the Holston river; thence down the Holston to the beginning, including all waters of the Watauga, part of the waters of Holston, and the head branches of the New river or Great Canaway, agreeable to the aforesaid boundaries."[16]

The Cherokee did not accept the additional offer right away and ended the sessions. Once they were concluded, Dragging Canoe made one last vow. He said to Richard Henderson: "We have given you this (pointing out the Cumberland area), why do you ask for more? You have bought a fair land. When you have this you have all. There is no more game left between the Watauga and the Cumberland. There is a cloud hanging over it. You will find its settlement dark and bloody."[17]

The ancestral hunting grounds were now gone. The Cumberland area was a hunting paradise that had been contentious between the Cherokee and the Shawnee as far back as any of the living older chiefs could remember. It was the last hunting ground the young Cherokee warriors had left. The many salt licks were not only desirable for the settlers, but were great draws for the abundant game. They were created by sulfur springs which overflowed in the spring and deposited salt on the surface as they dried.

Dragging Canoe became a very popular leader with the young warriors when he refused to buckle to the older chiefs. He was adamant that he would not sign the treaty and would defend the young warriors' rights to the hunting grounds. The treaty of Sycamore Shoals caused the worst split the Cherokee Nation had ever experienced with the revolt of the young warriors. It had to happen. It was the only chance the nation had to retain its identity, and Dragging Canoe would attack white settlements for the next two decades. He refused to trade with most white traders, the only exception being Tories like Richard Pearis.

It would become a noble effort on the part of Dragging Canoe, Doublehead, and the other young warriors; however, it would prove to be far too late.[18]

One of the white visitors to Sycamore Shoals was John Carter. The Cherokee owed Carter a large trade debt of between £600 and £700. He knew the Cherokee were poor, so he hoped to receive land in payment. It had become a common practice for the British traders to run up individual Cherokee debts that the Indians could not repay and then receive tracts of land as compensation. The traders became land speculators.

Carter openly offered to buy his tract of land by canceling the Cherokee debt to him.

He further agreed to furnish additional trade goods beyond what the Transylvania Company had already provided. The council of headmen met to consider his offer, and after some discussion, declined to accept it. They seemingly did not trust Carter to forgive the debt. Richard Henderson then approached the council and offered to personally destroy the Carter account books that contained the mark (the "x" signatures) of the individual Cherokees, to personally deliver the goods Carter had offered, and to supply additional trade goods in return for the tract to Carter and the strip that Henderson had requested at the end of the conference. This offer was accepted by the council, and a deed was drawn to cover it, which since that time has been known as the Path Deed.

On March 19, 1775, deeds were drawn up by the Transylvania Company. The Cherokee made a deed to John Carter and Robert Lucas, conveying various lands that extended from Cloud's Creek to Chimney Top Mountain, and embraced Carter's Valley (the land where Carter had settled and established his store), in compensation for the robbery of Parker and Carter's Store by Cherokee Indians, and in further consideration of the payment of a sum of money. (Cloud's Creek is located on the eastern slope of Clinch Mountain and three miles northeast of present-day Mooresburg, Tennessee, in Hawkins County. Carter's Valley is also located in present-day Hawkins County, Tennessee. Chimney Top Mountain is located one mile southwest of present-day Frozen Head State Natural Area in Morgan County, Tennessee.)

A deed was made assigning for fee simple to the Watauga Association, Charles Robertson, trustee, for lands on Watauga River (which had been leased in 1772—see earlier this chapter), in consideration of £2,000. Oconostota, Attakullakulla, Willenawah, and Tenase Warrior made their marks for the Cherokee. (Fee simple provides absolute title to land, free of any encumbrances, which one can sell or pass to another by inheritance. The usage is intended to show the fee is not conditional and is often used to transfer property titles.)

On March 25, 1775, two additional deeds were executed by the Cherokee to Jacob Brown for consideration of 10 shillings. Jacob Brown was a trusted trader with the Cherokee who had lost his land in Cherokee country in 1772 (see earlier this chapter). One deed provided him the tract where he had previously located his general store and repair shop, while the other conveyed an additional tract, known as Brown's Second Purchase. (Jacob Brown's home was located near present-day Jonesborough, Tennessee, on the north bank of the Nolichucky River near the mouth of Cherokee Creek.)

Such transactions were contrary not only to traditional Cherokee policy, but also totally illegal per the Proclamation of 1763. Chief Attakullakulla, who originally believed the Transylvania Purchase would take the settlers out of the Nolichucky, Watauga, and Holston settlements to Kentucky, seemed to have resigned himself that existing overmountain settlers were not going to leave. Attakullakulla is estimated to have been 80 years old at that time, and it was a hard 80 years. This likely contributed to his miscalculations even though he had been warned in no uncertain terms of the result by his son, Dragging Canoe. Shortly after the Treaty of Sycamore Shoals, and all of the land transactions that immediately followed, new settlers swarmed to the Watauga River Valley to the dismay of the Cherokee people. Daniel Boone, himself, was encouraging more settlements, not just in the Cumberland region, but on the Nolichucky and Holston Rivers as well.

In the meantime, the colonial agitation against Britain was beginning to grow. Colonial royal governors were beginning to abandon their posts to govern from the safety of British ships off coast. The British superintendent of Indian Affairs in the Southern Department, John Stuart, departed for Florida and left Alexander Cameron to see to the affairs of the Cherokee.

On July 23, 1775, Provincial congressman William Henry Drayton was sent to the backcountry of South Carolina to promote the Patriot (Whig) agenda. The British, working through John Stuart and Alexander Cameron, were trying hard to win the Cherokee over to the British side against the backcountry Whigs and were achieving a modicum of success with the young warriors. Drayton met with Cherokee headmen from the Lower Villages at Congaree Store on September 25, 1775, and stated that the Whig position was in the interest of the Cherokee. He tried to explain that the British tax on tea would raise the cost of trade goods which would require more deer skins.

> Drayton started eastward ... he stopped at Congaree Store on September 25 to meet five leaders of the Cherokee Indians, who had been waiting several days to see him. His address ... was extremely patronizing ... giving them an explanation of the conflict with Great Britain ... Drayton's contact ... did no lasting good.... He realized that ... [the Cherokee were firm in their alliance] ... with Great Britain ... and that Alexander Cameron (who boasted that the Cherokees would all die for him if necessary), was vigorously disseminating counterpropaganda.[19]

Drayton tried hard to convince the Cherokee that the British were treating the colonists harshly and that the Cherokee could expect no less. He said: "If they [the British] use us, their own flesh and blood in this unjust way, what must you expect; you who are a Red People; ... You see by their treatment of us that agreements even under the hand and seal go as nothing with them."[20]

The Cherokee were steadfast in their support of Britain. Shortly, the Cherokee would see Drayton's warning come to pass. Soon thereafter, Drayton visited with Tory (British Loyalist) Captain Richard Pearis who admitted that Indian agents John Stuart and Alexander Cameron were riling the Cherokee.

South Carolina royal governor Lord William Campbell had sent an order to Stuart at St. Augustine, Florida, that the Indian agents should enflame the Cherokee against the Patriots. He wanted the Indians to provide a second front against the Whigs in the event the British Army attacked South Carolina on the coast. Stuart received the order on September 25, 1775.

Subsequent to his visit with Pearis, Drayton wrote Alexander Cameron from Congarees on the 26th stating:

> It gives me great concern, sir, to be under a necessity of telling you, that from your connection with the King's government, and our knowledge of your incapability of betraying your trust, we look upon you as an object dangerous to our welfare; and, therefore, as an object, that we ought to endeavor to remove to a distance from your present residence ... I do, therefore sir, in the name of the Colony request, that you will forthwith remove to such a distance, from the Cherokee Nation, that will satisfy us that you cannot readily exercise the functions of your office among them, and thereby remove our apprehensions.[21]

Stuart developed a plan to implement Governor Campbell's order. He sent Moses Kirkland, a disaffected Whig turned Tory, to Boston on October 3, 1775, to present the plan to Major General Thomas Gage, the commander of the British Army in America. The British ship that transported Kirkland was seized en route by the Patriots, and Kirkland was captured. So were his dispatches. Kirkland was jailed, and his papers, that addressed inciting the Cherokee against the backcountry settlers, were printed and widely circulated.[22]

On the 16th, Indian Agent Alexander Cameron responded to Drayton from Keowee:

> I received your letter of the 26th ultimo [meaning the previous month], which I have maturely considered ... the concern you express for requesting me to remove to some distance from my present residence ... I cannot find myself at liberty to comply with it ... while I have the honor to serve in my present office, I must implicitly observe the directions and orders of my superiors, and cannot recede from my part without first obtaining their leave.[23]

He then withdrew to the safety of the Cherokee Upper Villages where he awaited further orders from John Stuart. Stuart needed to act quickly. He expected that the army would attack the southern colonies within a few months, and the Whigs in South Carolina were flexing their muscles against the Tories.

The first Siege of Ninety Six occurred in November of 1775. In that skirmish, nearly 600 Patriot militiamen under Ninety Six major Andrew Williamson, upon hearing of the approach of a large Tory militia unit, set up a defensive position at Savage's Old Fields. They quickly built a palisade that connected several of John Savage's outbuildings across the Spring Branch feed to Henley's Creek from the village of Ninety Six, South Carolina. Soon, Major Joseph Robinson and 2,000 Tory militiamen invaded the town and surrounded the fortified Whigs. After some sniping and negotiating, the affair ended on the 22nd with the Articles of Secession of Ninety Six. Some notables involved were Captain Richard Pearis of the Tories, Major James Mayson, Captain Andrew Pickens, and Captain Robert Anderson of the Whigs.

Meanwhile, on November 8, 1775, Camden Militia colonel Richard Richardson left his provincial congressional seat under orders to apprehend notorious Tory captain Patrick Cunningham. He mustered a force of 2,500 militiamen and headed for the backcountry. First, he moved on the estate of Tory captain Evan McLauren where, on December 2, 1775, he and Orangeburg Militia colonel William Thomson captured several notorious Tories including Colonel Thomas Fletchall and Captains Richard Pearis and Daniel Plummer. Spartan Militia colonel James Thomas, New Acquisition Militia colonel Thomas Neil, Colonel James Lyles of Fairfield, South Carolina, and North Carolina Militia colonel Thomas Polk were a part of the expedition.

After Colonel Richardson detached his son, Captain Richard Richardson, to escort the prisoners to Charles Town, the colonel led his expedition to Hollingsworth's Mill on the 20th. There he was joined by North Carolina Militia colonels Griffith Rutherford and Joseph Graham and Lieutenant Colonel James Martin. Then Beaufort Militia colonel Stephen Bull and Ninety Six major Andrew Williamson arrived. This brought Richardson's force to 5,000 militiamen. Soon he heard that Patrick Cunningham and his Tory allies were camped 50 miles away on the Reedy River. He detached Colonel William Thomson and 1,000 men to attack the camp. The Ninety Six Militia under Major Williamson was involved in the effort. They attacked at dawn on the 22nd, and while Cunningham was totally surprised, he escaped on horseback without being fully clothed. The Whig militia captured 130 Tories and killed six in what was called the Battle of Great Cane Brake or the Reedy River Fight. Colonel Thomas escorted the prisoners back to Hollingsworth's Mill where Colonel Richardson dispatched his adjutant, Captain Thomas Sumter, to take the prisoners to Charles Town. Before they could leave, and before the rest of the militiamen could be released from their musters, it began to snow—hard. The entire group, including Sumter and the prisoners, arrived at Congarees on January 1, 1776. The snow was two feet deep. Richardson wrote the South Carolina legislature on the 2nd: "Eight days we never set foot on the earth or had a place to lie down, till we had spaded or grabbled away the snow ... many are frostbitten, some very badly."[24]

Thus ended what became known as the Snow Campaign.[25] (Hollingsworth's Mill was located six miles due east of present-day Union, South Carolina, on Browne Creek just before it empties into the Broad River where that river makes a loop westward. The Battle of Great Cane Brake was fought along a small creek that feeds into the Reedy River near Simpsonville, South Carolina. A marker locating the spot is found west of Interstate 385 and north of State Route 418 on State Route 146, just south of its intersection with Old Hundred Road. The marker reads: "Here along the south side of the creek to Reedy River was fought, Dec. 22, 1775, the Battle of Great Cane Break [sic], between a force of South Carolinians under Colonel William Thompson and a band of Tories under Patrick Cuningham. The Tories were completely routed and Cuningham himself narrowly escaped." The marker had originally been located on State Route 12, or South Harrison Bridge Road, just southeast of State Route 542, or New Harrison Bridge Road.)

John Stuart, British superintendent of Indian Affairs in the Southern Department, was still in St. Augustine, Florida, where he had recently fled when Continental Army major general Charles Lee arrived at Charles Town. Stuart sent a letter to the Cherokee headmen that explained, from the British viewpoint, the division between the Loyalists and the Rebels. He further explained that Lee was in control of Charles Town, that Royal Governor Lord William Campbell was in exile, and that arms and ammunition shipments to the Cherokee from Charles Town had ceased. In January, 1776, 62 chiefs traveled to St. Augustine to meet with Stuart to pledge their loyalty and ask for more help from the British. Stuart told them he would send some guns and ammunition to them, but they were not to attack the Watauga settlers. Stuart did not want the Cherokee distracted when he would need them to attack the Carolinas. Before they left, he told them he would let them know when the time was right and where they should attack.

John Stuart loaded 60 pack animals with guns and ammunition. He sent his brother, Henry Stuart, to escort the chiefs to Chota. Chief Dragging Canoe met them partway and escorted them into Chota with 80 warriors. They arrived on April 24, 1776. Nine of the laden animals had been stolen by Illini Indians on a raid before Dragging Canoe joined the caravan. Dragging Canoe was not happy with the delay. He was eager to attack the overmountain settlers. He was further disturbed when he learned that, while in Florida, the chiefs had promised to attack backcountry settlements in the Carolinas instead of those at Watauga.

Henry Stuart, under instructions from his brother, iterated to the chiefs, including Dragging Canoe, that they were not yet to attack the Watauga settlers. Some have recorded that the British agents magnanimously wanted the Cherokee to remain neutral in the coming war. However, typically the British welcomed any allies they could muster. They would, in fact, bring in Hessian Jägers (elite German troops) before the American Revolution would end.

It is more likely that the British did not want distractions in the Upper Village region, when they would need all of their resources in the backcountry of the Carolinas. If the British were favorable to a neutral Cherokee Nation, they would probably not have supplied the arms and ammunition from Florida. In fact, Stuart was still diligently working to plan Cherokee attacks against the backcountry settlements. No, Cherokee neutrality was not on the minds of the British. However, using the Cherokee for the benefit of the British was. They especially did not want the Cherokee to waste the ammunition they had just provided before the backcountry attacks were to begin. Additionally, the British recognized that there were useful Tories in the Watauga settlement, and they wanted to protect them.

At Big Island Town, Dragging Canoe made preparations with his warriors to attack the encroaching settlers. Beloved Woman Nancy Ward, Principal Chief Attakullakulla, and War Chief Oconostota implored Dragging Canoe to wait until they, Henry Stuart, and Alexander Cameron had the opportunity to convince the settlers to leave peacefully. Dragging Canoe was not a big fan of the British, but they were enemies of his enemy, so he reluctantly agreed. This was a different strategy for Attakullakulla who had signed the original agreements at Sycamore Shoals that turned the settled land over to the encroachers. It is likely that he was losing his influence in the council sessions with the other headmen. The headmen met in council with Henry Stuart and Alexander Cameron to officially request them to evict the settlers.

On May 7, 1776, Henry Stuart and Alexander Cameron sent a letter to the leaders of the Watauga and Nolichucky River settlements that demanded the settlements be vacated within 20 days. They suggested other locations to inhabit such as western Florida. However, the settlers, who had expended eight years of effort improving their land, were not inclined to just pack up and leave—especially after Chief Attakullakulla had sold or leased the land to them in conjunction with the Treaty of Sycamore Shoals. A few settlers feared the Cherokee warriors enough to flee to Virginia; however, most hardened woodsmen determined to fight for their property.

This was neither a new issue nor one easy to solve. Dragging Canoe had never been inclined to cede the land to the whites, and he was more resolved now than he had ever been to regain the ancestral Cherokee hunting grounds.

Meanwhile, a 14-man delegation of northern Indians composed of Shawnee, Mohawk, Ottawa, and Delaware headmen led by Shawnee principal chief Cornstalk, arrived in Chota. They asked to speak in the Chota Council House and gave Attakullakulla 10 days to gather everyone. When the day arrived, 700 Cherokee headmen and several Tory leaders had assembled.

The visitors were adorned with traditional black war paint, and they announced that the British would soon be attacking from the coast. They suggested that the Cherokee join them and other tribes as they formed a new confederation of eastern Indian nations to help the British defeat the rebellious settlers. They indicated this would help stem the tide of white encroachment. Eager young Cherokee warriors began to apply their own war paint as they anticipated the joint effort.

Chiefs Attakullakulla and Oconostota, as well as other older headmen, listened to the presentation in silence. The Mohawk leader spoke first and offered his war belt. He was followed by the Ottawa chief who did the same. Each of their belts was accepted by Chief Dragging Canoe after they had been refused by Attakullakulla and Oconostota. Then the Delaware headman spoke and offered his war belt, which was accepted by Raven of Chota.

Interestingly, that represented a change of position because Raven was one who had signed the Treaty of Sycamore Shoals. The last to make a presentation was Chief Cornstalk. He said:

> In a few years, the Shawnee, from being a great Nation have been reduced to a handful. They once possessed land almost to the seashore, but now have hardly enough ground to stand on.
> The lands where the Shawnee have but lately hunted are covered with forts and armed men. When a fort appears, you may depend upon it there will soon be towns and settlements of white men. It is plain that the white people intend to wholly destroy the Indians. It is better for the red men to die like warriors than to diminish away by inches. The cause of the red men is just, and I hope that the Great Spirit who governs everything will favor us.
> Now is the time to begin; there is no time to be lost.[26]

He added that it was an appropriate time for war while the whites fought with each other. He also suggested that the Cherokee concentrate on the settlements near the Upper Towns and let the British take care of the coastal settlements. Cornstalk then presented a magnificent purple war belt that was nine feet long by six inches wide. He theatrically poured red paint over the belt to demonstrate his eagerness for war. He offered his war belt to Henry Stuart, who replied that he had no authority to speak for war. Dragging Canoe then accepted the belt. Some have suggested that Chief Doublehead and Young Tassel (John Watts, Jr.) had accepted two of the belts attributed to Dragging Canoe. Others have indicated that Bloody Fellow had accepted one of them. It is likely that each belt was accepted by a different headman to give the ceremony more significance; however, it is also probable that each belt had been handled by more than one of those headmen to further incite fervor for war. Each headman who handled the belts struck the war pole in the Council House with his tomahawk.

Chief Cornstalk's belt was handed to Osioota of Chilhowie who whooped and raised it for all to see. He then struck the war pole with his tomahawk, began his war chant and his war dance. He waved the belt as he circled the fire and enticed other young warriors to follow.

Before the session ended, the council received a threatening letter from Virginia. Isaac Thomas, a 41-year-old scout who had been living in the settlements, delivered the letter and interpreted it to those in the Council House. The letter suggested the Cherokee should not fight for the British as did the Tories and other Indians. It went on to warn that, if the Cherokee were to fight for Britain they would be destroyed, and that 6,000 Virginia militiamen already prepared to fight the redcoats, would instead attack the Upper Villages.

Apparently, John Carter of the Watauga settlement had received Stuart's letter and responded with one of his own wherein he stated the settlers were stunned by the demand and needed more time for deliberation. He reminded Stuart that many Loyalists resided in the settlements. Henry Stuart seems to have allotted an additional 20 days because some report that the Wataugans had 40 days to act. The Wataugans took advantage of the additional time and wrote to Virginia governor Edmund Pendleton asking for military support. The settlers constructed many small palisaded forts on private land for defense. (Pendleton was actually president of the Committee for Public Safety who acted as governor between the last royal governor, John Murray, 4th Earl Dunmore, and the first Whig governor, Patrick Henry.)

It was charged that the Wataugans forged new letters over Cameron's and Stuart's signatures. The new letter supposedly asked Watauga Loyalists to enter the war as Cherokee allies against the settlements, and also claimed that a British army was headed for the overmountain settlements with 1,500 Creek, Chickasaw, and Choctaw warriors to assist the Cherokee.

Dragging Canoe was furious when he learned that Virginia was threatening to attack the Cherokee Upper Villages. He immediately gathered a handful of his warriors and left the Council House. He ordered that British traders Isaac Thomas, William Fawling, and Jarrett Williams be detained at Chota and their trade goods be seized.

Dragging Canoe was ready to launch a major attack against the overmountain settlements. He ran into Henry Stuart who, representing the British, was more interested in the backcountry of the Carolinas and Georgia and not in helping the Cherokee with their objective. Henry Stuart explained that there were many in the overmountain settlements who were loyal to Britain. Dragging Canoe sneered and said: "White men have almost surrounded us, leaving now only a little spot of ground to stand upon. It seems the Unakas [white people] want to destroy us as a nation."[27]

Stuart responded: "I understand you, brother. But was it not the Cherokees themselves who sold land to the Unakas?"[28]

Stuart ignored that the old chiefs no longer spoke for the Cherokee Nation. The younger chiefs had garnered much support and were going to carry the fight without agreement from the older chiefs. Dragging Canoe firmly stated:

> I had nothing to do with making that bargin [sic]. That was the work of old men without teethe [sic], too old to hunt or fight. I and my warriors are young, and we will have our ground. It would have been better to have attacked the Wataugans at once, without writing those letters. The letters served only to put them on guard, and caused them to prepare to come against the Cherokee. By this time they will have all their people removed. YOU TOLD U.S. [sic] TO ASSIST THE KING. Now when there is a white army planning to come against our towns, we want to keep them back.[29]

Dragging Canoe immediately led his warriors, who had been listening attentively to the exchange, to the Wilderness Road that ran from Fort Chiswell, Virginia, to the Cumberland Gap, and continued into present-day Kentucky. (The Wilderness Road generally followed westward from near present-day Kingsport, Tennessee, through Powell's Valley, Virginia, to the Cumberland Gap near present-day Middleboro, Kentucky, and northward along present-day U.S. Interstate 75, ending at Boonesborough, Kentucky). They returned before the northern delegation left Chota, and Dragging Canoe presented the visiting headmen with four freshly-removed white scalps that indicated their willingness to fight. Because of his agitation, Dragging Canoe assumed the responsibility normally asserted by the Cherokee principal war chief. He accepted the first war belt from the delegation, struck the war pole, killed whites and removed their scalps. He seemed to be the first Cherokee chief to understand that there was no reciprocity on the part of the British in their alliances with the Cherokee, and the Cherokee were on their own against the Virginia encroachers.[30]

The overmountain settlers built more small stockades. Two companies of Whig militia visited 70 Loyalist families and demanded they swear allegiance to the Patriot cause; otherwise, they had two alternatives—leave the area or be executed. Henry Stuart sent British

Chickasaw Indian agent James Colbert to John Stuart in Florida to obtain 100 packhorses laden with ammunition for the Cherokee.

While the Cherokee prepared for war, a parallel event was occurring: William Bartram was planning a visit to the area. (Bartram was introduced earlier in this chapter when he attended the Treaty of Augusta.) Bartram was 37 years old when he made this amazing journey and gave a marvelous description of Cherokee villages and inhabitants that included an encounter with a famous Cherokee chief.

Bartram left Charles Town for Cherokee country on April 22, 1776, by traveling the South Carolina side of the Savannah River. On the 25th, he crossed to the Georgia side at Three Sisters Ferry (located one mile south of where present-day South Carolina State Highway 119 crosses the river, seven miles south of present-day Robertville, South Carolina) where he spent the night. He remarked in his journal: "I found these people, contrary to what a traveler might think ... from their ... remote situation ... to be civil and courteous: and though educated as it were in the woods."[31]

A few days later he recrossed the Savannah River to South Carolina 13 miles south of Augusta, Georgia, at Sand Bar Ferry. Bartram stayed at Silver Bluff Plantation which was owned by George Galphin of whom Bartram wrote: "The property and seat of G. Golphin, Esquire, a gentleman of very distinguished talents and great liberality, who possessed the most extensive trade, connections, and influence, amongst the South and South-West Indian tribes ... of whom I fortunately obtained letters of recommendation and credit to the principal traders residing in the Indian towns."[32]

(The property was Galphin's Fort, which would later be captured by Henry "Lighthorse Harry" Lee, who was working with Brigadier General Andrew Pickens during the Siege of Augusta, May 21, 1781. George Galphin was a Tory officer. The property had also been the site of Old Fort Moore.[33])

While he was at Augusta, William Bartram secured credentials from businessmen to present to traders once he arrived in Cherokee country. Bartram wrote that he next set out for "Fort James Dartmouth," meaning Fort James near Dartmouth. (He later properly referred to it as Fort James. Dartmouth was named such when it was developed because it sat at the confluence of the River Dart and the Savannah River. The River Dart became the [Georgia] Broad River by November 1773.)[34]

Apparently, Fort James and Dartmouth were north of the Broad River because Bartram wrote: "Toward evening I crossed the Broad River at a good ford, just above its confluence with the Savanna [sic], and arrived at Fort James."[35]

Bartram described Fort James as:

> a four square stockade, with salient bastions at each angle [corner], mounted with a blockhouse, where are some swivel guns, one story higher than the curtains, which are pierced with loop-holes, breast high, and defended by small arms. The fortification encloses about an acre of ground [about 200 foot square] ... the fort stands on an eminence in the forks between the Savanna [sic] and Broad Rivers, about one mile above Fort Charlotte [Fort Charlotte, 6.6 miles southwest of Mt. Carmel, South Carolina] ... on the Carolina side....
> The point or peninsula between the two rivers, for a distance of two miles back from the fort, is laid out for a town, by the name of Dartmouth.[36]

(Dartmouth and Fort James were, therefore, on the site of present-day Bobby Brown State Park peninsula, downriver of the R. B. Russell Dam. Dartmouth is also the site of the later community of Petersburg, Georgia. Sometime after Dartmouth disappeared, Petersburg sprang up around a tobacco warehouse, and that site is under the waters of Strom Thurmond Reservoir in the vicinity of Bobby Brown State Park. The foundations of Petersburg may be seen during times of low water.)

It was during his stay at Fort James that he encountered his first real Indian sign.

> I made a little excursion up the Savanna [sic] River, four or five miles above the fort, with the surgeon of the garrison, who was so polite as to attend me to show me some remarkable Indian monuments.... These wonderful labours of the ancients stand in a level plain, very near the bank of the river, now twenty or thirty yards from it. They consist of conical mounts of earth and four square terraces, &c. The great mount is in the form of a cone, about forty or fifty feet high, and the circumference of its base two or three hundred yards [200 to 300 feet diameter].[37]

(This site is likely under the waters of Russell Lake as it was situated a little above R. B. Russell Dam. In support of this, Bartram continued: "It is altogether unknown to us, what could have induced the Indians ... the ground for a great space around being subject to inundations, at least once a year.")[38]

On May 10, 1776, Bartram met a man heavily involved with the Cherokee:

> Sat [sic] off again, proceeding for Keowe [Keowee]; rode six or eight miles up the river above the fort; crossed over into Carolina ... travelled thirty-five miles, and arrived in the evening at Mr. [Alexander] Cameron's, deputy-commisary for Indian affairs for the Cherokee nation to whom I was recommended by letters from the honourable John Stewart, superintendent, residing at Charleston ... I was prevailed upon by Mr. Cameron to stay at his house a few days, until the rains ceased and the rivers could be more easily forded.[39]

Bartram met with Stuart when the Indian agent secretly stopped over in Charles Town on his way to the Upper Villages. Stuart initially was going to help his brother Henry and Alexander Cameron to supervise the Cherokee's war effort against the backcountry; however, he knew the British army would be attacking Charles Town soon, and he had to first make more detailed preparations. John Stuart had sent messages to various chiefs to advise them he was in Charles Town if they wanted to visit; however, they had to come singly and not en masse so as not to expose him to danger.

On May 15, Bartram continued his trip:

> The weather now settled and fair, I prepared to proceed for fort Prince George Keowe [Fort Prince George at Keowee], having obtained of the agreeable and liberal Mr. Cameron, ample testimonials and letters of recommendation to the traders in the nation: this gentleman also very obligingly sent a young Negro slave to assist and pilot me as far as Sinica [Seneca] ... I left Lough-abber [Lochaber], the seat of Mr. Cameron ... crossed several rivers ... all branches of the Savanna, now called Keowe [the Keowee River], above its confluence with the Tugilo [the Tugaloo River].[40]

This is the same Lochaber that hosted the Treaty of Lochaber (see Chapter 5). Bartram gave us a description of Seneca: "The Cherokee town of Sinica is a very respectable settlement, situated on the East Bank of the Keowe river, though the greatest number of Indian habitations are on the opposite shore, where likewise stands the council-house ... the chief's house, with those of the traders ... are seated on the ascent of the heights on the opposite shore ... as it overlooks the whole settlement."[41]

He further described Seneca as a new settlement that had been rebuilt since the 1759-to–1761 war. He then traveled 16 miles to Keowee: "Keowe [sic] is a most charming situation, and the adjacent heights are naturally so formed and disposed ... to be rendered almost impregnable."[42]

Bartram found a moment of solitude to opine about the troubles between the Cherokee and the Virginians and his own situation: "Heretofore somewhat dejected and unharmonized: all alone in a wild Indian country ... a vast distance from any settlements of white people. It is true, here were some of my own colour, yet they were strangers; and though friendly and hospitable, their manners and customs of living so different ... some hundred miles yet to travel; the savage vindictive inhabitants lately ill-treated by the frontier Virginians ... and the injury not yet wiped away by formal treaty."[43]

Bartram identified Mr. D. Homes as the principal trader at Keowee, and said: "The old fort Prince George now bears no marks of a fortress, but serves for a trading house."[44]

Bartram proceeded alone toward the Upper Villages, crossed the Cherokee Mountains and described:

> I began to ascend the Occonne [Oconee] Mountain. On the foot of the hills are the ruins of the ancient Occonne town ... the Cherokee mountains ... separate the waters of Savanna river from those of the Tanase [present-day Little Tennessee River] or greater main branch of the Cherokee [present-day Tennessee] river. This running rapidly a North-West course through the mountains, is joined from the North-East by the Holstein [Holston River].... On these towering hills appeared the ruins of the ancient famous town of Sticoe [Stecoah]. Here was a vast Indian mount or tumulus and great terrace, on which stood the council-house ... here were also old Peach and Plum orchards.[45]

William Bartram continued:

> After riding about four miles [from Fort Prince George] mostly through field and plantations, the soil incredibly fertile, arrived at the town of Echoe, consisting of many good houses, well inhabited. I passed through, and continued three miles farther to Nucasse [Niquasee or Nikwasi], and three miles more brought me to Whatoga [Watauga]. Riding through this large town, the road carried me winding about through their little plantations of Corn, Beans, &c. up to the council-house, which was a very large dome or rotunda, situated on the top of an ancient artificial mount and here my road terminated. All before me on every side, appeared little plantations of young Corn, Beans, &c. divided from each other by narrow strips or borders of grass, which marked the bounds of each one's property, their habitation standing in the midst ... chief of Whatoga [Watauga] ... esteemed by the whites for his pacific and equitable disposition ... exemplary virtues, just, moderate, magnanimous and intrepid ... tall and perfectly formed; his countenance cheerful and lofty ... brow ferocious, and the eye active, piercing or fiery, as an eagle. He appeared to be about sixty years of age, yet upright and muscular, and his limbs active as a youth.[46]

He spent some time at Cowee, which he described in detail, and he stayed with chief trader Patrick Galahan (sometimes spelled Callahan or Callihorn) whom he termed, contrary to typical traders, as

> esteemed and beloved by the Indians for his humanity, probity, and equitable dealings ... it is a fact, I am afraid too true, that the white traders in their commerce with the Indians, give great and frequent occasion of complaint of their dishonesty and violence.... The town of Cowe [sic] consists of about one hundred dwellings, near the banks of the Tanase [Little Tennessee River], on both sides of the river. The Cherokees construct their habitations on a different plan from the Creeks; that is, but one oblong four square building, of

one story high; the materials consisting of logs or trunks of trees, stripped of their bark, notched at their ends, fixed one upon another, and afterwards plastered well, both inside and out, with clay well tempered with dry grass, and the whole covered or roofed with the bark of the chestnut tree or long broad shingles. The council or town-house is a large rotunda, capable of accommodating several hundred people; it stands on the top of an ancient artificial mount of earth, of about twenty feet perpendicular, and the rotunda on the top of it being about thirty feet more, gives the whole fabric an elevation of about sixty feet from the common surface of the ground. But it may be proper to observe, that this mount, on which the rotunda stands, is of much ancienter date than the buildings, and perhaps was raised for another purpose.[47]

After spending two days at Cowee, he was disturbed that a guide, whom he had anticipated meeting, did not show up; so, he decided to travel to the Upper Villages alone. He was warned by the traders at Cowee that the Upper Cherokee were ill-humored because of the treatment they had received from the frontier Virginians, and that most of the traders of the Upper Towns had left. Patrick Galahan accompanied him, but only about 15 miles. Galahan departed for Cowee after they passed through Joree Town. Bartram then traveled toward the Upper Villages alone.

After he descended Joree Mountain, he encountered a young Cherokee man. Each man was quite startled to see the other, but the Indian was first to regain his composure. He approached Bartram, shook hands, and inquired about his travel. Bartram tried to explain where he was from and to describe his destination. They had some difficulty communicating because the Cherokee spoke the Upper Cherokee dialect. Bartram was hardly accustomed to even the Lower Cherokee dialect spoken where he had just visited. However, Bartram did manage to obtain the directions he required.

William Bartram then had an amazing encounter that he likely never forgot. He described:

Soon after crossing this large branch of the Tanase [Little Tennessee River], I observed, descending the heights at some distance, a company of Indians, all well mounted on horseback; they came rapidly forward: on their nearer approach, I observed the chief at the head of the caravan, and apprehending him to be the Little Carpenter, emperor or grand chief of the Cherokees, as they came up I turned off from the path to make way, in token of respect, which compliment was accepted, and gratefully and magnanimously returned; for his highness with a gracious and cheerful smile came up to me, and clapping his hand on his breast, offered it to me, saying, I am Ata-cul-culla [or Attakullakulla, Ada-Gal-Kala]; and heartily shook hands with me, and asked me if I knew it. I answered, that the Good Spirit who goes before me spoke to me, and said, that is the great Ata-cul-culla; and added, that I was of the tribe of white men, of Pennsylvania, who esteem themselves brothers and friends to the red men, but particularly so to the Cherokees.... To which the great chief was pleased to answer very respectfully, that I was welcome in their country as a friend and brother; and then shaking hands heartily bid me farewell, and his retinue confirmed it by an united voice of assent.[48]

During this encounter, Attakullakulla inquired of Charles Town and the health of John Stuart, who had been ill. Bartram replied that he had seen Stuart at Charles Town on the 21st of April. Bartram had a positive and welcoming encounter with Attakullakulla; however, he decided that, if Attakullakulla was going to be away, and considering the problems the Upper Cherokee had with the local Virginians, he should visit the Upper Villages another day. William Bartram reversed his line of travel and eventually made his way back to Charles Town. He did explore the Lower and Middle Cherokee Villages a few more days.[49]

Chief Attakullakulla continued his own trek to Charles Town and met with Stuart. The chief tried to regain his influence with the British; however, the relationship was strained. The Cherokee were in war mode (which was not sanctioned by Attakullakulla). Aware of the coming British assault on Charles Town, the British Indian agents desired to focus the Cherokee war chiefs' attention against the backcountry settlements rather than allow them to continue their vendetta against the encroaching Virginians. That meant dealing with new War Chief Dragging Canoe, Chief Doublehead, and Raven of Chota.

On May 2, 1776, British major general Sir Henry Clinton (Commander of the British Army in the south) and his second-in-command, Lieutenant General Charles Lord Cornwallis, landed at Cape Fear, North Carolina (20 miles south of present-day Wilmington, North Carolina), with 3,000 troops. They had been brought on a fleet commanded by Commodore Peter Parker. Royal Governors Lord William Campbell of South Carolina and Josiah Martin in North Carolina persuaded Clinton to attack the south. (Each of these governors had to rule in absentia due to the rebellion.)

The plan was for the North Carolina Loyalist Scots Militia, under the command of British brigadier general Donald MacDonald, to meet Generals Clinton and Cornwallis at their camp. Governor Martin and General MacDonald had expected the meeting to occur as early as February, so they began to muster their force at Cross Creek, North Carolina, on February 15, 1776. (Cross Creek was at present-day Fayetteville, North Carolina.) They began their march to the southeast to prepare a landing spot for the British Army; however, the Patriots had learned of their plans.

The First North Carolina regiment of the Continental Army was commanded by Colonel James Moore. Moore immediately marched his troops to Rockfish Creek (just south of present-day Fayetteville) while militia colonel Richard Caswell's North Carolina militia marched from New Bern, North Carolina, to Corbett's Ferry on the Black River (near present-day Ivanhoe, North Carolina) to block MacDonald.

Moore sent 100 North Carolina militiamen under Colonel Alexander Lillington and 150 Continental Army troops under Colonel John Ashe to Widow Moore's Bridge (present-day Moore's Creek National Battlefield) to protect Caswell's rear.

MacDonald found the blockades of Moore and Caswell, and circumvented them both. Caswell then withdrew from Corbett's Ferry and joined Lillington at Widow Moore's Bridge. The Patriot force then numbered 1,050 men. Caswell set up entrenched defenses on the Loyalists' approach (west) side of the bridge and had just completed the task when MacDonald arrived. MacDonald's forces had dwindled to 800 men through desertions.

When the Loyalist general arrived on the 26th, he sent a flagged messenger to demand the surrender of the American force. The true reason for this maneuver was to ascertain the American defensive strategy. When the messenger returned, he described the entrenchments to the general, who held a council of war with his officers that night. They decided to attack at dawn. MacDonald, ill and worn out from the march, assigned the battle command to Lieutenant Colonel Donald MacLeod.

During the night, Colonel Caswell decided that his position, the troops with their backs to the creek and a narrow bridge, might be ineffective. He repositioned his forces on the east side of the bridge, ordered the troops to remove several planks from the bridge surface, and then to grease the exposed plank supports. They finally built a defensive earthen berm at the east end of the bridge and mounted two small cannons off-center to the bridge. Those guns were likely three-pounders (grasshoppers) loaded with canister shot.[50]

In a foggy pre-dawn, MacLeod's Scots drew near the bridge. The Americans hailed the Scots, and British captain Alexander McLean responded that he was a friend of the king. Then McLean added a similar challenge—in Gaelic. No Americans responded, so McLean ordered his men to fire. That led to an exchange of sniping. Colonel MacLeod and Captain John Campbell followed with a company of soldiers who waved sabers and crossed the then-treacherous bridge surface.

The Patriot force opened up with the grasshoppers which had the effect of huge shotguns. A volley of rifle fire followed; MacLeod and Campbell were hit. Reportedly, MacLeod had been struck by 20 rifle balls. The attackers withdrew across the bridge, and the remaining Loyalists scattered. Caswell ordered a charge, and Patriot soldiers forded the creek on both sides of the bridge. Others replaced the planking, so the brunt of the American force could quickly give chase. The Patriots suffered one each killed and wounded while the Loyalists suffered a total of 50 killed and wounded. Over the next few days the Americans captured 850 Tories, some of whom were not in battle at the bridge.

Generals Clinton and Cornwallis, when they arrived at Cape Fear, North Carolina, were disturbed not to find the promised North Carolina Tory army. They decided they would not waste time with an attack into North Carolina, so they invited the South Carolina governor, Lord William Campbell, to meet with them aboard the *Bristol* while it was anchored. Campbell convinced the generals that the Georgia and South Carolina Tories were capable of assisting the British Army to take over the southern colonies. They decided to begin with Charles Town. Major General Clinton believed South Carolina could not successfully defend two fronts, so he sent a message to Alexander Cameron ordering the Indian agent to incite the Cherokee to attack the backcountry, beginning on July 1, 1776, to coincide with a British invasion of the coast.

The British fleet anchored off of Sullivan's Island on the 10th of June. Their first move was to offer a pardon for any Whigs who would lay down their arms and not defend Charles Town. Then Clinton made a military blunder. He had no intelligence that the defensive works in Charles Town were not completely constructed. He directed his attack at Sullivan's Island which was heavily defended. On the 28th, Clinton ordered Commodore Peter Parker to cannonade the island. The weather was blustery and not conducive to a successful attack. The fort on the island was built low, and its walls were earth-filled, double-thick palmetto wood which is soft and does not splinter on impact. The barrage lasted for 12 hours.

South Carolina militia colonel William Moultrie and Lieutenant Colonel Francis Marion returned fire with the fort's armament and struck the *Bristol*. Governor Campbell was killed; Commodore Parker suffered injuries, including a concussion, and General Cornwallis received lacerations. When Parker refused to accede to Clinton's demand that they put Charles Town under siege, the fleet withdrew.

An anonymous British historian recorded in 1779: "The ships ... were torn almost to pieces, and the slaughter was dreadful ... never did our marine in an engagement of the same nature with any foreign enemy suffer so rude an encounter."[51]

A British soldier wrote to his brother from New York after the fleet withdrawal:

CAMP, LONG ISLAND, 13th July, 1776.
DEAR BROTHER,
   With great difficulty I have procured this small piece of paper, to inform you of my being very well, notwithstanding the miserable situation we are in. We have been encamped on this island for this month past, and have lived upon nothing but salt pork and peas.... By this sloop-of-war you will have an account of the actions which happened on the 28th June, between the ships and the fort on Sullivan's Island. The cannonade continued for about nine hours, and was, perhaps, one of the briskest known in the annals of war. We had two 50 gun ships, five frigates from 24 to 30 guns playing upon the fort ... without success, for they did the battery no manner of damage; they killed about fifteen, and wounded between forty and fifty. Our ships are in the most miserable, mangled situation you can possible imagine.... Our killed and wounded amounts to betwixt 200 and 300. Numbers die daily of their wounds. The Commodore [Parker] is wounded in two different places; his captain lost his arm and right leg, and was wounded in different parts of his body. He lived but two days after the action. Captain Scott of the Experiment [ship], died of his wounds, and a number of officers. We are now [He is speaking of the time immediately after the battle] expecting to embark for New York, to join General Howe [Sir William Howe] with the grand army.[52]

The British had withdrawn prior to July 1, 1776, the date that the Cherokee were to open a second front on the west. However, the British were repulsed so rapidly that the backcountry militias had not been mustered to join the effort on the coast. That left the Cherokee holding the bag with no second front on the east.

The Cherokee complied with the directions of Alexander Cameron. They ignored their nemeses, the overmountain settlers, and concentrated on the backcountry settlements of the coastal colonies, especially South Carolina. The attacks were horrific.

The Cherokee fought well and had a time-proven battle tactic:
- They preferred to use superior numbers to surprise a small encampment or household, or to draw a small undermanned detachment into an ambush. This would result in hand-to-hand combat with tomahawks and knives, and the enemy would be defeated in minutes.
- Their next favored option was to surround, or draw into ambush, a larger enemy group. They pinned the enemy down with rifle fire from an elevated position until they obtained a greater advantage through attrition (i.e., the enemy suffered illness, starvation, thirst, deaths in the ranks, or depleted ammunition). While courageous and willing to risk the loss of braves, they were not willing to risk entire bands of warriors and did not initiate hand-to-hand combat until they were assured of victory.
- They were loath to encounter a large body of enemy on equal footing, and they would withdraw without incident if they could not secure a definite advantage, (i.e., an elevated position with plenty of cover, a proper siege situation). That was a lesson that several Continental Army Southern Department commanders had to learn the hard way. Several times the entire Southern Department was nearly wiped out during the American Revolution because the commanders risked the army in untenable situations.

The Cherokee did become distressed when mounted enemies, even if outnumbered, charged the war party (especially while brandishing sabers). The warriors could not perform rapid reload and fire maneuvers with their single-shot rifles with any accuracy or efficiency.

They could not defend such an attack with tomahawks and knives, so they would withdraw posthaste.

Ninety Six South Carolina militia major Andrew Williamson had been not only a land speculator, but also an Indian trader with the Cherokee. He held the illusion that he was most persuasive when dealing with the Cherokee. The Cherokee decided to take advantage of his misconception. On June 27, 1776, while at his White Hall Estate, he wrote Chief Justice William Henry Drayton:

> Dear Sir:
> The two Cherokee Indians returned to the nation on Wednesday week, seemingly well satisfied with their journey. I gave them a strong talk, the substance as follows: That I had, agreeable to the desire of the warrior of Sugar Town, accompanied them across the frontier settlements, and told them before I set out, that if they saw, and would show me any bad white warriors, who carried lies and bad talk amongst them from the settlements, that I would take them into custody, and punish; and in return demanded liberty to send some of our people into the nation to secure York, and other bad white people, who had carried lies and bad talk amongst them, and endeavored, by every method they could devise, to make them quarrel with us. If they complied with this proposal, I should then know they wanted to live in peace with us; but, if they denied us that liberty, I should believe they did not care to continue in friendship with us longer ... I desired them to remember—talk well, and tell it to the warriors, and return an answer soon, which I received yesterday by one Price, a half breed ... and returned an answer as follows: Thanked me for the good talk ... that the warriors of the lower towns would not interfere between the white people in their quarrel, and in future would not prevent me sending men into the nation, to take into custody such white people as went into the nation with bad talk and lies....
> I am, dear sir,
> Your most humble servant,
> A.WM.SON.[53]

It is uncanny that a man with Williamson's experience would lack an awareness of the Cherokee intellect and ability to run a ruse. They were simply setting up an elaborate ambush, a normal tactic. Francis Salvador, a backcountry settler and member of the South Carolina Provincial Congress, volunteered and was appointed (likely with a staff-position rank of captain) as aide-de-camp to Williamson. Salvador reported to Drayton by letter on July 19, 1776:

> Dear Sir:
> P.S ... Capt. McCall, with 20 men, was sent by Major Williamson to the Cherokees at Seneca, to make prisoners of some white men, by the encouragement of some Indians, who had been at the Major's. When the detachment got near, the Indians came out to meet them, spoke friendly to them, and invited the captain, lieutenant, and another man, to sup with them ... and, in a few hours after, in the night, the Indians returned, and suddenly attacked the detachment, which fled as fast as possible. They are all returned but the captain and six men.[54]

Captain James McCall remained a prisoner for several days before he successfully escaped. During that time, he was often taken to a place of torture to witness some of these events. One such presentation was the torture of a 12-year-old boy who was suspended, naked, upside down between two posts such that his head was about three feet off the ground. The braves then prepared splinters about 18 inches long that were pointed on one end and frayed on the other. They lit the frayed end and threw the splinters like lances at the boy, and the warriors whooped whenever the pointed end of a splinter stuck into his torso. This activity continued for about two hours until the child succumbed to the agony. The Cherokee thought they had McCall's attention, so Alexander Cameron sent an Indian woman to arrange a meeting. McCall refused. He then underwent periodic torture at the hands of the braves until he effected his escape.

These methods of torture horrified and frightened the settlers (even though these same settlers used some severely grotesque means of punishment of their own—hot tar with feathers, for example). It was recently explained regarding the Indians' practices:

> Their treatment of captives ... had more in common with the Pre-Columbian rituals of the Aztec and Maya. Excruciating tortures were inflicted to test the captive's soul ... "burning was a common element in torture. The victim was frequently made to walk barefoot over fires, as well as being slowly roasted in other ways.... Hot irons or splinters would be thrust through his limbs.... The whole village—men, women, and children—would usually participate."[55]

(The original practice of scalping was not rendered to obtain trophies. It amounted to a spiritual practice that was rarely used. When an enemy's scalp was taken, the Cherokee believed the enemy lost control of his soul and became socially and spiritually dead. The Europeans bastardized the practice in prelude to the French and Indian War as the settlers and soldiers of the two countries began to scalp each other, and each other's Indian allies. The colonies eventually offered bounties for enemy scalps. The promise of bounties caused the practice to grow between whites and Indians alike; among the tribes, scalping then became something different from its original spiritualistic practice, and trophies were collected.)[56]

Henry Stuart tried to delay the planned Cherokee attacks in the backcountry until the British Army had a chance to recoup. The mainstream Cherokee headmen agreed; however, the younger warriors and chiefs would not hear of it.

Robert Andrew Pickens, first cousin to future brigadier general Andrew Pickens, had a very close brush with the Cherokee about the same time as McCall's frightening experience. He lived and worked on his farm located at the Georgia side of the Savannah River, due west of the Long Canes settlement. A few Cherokee warriors, returning to the Lower Villages from Fort Charlotte, helped themselves to several settlers' horses, three of which belonged to Pickens.

Chief Skyuka (or Skiuka), the main chief of the Lower Villages and headman of Tugaloo Town, knew Robert Andrew Pickens very well. The chief arranged for a half-breed trader named Hughes to carry a message to Pickens. Pickens was invited to Tugaloo Village and told to bring two kegs of whiskey to ransom his horses. He complied with the message and, accompanied by a friend named John Welch, left with Hughes. As soon as Hughes reached his home in Tugaloo, he was notified by a young black boy that Chief Skyuka had come, taken all of Hughes' gunpowder, and gone to attack backcountry settlers.

Pickens and Welch were in a critical situation and spent the night at Hughes' home. The next morning Hughes told them to hide under a nearby river bank because Indians were approaching. Two warriors rode up to Hughes and asked him why two white men were staying there. He lied that they had come into the nation to join the Indians in their war against the Americans. The braves demanded to see the white brothers, so Hughes sent for Pickens and Welch. The Indians, who had apparently been drinking heavily, accepted them as brothers. Hughes then quietly advised Pickens and Welch to take two fresh horses and leave. They did as he suggested, and the Indians asked Hughes where they were going. He answered that he had sent them to collect his pastured horses so he could protect them during the coming war. The braves noticed that Pickens and Welch rode two of Hughes' horses, so they were satisfied.

Pickens and Welch had not gone far when they noticed they were being watched from behind a tree. When they saw a brave run toward Tugaloo, the men figured he was suspicious. Welch suggested they speed off, but Pickens decided it would draw attention to them since they were still within sight of Tugaloo. Pickens replied: "Wait till we descend the hill at hand and cross the creek at its base and then push to the utmost."[57]

After they had gone several miles, they struck the trail that led to the ford of Seneca River. Interestingly, they found Welch's coat at the ford. He had apparently left it there when he had come to Tugaloo.

They crossed the river near the village of Seneca and took the path toward the settlements. They had not gone far when they saw fresh signs that indicated substantial Cherokee activity. They took to the woods to avoid the trail and trekked until night. Welch was in pain and suffering from having traveled in miserable weather. He had required several breathers, so after dark the travelers rested. Welch urged Pickens to go ahead and get help at the settlement, but Pickens would not leave Welch behind.

The two men hobbled their horses and retired. Welch felt better the next morning. Once they regained the trail to the settlements, about half a mile from where they had bedded down, they discovered signs that an Indian war party had returned from a raid in the settlements while they slept. Had Pickens and Welch proceeded on, made a short rest rather than sleeping through the night, or even built a fire to ease Welch's discomfort, their lives would have been at great risk.

That day, the men reached Fort Independence on Rocky River, the extreme frontier of Abbeville District. On the way, they passed the house of settler Sam Marrow. Apparently, the same returning Cherokee party they had avoided as they slept had reduced the house to ruins. Sam, who lived alone, had escaped to Fort Independence. Pickens greatly feared for his own family and kindred, but his fear eased considerably when his wife ran out from the fort to meet him. The refugees in the fort were relieved to see that Pickens and Welch had not succumbed to a war party. Pickens was then told that some of his wife's relatives had been killed, and that all local families had come to shelter at Fort Independence. Sam Marrow's ruined house was the first visible evidence that Robert Andrew Pickens saw of the impending Cherokee attacks.

(This Fort Independence is not the well-known fort on the Georgia side of the Savannah. John Pickens, uncle of Andrew and Joseph Pickens and father of Robert Andrew Pickens, built this fort upon his land on Great Rocky Creek near Lowndesville, South Carolina. It was one of many small forts that had sprung up on private estates throughout the backcountry when the Cherokee went to war. The early settlers believed this fort was needed for protection against the Indians, as they were on the then-extreme frontier. The location is now under Lake Secession on Rocky River.)

Many of these smaller fortifications were simply modified houses or outbuildings that were altered with the addition of timbers. These structures often were named after the owners of the property. Fort Independence is mentioned in the pension applications of

Robert Andrew Pickens, William Pickens, and William Gabriel Pickens, all cousins of Andrew and Joseph Pickens.

Many families relocated to Fort Independence about July 1, 1776, as the Cherokee War of 1776 began. (Robert Andrew Pickens obtained a grant for the property in 1784, and it adjoined land he inherited from his father in 1770. His farm, mentioned in the experience he related to historian Lyman C. Draper, was in Georgia, directly across the Savannah River from Fort Independence.)

Chief Skyuka commanded a Cherokee war party that participated in those attacks on backcountry Whigs who were originally petitioned by the British to end their rebellion. The chief himself led raids down the Georgia side of the Savannah and killed many settlers. When he returned to Tugaloo, he found that Pickens had been there. Skyuka was sorry he had missed Pickens, and he thought he had probably been killed en route to the settlements. He regretted he could not have killed Pickens himself "in an easy death, for he loved him."[58]

(Tugaloo was a Cherokee town on the Tugaloo River, at the mouth of Toccoa Creek, six miles east of present-day Toccoa, Georgia, near the historic Travelers Rest Tavern located on Riverdale Road north of U.S. Highway 123 before it crosses into South Carolina.

(Chief Skyuka [Ground Squirrel] was a Cherokee chief who would later move west to the newly-created Chickamauga Cherokee villages that would be established by Chief Dragging Canoe near present-day Chattanooga, Tennessee. See Chapter 9.)

Alexander Cameron sent a message to Henry Stuart. The messenger caught up with Stuart in northern Georgia. Henry Stuart was made aware that war had broken out, and that Dragging Canoe had commandeered the 100 packhorses that bore ammunition. He further warned Stuart that Dragging Canoe intended to attack the Overmountain settlements.

While Nancy Ward attended a session in the Council House, she learned that War Chief Dragging Canoe was planning to attack the Watauga settlements, the Holston settlements near Long Island, and the Nolichucky settlements, on July 20, 1776. Dragging Canoe's brothers, Old Abram of Chilhowee and Raven of Chota (who had reconsidered his position regarding the Treaty of Sycamore Shoals) would lead some of the attacks.

On July 8, 1776, Nancy Ward performed her duties as Ghighau (Beloved Woman) and prepared the War Drink (or Black Drink) for the Cherokee warriors accompanied by a ritual as they prepared for war (see Chapter 5). Once the ceremony was fully underway, Nancy Ward quickly went to where traders Isaac Thomas, William Fawling, and Jarrett Williams were being detained (see earlier this chapter). She told them of Dragging Canoe's plans and helped them to escape their imprisonment in Chota. The three traders immediately spread the alarm, and settlers on the Watauga headed for the safety of Fort Caswell. The fort was commanded by Colonel John Carter, aided by Captain James Robertson, and Lieutenant John Sevier.

Chief Skyuka and Indian Agent Alexander Cameron concentrated on the backcountry settlements while Chief Dragging Canoe prepared his campaign against the encroaching Overmountain Virginians in the Holston, Watauga, and Nolichucky settlements.

Henry Stuart returned to the Upper Villages when he received Cameron's message; however, Chief Oconostota warned Stuart to leave forthwith to avoid being detained or killed. Stuart left to join his brother, John, in Florida on July 12, 1776.[59]

Dragging Canoe, still located in Big Island Town (Malaquo), carefully planned his campaign against the Overmountain settlers. He had a following of 700 warriors including a few Shawnee and some Creek who were followers of Chief Doublehead. (Doublehead was living in what had been Creek country near present-day Chattanooga, Tennessee.)

Raven of Chota split off from the main group with 200 warriors when they reached the Nolichucky River (near present-day Caney Branch, Tennessee, and 12 miles southwest of Greeneville). He headed north to attack the settlements in Carter's Valley (see information about John Carter earlier in this chapter).

Dragging Canoe and Old Abram, another of his brothers, continued on to Fort Lee, but they found it abandoned. After they burned the structures, Old Abram detached with 300 warriors to attack the settlements to the northeast on the Watauga River (near what is now Elizabethton, Tennessee). Dragging Canoe and his contingent of 200 warriors headed north for the settlements near Long Island of the Holston River (near today's Kingsport, Tennessee).

(Fort Lee was located at present-day Limestone, Tennessee, near Davy Crockett Birthplace State Park, on U.S. Highway 321/11E, 15 miles southwest of today's Johnston City, Tennessee.)

Dragging Canoe and his warriors established a campsite on the upriver end of Long Island on July 19, 1776. Scouts from Eaton's Station (a small stockade located six and one-half miles east of Kingsport, Tennessee, on U.S. Highway 11W) detected the presence of the war party; hence, the garrison's militia officers held a council of war that evening. Some captains desired to surprise the Cherokee, yet others thought it more prudent to defend the fort and the settlers within.

Captain William Cocke declared that if the militia did not challenge the Cherokee, the warriors would simply ignore the fort and destroy nearby settlers' cabins. The decision was to attack. Six companies of militia commanded by Captains John Campbell, James Shelby, William Buchanan, William Cocke, and Thomas Madison, and the ranking commander, James Thompson, left the fort at dawn on July 20 with 170 militiamen total. That was likely the same time that Dragging Canoe and a 20-warrior scouting party broke camp and headed for Eaton's Station. They hadn't gone far when the Indians met the militia's scouts. Behind the scouts were two columns of militiamen with outriders on the flanks.

The two advance groups skirmished with rifle fire that caused the militia scouts to take cover. The main body of militia charged; however, Dragging Canoe had already left to gather his main band of warriors, less than a mile behind. Dragging Canoe yelled at his war party: "Come on. The Unakas are running, come on and scalp them."[60]

The militia feared that the Indian scouts were the van of a large war party, so they withdrew toward Eaton's Station. After they removed a mile or so to Island Flats, they paused so the captains could discuss battle formations. The Cherokee then attacked them from the forest where the militia had just emerged. Captain Cocke and a few others ran for the fort, and the remaining militiamen formed a quarter-mile-long line. Dragging Canoe formed his warriors into a modified V with the ends curling toward the front. Dragging Canoe, at the point of the V, charged to split the militia line. The warriors at the curled ends of the V tried to surround the two militia line segments once it had split. Captain James Shelby led his company to a rise where his men and their rifle fire successfully forced the two flanks of the Cherokee to backtrack.

The battle developed into hand-to-hand combat. Eventually, the Cherokee withdrew.

A warrior named Big Sagwa was wounded with a rifle ball to the knee. He rolled into a depression in the ground where he could treat his wound and escape. Some militiamen spotted him, and one of them, Alexander Moore, full of bravado, laid his rifle down, drew his long hunter's knife, and jumped into the hole. Big Sagwa threw his tomahawk at Moore but missed and drew his own knife. As they tussled, Moore grabbed the warrior's knife by the blade and suffered a deep laceration to his left hand; however, with his right hand, he stabbed the large warrior several times. Then Charles Young, a 15-year-old militiaman, jumped into the hole and shot Big Sagwa in the head. Then other militiamen began to fire their rifles at the warrior from the rim of the hole.

The Eaton's Station militia suffered only four wounded; however, 13 Cherokee warriors were slain. The bodies of the Cherokee were scalped and grotesquely mutilated by the militiamen. Dragging Canoe was severely wounded with shots to both thighs. The wound to the right leg broke his femur. His brother, Little Owl, was also badly wounded by 11 rifle balls to his body, but he survived to participate in future battles alongside Shawnee allies. The Battle of Island Flats ended.

(The site of the Battle of Island Flats was within the city limits of present-day Kingsport, Tennessee. There is a marker at the corner of Memorial Boulevard and Jessee Street, near Fort Henry Mall, which reads: "In the area to the S.W. was fought this first battle of the Revolution in the West, July 20, 1776. Colonial Militia, under Capt. James Thompson, defeated a force of Cherokee under Dragging Canoe, in a short bloody struggle. It was also the turning point in the settlers' warfare with the Cherokee, who were British allies." This Eaton's Station is not to be confused with another by the same name near present-day Nashville, Tennessee.)

Dragging Canoe headed for Big Island Town and did not want to return empty-handed. He divided his band into several small war parties and ordered them to raid settlements along the Clinch, Powell, and Holston rivers. One war party is arguably credited with having swept up the Clinch River as far as Seven Mile Ford in Virginia. It then supposedly moved into the Wolf Hills settlement (near present-day Abingdon, Virginia) and attacked the Reverend Charles Cummings, a militant Presbyterian preacher. Cummings often rode to his appointments with his rifle on his shoulder and always placed his rifle on the pulpit before beginning church services.

The Reverend Cummings and four companions, including William Cresswell who had been at the Battle of Island Flats, were traveling to an appointment when the Cherokee warriors appeared. Cummings was killed and two others were wounded during the first volley from the Indians. Cresswell and his remaining two companions held the warriors off until relieved by some militiamen from Eaton's Station. (See the raids of Raven of Chota below for another opinion.) Dragging Canoe's warrior bands collected 18 white scalps for the return home.

The Watauga settlers had quickly constructed several small frontier forts on pieces of private property. They built a larger one called Fort Caswell (sometimes Fort Watauga) at Sycamore Shoals of the Watauga River (near present-day Elizabethton, Tennessee) that could protect several families of settlers. The militia hurriedly arrested several local Tories for fear they would join the Cherokee in the coming attacks. The British had sent a captain named Nathaniel Gist (father of George Gist or Sequoya) to enlist Tories for the coming war against the Patriots.

Old Abram (Ooskuah) of Chilhowee encamped his band of warriors on the North Bank of the Nolichucky River (near Jacob Brown's homestead. See earlier this chapter for information about Jacob Brown.) He led his braves toward the Watauga settlements on the 21st when the Cherokee were spotted by militia scouts a few miles from the settlement; 150 to 200 settlers then crowded into Fort Caswell. The fort's garrison consisted of 75 men under the command of John Carter (commissioner of the Council of Safety), with Captain James Robertson and Lieutenant John Sevier as subordinates. The Watauga settlement was not well prepared to enter into an open battle, so the militia intended to defend the fort.

Early July 21, 1776, several women went outside to milk cows. They were surprised and chased by some Cherokee. All made it inside the fort before the gate was closed, with one exception: Catherine Sherrill. She had been blocked from the gate by a large warrior. An athletic woman, she ran around the warrior and leaped for the wall to scale it. John Sevier had spotted her, caught her by the arm, and helped her over the wall. She later said she knew she must "scale the fort wall in spite of the bullets and arrows which came like hail. It was leap or die as I would not live a captive."[61]

"Bonnie Kate" married John Sevier in 1780.

The warriors attacked one wall that was uncovered by militia rifle fire and tried to set it ablaze. The women, using boiling water, organized a bucket brigade and poured the water on the Indians until they gave up the charge. The Cherokee lost an undetermined number of warriors in the assault thanks to accurate rifle fire from the fort's parapets. Old Abram placed the fort under siege for two weeks (some report for 20 days). At one point a man named James Cooper and a teenager named Samuel Moore believed it too quiet for Indians to be near, so they ventured out to get fresh water from Gap Creek near where it empties into the Watauga River. Cooper was shot, killed, and scalped, and Moore was captured. Old Abram raised the siege when messengers brought him word of Dragging Canoe's defeat on the Holston. He left with Moore and Mrs. Lydia Bean (wife of William Bean), another prisoner whom he had captured prior to the attack. Cherokee warriors (using a white trader who was traveling with them as an interpreter) threatened and interrogated Mrs. Bean for information. She replied that the settlers had enough guns, ammunition, food, and water to withstand a siege.

Raven crossed the Holston River and raided Carter's Valley. He found that the settlers were well protected by several small forts, so he burned a number of abandoned cabins and outbuildings while he looked for potential victims.

One of Raven's bands chased a Baptist minister, the Reverend Jonathan Mulkey, and his companion to the Holston River. Mulkey swam the river and escaped unharmed while his associate was scalped and left for dead. However, each eventually arrived at Eaton's Station. Another of Raven's bands had some success at Black's Station (*present-day Abingdon, Virginia*) where they killed one settler. (Some credit Raven's band with the attack on the Reverend Charles Cummings, William Cresswell, and their three other companions in the Wolf Hills Settlement near Abingdon. However, it is more likely to have been one of Dragging Canoe's small war parties. See earlier this chapter.) Raven withdrew when he was informed of Dragging Canoe's and Old Abram's lack of success.

Lydia Bean was held captive at Toqua, Chief Willenawah's village, near Chota while young Samuel Moore was imprisoned at Tuskegee near Tellico. Moore was tortured and burned at the stake. Lydia Bean had been sentenced to the same fate. She was dragged out of her confinement; her clothing was removed, her hair covered with clay, and her body painted. Furthermore, she had been jabbed with sticks, hit with rocks, and then secured to a pole with leather bonds. A warrior approached to light the brush that had been piled under and around her. Ghighau Nancy Ward had been warned of the impending action, and she arrived just in time with her swan's wing. She kicked the freshly-lit brush away, waved her swan's wing, and pronounced Lydia Bean to be pardoned. As Beloved Woman, Nancy Ward had the power to free any prisoner. The warriors were not happy and howled their protests. The Ghighau firmly declared: "It revolts my soul that Cherokee warriors would stoop so low as to torture a squaw. No woman shall be tortured or burned at the stake while I am GhiGau (Honored Woman)."[62]

Lydia Bean resided with Nancy Ward for a while and taught the Ghighau how to make butter and cheese from heavy milk. She also gave her instructions on the proper care of cattle. Nancy Ward later had her son, Fivekiller (Hiskyteehee), and her brother, Long Fellow (Tuskeegeetee), escort Lydia to the Watauga settlements.

Nancy Ward was influential in the failure of her first cousin's (Dragging Canoe) campaign. His planned invasion was a total failure. Had she not warned the whites of the coming attacks, the Overmountain settlers, who were widely scattered, would have suffered devastating losses.

The Beloved Woman's warning was not the only element that caused the botched action. The pro-settler policies of chiefs Attakullakulla and Oconostota had generated numerous delays that stymied the young warriors' actions for years. Each of the elders was nearing 80 years of age. Attakullakulla's sons, Dragging Canoe and his brothers, were all in their 30s and 40s. The politics of running an Indian nation and the energy to lead in times of war were a young chief's specialty. The elder chiefs continued to cede Cherokee land without a fight.

Dragging Canoe realized too late that the British were never going to help the Cherokee with their encroachment problem. The years of waiting for them to do so dearly cost the tribe.[63]

Alexander Cameron's decision to attack the backcountry settlements, regardless of John Stuart's orders for delay, was also costly to the Upper Villages. Chief Skyuka, the main chief of the Lower and Middle Villages, was a Dragging Canoe follower, and he would have gladly put off attacks in the backcountry to assist Dragging Canoe with the Overmountain settlers' encroachment had he been asked to do so. He would have realized that once the problem was resolved, Dragging Canoe would have directed the Upper Towns' young warriors to help the Lower Villages should the British regroup for another attack on Charles Town. The warriors from the Lower and Middle Villages were a necessary ingredient for Dragging Canoe to obtain a victory over the Virginians. The British left the Cherokee holding a weak bag, and the debacle wasn't over yet. The failure of Dragging Canoe's attacks was fatal to the Cherokee. The Overmountain settlers were still mindful of the danger, but they had become confident they could withstand a Cherokee attack.

Alexander Cameron was surely aware of John Stuart's desire to delay a backcountry invasion. However, he was apparently more interested in promoting himself with the more aggressive chiefs and warriors of the Cherokee. While Dragging Canoe was struggling against the encroaching Virginians, Cameron, along with his Tories, was monopolizing the warriors from the Lower and Valley Towns through Chief Skyuka. They launched devastating attacks through the South Carolina backcountry. They burned property, destroyed or stampeded livestock, and killed men, women, and children without distinction. The Chickamauga could certainly have used the aggressiveness of Skyuka's warriors in a united effort. However, Cameron had his way.

The backcountry settlers panicked and took refuge in the several stockades that had sprung up on private property. Some of the carnage that took place was recorded; one incident was included in Francis Salvador's report to Chief Justice Drayton on July 18, 1776, from Dewitt's Corner: "You would have been surprised to have seen the change in this country ... one of Capt. Smith's sons [John Smith] came to my house, with two of his fingers shot off ... I immediately galloped to Major Williamson's, to inform him, but found another of Smith's sons there, who made his escape, and alarmed that settlement."[64]

John Smith's father, Captain Aaron Smith of Long Canes, the captain's wife, five of their children, and one black servant were all slain. Only the two boys and two of their sisters, who were captured by the Cherokee, survived. The girls were returned after the Cherokee War was settled. Other examples of the attacks (ref. Landrum, pages 84–92):

- At the headwaters of the Tyger River, Anthony Hampton, his wife, one son (Preston), and a grandson were slain. The location was a holy place for the Cherokee, and they had been awaiting an opportunity to evict the Hamptons. Coincidentally, Anthony Hampton's married sons (Henry, Wade, Edward and John) who lived nearby, but a little farther toward the settlements, had been trying to arrange talks with the Indians to negotiate a peace treaty. These sons and their families somehow avoided the massacre.
- Concurrently, Mr. James Reed, who was visiting the Tyger settlement from North Carolina, "was attacked at the old ford on the North Tyger River, a short distance below Snoddy's Bridge." He was wounded through the breast and thigh. When a brave came to scalp him, he fought the Indian for his tomahawk, took it from him, and chased him away.
- Another Tyger area settler, Mr. Miller, had been visiting his neighbors. While he and two other men (a Mr. Leach and a Mr. Orr) were crossing Middle Tyger River, some Cherokee shot him. Leach and Orr tried to escape but were chased to a marsh by the Indians. Leach fell into the marsh and played possum while Orr jumped across and kept running. The Indians chased Orr and left Leach where he lay, as they thought him dead. When they caught up with Orr, they killed and scalped him. Leach, meanwhile, escaped. Orr was buried where he fell, and Miller was buried at the fork of the North Tyger and Middle Tyger rivers.
- The Cherokee killed a Mr. Bishop and captured his three children while Mrs. Bishop was away visiting friends. The children were returned after the end of the Cherokee War.
- The Hannon family lived on the North Pacolet River. A Cherokee war party killed Mr. Hannon and some of his family members as they planted corn. When he spied the Indians and saw them attack his family, ten-year-old Edwin Hannon grabbed his little brother, John, and ran for the North Pacolet with some of the braves close behind. At the river's edge, Edwin had to drop his brother to escape capture. As he was crossing the river, he heard the blows that ended John's life.

His eight-year-old sister, Winnie, had grabbed another little brother, William, and successfully hid in some nearby canebrakes until the Indians rode away.
- Cherokee surprised the Kemp family on the Broadmouth River. The Indians rapidly killed them, burned their house and outbuildings, and threw the dead bodies into the flaming structures. One young son was the sole survivor.

The slaughter and destruction were widespread and severe. The Reverend James Creswell wrote to Chief Justice Drayton from Ninety Six on July 27, 1776:

> Honored Sir: I make no doubt but you are anxious to hear how our affairs stand in this perplexed and unhappy district, since the heathen has broke in on our frontier.... The savages have spread great desolation all along the frontiers, and killed a great number ... Ninety Six is now a frontier. Plantations lie desolate and hopeful crops are going to ruin. In short, dear sir, unless we get some relief, famine will overspread our beautiful country.... Fences are thrown down, and many have already suffered a great loss. Such of us as are in forts have neither suitable guns nor ammunition, for the defence of our wives and little ones.[65]

Chief Skyuka's warriors, along with Alexander Cameron's Tory militia, experienced immeasurable success in the backcountry settlements. However, the Cherokee were hit with a double-whammy. Primarily, had that force joined War Chief Dragging Canoe in the Upper Villages, the war chief undoubtedly would have had a modicum of success against the settlements at the Holston, Watauga, and Nolichucky rivers. They might have even driven many of them out of the region. While Skyuka's and Cameron's methods seemed severe, they were not more so than those of Dragging Canoe and Doublehead. That approach was necessary in Dragging Canoe's mind if the Chickamauga were to successfully reclaim Cherokee ancestral lands and re-establish the old traditions. He and Doublehead hoped that, if they punished many of the encroachers severely enough, it would be an example for the others. This was the only way that these young leaders could see to instill a desire among the Overmountain settlers to leave the Cherokee lands, or at least to stem the desires of new arrivals from Virginia and North Carolina.

Secondly, Skyuka's and Cameron's attacks in the backcountry initiated a reprisal the like of which the Cherokee had never before seen. It would be far worse than had the 1759 to 1761 wars. Had they not listened to Cameron, and stayed out of the backcountry, the Carolinas and Georgia militias might well have opted to stay home and prepare to defend against possible future British invasions. There would have been no help for the Virginian Overmountain settlers against the onslaughts of Dragging Canoe, Doublehead, Skyuka, and their Tory allies. However, as things stood, there being no eastern front for the backcountry militias to worry about, there was nothing to keep Georgia, South Carolina, and North Carolina from delivering a vengeful blow to the Cherokee extending all the way into the Upper Villages. And they did so deliver.

Ninety Six Militia major Andrew Williamson began to muster forces right after the initial Cherokee incursion. Robert Andrew Pickens, in his interview with Lyman C. Draper, stated:

> General Williamson assembled his troops July 1, 1776 on a creek, a tributary of the Saluda River in Pendleton District, S.C. They numbered about 8 or 10 hundred me [sic]. There were two regiments. General Williamson was at the head of one and General Andrew Pickens at the head of the other. In Picken's [sic] regiment it is recollected that Capt. Norwood, Capt. Robert F. Anderson and Captain Joseph Pickens, the latter a brother of Gen. Pickens....[66]

(Williamson was actually a major, Andrew Pickens a captain, and Joseph Pickens a lieutenant at the time. Williamson did not have that many men so early in the campaign.)

Many of the militiamen wanted to protect their remaining family members who were holed up in the several makeshift forts that had sprouted on private Whig properties throughout the backcountry. Williamson had mustered only about 40 men by July 1, 1776. On July 3, 1776, Major Williamson began to move toward the Cherokee Nation with his small party; however, it grew as he traveled. (They would find out later that while they traveled this leg of their trek the Continental Congress had voted to declare independence from Britain on the 4th.) He stopped at DeWitt's Corner on Hogskin Creek on July 8; he had then marshaled 200 men. Williamson's march was concurrent with the devastation already described as the Cherokee war parties trailed him through the settlements.[67] (DeWitt's Corner was located at today's Due West, South Carolina.)

On July 14, 1776, several Whig families relocated to Lindley's Fort for protection and were joined there by a large militia force commanded by Major Jonathan Downs. A large band of Cherokee, accompanied by Tories dressed as Indians, attacked the fort on the morning of the 15th.[68] Williamson's army was camped at DeWitt's Corner on July 19, 1776, when Captain Francis Salvador completed a letter to Chief Justice Drayton that he had begun on the 18th. The addition included a description of the attack:

> I rode there [Lindley's Fort on the Saluda River] last Saturday, and found Col. Williams and Liles, and two companies from Col. Richardson's regiment, amounting to 430 men. They were attacked on Monday morning, by Indians and Scopholites [a variation of Schofieldites, an old Tory militia], but repulsed them, taking thirteen white men prisoners. The Indians fled the moment day appeared.... We have just received an account that two of the Cherokees' head warriors were killed in the late skirmish at Lindley's Fort.... P.S.—We, this day, increased to 600, all from the same regiment.... At Lindley's Fort ... the fort was attacked by ... eighty-eight Indians and one hundred and two whites.[69]

Major Williamson wrote a follow-up report of the incident from his camp on Baker's Creek on the 22nd:

> Exasperated at the behavior of Hugh Brown, and others, who have lately joined the Indians against us, thirteen of which were taken prisoners, a few days ago, and sent to Ninety-Six jail—four of which were found painted as Indians ... I understand last night, the Indians struck at North Carolina and Virginia the very day they commenced hostilities against our frontier. If these two colonies join heartily with us, I hope soon to ... reduce the savages to such a state, as to wish they had never broke their faith with us.[70]

The Reverend Creswell, on the 27th, also mentioned the affair in his letter to Drayton and included an estimate of the number of Indians and Tories involved: "The savages have spread great desolation.... On the 14th they attacked a part of Colonel Williams' regiment at Lindley's Fort, but were repulsed.... This attack was made by ninety Indians and 120 white men. Ten of the white Indians were made prisoners, nine of which were painted. They are now safe at Ninety-Six."[71]

(There are differences between the Reverend Creswell's account and those of Salvador and Williamson regarding the date of the action, the numbers of enemy combatants, prisoners, and prisoners dressed as Cherokee. The accounts of Salvador and Williamson are likely the more precise.)

Several Tories who had been working with Cameron and Skyuka, some of whom attacked Lindley's Fort, were sheltered at Tory captain Richard Pearis' property near the eastern boundary of the Cherokee Nation (proximate to the outskirts of what is now Greenville, South Carolina.) They used Pearis' place as a base camp while they continued to attack Whig settlers around the area.

Chief Justice Drayton was no fan of Richard Pearis, the Cunningham brothers, any other Tories, or the Cherokee. In a July 24 letter to Captain Salvador he stated:

> The discharge [release from prison] of [Captain] Robert Cunningham and his companions ... I must applaud your resolution to consider Cunningham "in future merely as an individual, and not as head of any party." Such is the station he ought ever to hold.... As for the fate of the thirteen white prisoners taken upon the repulse of the Indians—speaking as W.H.D. [William Henry Drayton] in private character, I think the republic would have received an essential piece of service had they all been instantly hanged.... For my part, I shall never give my voice for peace with the Cherokee Nation upon any other terms than their removal beyond the mountains.[72]

Colonel Ross and his Spartan Militia arrived at Pearis' property shortly before Captain John Hammond did from Ninety Six. There Ross' troops captured a large number of Tories and dispersed the remainder. Ross burned the structures, took Pearis' wife and daughters captive, and also took Pearis' cattle, horses, and personal effects. Ross' militia headed to Ninety Six with the prisoners and the loot. When the captain arrived at a Colonel Hight's place, he found a horrific scene of destruction and murder. The Tories had turned the only survivors, Mrs. Hight and her daughters, over to the warriors who headed for the Lower Villages.[73]

The coming war with the Cherokee would be handled differently than was Lieutenant Colonel James Grant's 15 years earlier (see Chapter 4). Grant was a British officer, and he moved with a full entourage that included wagons with food, artillery, ammunition, and extra clothing. This new incursion into the Cherokee Nation would be entirely a militia action. The militias (Whig or Tory) traditionally traveled lightly. Each man carried what he could in his saddle pack or on his belt. A militiaman was mounted and relied on a rifle, saber, small caliber pistol, knife, and tomahawk. He carried a powder horn, shot bag, and extra flints. He subsisted primarily on water (carried in a canteen or leather flask), jerked beef, and journey cake, a mixture of cornmeal and water, which was fried or baked until firm. (Journey cake was later called Johnnycake—the forerunner of hardtack in the old west.) He might also have carried his corn meal as mush boiled to the consistency of heavy bread and wrapped in corn husks or linen for flexibility, either eaten as was or sliced and cooked further into journey cake. Other backcountry travel fare might have been parched corn or dried pumpkin. The troops usually commandeered any other required subsistence, such as grain or fresh beef, from the properties of enemy sympathizers.

Militias primarily pressed an attack on horseback with small arms and rarely dismounted. When they did, they alit with their rifles, quickly staked their horses, fired from cover for a short time (as long as they had a suitable advantage), and then quickly remounted to chase a fleeing enemy or to retreat when necessary. It was a very similar tactic to what the Cherokee used.

On July 29, 1776, Williamson established his base camp with 1,150 men on a ridge beyond Six-and-Twenty Mile Creek, about 15 miles across the Cherokee Nation and South Carolina boundary. The time to press the enemy had arrived. On the 31st at 6:00 p.m. after he received intelligence regarding Alexander Cameron's supposed location, Williamson embarked across Eighteen Mile Creek with Captains Andrew Pickens, LeRoy Hammond, James McCall, and a 300-man regiment.

Major Williamson's objective was to move quickly and surround the enemy encampment at Oconee Creek by daybreak, August 1, 1776. The only direct route necessitated crossing the Keowee River at Seneca (near where Clemson University now stands, the village site now beneath present-day Lake Hartwell). Two Tory prisoners told the Whigs where Cameron allegedly was and led them toward the encampment. However, the Tories intended to lead Williamson into a trap at Seneca after they had assured him the village was deserted.[74]

Major Williamson split his regiment for the march. The commander took the point with Captain LeRoy Hammond and a 33-man advance party. Pickens, with his entire company, trailed behind the advance. McCall followed several miles back with the remainder of the force, a common arrangement to avoid exposure of an entire regiment to possible ambush. Pickens was to quickly support Williamson in the event of surprise, and McCall would join them at Oconee once Cameron's force had been located and surrounded.

Once again, however, Williamson had underestimated his adversary. From an encampment below Keowee, he penned to Drayton on August 4, 1776:

> I accordingly marched about six o'clock in the evening, with thirty-three men on horseback, (taking two prisoners with me to show me where the enemy were encamped...) intending to surround their camp by day-break ... the river Keowee lying on the route, and only passable at a ford at Seneca, obliged me (though much against my inclination) to take the road; the enemy ... laid themselves in ambush ... had taken possession of the first houses in Seneca, and posted themselves behind a long fence on an eminence close to the road where we were to march, and to prevent being discovered had filled up the openings betwixt the rails ... suffered the guides and advance guard to pass ... poured in a heavy fire upon my men ... which being unexpected, staggered my advanced party.[75]

Williamson and his advance party approached Seneca at 2:00 a.m. on August 1, 1776, and intended to pass quietly through the supposedly evacuated village. However, they had been watched since they left their base camp. A large group of Tories and Cherokee warriors, led by Chief Skyuka, ambushed them at the village. Cameron was not in the area as he had planned the ambuscade from the relative safety of Oconee. Williamson's army stiffened, and a fierce fight ensued. The combat around the fence, where a majority of the concealed party had waited, was especially intense, and vision was difficult in the darkness. (Some have reported that War Chief Dragging Canoe was involved in the ambush; however, Dragging Canoe was laid up from his injuries and was preparing to vacate the Upper Villages to avoid repercussions from the Virginians. See later this chapter.)

Several were wounded early in the battle, and Captain Francis Salvador, dressed in a very bright white uniform, was hit three times. The Cherokee had thought Salvador to be Williamson because of his finery; however, Williamson was plainly dressed in accord with common militia practice. A Cherokee brave approached and scalped Salvador who died less than an hour later. Captain John Smith, one of the two surviving sons of the massacred Aaron Smith family, was near Salvador. The Indian, however, had approached unusually slowly, and Smith thought him to be Salvador's servant.

Williamson's horse was shot out from under him, and he reportedly shouted to a subordinate: "Get me Salvador's horse! Damn you! Get me Salvador's horse!"[76]

In Williamson's letter of the 4th he continued: "Here Mr. Salvador received three wounds, and fell by my side; my horse was shot down under me, but I received no hurt. Lieut. Farar, of Captain Prince's Company, immediately supplied me with his. I desired him to take care of Mr. Salvador, but before he could find him in the dark, the enemy unfortunately got his scalp, which was the only one taken.... He died about half after two o'clock, in the morning, forty-five minutes after he received the wounds, sensible to the last."[77]

Captain LeRoy Hammond forged a critical saber charge at a gathering of Cherokee and Tories who were in a prime firing location. Hammond dispersed them with great effectiveness.

Captain Andrew Pickens' company reached the ford shortly after the initial attack. Having heard noise from the ambush, he urged his men across the creek and approached the fence. The captain ordered his men to dismount and "hitch if you can! If you can't, let the horses go and rush forward!"[78]

Chief Skyuka, his warriors, and his Tories dispersed and headed for the nearby forest, firing as they went. The Cherokee had suffered a heavy loss as evidenced by the amount of blood left behind, and by a constant mournful howling as they continued to retreat. This was the first defeat for the Lower Village warriors and their Tory allies since they had initiated their attacks. It would not be their last. Because of the misguided directions they received from British deputy agent Alexander Cameron, they had invited the horrific reprisals of a mass gathering of multi-colonial militias. The worst of it was the militias would not stop with the Lower Villages but would punish the Middle, Valley, and Upper communities as well. The only benefit that the Chickamauga would receive from Cameron's and Skyuka's rash assaults in the backcountry would be the collection of young refugee warriors that would trek to Chickamauga Town to join his collective. However, it would be some time before he could regain any momentum.

Williamson's entire regiment moved through the abandoned town and began to torch the cabins. The militiamen fed on Cherokee crops and destroyed what they could not use. They found twenty of their number had been wounded, six very severely. Militiaman James Noble was detached to take the more-seriously injured, some on litters, back to the settlements for care. Three men, including Salvador and Moore, had been killed outright during the battle. They were quickly buried near the village in a hole that was left by a fallen tree.[79]

Williamson would yet find stiff Cherokee opposition as he moved through Cherokee country; however, it would not be stiff enough. On August 8, Williamson, with a detachment of 640 men, left base camp at Seneca and proceeded to Oconee. The men found the site abandoned by Alexander Cameron and his force, which was outnumbered by four to one. After Williamson's militiamen destroyed the village, they did the same at Ostatoy and Tugaloo.

They bivouacked at Tugaloo, and on the 10th they crossed and proceeded up the Tugaloo River. The vanguard had a skirmish with a Cherokee war party at a shoal crossing on the 11th. As the militiamen plunged into the river, they were targets of an ineffective fusillade. The Cherokee took no militia casualties; however, they nearly eliminated Captain Andrew Pickens when they shot his horse from under him. Several warriors were killed in the scuffle, but once the advance party reached the shore, the Cherokee swiftly dispersed.

After the militia reached Little River, Captain Pickens and 25 of his company reconnoitered the vicinity on foot. They were armed with rifles since they were not mounted, but they also carried axes, knives, pistols, or some combination of the three in their belts. The choice depended on what was comfortable to each individual for close combat. After scouting for two miles, they reached an old crop field that had grown over with grass nearly five feet high. Some 200 Cherokee braves were ready. They watched from a nearby ridge and charged when the militiamen were in the middle of the field. According to the militia's mixed-blood guide, a man named Brennan, the Indian chief, likely Skyuka, yelled: "Rush in! Rush in! Tomahawk!"[80]

The chief apparently calculated, since the whites were so badly outnumbered, the braves should abandon their rifles and press for a quick hand-to-hand combat. The militia, though outnumbered, leveled a deadly and accurate barrage at the charging braves who withdrew to the ridge, retrieved their own rifles, and began to return the militia fire. The militiamen, however, had located better cover and were better shots, so more warriors were killed. Additionally, the Cherokee worked to retrieve their fallen comrades, so the militiamen had even more time to reload and carefully aim their devastating fire. Militia reinforcements arrived, and that was all the Cherokee needed to disperse. The militia lost 11 men, and the Cherokee 75, in what has famously become known as the Ring Fight. The Cherokee showed once again they were not ready to give up, but they were once more outmaneuvered.[81]

Williamson's forces proceeded up the Little River to Tomassee, camped, and found signs that the Cherokee had recently been there. Captains Andrew Pickens and Robert Anderson detached with some 60 men to reconnoiter the area and look for more Indian signs. They had gone a short distance when Anderson decided to take 25 men and investigate a creek that emptied into Little River. Shortly thereafter, Pickens' force came upon two braves who let out a few war whoops and galloped away. Pickens' men gave chase, apparently not fearful of a common Cherokee tactic for setting a trap. However, they were soon engaged with nearly 300 Indians, and the fighting was fierce. Major Downs, who had detached to reconnoiter another area with 25 men, heard the commotion. Anderson also heard the fray. He arrived on the Cherokee rear at the same time as Downs and began to engage the enemy. Hand-to-hand combat ensued for the most part. At one point, a stocky militiaman was engaging a brave. They were apparently unable to reload, so were using their rifles as clubs. Once they broke the rifle stocks, they began to grapple, and the militiaman gouged at the brave's eyes, forcing the brave to shout: "Canaly! Enough!"

The militiaman shouted back: "Damn you! You can never have enough while you are alive!"[82]

He callously tossed the surrendering brave to the ground, planted a foot on his head, and cruelly scalped the warrior before he killed him.

Williamson, on a foray with 150 men, was attracted to the battle, approached the enemy's back side and began to encircle the war party. The Cherokee still had the advantage of numbers; however, fighting while surrounded was not their favorite tactic. Hence, they smartly fled, unable to carry away all of their dead. The militiamen found 16 Cherokee bodies; the militia had lost two killed outright and 21 wounded, four mortally so. Captains Neel and Lacy were among those who later died as a result of their wounds. The Cherokee were taking a toll on the militia as it marched through their land, but Williamson's force had the momentum and would keep it.

After they burned Tomassee, the militia again broke into detachments and attacked some other Lower Villages. Jocassee, Chehohee and Eustash were burned by those troops; Pickens led a detachment to do the same at Estatoe. They burned crops of corn and peas and slaughtered livestock in each location. Williamson then led the militia back to his base camp at Seneca.

Colonel Ross' Spartan Militia made its way to the town of Estatoe and found indications that Pickens had been there. The militiamen looked for the Hight women but found the town deserted and burned. They burned Qualhatchee and Toxaway as they made their way toward Williamson's position. Some of Williamson's detachment joined Colonel Ross and his men at Keowee, and together they moved toward the village of Chatooga. There they captured a Cherokee woman and two black men who informed them the Hight women were being held at a Cherokee camp in the nearby mountains.

Colonel Ross' troops approached the camp and surrounded it. Cherokee defenders began to fire. The Indians successfully held the militia off until darkness fell, and the braves were able to slither away. The next morning Ross, with the combined militia, carefully entered the camp and found it deserted. They checked their personnel and found one soldier injured and one horse killed. They found Mrs. Hight's body one hundred yards out of camp. She had been stripped, killed, and left face-down in the dirt. After they buried her, they met Major Williamson at Seneca. The commander furloughed Ross' militia, so they could proceed to the settlements for fresh clothing and provisions. They were to rejoin him on August 28.

Williamson's campaign settled into a lull at Seneca where he ordered a crude, but strong, defensive structure built, called Fort Rutledge. Colonel Samuel Jack and his Georgia Militia destroyed structures and crops in abandoned Valley Towns along the Chattahoochee and Tulluluh Rivers up to the Tugaloo River. They then joined Major Williamson at Seneca as did Colonels Thomas and Neil with their regiments.[83]

Colonel Jack had entered into the conflict following Cherokee attacks in Georgia's backcountry settlements. Initially, a Georgia Militia company led by a Lieutenant Grant chased one band of Cherokee, and Grant was captured. He was tortured, tied to a tree, and scalped. His ears were removed, and a red-hot gun barrel had been thrust into his abdomen and fired. When he was found, 12 arrows protruded from his chest with a red war club lying on top of them. A decorated tomahawk was anchored into the tree above his head. The Cherokee showed that they, too, could formidably punish a captive.

Other militia regiments had participated in coordinated attacks in Cherokee country as described by Williamson in a letter to Drayton:

CAMP AT SENECA, August 22, 1776. DEAR SIR: This is to acknowledge the receipt of your favor of the 10th instant, acquainting me of the independence of the United States of America being declared, which I agree with you is a glorious event.... I have now burnt every town, and destroyed all the corn, from the Cherokee line to the middle settlements.... I have received letters from Gen. Rutherford, wherein he acquaints me that he will be in the middle settlements about the 4th or 5th of next month, with about 2,000 men. I have wrote him the day I am to move from home for the same place ... while Col. Lewis, from Virginia, attacks the Overhills, with about the same number.[84]

(Griffith Rutherford, as a colonel, had joined with South Carolina colonel Richard Richardson in an action against the backcountry Tories one year earlier. See earlier this chapter.)

Williamson had suggested to General Rutherford that they meet at Nikwasi (present-day Franklin, North Carolina) on September 9, 1776. Brigadier General Griffith Rutherford commanded the North Carolina Militia and was staging a parallel attack on the Cherokee from that province. North Carolina entered the fray because of Cherokee attacks along the Catawba River. Rutherford had advocated for a joint effort against the Cherokee and remarked: "If such a campaign can be mounted I have no doubts of the destruction of the Cherokee Nation."[85]

In mid–August, Rutherford led his 2,400 man militia across Swannanoa Gap (present-day Ridgecrest, North Carolina) of the Blue Ridge Mountains. When the North Carolinians crossed over the mountains, they approached a trader's cabin. One of the trader's slaves made a break for it, and Rutherford's chaplain, the Reverend James Hall, shot and killed him as they had mistaken him for a Cherokee warrior. Next they captured two Indian women and a boy. It was proposed to auction them off as slaves to members of the brigade, but one officer protested that their disposition should be left up to civil authorities after the war. Other militiamen chimed in that if they were not auctioned off on the spot, they would be killed and scalped. They were auctioned off and one of the soldiers bought them for twelve hundred dollars.

General Rutherford began his major attacks about September 7, with an assault on old Tuckaseegee and Stecoee (or Stecoah). (Those towns were near the junction of present-day U.S. Highways 74 and 141 South. The actual sites would have been on the Tuckaseegee River near today's Cullowhee and Sylva, North Carolina).

The Cherokee devised a surprise ambush against one company of Rutherford's force east of present-day Franklin, North Carolina, on the Cowee Divide. A second company rescued the primary company and dispersed the warriors.

When Major Andrew Williamson received word that the Declaration of Independence had been signed by the Continental Congress on August 2, 1776, he held a council with the other regimental commanders to apprise them of the event. (Though the Declaration of Independence had been adopted by Congress on July 4, 1776, it was not official until signed by most members of Congress on August 2.) Next, he met with his own regimental officers to offer them the same information who, in turn, passed the word of American Independence along to their respective companies. They would now fight not only for their defense, but also for a new country. The backcountry militiamen had a new fire for their vengeance to be exacted upon the Cherokee.

Chief Justice Drayton likely bent President John Rutledge's ear regarding Andrew Williamson because he was finally promoted to colonel. Colonel Williamson's next action would be to first attack the remaining Lower Villages of the Cherokee and then as many Middle Villages as he could prior to winter. However, he had to await the arrival of Major William Henderson who was en route with his rifle regiment. Colonel Thomas Sumter, who was also on his way with his regiment, had to recruit while on the move; thus, his progress was slower than Henderson's.

Colonel Ross and his regiment made a timely return, and on September 1, 1776, one of his companies made a short foray to scatter some Cherokee near the proximity of Fort Rutledge.

Major Henderson had already arrived at the fort by the time Colonel Sumter got there on the 12th. Williamson's force then numbered 2,300 militiamen. He planned to move out the next morning, Friday the 13th, and decided to leave 300 men to garrison the fort.

General Rutherford was late getting to Nikwasi, but Williamson was later. Rutherford's advance arrived at Watauga on the 8th, and he followed with the rest of his army on the 9th. On the 10th, Rutherford sent a detachment seven miles up the Little Tennessee River (southward) to burn Nikwasi. They went further south to burn Echoe, near where Colonel Montgomery had been ambushed in 1760. When they returned to Watauga, they informed Rutherford that there was no sign of Williamson's army.

On September 11, Rutherford sent a detachment north (downstream) along the Little Tennessee, burned Cowee, and did the same seven miles further at Alijoy on the 12th. Rutherford's entire army proceeded to Nikwasi on the 14th.

On September 15, 1776, scouts returned from the south and reported there was still no indication of the South Carolina militia. The officers held a council of war and decided to leave for the Valley Towns the following day. On the 16th, Rutherford left with 1,200 men, and he left the rest with the baggage at Nikwasi.

Williamson's army had left Fort Rutledge on the 13th and camped at Cane Creek after an eight-mile trek. They crossed the Oconee Mountains on the 14th after which they made camp. They had seen the tracks of Rutherford's scouts, so they assumed that Rutherford would be waiting for them at Nikwasi.

On the 15th, they marched to the mouth of Warwoman Creek on the Chattooga River. They followed the creek and made camp about halfway to its headwaters. They then generally followed the route of today's Warwoman Road to present-day Clayton, Georgia, where they headed north and passed through Rabun Gap in the direction of Nikwasi. (Rabun Gap is on present-day U.S. Highway 23/441 about two miles south of the North Carolina-Georgia border.)

Williamson warned his men to be prepared for an attack as they approached The Narrows just north of the Georgia-North Carolina border (where he had experienced a previous ambush while with the James Grant expedition in 1761); however, none occurred at that place. On the 17th, they reached Nikwasi, where they had hoped to meet General Rutherford; however, they missed him by nearly two days. Williamson made contact with Rutherford's baggage detail and camped at Canucca Village about two miles west by southwest on present-day Cartoogechaye Creek. Canucca was the location where two Indian trails separated going westward. The more southern trail that Rutherford took generally followed today's U.S. Highway 64 to modern Murphy, North Carolina.

The South Carolinians marched out on September 19 but did not follow Rutherford's track. Williamson decided to follow the primary, or main, Indian trail to the Valley Towns that passed through Wayah Gap. About midday, they found conflict, and plenty of it, at a place called The Black Hole on Wayah Creek, just east of Wayah Gap.

Some 600 Cherokee braves had carefully planned an ambush and fired on the militia from the forest. The warriors were well positioned on the flanks atop steep walls to force the militia to charge straight ahead into the middle of the gorge. Edward Hampton (a married son of the Anthony Hampton who was slain with some of his family in July) turned the battle as he and 30 men found the rear of the Cherokee, who were forced to withdraw after some measure of success. The warriors left 13 slain militiamen and 18 wounded. The Indians lost several warriors, but a count could not be taken. (The Black Hole is located on present-day Wayah Road, about 10 miles due west of Franklin, North Carolina. The specific location is a one and one-half mile long narrow valley east of, and at the foot of

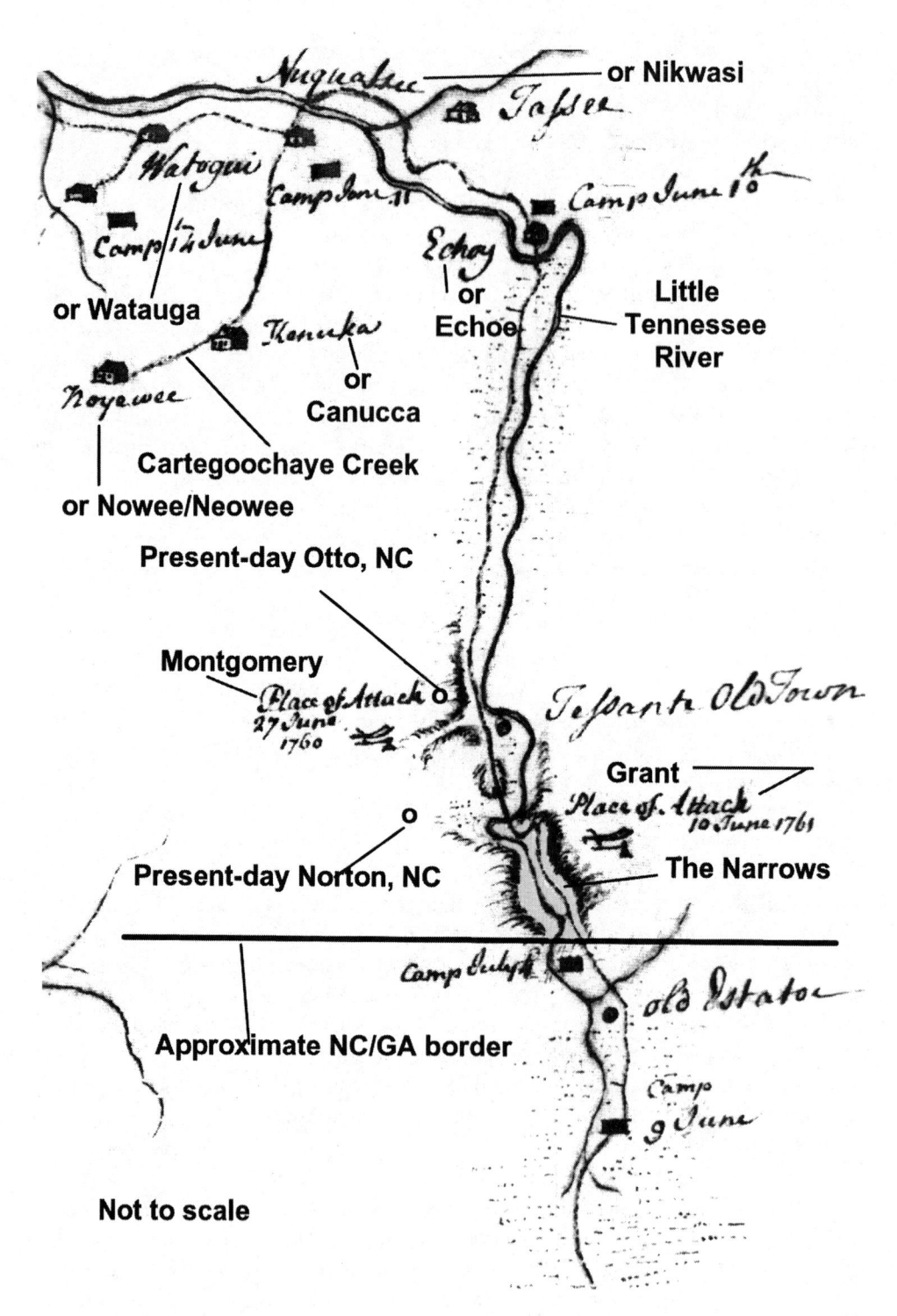

James Grant Expedition Map with notations by the author—Nikwasi (present-day Franklin, North Carolina) and Watauga were more directly north of Echoe than shown; Canucca and Nowe were more west by southwest of Nikwasi than shown; Williamson warned his men as they approached The Narrows from the south to be prepared for an ambush as he had been a member of Grant's expedition in 1761—however, the ambush did not occur there but later near Wayah Gap (not shown).

the climb to, Wayah Gap. See Appendix H for the research and maps regarding the location.)

The retreating warriors continued to snipe at Williamson's advance guard as it proceeded through the Nantahala Mountains. One such skirmish occurred on September 21, about two miles west of Wayah Gap. There they wounded a Cherokee warrior whom they found to be a woman. She was questioned by an interpreter and gave them information regarding the origination of the warriors who had ambushed them. She was wounded too badly to be moved and so was killed to put her out of her misery. (The location was on Jarrett Creek which feeds Nantahala Lake from the southeast near where Jarrett Creek Road departs Wayah Road. The incident is often attributed to Rutherford's force rather than Williamson's; however, those who have done so also wrote that Rutherford took the trail over Wayah Gap rather than the southern route to the Valley Towns.)

The terrain became more manageable, and Williamson's force gained momentum. It moved on Burning Town on September 25, then southward along the Valley River to Tomassee, Nowewee, and Little Tellico. Each town was destroyed in the same manner as those encountered the previous month.

(Rutherford's track from Nikwasi would have caused him to move northward on the Hiwassee River toward a juncture with Williamson.) On the 26th, Williamson found that Canusee and Ecochee had already been ruined by Rutherford. They followed Rutherford's track until they finally caught up with a company of the North Carolinians at Canostee and Nottely (near the present-day town of Murphy, North Carolina).[86]

General Rutherford had tired of waiting for Colonel Williamson at Brass Town, so he left the company of men and headed for Great Ecoche (Aquonatuste), where he deposited another company of men to remain while he started for the Hiwassee River Valley. He became lost and did not immediately find the valley. Williamson arrived at Great Ecoche, encamped his regiment, and detached a company that found Rutherford, who had circled aimlessly and wound up about three miles away. The detachment set General Rutherford straight with directions, then reported back to Williamson. Rutherford and his force went on to destroy some Hiwassee River villages. That confusion on the part of Rutherford provided the Cherokee warriors an opportunity, and they slew several militiamen in hit-and-run skirmishes. Williamson finally caught up with Rutherford at Hiwassee late on September 26, 1776.

One of Rutherford's detachments returned from Wolf Hills, Virginia (now Abingdon), with 11 warriors' scalps. The practice of scalping had been used with abandon throughout the Cherokee War of 1776. The South Carolina legislature had issued a bounty of £75 for each warrior scalp turned in and £100 for live captives.

They separated on the 27th, and Rutherford headed for home. Williamson went through Georgia burning lower Valley Towns as he went. They arrived back at Fort Rutledge on Monday, October 7, and the militiamen were dismissed. Williamson announced a truce to prepare for a peace conference to be held later.

During the Cherokee Campaign, Williamson lost 100 men, and the estimated Cherokee losses were set at 2,000. Over 30 villages were destroyed and five battles fought against large Cherokee war parties.

Rutherford's militia burned the structures and crops of every village on the Tuckaseegee, Oconaluftee, Hiwassee, and the upper portions of the Little Tennessee River to below where the Hiwassee joins the Valley River. It is estimated he destroyed 36 villages.

The situation deteriorated further for the Cherokee Nation because, while the militias from Georgia, North Carolina, and South Carolina attacked Skyuka's Middle and Valley villages, a parallel action was undertaken by the Virginia militia against the Upper Towns. In September 1776, Virginia lieutenant colonel William Russell, commander of the Fincastle Rangers, established Fort Patrick Henry at the upriver end of Long Island of the Holston River (near present-day Kingsport, Tennessee). The stockade wall, with bastions at the corners, enclosed three acres on a bluff overlooking the river. The site was at, or near, the location of old Virginia Fort Robinson (see Chapter 4).

Near the 1st of October, Virginia colonel William Christian entered the fort with 2,000 militiamen and planned his campaign. Among Christian's men was a North Carolina militia regiment from Surry County commanded by Colonel Joseph Williams and his second, Major Joseph Winston. He was also joined by the Holston settlements' militia commanded by Major Evan Shelby and Captain James Shelby. Virginia captain William Witcher's company would be assigned to garrison the fort while Christian and the main force would make their foray.

Sometime during the first week of October, Colonel Christian marched his troops six miles south from Fort Patrick Henry and camped at Double Springs near Chimney Top Mountain. He was joined by Captains James Robertson and John Sevier with their Watauga and Nolichucky militias, which brought the total field force to 1,800 men. (Double Springs was located six miles up Horse Creek from its confluence with the South Fork Holston River. That confluence is just upstream of where the South Fork Holston River joins the North Fork Holston River. Double Springs was farther up Horse Creek from where Lick Creek joins it. The reference to Chimney Top Mountain is a different mountain than the famous Chimney Tops Mountain that is located in Great Smoky Mountains National Park, along U.S. Highway 441 [Newfound Gap Road] eight miles south of Gatlinburg, Tennessee.)

In October 6, Colonel Christian wrote to Virginia governor Patrick Henry:

> I shall march in less than an hour and take with me thirty days' flour, and seventy days' beef. I hope to cross Broad River [meaning the French Broad] the 15th inst. [meaning October], where it is likely I shall be attacked or meet with proposals of peace. The men who have fled from the towns say the Indians will surely fight desperately; which they promised Stuart, the King's Superintendent, to do; and Cameron, his deputy, who remains amongst them is daily encouraging them to defend their country against a parcel of Rebels. I heartily wish they may attack me; and it is the wish of the army. Cameron, being an awful man, may invent measures to delay our march if the Indians will execute them with dexterity; but I still have no doubt of returning to the Island in five weeks from this time, six at fartherest.[87]

They soon left for the French Broad River, which Christian desired to cross in less than two weeks. After that, they would be in position to attack the main Upper Villages along the Little Tennessee River. The colonel expected that the Cherokee would have warriors waiting to ambush him at the river's crossing. However, the aged chiefs of the Upper Towns had not been favorable to either Chief Skyuka's or Chief Dragging Canoe's assaults on the Overmountain settlements or those of the backcountry. Apparently, the Upper Villages were about to be included in the punishment—unless they could convince Colonel Christian of their sincerity.

Just before the army reached the ford at the French Broad River, Colonel Christian established a campsite. Raven of Chota sent out Ellis Harlan and Nathaniel Gist, white traders who had married into the Cherokee clans. Harlan was a die-hard Tory, while Gist was simply suspected of being one. Harlan informed Christian that the Cherokee warriors would not attack unless he crossed the Little Tennessee River to the south bank. Gist added that over 1,000 warriors, who had been driven from the Lower and Middle Villages, had joined Dragging Canoe's band. Then the two visitors passed Raven's request for peace terms along to the colonel. William Christian guided Harlan and Gist through the camp so they could see the military capability of the army. Harlan was told to deliver the following message to the Cherokee chiefs:

> How can you expect peace before you have delivered up to me Alexander Cameron, that enemy of the white men and the red? How can you ask for peace when you have assembled your men to fight me should you dislike my terms?
> I shall cross the river and come to your towns. I will distinguish between those towns which have behaved well toward us, and those which have not.[88]

At night the militiamen ignited campfires. Colonel Christian did not trust the overt peace overture from Raven. He wanted it to appear as if the militia had settled in for the night. During the night, he sent a large contingent of his force downriver where they crossed the French Broad, then returned up the far bank to where the colonel had expected an ambush. However, there were no warriors to be found.

(Colonel Nathaniel Gist lived with the Cherokee at the time of Christian's expedition. Gist had fought for the British as a Virginia militiaman during the French and Indian War. He had later been Virginia's Indian agent to deal with local Cherokee people who lived within the colony's borders. More recently, he had worked with Alexander Cameron to arm the Cherokee for the British in 1776. However, he had backed Henry Stuart who admonished the Cherokee to not fight the Overmountain settlers until the British could gather themselves after their failure at Charles Town.

(Gist had one son, George Gist, also known as Sequoya, who later would create the Cherokee alphabet. Colonel Gist was often suspected of spying for the Indians, and many of Christian's militiamen wanted him hanged.)

Harlan left with Christian's message to Raven, and Gist remained with the militia in case the colonel might choose to send another communication.

On October 15, William Christian wrote Virginia governor Patrick Henry about Gist: "I judge the flag was only an excuse for him to get with me. I believe he is sorry for what he has done."[89]

The militia crossed the French Broad and arrived at the Little Tennessee River. They crossed it with no difficulty on the 18th, and completely destroyed Tuskegee and Toque as punishment for the torture and burning of young Samuel Moore. By the evening of the 19th, the attackers established their headquarters at Mialoquo (Big Island Town), Dragging Canoe's old center of operations.

In the meantime, the Cherokee headmen held a council. Chiefs Oconostota and Attakullakulla suggested they hold a treaty conference with Colonel Christian to save the Upper Towns. Dragging Canoe and Alexander Cameron argued against the older chiefs' proposal. Dragging Canoe declared that the Cherokee should vacate the Upper Villages, move south, and fight the settlers to the end. The Cherokee were again divided: the hawks and the doves, the young and the aged. The doves (the older chiefs) had accomplished little in their decades-old effort for peace with the settlers other than ceding away millions of acres of Cherokee ancestral land. The hawks (the young aggressive chiefs) were ready to right the wrongs in the old traditional way of standing up to the encroachers. Meanwhile, Alexander Cameron was his old wishy-washy self, wavering between advocating attacks and suggesting delays. Chiefs Attakullakulla and Oconostota declared that the problems were caused by the young warriors who listened to Alexander Cameron and Dragging Canoe. White trader Caleb Starr, after asking permission to speak, addressed the council and bravely stated: "Make peace with Christian. The Cherokee cannot hope to defeat such a large and well-armed force of Americans. The Great Spirit has fore-ordained that the White Men will triumph over the Red Men ... resistance will be futile."[90]

The council voted for peace. Dragging Canoe, as he had done at Sycamore Shoals the previous year, stormed out of the council session. He was through talking with his father, Attakullakulla, and with Oconostota.

Dragging Canoe led his followers, young warriors from the Upper, Middle, and Lower villages, to Chickamauga Creek at the foot of present-day Lookout Mountain. The Creek had called the mountain Chatanuga. (Chickamauga Creek enters the Tennessee River in present-day Chattanooga, Tennessee, immediately west of the intersection of Amnicola Highway and Route 319 [DuPont Parkway]. Amnicola Highway crosses over Chickamauga Creek near its mouth. Chickamauga Town was sited upstream on South Chickamauga Creek between the Brainerd Hills subdivision and the Chattanooga Airport. Little Owl's Village is claimed to be farther upstream [south] on South Chickamauga Creek at present-day Audubon Acres, south of where the creek crosses under I-75. Little Owl was a brother of Dragging Canoe.)

The British superintendent of Indian affairs in the South, John Stuart, had a deputy agent named John McDonald who had lived in the vicinity of Lookout Mountain for six years. There, McDonald had established a trading post, mill, and British commissary to store supplies for the Cherokee on the bank of Chickamauga Creek. Chickamauga Town was settled very near McDonald's residence. (McDonald's property site, later the Brainerd Mission, was located in today's Chattanooga at the parking lot of Eastgate Mall, 5600 Brainerd Road, Chattanooga, Tennessee, north of the junction of I-75 and I-24. The old Brainerd Mission Cemetery is preserved and available for visitors on weekdays. McDonald's father-in-law was William Shorey, the interpreter who died aboard ship on the trip to England with Lieutenant Henry Timberlake in in 1762. See Chapter 5.)

McDonald operated a trading post on his property, so he was thrilled to welcome the young Cherokee to the area. The new settlement was called the Chickamauga settlement and Dragging Canoe's band became known as the Chickamauga Cherokee. Dragging Canoe believed that his faction represented the traditional Cherokee beliefs and that he would be the savior of the Cherokee way of life.

Seven years earlier, Chief Doublehead had already relocated with another rebellious faction to the Muscle Shoals on the Big Bend of the Tennessee River in Alabama (near present-day Florence, Alabama). The two factions would come to be considered Chickamauga Cherokee. Although they often operated independently, they would at times join forces for an expedition into the settlements.

Dragging Canoe's relocation further divided the young warriors from what the whites considered the mainstream Cherokee Nation. However, many people followed the young war chief which traditionally would indicate the people could have declared him the headman of the nation. Several of Dragging Canoe's brothers followed him, including Turtle At Home, The Badger, Little Owl, and Old Abram (Raven would join them later), as did his first cousin Long Fellow (Nancy Ward's brother). They left the Upper Towns before Christian reached the Little Tennessee River.

Raven again sent Ellis Harlan with a message for Colonel Christian. He informed the colonel of the council's vote and of Dragging Canoe's departure from the Upper Villages. Harlan then added that Alexander Cameron was trying to arrange for someone to kill him and Nathaniel Gist, suspecting them of working with the settlers.

Christian was prepared to attack the Upper Towns, but he sent Harlan back with a reply to Raven requesting the mainstream chiefs to come in for a parley.

The colonel then penned to Governor Henry:

> I wrote The Raven that, as he wishes to speak to me, I was now here and found that his nation would not fight; that I was willing to hear him and other Chiefs; that I did not come to war with women and children but to fight with men; that his people had better be on their guard because if they did not comply with my terms after seeing me I should see them safe from camp and then consider them as enemies.... Tomorrow I expect The Raven, Oconostota, The Carpenter and many others of the Chiefs, and I suppose in three days I can open a treaty or begin to destroy the towns and pursue the Indians toward the Creeks. I know, sir, that I could kill and take hundreds of them and starve hundreds by destroying their corn, but it would be mostly the women and children, as the men could retreat faster than I can follow, and I am convinced that Virginia State would be better pleased to hear that I showed pity to the distressed and spared the suppliants rather than I should commit one act of barbarity in destroying a whole nation of enemies. I believe that all the old warriors and all the women of the nation this side of the Hills [Appalachian Mountains] were adverse to the war, and that the rest were led by Cameron, sometimes by bribing them and at other times threatening them.[91]

Attakullakulla, Oconostota, and Raven came right away. Colonel William Christian told them that he also desired to speak with the young warrior faction. Oconostota replied that Alexander Cameron had gone to Florida to see John Stuart, and that Dragging Canoe had left the nation with his young chiefs and warriors. Christian then demanded that Cameron and Dragging Canoe be handed over or Dragging Canoe's scalp be provided. Oconostota replied that those who remained had always been against the war, and that neither he nor Attakullakulla had influence or control over Dragging Canoe. He asserted that the Cherokee Council should not be held responsible for the young warriors' raids. Christian posted rewards of £100 each for the capture of Alexander Cameron and Dragging Canoe, either dead or alive.

Christian burned three more towns that he suspected of complicity with Dragging Canoe's raids. The colonel agreed to end his campaign when Attakullakulla and Oconostota promised that they would be willing to schedule treaty talks as soon as all Upper Village headmen could meet in the spring. Colonel Christian accepted the promise of the Cherokee to "surrender all their prisoners and to cede all the disputed territory ... in the Tennessee settlements [to Virginia]."[92] He then scheduled a treaty council session for June 1777 to be held at Fort Patrick Henry at the Long Island of the Holston River between the Cherokee and the states of Virginia and North Carolina. Then he suspended hostilities and prepared to withdraw back to the fort. He spared the primary Upper Village of Echota, which he had originally intended to destroy.

The army returned to the fort in mid–November, and Colonel William Christian furloughed the militias, except for a company to garrison the stockade. Several of Christian's officers were irritated with him for his leniency with the Cherokee. They wanted to see the Cherokee more severely punished for the death and destruction caused in the backcountry and Overmountain settlements during Dragging Canoe's campaign. It seemed to make no difference to them that the Cherokee who would be punished would be those who were not involved. Colonel Joseph Williams returned to Surry County where, on November 22, 1776, he wrote the North Carolina legislature, as recorded by historian John Preston Arthur, "enclosing documents which he claimed proved conclusively 'that some of the Virginia gentlemen are desirous of having the Cherokees under their protection,' which Williams did not think right as most of the territory was within North Carolina and should be under her protection."

Williams further stated that all they accomplished was to burn five towns and patch together a quick peace. However, as Arthur explained: "In this warfare every Indian was scalped and even women were shot down and afterwards 'helped to their end.' Prisoners were 'taken and put up at auction as slaves, when not killed on the spot.'"[93]

Christian left Fort Patrick Henry in December and protected Nathaniel Gist as they rode to Virginia. Gist appealed to Governor Patrick Henry and declared that he was a Patriot. He was sorry that so many of the militiamen didn't trust him, and that many wanted him to be hanged. However, he continued that he simply tried to do what was in the best interest of the Cherokee people, and that, as a resident of the Upper Villages, he was always under the scrutiny of Alexander Cameron, so he had to be very careful in his actions. Depositions were entered on Nathaniel Gist's behalf by several Overmountain settlement leaders, including Colonel William Russell, Major Evan Shelby, and scout and trader Isaac Thomas, that Gist was a friend of America and not a Tory. Upon inquiry of a state council, he was exonerated on December 17, 1776, of aiding and abetting the Cherokee during the war of 1776. (The following January 11, Gist would be promoted to colonel on the Continental Line by General George Washington, who would assign him to participate in the coming peace treaty negotiation with the Cherokee at Long Island of the Holston River.)[94] Following Colonel Christian's departure, Alexander Cameron returned to the Upper Villages and warned Attakullakulla and Oconostota not to sign any treaties with the colonies at the risk of losing British trade.

During the devastating Cherokee Campaign, Colonel Andrew Williamson's forces lost 100 men. That paled against the estimated tragic Cherokee losses set at 2,000. The Williamson Campaign was brutal. It paralyzed the Cherokee Nation. The total number of militiamen involved from South and North Carolina, Georgia, and Virginia was 6,000. More than 50 villages had been burned, the crops destroyed, and the cattle killed or driven off. Five major battles had been won against large Cherokee war parties. As historian John Preston Arthur noted above, Cherokee fatalities included warriors, women, and children. Also, those who were killed were scalped. Those who were wounded were finished off. Others died of starvation or exposure. Several had been captured and auctioned as slaves. Seventy to 80 Cherokee scalps were turned in to the South Carolina legislature for the £75 bounty. Those who escaped had to survive the winter in the mountains scavenging for acorns, chestnuts, and what game they could kill. Realizing their ammunition was in very short supply, they had to rely on their old art of using bows and arrows, which had not been the case for many years.[95]

Historian James Mooney stated a key point: "Realizing their common danger, the border states determined to strike such a concerted blow at the Cherokee as should render them passive while the struggle with England continued."[96]

The Cherokee had allied with Britain supposedly in return for protection against the Overmountain encroachment. However, as in the past, the affiliation was one-sided. The British were only interested in having the Cherokee attack the southern colonies' backcountry settlements. They played upon the young Cherokee warriors' ire with the Virginians and drew them toward the conflict in the Carolina backcountry by threatening to cut off arms and ammunition. The older Cherokee chiefs believed that the British would honor reciprocity by shooing the settlers out of the Cherokee Nation; however, the British had no inclination to spend valuable manpower on the Indians' problem. The Cherokee were left on their own.

The younger chiefs became fed up with the older chiefs' casual approach to white intrusion. They watched as four major treaties were made between 1768 and 1773, each one ceding more land to the whites. The Treaty of Sycamore Shoals in 1775 was the final straw. Cherokee custom required headmen to gather in council and give ear to all who wished to speak. The majority of chiefs present were younger and more aggressive. They were also the contingent most concerned with maintaining Cherokee tradition. They were willing to defend the land, but the older chiefs, who could no longer fight, gave it up anyway. The younger tribal members would have to live with the results of the elders' decisions, so the dynamic young warriors had no choice but to withdraw from the mainstream nation and act on their own. They were the only ones left who could stand up to the Watauga, Holston, Nolichucky, and Carter's Valley settlements.

King George's Proclamation of 1763 was designed to prevent encroachment onto Indian land; however, as sincere as the royal monarch may have been, his colonial representatives could not, and would not, enforce his edict.

Those Overmountain settlements in present-day Tennessee were located where no existing government had the manpower to govern. Indeed, one primary reason the settlers moved into those areas was to escape the thumb of colonial government, either British or American. Present-day eastern Tennessee had been settled mainly by Virginians who, supposedly, thought they were still within that colony's borders. North Carolina had, off and on, also claimed jurisdiction over the territory. Later, the region was officially declared a part of North Carolina, but North Carolina couldn't afford to administer it and tried to give it to the Continental Congress. The problem was the location. It was too expensive for either North Carolina or Virginia to govern as it was so far from the coast where the major population centers were at the time.

Neither of the colonies had sufficient manpower to expend on either civil law enforcement in that area, or on intercessions in conflicts between the settlers and the Indians. That echoed the British problem. The British didn't even have the manpower in the southern army to enforce laws in the Georgia or Carolina backcountry let alone the Overmountain settlements.

Historian James Mooney tried to justify Cherokee thinking for attacking the backcountry settlements for the British. He wrote: "There was good reason for this. Since the fall of the French power the British government had stood to them as the sole representative of authority, and the guardian and protector of their rights against constant encroachments by the American borderers."[97]

However, there is not one instance in the 13 years, from the time of the Royal Proclamation of 1763 to the beginning of the American Revolution, that the British government, or specifically the British military, ever came to the aid of the Cherokee Nation when settlers encroached. Additionally, these encroachers were not only the rebels but included many Loyalists. The primary reason this occurred was that the older chiefs had gained much influence over the years with their pro–British politics. Had these same chiefs given in to the backers of trade with the French or the Spanish, who were willing to offer it, they would not have retained their influence among the people. Other chiefs who favored different alliances were ignored and had not been able to sway the majority of the people. The influence of the younger chiefs, who recognized the folly of continually ceding land to the settlements in treaty after treaty, finally drew warriors and their families to resist. A conundrum developed because of the rift in the Cherokee community. The British colonial governments continued to deal with the older chiefs as the tribal authority; however, the Royal British Indian agents assisted the rebellious younger chiefs.

The mainstream Cherokee community was in a desperate situation. The young warriors could attack the encroaching Overmountain settlements, and the settlers were at liberty to punish the mainstream chiefs because they were recognized as the Cherokee leaders, but the prevailing older chiefs were no longer powerful enough to control the young rebellious leaders, so they suffered the price.

Mooney goes on to say that another good reason the Cherokee allied with the British had been that licensed British traders resided within the villages and intermarried, and thus became a part of Cherokee society. However, that is one Cherokee tradition that had been overdone. There had always been a tradition to allow members of other tribes to intermarry and become a part of the Cherokee Nation. In fact, it was a requirement if an outsider wanted to dwell within the nation for a time. Rather than a good reason for the alliance, it was really a good reason for avoidance of such close relationships with the British. The custom was in place so that permanent visitors would be assimilated into the Cherokee clans; however, since so many white traders took advantage of the practice for their own gain, the result was the Cherokee assimilated themselves into the British influence by broadening the practice.

The Cherokee war of 1776 was very bitter for the Indians. Had the Cherokee ignored the British regarding attacks in the backcountry of the Carolinas and Georgia, it is doubtful that those colonies would have moved against them. They had enough concerns of their own when they realized the British wanted to move against the south. The response of those colonies was so devastating for the Cherokee that they didn't totally ally with the British throughout the remainder of the American Revolution. The Chickamauga Cherokee factions did work closely with notorious Tories, such as, Colonel Thomas "Burn Foot" Brown, Captain Richard Pearis, and Captain William "Bloody Bill" Cuningham (sometimes Cunningham). Their enemies were the same settlers, so the Tories were happy to help the Chickamauga Cherokee.

The coming treaties (one between the Cherokee and the Virginians and North Carolinians; the other between the Cherokee and the South Carolinians) would not last because the Chickamauga Cherokee factions were not parties to them. In fact, chiefs Dragging Canoe and Doublehead had hardly begun to fight.[98]

Chapter 7

DeWitt's Corner and Long Island of the Holston

The Cherokee War of 1776 amounted to an expedition of punishment against the Cherokee Nation for British-inspired Cherokee attacks in the colonial backcountry. The British did not offer assistance to the Cherokee to eject encroachers from the northeast who were settling ever closer to the Upper Villages. The British had convinced the Cherokee to assist against the coastal colonies but declined to defend the Cherokee villages when the colonies exacted vengeance. Indeed, Major General Sir Henry Clinton had arranged for the Cherokee to initiate their incursion on July 1, 1776, which they did. The British pre-arranged to attack Charles Town from the sea at the same time to put a pincer move on the rebellious colony of South Carolina. The British were not there, and the Cherokee were left to their own devices. The British had launched their invasion early and had been expelled from the South Carolina coast before the Cherokee had complied with their agreement—on time. The British-Cherokee alliance had exhibited a lack of reciprocity at the expense of the Indians.

The harsh chastisement of the Cherokee was over by the end of 1776. Two treaties were signed between the colonies and the Cherokee Nation in 1777 to end the dispute. The parties, as in the past, were colonial authorities and the older Cherokee chiefs. The colonials, however, for the first time were Whigs and not the royal representatives. The younger, more militant chiefs boycotted the treaty sessions. They apparently understood that the Cherokee were not "children of the Great King" as Chief Attakullakulla had so often referred to them. The revolutionary colonists had learned that same lesson for themselves, but sadly, they would try to fill the void left by Britain in the coming accords and represent fatherhood to the Cherokee. Affairs did not improve. The older chiefs were frail and dying but continued to negotiate with the colonists. They persistently ceded more land. The younger chiefs had learned their lesson. They would try to deter a policy that would allow the new white leaders to adopt the same tactics as the British. Thus, the young warriors became more militant and totally estranged from the leaders in the Upper Villages.

Cherokee Chief Oconostota, who had been the most formidable and respected of the older Cherokee war chiefs, surrendered in October 1776. The chiefs of the Upper Villages presumed to speak for the entire Cherokee Nation and agreed to send a delegation to Long Island of the Holston River to sue for peace (meaning, more land cessions). There, on March 20, 1777, Principal Chief Attakullakulla led the representation to meet a contingent of Virginia commissioners. The group of 85 included several older chiefs. The meeting was adjourned because Dragging Canoe had boycotted the event.

The war had been fought on several fronts for the Cherokee, the earlier against South Carolina major Andrew Williamson, who led the South Carolina militias against the Lower Villages. Shortly thereafter, North Carolina general Griffith Rutherford staged a parallel attack against the Middle Villages, which assault was followed by Virginia colonel William Christian's foray against the Upper Towns. Then, Williamson and Rutherford united to extend their attacks against the Valley Towns. Hence, the Cherokee had to sue for peace with Virginia and North Carolina separately from South Carolina and Georgia. They really had no choice because the war had devastated the nation. They had no crops, their villages were destroyed, and they had no ammunition with which to fight. In short, they had no negotiating position.

In May, Principal Chief Attakullakulla and War Chief Oconostota, with 38 other Cherokee, visited Virginia governor Patrick Henry in Williamsburg. Henry asked the Cherokee to become their allies against the British; however, Attakullakulla stated they could not fight against "our Father, King George." He continued, "Colonel Christian promised that if we would make peace, we might remain neutral."[1] Some members of the Cherokee delegation told Governor Henry that, if they would schedule a follow-up treaty conference for June or July, Chief Dragging Canoe would likely attend. However, Attakullakulla privately informed Virginia commissioner Thomas Price that his son would never take part in such a meeting.

Concurrent to Attakullakulla's visit to Governor Henry, War Chief Ostenaco led a delegation of eight chiefs to DeWitt's Corner in South Carolina. Ostenaco, like Attakullakulla, had grown old, and this was to be his last major act. This Treaty of DeWitt's Corner was signed on May 20, 1777. Andrew Williamson, who had recently been promoted to colonel in the South Carolina Militia, was signatory for the colony of South Carolina along with Colonel Leroy Hammond, George Galphin, Esq., the Honorable William Henry Drayton, and Colonel Daniel Horry. (DeWitt's Corner was located on the Little River, just west of where present-day State Highway 20 crosses from Anderson to Abbeville County, north of the Little River Bridge, and 0.3 miles south of the junction of State Highway 20 with Sauer Farm Road. It was also recorded as Due's Corner, Dewes Corner, and Dewees Corner after a Tory-aligned Indian trader, named Robert Due or Dew, who had estab-

Chief Ostenaco, by Sir Joshua Reynolds, 1762.

lished a trading post at the location. DeWitt's Corner was also nearly on the old Cherokee-South Carolina boundary line that existed prior to the war.)

A Georgia delegation attended the conference; however, the articles of the agreement do not indicate any cessions by the Cherokee to that state. The articles itemized land cessions to South Carolina, provisions for South Carolina to provide trade goods to ease the suffering upon the badly-defeated Indian Nation, and a requirement for the Cherokee to deliver any and all white prisoners to the states of South Carolina, North Carolina, Georgia, and Virginia. The Cherokee ceded approximately one million acres to South Carolina at the signing. Historian Dr. J.B.O. Landrum briefly described: "In the conquest of 1776-'7, they ceded to South Carolina their lands east of the Unakaye Mountains, reserving to themselves the territory which now comprises, for the most part, the present county of Oconee."[2]

The South Carolina land retained by the tribe amounted to a very narrow strip along the Chattooga River. The Chattooga marks the boundary between northwestern South Carolina and northeastern Georgia before it joins the Tugaloo and heads for the Savannah. This loss included all of the major settlements of the Lower Villages except for the few along the Chattooga.

The Lower and Middle Town Cherokee were upset that the older Upper Town Chiefs had ceded the villages where they did not even live. Tradition held that each Cherokee town was self-reliant and each village's headman could negotiate its own treaties; however, in the case of the 1776 war, the Lower Villages had succumbed to the influence of British deputy Indian agent Alexander Cameron and attacked the backcountry of South Carolina. Apparently, that was sufficient for the Lower Villages to lose their negotiating authority. Thus, Ostenaco was the authority for the Cherokee at the conference. The Cherokee of the Lower Villages became refugees, and many of the younger warriors defected to Dragging Canoe's new community near present-day Chattanooga and followed the path of the Chickamauga Cherokee (see Chapter 8).

The prisoner exchange apparently resulted in the return of Anne Calhoun, Rebecca Calhoun Pickens' cousin who had been captured in the Long Canes Massacre of 1759 (see Chapter 4). It has often been reported that she was nine years old when returned, and sometimes 19 years old; however, she was born in May 1755, so was likely nearly 23. The timing seems appropriate regarding her age because she spoke no English and was well-established in Cherokee culture. Her marriage to Isaac Mathews did not occur until late 1784 when she was 29 years old. Andrew Pickens is often credited with negotiating the release of his wife's cousin. He was not a signatory at DeWitt's Corner but may have been on Williamson's staff. Regardless, he could have taken the articles of the treaty to negotiate for Anne's return. Likely Chief Skyuka (Skiuka) of the Lower Villages was involved in the treaty negotiation even though Chief Ostenaco from the Upper Villages was the Cherokee lead. Skyuka knew the Pickens family very well (see Chapter 6), and it is possible Andrew Pickens dealt with him on behalf of the Calhoun family. Skyuka likely had led the Long Canes Massacre in 1759.

Delegates began to arrive at Long Island of the Holston as early as April 1777. The Virginia commissioners were Colonels William Preston, William Christian, and Evan Shelby. Those from North Carolina included Colonels Waightstill Avery and Joseph Winston as well as state legislators William Sharpe and Robert Lanier. Several hundred Cherokee drifted into the area over the next few weeks. The commissioners began to meet with Attakullakulla in June, and Oconostota arrived on June 30, 1777. John McCormack, who lived north of the Holston, was to act as the interpreter.

On July 10, Raven of Chota (Colonah, the son of Attakullakulla and brother of Chickamauga Chief Dragging Canoe) arrived at the site. Chief Willenawah and his son Old Tassel (the brother of Chickamauga warrior Chief Doublehead) arrived the same day.

Principal Chief Attakullakulla, being aged, selected Old Tassel to speak for him. Oconostota selected Raven of Chota to be his orator for the same reason. Another aged chief, Ostenaco (Judge Friend), who had been handling the Treaty of DeWitt's Corner, did not attend the Treaty of Holston; rather, he retired to the Chickamauga country to live out his days with chiefs Dragging Canoe and Doublehead.

The conference nearly ended before it started. An unidentified white man killed a Cherokee named Big Bullet. The chiefs who were present, as well as those who arrived later, were distressed with that event. The white commissioners were angered and promised to do all they could to find the culprit and punish him. They also lavished many gifts for the clan of the deceased to fulfill the Cherokee policy of retribution. It is reported that the commissioners levied a reward of $600 for the capture of Big Bullet's killer. Big Bullet has been labeled as a Cherokee warrior and also as the 16-year-old half-blood son of John McCormack. Either or both of those descriptions could be accurate. Joseph Vann signed the final agreement as interpreter rather than McCormack (which would make sense if he were grieving).

The chiefs broached the subject of Big Bullet two or three times over the next several days. They interjected that they did not blame any one of the commissioners, only the perpetrator of the act, and they desired that the commissioners be successful in their search for the slayer. The prime suspect was a settler named Robert Young. His 15-year-old brother, Charles, had killed a wounded warrior named Big Sagwa when Dragging Canoe attacked Eaton's Station near Long Island of the Holston in July 1776 (see Chapter 6). Charles Young had been killed before the action ceased. Robert Young sought vengeance against any Cherokee he could. He was never apprehended.

Many years later, Robert Young admitted to Valentine Sevier that he did the shooting in revenge for his brother. Big Bullet had simply set up camp on an island well away from the main Indian encampment, so was an easy target. He was mending his moccasins when Young slew him.

On May 13, 1777, Colonel William Christian opened the conference. He stated that he was sorry that Ostenaco, Dragging Canoe, and Young Tassel (John Watts, Jr.) were not in attendance. (John Watts, Jr., aka Kunokeski or Young Tassel, was the mixed-blood son of Wurteh, sister to Chickamauga warrior Chief Doublehead and to Old Tassel, an orator at the conference. Watts was called Young Tassel in respect for his uncle, Old Tassel, to whom he was very close.)

On May 20, Raven rose and spoke. During his opening oration he stated that his grievances were years old; however, he admitted that he had received bad advice from Alexander Cameron and Henry Stuart. He regretted having followed it (apparently the advice to attack the Carolina backcountry).

Much oration and debate took place over the next few days. Raven and Old Tassel were reluctant to accept the proposed boundary proffered by the commissioners. On June 17, Old Tassel stood and spoke: "If this and another house were packed full of goods they would not make satisfaction. The giving up of this territory would spoil the hunting ground of my people. I hope you will consider this, and pity me; you require a thing I cannot do."[3]

Old Tassel went on to say, as translated by William Tatum (sometimes spelled Tatham or Tathum):

> It is a little surprising that when we entered into the treaties with our brothers, the whites, their whole cry is more land! Indeed, formerly it seemed to be a matter of formality with them to demand what they knew we durst not refuse. But on the principles of fairness, of which we have received assurances during the conducting of the present treaty, and in the name of free will and equality, I must reject your demand.
>
> Suppose, in considering the nature of your claim (and in justice to my nation I shall and will do it freely), I were to ask one of you, my brother warriors, under what kind of authority, by what law, or on what pretense he makes this exorbitant demand of nearly all the lands we hold between your settlements and our towns, as the cement and consideration of our peace.
>
> Would he tell me that it is by the right of Conquest? No! If he did, I should retort on him that we had last marched over his territory; even up to this very place which he has fortified so far within his former limits; nay, that some of our young warriors (who we have not yet had an opportunity to recall or give notice to, of the general treaty) are still in the woods, and continue to keep his people in fear, and that it was but till lately that these identical walls were your strongholds, out of which you durst scarcely advance.
>
> If, therefore, a bare march, or reconnoitering a country is sufficient reason to ground a claim to it, we shall insist upon transposing the demand, and your relinquishing your settlements on the western waters and removing one hundred miles back towards the east, whither some of our warriors advanced against you in the course of last year's campaign.
>
> Let us examine the facts of your present eruption into our country, and we shall discover your pretentions on that ground. What did you do? You marched into our territories with a superior force; our vigilance gave us no timely notice of your manouvres [sic]; your numbers far exceeded us, and we fled to the stronghold of our existence in the woods, there to secure our women and children.
>
> Thus, you marched into our towns; they were left to your mercy; you killed a few scattered and defenseless individuals, spread fire and desolation wherever you pleased, and returned again to your own habitations. If you meant this, indeed, as a conquest you omitted the most essential point; you should have fortified the junction of the Holston and Tennessee rivers, and have thereby conquered all the waters above you. But, as all are fair advantages during the existence of a state of war, it is now too late for us to suffer for your mishap of generalship!
>
> Again, were we to inquire by what law or authority you set up a claim, I answer, none! Your laws extend not into our country, nor ever did. You talk of the law of nature and the law of nations, and they are both against you.
>
> Indeed, much has been advanced on the want of what you term civilization among the Indians; and many proposals have been made to us to adopt your laws, your religion, your manners and your customs. But, we confess that we do not yet see the propriety, or practicality of such a reformation, and should be better pleased with beholding the good effect of these doctrines in your own practices than with hearing you talk about them, or reading your papers to us upon such subjects.
>
> You say: Why do not the Indians till the ground and live as we do? May we not, with equal propriety, ask, Why the white people do not hunt and live as we do? You profess to think it no injustice to warn us not to kill our deer and other game from the mere love of waste; but it is very criminal in our young men if they chance to kill a cow or a hog for their sustenance when they happen to be in your lands. We wish, however, to be at peace with you, and to do as we would be done by. We do not quarrel with you for killing an occasional buffalo, bear or deer on our lands when you need one to eat; but you go much

farther; your people hunt to gain a livelihood by it; they kill all our game; our young men resent the injury, and it is followed by bloodshed and war.

This is not a mere affected injury; it is a grievance which we equitably complain of and it demands a permanent redress.

The great God of Nature has placed us in different situations. It is true that he has endowed you with many superior advantages; but he has not created us to be your slaves. We are a separate people! He has given each their lands, under distinct considerations and circumstances; he has stocked yours with cows, ours with buffaloe [sic]; yours with hogs, ours with bear; yours with sheep, ours with deer. He has, indeed, given you an advantage in this, that your cattle are tame and domestic while ours are wild and demand not only a larger space for range, but art to hunt and kill them; they are, nevertheless, as much our property as other animals are yours, and ought not to be taken away without our consent, or for something equivalent.[4]

Eventually Old Tassel agreed to the boundary after some discussion with other chiefs. Also: "With a little variation the line proposed by Virginia, was agreed to by the Raven, after consulting with the other Indians. He wished it to be as a wall to the skies, so that it should [be] out of the power of all people to pass it."[5]

The Cherokee Chiefs, especially Raven, had lobbied for gifts in exchange for the ceded land; however, North Carolina offered no trade goods but declared the cession was payment for the expense of defending the state in the war that was started by the Cherokee. Virginia offered only 100 head of sheep and 200 head of cattle to alleviate the suffering of the Cherokee following the devastation.

Following the articles of the treaty, the following notations were made ahead of the signatures:

In testimony of all and singular the above articles and agreements the parties aforesaid have hereunto set their hands and seals in open treaty the day and year above written [July 20, 1777].

Read, interpreted and ratified in the Great Island opposite to the fort.

Memorandum before signing, That the Tassel yesterday objected against giving up the Great Island opposite to Fort Henry, to any person or country whatsoever, except colonel Nathaniel Gist, for whom and themselves it was reserved by the Cherokees.

The Raven did the same this day in behalf of the Indians and desired that colonel Gist might sit down upon it when he pleased, as it belonged to him and them to hold good talks on.[6]

(Nathaniel Gist had at one time been accused of being a Tory and militantly involved with the Cherokee against the Virginians during the war [see Chapter 6] but had been cleared and thereafter worked diligently on behalf of the Patriots during the American Revolution. He also worked tirelessly to assure peace between the settlers and the Cherokee. Nathaniel Gist was married to Wurteh Watts, daughter of Wurteh who was the sister of Doublehead and Old Tassel. Wurteh Watts was the sister of Young Tassel [John Watts, Jr.] and she was also married to Robert Due [of DeWitt's Corner], Bloody Fellow [Nenetooyah], and John Benge [father of Bench or Bob Benge who, along with Young Tassel, would become the future of the rebellious Chickamauga Cherokee]. Nathaniel Gist and Wurteh Watts were the parents of George Gist [Sequoya] who would be the creator of the Cherokee alphabet. Sequoya was then half-brother to Bench and to Nettle Carrier [Tahlonteskee].)

Article V of the Treaty of Holston specified the new boundary as:

That the boundary line between the state of North-Carolina and the said Overhill Cherokees shall forever hereafter be and remain as follows, (to wit:) Beginning at a point in the dividing line which during this treaty hath been agreed upon between the said Overhill Cherokees and the state of Virginia, where the line between that state and North Carolina (hereafter to be extended) shall cross or intersect the same, running thence a right line to the north bank of Holston river [sic] at the mouth of Cloud's Creek, being the second creek below the Warrior's ford at the mouth of Carter's Valley, thence a right line to the highest point of a mountain called the High Rock or Chimney Top, from thence a right line to the mouth of Camp Creek, otherwise called McNamas Creek, on the south bank of Nolichucky River, about ten miles or thereabouts below the mouth of Great Limestone, be the same more or less and from the mouth of Camp Creek aforesaid, a south east course into the mountains which divide the hunting grounds of the middle settlements from those of the Overhill Cherokees. And the said Overhill Cherokees in behalf of themselves, their heirs and successors, do hereby freely in open treaty, acknowledge and confess, that all the lands to the east, north east and south east of the said line, and lying south of the said line of Virginia, at any time heretofore claimed by the said Overhill Cherokees, do of right now belong to the state of North Carolina, and the said subscribing Chiefs, in behalf of the said Overhill Cherokees, their heirs and successors, do hereby in open treaty, now and forever, relinquish and give up to the said state and forever quit claim all right, title, claim and demand of, in and to the land comprehended in the state of North Carolina by the line aforesaid.[7]

The new boundary brought the total cession of Cherokee land between the two treaties (including DeWitt's Corner) to five million acres; a heavy price for following the desires of British Indian agents Alexander Cameron and John and Henry Stuart.

During the session, North Carolina appointed Watauga Militia captain James Robertson to be its temporary Indian agent and to

> repair to Chota in company with the warriors returning from the treaty, there to reside till otherwise ordered by the governor. He was to discover if possible, the disposition of the Dragging Canoe towards this treaty, as also, of Judge Friend, the Lying Fish and others, who did not attend it, and whether there was any danger of a renewal of hostilities by one or more of these chiefs. He was also to find out the conversations between the Cherokees and the southern, western and northern tribes of Indians. He was to search in all the Indian towns for persons disaffected to the American cause, and have them brought before some justice of the peace, to take the oath of fidelity to the United States, and in case of refusal to deal with them as the law directed. Travelers into the Indian nation without passes, such as the third article of the treaty required, were to be

Brigadier General Joseph Martin, **by Rembrandt Peale, 1780.**

secured. He was immediately to get into possession all the horses, cattle and other property, belonging to the people of North Carolina, and to cause them to be restored to their respective owners. He was to inform the government of all occurrences worthy of notice, to conduct himself with prudence and to obtain the favor and confidence of the chiefs; and in all matters with respect to which, he was not particularly instructed, he was to exercise his own discretion, always keeping in view the honor and interest of the United States in general, and of North Carolina in particular.[8]

On November 3, 1777, Colonel Joseph Martin was selected as agent and superintendent of Indian Affairs for the State of Virginia. He married Elizabeth "Betsy" Ward, daughter of Cherokee Ghighau Nancy Ward, and settled on Long Island of the Holston where he established a storehouse of supplies for the Cherokee. He also maintained a home at Chota.

The Cherokee chiefs who made their marks on the Treaty of Holston on July 20, 1777, were: "Oconostata [sic], of Chota; Reyetaeh, or the Old Tassel of Toquoa; Savanukah, or the Raven of Chota; Willanawas [sic], of Toquoa; Ootosseteh, of Hiawassee; Attusah, or the Northward Warrior of the mouth of Tellico River; Ooskuah, or Abram of Chilhowee; Rollowah, or the Raven from the mouth of Tellies River; Toostooh, from the mouth of Tellies River; Amoyah, or the Pigeon of Natchey Creek; Ootossetih, or the Mankiller of Hiwassee; Tillehaweh, or the Chesnut [sic] of Tellies; Queeleekah of Hiwassee; Annakehujah, or the Girl of Tuskega; Annecekah of Tuskega; Skeahtukah of Citico; AttaKullaKulla, or the Little Carpenter of Nachey [sic] Creek; Ookoonekah or the White Owl of Natchey Creek; Kataquilla or Pot Clay of Chilhowee; Tuskasah (Tuckaseh) or the Terrapin of Chilestooch; Sunnewauh of Big Island Town." (Savanukah and Abram were sons of Attakullakulla. Likely, White Owl was also Little Owl, another son of Attakullakulla. White Owl was the headman of Natchey Creek before he withdrew to the Chickamauga. Terrapin was a son of Oconostota, though some confuse the name with Attakullakulla's son, Turtle At Home. White Owl had been an earlier name for Attakullakulla and Little Owl was well enough known that Colonel William Christian would have noted his absence when he noted that of Dragging Canoe and Young Tassel.)[9]

The dynamics of the Cherokee relationship with the British and with the settlers was ever changing. In the 1730s, when Attakullakulla and his fellow chiefs were young, the expectation of having an alliance, whether for trade or military assistance, with the British was that the British would treat the Cherokee as equal partners as any neighboring Indian tribe would do for an ally. The British never did look upon the Cherokee as anything close to equals but more as a tool as they did in the French and Indian War. Even then, on the front lines in the north, the British officers held the Cherokee leaders in disdain. Some of those experiences led to the earlier wars with South Carolina of 1759, 1760, and 1761 when South Carolina governor William Henry Lyttleton, British colonel Archibald Montgomery, and lastly British lieutenant colonel James Grant launched devastating successive annual attacks on the Cherokee Nation (see Chapter 4).

This should have been the second clue to the Cherokee that something was amiss in their relationship with the British. The first was the obvious unsavory trade practice of many British colonial traders. Several of the Upper Village chiefs at that time tried to direct the associations of the Cherokee more toward the French and possibly the Spanish. The French actively pursued agreements with the Cherokee through the Creek, already French allies. The Creek had pointed out that the French were not encroachers as were the British.

Attakullakulla had been the impetus behind the continued pacts with the British. He truly believed that the British were well meaning and that kings George II and III were like fathers to the Cherokee. Attakullakulla was very dependent upon maintaining strong British relationships to preserve his influence with the Cherokee people. By the time he began to question the motives of the British colonial leaders, it was too late. The French and Indian War had ended, and France was relegated to holding only a small portion of land along the Mississippi River and could not offer the Cherokee the same level of support that would have been available earlier. They could still supply some ammunition but not on any scale that would be obvious to the British. Additionally, the Spanish were no longer in the picture. At the 1763 Treaty of Paris, Spain ceded its Florida rights to Britain in exchange for the rights to Havana and Manila.

Finally, though Attakullakulla had recently stated to Virginia governor Patrick Henry that he could not fight against the British and wished to remain neutral, Attakullakulla seemed to have had a change of heart. Overmountain trader and settler John Carter wrote a letter to North Carolina governor Richard Caswell on September 7, 1777, wherein he stated: "I just received intelligence of the Little Carpenter [Attakullakulla].... They declare the greatest friendship ... say they have five hundred young warriors ready to come to the assistance of Virginia or North Carolina ... to fight the English or any Indians."[10]

However, a few months later, John Stuart reported that Attakullakulla made a similar comment about fighting against the Americans. Attakullakulla would not live much longer.

At the beginning of the 1776 Cherokee War, it was becoming obvious to Dragging Canoe that the British were not the saviors of the Cherokee. He only tolerated Alexander Cameron and the Stuart brothers because they were his only source for ammunition. His relationship with them was tenuous at best. Those Indian agents needed to keep Dragging Canoe happy because he could be a valuable resource for them during the coming Revolutionary War. It was a game. The Indian agents wanted Dragging Canoe to leave the Overmountain settlers alone because a large number of them were valuable Tories. They also wanted the Cherokee to act against the backcountry Carolinians. Dragging Canoe was not interested in attacking the backcountry of the coastal colonies. He wanted the Overmountain settlers off of what he recognized as Cherokee land. The attacks that initiated the war in the backcountry were begun by the Lower and Middle Villages with assistance from the mainstream Upper Villages. Dragging Canoe launched his initial attacks (much to the despair of John Stuart and Alexander Cameron) against the Overmountain settlers in concert with attacks that the other Cherokee warriors were waging in the backcountry. This was futile. Had the Lower and Middle Cherokee warriors ignored Alexander Cameron and joined with Dragging Canoe, they would likely have met with some success in his 1776 attacks in the encroaching settlements. Additionally, had they done so, they likely would not have drawn the Carolinians and Georgians into the war of 1776.

One might suppose Dragging Canoe's source for ammunition would have dried up. It nearly did anyway, but he would not have needed as much support in that instance. Had he been successful in his 1776 attacks, the Chickamauga war against the encroachers may not have dragged on to no avail, as was about to happen. Eventually the Cherokee would have lost to the whites' ever-increasing interest in their land, but they would have demanded a severe price for it.

Dragging Canoe and Doublehead were about to intensify their separation from the

Upper Villages. They were disappointed in the older chiefs, but not antagonistic. There would be no war between the Chickamauga and the mainstream. Whether those in the Upper Villages wanted it or not, the Chickamauga took to heart the responsibility of returning the Cherokee Nation to its principles. Dragging Canoe believed that his father, Attakullakulla, and the other older chiefs were no longer capable of standing up to the encroachers. The Chickamauga would be joined by many young warriors from the Upper Villages as well as many refugee warriors from the Lower and Middle Towns.

Doublehead and Dragging Canoe would settle areas that were several miles apart and would lead separate factions of Chickamauga Cherokee. Doublehead's group was made up of his initial Cherokee followers plus a large group of disaffected Creek warriors. Dragging Canoe would be joined by his brothers, and by such youthful leaders as Young Tassel (John Watts, Jr.), Bench (Bob Benge), Bloody Fellow, and others. These two factions would not war with each other, would usually initiate separate expeditions, but sometimes would cooperate in joint actions. They would also be joined by several Shawnee warriors.

The time for the Chickamauga Cherokee to try and salvage the reputation, the hunting grounds, and the old traditions of the Cherokee Nation was at hand—as was Dragging Canoe's 1775 promise of a "dark and bloody settlement."[11]

Chapter 8

The Time of the Chickamauga

The Cherokee and the colonies had just negotiated the Treaties of DeWitt's Corner and Long Island of the Holston. Attakullakulla and Oconostota had initiated the latter when, in May 1777, they led a delegation of 40 Cherokee to Williamsburg, Virginia, to follow up on the requirements set by Virginia colonel William Christian at the end of the 1776 war (see Chapter 7). The delegation included several Cherokee headmen, some warriors, and a few women. (Some report that Savanooka [Raven of Chota] was a part of the delegation. He was still "rolling the thread from both ends" trying to keep his options open to join the Chickamauga or to make a move and take over the Upper Villages in place of aging chiefs Attakullakulla, Oconostota, and Ostenaco). They camped on the lawn of the Capitol and requested an audience with Governor Patrick Henry. The governor met with Attakullakulla and Oconostota who suggested the treaty be held at Holston. Attakullakulla indicated they would be willing to cede more Cherokee land in the interest of peace. Of course, the State of Virginia was elated at such a proposal. The two treaties were the first between the Cherokee and the Americans; however, that inauspicious beginning was no different than deals with the British colonies had been—peace would be contingent upon Cherokee land made available for the settlers.

It should have become apparent to Attakullakulla much earlier that his dream of a cooperative relationship with either the British colonists or the Americans had not panned out as he had hoped, that of the whites treating the Cherokee as equals, as the proud people they were. However, Attakullakulla had spent his life trying to make that happen, so he would not relinquish the idea.

Chiefs Doublehead and Dragging Canoe, on the other hand, had taken the burden upon themselves to force the whites to realize that the Cherokee were a people to be reckoned with and could not be dismissed so easily. They were about to put their hearts and souls into the effort.

Dragging Canoe continued his bloody raids against the Holston and Clinch River settlements. He had expanded his raids into present-day western Virginia which caught the attention of Governor Patrick Henry and influenced his decision to schedule the treaty.

Dragging Canoe (Attakullakulla's estranged son) openly declared his intention to ally with Deputy British Indian agent Alexander Cameron and fight the encroaching settlers (Watauga, Nolichucky, Holston, and Cumberland). However, reliance upon British assistance was a problem. Cameron could not supply any British soldiers, so it was still a one-sided alliance. He could supply a limited amount of ammunition and could lead Tories who would be willing to fight with Dragging Canoe anyway. Cameron had no remaining relationship with the Upper Village chiefs and had threatened to cut off British supplies and trade goods if Attakullakulla followed up on his recent declaration to assist the Americans against the British.

Dragging Canoe led "hundreds of the most warlike and implacable warriors."[1] in the Cherokee Nation. Certainly Attakullakulla could not raise a comparable force of fierce warriors to fight against anybody considering his recent promises to each side, the Americans and the British. After the severe losses in the 1776 war, the Chickamauga chief withdrew his band farther away from the Upper Villages during the winter and settled on Chickamauga Creek near present-day Chattanooga, Tennessee—the inspiration of the designation "Chickamauga Cherokee." Many young warriors were initially drawn to him and, in 1777, warriors from the impoverished Upper Villages, the Valley Towns, and the warrior refugees of the Lower and Middle Towns followed.

The mainstream Cherokee Nation thought of Doublehead's and Dragging Canoe's villages as simply another set of Cherokee settlements much like the Valley Towns and the Middle Towns. Mostly, the various communities operated independently. However, the distinction of the hawkish politics of the rebellious younger chiefs was vastly different than those of the nation's designated leaders, Attakullakulla and Oconostota. Even the newly-developing political identities in the Upper Villages, Old Tassel and Raven of Chota (Savanooka), were following Attakullakulla's direction of leadership. However, Raven would yet defect to the Chickamauga (see Chapter 9).

The American colonies still considered Attakullakulla and Oconostota the spokesmen for the entire Cherokee Nation even though the Upper Village Cherokee were listening to Chief Old Tassel and Raven. This gave the encroaching settlers of present-day northeast Tennessee the best of both worlds. They could resist Dragging Canoe's attacks and hold Attakullakulla and Oconostota accountable for not living up to their agreements. The settlers knew full well that the Upper Village chiefs could not control the Chickamauga. Indeed, Attakullakulla had admitted so during the treaty conference. Thus, the settlers could fight with the Chickamauga and pressure the Upper Village faction to sign away more Cherokee land as settlement. The absence of unity between the Upper Village and the Chickamauga factions, as well as between the older chiefs (Attakullakulla, et al.) and the younger (Old Tassel and Raven) of the Upper Villages compounded the collapse of the colonial Cherokee Nation. Dragging Canoe and Doublehead provided the only possible avenues to the nation's salvation, but they had an uphill battle without full unity of the nation behind them.

If the Cherokee had been still honoring their old traditions, there would have been a debate of opposing viewpoints at a much earlier time with each faction peacefully listening to the other. The people would then have followed whomever they thought held the wisest viewpoint. The adversary would then have submitted (not necessarily happily) and would have allowed the people to follow the chosen plan. It is hard to imagine that the younger chiefs' position would not have been the most popular, based on the historical dealings with the settlers, and treaty after treaty that involved land cessions. However, the older chiefs, apparently thinking they were doing what was best for the Cherokee people, began to make decisions for the nation without such rituals.

Such was the case in 1775 pertaining to Sycamore Shoals when Dragging Canoe presented an opposing viewpoint to his father's and the other older chiefs'. His perspective was seemingly very popular; however, the older chiefs relinquished the land to Henderson.

8. The Time of the Chickamauga

It is staggering how many peace treaties the older chiefs signed that ceded Cherokee land to the white settlers. It would have behooved the younger chiefs to have arisen earlier; however, they still had faith in the Cherokee traditions and thought they could be persuasive dealing with the aged chiefs.

Many young warriors agreed with Dragging Canoe's opinion that he represented and led the true Cherokee Nation in terms of the traditions. Their new location along Chickamauga Creek was perfect because they were in position to control traffic on the Tennessee River, which many settlers would attempt to use to settle in French Lick. (French Lick was present-day Nashville, Tennessee.) Aged chief Ostenaco lived out his days with Dragging Canoe's faction. Ostenaco (Mankiller, Judd's Friend, Judge Friend, Skiagusta) died in 1780 along Judd's Creek in the Chickamauga settlement.

Another well-known individual who lived with the Chickamauga faction at their new settlements was Scottish trader John McDonald. He had relocated to Chickamauga Creek about six years before Dragging Canoe (see Chapter 6). John McDonald was the grandfather of Chief John Ross who later would become principal chief of the Cherokee Nation.

British Indian agents John Stuart and Alexander Cameron supplied the Chickamauga with food and ammunition stored in McDonald's commissary building. Their hope was to use the Chickamauga Cherokee when it was time for the British Army to again attempt an invasion of the Carolinas and Georgia. The agents were diverting the British supply lines away from the Upper Villages and toward the Chickamauga Villages. Essentially, the British Indian agents were working with, and recognizing, the Chickamauga leaders while the North Carolina and Virginia Indian commissioners, Captain James Robertson and Major Joseph Martin, respectively, each considered a rebel or Whig, were dealing with and recognizing the Upper Village chiefs.

During Chief Dragging Canoe's attacks in 1777, he and his band stole ten of Captain James Robertson's horses while the Holston Treaty was being organized. Dragging Canoe also scalped a nearby settler named Frederick Calvitt. The chief was blamed for the August killing of Davy Crockett's grandparents, David and Elizabeth Hedge Crockett, near present-day Rogersville, Tennessee, just one month after the treaty signing. He killed several of their children and captured two sons, Joseph and James Crockett, who remained his prisoners for almost two decades. John Crockett, Davy Crockett's father, escaped both death and capture and married Davy's mother, Elizabeth Hawkins Crockett, just two years later. (The gravestone of the massacred Crocketts is located in Rogers Cemetery at Crockett Park on Rogan Road in Rogersville. The inscription reads, "Here lie David Crockett, and his wife, the grandparents of Davy Crockett who were massacred near this spot by Indians in 1777." GPS location is N36 24.238 W83 00.525.)

Stuart and Cameron had arranged for the Chickamauga to assist with the coming war effort in backcountry Georgia and South Carolina. Stuart had been assisting Henry Hamilton with a plan to pressure Whigs in the backcountry. Hamilton was the British governor of the Northwest Territory and had proposed that the northern Indians should attack the rebels from the northwest while the southern Indians would attack from the southeast. He hoped to crush the American rebels in the middle. Hamilton sent 300 packhorses of arms and ammunition to John McDonald who added the supplies to those already stored in the commissary for use by the Chickamauga.

Governor Hamilton was at Fort Vincennes, sometimes called Fort Sackville (in present-day Indiana), and spent the winter preparing his would-be intensive spring campaign. He planned to first destroy the army of Virginia colonel George Rogers Clark, sweep through the settlements in Kentucky, meet 500 Cherokee and Chickasaw warriors at the mouth of the Tennessee River, and rage through the Overmountain settlements.

However, Virginia governor Patrick Henry had ordered Colonel Clark to invade the Northwest Territory in the summer of 1778. He attacked and captured Fort Kaskaskia on July 4, 1778, and Fort Vincennes on February 22, 1779. Hamilton was captured and sent to Virginia, a prisoner of war. Clark captured a huge stockpile of goods that Hamilton had reserved for the Indians. Thus ended the only possible armed British assistance the Chickamauga would ever have received against the encroaching settlers. However, the Chickamauga leaders were more determined than ever before to attack the Holston, Nolichucky, and Watauga settlements. (The small present-day village of Kaskaskia, Illinois, is located 50 miles south of St. Louis, Missouri. It is unusual in that it is on the west side of the Mississippi River, surrounded by Missouri farmland. Vincennes, Indiana, is located at the junction of U.S. Highways 50 and 41.)

In March, Colonel Clark reached the conclusion that the only way to control the Illinois country was to withdraw from their present positions and center the army near the mouth of the Ohio River. He quickly constructed several small forts in the vicinity. As soon as the Chickasaw, who had become members of the Chickamauga confederation, learned of the new forts, they acted to defend what they considered their ancestral hunting ground. They lay siege to newly-constructed Fort Jefferson and destroyed the nearby settlement. The Chickasaw then invaded the frontiers of Kentucky and even penetrated as far as the Cumberland. Their success uplifted the Chickamauga leaders and fit right in with their plans to attack the Overmountain encroachers. As the Watauga, Holston, and Nolichucky settlements grew, they intruded further onto Cherokee land, despite the recent treaty that banned such further impingement.

Early in 1779, North Carolina agent James Robertson received word in Chota that 300 Chickamauga warriors were planning to invade the settlements. He immediately sent warnings to Holston and Watauga Valleys. Virginia agent Joseph Martin made a similar report to Governor Patrick Henry and recommended a preemptive attack on the Chickamauga. As further attacks became more likely, Henry initiated more action to protect the settlers. On January 8, 1779, he ordered Virginia colonel Evan Shelby to destroy the Chickamauga towns. Shelby worked for several weeks to muster 450 men, mostly from North Carolina and Virginia. Virginia colonel John Montgomery, a Holston settler, had commanded a regiment in Colonel Clark's expedition in the north. After the December 1778 fall of Fort Vincennes (Fort Sackville) in today's Indiana, Clark decided to return to the north and retake several important posts from the British. Before Montgomery led his regiment of 150 men to the north, he joined with Shelby's force to face the Chickamauga.

The troops assembled at Robertson's Station, located where Big Creek empties into the Holston River. They descended the Holston in canoes and pirogues on April 10 and continued down the Tennessee to surprise the Chickamauga settlements. On the 15th they reached the mouth of Chickamauga Creek, where they captured a Chickamauga warrior who was fishing. Shelby forced the fisherman to lead the army to the Chickamauga villages. The few warriors who were not on the raids to the white settlements fought a stiff delaying action until the women and children could withdraw to safety. The men then retreated to the slopes of Lookout Mountain. Shelby burned Chickamauga Town and 10 others, confiscated 20,000 bushels of corn, raided McDonald's Trading Post, and seized the stores of ammunition, food, and pelts. Shelby's force also took many Chickamauga horses and a large number of cattle. When Shelby returned to his settlements, Colonel John Montgomery used the pirogues and traveled up the Ohio River to rejoin Clark. The Virginia militia retreated a few miles up the Tennessee where a stream presently called Sale Creek joined the big river. There he held an auction for his militiamen who spent $125,000 on the spoils, including horses to replace the canoes for transportation back to the settlements.

The Chickamauga warriors, who had learned through runners that their towns had been destroyed, abandoned their campaign against the settlements and returned to rebuild their desolated homes. "Taken completely by surprise, their warriors swarmed like a nest of hornets, and finally settled again amid the ashes of their old homes at the mouth of Chickamauga Creek, still unconquered, and thirsting for vengeance."[2]

John Stuart died on March 21, 1779, and was replaced as agent to the Cherokee and the Creek by Colonel Thomas "Burn Foot" Brown who had been active around Augusta following the fall of Savannah. Alexander Cameron was assigned to the Chickasaw; however, he remained with Dragging Canoe at a rebuilt Chickamauga Town.[3]

Brown immediately sent an update to Lieutenant General Charles Lord Cornwallis:

> In consequence of letters sent to the Cherokee Nation, the Indians have agreed to attack Rebel Plunderers who have taken possession of their hunting grounds on the Watauga. Chiefs of 2,500 Cherokee warriors promise to continue the war during the winter if they are provided with arms and ammunition and their families are provided with clothing. No towns remaining friendly with the Rebels will receive any supplies.[4]

The settlers in the Watauga, Holston, and Nolichucky settlements continued to encroach further onto Cherokee land, irrespective of the treaties. White hunters further impinged upon Cherokee ancestral hunting grounds. The practice became perilous for frontiersmen because the Chickamauga factions of Dragging Canoe and Doublehead hunted another prey—the white hunters.

It is important to understand the 1779 and 1780 push to settle the Cumberland. It had an impact, upon not only the Cherokee but other Indian nations that claimed the hunting grounds in the vicinity. The movement to settle the area thrust the Chickamauga into action when a group of the settlers drifted right by the Chickamauga towns of Chief Dragging Canoe and the downriver settlements of Chief Doublehead.

The glorious accounts, given by the hunters on their return from what was called French Lick or Big Lick, caused a number of settlers who were already in the Overmountain communities to plan for relocation. A council of interested Watauga settlers decided a company of men should be sent to clear land, plant corn, and otherwise prepare for future transplantation of families.

In February 1779, Colonel James Robertson set out with fellow colonists George Freeland, William Neely, Edward Swanson, James Hanley, Mark Robertson, Zachariah White, and William Overall. James Robertson had carefully selected those men, all experienced woodsmen. After three weeks of hardship on their journey over mountains and through wilderness, they reached French Lick.

A few days later they were joined by a small company led by Kasper Mansker from the region of New River, Virginia. Robertson ordered crops of corn be planted near a sul-

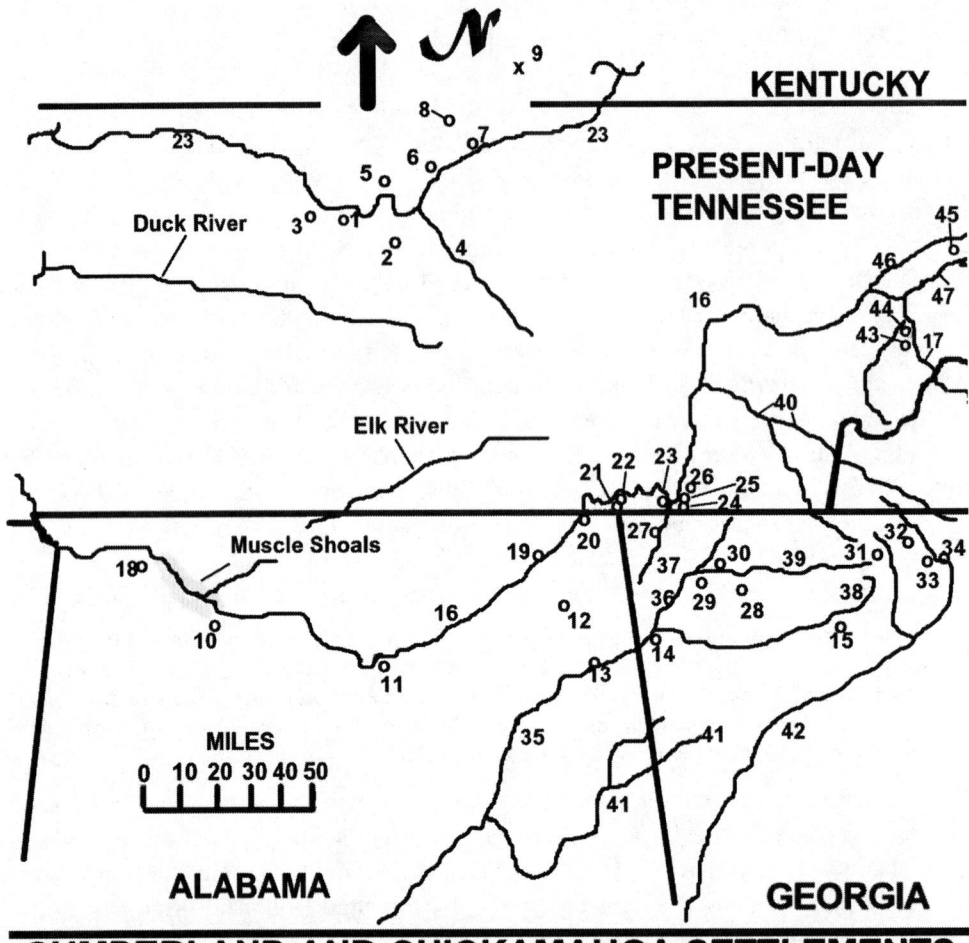

CUMBERLAND AND CHICKAMAUGA SETTLEMENTS

1. The Bluff
2. Buchanan's Station
3. Freeland's Station
4. Stones River
5. Eaton's Station
6. Mansker's Station
7. Zeigler's Station
8. Bledsoe's Station
9. Dripping Spring
10. Doublehead's Town
11. Creek Path Town
12. Will's Town
13. Turkey Town
14. Etowah
15. Long Swamp Town
16. Tennessee River
17. Little Tennessee R.
18. Cold Water Town
19. Crow Town
20. Long Island Town
21. Nick-a-jack
22. Running Water Town
23. Tuskegee
24. Chattanooga Town
25. Citico
26. Chickamauga Town
27. Lookout Town
28. Talking Rock
29. New Echota
30. Oostanaula
31. Frog Town
32. Notally
33. Nacoochee
34. Little Chota
35. Coosa River
36. Oostanaula River
37. Lookout Creek
38. Etowah River
39. Coosawattee River
40. Hiwassee River
41. Tallapoosa River
42. Chattahoochee River
43. Chota
44. Fort Loudoun
45. White's Fort
46. Clinch River
47. Holston River

phur spring. The parties labored to clear land, plant, and cultivate throughout the spring and summer of 1779. They built a crude fence to try and protect the crops from animals. (Sulphur Spring was within present-day Nashville, Tennessee, near the junction of Marilyn Road and Pennsylvania Avenue, to just south of the junction of present-day 60th Avenue North and California Avenue, one-half mile south of the Cumberland River.)

Swanson, White, and Overall volunteered to mind the crops while the rest of the men returned to the settlement to relocate the families. All, except for Robertson, retraced the original route. The colonel traveled via Kaskaskia, Illinois, where he sought advice on the Cumberland from General George Rogers Clark.

Robertson had thought French Lick to be within the extended boundary of Virginia, as had the original Overmountain settlers about their settlements. He did not think the original claims by Richard Henderson from the Sycamore Shoals conference of 1775 were legal, and he believed that Clark, the Virginia land agent, could provide land claims called cabin rights. Robertson wished to purchase such rights to avoid future legal issues. Clark, however, assured Robertson that was unnecessary as he thought the land was under the purview of North Carolina.

By mid–October, Robertson had collected 380 travelers from the Knoxville to New River, Virginia, settlements who were willing to relocate to the Cumberland. The plan called for the band to separate into two parties. James Robertson, himself, would lead most of the men overland. The route was the quickest, but the harshest. That party would arrive well ahead of the other and would prepare for the arrival of the second group, composed largely of families. The second group would be led by Colonel John Donelson, with Captain John Blackmore acting as his second in command. That assemblage was to proceed by boats down the Tennessee River to the Ohio and thence up the Cumberland to French Lick. Therein lay the rub! The Tennessee River flowed right by the Chickamauga community. The river travelers would be the first targets of the recuperated and eager Chickamauga Cherokee warriors.

The Cherokee numbered about 12,000 at that time, many of whom were on the move to relocate to the Chickamauga Town vicinity. Chickamauga chief Dragging Canoe's call for the young, disenchanted warriors to join him was bearing fruit. Dragging Canoe and Doublehead were building coalitions of allies. What had been the Cherokee's traditional enemies, the Creek of Alabama and Georgia, numbered about 20,000, and their warriors were joining Chief Doublehead's faction by the scores. The Chickasaw occupied present-day West Tennessee. They amounted only to about 4,000. They wafted between assisting the Chickamauga and the settlers. Some Iroquois and Shawnee would ally with the Chickamauga later (see Chapter 9).

In November 1779, Colonel James Robertson set out on his overland expedition with 200 skilled backwoodsmen to open the new settlement. They transported their supplies on packhorses. Soon after leaving Watauga, Robertson's party was overtaken by John Rains (sometimes spelled Raines) and a group from New River, Virginia, that was bound for Harrod's Station. (Harrod's Station was sited at present-day Harrodsburg, Kentucky.)

The Cumberland River was frozen solid when Robertson and his group arrived. As the entire party attempted to cross over, the ice made a loud cracking sound at midstream. The men crept along, fearful of being plunged into the icy depths; however, they attained safety on the far bank. Their landing was in the vicinity of the Bluff on what is believed to have been Christmas Day of 1779. They experienced no deaths on the 500-mile trek and were free of Indian attacks. The second party would not be so lucky. (The Bluff would become a major point of action between the settlers and the Chickamauga. The site is in Nashville at the vicinity of Broadway and Third Street, two blocks from the Cumberland River.)

One week later, another gaggle of settlers arrived led by Kasper Mansker, Daniel Frazier, and Amos Eaton. They had followed the tracks of Robertson's company. Shortly thereafter, a South Carolina group, directed by John and Alex Buchanan, Daniel and Sampson Williams, John and James Mulherrin, and Thomas Thompson, reached French Lick to join the new colony. There were a few women and children with Rains and Mansker; however, none had accompanied Robertson or Buchanan.

The settlers had not seen any signs of Indians on their arrival and had been unmolested on their journeys, so they were confident of their safety and began to scatter over the countryside, some extending themselves out to as far as 25 miles. Colonel Robertson did his best to counsel for the building of stockades, but many ignored his warning.

The primary stockade on the Bluff became headquarters for the colony. (The fort, called the Bluff Station and Fort Bluff, was located at the foot of present-day Church Street.) The main building in the Bluff's fort was a log structure two stories high with portholes around the walls on both levels. Other cabins were built, and all were enclosed by a circlet of cedar pickets driven firmly into the ground. The upper ends of those pickets were sharpened to a point, thus they were impractical to try and scale. The only entrance was gated and secured with a heavy chain at night.

On top of the fort was a lookout station from which sentinels might discover the approach and movements of an enemy. To the west and south beyond present-day Broad Street was a thick cedar forest. The bottom lands along the river and to the east and north were covered by a thick growth of cane from 10 to 20 feet high. The settlement was named Nashborough after General Francis Nash, an early military and political figure in North Carolina.

The treks of the colonizers proved Dragging Canoe to be a prophet. His words from over the past several years were quickly becoming facts. The Chickamauga warriors would be newly motivated to gather themselves and force their impressions upon the unwanted encroachers to the ancient ancestral hunting grounds so worshipped by young Cherokee men.

Such a large gathering of whites in the previously-unoccupied Indian territory had certainly attracted the attention of not only the Cherokee, but also the Creek to the south and the Iroquois Confederation and Shawnee to the north. They had all vied for hunting privileges in that same area for centuries; however, they now had cause to unite and free the land for their common use.

Colonel John Donelson's and Captain John Blackmore's vessels did not sail for nearly two months after the departure of the overland force because the waters were too low. Finally the voyage began. Donelson set out from Fort Patrick Henry, five or six miles above the North Fork Holston River on December 22, 1780, and the fleet commanded by Blackmore departed from Blackmore's Fort on Clinch River about the same time. The two convoys met at the mouth of Clinch River. Colonel Donelson was aboard the *Adventure,* the largest boat in the cavalcade. The colonel kept a journal in which he recorded all principal events of the journey from the time they set sail until they reached French Lick four months later.

The *Adventure* and the other boats drifted down the river to Reedy Creek, where they were stopped by more low water and excessive cold. (It is normally recorded that the flotilla comprised 30 boats. However, some raise the number to as high as 60 vessels. Donelson's Journal does not record the number of boats in his fleet, but James Cartwright, whose father, Robert Cartwright, was with Donelson on the *Adventure*, recorded that, when the boats from the Holston united with those from the Clinch, they were about forty in number. He wrote that the vessels varied from flat scows to canoes and pirogues, the latter having been hollowed out from the trunks of trees. Nearly all the boats had two or more families aboard. In the combined party there were 130 women and children, and about 50 men.)

The throng remained for several weeks at Reedy Creek and reached the tributary of Cloud's Creek on February 20, 1780. They passed the mouth of French Broad River on March 2. About noon that day, Hugh Henry and his family ran aground at William's Island, two miles above present-day Knoxville, and sank in the current. Much of their freight was lost. Colonel Donelson ordered a halt so the men of the party could bail and repair the boat, and also recover some of the cargo. Sunday morning, March 5, the fleet was underway before sunrise, and passed the mouth of the Clinch River by noon (near present-day Kingston, Tennessee.)

They reached the vicinity of Chickamauga Town on March 7, 1780. The first village they encountered had been evacuated. The next day they approached an inhabited village that belonged to a large body of Chickamauga. When the Indians spotted the boats, they clustered along the river and, pretending to be friendly, yelled to the voyagers. The Indians called the whites "brother" and invited the travelers to their village. John Donelson, Jr., and John Caffrey became intrigued, took a canoe, and rowed toward the town from the opposite shore. When Donelson and Caffrey made midstream, a half-breed, named Archie Coody, and a few of his associates rowed out to meet them. They warned the pair to return to their fleet. The young travelers did as warned, and were accompanied by Coody and his group. Colonel Donelson distributed presents to the Indians, and Coody and his companions appeared to be pleased.

A large body of armed warriors, painted red and black, embarked in canoes at the village. Coody ordered his friends to depart from the fleet as he remained with the whites and urged them to immediately drift away. They had scarcely done so when they observed the warriors coming down the river after them; however, the Chickamauga could not overtake them. Coody accompanied the fleet for some time; but then, after he had assured Colonel Donelson that he was safe, he rowed back toward the village. It is unknown what influence the kind-hearted Coody held at the village, or whether he was in trouble when he returned. Seemingly, the warriors would have been disappointed with his actions.

Soon, the whites came in sight of another Chickamauga town situated like the last on the south side of the river. It was nearly opposite a small island. The warriors repeated the promptings of the previous village's inhabitants by inviting their "brothers" ashore. The flotilla headed for the channel on the north side of the island. One of the warriors called in English to convince the whites that the north side was dangerous. When Captain John Blackmore's boat passed too close to the north shore, a small war party concealed nearby opened fire and killed a young man named Payne.

Thomas Stuart and his extended family of 28 had embarked with the company, but they suffered a smallpox outbreak. They agreed to keep well to the rear of the other boats. Donelson notified them each evening with a horn when it was time to camp. When they drifted past the Chickamauga towns, the Indians were gathered in large numbers and observed their plight. The warriors swarmed out in canoes, surrounded the boat, and killed and captured the entire crew. Their mournful cries were distinctly heard by the forward boats. Although the Chickamauga seemed to have achieved their goal, a cruel fate interceded. They became infected with the disease of their victims, and for many months thereafter smallpox raged—not only among the Chickamauga, but also the Creek and the mainstream Cherokee.

Jonathan Jennings ran a family boat in the procession that included his wife, daughter (Mrs. Ephraim Peyton, who was to join her husband at French Lick), a grown son, another young man, and an unidentified black couple. While on the way from Chickamauga Creek to Lookout Mountain, Mrs. Peyton delivered a child. Her father's boat lagged behind the others. The next day, the flotilla passed through the cut of the mountain. The Chickamauga had matched their progress by running down the south bank of the river. After they gained the lead, the warriors lined the bluffs overlooking them and, with their rifles, kept up a constant fusilade upon the boats.

John Cotton's canoe capsized nearby. Donelson's company, pitying his distress, landed on the north bank of the river and aided him as he recovered his cargo. When the Indians opened fire from the cliffs, the travelers withdrew to their boats and immediately moved out of range. Miss Nancy Gower and three others were wounded trying to escape. Her father, Abel Gower (sometimes reported as Russell Gower), lost his crew to injuries, so Nancy took the helm. As she steered through the narrows, under heavy warriors' fire, a bullet passed entirely through her body. Nancy made no outcry, but remained bravely at her post.

Colonel Donelson moved his boat to the relative safety of calm water beyond the Whirl of the Tennessee River near the mouth of Suck Creek. He turned and noticed that Jennings' boat was hung up on a rock that projected from the northern shore immediately at the Whirl. Donelson was too far along to assist, so he proceeded ahead. The warriors had focused their fire on Jennings' boat, and many bullets pierced the voyagers' clothing, especially that of Mrs. Jennings. Jennings ordered that his goods be thrown overboard to lighten the load, and he returned the Indians' fire. Rather than follow Jennings' orders, his crew (the two young white men and the black man) panicked and deserted the boat. The black man drowned, but the two white men were captured. One was burned to death and the other was ransomed later by a white trader. Jennings now had no other support than that of his heroic wife and the black woman. Mrs. Peyton and her infant were both a worry and a problem. After they had finished unloading the boat, Mrs. Jennings jumped into the water and shoved it off of the rock. When the boat was free, the current moved it so quickly that Mrs. Jennings struggled to regain its safety. Mrs. Peyton's newborn child was killed in the confusion.

After they had sailed Wednesday night and all day Thursday, March 9, 1780, the company was confident they were safely beyond the reach of the Cherokee. They camped at dusk on the northern shore, and about 4:00 a.m. on the 10th, they were aroused by a cry of "Help!" from the river. The call came from the Jennings boat, its occupants uncontrollably adrift. The campers discovered their fellow travelers by the reflections of their own fires.

The members of the Jennings group were redistributed among the remaining boats, and the voyage resumed.

Donelson's flotilla was not again molested by Indians until they reached Chief Doublehead's settlement at the Muscle Shoals of the Tennessee River. The Chickamauga could launch attacks from a strategic spot on travelers stranded in the rocks of the shoals. At the upper end of the shoals, the warriors fired on the flotilla but were off the mark. Two days later, a short distance below the shoals, the Chickamauga had better success. Some boats drifted too near the shore, and five people were slightly wounded. That night, they camped by the fire near the mouth of a creek and prepared to retire. One black man had already drifted off. The remaining members of the company, still awake, were unnerved by the persistent barking of their dogs, so they hastily returned to their boats. They drifted one mile downriver and camped on the opposite shore. The next morning, John Donelson, Jr., and John Caffrey were resolved to discover the cause of the previous night's alarm. They secured a canoe and rowed back to the first camp where they found the sleeping man untouched. They determined the alarm was false, and the three men returned to the boats. The Donelson party encountered no more Indians on their voyage, and arrived at Nashborough on April 24, 1780. Thirty-one people had been killed on the expedition.[5]

At first glance, the numbers might indicate that the Chickamauga failed in their first major attempt to stem the tide of settlers floating past their enclaves toward the Cumberland. Of 180, 150 or about 85 percent, successfully completed the journey. However, considering the warriors were just planning and preparing their spring and summer campaign, it was an adequate beginning. It is unlikely they expected such a large convoy to drift past their villages. Although some were painted for war (which could indicate they had been expecting Donelson's party), it is more probable the warriors were preparing for an expedition into the settlements. Had they been preparing for the flotilla, they assuredly would have had a fleet of canoes ready to dispatch at the first sign, so they could cut the trekkers off and successfully surround them. As it was, the Chickamauga did set an example that would be publicized throughout the settlements to announce the risk associated with such an excursion. It also provided a target for their first major mission—the Cumberland. (Some later historians, such as Edward Albright and John Preston Arthur, freely used the word "savages" as late as the early twentieth century to describe the actions of the Indians in the Cumberland and Overmountain settlement attacks in the late 1700s.)

Inexplicably, the Chickamauga did not join the Chickasaw for the initial harassment against the Cumberland settlers. Had the Chickamauga and the Chickasaw united at the beginning, they might have wiped out the new settlements. As a result, the attacks against the Cumberland, devastating as they were, would continue for a decade and a half. Not only was survival of the original onslaught to the advantage of the settlers, but so was the war of attrition. The warriors tried hard to evict the whites from the Cumberland. Historian Edward Albright noted: "We wonder that a single individual escaped such a terrible onslaught.... In the language of Judge John Haywood, it was indeed 'a period of danger and hazard; of daring adventure and dangerous exposure.'"[6]

The Indians deeply resented the sudden advent of so large a number of the whites onto their hunting grounds. The British on the north and the Spaniards on the south secretly urged the Indians to increase hostilities against the nearby outposts. Stragglers from the various Cumberland stations were picked off at will. The Chickamauga eventually joined the Chickasaw, as did some of the northern tribes and the Catawba and the Creek from the south and east. Following are some accounts of their attempts to make the encroaching colonists pay dearly for their settlements.

In May 1780, a Mr. Keywood rushed to Bluff Station to announce that his companion, John Milliken, had been killed on Richland Creek five miles south. The two men were trekking toward the Bluff settlement and had stopped at the creek for a drink when they were fired upon by a band of Indians who were hidden on the bank. Milliken was hit and died on the spot; however, Keywood had no injuries and hustled to the fort.

A few days later, as Joseph Hay was alone down on Lick Branch near Freeland's Station, a war party of reported Chickamauga, hiding in the nearby canebrakes, shot and scalped him. The warriors quickly withdrew with Hay's gun, hunting knife, shot pouch, and powder horn. Hay was buried in the open ground on a point of land east of Sulphur Spring by settlers from the Bluff.

Soon thereafter a man named Bernard was at work on his claim. He was so busily engaged in his efforts that he did not hear the approach of the warriors. The Indians easily shot him dead, after which they decapitated him and carried his head away.

(Freeland's Station was located in present-day Nashville. A marker designating the site is on Rosa L. Parks Boulevard [also called 8th Avenue North and U.S. Highway 41A] just south of its intersection with Garfield Street, GPS 36° 10.719' N, 86° 47.701' W. The war party that killed Joseph Hay may have been Chickasaw.)

When the warriors who killed Bernard retreated, they encountered three young men: two brothers named Dunham and a son of the previously-mentioned John Milliken. The brothers safely escaped to Freeland's Station; however, young Milliken suffered the same fate as had Bernard—head and all.

Also in May, two men were attacked at the Clover Bottom property owned by Colonel Richard Henderson who was erecting a cabin and outbuildings on the grounds. Henderson's servant and cook, a man named Jim, and a young man who had been left in charge of the half-faced camp not far from Colonel John Donelson's property were attacked by a war party while Henderson was visiting some Kentucky forts. The two men were about to canoe down the river to the Bluff. Warriors were hiding in the thick canebrakes on the bank and fired upon the pair. Jim was killed outright, but his companion was able to escape. (A half-faced camp was a variety of a lean-to that was used by settlers for a while before expending the time and effort to build a cabin. It was usually formed by finding a large downed tree, or felling one, that lay north to south. Then to the east 12 to 15 feet away, two smaller felled trees were set into the ground so that each was about eight to ten feet high, about 12 to 15 feet apart, and so that a line drawn between them would be parallel to the initial large tree. These were cut so that a fork existed at the top. Then a sturdy and straight log was secured across from one fork to the other. Then smaller trees were footed against the original downed tree and spanned to the log that ran between the forks forming the lean-to. The open end always faced east because of the prevailing westerly winds. Sometimes the other three sides would have a short wall two or three logs high, just tall enough so that a prone person would not be exposed to direct wind. The occupants would sleep with their heads toward the low end of the shelter, and a small fire was often built near the high end for warmth and safety from animals. Sometimes the logs that made the roof were chinked with mud or covered crosswise with smaller branches.)

8. The Time of the Chickamauga

In the month of June 1780, two settlers named Goin and Kennedy were clearing land somewhere between Mansker's and Eaton's Stations. A war party approached (through some brush piles the men had made) and killed the two men. The warriors removed the scalps of their victims and escaped into the forest. (Mansker's Station was twenty miles north by northwest of the Bluff settlement near present-day Goodlettsville, Tennessee. A restoration of the original station is located at 705 Caldwell Drive at the northwest perimeter of Moss Wright Park. A marker for Mansker's Station is in town near the junction of Memorial Drive and French Street, 36° 19.267' N, 86° 42.883' W. Eaton's [or Heaton's] Station was located one and one-half miles downstream of the Bluff Fort, in today's Nashville, north of the Cumberland at the junctions of Lock Road and Seminary Streets, 36° 11.995' N, 86° 47.259' W. This is not to be confused with the Eaton's Station near Kingsport, Tennessee [see Chapter 6].)

A band of Choctaw and Chickasaw attacked Renfroe's Station at the mouth of Red River in July. There Nathan Turpin was slain and scalped as was an unidentified companion. Renfroe's was abandoned out of fear, and the Turpin family decided to trek to Freeland's Station. The Turpins and the Freelands were related. The Johns family and others favored Eaton's Station for their destination. Both groups quickly embarked following the attack and took only a few necessities. They camped by the trail about dusk and ate supper. Some of the party opined about having left so many valuables, so they decided to return to the fort that night and recover what they could carry. The balance of the party continued the journey and arrived safely at their respective destinations. Those who returned to Renfroe's reached the station early in the morning, and by dawn had gathered up all they could manage. They headed out after daylight. That evening they made camp two miles north of Sycamore Creek on a small branch, ever since called Battle Creek.

In the predawn darkness, Joseph Renfroe made his way toward the spring for water. When he knelt to drink, a party of warriors fired on him from ambush and killed him. The settlers scattered through the blackness in every direction, but they were pursued and all killed—except a Mrs. Jones. Eighteen men, women, and children were tomahawked to death including Joseph Renfroe and the entire Johns family of twelve. A distraught Mrs. Jones followed the tracks of those who had gone on to safety the day before. Sometime after daylight, she encountered Henry Ramsey, a noted Indian fighter, who escorted her to Eaton's Station. When news of the above disaster reached Eaton's and the Bluff Fort, each sent a rescue party to Battle Creek. They found a few who had been mortally wounded, and they cared for them as best they could; however, they had to bury all 18. (Renfroe's Station was located near present-day Clarksville, Tennessee. There is a marker on State Highway 76, east of the Interstate 24 overpass, N 36° 32.084' N, 87° 11.848' W. The marker reads, "Established in 1780 as the first settlement in Montgomery County, Renfroe's Station was located 1.4 miles northwest of here, on the north side of the Red River at the mouth of Parson's Creek. Moses Renfroe's party broke from the John Donelson flotilla, which later settled in Nashville. Lasting only three months, the Renfroe settlement fell to Indian hostilities.")

Warriors struck Mansker's Station shortly after the Renfroe assault. They killed Patrick Quigley, John Stuckley, James Lumsley, and Betsy Kennedy. Mansker's was abandoned following the attack.

During the late summer months following the Renfroe Station attacks, several settlers were killed near present-day landmarks within today's Nashville. D. Larimer was shot, scalped, and beheaded near Freeland's Station. Isaac LeFeore was treated likewise on the west bank of the Cumberland River near the end of the Louisville & Nashville railroad bridge. Soloman Murry and Robert Aspey were fired upon and killed, then scalped, while at work near Fogg High School. Their comrade, Soloman Phillips, was mortally wounded but escaped to the fort at the Bluff. He died a few days later. Benjamin Renfroe, John Maxwell, and John Kennedy were fishing on the river bank near the mouth of Sulphur Spring Branch when warriors surprised them from behind. The men fought for a while but were overpowered by the number and the strength of the Indians. Renfroe was tomahawked and scalped, but Kennedy and Maxwell were taken captive. Phillip Catron was traveling from Freeland's Station to the Bluff along a buffalo path that ran through a thick cluster of undergrowth near the junction of Cedar and Cherry Streets. He was shot from ambush while in the midst of the thicket. He managed to retain his seat in the saddle and escape. John Caffrey and Daniel Williams, two occupants of the Bluff settlement, took a canoe up the river. When they returned, they tied the craft and were climbing up the bank near the foot of Church Street when a war party opened fire, wounding the legs of each. John Rains was on duty in the fort when he and others heard the commotion. They rushed out and chased the small band of warriors to Sulphur Spring.

Late in August, Jonathan Jennings (see the Donelson expedition above), while building a cabin, was killed by a reported band of Delaware (sometimes reported to be Chickamauga) near the river bank upriver from the Bluff. The warriors tomahawked his body into pieces and scattered the fragments over his property.

James Mayfield and a man named Porter were ambushed in plain view of Eaton's Station. A group from the fort hurried out, too late to save them, and the Indians rapidly escaped.

Ned Carver (sometimes reported to be Carvin) established a claim on some land four miles east of the Bluff. He had built a cabin for his family and established a garden along one wall. While he was hoeing one day, some warriors shot from a nearby thicket and instantly killed him. Mrs. Carver and their two small children escaped by a door on the opposite side of the cabin, then hid in some neighboring canebrakes. They made their way to Eaton's Station the following morning. Shortly thereafter John Shockley and Jesse Balestine were killed while hunting in the woods near the Carvers' cabin.

Brothers Jacob and Frederick (sometimes recorded as Edward) Stump, described as two Dutchmen, had a cabin on White's Creek, three miles north of Eaton's Station. Normally they took turns clearing the land while the other stood guard. For some unknown reason, they broke their habit one day and labored together. Indians had approached under cover of a clump of trees that edged the field. They fired upon the brothers and killed Jacob. Frederick realized he had no chance to defend his ground, so he ran toward the station with the warriors close behind. They chased over rolling hills and rock outcroppings, and through canebrakes and cedar thickets. About halfway to Eaton's, the pursuers closed the gap enough to hurl a tomahawk at Stump, who was not hit. The attackers were near enough to their quarry that the weapon hit the ground twenty or thirty feet past him. The warriors ended their chase at that point and were content to search for their hatchet.

Late in the summer of 1780, a party of hunters spent the night in a cabin at Asher's Station. A band of warriors learned the group was there, and during the night surrounded the cabin. At daybreak, the Indians poked their guns through cracks between the logs and fired at the sleeping white men. They killed a man named Payne and wounded another by the name of Phillips. They scalped Payne, captured all the horses at the station and, in single file, rode horseback on the buffalo path toward Bledsoe's Station. Suddenly they rounded a bend and were face to face with a hunting party of settlers, composed of Alex Buchanan, William Ellis, James Manifee, Alex Thompson, John Brock, William Mann, and others who were returning to the Bluff. Buchanan, who was riding at the head of his party, fired and killed the first Indian and wounded a second. The remaining warriors took flight, leaving the captured horses to the whites. A few of the hunting party chased the war party about 40 miles to Gordon's Ferry on the Duck River where a skirmish ensued, and several members of the war party were killed. The warriors did not flee from the hunting party out of fear, but were smart enough to know when the odds were against them and knew they could not win a war of attrition. (Asher's Station was located in the vicinity of present-day 709 Cole's Ferry Road, southeast of Gallatin, Tennessee.)

In the fall of 1780, Isaac and Anthony Bledsoe established Bledsoe's Station at present-day Castalian Springs, Tennessee. A band of Chickamauga killed and scalped William Johnson and Daniel Mungle near the station and fired several shots at the stockade. Then they shot several head of cattle, set fire to some outbuildings and fences, and rode away up the river toward Hartsville. They encountered Thomas Sharp Spencer who was returning alone from a hunting trip. He led two horses laden with bear meat and pelts. The warriors fired at Spencer and wounded him. Spencer dismounted, left the spoils for the attackers, ran through the woods, and escaped into Bledsoe's Fort. (In 1992, the Bledsoe's Lick Historical Association developed Bledsoe's Fort Historical Park. The nearly 80-acre county park, which includes the archaeological location of Isaac and Anthony Bledsoe's 1780 fort, is on State Highway 25 less than one mile east of Gallatin, Tennessee.)

Later in the fall, a war party approached Bluff Fort at night, stole a number of horses, loaded them with plunder, and rode away. The next morning Captain James Leiper led a company of 15 pursuers and overtook the assailants on Harpeth River. The warriors heard the posse approach and tried hard to escape, but they could not make headway with their heavily-laden horses. They fled and left the plunder to be recovered by Leiper's party.

Colonel John Donelson was well aware of the Indian attacks lower down the Cumberland, and he knew that they had destroyed Renfroe's Station. They had not yet bothered his property, Donelson's Station, at Clover Bottom. (Clover Bottom was at the present-day location of Clover Bottom Mansion on Stones River, 2941 Lebanon Road, Nashville, Tennessee. The site is now in the Donelson area of Nashville, right next to the Hermitage section. Hermitage was later the home of President Andrew Jackson, son-in-law of Donelson.) Donelson hoped to escape being a war party target; however, he was unprepared to defend against such an attack, and he reckoned one was looming. Donelson abandoned his property and took his family to Mansker's Station.

Colonel Donelson left the half-faced camp he had built for his family and servants. He had planted his corn in the bottoms on the west side of the river and a small patch of cotton on the east side.

On November 4, 1780, Colonel Donelson learned that the crops at Clover Bottom had matured, and were ready to harvest. He desired to reap the crops and share them with the settlers at the Bluff and at Mansker's Station where he and his family had been living. He proposed that a boat party from each of the two stations should meet at Clover Bottom and gather the corn and cotton. They met at Donelson's fields on November 1, 1780; twelve came from the Bluff, led by Captain Abel Gower. Colonel Donelson was not able to go, but his 26-year-old son, Captain John Donelson, Jr., led the group from Mansker's Station. The group included Hugh Rogan, Robert Cartwright, and several others, including a number of Donelson's slaves (including his personal body servant, Somerset). The group from the Bluff included Abel Gower, Jr., John Randolph Robertson, and William Cartwright. One of the groups, likely from Mansker's, had brought a horse to drag the corn sled to the boats and then to tow the laden boats down Stones River to the Cumberland.

The Mansker's Station party loaded their boat first, and they crossed the Stones to gather cotton. They began to pile bolls on top of the corn and expected they would soon be joined by the group from the Bluff. However, Captain Donelson was surprised to see the Bluff boat heading down the Stones River. When the captain hailed the boat, he was told by Gower that the hour was late and they wanted to reach the Bluff before nightfall. Captain Donelson yelled a protest. Captain Gower's boat then reached a narrow channel between a small island and the west bank. In the meantime, 200 Chickamauga had concealed themselves on the west bank opposite the island and opened an intense rifle fire upon Gower's boat. Several of the men jumped from the boat and waded through the shallow water to the shore, where they were hotly pursued by the warriors. Captain Gower, his son, John Randolph Robertson, and two others were killed. Their bodies floated toward the Cumberland River. Three were hit by the rifle balls and died atop the corn in the boat. Only one white man and two black men, who had evacuated the boat, survived.

The white man and one black slave wandered through the woods for nearly two days and finally reached the Bluff. The third survivor, a free black man named Jack Cavil, was wounded, captured, and taken prisoner to Chickamauga Town on South Chickamauga Creek. He later would become a notorious member of the Chickamauga (see Chapter 9).

Gower's boat, containing the bodies of the three slain, the corn, and two or three dogs, floated to the Bluff Fort during the morning of the next day where the garrison sighted and retrieved it.

When the assault on Captain Gower's boat had ended, the war party ran up the river to a point on the opposite shore from Donelson's boat. The water was too deep to ford. When Captain Donelson and several companions saw the attack on Gower's boat, they rushed down to their own craft for their rifles and shot-bags. When they returned, they found that the other members of their party had fled into the canebrakes. The captain and his men paused long enough to fire a volley across the river and then followed their companions into the cane. All of them eventually collected and held a council. They decided to abandon the boat and make their way through the woods east of the river and eventually to Mansker's Station. Mr. Cartwright was aged and infirm, so he was placed on the horse. They separated, to leave less of a trail than would a group, and traveled the remainder of the day. At dusk Captain Donelson signaled the men to join him in a fallen leaf-covered top of a large hickory tree where they slept.

Somerset, the servant, volunteered to ride the horse across the Cumberland River and then to Mansker's Station. He arrived safely, and several men from the station returned with him. They built a strong raft to cross the Cumberland, collect the refugees, and returned to Donelson's fields to gather the crops. The activity took three or four days, and they saw nothing of the war party. However, they were uneasy because the dogs constantly barked at night. During the last night of their stay, the dogs rushed madly about the camp. At daylight next morning, the hands went into the field to hastily gather and load the rest of the cotton. They quickly departed for Mansker's Station.

The settlers were in the midst of hunting season and needed salt to preserve meat. They obtained the seasoning from sulphur springs which evaporated in the late summer and left white granules all over the ground. The amount of salt needed was such that the settlers had to boil water from the springs and save the residue. It took an average of 800 gallons of spring water to accumulate a bushel of salt. (The amount of water required depended on the strength of the saline solution.)[7]

Mansker's Station had a nearby salt lick called Mansker's Lick; however, it was not very dependable for large amounts of the necessity. A party consisting of William Neely, his 16-year-old daughter, and several men went from that station to Neely's Lick, an adequate salt source on Neely's evacuated property. Later the site was known as Neely's Bend and was located up the Cumberland River, northeast from the Bluff. The group established a camp and was successfully gathering salt while Neely, himself, hunted for game daily. His daughter served as the camp cook. The salt kilns were located some distance from the camp, and the workmen experienced a false sense of security after several days with no problems.

One evening at dusk Neely brought a large buck into camp and lay down by the campfire to rest. Meanwhile, his daughter sang as she skinned the deer and prepared the venison for supper. A shot suddenly broke the serenity, and Neely, who had raised himself on an elbow, groaned and fell dead. Warriors rushed out from the forest, seized the girl, tied her hands behind her, grabbed Neely's gun and powder horn, then rode away with their captive. She was tethered to a mounted warrior on each side who forced her to run between them until late that night. They rested at a creek south of Bluff Station, and the next day they mounted the girl on a horse and traveled into the Creek Nation somewhere in Georgia.

The salt processors returned to camp shortly after dark, found Neely's body, and noted his daughter was missing. They arrived at Mansker's Station by dawn and informed Mrs. Neely of the tragedy. The settlers organized a posse to pursue the attackers and rescue the girl. They followed the tracks for 15 or 20 miles, then quit the chase when Kasper Mansker declared he was afraid the captors would kill the girl if they were pursued. Miss Neely remained a captive for several years, but she was eventually released. She later married a settler who resided at a Kentucky station. (There is a marker at Madison, Tennessee, near the junction of Gallatin Pike and Neelys Bend Road [36° 15.376' N, 86° 42.886' W] inscribed, "Two miles east on Cumberland River was Neely's Lick, later called Larkin Sulphur Spring. Here, in the fall of 1780 William Neely was killed and his daughter Mary captured by Indians. Carried by her captors to Michigan, she escaped after two years, and made her way to New York State, and thence eventually back to her home here.")

Many settlers abandoned the stations by the end of 1780 because of their inability to defend themselves against Indian attacks. Several relocated all the way to Kentucky and believed it to be a far safer location in which to settle. All stations on the Cumberland had been abandoned except the Bluff, Eaton's and Freeland's Stations. Colonel Robertson traveled to Kentucky to investigate other measures for defense, to see if he could hold peace talks with the Chickasaw, and to purchase ammunition. It appeared that Chief Dragging Canoe and his warriors from Chickamauga Creek were beginning to make good on the promise to rid the Cherokee ancestral hunting grounds of white encroachers. They had help: the Chickasaw and a few remaining young Upper Village warriors on the west, the Creek from the Muscle Shoals on the south with Doublehead, the Catawba from the east, and the Delaware from the north. By the first of December, only about 130 settlers remained in the Cumberland settlements. Those settlers who remained were despised by the Chickamauga Cherokee who intended to work even harder to evict the encroachers.

Chiefs Dragging Canoe and Doublehead were further enraged because the Cumberland settlers continued to take wildlife on the Cherokee ancestral hunting grounds. Late in the fall of 1780, a party of those hunters went in canoes up the Caney Fork River, and during a five days' hunt reportedly killed 105 bears, 75 buffalo, and 87 deer.[8]

In spite of their successes against the Cumberland settlements, Dragging Canoe and Doublehead missed an opportunity to severely damage the Overmountain communities, especially along the Watauga, Holston, and Nolichucky Rivers.

Since the Chickamauga focused their attention on the Cumberland, the settlers of Watauga and Holston had an opportunity to assist the Carolinas against the British. Their temporary absence from home likewise afforded the Chickamauga an opening to form a coalition with the Upper Village warriors of Oconostota for a second general invasion of the frontier settlements.

British lieutenant general Charles Lord Cornwallis, commander of the British Army in the South, had met with Major Patrick Ferguson on August 23, 1780, to explain the autumn campaign. It would begin with the army's march to Charlotte, North Carolina. Cornwallis had determined that Ferguson would disjoin from the army and take his detachment into North Carolina to the west of Charlotte. There Ferguson would guard Cornwallis' left flank, harass and punish active local Whigs, raid Whig farms for supplies, and deliver the supplies to the army. He would also recruit Tories to comprise local militia regiments and also to supplement his own provincial force.

Ferguson left Fair Forest Creek in South Carolina on September 2, and on September 8, General Cornwallis marched his army out of Camden. The general enthusiastically headed for Charlotte, North Carolina; however, his force was weakened as several men were down with malaria. Lieutenant Colonel Banastre Tarleton, his passionate brash young legion commander, was ill with yellow fever.

Major Ferguson arrived at Gilbert Town (present-day Rutherfordton), North Carolina, on September 7. He camped on a hill that overlooked Gilbert Town from the west, later referred to as Ferguson's Hill (present-day Ferguson's Ridge). Ferguson was an experienced British military officer with an excellent service record. He had been assigned to several command positions and was eager to embark upon his new assignment. He was aware of the Overmountain (or backwater) militiamen and knew they could pose a threat to Cornwallis' flank. On the 10th, the major tried to secure that flank as ordered by the general. He paroled prisoner Samuel Phillips, cousin to Colonel Isaac Shelby, with a message for the Overmountain men. Ferguson told them to stay on their side of the mountain and "desist from their opposition to the British arms, and take protection under his standard." If they did not, he threatened to "march over the mountains, hang their leaders, and lay their country waste with fire and sword."[9]

On the 12th, Ferguson took a detachment to try and locate North Carolina colonel Charles McDowell at his home, Quaker Meadows; however, McDowell had evacuated the area and had taken his militia over the mountains to locate Colonels Isaac Shelby and John Sevier. Samuel Phillips found Colonel Shelby at his home in the Holston settlements and reported Ferguson's warning. Shelby then located Colonel Sevier on the Nolichucky, and together they decided they could not allow Ferguson to get away with his threat. Sevier began to look for McDowell, whom he knew to be in the vicinity. Shelby agreed to contact Washington County, Virginia, Colonel William Campbell. Shelby and Sevier were laying plans to set up a massive rendezvous to take place in the near future.

Colonel Shelby's home was at Shelby's Fort (located on the South Fork Holston River near present-day Bristol, Tennessee, then a part of Virginia) near Samuel Phillips' home. Colonel Sevier's abode was on the banks of the Nolichucky River (10 miles south of present-day Jonesborough, Tennessee, then also claimed by Virginia). Colonel Campbell lived near a salt lick 60 miles further up the South Fork Holston River from Shelby (near present-day Marion, Virginia).

On September 25, 1780, Colonels Isaac Shelby and John Sevier arrived at Sycamore Shoals with 200 militiamen each. They were greeted by North Carolina colonels Charles McDowell and Andrew Hampton who had been camped at the shoals for several days with 450 men between them. Early the next day, Colonel William Campbell appeared with 200 more men to total 1,050. Colonel Sevier's troops included John Crockett, father of frontiersman Davy Crockett. (John Crockett's father, David Crockett, was killed by Dragging Canoe's warriors in 1777. See earlier this chapter.)

The Overmountain men, often called backwater men and screamin' or yellin' boys, were described by historian James Mooney as "led by leaders they trusted, they were wonted to Indian warfare, they were skilled as horsemen and marksmen, they knew how to face every kind of danger, hardship, and privation. Their fringed and tasseled hunting shirts were girded by bead-worked belts, and the trappings of their horses were stained red and yellow. On their heads they wore caps of coon skin or mink skin, with the tails hanging down, or else felt hats, in each of which was thrust a buck tail or a sprig of evergreen. Every man carried a small-bore rifle, a tomahawk, and a scalping knife. A very few of the officers had swords, and there was not a bayonet nor a tent in the army."[10]

Once Ferguson heard that the Overmountain militia was on its approach, he made his way eastward toward the safety of the army in Charlotte. He realized that, if he continued, it would signify that his warning was insignificant, so he changed his mind. On the evening of October 6, 1780, Major Patrick Ferguson organized his force on Kings Mountain in South Carolina. He prepared to make a stand. He walked among the exhausted men in his camp and inspired them by firmly stating that he was "on Kings Mountain, that I am king of that mountain and God Almighty and all the Rebels of hell can not drive me from it."[11]

General Henry "Light-horse Harry" Lee later wrote about Ferguson's position, "a position thickly set with trees, and more assailable by the rifle than defensible with the bayonet."[12] He was describing the approach up the sides of the mountain. Dr. J. B. O. Landrum wrote, "The crest of the mountain was bare, and the British, when in column, were unprotected."[13] Major Patrick Ferguson gave the backwater men from North Carolina no credit at all. He often referred to them as curs or mongrels. In reality, they were seasoned fighters and had been up against one of the best armies around—the Cherokee warriors. Ferguson's force would be no match.

Colonel William Campbell led his unit up the mountain as he yelled: "Here they are, my brave boys; shout like hell, and fight like devils!"[14]

Captain Abraham De Peyster, Ferguson's second in command, had been at Musgrove's Mill and remembered the sound well. He nervously told Ferguson: "These things are ominous—these are the damned yelling boys!"[15]

Ferguson's force was eliminated on October 7, 1780, and Cornwallis lost about 1,000 men, one-fourth of his command. Ferguson's ill-advised warning spoiled Cornwallis' move northward, so he returned to South Carolina. Ferguson missed a chance to ably assist Cornwallis and the Chickamauga. Rather than vocalizing his warning, which basically invited the entire Overmountain militia to the Carolinas, a better move would have been to surprise them with a coordinated attack of his own. Had he furtively alerted Alexander Cameron, Dragging Canoe, Oconostota, and Doublehead of such a plan, they could have simultaneously hit the Holston, Watauga, and Nolichucky settlements. He could have supported a siege, if required, for several weeks. The coalition would likely have been joined by Chief Skyuka with at least warriors from the Middle Villages when they realized that the move would greatly assist Cornwallis' efforts to gain control of North Carolina. The Creek allies of Doublehead might also have joined temporarily and left the Chickasaw alone to harass the Cumberland settlements.

Such a move would have put the encroaching settlers on the defensive (rather than exposing Ferguson's force at Kings Mountain) because the settlers would have been spread out among the various stations. He would have had the extra benefit of trapping McDowell's North Carolina militia at Sycamore Shoals as there would not have been room enough to support them at any of the settlers' small forts. It is highly possible such action would have resulted in the settlers being forced to an agreed truce, so they could move back into Virginia. Then Ferguson could have returned to Cornwallis. Oconostota could have put warriors on the passes of the Holston, and Dragging Canoe and Doublehead could have returned to pressuring the Cumberland settlements. Such a move by Ferguson might not only have freed the Cherokee lands from encroachers, but might have led the American Revolution in another direction.

Even though Ferguson did not organize an attack on the Overmountain communities, Dragging Canoe, Oconostota, and Doublehead could have taken advantage of the opportunity while such a large group of the backwater militia was in South Carolina. The Chickamauga could have immediately left the Cumberlands, joined the Cherokee warriors of Oconostota and Skyuka, and hit the Overmountain settlements. They might have succeeded to take the settlers' stations and set traps in the passes to await the return of the militia. In the worst case, they could have done considerable damage and then returned to their efforts on the Cumberland River before the militia returned. However, they were one month too late.

The exhausted victors of the Battle of Kings Mountain readied the camp for departure the morning after battle. On the night of October 15, 1780, the ragged troops arrived at Quaker Meadows, North Carolina, the home of Major Joseph and Colonel Charles McDowell. There was a parting of the ways next day. The South Carolina troops returned to their own state; Shelby's and Sevier's Overmountain men returned to their own valleys, and Colonel William Campbell took charge of the prisoners.

The return of the Overmountain men, less than one month after they had left, coincided with the beginning of a Chickamauga offensive, and Ghighau Nancy Ward warned Sevier of the coming attacks. Traders Isaac Thomas, Ellis Harlan, and Henry (or William) Springstone carried the warning. Springstone went to Long Island to warn Virginia major Joseph Martin, and Thomas and Harlan were at Sevier's home when he returned from Kings Mountain. He sent word to Virginia colonel Arthur Campbell and began to make plans. The militia needed to rest from the arduous trek to Kings Mountain and back. It would be December before the settlements would raise 700 volunteers from the ranks of the returning militiamen.

Sevier gathered 300 men at Swan Pond on Lick Creek and headed south. They crossed the French Broad River and camped at Boyd's Creek (near present-day Sevierville, Tennessee) three days later. On the morning of December 16, 1780, scouts reported nearly 100 Cherokee were camped three miles away.

Seventy Chickamauga set an often-used Cherokee warrior trap. They formed an arc and hid in the tall grass. Sevier took a vanguard to find the war party. Sevier's men spotted the trap. Before the Chickamauga could try to draw the militiamen into their semicircle, Sevier initiated attacks on each end of the Indians' formation. When Sevier's main force arrived, the warriors closed ranks and withdrew. Sevier tried to give chase but was hampered by swamps. Thirteen Chickamauga were killed, and the plunder they had already taken from some settlements was recovered. The militia suffered no losses.

Sevier received a message from Campbell asking him to wait for the northern units before attacking the Cherokee Upper Towns. Sevier retreated eight miles and camped.

On December 22, Arthur Campbell, Major Martin, and 400 militiamen joined Sevier. They moved on the Upper Villages, mostly abandoned, and destroyed the towns and crops. They killed 29 warriors. They also captured 17 Cherokee, mostly women and children.

Nancy Ward directed some Cherokee men to drive a herd of cattle to Chota to feed the army. Georgia colonel Elijah Clarke led a detail to slaughter the cattle. Major Martin rode up and discovered Ward's cattle being butchered. He was unaware of his mother-in-law's action, and he challenged Clarke. A fistfight erupted which caused a rift between Sevier's and Martin's forces. Martin demanded payment for the cattle. (Colonel Clarke had led a party of Whig families from Georgia to the Overmountain settlements in October to escape tyrannical backcountry Tories who had come into power after the fall of Savannah one year earlier He temporarily associated his militiamen with those of his host, John Sevier.)

The combined militia crossed the Little Tennessee River three miles below Chota as warriors watched from a distant ridge. The force divided into two bodies and began to destroy towns along the river (being Upper Villages, these were not Chickamauga towns). The chiefs sent Nancy Ward with a peace message, but Sevier would not parley. He continued to the lower Hiwassee River with plans to destroy towns that allied with Dragging Canoe. They devastated Hiwassee and Chestowee along with their stores and provisions. They did not, however, penetrate as far south as Chickamauga Town on the lower Tennessee River.

On January 1, 1781, the militia began its return journey. Sevier had destroyed ten principal villages including the capital, Chota, and several smaller villages. Over 1,000 dwellings and 50,000 bushels of corn were ruined. Even Chief Oconostota had to take shelter in the mountains. Sevier sent a message to the older chiefs to make peace or suffer a worse invasion. Again, the older chiefs had worked their way into an awkward position. They had sued for peace many times, and always at a cost of land cessions. When the young warriors tried to defend the Cherokee land, as in this case, the militia would take it out on the Upper Towns, the older chiefs, and their followers because they presented themselves as the ones who spoke for the nation. During the return trip, Sevier was met at Chota by several Cherokee who surrendered many white captives and wanted to hold peace talks.[16]

Two weeks later, Colonel Sevier wrote to Major Martin to offer payment for Nancy Ward's cattle, per a demand by Martin:

> TO MAJ. JOSEPH MARTIN   Jan. 14, 1781
> Dear Sir: I received yours of the 12th. According to your request, have sent Nancy Ward the certificate. I thank you for your kind offer to serve me in carrying down any demands of mine. I have got a person to take down some letters. Am glad you are agoing [sic] down, as you can inform them fully of any particular circumstances relating to our campaign. I am, sir, with esteem and your most obedient servant,
> John Sevier[17]

About the first of January 1781, warriors fired upon John Tucker and Joseph Hendrix near Sulphur Spring. They were returning to the Bluff from Freeland's Station by the buffalo trail. Each suffered a broken arm, but they reached the fort ahead of their pursuers.

On the evening of January 11, 1781, James Robertson returned to the Bluff from his trip to Kentucky. Earlier that same day, a small party of Chickasaw had appeared in the neighborhood. While David Hood was passing from Freeland's Station to the Bluff, the band fired upon him from ambush near Sulphur Spring (where Hendrix and Tucker had been attacked a few days earlier). Three balls hit Hood and knocked him from his horse. The warriors rushed up, and one of them began to scalp him. The knife was dull, and the scalp did not remove easily. The Indian sawed on Hood's head until he could pull the trophy away. Hood withstood the ordeal without exhibiting any sign of life. The brave then stomped upon him so as to break his neck and left him for dead. Once the Chickasaw disappeared, Hood cautiously looked around to be sure he was in the clear. He arose and, weak from the ordeal, slowly traveled towards the Bluff. On his way, he encountered the same war party. They laughed at his predicament from the top of a ridge. He ran as they fired upon and slightly wounded him. They did not track him, and he collapsed into the brush. Some men at the Bluff Fort heard the shots and ventured out. They found him and, thinking he was dead or near so, placed him in an outhouse. That night the Chickasaw assaulted Freeland's Station, and the militia from the Bluff hurried to assist.

When Colonel Robertson arrived that same evening, he discovered that his family was at Freeland's Station. When he arrived there, he learned that his wife had given birth earlier in the day. About midnight, Robertson heard a sound at the gate, seized his rifle, then yelled, "Indians!"

The party of Chickasaw, then numbering 150 warriors, had dislodged the gate bar and were entering the station. All eleven men in the stockade rushed to the defense. Major Robert Lucas, who occupied a house with unchinked cracks, rushed out and was mortally wounded. One of Colonel Robertson's slaves had been in the house with Lucas, and he was also killed. They were the only fatalities in the skirmish. Lucas had been a party to the Treaty of Sycamore Shoals and to the Cherokee deed to a part of Carter's Valley. A specific partial fulfillment of Dragging Canoe's warning at Sycamore Shoals had come to pass.

The gunfire from the attack had been so loud that people as far away as Eaton's Station and the Bluff had been awakened. The militia at the Bluff fired the cannon and the Chickasaw, realizing that help was on the way, withdrew. One warrior was killed. Soon thereafter Colonel Robertson held talks with Chickasaw chief Piomingo, and formed an alliance. The Chicaksaw had been long-time enemies of the Cherokee. Though they had recently allied themselves with the Chickamauga, they permanently switched allegiance to the white settlers. (Historian James Mooney recorded that the attack actually occurred four days later, on the 15th.)

(Piomingo was a striking figure described as medium in height, well-proportioned in body, and intelligent in countenance. He is said to have been more than 100 years old when he parleyed with Robertson, but he strode the earth as he did in his prime. He dressed in white buckskin and wore his white hair in a scalp-lock.)

Robertson returned to the Bluff and went out to see David Hood in the outhouse. The colonel found him alive and asked how he was doing. Hood answered that he was still alive and believed he could recover. Robertson dressed Hood's injuries, including the horrendous scalp wound. The colonel had learned a treatment for scalped victims from a traveling French surgeon on the Holston. He took a pegging awl and punched holes throughout the entire scalped portion. That procedure allowed granulation to arise through the holes and gradually spread until it formed a coating over the skull. The operation became so common that there were persons in every settlement station who could perform it. As late as 1796 there were still twenty persons reportedly still living on the Cumberland who had lost their scalps.

Hood, a tall and lanky young cooper and a bachelor, recovered and lived in Nashville to an old age.

At the beginning of 1781, the entire population of the Cumberland settlements was concentrated in three central stations not over two miles apart: Eaton's on the north side of the Cumberland, and the Bluff and Freeland's on the south. The settlements had suffered the retirement of many families to Kentucky and Illinois.

Three months after the January 11, 1781, Chickasaw attack on Freeland's Station, the Chickamauga directed their attention toward the Cumberland. They had concentrated on the Holston late in 1780, but were driven out by Colonels Sevier and Arthur Campbell, and Major Martin, who destroyed the Upper Towns of the Cherokee and the Valley Towns on the Hiwassee. They had mistakenly assumed that most of the Chickamauga had taken refuge along the Hiwassee after the destruction of Chickamauga Town by Colonel Evan Shelby in 1779 (see earlier this chapter). Sevier seemed to have considered Chickamauga Town to be either abandoned or of little consequence, so he did not pursue an invasion. After Sevier reached a peace agreement with the Cherokee of the Upper and Valley Towns, the Chickamauga turned their arms against the weaker settlements on the Cumberland.

The strongest of the three Nashborough stations was the Bluff, still the home of Colonel James Robertson; consequently, the Chickamauga campaign of 1781 was directed mainly against that site. The result of that campaign would decide the fate of the settlement. If the Bluff were to fall, Freeland's and Eaton's Stations would be unable to resist the warriors, and the whites would be evicted from the Cumberland. Dragging Canoe and Doublehead had developed a smart campaign, and the Battle of the Bluff was brilliantly planned.

The garrison had been on alert since the assault at Freeland's Station. The settlers dared to leave the stockade only when absolutely necessary. In the summer of 1780, John and Daniel Dunham had located a property near the Bluff (present-day Belle Meade). They had built a log house and made some other improvements, but relocated their families to the fort at the Bluff for protection. One day, a Mrs. Dunham sent her daughter 300 to 400 yards from the fort's enclosure for an armful of wood chips. There were Indians concealed in a fallen treetop nearby. They grabbed the girl by the hair, and tore off her scalp. Her mother heard her cries. Terrified, she ran to her assistance and was shot down. Before the men from the fort could reach the scene, the warriors, having scalped the girl, disappeared. The mother and the daughter recovered. Near the end of March, Colonel Samuel Barton rode down to Wilson's Spring Branch in search of cattle. He was fired upon and wounded in the left wrist. He escaped, but was unable to take part in the approaching battle.

On the night of April 1, 1781, 400 Chickamauga surrounded Bluff Fort. Sentinel James Menefee (sometimes Manifree) fired upon one Indian scout. About 200 of the party concealed themselves in the brush and cedars which grew on the hillside (along present-day Cherry Street in Nashville, between Church and Broad Streets). The remainder of the band went down and lay along the bank of a small stream (which ran south of Broad Street, near to and parallel with today's Demonbreun Street, and into the Cumberland River near the foot of Broad).

Three warriors ran toward the fort at dawn on the 2nd, fired at the sentry, and withdrew. Since the militiamen were aware of how well the Cherokee could plan an ambush, they figured the three braves were trying to draw them out. Regardless, after some prodding by his junior officers, Colonel James Robertson took 20 men and gave chase. The baiters stopped on the bank of the Wilson's Stream Branch (near the intersection of today's College and Demonbreun Streets). Soon they faced a small band of Chickamauga, dismounted, and skirmished near Broad Street. A larger band of warriors emerged from the creek bed, cut the militiamen off from the fort, and fired upon them from the rear. An even larger group emerged closer to the fort. The militiamen's horses were startled and stampeded uphill toward the gates. The braves chased the horses, and the militiamen tried to work their way back as the Indians had been distracted. The horses found the gates closed and veered away with the warriors hot on their trail. Most of the horses wound up at Sulphur Spring.

The skirmish continued. Captain James Leiper, Peter Gill, Alex Buchanan, and John Kennedy had been killed; Kasper Mansker, James Manifee, and Joseph Moonshaw were wounded. The survivors fought desperately to make their way toward the fort. They dragged their wounded comrades with them.

Mrs. Robertson, with an axe in her hand, was watching the fray from the parapet. A pack of 50 watchdogs were shut up in the fort. They had reportedly been trained to hate the scent of Indians, so, during the progress of the battle, ran amok around the enclosure as they desired to join the fray.

The confusion and excitement of the chase was witnessed from the fort, and Mrs. Robertson observed the fury of the dogs. She directed the sentinel to open the gate and turn the pack loose on the already broken and confused ranks of warriors.

The dogs ran furiously down the hill, made straight for the Indians, and attacked them with great ferocity. The warriors were then busy defending themselves. As soon as the warriors' attentions were diverted by the attack of the dogs and the chase after the horses, the white skirmishers, still dragging the wounded, ran for the fort.

Isaac Lucas, brother of Major Robert Lucas, who had been killed at Freeland's, was shot down during the scramble back to the fort. His thigh was shattered. He was in the rear and the other members of the party did not realize he was down until they had safely passed through the gate. He turned his face toward the approaching warriors as he fell, determined to fight to the death. He quickly primed his gun, took aim at a huge brave at the fore of the pursuers, and shot him dead in his tracks. Some of the militiamen saw Lucas' dangerous position and began to fire at the warriors, whereupon they withdrew. Lucas dragged himself to safety near the fort.

A courageous warrior overtook Edward Swanson within twenty yards of the gate and struck him on the shoulder, causing him to drop his gun. Swanson turned and seized the gun of his adversary, but the larger and stronger Indian wrenched it back and knocked Swanson to his knees. The militiamen on the parapet were afraid to fire lest they hit Swanson; however, the Indian tried to shoot him. The gun misfired. John Buchanan, Sr., saw Swanson's danger, rushed out the gate, fired, and killed the warrior. The surviving whites had all reached the stockade and maintained a brisk barrage upon the Chickamauga to protect the wounded Lucas. Soon thereafter, he and Swanson were brought into the fort, and the attackers withdrew.

It is said that Mrs. Robertson stood at the gate after the battle, patted each dog on the head as he came into the fort, and she "thanked God that he had given Indians a love for horses and a fear of dogs."[18] It is more likely that the dogs had a prejudice against strangers causing a ruckus than specifically against Indians. Certainly, the dogs were so well acquainted with the inhabitants of, and refugees visiting, the fort that they became agitated at the sight of unfamiliar people attacking familiar faces. At times during the commotion, a dog mistakenly attacked settlers involved in the melee. Those animals were shot by other militiamen before doing severe damage.

Thus the Battle of the Bluff, sometimes called the Battle of the Horses and Hounds, came to an end. The warriors scalped the settlers who had been left dead on the field, confiscated such guns and ammunition as had been abandoned, and withdrew to the woods at about 10 a.m. Just how many of the attacking party were killed is not known; however, several bodies were found at various places in the nearby forest. It is supposed that a number of the warriors dead and wounded were carried away per Cherokee custom. Later in the battle, John Kesenger, Zachariah White, and George Kennedy joined those previously listed as killed.

Warriors attempted a feeble attack at dusk, presumably by a war party that was late to the battle. They were plainly seen gathered several hundred yards west of the station. They had fired only a few rounds when Colonel Robertson determined to give them a shot from the swivel gun. Some of the men protested that they could not spare the powder and that there were no cannon balls in their stock of ammunition. However, over these objections the piece was loaded with broken horseshoes, scraps of lead, and bits of broken pottery. One heavy charge of powder was used as each militiaman contributed a small amount from his flask. Everything being in readiness, the spark was applied. The little cannon made a massive report, and the warriors retreated. Supposing the shot was a signal for help, a party from Eaton's Station soon arrived on the opposite bank of the Cumberland and called for boats to bring them over. Two men quietly slipped down the bank behind the fort and, after making the round-trip in safety, they brought their friends into Bluff Station. There the visitors spent the night and took their turn on watch in the tower until daylight.

The Battle of the Bluff, as a tribute to the Chickamauga, was the most formidable invasion ever undertaken against the Cumberland stations. The settlers were distressed afterward; however, it marked the beginning of the end for the Chickamauga, though it would not come for many bloody years. A few days later William Hood was killed near Freeland's Station and Peter Renfroe between Freeland's and Sulphur Spring.[19]

Attakullakulla died sometime around 1780. His influence had waned so much that the exact date of his death was not recorded. In recent years, he and Oconostota had generally been accepted as leaders of the Cherokee Nation but were little more than chiefs emeriti. Oconostota carried on as principal chief after Attakullakulla's death; however, Old Tassel and Raven, since they spoke for the two aging chiefs at the Treaty of Holston in 1777, had been the real powers in the Upper Villages. They cooperated with each other but also competed for prominence. Old Tassel had imposed himself as the advocate for peace with the American colonists. Raven, on the other hand, acted as the emissary to the Chickamauga factions and drifted further away from Old Tassel's policies.

It was relatively quiet throughout 1781 with a few skirmishes between the Chickamauga alliance and the settlers. Two events served to keep a lid on things: the unsuccessful attack of the Chickamauga on the Bluff after so much energy had been invested, and a warning by Virginia colonel Arthur Campbell when he left Chota after he and John Sevier had completed their punishing attacks. Campbell sent an ultimatum to the Upper Village Cherokee chiefs and demanded they meet at a peace conference with Major Joseph Martin before summer, or else the army would return and pour out even more devastation upon the villages.

Campbell also sent a report to Continental Army Major General Nathanael Greene, commander of the Southern Department. Greene, who was preparing for his return to South Carolina after the Race to the Dan, sent orders to appoint Virginians Joseph Martin, William Preston, William Christian, and Arthur Campbell, and Overmountain settlers Evan Shelby, Joseph Williams, and John Sevier as commissioners for the treaty conference—any five to make a quorum.

The treaty conference began July 26, 1781, at Long Island of the Holston. The commissioners intended to require another cession of land—all of it that lay north of the Little Tennessee River. First, the commissioners reminded the chiefs that the British had not been able to adequately support their war efforts and would not be able to provide aid in the future.

Old Tassel rose and spoke: "We were opposed to this war and tried to restrain the young chiefs but they would not listen. I know that you (speaking to Sevier) are a man and a warrior. I have heard different talks by different people quite different from what I expected. I fear you must have been angry and that it was caused by some evil persons.... You have risen up from a warrior to a Beloved Man. I hope your speech will be good."[20]

Sevier replied that he held no animosity for the Cherokee people.

The Ghighau, Nancy Ward, stood as head of the Women's Council and made a now-famous oration that included: "You know that women are always looked upon as nothing; but we are your mothers; you are our sons. OUR CRY IS FOR PEACE; let it continue. This peace must last forever. Let your women's sons be ours; our sons be yours. Let your women hear our words."[21]

Nancy Ward believed the Cherokee should begin to adjust to the white man's world because assimilation was unpreventable. She was prophetic and had inherited her Uncle Attakullakulla's sensibilities.

Colonel William Christian was visibly touched as he replied: "Mothers; we have listened well to your talk; it is humane.... No man can hear it without being moved by it. Such words and thoughts show the world that human nature is the same everywhere. Our women shall hear your words, and we know how they will feel and think of them. We are all descendants of the same woman. We will not quarrel with you because you are our mothers. We will not meddle with your people if they will be still and quiet at home and leave us in peace."[22]

Peace was established between the Overmountain settlers and the Upper Villages—for the time being. The settlers were unhappy with General Greene's requirement that no Americans would pursue further encroachment onto Cherokee lands. However, they likely realized that article of the treaty would be no more enforceable than King George's Proclamation of 1763 had been. General Greene was certainly too busy with the British to provide any troops to the Upper Villages. It was the same old tale; the Cherokee would have to rely on assistance from the Overmountain militias. They would have a long wait.

Chiefs Dragging Canoe and Doublehead continued to attack travelers, especially along the Wilderness Road, and they kept the pressure on Nashborough. As they hid in ambush by every path and along every trail, it was perilous for settlers to attempt passage from one fort to another. War parties hovered around and shot cattle, killed and drove the game away, and destroyed crops in an effort to exhaust the food supply for the encroachers. The Chickamauga actions in 1780 and 1781 were necessary to continually warn the settlers they were not welcome and needed to leave. Doublehead and Dragging Canoe were not done and would yet make themselves heard throughout the region.

In the fall of 1781, British Indian agent Thomas Brown at Augusta began to deal more with the Chickamauga Cherokee than the Upper Village chiefs. He had already been working with the Creek. Raven of Chota became Brown's envoy to Chief Dragging Canoe and Deputy Indian Agent Alexander Cameron. Raven undertook to supplant Oconostota, who had been his mentor in the councils of the Cherokee Nation. Raven went to Georgia in 1781 and grovelled before Brown. The British agent nominated him as principal chief of the Cherokee and gave him a medal as the symbol of his authority. Raven returned to Chota and declared he was done with the Americans and would deal only with the British. His announcement, however, had no impact with the people, and Old Tassel solely held the power in the Upper Towns. Raven's defection had only strengthened the position of Old Tassel, so Raven was forced to join his brother, Dragging Canoe, in a subordinate role.

More young Cherokee warriors in the Middle and Valley Villages, and some along the Little Tennessee River, aligned themselves with the Chickamauga. Those, led by Chief Skyuka, and their Tory allies were very active and, in November, 1781, attacked backcountry settlements in Georgia and South Carolina that lay along the Savannah River. One of the Tory bands, commanded by William "Bloody Bill" Cuningham (sometimes spelled Cunningham), sowed seeds of destruction and vengeance in the backcountry of South Carolina.

On December 7, 1781, Captain John Crawford of Cuningham's regiment rode past General Andrew Pickens' blockhouse. He then headed east toward Ninety Six. As luck would have it, Crawford came upon a convoy of wagons being escorted by South Carolina

Patriot Militia captain Moses Liddell and his company. The Tories drove the escort away and killed several in the process. Crawford captured the wagoners, one of whom was John Pickens, the younger brother of the general.

"Bloody Bill" knew he would be the focus of a huge manhunt, so he split his forces. He and 50 of his closest comrades returned to Charles Town, while the larger group of 250 men sought protection in the Cherokee villages on the Georgia side of the Savannah River. John Pickens and the other prisoners were in the custody of the latter group. When they reached the villages, the captives were turned over to the Cherokee and tortured for several days.

The Cherokee eventually scalped John Pickens and then burned him to death on a pile of lightwood while Cuningham's Tories watched with pleasure. It is likely that Andrew Pickens' first cousin, John "The Tory" Pickens, was present at young John Pickens' death. John "The Tory" Pickens had worked closely with the Lower, Middle, and Valley Towns' Cherokee warriors as early as the 1776 war, and maybe earlier. He was later apparently quite friendly with Chickamauga leader Bob Benge (known by the whites as Chief Bench), because Bench named one of his children Pickens Benge. There will be more about John "The Tory" Pickens later.[23]

The Chickamauga were making big plans for an offensive intended to bring the encroaching settlers to their knees. They would be even harsher than they had been the previous two years. Time was running out, and they could spare no effort.

CHAPTER 9

The Chickamauga Continue to Defend the Cherokee Nation

In 1782, Oconostota resigned his nominal leadership in favor of his son, Terrapin (Tuckasee). When Virginia governor Benjamin Harrison sent a medal to Old Tassel, Tassel gave it to Terrapin. As de facto first beloved man and white (Peace) chief, Old Tassel had the consent of the Chota Council. The action signified that Terrapin would replace his father in the position of red (War) chief of the Cherokee Nation since Raven had withdrawn to Dragging Canoe's faction of the Chickamauga. Old Tassel would not yet become the official principal chief for another three years. Oconostota would continue to fill that position in name, more so a principal chief emeritus.

Old Tassel's communications exemplified him as a man with high intellect. His descendants were becoming very powerful in the Chickamauga faction. His nephew, Young Tassel (John Watts, Jr. or Kunokeski) would yet become a famous Chickamauga leader as would his grand-nephews, The Bench (Robert Benge, Captain Benge), The Tail (Martin Benge), and Nettle Carrier (Tahlonteskee). His nephew, White Man Killer (Unacata or Malachi Watts), would also become a well-known warrior. The maternal uncle-to-nephew relationship is strong in Cherokee culture and none more so than that of Young Tassel to Old Tassel. Of course, Old Tassel's brother was none other than notorious Chief Doublehead (Incalatanga, Taltsuska) who, at first, worked independently of the Chickamauga for the same purpose. That closeness, however, gave Old Tassel little influence over the direction the Chickamauga were taking. After all, during the years their Uncle Attakullakulla was a man of influence, the politics that he espoused had disappointed them.

The Cherokee had suffered greatly from the wars of 1776 and 1780, and Old Tassel was convinced he could not retain his influence in the nation by advocating further conflict. He, like Attakullakulla had done, decided his best approach to continue peace advocacy would benefit the Cherokee. He not only believed he could rely upon the white men's sense of justice and fair play to protect treaty boundaries, but also trusted that encroachment onto the ancestral hunting grounds would stop. How mistaken he was. He seemingly ignored that the warriors were defecting to Dragging Canoe's and Doublehead's factions in droves. The political power in the Cherokee Nation at that time rested with those two Chickamauga chiefs. Each was a charismatic leader and resided along the lower Tennessee River: Dragging Canoe at Chickamauga Town (present-day Chattanooga, Tennessee) and Doublehead further downriver at Muscle Shoals of the Tennessee. Doublehead was the more notorious of the two and could be labeled a bully. He had withdrawn to the Tennessee River in 1770, well before Dragging Canoe had in 1775. Dragging Canoe was a formidable warrior and could punish an enemy with the best of war chiefs; however, he did at times exhibit fairness to captives.

In early 1782, Georgia Militia major John Cunningham eagerly joined Brigadier General Andrew Pickens to quell recent attacks by Tories and Creek and Chickamauga Cherokee warriors. Pickens had lobbied in January for a large Georgia force under Colonel Elijah Clarke and for an equally strong North Carolina force to be led by Brigadier General Griffith Rutherford. However, Clarke and the Georgia State Troops were assigned to Continental Army major general Anthony Wayne to surround Savannah, the last place of refuge for the British that still remained in Georgia. Continental Army major general Nathanael Greene had surrounded Charles Town in a similar effort. The final departure of the trapped British and Tories aboard British ships from Savannah and Charles Town would occur in July and December respectively. Britain stalled their withdrawal from American territory because, once peace dialogues began, the power of the British negotiating position would be dependent upon which land they still controlled.

The Georgia backcountry settlers lobbied the Georgia legislature for help against the intensified attacks by Tories and Indians. Georgia governor John Martin contacted the Creek and suggested they and the Chickamauga should end their attacks in the Georgia backcountry. He emphasized that the British had been defeated, and that the French would no longer be able to supply their needs; consequently, they should realize that their only trade partners would be those in the states of Georgia and South Carolina. On January 19, the legislature prepared an order to increase the support of Wayne's army; however, Governor Martin convinced the solons to support Pickens' effort. The legislature, in turn, ordered Clarke to assist. He detached Major John Cunningham and one-half of the Georgia militia to meet Pickens. General Rutherford was too busy in the North Carolina backcountry to participate.

Pickens and Cunningham, however, became too involved scouting the backcountry of their states for marauding bands of Tories. They compounded that effort in early February, but they were never able to engage the Loyalists. The Tories melted away to rejoin the Chickamauga in the very towns that Pickens wanted to attack. On March 1, 1782, South Carolina governor John Matthews ordered Pickens to resume his planned invasion. Much organizing had to be done. The sieges of Charles Town and Savannah had to continue, and the backcountry could not be exposed to the Tory bands.

Andrew Pickens left Colonel LeRoy Hamilton with a regiment to patrol the backcountry of South Carolina, and Colonel Clarke did the same in Georgia with Captain Patrick Carr assigned to the task. Pickens was then able to begin the expedition with John Cunningham, who was promoted to lieutenant colonel, and South Carolina colonel Robert Anderson.

The troops first moved on Little Chota, which had been a Tory stronghold. They found and buried the skeletons of 11 captive militiamen. (Little Chota was in the vicinity of present-day Sautee Nacoochee, Georgia, on State Highway 17 between Clarkesville and Helen, near the juncture of Sautee Creek and the Chattahoochee River.) They burned several abandoned towns where Pickens was sure the inhabitants had abetted the Tories. They had one skirmish with warriors whom they surprised at Catoogajoy, and they burned Quawasee. Colonel Anderson had another skirmish with some warriors across the river from the town. They proceeded through a severe snowstorm to Horse Shoe Town where another fight resulted in the capture of prisoners, one being a Tory. The Tory told General Pickens that the warriors were gathering and might attack that night. Because of the weather, however, the attack did not come. Pickens and his officers met in council and decided to return to the backcountry. The warriors they had expected to attack at Horse Shoe Town assaulted them from the rear on the second day of their return march. They repulsed the band and continued on their way.

Pickens likely had vengeance in the back of his mind at the onset of the expedition as he was sorely troubled over the death of his younger brother, John. However, he may have blamed the Tories of "Bloody Bill" Cuningham more than he did the Cherokee since "Bloody Bill" had riled the Indians to attack the backcountry settlements of the Carolinas and Georgia. After Cornwallis had been defeated, the Tory militias became outlaws. Hence, they were primary targets for the Americans to effectively attack and end depredations on the settlements. Pickens seemingly realized that the Cherokee were fighting for their existence, but he was determined to continue and abolish the source of the problems to the backcountry, and that included punishment for those who made the attacks. Pickens and John Cunningham had killed 40 warriors and captured or wounded 40 more before the end of the excursion.

General Pickens was then given command of the retired Brigadier General Thomas Sumter's old 1st Brigade of State Militia in addition to his own 3rd Brigade. He had hoped that his recent foray would end warrior incursions into the backcountry, so he joined Major General Greene at Charles Town.

On May 23, 1782, Tories, Creek, and Chickamauga attacked a blockhouse in northeastern Georgia. A company of militia that patrolled the area chased the war party, but they could not keep up. This unnerved Governor Martin who sent an urgent message to apprise General Pickens in South Carolina saying: "For God's sake exert yourself and come to our timely aid, as delays are dangerous."[1]

Indian trader Jesse Spears had gingerly made his way from Georgia into South Carolina to look for General Pickens; however, Pickens was busily engaged at Charles Town, so Colonel Robert Anderson received the warning that a combined party was invading backcountry Georgia. Anderson decided to take a regiment and assist Colonel Clarke. They met on the Oconee River on June 1. British Indian trader William McIntosh was on his way with more than 400 Chickamauga, Creek, and Tories. Spears had given Anderson enough detail that they established a proper ambush and surprised the large force. Both sides experienced some casulaties before the Loyalists and warriors withdrew. Anderson and Clarke captured two Tories: Indian trader Daniel Murphy and a man named Adam Luny. At Big Shoals of the Oconee, Colonel Clarke held court; the two prisoners were found guilty of treason and therefore hanged. Their bodies were left in place dangling from a hickory tree on the east bank of the shoal to warn future invaders of the backcountry they were not welcome. (Daniel Murphy is the likely grandfather of Mary "Polly" Murphy and 6th great-grandfather of the author. See Appendix A and Chapter 3.)

Late in August 1782, Simon Burney and two Chickasaw warriors approached Lieutenant Colonel John Logan near Fort Jefferson under a flag of truce. They brought a talk signed by Chickasaw leaders Poymace Tankaw, Mingo Homaw, Tuskon Patapo, and Piomingo who desired to negotiate a treaty with the settlers. They admitted their past attacks not only those in Kentucky, but near Nashborough as well. They had been irked that Colonel George

Rogers Clark had built Fort Jefferson on their hunting ground. Clark had constructed the fort in 1779 to be used as a muster post for his Rangers from which they initiated their forays into the northern theater of the war. The then–Virginia governor, Thomas Jefferson, had ordered Clark to purchase the site from the Chickasaw; however, Clark moved in without their consent. The fort, deemed no longer necessary, was abandoned in the summer of 1782; therefore, the Chickasaw desired to defect from the Chickamauga confederation and end hostilities. Colonel John Donelson had moved to Kentucky after his property at Clover Bottom was destroyed in 1780. Colonel Logan presented the message to Donelson, who wrote Virginia governor Benjamin Harrison V. Colonel Donelson suggested the governor appoint a treaty commission to meet the Chickasaw leaders at the Nashborough settlement. (Fort Jefferson was located on present-day U.S. Highway 51/62 [Westvaco Road]. The site has a 20-foot-tall cross that can't be missed from the highway. There is a marker in Wickcliffe, Kentucky, on the same highway about one mile north of the site. The marker is at 36° 57.342' N, 89° 5.469' W.)

Late summer of 1782 was also a perilous time for the entire Nashborough settlement. It extended to the complacent settlers in the vicinity of Kilgore's Station, 30 miles to the north. Heretofore ignored by the warriors, the serenity ended when residents Samuel Martin and Isaac Johnson were captured outside of the fort. The Creek allies of the Chickamauga transported the pair to the Creek Nation. Though Johnson soon escaped, Martin assimilated and reportedly raided the Nashborough settlers with Creek war parties. Historian Edward Albright stated regarding Martins eventual return to the settlements: "He came home elegantly dressed, silver spurs on his boots, and bringing with him two valuable horses."[2]

Shortly thereafter, two young men, brothers by the name of Mason, had concealed themselves in their deer blind at Clay Lick. Salt licks were excellent locations for settlers and warriors alike to waylay unsuspecting game. The Masons soon spotted seven Chickamauga hunters who had planned to use the same location. The two white men ambushed the Indians and killed two of them. After the survivors withdrew, the brothers then returned to the fort and summoned three friends. Once they were comfortable that those who escaped would not return, they scalped the two victims of the ambuscade.

Travelers John and Ephraim Peyton of Bledsoe's Station spent that night at Kilgore's Station. Warriors, likely those that had survived the earlier ambush, hustled several horses overnight including those that belonged to the Peytons. Kilgore Station's militia overtook the war party at present-day Peyton's Creek. The militia recovered the horses and killed one warrior in the process. After they had camped for the night, the militiamen were waylaid by the war party that had circled to get ahead of them. The ambushers killed Josiah Hoskins and one of the Masons. (A varied account is found on pages 231–232.)

All of the Cumberland stations' residents were unable to safely farm and tend to livestock. They dared not to venture out for water without extra precautions. They increased their sentries to keenly watch for war parties. The inhabitants of Kilgore's Station became so concerned over safety that they quit the fort and moved to the Bluff Fort at Nashborough. The Chickamauga plan of a strong offensive to drive the settlers from their land seemed to be working. All of the stations near Nashborough had been closed but three: the Bluff Fort, Eaton's Station, and Freeland's Station. (Kilgore's Station was located at present-day Cross Plains, Tennessee, on State Highway 25, south of the Kentucky border, just west of Interstate Highway 65, northeast of Springfield, Tennessee.)

Colonel James Robertson called a general council to discuss the safety of the settlements. Some settlers declared their intentions to relocate to the Overmountain settlements or to Kentucky. Colonel Robertson pointed out that the Chickamauga expected just such a reaction and would alertly watch all roads and waterways leaving the Nashborough settlements. He continued that any such travelers would not survive well-organized war party attacks. Robertson's admonition convinced the settlers to remain at Nashborough.

Meanwhile, Tory colonel Thomas Waters led a band of Loyalists and Chickamauga from their base in Georgia to attack the backcountry settlements of Georgia and South Carolina. Those attacks were not planned by the Chickamauga, but were Tory initiatives. This repetitive action, of allowing the British or Loyalists to focus the warriors' attention on the backcountry, again detracted from the Chickamauga focus on the Overmountain and Nashborough settlements. They had once more invited severe retribution from the coastal states' militias.

On September 5, 1782, South Carolina governor John Matthews ordered Brigadier General Andrew Pickens to go after Waters, his Loyalist band, and his allied Chickamauga warriors. Pickens, in turn, sent a message to Georgia colonel Elijah Clarke and asked him to take part. Pickens and 316 men from four companies of South Carolina militia crossed Cherokee Ford of the Savannah on the 10th where they were joined by Colonel Clarke with 98 Georgia militiamen.

The combined militia crossed the Chattahoochee River on the 24th. The militiamen carried rifles in their saddle scabbards, sabers at their sides, and tomahawks and knives on their belts. They rode on seldom-traveled trails to avoid Indian and Tory patrols. Their plan was to use the rifles only when they scouted the Cherokee positions. When it came time to fight, they would surprise their foe with a charge on horseback while flashing sabers and tomahawks. This militia technique usually awed enemies taken by surprise, especially if they were armed only with single-shot rifles. They could not cope with a quick blitz by men on horses. The shortage of ammunition did not affect Pickens' plan of action. He had the utmost confidence in the use of sabers, tomahawks, and knives as cavalry weapons when fighting.

Before reaching the Chattahoochee, the troopers captured two warriors who warned Pickens that a spy had been in his midst and escaped to warn Waters of his presence. Pickens skirted where he thought Tory patrols were working to the north, and he, guided by the two prisoners, followed a seldom-used trail straight west to Long Swamp Town, Waters' base of operation.

The militia traveled through the night and reached the vicinity of Long Swamp Town in the darkness of the early morning on the 25th. Pickens warned his militia as he described later to General Henry Lee: "To endeavor to put a stop to the cruel murder of women and children which had been long practiced both by the white people and the Indians in their war on each other I issued positive orders that no Indian woman, child or old man or any unfit to bear arms should be put to death or [i.e., upon] pain of death on the perpetrator, giving at the same time the object I hoped to obtain by it. This order was readily obeyed and the Indians soon followed the example."[3]

Pickens sent Colonel Clarke around to the north end of the town, and the South Carolina militia attacked from the south. The warriors and Tories were taken completely by surprise and were devastated. Waters, however, had escaped the onslaught as he had left the previous day. Several militiamen were overly exuberant with their sabers and beheaded several Tories and warriors as they rode through the town. One such example was a militiaman named Parata:

> One Indian headed for a deep ravine as he carried his rifle. General Pickens gave chase, but the ravine was inaccessible by horse. The General and others fired a few rounds into the ravine to no avail. A militiaman, identified only as Parata, jumped into the ravine with his rifle and sword. He and the brave came to within 30 yards of each other and fired as they dodged from tree to tree. The warrior charged and swung his rifle at Parata who parried with his saber and yelled, "Now—damn ye, it's my turn!" They continued to swing their weapons at each other. Finally, Parata sliced the brave's throat with his saber, and the Indian went down. Parata cursed with each blow as he decapitated the warrior. General Pickens said loudly, "Parata acts like a fool!" Parata climbed out of the ravine with his own weapons and the brave's rifle and shot pouch. He haughtily said, "General you 'lacked' to have lost the best soldier you have!" Andrew Pickens gave Parata a stern glare and turned away with a "Huh!"[4]

Pickens wrote Lee about the reason for the action and the result:

> When they evacuated that [Ninety Six] some of the worst tories [sic] went to the Cherokees and were almost contiually [sic] harassing and murdering the frontier inhabitants and made no distinction of sexes.... You know the scarcity of ammunition which prevailed after being reduced to Four rounds per man. I met Clark [sic] at the place appointed. We proceeded with about 500 men all mounted and nearly one third with swords. I had not more than five or six rounds of ammunition for each man. It may be thought rash to have gone with so little ammunition against a powerful tribe of Indians, aided by a banditti of desperadoes. We went the whole way through the woods unexplored by any of us before. We intirely [sic] evaded their spies and completely surprised one of their towns and made prisoners of more than 50 women and children with a few men. We had marched the whole night before, guided by two Indians who we accidentally met with the day before and made prisoners of. They faithfully performed the task allotted them. After surprising the town and making the prisoners in the evening I sent out three of the most active Indian men that we had taken and told them to go tell their people that I was there, that I did not blame the Indians so much as the white men that was amongst them, I would go no further nor destroy any more of their towns and would release all their prisoners on their delivering to me all their prisoners they had of ours including the negroes they had taken, that I would [remain there] two days and that if they refused to comply I would proceed and as far as I could I would destroy as many of their towns and as much of their provisions as possible and if they wished to fight they knew where to find me. The next day they sent in a flag, they said they had heard my talk and would comply with my demands as far as in their power but asked for a few days longer time. I gave them three days longer. On the evening of the last day I had given them their principal chief, with 8 or 10 warriors came in with six white men tied who had been very active with them. We remained in their nation till we had collected a number of their chiefs and warriors and had matters so settled with them that the depredations of the Cherokees on the frontiers of Georgia and South Carolina ceased from that time.[5]

No Patriots were killed, but two were wounded in the campaign. Five Tories were captured; one was hanged, and Clarke took the others to Augusta for trial. Forty warriors had been killed and 13 villages destroyed, including Long Swamp Town. The other 12 towns were destroyed as Colonels Clarke and Robert Anderson rode up and down the territory looking for Waters.

On the 30th, Chief Terrapin (son of Chief Oconostota) and Chief Wolf went to Pickens on Long Swamp Creek with six Tories and some horses that had been taken from the settlements. They asked for more time, and the general reluctantly gave it.

Finally, 12 chiefs and more than 200 warriors arrived at Pickens' camp on October 17, 1782. They negotiated after Pickens explained that the British were leaving and the Tories would not be able to help the Cherokee. He further stated that he did not blame the Cherokee but did blame the Loyalists in their midst. On the 22nd, they signed the Treaty of Long Swamp Creek which required the Cherokee to deliver within 20 days all Tories and property taken from backcountry settlements to some of Pickens' militiamen at Frog Town. After that treaty, there was very little to report regarding raids into backcountry South Carolina or Georgia. The Chickamauga then could focus on their prime targets—the Overmountain and Cumberland settlements. (Long Swamp Town was located where Long Swamp Creek enters the Etowah River, 50 miles west of Big Shoals of the Oconee and 20 miles west of the Chattahoochee River, 34°19'10.49" N 84°20'31.56" W. Frog Town was located on the Chestatee River, 30 miles northeast of Long Swamp Town and 30 miles due west of the westernmost point of South Carolina.)[6]

Before General Pickens had embarked on his expedition, he wrote to Colonel John Sevier in the Overmountain settlements and asked him to coordinate a similar action from the north.

North Carolina governor Alexander Martin ordered Sevier to attack the Chickamauga to relieve the pressure from the Upper Village Cherokee. Sevier received Martin's and Pickens' messages and, on September 3, 1782, mustered his militia at the bend of the Nolichucky River. They met a number of militiamen from Colonel Arthur Campbell's Washington County regiment and set out for Chickamauga country.

Sevier and 200 men went to Chota where the Cherokee provided a guide. They destroyed several towns on the Tellico River where known allies of Dragging Canoe resided.

Next the militia marched on Chickamauga Town, Dragging Canoe's center of operation; however, Chickamauga Town was deserted. They burned the village and then did the same with the other villages along Chickamauga Creek.

On September 20, 1782, Sevier met a small band of warriors led by Chief Skyuka, a refugee from the Lower Towns who had joined Dragging Canoe's faction. The skirmish did not amount to much as most of the Chickamauga were on raids in the Cumberland settlements.

In a letter dated August 19, 1839, James Sevier recalled:

> We set out for the Indian country in the month of September, 1782. On the Highwassee [sic] river and Chiccamauga [sic] creek we destroyed all their towns, stock, corn & everything they had to support on. We then crossed a small range of mountains to the Coosa river, where we found and destroyed several towns, with all their stock, corn & provisions of every kind. The Indians eluded our march and kept out of our way in the general, although a few men, women and children were surprised and taken. We left the Coosa river for home about the last of October.... Thus ended the war of 1782. We all set out for our homes without the loss of a single man.[7]

(A marker is erected in the town of Lookout Mountain, Tennessee, at the intersection of Lookout Mountain Scenic Highway [State Highway 148] and Jo Conn Guild, on the right heading north on Lookout Mountain Scenic Highway, 35° 1.124' N, 85° 20.313' W. See Chapters 5–8 for more background on Chief Skyuka.)

While Pickens' and Sevier's missions were underway, Chief Old Tassel wrote a message to North Carolina governor Martin and sent it by Colonel Joseph Martin. The letter, or talk, was dated at Chota, September 25, 1782. Chief Old Tassel said:

> Brother: I am now going to speak to you. I hope you will listen to me. I intended to come this fall and see you, but there was such confusion in our country, I thought it best for me to stay at home and send my Talks by our friend Colonel Martin, who promises to deliver them safe to you. We are a poor distressed people, that is, in great trouble, and we hope our elder brother will take pity on us and do us justice. Your people from Nollichucky [sic] are daily pushing us out of our lands. We have no place to hunt on. Your people have built houses within one day's walk of our towns. We don't want to quarrel with out elder brother; we, therefore, hope our elder brother will not take our lands from us, that the Great Man above gave us. He made you and he made us; we are all his children, and we hope our elder brother will take pity on us, and not take our lands from us that our father gave us, because he is stronger than we are. We are the first people that ever lived on this land; it is ours, and why will our elder brother take it from us? It is true, some time past, the people over the great water persuaded some of our young men to do some mischief to our elder brother, which our principal men were sorry for. But you our elder brothers come to our towns and took satisfaction, and then sent for us to come and treat with you, which we did. Then our elder brother promised to have the line run between us agreeable to the first treaty, and all that should be found over the line should be moved off. But it is not done yet. We have done nothing to offend our elder brother since the last treaty, and why should our elder brother want to quarrel with us? We have sent to the Governor of Virginia on the same subject. We hope that between you both, you will take pity on your younger brother, and send Colonel Sevier, who is a good man, to have all your people moved off our land. I should say a great deal more, but our friend, Colonel Martin, knows all our grievances, and he can inform you.[8]

The plight of the Cherokee was pitiful. Chief Old Tassel relied on the graciousness of the whites to stop encroachment in the Overmountain and Cumberland vicinities. Governor Martin relied on Overmountain colonel John Sevier to police the treaties with the Cherokee. The Chickamauga attacked the Overmountain and Cumberland settlements, which often resulted in Sevier's militias attacking peaceful Cherokee villages. The mainstream headmen of the Cherokee Nation had no control over the Chickamauga, and the encroachment was getting worse.

After Sevier destroyed the Chickamauga towns (the second time they had been devastated) Dragging Canoe decided they needed to move to a more defensible location. He moved downstream near the Whirl (or the Suck) of the Tennessee River. There he organized what has become known as the Five Lower Towns. These were Nickajack Town (present-day Shellmound, Tennessee), Running Water Town (near Hale's Bar Dam), Long Island Town (Bridgeport, Alabama), Crow Town (Stevenson, Alabama), and Lookout Town (on Lookout Creek in Georgia). Dragging Canoe used Lookout Town as his center of operation. He met there often with such Chickamauga leaders as Bob Benge (The Bench), John Watts, Jr. (Young Tassel), Bloody Fellow (Nenetooyah, a husband of Wurteh Watts [Doublehead's niece, sister of Young Tassel]), Glass, Little Owl (Wyukah) and Turtle At Home (three of Dragging Canoe's brothers; Attakullakulla's sons), Nettle Carrier (Tahlonteskee, brother of Bench), and the Badger (Ocuma, also Dragging Canoe's brother). Sometimes he met there with Doublehead and Pumpkin Boy (Iyahuwagiatsutsa, Doublehead's brother) who usually led expeditions independent of the early Chickamauga. Even Shawnee warrior, Tecumseh, and his older brother Cheeseekau (The Shawnee Warrior) would join Dragging Canoe in the Five Lower Towns. Alexander Cameron and trader John McDonald relocated to Running Water Town.

One intriguing leader among the Chickamauga was a free black man named Jack Cavil who was taken captive in the Cumberlands (see Chapter 8). Cavil assimilated into the Chickamauga culture and led many war parties into the settlements. He dwelt at the village of Nickajack, which was named after him. The Chickamauga referred to Cavil and the town as "Nigger-Jack." Not far from that town was Nickajack Cave which contains a stream that flows so well before it empties into the Tennessee River that Chickamauga canoes could be paddled two or three miles inside Lookout Mountain. The cave housed some smaller communities, mostly temporary, that were likely used for housing recent captives. (The cave was partially flooded by Lake Nickajack in 1967; the entrance is presently about 140 feet wide by 25 feet high, and the water depth at the mouth, about 30 feet. There is a marker on eastbound Interstate 24 in Jasper, Tennessee, in the rest area at mile marker 160, 35° 1.441' N, 85° 33.512' W. It reads, "5¼ miles southeast was the town of Nickajack or Anikusatiyi, destroyed by Ore's force, Sept. 14, 1794. The town occupied a space between the river and the cave in which was a storehouse for plunder. It was also used by the Confederacy during the War Between the States as a source of saltpeter.")

Late in the fall of 1782, General Daniel Smith, Hugh Rogan, and William McMurry were traveling the buffalo trail that ran from the abandoned Bledsoe's Station to Mansker's Lick. A war party fired on them in the vicinity of Castalion Springs. (Five miles east of present-day Gallatin, Tennessee, on State Highway 25. The exact location was near the site of Cragfont Mansion.) McMurry was killed, and Smith, who had dropped his gun, was wounded. He quickly regained control of the rifle and joined Rogan who had begun to return fire. The warriors dispersed into a canebrake.

Also in fall of 1782, Colonel Joseph Martin took his wife, Betsy, Ghighau Nancy Ward, and Chief Oconostota to live out the winter on Long Island of the Holston. Oconostota was aged and suffered from poor eyesight. William Martin, son of Joseph Martin, later wrote: "I am of the opinion that Oconostota was one of the noblest and best of humankind. He had a powerful frame, and in his prime must have weighed more than two hundred pounds, with a head of enormous size. He was, when I saw him, very lean, stooped, and emaciated."[9]

The Cherokee warriors had mostly relocated to the Fiver Lower Towns of Chief Dragging Canoe, and a few to Muscle Shoals of the Tennessee with Chief Doublehead. A Moravian missionary reported that Chota, the mother town, consisted of no more than 30 dwellings in 1784 and was the largest of the Upper Villages.

The Cherokee had experienced constant warfare since 1776, mostly inspired by the British, the Tories, and the influx of Virginia settlers onto the Cherokee lands. The Tories were a roadblock for the Cherokee rather than a help. Every time the warriors extended their warfare into the Carolina and Georgia backcountry settlements for the British, the Cherokee Nation was decimated afterward by those states' militias. Those colonies mounted severe reprisal attacks. That cycle only served to transfer warrior manpower from the Cherokee's immediate problem—that of encroachment from the northeast into the vicinity of the Upper Towns and onto the ancestral hunting grounds along the Cumberland River.

The Cherokee certainly received no help from the British in terms of manpower to end encroachment, almost 20 years since King George III's proclamation of 1763. The Chickamauga effort seemed to be succeeding on the Cumberland, and chances were never better for them to drive the Nashborough residents away. The influence that the Tories seemed to have over the Chickamauga had been broken. No more distractions.

The successes the Chickamauga had experienced along the Cumberland had not been repeated in the Overmountain settlements, those along the Holston, Watauga, and Nolichucky rivers. They had already wasted their opportunities in that vicinity, such as when the Overmountain militias went after Major Patrick Ferguson in South Carolina one year earlier. Ferguson sent a threatening letter to the Overmountain militias ordering them to remain there (essentially giving them permission to abide in Cherokee country) or face desolation of an attack from Ferguson's provincial force. Several hundred militiamen from the settlements then went after Ferguson. That would have been an opportune time for the warriors to attack the Overmountain community.

Better yet, it might have made more sense had Ferguson, rather than send an ignominious warning, launched a surprise attack from the southeast, coordinated with a Chickamauga attack from the southwest. It is possible the settlers could not have withstood such an onslaught and would have withdrawn up the Holston and Watauga valleys. If they had taken care of the Watauga, Holston, and Nolichucky settlements, Ferguson could then have withdrawn to Gilbert Town; the Chickamauga could have placed ambush patrols on the passes from the east, and then could have attacked the Cumberland settlements in the west. The same old story: the British left the Cherokee out to dry. Seventeen eighty-three would hold more promise for the Chickamauga warriors.[10]

However, there was a lapse in hostilities early in 1783. The respite was likely due to the destruction of Dragging Canoe's initial villages by John Sevier's militia and by the Treaty of Long Swamp Creek by Pickens and several Cherokee and Chickamauga headmen. It would have taken some time for Dragging Canoe to relocate his faction to the Five Lower Towns. The treaty with Pickens was attended by many warriors led by Chief Terrapin (Tuckaseh), the unofficial red (war) chief of the nation, and well-respected son of Oconostota. While a necessary break, the lull would give the Cumberland settlers such a boost of confidence that they could withstand whatever the Chickamauga could throw at them. New settlers began to arrive in the Nashborough neighborhood and the settlement began to experience some prosperity. The breather, however, would not last.

In early 1783, Jeremiah Jack and William Rankon of the Nolichucky settlements visited the Upper Villages. The Nolichucky residents needed food, especially corn, and the two settlers came to trade. Their canoe was laden with trade goods, but the warriors of Coyatee refused to help. One of them noticed that the visitors had their rifles hidden and threatened the settlers' lives. Nancy Ward happened to be at Coyatee and interceded on behalf of the settlers. The braves accepted the trade goods and filled the canoe with corn.

Nancy Ward, Old Tassel, and Terrapin were the leaders of the mainstream Cherokee Nation in the Upper Towns. They were still advocates of peace, but the split between them and the factions of Doublehead and Dragging Canoe was growing. The Chickamauga were gaining strength and a stronger identity. They were no longer under any form of British or Tory leadership. In addition, the departure of their old allies from America also meant they had to seek arms and ammunition elsewhere. However, the pros of the British exodus far outweighed the negatives.

Regardless of what Georgia governor John Martin had told the Creek, the Spanish were open to fill the void position of arms supplier for the Cherokee Nation.

Meanwhile, more settlers eyed present-day Kentucky and Tennessee land as open for development. The Overmountain communities were encroaching as far south as Pigeon River below the French Broad. That action had prompted Old Tassel's letter to North Carolina governor Alexander Martin the previous September.

In the Cumberlands, several of the older abandoned stations were reopened, such as Asher's Station near present-day Gallatin, and new stations established exemplified by Kasper Mansker, and his friends, which new location on the east side of Mansker's Creek was one mile upstream of their original abandoned fort.

In the meantime, a party of French adventurers from a settlement on the Wabash River (a tributary of the Ohio in present-day Indiana) began to aggressively pursue an alliance with Doublehead's faction of the Chickamauga. They settled in a town called Coldwater (Oka Kapassa), which had been founded by Chief Doublehead in late 1769 or early 1770, well downriver of the Five Lower Towns of the Chickamauga. It was developed at the mouth of Coldwater Creek at the present-day town of Tuscumbia, Alabama. The combined force garrisoned the town with 35 Chickamauga, ten Creek, and nine Frenchmen. They kept the existence of the village so quiet it was not discovered by the whites for four years. Chief Doublehead resided there for some time and made it his temporary center of operations.

Early in 1783, Major John Buchanan and a family by the name of Mulerrin settled four miles east of the Bluff. They built a fort called Buchanan's Station.

North Carolina selected Anthony Bledsoe, Absalom Tatom, and Isaac Shelby to act as commissioners and sent them to the Cumberlands to lay out parcels of land to be awarded to veterans of the American Revolution. Bledsoe brought his family and settled permanently. In the fall he established a station (present-day Greenfield, Tennessee, 36°9'25" N, 88°48'5" W), two and one-half miles north of Isaac Bledsoe's Station.

About the same time, new Cumberland settlers James McCain, James Franklin, Elmore Douglass, and Charles Carter built a station on the west side of Station Camp Creek (located just south of where State Highway 174 [Long Hollow Pike] crosses Upper Station Camp Creek Road, five miles west of Gallatin, Tennessee. It was near the Douglass Chapel.)

The confidence level regarding the safety of Nashborough had risen so much that the Nashborough Court of Triers, a civil and criminal court created in 1781, began to hold regular sessions beginning on January 7, 1783. The following judges were present at that first session: James Robertson, George Freeland, Thomas Molloy, Isaac Lindsay, David Roundsevell, Heydon Wells, James Maulding, Ebenezer Titus, Samuel Benton, and Andrew Ewing. Isaac Bledsoe and Captain John Blackmore were seated on January 18 to fill the vacancies.

They also appointed a sheriff at their February 5, 1783, meeting. A white man named James Logan Colbert led a gang of pirates along the Cumberland River and its tributaries. The new sheriff, John Montgomery, was found to be in cahoots with the criminals, so he was replaced by Thomas Fletcher. Historian James Adair wrote that James Colbert, born about 1721 somewhere in the Carolinas, was raised among the Chickasaw.[11] He married three times to Chickasaw women and raised four sons who joined him on raids in the Cumberland settlements. His sons became respected chiefs within the Chickasaw Nation.

The settlements paid six men to be fulltime spies, which amounted to being scouts.

They were to continually ride through the forests and look for signs of war parties. Colonel James Robertson and Isaac Bledsoe acted as their superiors. The outriders were paid 75 bushels of corn per month at a value of $50 per bushel. That was a high salary for those days; however, theirs was a particularly risky venture.

In March 1783, Colonel Robertson was elected to the North Carolina Legislature. Virginia governor Benjamin Harrison appointed Colonels John Donelson, Joseph Martin, and Isaac Shelby to a commission to treat with the Southern Indians. Major John Reid was to mediate the event. He visited the governor at Richmond to receive instructions, delivered Donelson's and Shelby's commissions to them in Kentucky, carried instructions to Martin at Long Island of Holston River, and arrived to meet with Colonel James Robertson in Nashborough on May 2, 1783. Robertson opposed assembling the Chickasaws in the Cumberland settlements and refused to allow Major Reid to met with them until the Cumberland settlers could be polled.

The settlers became indignant when they heard that Virginia wanted to force a treaty on what was then considered a part of North Carolina. They were very hesitant to invite large numbers of warriors, whom they considered not only savages but also their enemies, to gather around the stations. The Cumberland settlers were also reluctant to furnish food for so large a congregation at a council session for an indefinite time period. There were a few Nashborough residents who thought positively. They argued that such a meeting might bring about a long-sought peace.

An election was held on June 5, 1783, to determine the people's desire. Colonel Robertson and other leaders generally voted against the proposition, but a majority of the settlers was favorable. Colonel Robertson, then, invited the commissioners to proceed.

The results of the poll were (several stations were included in each group of the largest station in their area):
- Freeland's Station, no treaty here, 32.
- Heatonburg, no treaty here, 1; treaty here, 54.
- Nashborough, no treaty here, 26; treaty here, 30.
- Total, no treaty here, 59; treaty here, 84.
- The other stations of Mansker's and Maulding's failed to return their votes.

Major Reid was then allowed to consult with the Chickasaw who asked that the session be held at French Lick (Nashborough) beginning with the October full moon. Late in June, Nashborough's leaders agreed to the Chickasaw request.[12] Colonel Robertson offered his claim, the site of his future home at the sulphur spring four miles west of the Bluff (near present-day Robertson Avenue and White Bridge Road, just north of Interstate 40).

The Chickamauga began to look northward again in the summer of 1783. They reminisced about their successes of 1782 and were aware of the expansions occurring in the Nashborough area. Indeed, the warriors had lost their previously-acquired gains. They resumed their previous concentration on the Cumberland settlements with several quick raids:
- Roger Top was killed and Roger Glass wounded at Rains' Station.

(Rains' Station was located in the present-day historic Waverly Place district of Nashville, roughly bounded by Beech, Douglas and Bradford Avenues, 10th Avenue South, and Acklen Avenue, 36.135593° N, 86.799619° W.)
- William, Joseph and Daniel Dunham, Joshua Norrington, and Joel Mills were

prospecting on Richland Creek when they were ambushed and killed by a small Chickamauga war party.
- Patsy Rains, daughter of John Rains, was riding double on horseback with a friend, Betsy Williams, west of Nashborough when they were fired upon by warriors from some nearby brush. Betsy was killed, but Patsy escaped safely to Bluff Fort.
- Chickamauga braves killed Joseph Nolan while he was exploring the forest outside of Nashborough. Joseph's father, Thomas Nolan, was later killed while looking for him.
- A war party furtively approached Buchanan's Station and killed sentries Samuel Buchanan and William Mulherrin.
- William Overall and Joshua Thomas were ambushed, shot, and killed while en route from the Cumberland Settlement to Kentucky.
- A party of Chickamauga approached Nashborough Fort on the Bluff after dark one night. They stole all horses in the area that were not safely corralled within the fort. They quickly headed south, and shortly thereafter Captain William Pruett led a company of 20 militiamen in pursuit. They overtook the warriors south of Duck River and fired a volley that caused the Indians to disperse. The militia recovered all of the stolen horses and headed for home. They camped for the night in a canebrake on the north shore of Duck River. The Indians followed their trail in the darkness and attacked the encampment at dawn. Moses Brown was killed with the first shots. The surprised militiamen quickly withdrew on foot to higher ground. They re-formed in an open area and awaited the approach of the warriors. The Chickamauga, with the advantage of size, approached, and a fierce battle ensued. Captain Pruett's force was demolished, and the survivors hastily dispersed and fled for the Bluff. Daniel Pruett and Daniel Johnson had been killed. Morris Shine was one of several wounded who escaped. The war party reacquired the stolen horses, supplemented by those left behind by the surviving militiamen, and resumed their trip south. Captain Pruett had come only recently to the settlement. He was an accomplished soldier but was inexperienced in Indian warfare. The Chickamauga were skilled in the old ways and not only knew how to create an advantage, but to make the most of it. Many backcountry militiamen had trained themselves in Indian-style combat over the years; however, those who were not yet experienced were detriments to their comrades. At the beginning of the attack, Pruett rebuked his men for sniping from behind rocks and trees. He insisted that they line up in the open and fight as men, á la European-style warfare. They obeyed his command, came out in the open, and were exposed to the imposing warrior army.

Thus, the Chickamauga warriors were off to a successful beginning. New settlers, however, were still moving in faster than the warriors could remove them.[13]

In October 1783, the treaty negotiation with the Cumberland settlers, the Virginia commissioners, and the Chickasaw took place as planned. The Chickasaw contingent, led by Chief Piomingo, arrived on time ten days in advance of the commissioners: Colonels John Donelson and Joseph Martin. Colonel Isaac Shelby did not attend. One of his brothers had recently been killed by a war party in Kentucky. The treaty was concluded November

12, 1783. The Chickasaw ceded a large body of land on the south side of Cumberland River, which would be confirmed at the Treaty of Hopewell in 1785.

Some record that chiefs from the Creek, Cherokee, and Choctaw attended as well; some indicate only the Chickasaw and the Chickamauga were there. However, the treaty negotiations appear to have been only between the whites as listed above and the Chickasaw. The headmen were accompanied by many warriors, women, and children. Historian Edward Albright adds: "As is the latter-day custom of these tribes in the West on such occasion, they brought with them ... dogs, cats, chickens, geese, and other domestic animals and fowls, such as they happen to possess."[14]

While likely an exaggeration, there were definitely many observers.

The white settlers received the Chickasaw cordially and acted the good hosts, which was somewhat surprising considering "savage" was a primary white synonym for "Indian." There were many recreational activities, such as footraces, ballgames, and other contests. The Chickasaw appeared to be pleased with their treatment.

The land ceded by the Chickasaw extended 40 miles south of the Cumberland to the Elk and Duck Rivers and their tributaries. The session went well; however, the treaty was between a state and a tribe. The United States was not involved, and other nations, such as, the Cherokee, claimed the same land. The primary benefits were the new friendships that developed between the settlers and the Chickasaw, and the potentially irreversible wedge that was driven between the Chickasaw and the Chickamauga. Dragging Canoe, until the time of his death, would try unsuccessfully to convince the Chickasaw leaders to rejoin the Chickamauga confederation. War Chief Piomingo honored the treaty for the rest of his life. (There is a marker in Nashville that denotes the treaty and its location. The marker is found by proceeding north from Interstate 40 exit 204. Drive 0.2 miles and turn right onto Urbandale Avenue. Then go one-fourth of a mile and turn left onto Morrow Road. After 0.8 miles, the marker will be on the left in front of the West Park Community Center [6105 Morrow Road]. Turn left onto Terry Road and find a parking area on the left. The marker reads, "CHICKASAW TREATY In 1783, Chickasaw chiefs met with white settlers at a spring 100 yards north and agreed on land rights—the Cumberland country for the settlers, the Tennessee River lands beyond the Duck River ridge for the Chickasaw. This tribe became firm friends of James Robertson and his people, but the settlements suffered many more raids by the Cherokees and the Creeks.")

The marker is telling. The settlers had a ray of hope that they could live in peace; however, the agreement with the Chickasaw did not commit the Creek or the Chickamauga factions to anything. Indeed, the agreement angered both Chief Doublehead and Chief Dragging Canoe. The two Chickamauga factions were more resolved than ever to drive the white men from the Cherokee ancestral lands.

Doublehead's warriors, including his Creek allies, became extremely aggressive in the Cumberland settlements. They were operating out of Coldwater Town near Muscle Shoals. Colonel Robertson and the other leaders were ignorant of Coldwater Town's existence. They blamed Dragging Canoe and the Chickamauga for several depradations that had occurred within Nashborough. Robertson raised a militia and marched toward the Five Lower Towns, but he thought that a demonstration would serve the purpose. Once he knew that Dragging Canoe's warriors had seen his army, he returned to the Cumberlands. The colonel sent an offer of peace to Dragging Canoe who sent a cluster of Chickamauga chiefs to Nashborough. Dragging Canoe's brother, Little Owl, led the group to talk with Colonel Robertson. Several men were killed near Nashborough (one near the assembly) by a war party while the peace conference was in session. Robertson thought that his guests were the instigators, but Little Owl explained about the Coldwater warriors.

The Cherokee needed a source of ammunition since their British sources had dried up and the French were inconsistent. The Spanish were likely candidates. On May 10, 1781, during the American Revolution, British general John Campbell surrendered Florida's Fort George to the Spanish. One of the Spanish officers, Arturo O'Neill (actually an Irishman in the Spanish Army), participated in the surrender ceremonies and, on June 4, 1781, was named the Spanish governor. He served in the office at Pensacola. Don Esteban Rodriquez Miró y Sabater, who had been the acting Governor of Louisiana since January 20, 1782, worked closely with Governor O'Neill to further Spain's sphere of influence with the southern tribes. About that same time, Alexander McGillivray (Hoboi-Hili-Miko) had become the chief of the Upper Creek, allies of the Chickamauga.

On January 1, 1784, McGillivray wrote to Governor O'Neill, the Spanish governor of Pensacola, and proposed a trade alliance with the Spaniards. The chief advised the governor that United States citizens were spreading westward toward the Mississippi. He further suggested that, if American settlements were to develop on that river, it would be disastrous for Spanish commerce. Chief McGillivray continued that the Spanish should grant his nation and his Chickamauga allies trade advantages and other privileges so they could counter the Americans' aggressive actions.

Shortly thereafter, Shawnee representatives visited the Five Lower Towns to promote an alliance with Dragging Canoe. They presented: "Brothers; We are glad to see so many of our friends, the red people. We shall let you know everything that is passing amongst us. We have the war hatchet still in our hands, but are going to lay it down, and we want our brothers who fought with us in this war to lay it down with us. We do not expect that it will be still very long, as we will then assist you, and you shall want for nothing. In the meantime, visit all our brothers, the red men, and make everything straight and strong."[15]

On January 6, 1784, the Court of Pleas and Common Sessions in Nashborough reorganized the militia. Anthony Bledsoe was chosen as colonel. The North Carolina Legislature changed the name of Nashborough to Nashville in May. At that time, Chief Old Tassel was the principal chief and his brother, Chief Hanging Maw (Uswaliguta), the war chief of the Upper Villages. They represented the small remainder of the dovish portion of the Cherokee Nation, and they continued to appeal to the good nature of the white settlers. During 1784, however, 500 more families encroached further into Cherokee country and settled on Boyd's Creek. (Boyd's Creek empties into the French Broad River five miles north of present-day Sevierville, Tennessee.) That put the white settlers only 35 miles from the Cherokee Mother Town of Chota. North Carolina governor Alexander Martin disclaimed any responsibility for the encroachment and placed the blame upon John Sevier to whom he referred as a "freewheeling individualist." Martin recalled that nearly two years earlier he had ordered Sevier to clamp down on encroachment onto Cherokee lands.

Nicholas Trammel and Philip Mason had been hunting on a tributary near White's Creek, northwest of present-day Goodlettsville, Tennessee. They had left their blind to process a deer carcass when noticed by a large war party. The warriors fired and wounded Mason. Trammel escaped and sought reinforcements at Eaton's Station. Mason treated his wound and joined Trammel who had returned with four men to pursue the Indians who had absconded with the venison.

The posse chased the warriors and overtook what they assumed to be the entire war party, but it was only a portion of the group, the militiamen dismounted and killed two warriors. The remainder of the war party arrived, captured the militia's horses, and attacked the trapped white men. This time Mason received a mortal wound, and the four reinforcements from Eaton's Station dispersed into the forest. Trammel loudly conveyed his ire over their departure; however, they called back that they were too badly outnumbered. Trammel joined them and the group encountered Josiah Hoskins, a reported expert woodsman. The appearance of Hoskins buoyed the party, and they continued the chase. Things went well for the militia as they properly attacked under Hoskins's leadership and killed three warriors. However, Hoskins made a critical error in judgment as he and Trammel foolishly moved onto the open thinking the Indians would bolt. The two were instantly slain. The remaining militiamen and warriors fired at one another to no avail until they all dispersed.

In May, Nashville settler Cornelius Riddle hunted between Buchanan's Station and Stones River. He killed two wild turkeys, hung them from a tree in a clearing and went after more. While he was gone, a small party of Chickamauga heard the reports from his rifle and found his prey. They lay in ambush in some nearby brush and mortally wounded Riddle when he returned. They scalped him and took all the turkeys.

Since the war had ended in 1783, Governor O'Neill had given individual attention to the Indians. He and Louisiana governor Esteban Rodriguez Miró hosted a conference with the Creeks and the Chickamauga in Pensacola from May 31 to June 1, 1784, that concluded with a treaty of friendship.

Miró reportedly told the headmen: "Do not be afraid of the Americans. You our brothers, the red men, are not without friends. The Americans have no King, and are nothing of themselves. They are like a man that is lost and wandering in the woods. If it had not been for the Spanish and the French, the British would have subdued them long ago."[16]

Miró then reportedly advocated that Dragging Canoe and his warriors expand their aggressive campaign on the encroaching settlers—which they did with vigor. A similar agreement was made on June 22 at Mobile in present-day Alabama between the Spanish and the Chickasaw, Alabama, and Choctaw. Chief Piomingo and the Chickasaw refused to attend. (It is more likely to have been Governor O'Neill who orated to the headmen and to Dragging Canoe. He was the more senior of the two governors, was host for the session, and it was to him that Chief Alexander McGillivray had originally written. The session is more often written as having occurred in 1783, but actually occurred in 1784.[17])

Historian Edward Albright recorded: "During the summer George Espie, Andrew Lucas, Thomas Sharp Spencer and a scout by the name of Johnson left the bluff on horseback for a hunting expedition on Drake's Creek, in Sumner County. As they crossed the creek their horses stopped to drink. A band of Indians who were in ambush along the bank opened fire upon the party while they were yet in midstream. Lucas was shot through the neck and also wounded in the mouth. He rode to the bank, dismounted, and attempted to return the fire, but the blood gushed from his mouth and wet the priming in his gun. Seeing that the weapon was thus useless he crawled away and hid himself in a bunch of briers. Espie alighted from his horse and at the same moment received a shot which broke his thigh, but he continued to load and return the fire. Spencer and Johnson made a gallant stand in defense of their comrades and for a time held the enemy at bay. Finally, however, a bullet broke Spencer's right arm and they were obliged to leave the wounded men to their fate. Espie was killed and scalped, but the savages failed to find Lucas, who escaped and returned to the fort."[18] (Explorer Thomas Sharp Spencer became a legend among Indians and whites. See Appendix C.)

North Carolina was becoming discouraged. Debts were high as the colonial officials tried to govern the settlements which they decided were too far away to properly oversee. The legislature did not have enough manpower to enforce the laws east of the mountains let alone try to control what the Cherokee were demanding as their ancestral land. The Continental Congress was pressuring North Carolina to do something. The state legislature officially ceded its lands west of the Appalachian Mountains to the United States government. It had become to large of a financial burden for the state; however, Congress was not expecting the cession and delayed any approval action. Suddenly, in June of 1784, the Overmountain and Cumberland settlers had no official representation. In reality, the settlements experienced no physical difference as far as any change in the quality of life. The official lack of representation did, however, create an opportunity. In August John Sevier was named president of a convention to be held at Jonesborough, a village that was created in present-day eastern Tennessee in 1779. This was the impetus for the movement to create a new state to be called Franklin.

North Carolina rescinded the cession in October thus competing with the Franklinite movement for control of present-day Tennessee. Sevier, who was offered a promotion to brigadier general by the North Carolina legislature if he would back the state's action, istead succumbed to William Cocke's overtures and sought to lead the Franklinite movement. On December 17, 1784, the delegates officially declared the region to be Franklin, acclaimed Sevier to be the acting governor, and established Jonesborough as its capital. Sevier would become elected as governor the following March. Franklin would function as a state for four years but would not be admitted to the Union. (William Cocke had been a comrade of Daniel Boone during some of his early explorations, and was a Virginia officer in the Cherokee War of 1776.)

Many differences arose between the Franklinites and those who supported remaining a part of North Carolina. The Continental Congress tried to arbitrate, but the animosity grew. Chiefs Old Tassel and Hanging Maw had no idea who was in charge of the white settlers or what the outcome would be for the Cherokee Nation, but they were not confident. The Spanish saw that as an opportunity to expand their influence. Dragging Canoe and Doublehead perceived the obvious: the settlers were determined to be permanent.

Sevier had much popular support; however, rival John Tipton led the lobby to retain North Carolina. Two parallel governments were developing, one loyal to Franklin and one to North Carolina. They each elected public officials. Relations between the two were openly cordial at first, while behind the scenes there was bitterness, especially between Sevier and Tipton. Each group eventually raided the other's courthouse and destroyed political papers and other property. At one point, Sevier and Tipton had a fistfight in Jonesborough. (John Tipton was an activist and would later be elected to the North Carolina Senate. He is not to be confused with his brother, Jonathan Tipton, who fought at King's Mountain and signed the Watauga Petition of 1776.)[19]

Early 1785 was a provocative period. The confidence that had sprung up in the Cumberland settlements was waning. The withdrawal of the Chickasaw from the Chickamauga alliance was definitely a plus; however, the confederation was not weakened by their absence. Dragging Canoe and Doublehead, along with their remaining allies, had increased their efforts with vigorous attacks.

The Bench (Bob Benge), 25-year-old nephew of Young Tassel (John Watts, Jr., Kunokeski), and grandnephew of Doublehead, Old Tassel, and Hanging Maw, is credited with living at Lookout Town and at Running Water Town. He became a formidable Chickamauga minor chief about that time. He was apparently a close associate of John "The Tory" Pickens, first cousin of Brigadier General Andrew Pickens, because in 1785 he gave a newborn son the name of Pickens Benge. He also worked closely with allied Shawnee warriors in the coming years.

The Bench, and his brother, The Tail (Martin Benge), were sons of white trader John Benge and Wurteh Watts, sister of Young Tassel. John Benge was well respected throughout the Cherokee Nation including the Chickamauga. Chief Dragging Canoe often sent warriors to protect him and his family in times of difficulty with the whites, such as the war of 1776. John Benge died about 1779.

Oconostota died in the spring of 1785. His death, and Attakullakulla's three years earlier, were discussed later in the year at the Treaty of Hopewell.[20] Old Tassel's and Hanging Maw's positions then become official within the Cherokee Nation.

Things were not going well for the Cherokee Upper Villages. The Overmountain settlers had exhibited their new-found authority in their presumed upstart State of Franklin. The Cherokees found the concept of the two opposing governments of Franklin and North Carolina confusing, to say the least. The Franklinites invited Cherokees to Dumplin Creek on May 1, 1785, to negotiate yet another treaty. Old Tassel refused to personally attend, so he sent a chief named Ancoo. (Ancoo is possibly Anakanoe, an older chief from Tellico. However, some have identified him as Old Abram [Oskuah] since Ancoo had been designated as the chief of Chota.) Ancoo signed a treaty on June 10, 1785, but apparently did not understand that he was ceding Cherokee land. He agreed that the boundary between the whites and the Indians would become the ridge that divides the watershed of Little River and the Tennessee River. That resulted in a cession of all Cherokee land east of the ridge that lay south of the French Broad and Holston Rivers. Old Tassel protested the treaty in a letter to North Carolina governor Alexander Martin that claimed the Franklinites and their interpreters did not even mention the land cession before acquiring Ancoo's mark. Martin's response was, as it had been in 1784, to blame Sevier. Martin pointed out that he had assigned responsibility to Sevier in 1782 to police the Cherokee Upper Villages and protect them from further encroachment. He again referred to Sevier as a freewheeling individualist. This time Martin was right about Sevier who was now the acting governor of a new state and did not believe he owed any allegiance to North Carolina. He had the perfect situation to absorb all of the Cherokee land he desired into the Overmountain settlements. (A marker is located in Kodak, Tennessee, at the intersection of Winfield Dunn Parkway [State Highway 66] and West Dumplin Valley Road, 35° 58.837' N, 83° 36.48' W. It reads, "About 2 mi. E., at mouth of Dumplin Creek, was Henry's Station, founded by Maj. Hugh Henry. Here, the state of Franklin, John Sevier, and the Cherokee Nation, represented by Ancoo, Chief of Chota, signed, on June 10, 1785, the treaty opening a large area south of the French Broad and Holston Rivers to settlement.")[21]

Meanwhile, there was also action around Nashville. In the spring of 1785, Moses Brown erected a station at present-day Richland two and one-half miles west of Bluff Fort. He had barely completed the construction when Chickamauga warriors killed and scalped him. His family immediately retreated back to the Bluff. Nearby, a hired man who worked for William Stuart was killed at the forks of Mill Creek near Buchanan's Station. (Brown's Station was about one mile east of the Chickasaw Treaty site of 1783.)

During the summer, Colonels James Robertson, Robert Weakely, and surveyor Edmund Hickman went to Piney Creek to plat some tracts of land. A small war party surprised them, and Hickman was killed during the skirmish. Robertson and Weakely retreated safely to the Bluff Fort.

In August 1785, Spanish governors O'Neill and Miró decided they had not progressed quickly enough to gain a foothold into the Cumberland and the Ohio. They needed to either win the allegiance of the settlers or use the Chickamauga to destroy the settlements. They acted to prohibit navigation of the Mississippi River through Louisiana, the only outlet for the settlers to export corn and tobacco. Colonel Robertson traveled to North Carolina to lobby the state legislature about the importance of the Cumberland settlement. The legislature would merely commit to ineffective assistance, and only then if the settlement would cover the costs. It would not commit any military and would solely supply ammunition and arms if the cost was in no way taken from the state treasury.

Robertson appealed to the United States government for protection against the pressure of Spain and the Chickamauga alliance, but his efforts were futile. The United States was negotiating a treaty with Spain and feared that a show of force to keep the Mississippi open would offend the Spanish. The governments effectively told the Nashville settlers that they assumed their dangerous situation by their own initiative and must solve the problem themselves.

Hopewell, Estate of Andrew Pickens.

William Hall, his wife, and children arrived at Bledsoe's Station late on November 20, 1785. William Hall, Jr., would become a future governor of Tennessee.

On November 17, 1785, the United States opened its first treaty meeting with the Cherokee at Andrew Pickens' estate, Hopewell. (Hopewell was located on the orchard of present-day Clemson University near the site of the old Lower Village of Keowee.)

On the 22nd, Commissioners Benjamin Hawkins, Andrew Pickens, Joseph Martin, and Laughlin McIntosh, presented their opening statement to the 37 Cherokee leaders that were present and the additional 881 Cherokee observers. The commissioners said:

> Head-men and warriors of all the Cherokees: We are the men whom you were informed came from Congress to meet you, the head-men and warriors of all the Cherokees, to give you peace, and to receive you into the favor and protection of the United States; and to remove, as far as may be, all causes of future contention or quarrels. That you, your people, your wives and children, may be happy, and feel and know the blessings of the new change of sovereignty over this land, which you and we inhabit.
>
> We sincerely wish you to live as happily as we do ourselves, and to promote that happiness as far as is in our power, regardless of any distinction of color, or of any difference in our customs, our manners, or particular situation.
>
> This humane and generous act of the United States, will no doubt be received by you with gladness, and held in grateful remembrance, and the more so, as many of your young men, and the greatest number of warriors, during the late war, were our enemies, and assisted the King of Great Britain in his endeavors to conquer our country.
>
> You, yourselves, know, that you refused to listen to the good talks Congress sent you; that the cause you espoused was a bad one; that all the adherents of the King of Great Britain are compelled to leave this country, never more to return.
>
> Congress is now the sovereign of all our country, which we now point out to you on the map.* They want none of your lands, or any thing else which belongs to you; and as an earnest of their regard for you, we propose to enter into articles of treaty perfectly equal, and comfortable to what we now tell you.
>
> If you have any grievances to complain of, we will hear them, and take such measures, in consequence thereof, as may be proper. We expect you will speak your minds freely, and look upon us as the representatives of your father and friend, the Congress, who will see justice done you. You may now retire, and reflect on what we have told you, and let us hear from you to-morrow, or as soon as possible."
>
> "* We used McMurray's map, and explained, with great pains, the limits of the United States as well as the occurrences of the late war; and we believe they comprehend us. Some of the Indians had visited the Six Nations; some had been up the Wabash and down the Miami, to lake Erie; and others had been at fort Pitt, the Natchez, Pensacola, St. Augustine, Savannah, Charleston, and Williamsburg. B. H. [Benjamin Hawkins]"[22]

Old Tassel agreed to respond the next day, and the chiefs retired to ponder. They had a lot to consider. The commissioners talked about equality; however, no parity had been exhibited thus far. The Overmountain settlers keep moving onto Cherokee lands and forcing the nation into more treaties to cover the encroachment. If they were truly equivalent, would the Holston settlers move into the Watauga Valley and take the land from the Watauga settlers, or vice-versa? No, the Overmountain settlers would just move in on the Cherokee whom they did not believe were justified in holding onto lands as were their fellow white settlers.

The commissioners made a point of dwelling on the matter that their former enemies, Great Britain and Tories, were being required to leave, but the Cherokee magnanimously were not.

Congress promised to look out for the Cherokee interests, treat them fairly, and stated that they did not want Cherokee land or anything else belonging to the Cherokee. Yet, the encroachers kept coming.

They vowed justice, but could they control those who were creating their own political state to strengthen their powers to grab Cherokee land? Yes, the chiefs had a lot to contemplate for their answer.

The next day, November 23, 1785, the Cherokee headmen met the commissioners as promised. The chiefs sat in silence for quite some time. Then Old Tassel rose and delivered one of his wise orations. (The interpreters were James Madison and Arthur Coody. The citations of the Cherokee are only as accurate as the interpretations by those two white men. It was likely difficult to keep up with a transcription in English as the Cherokee spoke. Notice they refer to themselves as "red men." Initially, the Cherokee had addressed themselves that way because of their propensity for red body paint. However, over the years the label stuck, and they used the term freely to distinguish themselves from white men when speaking in mixed company.) Chief Old Tassel said:

> I am going to let the commissioners hear what I have to say to them. I told you yesterday I would do this today. I was very much pleased at the talk you gave us yesterday; it is very different from what I expected when I left home; the head-men and warriors are also equally pleased with it.
>
> Now, I shall give you my own talk. I am made of this earth, on which the great man above placed me to possess it; and what I am about to tell you, I have had in my mind for many years.
>
> This land we are now on, is the land we were fighting for, during the late contest, * and the great man made it for us to subsist upon. You must know the red people are the aborigines of this land, and that it is but a few years since the white people found it out. I am of the first stock, as the commissioners know, and a native of this land; and the white people are now living on it as our friends. From the beginning of the first friendship between the white and red people, beads were given as an emblem thereof: and these are the beads I give to the commissioners of the United States, as a confirmation of our friendship, and as proof of my opinion of what you yesterday told us. (A string of white beads [was presented].)
>
> The commissioners have heard how the white people have encroached on our lands, on every side of us that they could approach.
>
> I remember the talks I delivered at the Long Island of Holston, and I remember giving our lands to Colonel Christie and others, who treated us, and in a manner compelled me thereto, in 1777. I remember the talks to Colonel Christie, when I gave the lands at the mouth of Cloud's creek, eighteen springs past. At that treaty, we agreed upon the line near the mouth of Lime Stone. The Virginia line, and part from the mouth of Cloud's creek to Cumberland mountain, near the gap, was paid for by Virginia.
>
> From Cloud's creek, a direct line to the Chimney-top mountain, thence, to the first mountain about six miles from the river, on a line across the sun, was never paid for by the Carolina which joins the Virginia line. I wish the commissioners to know every thing that concerns us, as I tell nothing but the truth. They, the people of North Carolina, have taken our lands for no consideration, and are now making their fortunes out of them. I have informed the commissioners of the line I gave up, and the people of North Carolina and Virginia have gone over it, and encroached on our lands expressly against our inclination. They have gone over the line near Little River, and they have gone over Nine-mile Creek, which is but nine miles from our towns. I am glad of this opportunity of getting redress from the commissioners. If Congress had not interposed, I and my people must have moved. They have even marked the lands on the bank of the river near the town where I live; and from thence, down in the fork of the Tennessee and the Holston.

I have given to you a detail of the abuse and the encroachment of these two States. We shall be satisfied if we are paid for the lands we have given up, but we will not, nor cannot, give up any more—I mean the line I gave to Colonel Christie.

I have no more to say, but one of our beloved women has, who has born and raised up warriors. (A string of beads.)

* Hopewell is fifteen miles above the junction of the Keowee and Tugalo [sic]; it is a seat of General Pickens, in sight of Seneca, an Indian town at the commencement of the late war, inhabited by one hundred gun-men, but at present a waste. Dewit's corner is forty miles east of this, and that was the eastern boundary, till the treaty of 1777. B. H. [Benjamin Hawkins].[23]

The chief, tactful as always, put it on the line. He spoke of the encroachments and asked that Congress do something about it. However, in line with his liberal politics, he did not demand that the encroachers be removed, but rather that the Cherokee be paid for the land already absorbed by the settlers. That had no teeth and left the Cherokee exposed to continued treatment by the Overmountain white establishment. Those whites had no fear of Congress.

Nancy Ward, the Ghighau or First Beloved Woman of the Cherokee Nation and mother-in-law of Commissioner Joseph Martin, spoke next:

The War-woman of Chota then addressed the commissioners:

I am fond of hearing that there is peace, and I hope you have now taken us by the hand in real friendship. I have a pipe and a little tobacco to give the commissioners to smoke in friendship. I look on you and the red people as my children. Your having determined on peace is most pleasing to me, for I have seen much trouble during the late war. I am old, but I hope yet to bear children, who will grow up and people our nation, as we are now to be under the protection of Congress, and shall have no more disturbance. (A string, little old pipe, and some tobacco.)

The talk I have given, is from the young warriors I have raised in my town, as well as myself. They rejoice that we have peace, and we hope the chain of friendship will never more be broken. (A string of beads.)[24]

The commisioners kept pushing the chiefs to mark a map to indicate what the boundary of their lands should be, and promised that once that was done they would not permit any encroachment.

On November 26, Old Tassel stated firmly that Henderson had forged Oconostota's mark on the paper from the Treaty at Sycamore Shoals in 1775, and he further declared Henderson to be a liar. He went on to say that the United States should remove the 3,000 settlers that resided at the fork of the French Broad and Holston rivers. Then he declared that the Chickasaw had no right to give the Cumberland area to the western settlers because the area had always been declared as hunting grounds for several nations. He suggested they await the Chickasaw to arrive and straighten it out.[25]

The commissioners pointed out that the settlers moved into the French Broad and Holston area while the Cherokee were allies of the British, who had control of the land. They pointed out that the alliance the Cherokee had with the British should have led the British to remove the settlers from the Cherokee lands when they first moved in. They told the Cherokee they needed to make allowance for the settlers in that area when they marked their map. They further stated they expected the Chickasaw to not come to the Cherokee treaty meeting and that the Cherokee would also have to account for the Cumberland settlers. Lastly, the commissioners stated that Oconostota, Henderson, and Attakullakulla were dead and nothing could be done about the provisions of the Treaty of Holston.[26] (It was apparent by November 1785 that the British had allied with the Cherokee solely for the benefit of the British—to fight against the rebels in the backcountry of the Carolinas and Georgia. The British never had any intention of diverting manpower to assist the Cherokee to counter encroachment.)

Old Tassel was exasperated. However, he, as always, maintained control of himself. He answered: "I have shown you the bounds of my country on my map which I drew in your presence, and on the map of the United States. If the commissioners cannot do me justice in removing the people from the fork of French Broad and Holston, I am unable to get it of myself. Are Congress, who conquered the King of Great Britain, unable to remove these people?"

This was his chance to really apply pressure; however, Old Tassel continued: "I am satisfied with the promises of the commissioners to remove all the people within our [marked] lines, except those within the fork of Holston and French Broad; and I will agree to be content, that the particular situation of the people settled there, and our claims to the lands, should be referred to Congress, as the commissioners may think just, and I will abide by their decision."[27]

The Treaty of Hopewell was then signed on November 28, 1785, by the commissioners already identified, and by the marks of the following headmen of the Cherokee Nation:

> Koatohee or Corn Tassel of Toquo; Scholauetta or Hanging Man of Chota; Tuskegatahu or Long Fellow of Chistohoe; Ooskwha or Abraham of Chilkowa; Kolakusta or Prince of Noth; Newota or the Gritzs of Chicamaga; Konatota or the Rising Fawn of Highwassay; Tuckasee or Young Terrapin of Allajoy; Toostaka or the Waker of Oostanawa; Untoola or Gun Rod of Seteco; Unsuokanail Buffalo White Calf of New Cussee; Kostayeak or Sharp Fellow of Wataga; Chonosta of Cowe; Chescoonwho or Bird in Close of Tomotlug; Tuckasee or Terrapin of Hightowa; Chesetoa or the Rabbit of Tlacoa; Chesecotetona or Yellow Bird of the Pine Log; Sketaloska or Second Man of Tillico; Chokasatahe or Chickasaw Killer of Tasonta; Onanoota of Koosoate; Ookoseta or Sower Mush of Kooloque; Umatooetha or the Water Hunter of Choikamawga; Wyuka of Lookout Mountain; Tulco or Tom of Chatuga; Will of Akoha; Necatee of Sawta; Amokontakona of Kutcloa; Kowetatahee of Frog Town; Keukuck of Talcoa; Tulatiska of Chaway; Wooaluka or the Waylayer of Chota; Tatliusta or Porpoise of Tilassi; John of Little Tallico; Skelelak; Akonoluchta or the Cabin; Cheanoka of Kawetakac; Yellow Bird.

Regarding the designations, Old Tassel (Corn Tassel) signed as Koatohee on the Treaty of Hopewell, but had signed as Reyetaeh on the Treaty of Long Island in 1777. Hanging Maw is represented as Hanging Man, which is likely a misinterpretation of what he had spoken. Long Fellow was the brother of Nancy Ward. Abraham was Old Abram, brother of Dragging Canoe. Terrapin of Hightowa was the son of Oconostota. Wyuka of Lookout Mountain is sometimes listed as Wyuka of Chickamauga; likely he is Little Owl, the son of Attakullakulla, though some think him to be Skyuka, the Lower Village refugee chief who had joined Dragging Canoe's settlements after the War of 1777 and fought against John Sevier in 1782.

Article IV of the treaty reads:

> The boundary allotted to the Cherokees for their hunting grounds, between the said Indians and the citizens of the United States, within the limits of the United States of America, is, and shall be the following, viz. Beginning at the mouth of Duck river, on the Tennessee;

thence running north-east to the ridge dividing the waters running into Cumberland from those running into the Tennessee; thence eastwardly along the said ridge to a north-east line to be run, which shall strike the river Cumberland forty miles above Nashville; thence along the said line to the river; thence up the said river to the ford where the Kentucky road crosses the river; thence to Campbell's line, near Cumberland gap; thence to the mouth of Cloud's creek on Holstein [sic]; thence to the Chimney-top mountain; thence to Camp-creek, near the mouth of Big Limestone, on Nolichuckey [sic]; thence a southerly course six miles to a mountain; thence south to the North-Carolina line; thence to the South-Carolina Indian boundary, and along the same south-west over the top of the Oconee mountain till it shall strike Tugaloo river; thence a direct line to the top of the Currohee mountain; thence to the head of the south fork of Oconee river.[28]

Article V specified:

If any citizen of the United States, or other person not being an Indian, shall attempt to settle on any of the lands westward or southward of the said boundary which are hereby allotted to the Indians for their hunting grounds, or having already settled and will not remove from the same within six months after the ratification of this treaty, such person shall forfeit the protection of the United States, and the Indians may punish him or not as they please: Provided nevertheless, That this article shall not extend to the people settled between the fork of French Broad and Holstein rivers, whose particular situation shall be transmitted to the United States in Congress assembled for their decision thereon, which the Indians agree to abide by.[29]

Historian James Mooney tried to clarify the land allotted to the Cherokee in Article IV:

The general boundary followed the dividing ridge between Cumberland river and the more southern waters of the Tennessee [similar to how the Continental divide separates the eastern flowing waters from the western] eastward to the junction of the two forks of Holston, near present Kingsport, Tennessee, thence southward to the Blue ridge and southwestward to a point not far from present Atlanta, Georgia, thence westward to the Coosa river and northwestward to a creek running into the Tennessee river at the western line of Alabama, thence northward with the Tennessee river to the beginning.[30]

Article V is an indication that the commissioners wanted encroachment to end; however, they were apparently under orders of Congress to not commit government resources toward policing the Cherokee lands. A huge factor was the lack of treasury funds. The new nation had no money to support a large standing army now that the American Revolution was over. There was still not money enough to pay all of the regular army veterans what was owed them. The one salvation of the United States was unsettled land that could be used for veterans' land grants to compensate them for their service. Each state had problems and would have appreciated federal support, but it just was not possible. The same was true regarding the Cherokee Nation. Enforcement of treaties, even this new one that was a federal treaty, fell upon the states. Each state had its own Indian agents; however, putting the fox in charge of the poultry house is never a good idea. The Franklinites were the winners for the most part.

The treaty protected the Middle and Upper Villages as well as those along the Coosa River from further encroachment. While the commissioners gave some flexibility to the Watauga and Holston settlers, they did provide that the Cherokee could retain a large portion of their hunting grounds. The Treaty of Hopewell required that encroachers within the line drawn by Old Tassel needed to remove themselves or be subject to removal by the

Cherokee warriors. Georgia and North Carolina observers protested that these lands had been legally ceded for land grants to war veterans. The treaty protected whites in the Cumberland settlement by setting the boundary outside of their lands, and it also protected the Overmountain communities. However, those who quickly settled west of the French Broad on land covered by the treaty of Dumplin Creek were required to evacuate and would not be protected by the United States if they remained.

Congress made it quite clear they would not protect either the Cherokee or the whites. The two sides were expected to resolve their own issues, so basically things had not changed resultant of the treaty. The Franklinites especially could continue to encroach and had no real incentive to vacate the Dumplin Settlement.

The one caveat in the treaty was Article V. The United States was clear it would not intercede should the Cherokees retaliate against encroachers as defined by the articles. The sole gladiators of the Cherokee were the Chickamauga led by chiefs Dragging Canoe and Doublehead. Chief Old Tassel continued to hang onto his politics of peace and to rely on the generosity of white settlers. The mainstream chiefs still did not recognize the Chickamauga as their representatives even though their own political policies had not worked since the days of Attakullakulla and Oconostota. Discouraged with treaties, Chief Hanging Maw would, at times, join his brother, Chief Doublehead, in war against the whites. (The Second and Third Treaties of Hopewell were signed on Pickens' estate January 3, 1786, with the Choctaw, and January 10, 1786, with the Chickasaw respectively.)

Old Tassel was unable to stem the tide of encroachment with diplomacy. The white settlers paid no attention to the specified boundary and kept pushing the Cherokee southwestward. Chickamauga warriors began to honor Article V and punished intruders at will. However, the settlers fought back, punished the Upper Villages, and impinged even further. The Overmountain militia leaders realized there would be no interference from the federal government or from that of North Carolina. The Franklinites had become very confident that they could withstand the onslaught of the warriors which, though intense, had not successfully devastated the settlements during years of attempts. They had been able to hold their own by fighting a similar style of combat as the warriors. The Overmountain settlers developed a hatred for all Cherokee and considered them as savages. One such settler declared to Moravian missionary John Heckewelder: "An Indian has no more soul than a buffalo. To kill either is the same thing, and when you have killed an Indian you have done a good act and have killed a wild beast."[31]

The Chickamauga hated the white settlers just as intently and would continue to champion the cause of the Cherokee Nation with or without Chief Old Tassel's support. Indeed, chiefs Dragging Canoe and Doublehead would not only increase their efforts, but would coordinate with each other more often in the coming years to become more efficient.

Colonel John Donelson was killed in the fall of 1785. He had been in Virginia to conduct business and had returned to his home at Davis' Station in Kentucky. A short time before, his family, together with that of his son, John Donelson, Jr., had left Kentucky and returned to Mansker's Station near Nashville. Donelson rested a few days at Davis' and headed south to rejoin his family.

Before he departed, two young men at the station asked permission to accompany him on the journey. They said they, too, wished to settle near Nashville. The two young men appeared alone at the gate of Mansker's Station two days later, and declared in substance:

On the morning of their departure from the Kentucky station they had traveled with Colonel Donelson until the heat of the day. Coming at that time to a spring by the roadside they stopped for a drink. Colonel Donelson did not tarry with them, but rode on, saying that he was anxious to reach home. He had not gone far when they heard several shots. Their impression at the time was that his sons had met him on the way and were firing a salute. After some delay at the spring they had resumed their journey and at length overtook him, severely wounded and in great agony, but still riding along the road. Their supposition now was that he had been shot by Indians. They had camped together at sundown on the north bank of Barren River, and during the night Colonel DONELSON died. On the following morning they had buried his body beside the stream, and taking his horse, saddle and saddle-bags, started toward Nashville, but in crossing the river the saddle-bags had washed off and floated away.[32]

Colonel Donelson's sons accompanied one of the young men to the designated ford on the Barren River and searched for their father's remains. They not only wished to give him a proper burial, but to search for evidence of possible foul play. They found Colonel Donelson and his personal papers that were inside his saddlebags but saw no sign of the large sum of money they expected, resultant from his business venture.

Donelson's sons placed the young men under arrest. Each was charged with murder, but the evidence was circumstantial. No one else was ever charged with Colonel John Donelson's death.

The Spanish and the French still courted the Cherokee. Spanish governors Miró and O'Neill especially desired to trade with the Chickamauga and provide covert assistance. It would have been a good situation for the Cherokee had it occurred years earlier, before the Cherokee were decimated by war and the lands around the Upper Villages swallowed by white settlements. The end was in sight, but it would be preceded by years of bloody conflict—and the United States would be no more help than was Britain.[33]

The year 1786 began with the Cherokee concentrating on the Cumberland region. The settlements around Nashville were supposedly protected by the Treaty of Hopewell; however, the Chickamauga did not sign on to the agreement. Indeed, new settlers constantly arrived and spread white settlements. Some of these were from the Overmountain communities, but most were from east of the Appalachians. Captain John Morgan, a cousin of Revolutionary War General Daniel Morgan, established a new station at the mouth of Dry Fork Creek, two and one half miles northwest of Bledsoe's Station. (Morgan's Station was located on Bledsoe's Creek near present-day Rogana, Tennessee. Rogana is located between U.S. Highways 31E and 231, northwest of Gallatin, Tennessee, and due north of Castalion Springs.)

In January 1786, Chickamauga warriors killed Peter Barnett and David Steel on Blooming Grove Creek. Near the same place, about one week later, the war party captured William Crutcher. They stabbed him in the abdomen with a rusty hunting knife and hit him on the skull to render him unconscious. They withdrew and left the knife in place so he would suffer. Crutcher later came to and crawled to the cabin of a neighboring settler where he eventually recovered. (Blooming Grove Creek empties into the Cumberland River from the north at a point eight miles southwest of Clarksville, Tennessee.)

Another band of Chickamauga was operating around Bledsoe's Station in January. Warriors stole 12 horses from an enclosure near William Hall's house one night. Hall removed his family to the safety of Bledsoe's Station, and they did not return to their property until fall.

According to historian Edward Albright, about the first of February, a hunting and surveying party camped on a creek north of present-day Carthage, Tennessee. The members of the group were brothers John, Ephraim, and Thomas Peyton, John Frazier, Thomas Pugh, and Esquire Grant. They built a fire on snow-covered ground. A fire at night would quickly draw warriors. About ten o'clock that night, their dogs began to bark and run amok, but the men assumed that wild animals were nearby. They had hung and bled fresh meat from the trees on the edge of the camp. John Peyton raised himself on his elbow and scolded the dogs, and a band of 60 Indians, reportedly led by Chief Hanging Maw, fired a volley. The initial barrage broke John Peyton's arm in two places and also hit Thomas Peyton's shoulder and Esquire Grant's thigh. John Frazier was wounded in his calf. Ephraim Peyton escaped injury until he dislocated his ankle when he leaped off a bluff into the creek. At the onset of the attack, John Peyton threw a blanket over the fire, and the little group dispersed through their attackers' line in the darkness. They abandoned their horses, saddles and bridles, surveyor's compass, and other equipment to the warriors. Each man separately reached Bledsoe's Station and reported that his comrades were either killed or captured. They were pleasantly surprised to be reunited.

Interestingly, Ephraim Peyton used a crooked stick as a crutch for 20 miles until he slipped. When he fell, near present-day Hartsville, his ankle corrected itself, and he walked normally to the fort from there.

(The stream was later named Defeated Creek because of that event. Defeated Creek empties into Hull Lake from the north, five miles north by northwest from Carthage, Tennessee.)

Apparently, someone in the party had recognized Chief Hanging Maw. One year later, John Peyton sent Hanging Maw a message and demanded that he return the horses and compass he had stolen. Hanging Maw reportedly answered the message and declined to return any property. The chief reportedly declared: "You, John Peyton, ran away like a coward and left them. As for your land stealer, I have broken that against a tree."[34]

In 1834, Ester Morris wrote an essay about the Defeated Creek event. John Peyton, who had died in 1833, personally related the story to her. She corroborated Mr. Albright's version except for a few small variations regarding the wounds the men experienced. The primary difference in the story is that the Cherokee chief who led the war party is identified as Chickamauga chief Fool Warrior. Morris makes no mention of an exchange of letters. She also added that it took the dispersed group four days to reunite at Bledsoe's Station after separately following circuitous paths of about 70 miles each.[35]

By the spring of 1786, a land office had opened that offered tracts for all of the land north of the Little Tennessee River, and the white frontiersmen were actually settling on the northern banks of the river. The white settlers and the Upper Cherokee were then closer neighbors than they wanted to be, and only the Little Tennessee River separated them.

Old Tassel continually engaged himself in peaceful negotiations; however, the Chickamauga, which now included warriors in some of the more remote Upper Villages, took another approach—war!

Colonel Joseph Martin had become the Indian agent for both Virginia and North Carolina. He constantly patrolled the Upper Villages and reported that the Upper Cherokee were mostly peaceful, but the Chickamauga were not.

However, historian James Mooney declared that a party of Upper Cherokee was sent out to avenge the settlers' killing of four Cherokee. The warriors killed and scalped 15, and then sent a message to John Sevier that they wanted peace. They continued that they would, however, defend themselves if the settlers desired war. Captain William Fayne had been drawn into an ambush at Citigo Town, and several militiamen were killed. The Indians, likely Chickamauga led by Young Tassel, chased the survivors to Knoxville and attacked a station near present-day Maryville, Tennessee. Sevier drove the attackers off, mounted an attack on the Cherokee Valley Towns, and destroyed three villages. He withdrew when he was warned that chiefs Dragging Canoe and Young Tassel defended the other Valley Villages and had gathered many warriors to face him.

Virginia colonel William Christian, referred to as Colonel Christie by Old Tassel at the Treaty of Hopewell, was killed in a battle with Wabash Indians in Illinois country on April 9, 1786.

Less than one year after the Treaty of Hopewell, the whites had passed the line not only established by that treaty, but they had also reclaimed the secured the area of the Dumplin settlement. The Franklinites were determined to acquire all Cherokee land around and including the Upper Towns.

John Sevier, acting governor of the illegal state called Franklin, ordered his militiamen under the leadership of Colonels Alexander Outlaw and William Cocke to march on the Mother Town, Chota, and face Chief Old Tassel. Apparently, two young men had been killed on July 20, 1786, by two or three young braves who had been hired by an old warrior from Chickamauga. The Chickamaugan supposedly wanted revenge for the death of two sons who had been killed by white people in the spring.

Outlaw and Cocke, at the head of 250 militiamen, marched to Chota Ford, and sent for the headmen of the Upper Towns. Chiefs Old Tassel and Hanging Maw appeared. The militia colonels charged them with breaking the treaties and murdering the young men. Old Tassel declared his people were not responsible. He said the men who did the murder were Chickamauga followers and lived 20 miles away in Coyatee, at the mouth of Holston River.

Colonels Outlaw and Cocke marched their force to Coyatee and killed the two warriors that committed the murder. They then destroyed the town house and the guilty warriors' homes. The militia returned to Chota and, on August 3, renewed their conference with Old Tassel and Hanging Maw. After they again accused the chiefs of breaking the treaty, they charged them with the murders of Colonels Donelson and Christian. Old Tassel responded: "My brother, William Christian, took care of everybody, and was a good man; he is dead and gone. It was not me nor my people that killed him. They told lies on me. He was killed going the other way, over the river."[36]

Colonels Outlaw and Cocke then declared: "We now tell you plainly that our great counsellors have sold us the land on the north side of the Tennessee [the Little Tennessee] to the Cumberland Mountain, and we intend to settle and live on it, and if you kill any of our people for settling there, we shall destroy the town that does the mischief."[37]

Old Tassel disputed the claim: "You say that North Carolina sold you the land over the river ... I never heard of your great Council selling you the land you speak of. I talked last fall with the Great men from Congress, but they told me nothing of this."[38]

Old Tassel and Hanging Maw were coerced into signing the "Treaty of Coyatee."

While Old Tassel was powerless to prevent their taking possession of the land, he hoped they should live on it together as friends and keep their young men at peace. The Franklinites had no desire to cohabitate with the Cherokee. Judge David Campbell of the Franklinites reportedly said: "No people are entitled to more land than they can cultivate. People will not sit still and starve for land when a neighboring Nation has more than it needs."[39]

Such was the Treaty of Coyatee!

Old Tassel opined: "We have held several treaties with the Americans when boundaries were fixed and fair promises made that the white people would not cross over, but we always find that after a treaty they settle much faster than before. Truth is if we had no land we should have fewer enemies."[40]

Joseph Martin, still representing both North Carolina and Virginia, was residing in Chota. He tried to arbitrate on behalf of North Carolina; however, Outlaw and Cocke declared that North Carolina had no jurisdiction in Franklin.[41]

(The Treaty of Coyatee is variously reported as happening anywhere between 1786 and 1788; however, the timing of surrounding events establishes 1786 as the proper year of the event.)

Meanwhile, in December 1786, Colonel Robertson (a member of the North Carolina legislature) successfully lobbied for the passage of an act to station a North Carolina State Militia battalion around Nashville. The 300-man force was to protect its inhabitants and to cut a road between Nashville and the Clinch River. This battalion, commanded by Major Nathaniel Evans, reached the Cumberland in several detachments during 1787. They were divided into companies and sporadically stationed to react to emergencies as required.

Colonel Robertson used local militia as roving scouts. This was a setback for the Chickamauga, as the war parties were suddenly exposed. Once the weather warmed, the cane and weeds became thick, and the warriors adjusted their methods. They could work in much smaller bands, use the cover, sneak upon someone exposed, and either kill or capture a settler with ease.

One band of Indian warriors, led by well-known Chickamauga chief Big Foot, was chased from the settlement by a company under command of Captain John Shannon. Luke Anderson, noted scout Jacob Castleman, William Pillow, and a few others accompanied him. The warriors were preparing to cross the Tennessee River on their way south. When the white posse caught up to the Indians, some were eating on the north bank while Big Foot and some others were looking for a place to ford. Captain Shannon and his party fired on the warriors and then rushed the ones lounging on the bank. Big Foot hurried back to reinforce his warriors, and the two sides were about equal in numbers, so a hand-to-hand conflict ensued. Castleman and Pillow each killed a Chickamauga brave and then spotted Big Foot. He was engaged with the much smaller Anderson and had just wrested the white man's rifle away from him. Just as Anderson was hurled to the ground, Pillow planted his tomahawk in the chief's head. The surviving warriors withdrew and left the bodies of Big Foot and four others of their band.

The Nashville settlements continued to grow as new settlers steadily arrived. However, the physical dimensions of Nashville did not enlarge as the Chickamauga were still surreptitiously active on the outskirts. A man by the name of Price (or Prince), his wife, and children were killed on the creek just south of Gallatin. Judge Haywood recorded that, during the incident, the family members were mutilated and their body parts spread about the property. John Beard was killed on Big Station Camp Creek in the vicinity of Bledsoe's Station.

Chickamauga warriors raided Morgan's Station at the mouth of Dry Fork and stole some horses. The Indians made a circuit through the hills and apparently were headed to recross the Cumberland River at Dixon Springs. One of the horses wore a bell that attracted pursuers from the station. The settlers killed one warrior and recovered the horses.

Major William Hall had been a magistrate in the new Sumner County since 1786. On June 3, 1787, Colonel James Robertson held a council in Nashville with Chief Little Owl, Dragging Canoe's brother, and a few other Chickamauga chiefs. He requested that Major Hall attend.

While Hall was gone, his sons, James and William, Jr., left their barn and trekked through a wooded tract to a nearby field to retrieve some horses. Fifteen Chickamauga prepared an ambush beside the path: ten behind a log pile, and five a little further along in the branches of a fallen tree. After the boys passed the first group, the warriors attacked James, who lagged behind William. William heard the commotion and turned to see that his brother, with two tomahawks buried deep in his forehead, was being held by a warrior. William fled down the path toward the horses but encountered the second party of Indians. They rushed toward him, and one of them raised a tomahawk. William, suddenly, darted off the path into a canebrake. Two warriors chased him, but he flitted in different directions until he reached his home. The warriors did not stop until they were within 100 yards of the structure.

Half a dozen young men, with their girlfriends, had just arrived at Major Hall's when William rushed up. Being armed, they at once dismounted, and followed him to the scene of the attack. They found James' body and brought it to the house; the warriors had scalped him, and withdrawn. One of the visitors carried news of the attack to Bledsoe's Station two miles away. Major James Lynn led five other men in pursuit of the war party. The Indians had retreated down a buffalo trace to Dickson's Lick. The settlers decided to take a different route to avoid an ambush. The trails joined at Goose Creek Ford, and the stalkers fired upon the fleeing band. They wounded two warriors, but all escaped. The Indians left their guns, tomahawks, and loot that was in their possession, so they could move more quickly. The settlers took all of it to Bledsoe's Station. Once they arrived, they discovered that James Hall's scalp was tied to a leather bag.

It was believed that the attack was by the same warriors who had stolen the Morgan's Station horses a few weeks earlier. The settlers assumed that Hall was killed in revenge for the subsequent pursuit by the Morgan's Station party.

Major Hall was told of the incident when he returned from Nashville. He immediately met with neighbors, men named Gibson and Harrison. They considered whether they should remain in place until the crops were in or withdraw to Bledsoe's Station. They decided to stay, but they would collectively hire six outriders for the remainder of the season.[42]

Early in June, two young Chickasaw warriors, one named Toka, were hunting along the Tennessee River in Alabama. During their expedition, they unexpectedly approached Coldwater Town. That secluded village had been a closely-guarded secret by the Chickamauga. The Chickasaw were treated kindly and spent the night. While there, they heard the Coldwater warriors discuss a relationship with the French who supplied them with arms and ammunition. They also heard tails of raids into the Cumberland settlements. When the two returned to the Chickasaw villages (near present-day Memphis, Tennessee), they informed Chief Piomingo of their findings. The chief immediately sent them to Colonel James Robertson at Nashville. Piomingo recommended that he destroy Coldwater Town as quickly as possible. Colonel Robertson, stunned to hear about the secret village, was irked that French traders had supplied the Chickamauga. On June 12, 1787, he and Colonel Anthony Bledsoe jointly wrote North Carolina governor Richard Caswell and asked for permission to attack the town. He reported that the inhabitants included 35 Cherokee warriors, 10 Creek, and nine Frenchmen.

The next day near Nashville, Chief Doublehead's faction killed Mark Robertson, the colonel's younger brother. Mark Robertson had been captured in a canebrake on Richland Creek and brutally cut to pieces with tomahawks and knives. The broken cane and blood on the surrounding shrubbery was evidence of a fierce tussle. Colonel James Robertson chose not to await Caswell's reply, but raised a militia of (variously reported) 120 to 130 men, under Lieutenant Colonels Robert Hays and James Ford. Colonel Robertson assumed chief command himself. He immediately trailed the warriors and sent (also variously reported) 20 to 50 more men, led by Captain David Hay, to the mouth of Duck River to prevent retreat, especially by the French.

It took the militia several days to locate the village. None of the settlers had ever been this far south, so Colonel Robertson employed the two Chickasaw messengers to guide them. They followed a circuitous route, up Turnbull Creek to its head, and then down Lick Creek. They descended the Duck River and ascended Swan Creek to its head. They followed Blue Water Creek downstream but stopped before the spot where it empties into the Tennessee River one and one-half miles upriver of the lower end of Muscle Shoals. They departed Blue Water Creek to their left, hurried on, and immediately encamped when they could hear the sound of Muscle Shoals. Robertson sent scouts to reconnoiter. They returned at midnight and reported the militia was still ten miles from the shoals. The company broke camp at dawn the following morning and cautiously approached the river. They crossed as quietly as possible. They quickly ate breakfast on the south bank, dried their clothes, mounted their horses, and galloped toward the village 18 miles downstream. The colonel halted the force after 40 minutes and held a council of war.

The village was located on a sharp rise a few hundred yards west of Coldwater Creek. The attackers found a ford upstream from the village, and Robertson broke the group into two detachments. He led the larger portion of the force and approached the village from behind on the rise. Captain John Rains furtively inched along the creek bank to the ford to cut off any retreat. The colonel ordered a charge, but the inhabitants were already darting for the ford. Rains and his men shot and killed 26 as they approached his position. The survivors of that onslaught hastily dispersed in every direction, unarmed, as they had left their weapons in the village. Six of the dead were Creek warriors; three were Frenchmen, and one was a Frenchwoman who had come with them. There were 15 more inhabitants than when the Chickasaw first found the town several days earlier. The surviving 24 Indians and Frenchmen were captured.

It was agreed that Captain David Hay's company should carry an extra supply of provisions. They rigged a large boat called *Piragua* and two smaller boats. Hay was assisted by Moses Shelby, brother of Isaac Shelby. Hugh Rogan, Josiah Renfroe, Edward Hogan and

John Top (sometimes Topp) were among the crew. Their orders were to proceed down the Cumberland and up the Tennessee as far as Colbert's Landing. If Robertson's group were to have a problem crossing the Tennessee, then Hay's crew was to continue on and ferry them across.

Hay's company was not as successful as Robertson's force. Their movements were observed by a band of Chickamauga. When the whites reached the mouth of Duck River, they noticed a seemingly empty canoe fastened to its bank. Captain Moses Shelby rowed his boat out of the Tennessee River and into the Duck. When he approached, he wished he had not done so. It was a trap! A few of the Chickamauga had simply hidden themselves in the canoe, and the others were concealed in some thick brush along the bank. When Shelby neared, the warriors arose and fired on the craft. Josiah Renfroe was killed with the first volley. Hugh Rogan, Edward Hogan, John Top, and five others were severely wounded.

Shelby struggled to row back to the others in midstream, and a council was held to determine the best course of action. They decided to withdraw to Nashville and seek medical attention for the wounded.

Robertson's force looted Coldwater Town, burned the cabins, and camped by the ruins for the night. At dawn the next day, they placed the captives and the goods into several captured canoes. The French traders' goods consisted of tafia (a cheap rum), sugar, coffee, cloths, blankets, handkerchiefs, beads, paints, knives, tomahawks, tobacco, and gunpowder. They were caravanned down the Tennessee River under guard led by Jonathan Denton, Benjamin Drake, and John and Moses Eskridge. They met Robertson and the others at an agreed-upon place. They released the prisoners with instructions to hurry back up the river, which they did in haste. The group in the canoes, along with the captured goods, proceeded along the rivers to Nashville. The two Chickasaw were discharged to report to Chief Piomingo. The colonel awarded each a captured Chickamauga horse, a gun, and several blankets in appreciation for their efforts.

The boats proceeded down the Tennessee, and after a few days the travelers met five Frenchmen from Kaskaskia in Illinois country, with two boats full of trade goods. The French traders believed Denton and his men were other Frenchmen from Coldwater Town come to greet them. The traders fired their loaded cannon in salute. The Cumberland boatmen pointed their own charged guns at the French and took them captive. The captors escorted their new prisoners and their spoils up the Cumberland River near Nashville. They proposed that the Frenchmen could continue on with them and stand trial, or they could return to Kaskaskia without their goods. They chose the latter. Denton gave them a canoe and sent them on their way. All of the spoils captured on the trek were delivered to Eaton's Station where they were auctioned off, and the proceeds were divided among the militia. Colonel James Robertson's force returned to Nashville without the loss of a single man during the action at Coldwater Town. (Coldwater Town was in the vicinity of present-day Tuscumbia, Alabama.)[43]

What became known as The Coldwater Expedition was a setback for the Muscle Shoals Chickamauga faction; however, Chief Doublehead was apparently not in Coldwater Town at the time. The Chickamauga were led by strong, charismatic chiefs who would not be down long. They would, in fact, interpret it a weakness of the whites that they did not hang their captives after the depredations that faction had performed in the Nashville area—especially the slaughter of Mark Robertson. The restraint that Colonel James Robertson had exhibited was remarkable.

9. The Chickamauga Continue to Defend the Cherokee Nation

Also in June, Virginia governor Edmund Randolph wrote to Chief Old Tassel. The governor accused, that the Cherokee warriors had burned a white woman at the stake in the Five Lower Towns, and thus threatened revenge. Old Tassel denied the charge and replied that no one had been burned at the stake in over ten years. He accused the Virginia settlers of a frame to justify a new war against the tribes and gain more Cherokee land.

Nancy Ward's brother, Chief Tuskeegeetee (Long Fellow) then threatened the governor. He declared he had once been a Chickamauga warrior, but Colonel Joseph Martin had convinced him to rejoin the peaceful Cherokee six years earlier. Long Fellow avowed that should the governor continue to ignore encroachment onto Cherokee land, he would take many warriors, return to Dragging Canoe's force, and wreak destruction on the settlements. Randolph sent trade goods to the Upper Villages to calm Long Fellow.

General Pickens continued as South Carolina's de facto Indian agent for several years following the 1785 Treaty of Hopewell. In 1787, Chief Hanging Maw sent Joseph Martin to speak with Pickens and protest because white men were not abiding by the treaty and had settled on Cherokee lands. The message stated: "We have been told by people a great way off that the Americans only meant to deceive us.... They [the Northward tribes and the Creeks] want us to join them also [to strike the Americans]. But, I remember your talks and will hold them fast."[44]

The Chickamauga resumed their offensive after a short lull following the Coldwater Expedition. On August 2, 1787, scouts reported that a war party of 30 Chickamauga was roaming the area. Major William Hall and his family began moving to Bledsoe's Station two miles away early the next morning. (They had postponed the move after their son, James, had been killed in June. They had remained to work their crops.) They transported their belongings on a sled pulled by a brace of horses. Mrs. Hall worked in their cabin packing, with help from the younger children by her side. The oldest daughter had gone to the fort early to receive and unpack the household goods as they arrived. They worked all day to transfer three sled loads. The major, Mrs. Hall, a younger daughter, and three sons, including William Hall, Jr., accompanied the fourth and last load late in the afternoon. Charles Morgan, husband of the older daughter and son of John Morgan of Morgan's Station, a Mr. Hickerson, and Hugh Rogan assisted.

The Chickamauga attacked them when halfway to the fort, in the vicinity of Defeated Creek. The warriors had apparently seen an earlier trip and laid ambush from brush that extended for one hundred yards on each side of the road. The Indians arose at an opportune time and poured a volley into the travelers. Richard Hall, the oldest son, was the vanguard and was killed with the first shots. He fell into the brush on the side of the lane. Hickerson, who was a short distance behind, had triggered his gun, but it misfired. He was mortally wounded by six rifle balls that hit him all at once. Mrs. Hall's horse shied and dashed through the warriors. It did not stop until it reached the fort.

Thirteen-year-old William Hall, Jr., was driving the sled, and he dropped the lines with the first shots. He bravely ran back to protect his little brother, John, and little sister, Prudence. Major Hall ordered the children to scatter into the woods while he and Morgan covered their escape. Hall and Morgan stood their ground and accurately returned fire. However, as Morgan was severely wounded, he followed the children through the forest to the fort. Major Hall was felled in the middle of the road by thirteen rifle balls. The warriors scalped him, took his rifle and shot pouch, and withdrew.

William directed John and Prudence to run back to the house while he hid to await the results of the fight. When he heard the discharge of his father's heavy rifle, followed by the whoops of the warriors, he knew that the fight had been lost. He started for the fort. When John and Prudence reached the house, the noise of the battle ceased. The two retraced their steps through the woods to the scene of the slaughter. Rogan had apparently escaped. John found and picked up Rogan's hat while Prudence grabbed a pail of butter from the overturned sled. They walked heedlessly down the road towards Bledsoe's Station, which was one mile away. Men from the fort, who had been alerted by young William, met them. A few took the children to the fort and the rest went to the site of the battle. Major Hall's death was a tragedy for the settlements, but a great coup for the Chickamauga.

Soon thereafter, John Pervine was killed two miles northeast of Gallatin, and John Allen was ambushed and shot in the abdomen a short distance north of Bledsoe's Station. Allen survived.

Randal Gentry was surprised and killed near Bluff Fort, and Curtis Williams, Thomas Fletcher, and Fletcher's son were slain as they explored around Harpeth River, apparently scouting hunting locations 20 miles west of the Bluff.

On August 5, 1787, Colonel Anthony Bledsoe wrote Franklin acting governor John Sevier and asked him to forward it to North Carolina governor Richard Caswell. In the letter, Bledsoe urgently requested assistance to bring the Chickamauga under control.

Captain John Morgan's father was killed just outside the stockade at Morgan's Station. Two companies of militia gathered to pursue the warriors. Major George Winchester and Captain William Martin commanded the companies. After they lost the trail, each group searched separately through the canebrakes near Bledsoe's Station for signs of the war party. One of Winchester's men heard a sound and, thinking he had come upon the Indians, fired into Martin's party and killed William Ridley. The troops immediately abandoned the effort.

In September 1787, Captains John Shannon and John Rains were ordered to scour the country around the Duck and Elk rivers. Captain Shannon's company was the vanguard and passed near a recently-abandoned Indian camp without discovering it; however, Captain Rains noticed buzzards circling overhead. His group encamped nearby and discovered a recently-killed deer. He found a war party's trail the next morning, and later that day one of his scouts discovered and fired upon one of the warriors.

Rains and his company rushed in at the sound of the rifle shot, and Rains spotted and pursued the warrior running a ridge. He yelled for the Indian to stop, which he did. However, he quickly resumed his flight. Rains fired and wounded the man. Reuben Parks and Beverly Ridley joined the pursuit. The Indian fired at Ridley but shot high. The group caught up to the warrior, knocked him off his feet, and Ridley stabbed him to death. John Rains, Jr., and Robert Evans outran and captured a young warrior not yet 20 years old. He was held in the settlements for a year or more; then he was released to return to his home.

On September 19, 1787, Chief Old Tassel sent a letter, to no avail, to the governors of North Carolina and Virginia pleading for them to be decisive against encroachment onto Cherokee lands. The governors were apparently in a quandary as to how to handle the governor of Franklin, John Sevier. During the fall, Sevier continued to attack some Upper Villages to punish the Cherokee for the aggressiveness of the Chickamauga warriors. The Chickamauga, then, sought additional revenge. Tit for tat activities would continue for years—and they would get worse.

During the winter of 1787, Charles Morgan (who was wounded when his father-in-law, Major William Hall, was killed a few months before) had left Bledsoe's Station on his way to Greenfield Station. He was accompanied by Jordan Gibson, and, as they neared the Hall family property, they were ambushed by Chickamauga. Gibson was killed outright: Morgan was mortally wounded. Each was scalped. Before Morgan died he identified the warrior who scalped him as harelipped. He was believed to have been Chief Moon, who was known to have had a cleft lip.

Young Tassel (John Watts, Jr.) had not yet taken up arms for the Chickamauga. He had, however, refused to take part in the Treaty of Holston in 1777 and withdrew from the Upper Villages. Indeed he worked hard to establish peace between the settlers and the Cherokee. Historians Albert V. Goodpasture and J. G. M. Ramsey stated respectively: "The first glimpse we have of him is in the capacity of a diplomat. When Campbell and Sevier invaded the Indian country in 1780, Watts, and a chief called Noonday, afterwards killed by rangers near Craig's Station, met them at Tellico and proposed terms of peace. Ramsey says it was granted to Tellico and the adjacent villages, but Campbell, in his official report, expressly states that Tellico was burned." And: "Here, also, John Watts, who afterwards became a distinguished chief in his tribe, was engaged to accompany the expedition, to effect, by friendly negotiation, an arrangement for peace with the entire nation."[45]

The Chickamauga Cherokee and their Creek and Shawnee allies attacked again throughout Tennessee in 1788. The Virginia and North Carolina Indian agent, Colonel Joseph Martin, again reported that the Cherokee, except for the Chickamauga, greatly desired peace; however, the Franklinites used the Chickamauga attacks as justification to pressure the Upper Cherokee Nation. Sevier led an army through the villages along the French Broad River.

Sevier's rival, Colonel John Tipton, had originally favored separation from North Carolina. However, he opposed an official organization of Franklin until North Carolina could address the settlements' complaints. As his relationship with Sevier deteriorated, Tipton was selected by North Carolina to suppress Sevier's unofficial government. The North Carolina courts issued a writ against Sevier's estate for taxes due, and the sheriff seized Sevier's slaves. The sheriff took them to Colonel Tipton's estate on Sinking Creek. Sevier mustered 150 militiamen and, with a light field cannon, besieged Tipton's home. Tipton and 30 to 40 of his own militiamen defended the buildings for two days. Three men were killed or wounded. A Sullivan County militia lieutenant arrived with 180 militiamen to reinforce Tipton. They reached Tipton's at dawn on February 29 and surprised Sevier. They killed two of Sevier's men and took two of Sevier's sons captive. Tipton was eager to hang the two young Seviers; however, cooler heads prevailed, and he was dissuaded. The young captives were eventually released. This skirmish became known as the Battle of Franklin and, for all practical purpose, ended the viability of that would-be state. Sevier fled back to his settlement and re-engaged in war against the Cherokee.

One day in March 1788, the Chickamauga stealthily approached a camp near Colonel James Robertson's residence (where the Chickasaw Treaty was held in 1783). The colonel's son, Peyton, John Johnson, and other young friends were engaged with processing sap into maple sugar. One of the young men spotted the warriors between them and the Robertson house. The boys dispersed into the woods. Peyton Robertson was killed, and John Johnson was taken captive. The rest of the boys escaped.

In April 1787, William Montgomery's sons, John, Robert, and Thomas, were killed near their father's house on Drake's Creek, three miles below Shackle Island. The oldest, John, had suffered a broken thigh in an Indian attack one year earlier and still used crutches. He watched as his brothers trimmed apple trees in their orchard. Warriors rushed out from a nearby thicket, killed the three, scalped them, and stacked their bodies on a brush pile. (Shackle Island is eight miles west of present-day Gallatin, Tennessee, near the junction of State Highways 25 and 258.)

Shortly thereafter, Mrs. Neely, widow of William Neely, was killed at the salt kilns where her husband had been slain a few years earlier. Robert Edmonson was hit by a rifle ball that broke his arm, but he escaped into nearby canebrakes.

Robert James was killed two miles east of present-day Gallatin, Tennessee. Jesse Maxey was wounded while traveling along a road near Asher's Station. He saw no means of escape so fell face down on the ground. The warriors scalped him, stabbed him with a hunting knife, and left him to die. He survived.

The Cumberland settlers strongly believed the Spaniards were responsible for the hostilities of the Creek. The Creek never had owned or claimed any land on the Cumberland River, so they had no incentive to assist the Chickamauga Cherokee in their attacks. Creek chief Alexander McGillivray admitted:

> I will not deny that my nation has waged war against your country for several years past, and that we had no motive of revenge for it, nor did it proceed from any sense of injuries sustained from your people; but, being warmly attached to the British, under their influence our operations were directed by them against you, in common with other Americans. After the general peace had taken place you sent us a talk, proposing terms of peace, by Samuel Martin, which I then accepted and advised my people to agree to, and which should have been finally concluded in the ensuing summer and fall. Judging that your people were sincere in their professions, I was much surprised to find that while this affair was pending they attacked the French traders at Mussel [sic] Shoals, and killed six of our Nation who were there trafficking for silverware. These men belonged to different towns, and had connections of the first consequence in the Nation. Such an unprovoked outrage raised a most violent clamor, and gave rise to the expedition against Cumberland which soon took place.[46]

Historian Albert V. Goodpasture commented:

> This explanation of the great Indian diplomatist contained only a half-truth. The habit of fighting the American pioneers undoubtedly had a great influence. For that reason the people of Cumberland hailed with joy the transfer of Florida from Great Britain to Spain, who had acted with America in the Revolution. Not only the Creeks, but the Cherokees, and Chickasaws, had all, at some time during the war, allied themselves with the British, and made war on the southwestern frontiers. It was hoped that the withdrawal from Florida of the British agents, to whom the Indians had looked for arms, ammunition and supplies, would bring with it a cessation of Indian hostilities. For a time it seemed to have had that tendency, but the development of the Spanish policy finally resulted in such new Indian depredations as made the Spanish more detested on the frontiers than the British had ever been.[47]

At the end of the American Revolution, Spain had feared the spread of American institutions and ideas. At the Treaty of Paris in 1782, Spain secured the cooperation of France in an effort to limit the western boundary of the United States to the Allegheny Mountains, and convert the entire western country into an Indian reservation. This would have been great for the southern tribes, but the entire area west of the Alleghenies was impractical to enforce. Spain wanted to divide the west into three parts: north of the Ohio River under the protection of England; between the Ohio and Cumberland, including a narrow strip west of the Carolinas and Georgia, under the protection of France; south of the Cumberland under the protection of Spain. That arrangement would create a barrier between the United States and West Florida. Great Britain honored the treaty, so the agreement failed.

Spain subsequently sought to accomplish the purpose by causing the western settlements to withdraw from the Union or, with the assistance of the Creek, destroy the settlements entirely. The eighth article of the Treaty of Paris expressly declared that the navigation of the Mississippi River, from its source to its mouth, would remain open and free to the subjects of Great Britain and the citizens of the United States. However, Spain had closed it against American commerce to discourage emigrants from settling the western rivers by denying the only outlet that existed for their export. Thus, Spain thought the western settlers would cooperate.

Spain had succeeded in monopolizing the trade of the southern Indians and influenced them to intimidate the Cumberland settlements.[48]

The Chickamauga continued to be active, and a family of settlers literally walked into their hands. In 1783, Colonel James Brown, an American Revolution veteran from North Carolina, had been given tracts of land as a grant in the disputed territory. He and his oldest sons, William and Daniel, traveled to the Cumberlands late in 1787 and claimed a tract at the mouth of White's Creek on the Cumberland River (near present-day Columbia, Tennessee). The boys stayed on the land to erect a cabin and clear a field for crops while the colonel returned to North Carolina. He also had new tracts on the Duck River. He and his wife, Jane Gillespie Brown, had nine surviving children of 16.

Colonel Brown had to decide on one of three routes to take to the new land. The first choice was to retrace the steps of Colonel Robertson overland through Cumberland Gap. His second option was a newly-opened road that ran from Clinch Mountain to Nashville. Of course, he could select the river route followed years earlier by Colonel Donelson when he met up with Colonel Robertson at, then called, French Lick.

He selected what was seemingly the most dangerous alternative of the three from a Chickamauga point of view, and started to build a large boat near Long Island of the Holston River. He had feared going overland because of snow; however, he did not leave until midspring. His large boat was well constructed. The walls were lined with two-inch-thick oak planks. He drilled portholes for defense and mounted a swivel gun on the stern.

On May 4, 1788, James Brown cast off on his perilous journey accompanied by his wife, his grown sons, James and John, 15-year-old Joseph, George, who was nine, Jane, aged ten, seven-year-old Elizabeth, and Polly, four. Five young men, J. Bays, John Flood, John Gentry, William Gentry, and John Griffin, and an unidentified black woman were also along on the trek.

They passed Chickamauga Creek at dawn on Friday, May 9, 1788, and reached Tuskegee shortly thereafter. Tuskegee was the first town encountered in the Lower Villages of the Chickamauga, and it sat on the north bank of the Tennessee downriver from present-day Chattanooga.

The headman of Tuskegee, Chief Coteatoy, canoed out to the boat with three warriors. They waved and seemed friendly, so Brown allowed them to come aboard. The purpose of the visitors was to obtain information about how many white men were aboard, how they were armed, and what goods these interlopers had with them. Although they were courteous, the last things the Chickamauga wanted to see were boatloads of whites pouring into the ancestral land of the Cherokee, and they intended to make examples of these that were before them. When Coteatoy reached the shore, he sent runners to Nickajack and to Running Water Town to alert the warriors there.

About one hour later, Brown's boat arrived in the vicinity of Nickajack. John Vann, who was a half-blooded Cherokee and spoke excellent English, led 40 warriors aboard four canoes to intercept the boat. They were apparently unarmed. The warriors bore white flags in each canoe; however, they had carefully concealed guns and tomahawks in the bottoms of their boats. Colonel Brown became suspiscious because too many boats were coming too quickly. He warned them to stop, turned his boat around, and pointed the swivel gun at the canoes. John Vann begged Brown not to shoot and insisted that his companions desired to trade goods with the voyagers.

During this parley, the Chickamauga continued to advance. They had soon surrounded Brown's boat and climbed over its sides. Seven or eight other canoes, heretofore hidden in the cane along the banks, quickly approached. Vann's party appeared friendly until the other canoes arrived, and the warriors transferred goods from the boat to the canoes. Brown asked Vann for protection, but was told that he must await the return of Breath (Unlita), the headman of Nickajack. Breath was away from home, but he was expected back that night. Vann promised that Breath would require the warriors to return the goods and would provide a guide to pilot his boat over the dangerous rapids of the Muscle Shoals. In the meantime, the boat had been completely ransacked, and the warriors pointed it for the mouth of Nickajack Creek. (Vann spoke the truth when he told Brown that Breath was away when the attack took place. He had visited another village fifteen miles from Nickajack. When he returned, he was displeased with the massacre. Breath claimed that he had never "stained his knife in the blood of a white man.")[49]

Suddenly, a large warrior seized Joseph Brown by the arm and violently pulled him to one side. The colonel grabbed the Indian and scolded him. The warrior released Joseph and directed his attention to his father. As soon as Brown had turned his back, the Chickamaugan drew a previously captured saber and, with one stroke, beheaded the colonel. After the attacker threw the body overboard, Joseph Brown ran to the bow and told his brothers their father had drowned. Joseph had not seen the fatal blow.

A band of Creek who were among the party stashed Mrs. Brown, her youngest son, George, and the three little girls, into their canoes. Then, as the Chickamauga Cherokee deliberated the fate of the men, the Creek quickly departed for the Coosa and Tallapoosa rivers. The Chickamauga discovered the departure the next morning, pursued the Creek band, and forced them to deliver up Jane and Polly. The Chickamauga returned to Nickajack with the two youngsters and allowed the Creek to keep Mrs. Brown, nine-year-old George and seven-year-old Elizabeth.

That day, Kiachatalee, a warrior of Nickajack, asked young Joseph Brown to get into his canoe and go with him. Joseph did not yet understand that he was a prisoner and refused to go. Kiachatalee returned with his stepfather, Tom Tunbridge, who could speak English. Tunbridge asked Joseph to spend the night at his house which was one mile east of town on the Running Water Road. Joseph asked his older brothers for permission, and they consented. (Kiachatalee was the son of a Cherokee warrior and Polly Mallett, a French woman who had been reared among the Indians. When Kiachatalee was six years old, Polly married Tom Tunbridge, an Irish deserter from the British army, who had taken up his residence among the Cherokee before the American Revolution. At the time of the attack on Brown's boat, Tunbridge had lived with Polly for sixteen years.)

Coteatoy of Tuskegee arrived in Nickajack and took the black woman as his captive, put her aboard his canoe, and had a warrior take her to Tuskegee.

As the other captives had been accounted for, the seven young men were the only ones who awaited disposition. They were told they could spend the night at a house in town. However, they were later directed to a supposedly better one at the lower end of the village. A young warrior was sent to lead them to the cabin. About two o'clock in the afternoon, they boarded a canoe and went down the creek to the house. A party of Chickamauga ambushed them from the canebrake along the creek. Three of the whites were shot and killed during the initial volley. The others quickly abandoned the boat for the creek, but the warriors, armed with knives, tomahawks, and rifles, pursued and killed them all. The bodies were mutilated.

Tom Tunbridge hurried Joseph Brown away from the town. As they traveled to the Tunbridge home, they could hear gunshots from Nickajack Creek. They reached the home shortly thereafter. Coteatoy's mother, a very large woman, came rushing up to the house. She upbraided Tunbridge for not killing the prisoner as he had the other men. She pointed out that he was nearly grown and could take revenge. She added that she was sure Coteatoy would kill him. Tunbridge arose, went to the door, and looked toward the village. Coteatoy emerged out of the nearby canebrake and asked Tunbridge if he had a white man in the house. Tunbridge answered that there were no white men in his house, but there was a white boy. Coteatoy averred that he knew how big the lad was and that he must be killed immediately. Tunbridge answered that it was not right to kill women and children, that the boy was Kiachatalee's prisoner, and he must not be killed. Coteatoy was irate, and Tunbridge feared for his wife and himself. He stepped back and told Coteatoy to take the boy.

Coteatoy entered the cabin with his knife and tomahawk both drawn. Polly Tunbridge begged Coteatoy not to kill the boy in her house. He yanked the lad out of the cabin. Eight or ten of Coteatoy's warriors were there, fully armed with guns, knives and tomahawks. Joseph Brown saw they displayed two scalps from poles. He sadly recognized one as being that of one of his brothers. He asked Tom Tunbridge to beg for 30 minutes so he could pray. Tunbridge told him that Coteatoy had his mind made up, and that no time remained. The warriors began stripping Joseph's clothes, and Mrs. Tunbridge again pleaded with them not to kill him there, nor on the road to their spring. Coteatoy agreed to take him four miles to Running Water Town where they could celebrate with torture.

Coteatoy and his warriors headed for Running Water Town with their captive; however, it occurred to him that the Kiachatalee might demand the same treatment of Coteatoy's captive black woman. He stopped the procession and admitted his thoughts to his warriors. Joseph had no idea what Coteatoy was saying, but he took advantage of the respite to kneel and pray. Ten minutes later, he looked up to see smiles rather than scowls. Coteatoy's mother took a lock of Joseph Brown's hair, which she shaved off with a dull knife and kicked him once. Coteatoy then called to Tom Tunbridge and told him to take the captive back to the cabin. Coteatoy stated that he loved the boy but would not make friends with him. He said he would return to Nickajack in three moons, and if Joseph still lived, he would then make friends with him.

On Saturday, May 10, Kiachatalee and his mother went in to consult with Chief Breath about their young prisoner, and were told to bring the boy the next day. On Sunday, Mrs. Tunbridge took him to Breath. The chief shook hands with him, and then explained to him that, according to their customs, no one was required to protect a captive; but if Joseph would adapt to a Cherokee lifestyle, and if Tom Tunbridge would agree to adopt Joseph into his own family, then the laws of clan revenge would apply to Joseph as well as the Tunbridge's own blood family. Chief Breath then told Joseph to call him uncle and Kiachatalee brother. Joseph Brown complied. He had his long hair shaved off, except for a scalp lock, donned a breach clout, and joined the Tunbridge family.

Meanwhile, Mrs. Brown, young George, and little Elizabeth eventually had to leave the canoes and travel overland for days. During the long journey, they were not allowed to stop even to remove gravel from inside their shoes.[50]

After the Brown family incident, Chief Old Tassel apparently admitted that he had no control over the Chickamauga and recommended their towns be destroyed. On February 2, 1789, Colonel Joseph Martin wrote of the late chief to Secretary of War, Henry Knox. He said:

> In the month of May last [1788], a boat, richly laden, was going down the Tennessee to Cumberland, the crew were decoyed by the Chicamoga Indians and Creeks together, all of which crew were killed and taken prisoners; after which doings, the Corn-tassel informed me of the cruel murder they had committed, also the repeated murders and robberies they were constantly committing on the frontiers of Cumberland and Kentucky, also on the Kentucky road, in the company of the Creeks. There was not the least hopes of reclaiming them as long as they lived so far detached from their nations. That the Corn-tassel had talked to them until he found it was of no use; that he, with the other chiefs, advised and thought it best to go, against them and burn their towns, by which means they would return to their allegiance; that then they would have it in their power to govern them.[51]

After such episodes as the Treaty of Coyatee, Old Tassel still placed blame on the young warriors who were trying to defend the ancestral Cherokee lands to the best of their abilities. Old Tassel's stated positions, and his overtures to the settlers, had no effect on the actions of Colonel John Sevier and his men. As mentioned above, he effectually invited the whites to invade Cherokee country, and they would not be able to distinguish between Upper Cherokee and the Chickamauga. That would soon be Old Tassel's undoing.

In May 1788, Governor Sevier and Major James Hubbard warned the settlements of an impending Cherokee invasion:

> Major Houston's Station, 8th of July, 1788.
> To the inhabitants in general: Yesterday we crossed the Tennessee with a small party of men, and destroyed a town called Toquo. On our return we discovered large trails of Indians making their way towards this place. We are of the opinion their numbers could not be less than five hundred. We beg leave to recommend, that every station will be on their guard; that also, every good man that can be spared will voluntarily turn out and repair to this place, with the utmost expedition, in order to tarry a few days in the neighborhood and repel the enemy, if possible. We intend waiting at this place some days with the few men now with us, as we cannot reconcile it to our own feelings, to leave a people who appear to be in such great distress.
> John Sevier.
> James Hubbert.

N. B. It will be necessary for those who will be so grateful as to come to the assistance of this place, to furnish themselves with a few days' provisions, as the inhabitants of this fort are greatly distressed with Indian.[52]

Many families were concerned by the warning and removed to safety into neighboring forts or stations. However, the Overmountain men were generally such hardened frontiersmen, so inured to the perils and dangers of the situation they were in, that they had seemingly lost the sense of fear. They had grown familiar with the Cherokee in the Upper Villages, so they were not intimidated by any of them. Even though they constantly punished these neighboring Indians for the Chickamauga attacks, they knew they had nothing to fear from Old Tassel and his people. The settlers knew many warriors by name and trusted them. They expected the Indians who seemed friendly to always be friends in terms of white relationships; however, as has been discussed in previous chapters, the warriors would go to war based on necessity. Consequently, it would make no difference how familiar they were with any specific white people.

As an example: during the events leading to the Cherokee War of 1776, Lower Village headman Skyuka stated he regretted he could not have killed his friend, Robert Andrew Pickens (*a cousin of General Pickens*), himself "in an easy death, for he loved him." (See chapter 6.)

A more pertinent illustration occurred in May. John Kirk had settled on Little River, 12 miles south of present-day Knoxville, Tennessee. He and his son, John, Jr., were away hunting one day, and a warrior named Slim Tom of Chilhowie appeared at the Kirk property. He was very familiar to the Kirk family as they had often fed him and thought of him as a friend. He asked Mrs. Kirk for food. The family fed him and he noticed they were ill defended with the absence of Mr. Kirk and his son. Slim Tom took his leave but soon returned with a small war party that had been hiding in the nearby brush. They killed every member of the Kirk family present, 11 in all.

Though Slim Tom, the perpetrator of what has been called the Nine Mile Creek Massacre, had been friendly in the past, he was becoming notorious as far away as Nashville. The preceding spring, a small band of Chickamauga attacked the house of Joseph Hinds, killed and scalped his son, and absconded with a number of horses. Cumberland militia hotly pursued and surprised the Indians in their camp. The warriors fled into the canebrake and left their property behind. Colonel James Robertson identified one of the captured guns as the property of Slim Tom's son. Colonel Robertson had seen it in the warrior's possession the previous fall.[53]

When John Kirk returned home and discovered his slain family, he gave the alarm throughout the nearby stations. In June, Colonel Sevier mustered his militia at James Houston's Station at the mouth of Nine Mile Creek where it empties into the Holston River from the south. John Kirk, Jr., was a member of Major James Hubbard's militia company. Colonel Sevier led the militia to the Hiwassee River and, early in the morning, came upon a town which had been burned in 1779. Many of the Cherokee inhabitants bolted to the river while Sevier's men killed others at the village. The militia then fired upon and killed many of those in the river as they fled for their lives. Sevier's force first captured a few who survived the onslaught, then burned the town, and returned to Houston's Station.

The next day the militia burned several villages on the Little Tennessee River and killed the inhabitants. The Indians fled from the different towns into the mountains; however, they were pursued by the militiamen and many were killed.

Sevier detached Hubbard to Chilhowie to set up a meeting with Old Tassel while Sevier took care of business at Houston's. (The confrontation between Major Hubbard and Chief Old Tassel is variously reported to have been at Toquo, Chilhowie, and Chota. Chilhowie is more likely since it was in Old Abram's cabin, and he lived at Chilhowie. Chota is possible as it was still considered the mother town; however, the Upper Cherokee were seemingly gathering in other villages with the encroachment nearing Chota.)

Old Tassel flew the United States flag in front of his cabin. It was the one that was presented to him at the Treaty of Hopewell. Major Hubbard was a known Indian hater (some of his relatives were reportedly killed by warriors in an earlier incident). Chief Old Abram had publicly declared that, if the Cherokee warriors went to war, he would remain at his own house. When the troops came to Chota, they approached Old Abram's cabin. Hubbard asked Old Abram and his son to cross the river and return with Old Tassel and other chiefs to await Colonel Sevier's arrival. The militiamen held a white flag and seemed sincere. The chiefs were confined to Old Abram's small cabin to await the conference.

In Sevier's absence, Hubbard permitted a pleading John Kirk, Jr., survivor of the massacred Kirk family, to enter the cabin with a tomahawk. Kirk stuck his tomahawk into the head of one chief who fell dead at his feet. Major Hubbard and those on guard duty watched from the door. The other chiefs understood their fate and stared at the ground. One by one, each received a fatal tomahawk blow to the head at the hands of Kirk.

Once Sevier returned and saw the tragedy that had occurred, he reportedly protested the act. Kirk, who was backed by quite a few of the militiamen, told Sevier that if he had suffered the loss of his family, he, too, would have acted accordingly. Sevier was unable to disagree and refused to punish John Kirk, Jr. The Cherokee chiefs that were killed were Old Tassel (brother of chiefs Hanging Maw, Doublehead, and Standing Turkey), Old Abram (brother of Dragging Canoe, Little Owl, Turtle at Home and Raven of Chota), Fool Warrior, and Tassel's son.

Hanging Maw immediately left the Upper Villages for the protection of Young Tassel (John Watts, Jr.). Watts acted as scribe for Hanging Maw and wrote a letter to General Andrew Pickens, dated June 25, 1788, in which he complained of the events and asked Pickens to write John Sevier to request he stop making attacks. A second talk was added from Black Dog of Notoly in which he stated his friends the chiefs were "treacherously murdered."[54]

(The massacre of the chiefs is reported by various historians to have occurred sometime between the middle of June to August 3, 1788; however, since the letter from Hanging Maw, John Watts, and Black Dog of Notoly was written June 25, the murders must have occurred before that date.)

The Overmountain leaders had shown their true colors. They had killed the only Cherokee chiefs that were settler friendly. This would greatly impact the strategy of the Chickamauga leaders, most of whom were closely related to the Upper Village chiefs. Only Nancy Ward and her son-in-law, Colonel Joseph Martin, stood between the two sides to lobby for peace. The Chickamauga were scathed for killing or capturing settlers who invaded what the warriors considered Cherokee land, but the militiamen's slaughter of the friendly Upper Village chiefs was viewed as an allowable defense of the settlements.[55]

Historian Dr. J. G. M. Ramsey stated:

> Sevier, unable to punish him [John Kirk, Jr.], was obliged to overlook the flagitious deed, and acquiesced in the reply.

It is much to be regretted, that history, in the pursuit of truth, is obliged to record, to the shame and confusion of ourselves, a deed of such superlative atrocity, perfidy, cowardice and inhumanity. Surely something is due to wounded feelings, and some allowance is to be made for the conduct of men acting under the smart of great and recent suffering. But never should it be forgotten by an American soldier, that his honour must be unspotted; that a noble generosity must be the regulator of his actions; that inviolable fidelity, in all that is promised an enemy, is a duty of sacred obligation, and that a beneficent and delicate behavior to his captive, is the brightest ornament of his character.[56]

Many have written that Sevier would not have allowed the massacre to happen had he been at the site; however, the condemnation of Sevier regarding the action is that he, knowing the disposition of Major James Hubbard toward Indians, and that of John Kirk, Jr., toward the Cherokee, allowed them to go ahead and take charge of the initial contact with the peaceful chiefs. After all, John Sevier had bragged to Joseph Martin that he would drive all Cherokee from the region.[57] His absence was, to say the least, an oversight of convenience for his reputation's sake.

Historian John Preston Arthur wrote of the murder of the chiefs:

Such was the indignation with which this deed was received by the better class of backwoodsmen that Sevier's forces melted away, and was obliged to abandon a march he had planned against the Chickamaugas. The Continental Congress passed resolutions condemning such acts, and the justices of the court of Abbeville, S. C., with Andrew Pickens at their head "wrote to the people living on Nollechucky, French Broad and Holstein" denouncing in unmeasured terms the encroachments and outrages of which Sevier and his backwoodsmen had been guilty. "The governor of North Carolina, as soon as he heard the news, ordered the arrest of Sevier and his associates [for treason] doubtless as much because of their revolt against the State as because of the atrocities they had committed against the Indians.... The Governor of the State had given orders to seize him because of his violation of the laws and treaties in committing wanton murder on friendly Indians; and a warrant to arrest him for high treason was issued by the courts."[58]

(Apparently, militia general Richard Winn forwarded a copy of the letter from Andrew Pickens to Secretary of War Henry Knox. That may have provided the impetus for the actions of the Continental Congress described above by historian John Preston Arthur.)[59]

According to Colonel Joseph Martin, the settlers would not stop with the murder of the chiefs. In his February 9, 1789 letter to Secretary of War Henry Knox, Martin stated:

I have certain accounts that some designing men on the Indian lands have assembled themselves to the number of fifteen, and call themselves a convention of the people, and have entered into several resolves, which they say they will lay before Congress; one of which resolves is, to raise men by subscription to defend themselves, as the Legislature of North Carolina refuses to protect them on the Indian lands, but, on the contrary, have directed and ordered these people off the Indian lands. A certain Alexander Outlaw by name, I am informed, is to wait upon Congress on behalf of this new plan. I think it is my duty to say the truth of him: Shortly after the murder of the Corn-tassel ... this said Outlaw collected a party of men and went into an Indian town called Citico, where he found a few helpless women and children, which he inhumanely murdered, exposing their private parts in the most shameful manner, leaving a young child, with both its arms broken, alive, at the breast of its dead mother ... Mr. Outlaw has done everything in his power to drive the Indians to desperation.... It will now be our own faults if we do not make that race of Indians our friends.

So great the thirst for Indian lands prevails, that every method will be taken by a party of people to prevent a treaty with the Indians. They are now laboring to draw some of the Indians to a treaty, as they may purchase their country: this party say, if they can purchase of the Indians, they will have it without the consent of any other power ... that if they could only prevail on a few of the lower class to come into their scheme, they would get conveyances made and contend for the right. This I have heard from them.[60]

The Chickamauga would offset that and launch an unimaginably bloody retaliation.

Chapter 10

The Final Onslaught

The mainstream Cherokee moved their capitol from Chota to Ustanali (present-day Calhoun, Georgia) following the chiefs' slayings. The nation had, for all practical purposes, given up on a peaceful coexistence with the white settlers.

The Cherokee selected Chief Little Turkey to be the principal chief upon the death of Chief Old Tassel. Little Turkey had already been living in Turkey Town on the Coosa River (present-day Centre, Alabama, 25 miles northeast of Gadsden on U.S. Highway 411.) Trader John McDonald, who had lived near Lookout Mountain for nearly 10 years, moved to Turkey Town to support the young warriors.

Many such young warriors left the Upper Villages to join Chief Dragging Canoe, who had become their militant hero. The general feeling throughout the nation was that Chief Dragging Canoe, and Chief Doublehead, had been right all along.

Creek principal chief Alexander McGillivray was greatly irritated by the assassinations and renewed Creek support of their allies, the Chickamauga. The chief referred to Sevier as a barbarian and continued: "[Sevier] I am told, is meditating another expedition for accomplishing the total extirpation of the Cherokees ... I don't know what to think of a government that is compelled to wink at such outrages."[1]

A 1789 exchange of letters between Chief McGillavray and a commission working to arrange a treaty with the Creek exhibits exactly the lack of trust between the frontier settlers and the Indians. It also gives an insight to McGillivray and shows what high intellect the Creek and Cherokee chiefs possessed. They maintained a perfect understanding of the situation, and the settlers still believed them to be ignorant savages.

> NINETY-SIX, August 28.
> To Alexander McGillivray, Esq, and others the chief men and warriors of the Creek nation
> Our last to you, dated at Fort Charlotte, July 16, 1788, appointing the 15th next month for holding the treaty & every effort on our part has been exerted to effect it by that time, but from very cogent reasons we find it impossible; two powerful ones are—the necessary dispatches from the present congress not arriving in time, without which the supplies for putting the treaty into execution, upon a liberal footing, would be entirely insufficient—next the change of government taking place since; and the probability of our receiving instructions very shortly under the auspices of the new congress, whose fiat in this, as well as in every other case, will be more permanent than that of the expiring one. Other circumstances might be urged, but these, we think, will have their due weight with you for prolonging the time of treaty, which we wish to make agreeable to both parties. We have no objection to put it off to the spring of next year, which we hope will meet your approbation.

In the interim, we await your answer, and can assure, hostilities will cease on the part of Georgia against your nation; the same, we expect will be mutually observed on your part, as it appears to be the wish of your people, as well as ours, to come to a peace.

We subscribe ourselves,
Your humble servants,
RICHARD WINN
ANDREW PICKENS
GEORGE MATHEWS

N.B. We inclose [sic] you a Georgia paper—in it you will see the governor's proclamation respecting the treaty.

Little Tallasee, Sept. 15.
Gentlemen,

I have received your letter of the 28th of August, wherein you desired that the proposed treaty between us may be deferred until the spring of the next year. The reasons you give us for that measure are good, and to which we give our assent, hoping that a new congress, acting on the principles of the new constitution of America, will set everything to rights between us on the most equitable footing, so that we may become real friends to each other, settling on the same land, and having but one interest.

We expected that on Mr. Whitefield's return, a truce of arms would have been immediately proclaimed in Georgia, and cannot account for the delay of that measure—in fact there has been no observance of it, from that time till now; they have been driving our hunting camps and plundering them of horses, skins, &c. and it is but lately that a Cowetan Indian brought me a paper, which he found stuck upon a tree near Flint river, and which, upon a close examination, I found to be a threatening letter addressed to me; it was wrote with gun-powder on the back of an advertisement, and a great part of it has been effaced whilst drying and by carrying it. It is expressed somewhat concerning "war" and "your savage subjects"; it proceeds thus—"An establishment of peace you must not expect until all our damages are made good at the treaty; and satisfaction we will have for our grievances";—from all which I foresee great difficulty in attempting to preserve a strict suspension of hostilities, and can only assure you, that we shall regulate ourselves by the conduct of the Georgians, and act according to circumstances.

The Writing which I mentioned is signed Sam. Alexander, 5th August, 1788. The Cherokees are daily coming into me, complaining of acts of hostility committed in the most barbarous manner by the Americans: numbers of them are taking refuge within our territory, and are permitted to settle and build villages under our protection.—Such acts of violence committed, whilst congress through you, is holding out to all nations and tribes profession of the most friendly nature, make it appear to all, that such professions are only deceitful snares to lull them into a security whereby the Americans may more easily destroy them. Be not offended, gentlemen, at the remark, it is a truth that is universal among the Indians.

I am, with great respect,
Gentlemen,
Your most humble servant,
ALEX. McGILLIVRAY[2]

Young Tassel (John Watts, Jr.) and his nephew, Bench (Bob Benge) were quick to swear vengeance for the death of their Uncle Tassel. Their Uncle Doublehead was also eager to avenge his brother's slaying. The younger two were just making names as Chickamauga leaders, and the three were formidable warriors. Young Tassel and Bench were led by Dragging Canoe, who was also intent upon revenge for the death of his brother, Old Abram.

Young Tassel apparently wrote a threatening letter to John Sevier. While John Kirk, Jr., had deep feelings regarding the murder of his family, and even in the Cherokee culture would have the right to clan revenge, he exercised that vengeance against innocent and peaceful Cherokee. Sevier, as the overall commander of the militia, was responsible for putting Kirk in that position. Kirk sent the following response to Young Tassel's letter:

Copy of a letter from young Kirk, the noted Indian Killer, to John Watts, new chief war captain of the Cherokee nation.

SIR,
I have heard of your letter lately sent to Chudkey John*—You are mistaken in blaming him for the death of your uncle. Listen now to my story. For days and months, Cherokee Indians, little and big, women and children, have been fed and treated kindly by my mother. When all was peace with Tenale towns, Slim Tom, with a party of Satigo and other Cherokee Indians, murdered my mother, brothers and sisters, in cold blood, when the children just before was playful about them as friends, and the very instant some of them received the bloody tomahawk, they were smiling in their faces.—This begun the war, and since I have taken ample satisfaction, and can now make peace, except with Slim Tom. Our beloved men, the congress, tells us to be at peace—I will listen to their advice, if no more blood is shed by the Cherokee; and the head men of your nation take care to prevent such beginnings of bloodshed in all times to come. But if they do not, your people may feel something more, to keep up the remembrance of

JOHN KIRK, jun.
Captain of the Bloody Rangers
To Captain John Watts
October 17, 1788
*Chudkey John—The Indian name for John Sevier.[3]

The letter from Kirk likely served to provide more incentive for Young Tassel to make war. The young warriors raised their hatchets, and Young Tassel took the lead. He was deeply affected by his uncle's death; indeed, when he would speak of it at the future treaty of Holston, he would be so overcome that he had to request Chief Bloody Fellow to finish the oration.[4] An additional incentive was the old law of clan vengeance. Young Tassel believed it his duty to take satisfaction for his mother's clan.[5] He was ready to lead some 200 to 300 warriors into the settlements.

Chief Doublehead and his brother, Chief Pumpkin Boy, declared a dark and bloody vengeance in the name of their brother, Chief Old Tassel.

Severe retaliatory raids were launched against the Overmountain settlements; hence, the militias responded with a vengeance.

On July 20, 1788, Doublehead attacked Bledsoe's Station in the Cumberlands. This fort was built in the form of a rectangle. It was completely enclosed by a stockade, running from cabin wall to cabin wall, except for an access between two cabins that nearly abutted. This access was referred to as a double-cabin. Colonel Anthony Bledsoe and his family had abandoned their own station at present-day Greenfield, Tennessee, to seek the safety of his brother Isaac's fort. The two brothers each occupied a room of the double cabin with their respective families.

Historian Edward Albright excellently described the action:

The Indians, as was their custom, chose a beautiful night for the attack. From out the depths of a cloudless sky a full moon flooded the landscape with its glorious light. No signs of danger having recently appeared, there were but few men within the fort. These had gathered into the quarters of Col. Anthony Bledsoe and until a late hour were making merry with story and song. The Indians from afar had spied out the situation during the day. Now, while all within were happy in their supposed security, the savages were creeping up to the fort, secreting themselves around the stockade and awaiting an opportune moment for the onslaught. George Hamilton, who at last time was conducting at the Lick the first school taught in Sumner County, was singing for the entertainment of the company. The Indians, opening the attack, poked a gun through a hole in the back of the fireplace and shot Hamilton in the mouth. Just at this juncture, doubtless by pre-arrangement, several of the attacking party galloped down the road in front of the cabin. Alarmed by the shot and noise, Col. Anthony Bledsoe and his Irish servant, Campbell, rushed out into the moonlit passway and received each a mortal wound. These shots came from Indians who were concealed in the fence corners on the opposite side of the road.

With a whoop the savages now sprang as if by magic from their hiding places and began a vigorous assault in an effort to reach the inside. With their tomahawks they chopped through the window shutters of one of the cabins. Hugh Rogan was waiting for them on the inside and fired into their ranks the contents of a heavily loaded musket. Frightened by this shot they ran from that part of the stockade, and going around to the other side, made an assault on the cabin of William Donahoe. Through the cracks they fired a number of shots at the occupants, but killed only a large dog which lay stretched out on the floor. Donahoe blew out the light, leaving the room in darkness. At length, finding their efforts to enter the stockade futile, the Indians withdrew.[6]

Colonel Anthony Bledsoe, who was severely wounded, had written no will, and the North Carolina law at the time did not provide for his seven daughters. Mrs. Isaac Bledsoe interceded on her nieces' behalf and asked James Clendening to record a will for Anthony Bledsoe's signature.

Colonel Bledsoe died the next morning and was buried at present-day Bledsoe Academy Cemetery, seven and one-half miles from Gallatin, Tennessee, and seven-tenths of a mile west of Castalian Springs at Bledsoe Pioneer Memorial.

Many settlers mourned Colonel Bledsoe's death; however, it was a real coup for Chief Doublehead even though he failed to gain control of the fort. (Some historians set the date of this attack one year later, in 1789; however, most specify a date of July 20, 1788.)

Campbell, Colonel Bledsoe's servant, died on the second morning following the attack.

In August, warriors shot, killed, and scalped a man named Waters who was fishing on Bledsoe's Creek. They also mutilated his body with their hatchets. Near the same time, militia Captain John Fain led 31 men into Settico to pick fruit from an orchard. Young warriors attacked, killed, and wounded several men.

After the capture of Brown's boat, Chief Old Tassel admitted his inability to restrain the Chickamauga and advised Joseph Martin to invade their country and burn their towns. (See Chapter 9.) Martin was not only an Indian agent, but also a brigadier general in the North Carolina State Militia. In August, the North Carolina legislature ordered him to lead an army against the Chickamauga. Many of Sevier's militiamen neither liked Martin nor trusted him, but he raised a force of 500 men in August. There were three regiments commanded by Colonels Daniel Kennedy, Love, and George Dougherty (sometimes Doherty). Three companies of light-horse were led by Captains Miller, Richardson, and Hunter and commanded by Major Tom King.

They mustered at White's Fort, crossed the Tennessee River 20 miles downriver, and crossed the Little Tennessee. They followed the Hiwassee River to its mouth and arrived on the evening of the third day out. The troops galloped to surprise those at Chattanooga Village (on the east side of the north end of Lookout Mountain), but only four warriors were there, one of whom they shot and killed. Several burning fires at the deserted cabins indicated the Chickamauga residents had been warned of their coming and had quickly withdrawn. General Martin established his camp at the village.

Early the next morning, the officers recruited volunteers for a scouting mission to reconnoiter the trail. Captain Richardson led the 50 volunteers up the path. Most of the more-experienced men understood the futility and refused to volunteer, including Captain George Christian (a nephew of the late William Christian). Captain John Beard and another man somehow got separated. They missed the trail and actually rode almost straight up the mountain to arrive at a point on the trail ahead of their comrades. The scouting party had stuck to the trail and was so surprised by the sudden appearance of the two men that a skirmish ensued. Beard's horse was shot through the body but still carried his rider as the two men scurried back toward camp.

The scouting party continued on. They could not travel in regular order through the large jagged boulders, but had to zigzag in single file. Lookout Mountain is quite steep where it abuts the Tennessee River. The trail traversed a pass on an east-west route and leveled off to a 40-yard-wide bench halfway up the mountain. The path wound through the terrain, with a steep uphill rise to the south and a sheer downhill fall to the north that overlooked the river. Along the south side of the path lay huge boulders that had tumbled down from the rise to rest above the trail.

The men in camp at Chattanooga Town heard the firing and assumed an Indian attack was underway. Colonel Dougherty gathered a rescue party which rode to the foot of the mountain path, and dismounted there. They were met by Captain Beard and his companion, and then led their horses up the mountain. They had separated into two groups. Colonel Kennedy led the majority of the party off the path and up the mountain to the left following Captain Beard's route. Major Joseph Bullard and Captains John Harden and George Vincent led the remainder (including George Christian) uphill by staying on the path.

The Chickamauga had heard the original internal skirmish of the scouting party, and a few advanced up the hill from Tuskegee Town to engage the primary portion of the scouting party. They were led by notable chiefs Little Owl, The Badger, Bloody Fellow, and Glass. The rescue party came into view, and the warriors, who had plenty of cover among the rocks and trees, poured a devastating volley upon them. The Chickamauga shot and killed several, including Major Bullard and Captains John Hardin, Fuller, and James Gibson. Five, Captain Vincent among them, were wounded.

The Chickamauga warriors withdrew when they were fired upon by the remainder of the rescue party who then removed the casualties and returned to camp. General Martin was unable to turn his men, who declared it a folly to try again. They buried their dead in an old Indian Council House and set it afire to conceal their graves.

General Martin wanted to organize another attack, but some of Sevier's militiamen accused him of leading them into an ambush. Some wanted to kill him. Thus ended the expedition, and all returned to the settlements. (White's Station was in present-day Knoxville, Tennessee, at 205 Hill Avenue SE, across Hall of Fame Drive from the Women's Basketball Hall of Fame.)

This was the last expedition undertaken against the Chickamauga during the life of Dragging Canoe. Though he lived nearly four more years, little is known of his personal movements during that time. He continued his friendly relations with the English, and traded with them at Fort Detroit. His brother, Little Owl (often called the White Owl's Son—White Owl [Okoonaka] was an earlier name for Attakullakulla), would brag of valuable gifts presented to him and Dragging Canoe by the British at Detroit in the winter of 1791 and 1792. He received a pair of small, and a pair of large, arm bands, three gorgets for his brother and four for himself, a pair of scarlet boots and clothing, blankets, and powder and lead. (An 18th century gorget was a large ornament of metal or shell that hung from the neck and covered either the throat or the upper chest.)

(There are varying historical accounts of General Martin's expedition that conflict concerning numbers of men in each action, order of action, numbers of men killed and wounded, and even which Captains were either killed or wounded. The account above is a common-sense description based on those versions.)[7]

General Joseph Martin came under fire from the North Carolina legislature, which apparently also overruled the arrest order for John Sevier issued by the governor and the courts after the murder of the chiefs (see Chapter 9). The following anonymous extract printed in *The Maryland Gazette* was likely written by a member of the legislature who favored the Franklinites:

> Extract of a letter from Fayetteville, December 6, 1788, to the Printer hereof.
>
> Our session is dragging near a close; and we have taken care to pay some attention to our western frontier. Martin is reprimanded for his injudicious management in your district last summer. Sevier is indemnified, and probably soon will be placed at the head of the militia, as brigadier-general, if he will accept of the offered terms. Drumgole is appointed a commissioner to treat with the Cherokees, and give assurances that hostilities will shortly cease. His particular connexion with one of John Watt's sisters, will place him in an advantageous situation for negotiation. Colonel Steele, of Salisbury, is appointed to purchase of the Indians, their claims to the lands in dispute; and offer pre emptions to other lands, within our charter limits, to such Indian families as will choose to join the state as citizens. This is judged to be a more wise path than sending an army to cut their throats. Measures will be taken to prevent vagabonds and fugitives from justice, from taking sanctuary among the Indians.
>
> It will give joy to many, when they hear of the safe passage of so great a number of emigrants, through the wilderness, both on the Kentucky and Cumberland paths; and whether under Providence it has been brought about by the active exertions of Sevier and his armed volunteers, or the timeous negotiation from Virginia, it is immaterial; in either case, much gratitude will be due from those who have received so singular a boon. And not a little will be the self satisfaction of those benevolent minds, who in any degree contributed to the happy event.[8]

In October 1788, Daniel and John Dunham, and another man named Astill, were killed near Dunham's Station which was then abandoned by surviving family members who relocated to Bluff Fort. (Dunham's Station was located at present-day Belle Meade Plantation, 110 Leake Avenue Nashville, Tennessee.)

On October 15, 1788, chiefs Bloody Fellow, Glass, and Young Tassel attacked Colonel George Gillespie's Station on the Holston River near its juncture with Little River. Their demand for surrender was refused, so they stormed the outpost.

> Extract of a letter dated Greene county, (North-Carolina) October 25, 1788.
> ... On the 17th instant, Gillespy's [sic] Fort ... a little after sunrise was furiously attacked by about 300 Indians, under the command of John Watts. The few men in the Fort ... being over-powered by numbers, and their ammunition being expended, the Indians

rushed over the walls, or rather the roofs of the cabins, which made part of the Fort.... The best accounts say our loss is 28 persons, mostly women and children, as several of the men belonging to the Fort, were abroad at the time.

This body we are told, is a part of a much larger body now encamped at Chota, composed of both Creeks and Cherokees, said to be under the direction of Alexander McGillivray. And I am just now informed, that one thousand Indians have crossed the Tenasee, in two divisions, and that one of them had attacked major Houston's fort, and the other was near captain White's on the north side of Holstein.[9]

This was in the area of the controversial Dumplin Settlements (see Chapter 9).

Bloody Fellow left a rare message addressed to John Sevier and Joseph Martin which stated that the killing of the women and children was unintended. He continued: "The Bloody Fellow's talk is that he is now upon his own ground ... you beguiled the head man [Old Tassel], that was your friend and wanted to keep peace; but you began it, and this is what you get for it. When you move off the land, then we will make peace."[10]

He then declared that the young warriors numbered 5,000 men. Glass and Young Tassel (John Watts, Jr., nephew of Old Tassel) cosigned the message. (Gillespie's Station was located near present-day Rockford, Tennessee. A marker is affixed on State Highway 33 [the Old Knoxville Highway] near Rockford.).

On January 15, 1789, Joseph Martin sent a letter to Secretary Henry Knox of the attack. He also stated he had been negotiating regarding peace with Hanging Maw, who was still a leader in the Cherokee Nation. They were unable to act quickly enough to stop the action at Gillespie's Station. He said:

> I am well assured that, with prudent means, we may have the Cherokee Indians our friends; but it is to be feared there is a party that has such a thirst for the Cherokee lands, they will take every measure in their power to prevent a treaty. You will observe, in the talks sent on in October last, that the Hanging Maw said, all hostilities should cease. Before he reached the nation, 400 Creek Indians were come out, were joined by 1200 Cherokees, had marched against the frontiers, and had stormed a fort and took 28 prisoners before the runners overtook them.[11]

Martin verified the number of 28 captives. There were an unknown number of those killed, though some accounts say 15, mostly women and children.

(Hanging Maw was in contention for principal chief of the Cherokee Nation versus Little Turkey, who was initially chosen.)

Late in 1788, after Young Tassel and Bloody Fellow had taken captives and killed others at Gillespie's Station, they took winter refuge on Flint Creek in Rocky Ford Gorge at Greasy Cove (present-day Unicoi County, Tennessee). It was secluded with few passes, and the Cherokee posted small bands at each access.

John Sevier's scouts reported the Indian encampment to be some 30 miles away. On January 10, 1789, he led 450 militiamen toward the camp through snow that grew deeper as they climbed in elevation. He detached a General McCarter, of the same Bloody Rangers in which John Kirk, Jr., was a captain, around the terrain (up Devil's Fork Pass) to seal off the upper egress. Sevier and the remainder of the force positioned themselves at the lower entrance. Sevier began firing loads from several grasshopper cannons into the Cherokee camp; however, the warriors had spread themselves throughout the higher terrain and were leveling a heavy volley of rifle fire at the militia. Sevier ordered his militia to mount and draw sabers. They charged through Chickamauga warriors with sabers and tomahawks. Several bloody skirmishes ensued.

Sevier reportedly buried 145 warriors at the scene, while five militiamen were killed and 16 wounded. Sevier wrote that the Battle of Flint Creek was the bloodiest of all 35 of his Indian battles. During the expedition he captured (variously reported) 27 to 29 women and children, a daughter of Little Turkey among them. They may have been at the winter camp; however, it is more likely they were at a nearby village on the Coosa River. Sevier treated them as hostages and traded them for Cherokee captives, i.e., those captured at Gillespie's Fort.

Joseph Martin continued in his letter of January 15: "which actings of Mr. Sevier made great confusion again, but by the early intervention of General Pickens and some others, that affront was allayed, alleging those Indian prisoners taken by Mr. Sevier were to be exchanged for those taken by them."[12]

Many historical accounts state the Cherokee proposed an exchange of prisoners, and General Sevier demanded the prisoners taken at Gillespie's and all white prisoners in the Lower Towns including the Brown family (see Chapter 9). Chief Little Turkey was said to be unable to negotiate further, so he agreed to the terms.

It is likely that Sevier had such an exchange in mind; however, may have received too much credit for the release of those prisoners in the Lower Villages. According to Joseph Martin's letter, Brigadier General Andrew Pickens of South Carolina had become involved in the negotiations.

Accordingly, Joseph and Polly Brown were brought into the Chickamauga village of Nickajack. The Indian woman who had the care of Polly seemed as close to her as to her own children. The affection was apparently reciprocated. When Joseph told his sister they were to leave, she ran to her Cherokee mother and clasped her arms around her neck. Joseph had to take her away by force to Running Water Town.

Their sister, Jane, had been held in Crow Town 30 miles away and had not been brought in by the time they were to leave Running Water Town. Joseph steadfastly would not leave without both girls. He had been able to visit with each periodically during their captivity.

A young warrior was immediately sent from Running Water Town to retrieve Jane; however, he returned empty-handed two days later. He said her warrior captor would not release her without a handsome ransom. Chief Bench happened to be sitting nearby. He took his saber from the wall, mounted his horse, raised his tomahawk, and said, "I will bring her, or his head."[13]

Bench returned the next morning with Jane and without comment. The group left immediately for Coosawatee. The final prisoner exchange was completed on April 25, 1789, and the Brown children were delivered to their uncle Joseph Brown in South Carolina. Mrs. Brown, young George, and Elizabeth were still captives of the Creek.[14]

On November 1, 1788, several chiefs of the reorganized Cherokee Nation sent a message to Brigadier General Joseph Martin, expecting his assistance. They had no way of knowing that his star would soon fall. They wrote:

> Friend and Brother:
> We hear that you are at Tascola, and that you are the great warrior of North Carolina and the new State. Your people provoked us first to war, by settling on our lands and killing our beloved men; however, we have laid by the hatchet, and are strongly for peace.

10. The Final Onslaught

Now we have heard from our brother, also from Congress, likewise the Governor of Virginia, who tells us that the people settled on our hunting grounds shall be removed without loss of time, which gives us great satisfaction. As we told you before, we are strongly for peace; we do not want any more war; we hope you will keep your people now at peace, and not to disturb us as they have done. When these people move, we shall all be friends and brothers. There are a great many Creeks out: if they should do your people any injury we hope you will not lay the blame on us, for all our head-men and warriors will prevent our young people for the future to do the white people any injury, but they expect they will move off their land.

The talk from Congress, and the talk likewise from the Governor of Virginia, we have taken fast hold of, and will remember, because they are good, and strongly desirous to live in the greatest friendship with their red brothers. We should be glad to receive a talk from you, if it is a good one, and for hereafter to live in peace and friendship. We desire you will let our friends and brothers in North Carolina hear this talk, which we hope will be the means to procure that peace and friendship we so strongly desire. We are your friends and brothers.

The badger, the Crane, Bloody Fellow, Jobber's Son, Killugiskee, Yellow Bird, Bear coming out of the tree, Thigh, Pumpkin Vine, Chesnut, Hanging Maw, The Lyin Fawghn, The Englishman, &c.[15]

The publicity of so many attacks and so much killing, both on the part of the Chickamauga and the Overmountain militiamen, and the high-profile talks of congressional interest in solving the issues, led to a relatively peaceful coming year.

The year 1789 was regarded as one of comparative peace. Colonel PUTNAM, in his historical account of this period, boasts of the fact that during the year only thirty persons were killed, a few scalped and wounded and one-half of the horses stolen. It is estimated that from the establishment of the settlement up to this time about one thousand horses had been captured and carried away.[16]

Many scouting parties periodically ranged the forests in all directions where war parties were likely to pass. They did not always overtake or intercept a scalping party; however, the Creek and the Chickamauga became aware of the risks. This feeling greatly reduced the number and strength of the Indian attacks in the Cumberland settlements.

On January 20, 1789, warriors killed Captain Hunter and wounded Hugh F. Bell outside of Isaac Johnson's Station, near Nashville. A posse gathered and overtook the band one hour later. A skirmish followed and Major Kirkpatrick was killed. John Foster and William Brown were wounded.

Hugh Webb and Henry Ramsey, the latter one of Colonel James Robertson's scouts, had gone to Kentucky for a supply of ammunition and salt. On the trail between Morgan's Station and present-day Greenfield, Tennessee, they were ambushed and killed.

In February 1789, John Helin was working a field near Johnathan Robertson's property, six miles downriver of Nashville. A band of Creek shot Helin, stole horses from a nearby field, and withdrew. Captain Murry led a company in pursuit. Members of the group included Thomas Cox, Robert Evans, Jacob Castleman, Luke Anderson, and William Pillow. (Castleman, Anderson, and Pillow had accompanied Captain Shannon on the expedition to the Tennessee River during which the chief Big Foot was killed. See Chapter 9.)

They crossed Duck River five miles below present-day Columbia, Tennessee. They caught up with the band of warriors at the Tennessee River in Alabama the next day.

Captain Murry and his men stealthily surrounded the Indians, who were trapped against the river. Scouts climbed a nearby knoll and opened fire. One warrior died and several of the others jumped into the river to escape. Militiamen, who were prepared for such a tactic, fired at the swimmers and killed several. The remaining Creek were slain in a skirmish at their campsite. Eleven warriors were dispatched and those taken captive were later released.

Men named Brown and Southerland Mayfield established stations one mile apart on Mill Creek at present-day Nashville. On March 10, 1789, Mayfield, his two sons, and a helper named Benjamin Jocelyn worked on some outbuildings. They propped their guns against a nearby tree, and while they worked a soldier named Andrew Martin guarded the operation. The sentry took a necessary break, and a band of Creek, who had been spying from some nearby brush, quietly maneuvered themselves between the guns and the workers and attacked. Mayfield, his son William, and Andrew Martin were killed. The other Mayfield son, George, was captured and kept prisoner for ten years. Jocelyn hastened safely away. Surviving residents abandoned the property and relocated to John Rains' Station.

Brown's Station experienced a similar attack one week later. James Haggard, a man named Adams, two sons of Mr. Stoval, one son of Mr. Denton, and one of Brown's sons were all killed. Surviving occupants of the property likewise retreated to Rains' Station.

On May 19, 1789, the headmen and leading warriors of the Cherokee Nation met in the Council House in Chota. Chief Taken Out of the Water was selected to draft a letter to the president of the United States. He wrote:

> Great Brother: … There are a great many towns of us that live on Tennessee, Highwassee, Telliquo, and Ammoah, who are near neighbours to the white people, and we wish to live in peace with them.… At our last treaty, held in South Carolina, we gave up to our white brothers all the land we could anyhow spare, and have but little left to raise our women and children on, and we hope you wont [sic] let any people take any more from us without our consent. We are neither birds nor fish; we can neither fly in the air, nor live under water; therefore we hope pity will be extended towards us. We are made by the same hand, and in the same shape with yourselves.… We hear that Congress have got strong powers now, and nothing can be spoiled that you undertake to do.… We wish you to appoint some good men to do the business between us and our elder brothers. Let us have a man that don't speak with two tongues, nor one that will encourage mischief or blood to be spilt. Let there be a good man appointed, and war will never happen between us. Such a one we will listen to; but such as have been sent among us, we shall not hear, as they have already caused our nation to be ruined, and come almost to nothing.[17]

Much may be read into the polite wording of the letter. The chief refers to the Overmountain settlers as "older brothers," so it is evident that no effort had been made to treat the Cherokee as equals. Written language of white settlers of the time is full of references to "savages," and the term is used regularly by older historians as late as the turn to the twentieth century. The chief's verbiage near the end is apparently referential to John Sevier, especially that of the last sentence.

On July 7, 1789, Secretary of War Henry Knox wrote President Washington and referred to inequities in past dealings with the Cherokee, and of the united front exhibited by the Southern Indian Nations. This was apparently the continuation of a report that Knox had started earlier. He wrote:

> It will appear that the interest of all the Indian nations south of the Ohio, as far as the same may relate to the whites, is so blended together as to render the circumstances highly probable, that, in case of a war, they may make it one common cause.

Their situation, entirely surrounded on all sides, leads naturally to such an union, and the present difficulties of the Creeks and the Cherokees may accelerate and complete it. Already the Cherokees have taken refuge from the violence of the frontier people of North Carolina [to] within the limits of the Creeks, and it may not be difficult for a man with Mr. [Chief Alexander] McGillivray's abilities to convince the Choctaws and the Chickasaws that their remote situation is their only present protection; that the time must shortly arrive when their troubles will commence ... the policy of the Spaniards ... will, therefore, endeavor to form such an union of the Southern Indians ... Spain actually claims a considerable part of the territory ceded by Great Britain to the United States ... the negotiation should be conducted by three commissioners ... invested with full powers to examine into the case of the Cherokees, and to renew with them the treaty made at Hopewell in November 1785, and report to the President such measures as shall be necessary to protect the said Cherokees in their former boundaries.

But all the treaties with the Indian nations, however equal and just they may be in their principles, will not only be nugatory but humiliating to the sovereign; unless they shall be guaranteed by a body of troops.

The angry passions of the frontier Indians and whites, are too easily inflamed by reciprocal injuries, and are too violent to be controlled by the feeble authority of the civil power ... the commissioners concluding a treaty, the boundaries between the whites and the Indians must be protected by a body of at least five hundred troops....

The disgraceful violation of the treaty of Hopewell, with the Cherokees, requires the serious consideration of Congress. If so direct and manifest contempt of the authority of the United States be suffered with impunity, it will be in vain to attempt to extend the arm of Government to the frontiers. The Indian tribes can have no faith in such imbecile promises, and the lawless whites will ridicule a government which shall, on paper only, make Indian treaties, and regulate Indian boundaries....

The expense of such a conciliatory system may be considered as a sufficient reason for rejecting it; But when this shall be compared with a system of coercion, it would be found the highest economy to adopt it.[18]

Secretary Knox exposed much in his letter. He obviously believed the Overmountain leaders had taken considerable advantage of the Cherokee, and that the Treaty of Hopewell had hardly ever been considered. He pointed out that the examples set by those leaders were an indication that local government could not be relied upon for an adequate enforcement of such a treaty—basically the fox and the henhouse adage exhibited by past events. Although he, President Washington, and the administration were concerned with the treatment of the Cherokee, there were some definite problems within the United States government that would prohibit installing his recommendations. He alluded to one in his final remarks as he addressed the expenditures. The United States was broke. It had not yet met its financial obligations from the war, including the payment of veterans. The second major problem was congressional support. Congress was made up of many idealistic people, and a big portion of its members glorified people such as John Sevier and their situation of settling the frontiers.

Knox also made references to the influence of the Spanish, who continued to supply the Creek and the Chickamauga. The Spanish actually had a treaty in force with the Creek where they guaranteed to protect Creek hunting grounds from encroachment. The Spanish, but even more so the French, seemed to have more success fulfilling treaty obligations than did Great Britain or the United States.

Indian agent James Seagrove later added: "It is to be regretted that the insatiable rage of our frontier brethren for extending their limits cannot be checked and kept within the bounds set for them by the general government. The United States, like most countries, is unfortunate in having the worst of people on her frontiers, where there is the least energy to be expected in civil government, and where, unless supported by military force, civil authority becomes a nullity."[19]

In the meantime, late June 1789, Colonel James Robertson led a work force in a field half a mile from his cabin. An armed sentinel had been stationed at the edge of the nearby forest to keep a lookout for any sign of trouble. At 11 a.m. a suspicious noise in a proximate thicket caused him to sound the alarm. Colonel Robertson started toward the sentry but was shot through the foot. Other shots were fired but caused no harm.

The group organized a pursuit of the snipers and Robertson, suffering from his wound declared, "Oh, if I only had Old Captain Rains and Billie here!"[20] The colonel was speaking of Captain John Rains from Rains' Station and William Robertson, his own brother, who were both away on business.

Lieutenant Colonel Elijah Robertson, another brother of James, was selected to lead a 60-man volunteer posse. Future United States president Andrew Jackson, a young lawyer, had recently settled in the Nashville vicinity and was one of the volunteers. Something detained Elijah from going, so Captain Sampson Williams commanded the expeditionary force which rode out the next morning. They followed the trail of an apparently small war party through McCutcheon's Trace to the highlands along Duck River Ridge. They decided that they had not gained ground on their prey, so Williams chose twenty men, including Jackson, to follow him more quickly than the larger group had thus far done. Eventually, due to the rugged terrain, two men remained with the horses, and 18 proceeded on foot. They followed the Duck River and came into view of the Indian camp just at dusk. The warriors were on the opposite side, the south bank, of Duck River. The militia quietly detoured one and one-half miles upriver, crossed it in the dark, and cautiously approached the war party. The canebrake, however, was thick so they stopped for the night. At dawn, after advancing 50 yards, Captain Williams spotted the Creek 100 yards ahead of him. There before them were 30 warriors, some of who were preparing breakfast while others slept. Captain Williams immediately ordered a charge, and the troops opened fire from fifty yards out. They initially killed one and wounded six. The surprised warriors quickly carried their wounded as they fled across the Duck River. They abandoned 16 guns, 19 shot pouches and all of their blankets, moccasins, bearskins, and camp utensils. The militia gathered the loot, regained their horses, and returned to the settlements.

(Considerable space is herein devoted to the preparations and the final resolution of the treaty with the Creek Nation, because it not only affected the Cherokee, as is shown below, but is not as simple as most historians have recorded. The time devoted to the Creek treaty indicates the attitude of President Washington regarding the importance of such a treaty. It took over one year to resolve the treaty as is hereafter shown in transcriptions of pertinent correspondence. The end notes listed at the citations, and at the other related paragraphs, refer to many relevant documents in the American State Papers, Indian Affairs.)

In August and September of 1788, a commission composed of Richard Winn, Andrew Pickens, and George Mathews exchanged correspondence with Creek chief Alexander McGillivray (see earlier this chapter). They mutually agreed to readdress the attempt to treat in the spring of 1789.

In April 1789, President George Washington sent Colonel Marinus Willett to Andrew

Pickens to enlist his help with an elusive agreement with the Creek Indians. Pickens addressed a letter to Chief McGillivray on April 20, 1789. He wrote:

> A talk, lately sent by the Commissioners of Indian Affairs in the Southern Department, to the Creeks' correspondent.
> TO THE HEAD-MEN, CHIEFS, AND WARRIORS, OF THE CREEK NATION
> We last year appointed a time and place for holding a treaty with you, to establish a lasting peace between you and us, that we might again become as one people; you all know the reasons why it was not held at that time.
> We now send you a talk, inviting you to a treaty on your bank of the Oconee river at the rock landing. We wished to meet you at that place on the 8th of June, but, as that day is so near at hand, you might not all get notice. We therefore shall expect to meet you on the 20th of June.
> We have changed the place of meeting from that of the last year; so that none of you should have reason to complain; it is your own ground, and on that land we wish to renew our former trade and friendship, and to remove every thing that has blinded the path between you and us.
> We are now governed by a President, who is like the old King over the great water; he commands all the warriors of the thirteen great Fires. He will have regard to the welfare of all the Indians; and, when peace shall be established, he will be your father, and you will be his children, so that none shall dare to do you harm.
> We know that lands have been the cause of dispute between you and the white people; but we now tell you that we want no new grants; our object is to make a peace, and to unite us all under our great chief warrior and President, who is the father and protector of all the white people. Attend to what we say: our traders are very rich, and have houses full of such goods as you used to get in former days; it is our wish that you should trade with them, and they with you, in strict friendship.
> Our brother, George Galphin, will carry you this talk; listen to him; he will tell you nothing but truth from us. Send us your answer by him.
> Andrew Pickens,
> H. [Henry] Osborne
> Commissioners of the United States for Indian Affairs, in the Southern Department.
> April 20, 1789[21]

On the 18th of May, Chief Alexander McGillivray responded from Little Tallassee to George Galphin. The news was discouraging.

> DEAR SIR:
> I have this moment received your letter, enclosing a talk of invitation to the chiefs and warriors of the nation to meet the commissioners of Congress the 20th June next.
> I wish that you could have been up, while I was in the Lower towns; the great fatigue which I have undergone this spring, prevents my seeing the Lower chiefs on the occasion.
> I have received a letter from the commissioners and superintendent last winter, in which they declared, in the most pointed manner and unequivocal terms, that it was impossible to make the restitution of territory the basis for a peace between us and Georgia, which we demanded as a first measure to be complied with by them, to lead the way to a lasting peace.
> At our late convention, I explained the letter to the chiefs, who were much dissatisfied at the declaration, and observed, that it was in vain to talk of peace while an obstacle of such magnitude was suffered to remain in the way of it, on the part of the Georgians; and the warlike preparations, which you notice in your letter, are carrying on to make another trial to accomplish by force, what can't be obtained by peaceable methods. Our excursions, hith-

erto, have been made with no other view than to warn the Georgians to desist from their injustice, and to induce them to listen to reason and humanity. It is well known, that, if any other was our motive, that our force and resources are equal to effect [sic] their destruction.

On the present occasion, the chiefs, having sent for my opinion and advice, I have wrote to them, to be explained by [the interpreter] Mr. Derezeoux. I have left the matter to their own choice; if they agree to meet, I will likewise go, though I have the best reason against it. Yet apprehensions for personal security shall not deter me from fulfilling the duty which I owe my country.

I am, sir, your humble servant,
ALEX. McGILLIVRAY.
Mr. GEO. GALPHIN, at Cussetahs[22]

An excerpt of a May 27 letter from Geo. Galphin to "The Hon. And'w Pickens and H'y Osborn, Esq.," stated:

The whole Upper and Lower Creeks, down as far as the Seminoles, were ready fitted off to go out to war ... upwards of three thousand would have been out, and intended to have drove [the settlers from] Ogeechee [River] from the mouth to the head ... by consent of Mr. McGillivray, after a general meeting of the chiefs and head men of the whole Upper and Lower Creeks; and, being informed by him they were not to have their lands on the Oconees restored to them again, he acquainted them that the Spaniards had provided for them, for the purpose of defending their rights to their lands, fifteen hundred stand of arms and forty thousand weight of ammunition.[23]

Galphin continued that he had talked with the chiefs and persuaded them to await further talks from Congress before they would go to war.

On June 16, Chief McGillivray wrote to George Galphin and requested him to be at Rock Landing on the 20th to tell the commissioners that the Creek would not attend the meeting. He stated that several of the war parties had been out before they could be stopped, and had returned with scalps, and the chiefs wished to let time pass so things could cool down before they received another treaty talk. McGillivray promised that the chiefs would control the warriors in the interim.[24]

The commissioners were dejected and somewhat miffed. They followed up with a tactful letter to the chief:

To the Head men, Chiefs, and Warriors of the Creek nation.
Rock Landing on the Oconee, June 29th, 1789.
BROTHERS:
We came to this place expecting to meet you agreeably to our invitation, which we sent to you by Mr. George Galphin. We are sorry any thing should have happened to prevent your coming. We have heard your reasons from your chief speaker, Mr. McGillivray, with which we are satisfied. We have consulted your beloved man, Mr. John Galphin, and have fixed the time for meeting you all at this place, to be the 15th of September next. We hope you will be punctual in coming that all disputes may be settled, and we may again take you by the hand as friends and brothers.

As a mark of your good intentions, we shall expect all the prisoners in the nation, both whites and blacks, will be sent to this place as soon as possible, where one of us will remain to receive them.

We have strictly charged our people not to cross over to your side of the Oconee, and we expect your people will not come on this side, except at this place, before the time for holding the treaty.

We shall expect that all your people will be prohibited from committing any kind of depredation against ours, so that peace may be preserved, and all of us meet at the appointed time, as friends and brothers.
ANDREW PICKENS,
H. OSBORN.[25]

On August 29, 1789, President George Washington and Secretary of War Henry Knox wrote a letter of instructions to a special commission to treat with the Creek at the appointed time, September 15, set by Andrew Pickens and Henry Osborn with Chief McGillivray. The commissioners were Benjamin Lincoln, Cyrus Griffin, and David Humphreys. The first important accomplishment was to arrange peace between the white inhabitants of Georgia and the Creek Nation. They were next told to investigate the matters of previous treaty negotiations between the Creek and Georgia from the terms of fairness. They were to determine, based on the current fair value of the previously ceded land in question, whether the Creek had more coming to them from Georgia. They were to have a representative of the governor of Georgia attend to effect the commissioners' decisions in that regard.

Another important stipulation involved Creek trade with Great Britain in the Bahamas. The trade ships navigated up the Mississippi River and were subject to Spanish tariffs with which Chief McGillivray was unhappy. The commissioners were to negotiate a port in the United States, convenient for the Creek to use free of charge, to export and import to the Bahamas. This was intended to help break the hold that the Spanish had among the southern Indian nations.

In that same regard, the president told the commissioners that the Spanish had given Chief McGillivray a military relegation of either colonel or lieutenant colonel. The commissioners were to offer an assignment with pay that would outrank the one presented by the Spanish.

The president instructed the commissioners about how issues should be handled. However, the commissioners were given authority to alter the provisions of the proposed treaty.[26]

The commissioners kept a journal that fully documented every step leading to a final treaty. They involved the existing Indian commissioners of the Southern Department.

On September 11, 1789, from Savannah, the commissioners wrote a letter addressed to the governor of Georgia that requested his assistance to provide for the large group of Indians expected at Rock Landing on the Oconee River.[27]

The same day, they also wrote to Andrew Pickens and H. Osborne who were already at Rock Landing. They said:

GENTLEMEN:
Having been appointed commissioners plenipotentiary by the Supreme Executive of the United States of America, for concluding treaties of peace and amity with the Indian nations, South of the Ohio, we thought proper to give you the earliest possible notice of our appointment. The reasons why that the characters employed in the execution of this business should not belong to any of the States bordering on those tribes of Indians with whom the treaties are proposed to be formed, will be fully, and, we suppose satisfactorily explained to you by the letter from the Secretary of War, which we shall have the honor of delivering into your hands.
We have also to inform you that we shall set off from this place as early as we can make the necessary arrangements, and reach you as soon as may be. In the mean time, we

earnestly hope and expect that you will not remit your endeavors to have everything in readiness to give despatch and success to the negotiations; and you will please to communicate every necessary information to the Creek nation on the subject. We are convinced this will be the case, because the interest and happiness of the State of Georgia, not less than the dignity and honor of the United States, seem to require it.

On our part, you will be assured, gentlemen, that we shall always take a particular pleasure in doing justice to your merits by making the most favorable representations of your public service,

Being, with the greatest respect and esteem, gentlemen, your most obedient humble servants,

B. Lincoln
C. Griffin
D. Humphreys
The Honorable ANDREW PICKENS and H. OSBORNE, Esquires, Rock Landing.[28]

That letter was answered on the 16th with:

Rock Landing, 16th Sept., 1789.
GENTLEMEN:
We had, this day, the honor to receive your joint letter of the 11th instant. Every arrangement that was in our power to make, preparative to the treaty, has been completed for two weeks past, and the Indians have been encamped at the distance directed by the Secretary of War, during the same period.

We have used every exertion to keep the Indians together, and in a good humor, which has hitherto been done with great difficulty. The same zeal and industry shall be continued on our part, for their continuance, but at the same time it is necessary to give you the earliest information, that the Indians will not remain after Friday next, unless you arrive here before the expiration of that day; this Mr. McGillivray informed us yesterday, though it is his wish to remain longer.

We have the honor to be, gentlemen, with due respect, your obedient servants,
ANDREW PICKENS
H. OSBORNE
The Hon. B. LINCOLN, C. GRIFFIN, D. HUMPHREYS, Esqrs.[29]

The commissioners arrived on the 20th and exchanged short messages of greeting with Chief Alexander McGillivray. They had preliminary discussions that lasted until the 24th when Chief McGillivray invited the commissioners to witness the ceremony of the Black Drink (see Chapter 5), all faithfully recorded with correspondence.[30]

The commissioners presented a draft treaty to the Creek by the end of the day on the 24th, and the following day the Creek answered that they were not satisfied. Exchanges of written communications continued from the 25th to the 28th. Then the Creek left without a treaty but did express that they departed in peace.[31]

The dejected commissioners wrote reports of the events to the secretary of war and the governor of Georgia and continued to exchange correspondence with all involved at least through November 20, 1789. At that time they reported that the Creek refused to conclude a treaty.[32]

It would be almost one year before the treaty could be concluded. On August 6, 1790, President George Washington sent a communique to the Senate to attain approval for Henry Knox to conclude a treaty with the Creek chiefs who were then in New York. On the next day, August 7, 1790, the finalized signed treaty was presented to the Senate for approval. The signatories were Henry Knox, Alexander McGillivray, and 23 other chiefs and warriors of the Creek nation.[33]

The president and Henry Knox also allowed magnanimous terms for the Creek that included commerce agreements and $100,000 annually for the chiefs of each group. Washington ceremoniously appointed Chief Alexander McGillivray a brigadier general with an annual salary of $1,200.

The treaty with the Creek affected the president's attitude toward the Cherokee situation. On August 11, 1790, the president had the following exchange of correspondence with the Senate:

> Gentlemen of the Senate:
> Although the treaty with the Creeks may be regarded as the main foundation of the future peace and prosperity of the southwestern frontier of the United States, yet, in order fully to effect so desirable an object, the treaties which have been entered into with the other tribes in that quarter, must be faithfully performed on our parts.
> During the last year, I laid before the Senate a particular statement of the case of the Cherokees. By a reference to that paper, it will appear that the United States formed a treaty with the Cherokees in November, 1785: That the said Cherokees thereby placed themselves under the protection of the United States, and had a boundary assigned them:
> That the white people settled on the frontiers openly violated the said boundary by intruding on the Indian lands:
> That the United States, in Congress assembled, did, on the first day of September, 1788, issue their proclamation, forbidding all such unwarrantable intrusions, and enjoining all those who had settled upon the hunting grounds of the Cherokees, to depart with their families and effects without loss of time, as they would answer their disobedience to the injunctions and prohibitions expressed at their peril.
> But information has been received, that, notwithstanding the said treaty and proclamation, upward of five hundred families have settled on the Cherokee lands, exclusively of those settled between the fork of French Broad and Holston rivers, mentioned in the said treaty.
> As the obstructions to a proper conduct on this matter have been removed since it was mentioned to the Senate on the 22nd of August, 1789, by the accession of North Carolina to the present Union, and the cessions of the land in question, I shall conceive myself bound to exert the powers entrusted to me by the constitution, in order to carry into faithful execution the Treaty of Hopewell, unless it shall be thought proper to attempt to arrange a new boundary with the Cherokees, embracing the settlements, and compensating the Cherokees for the cessions they shall make on the occasion. On this point, therefore, I state the following questions, and request the advice of the Senate thereon:
> 1st. Is it the judgment of the Senate that overtures shall be made to the Cherokees to arrange a new boundary, so as to enhance the settlements made by the white people since the Treaty of Hopewell in 1785?
> 2nd. If so, shall compensation, in the amount of,——dollars, annually, or of——dollars, in gross, be made to the Cherokees for the land they shall relinquish, holding the occupiers of the land accountable to the United States for its value?
> 3rd. Shall the United States stipulate solemnly to guaranty the new boundary which may be arranged?
> GEO. WASHINGTON

The Senate's response:

The Senate thereupon adopted the following resolution:
Resolved, that the Senate do advise and consent, that the President of the United States do, at his discretion, cause the treaty concluded at Hopewell, with the Cherokee Indians, to

be carried into execution according to the terms thereof, or to enter into arrangements for such further cession of territory, from the said Cherokee Indians, as the tranquility and interest of the United States may require: Provided, The sum which may be stipulated to be paid to the said Cherokee Indians, do not exceed one thousand dollars annually; and Provided further, That no person that shall have taken possession of any lands within the territory assigned to the said Cherokee Indians, by the said treaty of Hopewell, shall be confirmed in any such possessions, but by compliance with such terms as Congress may hereafter prescribe.

Resolved, In case a new, or other boundary than that stipulated by the treaty of Hopewell, shall be concluded with the Cherokee Indians, that the Senate do advise and consent solemnly to guaranty the same.[34]

Obviously, the United States desired to make further restitution to the Creek and Cherokee nations rather than to return the prime hunting grounds to either the Creek or the Cherokee, or to go to the trouble of removing the illegal settlers. Such restitution could never really compensate the tribes for the loss of their prime ancestral hunting grounds, for either the emotional or the actual value. That was the stipulation that turned the Creek chiefs off and caused them to not attend the treaty meeting set for June 20, 1789.

In the meantime, late in the fall of 1789, General James Winchester led a scouting party on Smith's Fork. A fresh trail indicated a small band of warriors was in the vicinity. The militia began pursuit along a buffalo path down the creek. The Indians discovered they were being followed, and set up an ambush where the path crossed a stream. There was a thick canebrake on the far side that was perfect. Joseph Muckelrath (or Meckelrath) and John Hickerson were General Winchester's vanguard. Just as the militia scouts exited the ford and passed the cane, the warriors fired and killed Hickerson. Muckelrath escaped and met Winchester and his men advancing to the rescue. A skirmish ensued and Frank Heany was wounded. The war party had the advantage, and Winchester retreated. The Indians refused to follow lest they be drawn into a trap. Two brothers, John and Martin Harpool, were members of the group. John, the older, was very intelligent and prudent; however, Martin tended to be reckless. The Harpools were still engaged with the warriors as Winchester withdrew, and John told his brother to go down and drive them out where he, John, could get good shots. Martin whooped, charged through the cane, and made as much racket as he could. The warriors thought that Winchester had led the group back to encircle them, so they fled. The Indians later reproached the settlers for having what they termed a "fool warrior" on this expedition. Martin Harpool became known throughout the settlement as the "fool warrior" from that time on. It was in this skirmish that Captain James McCann killed Chief Moon, the warrior said to be "harelipped" who supposedly mortally wounded and scalped Charles Morgan near Bledsoe's Lick (see Chapter 9).

North Carolina ratified the United States Constitution on November 21, 1789, and ceded the Western Territory (present-day Tennessee) to Congress. The act of Congress making such a cession was introduced by North Carolina senators Samuel Johnston and Benjamin Hawkins in December 1789. It passed the Senate on February 25, 1790, and was formally approved by Congress on April 2nd following. About April, Colonels John Sevier and James Robertson were appointed brigadier generals for the Washington and Mero Districts of the area that was about to be included in a new territory of the United States. The Mero District was named after the Spanish governor of Louisiana, Esteban Rodriquez Miró.

Secretary of War Henry Knox instructed the new brigadiers to treat the Spanish with politeness, to only act defensively, and to show no aggression toward the Indians lest they offend the Spanish, who were protective of the Indians.

Thus, the region embracing the Watauga and Cumberland Settlements became the Southwest Territory, separate and apart from the parent state of North Carolina. President Washington appointed Watauga settler William Blount to be the new territorial governor on June 8, 1790.[35]

Mrs. Brown was confined to a small Creek village after she was captured in the attack on the family's boat along Muscle Shoals in 1788 (see Chapter 9). Nearby lived Benjamin Durant and his wife, Sophia, who was a sister of Chief Alexander McGillivray. Sophia was as charismatic as her brother, and she was just as humane. She gained a friend in Mrs. Brown and acted on her behalf. Sophia advised Mrs. Brown to apply to Alexander McGillivray for mercy; she even helped her make the trek to his house at Little Tallasee. Chief McGillivray was cordial and, later, ransomed her from her captor. The chief then kept her at his house, as a member of his family, for more than a year.

Mrs. Brown won the confidence and respect of her Creek friends and especially that of General McGillivray. He next ransomed young Elizabeth from her captor and restored her to her mother. At the same time he brought Mrs. Brown information of her young son George, whom he would also have ransomed, but the warrior owner was not willing to part with him on any terms. In November 1789, Chief McGillivray had gone to Rock Landing, Georgia, on public business. He carried Mrs. Brown and Elizabeth with him, and delivered them to her older son, William, who had gone there seeking information of her. (William was one of two sons who was already in the Cumberlands preparing the land for the arrival of the family in 1788 before they were attacked en route.) After 18 months of captivity, Mrs. Brown visited with relatives in South Carolina. Then she returned to visit with her old friends at Guilford Courthouse, North Carolina.

Chief McGillivray, on his way to New York with Andrew Pickens and others to meet with President Washington, stopped in Guilford Courthouse in late June 1790. When Mrs. Brown heard of his arrival, she rushed through the large assembly at the courthouse, and with a flood of tears warmly expressed her admiration and gratitude. Her brother, Colonel George Gillespie, offered to pay Alexander McGillivray any sum he might desire as a ransom for Mrs. Brown and her daughter, but the chief refused any compensation. He also assured Mrs. Brown that he would use his best efforts to liberate her son, George.

(It would be more than eight years of captivity before George Brown would be restored to his white family. General Pickens would receive him from Superintendent Seagrove and deliver him to his uncle, Joseph Brown of South Carolina, in September 1796.)[36]

A land company tried to settle over 3,000,000 acres near the Muscle Shoals area from 1788 to 1791. President Washington and Secretary of War Henry Knox warned them that the settlement was purchased illegally and, that as far as the United States was concerned, the Indians would have the right to retaliate—which they did.

NEW-YORK, July 3 [1790]
    It is with sincere pleasure we inform the public, that Major [John] Doughty, who was reported to have been killed by the Indians on the river Tenasee, safely arrived … on the Ohio on the 15th of last month.… While ascending the Tenasee, on the 21st of May last, he met a party of 40 Indians, in three canoes, having a white flag hoisted. This party were a banditti of Cherokees and Shawanese, with three Creeks.

The major was in a barge with ensign Sedam and fifteen non-commissioned officers and privates. The Indians appeared very friendly, and their chief, and several others, even came on board the barge.... They endeavored ... to persuade the major to land, and pass the night with them ... but he, being suspicious of their designs, evaded their entreaties. After ... an hour, they shook the major by the hand, and left him: but the men had scarcely took to their oars, before they received from the Indians a severe fire, which was instantly returned, and the boat put about ... an incessant fire ensued for four hours ... the major had five of his party killed, and six wounded, one of which died thereafter.[37]

A man named Hubbard led a party of 16 men to assist Zachariah Cox of the land company to take possession of the property at Muscle Shoals. They built a blockhouse and a stockade on a small island at the Shoals. Chief Glass led 60 warriors from Running Water Town and ordered the party to leave. The crew had to abandon their equipment and structures, which were burned. Hubbard and his men were at the mercy of Glass who, according to Chief Richard Justice in a May 1792 letter to Governor Blount, might have killed them, but instead of doing so, he "lifted them up and told them to go in peace."[38] (This was likely Major James Hubbard who was in the Bloody Rangers and involved in the assassination of the old Upper Village chiefs.)

The Chickamauga and their allies completely disrupted river traffic, and the land company withdrew.

Because so much effort was devoted to treaties, 1790 was relatively peaceful compared to previous years; however, the Chickamauga were true to their issues and kept up the pressure on the settlements. Henry Howdyshall and Samuel Farr were ambushed and killed while fishing on the Cumberland River.

(Several accounts of Creek and Chickamauga attacks over the next few years are reported herein, and they may seem severe. However, it was a harsh period. The Indians were fighting to regain their land and to not lose any more. They strongly felt that the settlers took extreme advantage of them and encroached knowing the government had no control over such actions. A European type of warfare, with courteous paroles, fair tactics, and gentle treatment of prisoners, was out of the question. The only chance the Indians had to meet their aims was to use a bloody form of warfare that would make the settlers regret having moved onto Indian lands enough to want to leave. This was a familiar war tactic for the Indians, and they would use it to their best advantage. They were, after all, fighting for life as they knew it, and had been susceptible to ill treatment almost from the time of their first white contacts. Enough had become enough.)

Benjamin Williams, who had settled on a tract of land about two and one-half miles north of present-day Gallatin, Tennessee, was killed one night along with his wife, children, and two slaves. One young black boy hid in the chimney over the fireplace and escaped harm.

Samuel Wilson, who lived one mile nearer present-day Gallatin, was out on the trail the next morning to look for his horse in Williams' neighborhood. He heard someone riding toward him and hid behind a tree. Soon, a warrior on horseback appeared. Wilson, who had not yet heard of the attack on the Williams family, drew a bead on the Indian and killed him. Thinking the warrior might be a scout for a party, he loudly shouted "Surround them, boys; surround them!" He heard the war party withdraw, and he did the same—in the opposite direction. A few days later John Edwards was killed in the same vicinity.

About 300 Chickamauga warriors attacked Houston's Station near present-day Maryville, Tennessee. Houston's was a small and stout log cabin with firing ports. Several families had gathered there for protection. Seven marksmen manned the apertures. The Chickamauga drew near as they had not yet drawn the fire of the settlers. The marksmen opened up when the warriors were very close and killed several before the Indians withdrew.

In midsummer, Alexander Neely was killed along with his two sons, James and Charles, one mile north of Bledsoe's Station.

About the same time, Benjamin and Robert Desha, sons of Robert Desha, Sr., were killed four miles northwest of Bledsoe's Station on a creek which later was named Desha Creek.

Henry Ramsey was shot from ambush and killed while he rode from present-day Greenfield to Bledsoe's Station. His companion, Mr. Hicks, was wounded.

Shortly thereafter, William Ramsey left his home on White's Creek to settle Henry's estate. As he returned, he was ambushed and killed, along with his horse, near Bledsoe's Station.

The Indians attacked Brown's Station and killed John Everett, Miss Norris, and one other person. They also scalped three of Everett's children. They then attacked Mayfield's Station and killed John Glen. He had married the widow of previously-killed Southerland Mayfield. They also slew a few settlers at a nearby mill.[39]

Seventeen ninety-one continued the relatively uneventful atmosphere of 1790. "A census of the Mero district taken this year shows a population of seven thousand and forty-two. One thousand of these were males capable of bearing arms. The population of the Indian tribes surrounding the Territory at that time is variously estimated at from twenty-five to fifty thousand."[40]

The new treaty with Chief, and new general, Alexander McGillivray of the Creek was the basis for much optimism on both sides. The United States wined and dined the Creek delegation while they were in New York. However, the real test, as far as the Creek were concerned, was the primary issue of that portion of their ancestral land, along the Ogeechee and Oconee Rivers, of which they believed they had been cheated. The finalized treaty restored a large tract of wilderness to the Creek. In a portion of the treaty that was secreted from the Creek warriors, Chief McGillivray was awarded $100,000 in return for an alleged destruction of personal property by the colonial militia.

Shortly thereafter, Governor Blount visited tribes in all parts of the territory, especially near the Cumberland settlements. He assured the people of his friendship and urged peace with their white neighbors. Some, especially the Chickasaw, occasionally took venison and furs to the settlers and traded for powder, lead, blankets, calico, tomahawks, knives, and beads.

Chief Piomingo of the Chickasaw had hoped the white settlers could develop a good relationship with the Creek based on the good report that had existed between the settlers and his own nation.

Piomingo had been a friend of the Cumberland settlers for quite a few years, and the recent treaty with the Creek led Governor William Blount to hope that it would be easy to pacify the Cherokee.

Early in 1791, Governor Blount invited Hanging Maw and Little Turkey to take part in peace talks. Hanging Maw was the de facto leader of those Cherokee still living in the Upper and Middle Villages. Little Turkey, however, was considered the southern peace chief and the principal chief of the Nation. Blount proposed White's Fort as the location for the talks. (This was the original James White's Fort at present-day Knoxville, Tennessee, as opposed to the new station he would build three miles northeast of Gallatin, Tennessee.)

There were some Indian traders and land speculators who opposed peace talks lest any treaty should cut into their profits. They spread a rumor among the Cherokee, especially the Chickamauga, that Blount had prepared a trap to assemble the warriors and headmen in one place where they could be surrounded by troops and slaughtered.

Governor Blount identified which traders were responsible for the distraction, revoked their licenses, and ordered them from the Cherokee Nation. He countered the damage by sending General James Robertson to represent the United States. Blount relied heavily on Robertson's discretion in dealing with the Indians. It was not lost on the Cherokee that, after the death of his brother, when Robertson invaded Coldwater Town (Oka Kapassa), he released his captives from that expedition without harm.

Robertson immediately set out on horseback from Nashville to Chota, the old beloved capital and Mother Town of the Cherokees. He found it nestled beautifully among the foothills of the Chilhowee Mountains east of present-day Madisonville, Tennessee. The Cherokee still considered Chota to be a city of refuge. (The Cherokee have a story of an English trader who, a few years later, took refuge there after having murdered a Cherokee warrior following a disagreement. He remained in the village for years and eventually desired to return to his trading post. He was warned that he would certainly be killed the minute he would leave Chota.)

Hanging Maw warmly welcomed General Robertson, as did Little Turkey who had arrived a few days earlier. Each chief had a contingent of headmen and warriors in their company. It took Robertson a few days, but he successfully convinced the Cherokee that the proposed treaty session was nothing more than that. He then arranged for the council at White's Fort. A treaty was established and was called, as were several others before it, the Treaty of Holston, also Blount's Treaty. It was signed on July 2, 1791, and on November 9, ratified by the United States Senate. The Cherokee, in consideration of trade goods and an annual payment of $1,000, released their claims to the central portion of East Tennessee. The Cherokee supposedly committed to cease attacks on the Cumberland.

One week prior to the signing, Young Tassel orated: "I know that the North Carolina people are headstrong. Under the sanction of a flag of truce they laid low my Uncle, Old Tassel. It is vain for us to contend about a line. The North Carolina people will have their way, and will not observe orders of Congress or anyone else.... When you North Carolinians make a line, you tell us it is a standing one, but you are always encroaching on it and we cannot depend on what you say."[41]

Governor Blount replied: "The lands were taken from the Cherokee in time of war, and I do not consider the settlements to be encroachments."[42]

Forty-two chiefs signed the new treaty, including Hanging Maw who had fought with the Chickamauga at times, as did some of the other signatories: Bloody Fellow (who had left the Chickamauga for a time), Young Tassel (John Watts, Jr.), the notorious Doublehead (Hanging Maw's brother), and Terrapin (son of the late Oconostota). A man named John D. Chisholm witnessed the signing. (John D. Chisholm, an advisor to the chiefs, was the grandfather of Jesse Chisholm, who developed the Old Chisholm Trail.)

However, Chickamauga chief Dragging Canoe was not any more impressed than he had been with previous treaties. This was just another where the appointed headmen ceded precious ancestral land for a piddling amount. One thousand dollars per year was such a meager sum that it could not even be distributed throughout the nation. The Chickamauga would yet be heard from again, and some of the above signatories would be involved as suggested by Chief Young Tassel's exchange with Governor Blount.

Although Young Tassel was a signatory, he did not officially represent the Chickamauga at that time and did not accept any of the gifts or the annuity on behalf of Dragging Canoe. Doublehead likely did, although his faction was not officially labeled Chickamauga. He had settled on the lower Tennessee River many years before and, up until 1792, did not really take part in joint expeditions with Dragging Canoe's faction. However, his forays were as pointed against the settlers as were those of the Chickamauga.

One week after the signatures, all land within a triangular section of Tennessee and North Carolina, extending from the Clinch River to near the Blue Ridge, and including almost all of the French Broad and lower Holston rivers, was ceded to the settlers. Included were the sites of present-day Knoxville and Greeneville, Tennessee, as well as Asheville, North Carolina, which had already been illegally settled by the whites. Permission was also given the settlers for a road from the eastern settlements to those of the Cumberland, with free navigation on the Tennessee River.

In the meantime, peaceful conditions existed, and the Nashville settlements expanded. New settlers arrived, and more stations were established. In the early spring of 1791, Major James White added a new station three miles northeast of Gallatin (not to be confused with his station that was the origination of Knoxville).

Colonel James Saunders built a fort on the west side of Desha Creek two and one-half miles east of White's Station. Captain Joseph Wilson located three miles southeast of Gallatin at Walnutfield Station. Jacob Ziegler built a fort one and one-half miles north of present-day Cairo, Tennessee, on the western branch of Bledsoe Creek. (Ziegler's was in the vicinity of present-day Bledsoe Creek State Park.)

The Chickamauga then went to work to counter the expansion. Scarcely had Colonel Saunders completed his fort on Desha Creek and moved his family in when Chickamauga warriors ambushed, shot, and killed his two young sons who had wandered outside the gates.

In May 1791, Bench attacked and killed James Patrick in Poor Valley near present-day Rogersville, Tennessee. Soon thereafter, James Dickinson was killed while riding from Saunders' Station to White's Station. On June 2, 1791, John Thompson was shot and killed while hoeing in his cornfields south of Nashville. Later in the summer, a band of Creek killed Mr. Miller, his wife, and five children over on Rolling Fork of the Cumberland.

On June 14, John Gibson was also killed near Nashville. Later in June, Benjamin Kirkendall was killed at his home near Bledsoe's Station. Three were killed, and another three mortally wounded, while they traveled the Natchez Trace from Natchez, Mississippi, to Nashville. Then, Thomas Fletcher was one of three killed and scalped near the mouth of the Red River, near Clarksville, Tennessee. (Clarksville had been incorporated since 1785, is located about eight miles south of the Kentucky border on U.S. Highway 41A, about 35 miles northwest of Nashville.)

In Running Water Town during the summer of 1791, shortly after the Treaty of Holston was signed, young Chief Bench announced he would plan raids into the southwest Virginia settlements. At that time, he had a following of five warriors so would keep the raids relatively small but devastating.

On August 23, his band moved against the large cabin of William McDowell and Benjamin Pendleton. (The house was located at the southwest end of Clinch Mountain near present-day Moccasin Gap, Virginia, 10 miles northwest of Abingdon on U.S. Highway 19.) Mrs. McDowell and Pendleton's 17-year-old daughter, Frances, were killed and scalped; young Reuben Pendleton was wounded. Mrs. Pendleton and an eight-year-old boy were taken captive.

Nearby, three days later at 8:00 a.m. Bench's band attacked the home of Elisha Farris (sometimes Ferris), then killed and scalped Mrs. Farris, Mrs. Livingston, and Livingston's three-year-old child. They mortally wounded Mr. Farris and took his 19-year-old daughter, Nancy, captive. Bench's band then took their prisoners and headed for Running Water Town.

The settlers gained a healthy respect for Bench's abilities. They described him as sly, intelligent, strong, durable and very quick. Virginia offered a reward for his capture dead or alive.

Bench then gathered his band and, a few days later, ambushed seven men, four women and one young boy who were on their way to the Nashville settlements from present-day South West Point. (South West Point is near Kingston, Tennessee, 30 miles west of Knoxville.) One of Bench's young warriors fired early and alerted the travelers. The men then abandoned the women and ran. Bench then approached the women and, in perfect English, told them they would not be harmed. He shook hands with each of them, gathered their horses for them, had one of his warriors build a fire, and the band left. Three of the men returned for the women after they were sure the Cherokee were gone.

According to a deposition filed by Daniel Thornbury on April 10, 1792,[43] Chief Doublehead led 28 men on a hunting expedition in the fall of 1791. The party also included several women and children. The chief, during the excursion, took seven warriors, moved up the Cumberland River, and took scalps as they went. They killed several men and stole their clothing. The band came upon and captured a salt boat after killing one man and then proceeded as far as Clarksville, Tennessee, where they fired upon some houses but did not attack. Then Doublehead returned to camp.[44]

The Treaty of Hopewell had provided that the Cherokee could send a deputy to Congress whenever they deemed necessary. After discussing the matter among themselves, the Cherokee headmen became dissatisfied with the boundary that had been set at the Treaty of Holston. On December 28, 1791, they surprised the government at Philadelphia with a delegation headed by Chief Bloody Fellow.

> The following Cherokee Chiefs and warriors arrived at Philadelphia on the 28th of December, 1791, by the way of Charleston, South Carolina, bringing with them evidence [letters] from Governor [Charles] Pinckney and General Pickens, of the authenticity of their mission, to wit:
>
> Nenetooyah, or Bloody Fellow, Chutlow, or King Fisher, Nontuaka, or the Northward, Teesteke, or the Disturber, Kuthegusta, or the Prince, George Miller, and James Carey, Interpreter.
>
> They were, on the 4th of January, 1792, introduced to the President of the United States, who desired them to communicate their business to the Secretary of War. They were assembled for this purpose, at his house, on the 5th.[45]

Bloody Fellow orated from Thursday, January 5, through Monday, January 9, (meeting every other day) about the shortcomings of the Treaty of Holston.[46]

On Wednesday, January 7, 1792, Henry Knox responded: "BROTHERS: I am heartily glad that you have disburthened your hearts in your own way.... You have mentioned some uneasiness about your treaty with Governor Blount; but the President, and the Senate of the United States, who are his council on this business, believing that this treaty was a good and satisfactory treaty, as well for the red as the white people ... and, if any bad white people should encroach upon your grounds, or do any thing contrary to that treaty, they would be immediately punished."[47]

Bloody Fellow then covered the main issues:

> At the time of the treaty, we objected to giving up so much land; but for the sake of peace and quietness, we did it. But we object to the little money given for so much land. We request, therefore, that something further may be done in this matter, so that all our people may be quiet in their minds.
>
> Instead of one thousand dollars a year for our lands, give us half as much more; that is, fifteen hundred dollars a year, and we shall be perfectly satisfied.
>
> If this could be done for us, we do not require it in money, but in goods, bought in Philadelphia, where they are cheapest; and to be sent to General Pickens, by the way of Charleston.
>
> I shall now speak on a matter of great importance. The ridge, which divides the waters of Little river from the Tennessee, is the boundary fixed by the treaty. But the white people are already over it, and their numbers have increased since the treaty. Remove these back, or our people will not be quiet. We speak strongly on this point.
>
> Governor Blount spoke very much to us, that a trading house should be established at Bear creek, below the Muscle Shoals, on the Tennessee. We could not consent to this. After we returned home we talked among ourselves on this matter, and it would be very disagreeable to our nation. But we have heard that this matter is still going on. We desire that ... you ... should prevent this settlement on the Muscle Shoals.[48]

Then, on January 18, 1792:

> Gentlemen of the Senate:
> I lay before you the communications of a deputation from the Cherokee nation of Indians, now in this city, (Philadelphia) and I request your advice whether an additional article shall be made to the Cherokee treaty, to the following effect, to wit:
> That the sum to be paid annually by the United States to the Cherokee nation [sic] of Indians, in consideration of the relinquishment of lands, as stated in the treaty made with them on the second day of July, 1791, shall be one thousand five hundred dollars, instead of one thousand dollars, mentioned in the said treaty.
> GEO. WASHINGTON
> UNITED STATES, January 18, 1792.
> On the 20th January it was
> Resolved, two-thirds of the Senate present concurring, that they advise and consent to the additional article in the form above proposed.[49]

It is often recorded that the president, at this time, changed Bloody Fellow's name and gave him a military rank. Those actions would actually take place later (see below).

About this same time, McGillivray was falling into disfavor within the Creek community. It became known that he had received $100,000 by a secret clause in the Treaty of New

York. The headmen of his nation wanted to correct the matter. Charismatic William Augustus Bowles, born in Maryland, and later captured by the Creek, had, in 1781, fought with the British and the Creek against the Spanish in Florida. He worked to develop an American Indian state and was commissioned by King George III to be the chief ambassador to the Creek. He married a daughter of Chief McGillivray and was in place to step in when McGillivray was exposed. He denounced McGillivray and, as the ambassador, asserted that the Chief had been bribed and cheated at the treaty. (This Bowles is not to be confused with Chief Bowles of the Cherokee Nation.)

Bowles then announced that, while visiting in England, he was empowered by the British government to declare void all treaties between the Creek and the whites, and he assured the headmen that all lands previously claimed by them would be restored. He began to act as the Creek chief by acclamation and directed their invasions into the settlements.

Early in 1792, Bowles sent Coteatoy with a message to visit General James Robertson at Nashville. In the message, Bowles professed feelings of friendship for the settlers. Robertson kindly hosted Coteatoy; however, the general carefully watched the warrior, whom he thought might be reconnoitering the settlements. Jonathan Robertson, James' son, was assigned to be Coteatoy's guide.

Shortly thereafter, Young Tassel led a small delegation of Cherokee chiefs to Nashville. General Robertson thought that visit might also have been a spy mission. When Young Tassel's party departed, they requested to be able to hunt as they passed over the white man's land.

The visits put General Robertson so on guard, that he expected a series of attacks. He ordered the militias to make preparations. The companies were to garrison the various stations, and a 500-man force was put on alert to react as needed. Captain John Rains commanded a band of rangers with headquarters at Rains' Station. He always had two men on guard duty ready to sound a horn should the force be called to action. Additionally, Southwest Territory governor William Blount placed militia major Sharpe and his 190-man infantry and cavalry at the disposal of General Robertson.

Colonel Valentine Sevier, brother of General John Sevier, lived in the Cumberlands at his station near the mouth of the Red River. (The blockhouse still stands in the downtown Boot Hill section of Clarksville in New Providence, and is located at 326 Walker Street.) He and his wife had five sons, and several other relatives, including Messrs. Price and Snyder who resided at the station.

When General Robertson called for volunteers to act as scouts and outriders, Colonel Sevier gave permission to his sons, Robert, William and Valentine, Jr., to enlist. They were to travel to Nashville with friends John Price, John Curtis, and three others. Colonel Sevier did not have enough horses to spare, so they decided to travel by a large canoe.

They ascended the Cumberland River on January 18, 1792 (the same day that the United States Congress acceded to Chief Hanging Maw's demands in Philadelphia). They were spotted by Chief Doublehead, who had been watching the station for just such an opportunity. The chief led his band of warriors to a sharp bend in the river, south of the station, where he set up an ambush. The Indians fired upon the canoe as it drew near, and the three Sevier brothers were all killed with the first volley, along with Curtis and another of their friends.

While the warriors reloaded their guns, Price and the other survivors turned the canoe around and raced downstream; however, Price saw that they would be cut off. Doublehead had crossed over a peninsula to get ahead of the travelers. They rowed to the opposite shore from the Indians who were awaiting them. They then abandoned their canoe, set it adrift, and darted into the forest. They reached the bank west of Clarksville where nearby settlers took them in. The rescuers delivered news of the attack to Colonel and Mrs. Sevier. (The attack took place at present-day Seven Mile Ferry. Seven Mile Ferry Road is south, across the Cumberland River from Clarksville, and exits off of Marthas Chapel Road.)

Once Price and his canoe mates had escaped, the warriors boarded the craft, scalped the five dead men, and threw their bodies into the river. They withdrew with guns and provisions from the boats, including clothing and boots from the corpses.

This was a high point for Doublehead to have killed members of the prestigious Sevier family. He had no respect at all for their uncle, General John Sevier.

A week later, three of Doublehead's warriors killed a man named Boyd in the same vicinity, after which he withdrew his band to the hunting camp. On January 12, 1792, Thomas White was killed on Cumberland Mountain, likely by Doublehead and his band. The smaller forts in the Clarksville neighborhood were mostly abandoned after the attacks; the occupants had sought refuge at Valentine Sevier's Station.

Several small forts had been established near present-day Springfield, Tennessee. The Creek made a series of attacks on them about the time of Doublehead's exploits near Clarksville. John Titsworth, Thomas Reason and his wife, and Mrs. Roberts were killed. The entire family of Colonel Isaac Titsworth was also killed, except for the colonel, who was away, and an older daughter, who was taken captive. The warriors destroyed the house and withdrew. The Creek kept their captives at a camp near the mouth of the Cumberland, at the Tennessee, until the first of June. Then they took the prisoners to the Creek Nation. Miss Titsworth remained for the next three years until her father discovered her location and negotiated her release.

In 1791, a Cherokee warrior, identified as White Owl's son, had gone north to help the Shawnee fight General Arthur St. Clair (governor of the Ohio Territory). St. Clair had attacked several Miami, Delaware, and Shawnee villages near present-day Fort Wayne, Indiana. The militia forces that were traveling with his army deserted him, and many of his regular soldiers had become ill. On November 4, 1791, St. Clair and 1,400 men camped along the Wabash River. Miami war chief Little Turtle led 1,200 warriors, who had united from several tribes, in a surprise dawn attack on St. Clair's camp. Half of the army had been killed by noon. The survivors withdrew and left the dead and wounded for their conquerors. The Indians suffered only 21 killed.

White Owl's son (likely Dragging Canoe's brother, Little Owl) presented a Shawnee war pipe to Chief Dragging Canoe to unite the two tribes in their cooperative effort against the whites. Little Owl's expedition to the north was a great public relations move on the part of the Chickamauga. (Little Owl's father, Attakullakulla, had once been known as White Owl.)

In 1792, Dragging Canoe was looking for allies. He had reached out to the Creek and the Chickasaw to join him in a new offensive. General Bowles was willing and took an active part; however, Chief McGillivray was already regaining his influence among the Creek headmen. Chickasaw chief Piomingo would have nothing to do with the alliance. He was satisfied with the existing treaty. The Shawnee would make a welcome ally.

A Shawnee war chief named Pukeshenwa was killed years earlier, on October 10, 1774, at the Battle of Kanawha, later known as the Battle of Point Pleasant. (See Chapter 6.) His 15-year-old son, Cheeseekau, had aided him, much as a page would have done for a knight in Europe.

In 1792, 32-year-old Cheeseekau moved to Running Water Town to aid the Chickamauga; he was joined there by his new friend, Chief Little Owl. Cheeseekau brought 150 warriors, of which 30 were hardened veterans of major battles in the north. He called himself Pepquannakek (Gunshot), but the Cherokee were so impressed with him that they called him the Shawnee Warrior. One of Cheeseekau's sub chiefs was his 23-year-old brother, Tecumseh, who led 10 or 12 young warriors. Shawnee Warrior and Little Owl would lead a formidable combined force in deadly raids against the settlements. Dragging Canoe implicitly trusted Shawnee Warrior to carry out important expeditions.

Shawnee Warrior introduced himself to some settlers in February 1792 when their boats drifted on the Tennessee near Running Water Town. He and his braves tried to hail the vessels as if they were friendly, but the settlers did not take the bait. The warriors fired upon the craft as they floated past.[50]

James Thompson, his wife, and two teenaged daughters lived in a log cabin four miles south of Nashville. Peter Caffrey, his wife, and their two-year-old son resided with them. On what has been variously reported from February 25 to March 1, 1792, on a cold and snowy evening, Caffrey ventured out to feed the stock, and Thompson went for the night's firewood. Thompson split some logs and carried several armfuls to the yard fence. He tossed them over near the cabin.

A Creek war party had been watching Thompson from some nearby brush. They shot and severely wounded him, but he was able to enter the house and bar the door. The warriors chipped chinking from between the logs with their knives and tomahawks and shot at the family through the gaps. They killed Thompson and his wife and wounded his younger daughter. The war party then broke the door out and took the two Thompson girls captive, along with Mrs. Caffrey and her son. The wounded teenager was so badly hurt that she could not keep up with the warriors, and they scalped her after they had gone some distance. She lay in the snow all night but was still alive when neighbors found her next morning. They carried the unconscious girl to a house where she soon died.

The Indians took Alice Thompson, Mrs. Caffrey, and the Caffrey boy toward the Creek Nation.

Colonel Elijah Robertson wrote to Governor William Blount three days later:

SIR:
I this moment received information that the Indians, a few hours ago, killed James Thompson, and family; also Peter Caffey's [sic] family, within about five miles of Nashville. It appears that, in the evening, they killed Mr. Thompson in the yard, and jumped into the house and killed all the women and children, except two small ones, who they spoke to in English, and told them to grow up, and then they would come and kill them. I am raising a party to pursue them.
I am, &c.[51]

Note that there are discrepancies in numbers between the historical accounts and the details within Colonel Robertson's letter. The Thompsons may have had two younger children. Such inconsistencies are to be expected with the manner of communications being what they were in those times. It was not until May 17 that Blount would write to Chief Alexander McGillivray of the incident:

> SIR:
> I am already informed that the murders and horse stealings lately committed by the Creeks, may, in a great degree, be charged to the attention they paid to the pernicious counsels of Mr. Bowles. Nevertheless, I conceive it essential, they should be known to you ... [Several incidents were detailed in this communication.] Early in March, a party of Indians attacked the house of Mr. Thompson, within seven miles of Nashville; killed and scalped the old man and others of the family, and made prisoners Mrs. Caffray and Miss Thompson, and a child.
> A few days since, some Cherokee chiefs were here with me ... who informed me ... about the last of March, they came to a camp of the Creeks ... where they had prisoners two women and a child about two years of age.
> The description of the prisoners taken, and those seen by the Cherokee chiefs, and the time when taken and when seen, afford a violent presumption that it was Mrs. Caffray, Miss Thompson, and the child taken with them....
> P.S. I am since informed that the Creeks who had two women and the child prisoners, belonged to the Oakjoys ... the white men with the Cherokee chiefs ... also saw the women and child, and one of them conversed with one of the women on the fatigue she suffered with walking.... They mention that they heard one of the women complain to one of the Indians that she was tired of walking, and the Indian answered, that he would get briars and scratch her thighs, and that would make her walk fast.... These circumstances are mentioned, the better to convince you that Mrs. Caffray, Miss Thompson, and the child, have been made prisoners by a party of the Creeks; and prove, that they also killed Miss Thompson's father, and the rest of the family.[52]

There were more contradictions in this letter with what was written by Colonel Robertson and what has been historically recorded. In the first place, it did not occur early in March as stated, since the letter Robertson had addressed to Blount regarding the matter was dated February 28.

There could be a misunderstanding regarding the scratching of the woman's thighs to make her walk more quickly. Rather than a threat, it was more likely a known remedy in the southern nations to improve circulation when taking long treks to gently scratch the legs, but not to the point of injury.

The captives were first kept in Kialiages, a Creek town on the Tallapoosa River. John Riley, an Irish trader, offered to ransom them at the price of a black slave for each, but the warriors vehemently refused, stating they did not take captives to let them go back to the settlements. They further declared that all captives were there to work.

James Ore made a deposition that included a visit to that village on the 16th of March where he spoke with Riley. He deposed:

> [After Riley's initial offering to ransom the captives, the Creek told him] that if he was not so great a friend of theirs, they would knock him in the head for the proposal, and requested him never to talk so to them any more.
> This deponent further saith, that he was informed that the Indians had put Miss Thompson and the other woman into the fields to work. Miss Thompson cried, and they put her into the house again to pound meal; and that the child was taken from the mother by one of the captors, and taken to another town, where he committed it to a Mrs. Williams, who has been a prisoner with the Creeks for some years, and treated with the greatest degree of barbarity, and with much severity, having been often beat until she was black and blue....

> He further saith, that he saw one party, consisting of five, and was informed there were several other parties on their way to Cumberland, with an express intention to take hair or scalps, and to steal horses....
> The general talk in the Creek nation was, that they would never be at peace with Cumberland, for it was their particular hunting ground.[53]

Riley was touched by Alice Thompson's plight. He eventually bargained her release with dressed deer skins valued at $260. She still remained at the town but was treated much better. Mrs. Caffrey was still required to work the fields and pound meal. She was reportedly often punished by having her back, legs, and arms scratched with gar's teeth. Historian A. V. Goodpasture recorded in a footnote: "This probably was not intended as punishment. Colonel Joseph Brown, who was for nearly a year a prisoner among the Chickamaugas, says they performed this operation twice a year, both on themselves and on their prisoners. They called it 'scratching to keep them healthy.' Colonel Brown's Narrative, *Southwestern Monthly*, Vol. 1, p. 72."[54]

(Mrs. Caffrey and Miss Thompson were released early in May 1794; however, the Caffrey boy was retained by the Creeks. The boy was released three years later, and it is recorded that Abram Mordecai retrieved him with great difficulty. The seven-year-old boy had adjusted well to Creek life and physically resisted being taken from his Creek playmates.)

The Creek and the Chickamauga continued to control river traffic through the Muscle Shoals of the Tennessee. They attacked a boat in February 1792 as deposed by Ezekial Abel the following April 16:

> This deponent saith, that the ____ day of February last, on his passage down the Tennessee river, in company with Colonel Harry Hunter, their boat lodged on the Muscle Shoals; that this deponent, in company with one Mr. Wilson, (Who had a pass from his Excellency William Blount, Esq., in his care, granted Colonel Hunter) went to shore in a canoe, to a party of Indians, in order to get assistance over the shoals; that five Indians went into the canoe, apparently very friendly, but, after going some distance up the river, one of the Indians, who stood behind this deponent, gave him (the deponent) a blow on the neck, aimed, as he supposes, at his head, with a tomahawk, which the said Indian had concealed under his watch coat; by the force of which blow the deponent fell into the water; the other Indians, or a part of them, fell on Mr. Wilson with tomahawks, which they had concealed in the same manner as above. This deponent saith, that the canoe oversat in the time of the engagement; that Wilson was, after repeated blows given him while in the water, killed, scalped, and stripped, but that he (the deponent) made his escape after receiving several blows. The deponent further saith, that the Indians, at all the towns the boats passed, fired heavily on them, and that a number of balls struck heavily in the boats: he also saith, that every part of the Indians' conduct to them, during their passage, seemed inimical. And, finally, this deponent saith, that he is well convinced that one of the Indians who killed Wilson, was a Cherokee, as he had last summer seen him at the treaty, and knows him by a remarkable scar on one of his thighs.[55]

(It seems unbelievable that, after years of publicized aggression by the Chickamauga and the Creek, people would think it safe to travel through the Five Lower Villages, safe to simply canoe over to the inhabitants for help, and be surprised that the warriors were ill-disposed.)

Chief Dragging Canoe had obtained Spanish arms and ammunition through trader John McDonald. Chief Bloody Fellow was his main point of contact for that trade. Dragging Canoe also busily promoted the formation of a confederacy of southern Indian nations to drive the white community back to the coastal states. He believed the current western boundary, resultant from treaty after treaty, was entirely unacceptable and had been unfairly obtained. He had just returned on the last of February from the Chickasaw Bluffs where he had failed to enlist Chickasaw chief Piomingo in the effort.

Chiefs Glass (Tauqueto) and Turtle At Home (Dragging Canoe's brother) had just come back from leading 60 warriors on successful raids into the Cumberland settlements. They brought many white scalps. Little Owl had also returned from successful raids into the settlements.

The warriors, including Chief Dragging Canoe, celebrated all night with scalp dancing, and an Eagle Tail Dance tribute to the 60-year-old chief. Some report the celebration occurred at Lookout Mountain Town (Stecoyee) and others that it happened at Running Water Town (Amogayunyi). The former is the more likely.

Chief Dragging Canoe died the next morning, March 1, 1792. Some say he died of battle wounds that had festered, and others that he died from the night of celebration; however, the fact is that he died and was buried at Running Water Town. (The sites of Running Water Town and Chief Dragging Canoe's grave, which were inundated in 1967, were located near where Interstate Highway 24 crosses Nickajack Lake.)

Historian E. Raymond Evans paid tribute to the great chief with:

At the beginning of the American Revolution it had seemed that the Cherokee might be completely exterminated, or at best survive only as a beaten and degenerate people like the Catawba. This disaster was avoided by the firm holding action fought by Dragging Canoe. It was his determined resistance that made the Treaty of Tellico Blockhouse workable. Having felt the strength of the Cherokees, the whites respected the treaty for more than a generation. This period of peace made possible the brilliant flowering of Cherokee culture during the first quarter of the nineteenth century.... The Cherokee culture which Dragging Canoe and the Chickamauga Cherokee devoted their lives to saving is still very much alive. Today their descendants in Oklahoma and the mountains of North Carolina can still repeat with great pride Dragging Canoe's statement to the Shawnee delegation: "we are not yet conquered."[56]

Chief Young Tassel (John Watts, Jr.) is most often reported as being in the company of Governor William Blount, negotiating a treaty at Chota in March 1792, when he was reportedly notified not only of Chief Dragging Canoe's death, but also that he had been selected by the council to succeed as the chief of the Chickamauga. That is not entirely factual:

Information by Governor Blount, respecting the Cherokee Chiefs whose names are mentioned in the narrative given by Richard Finnelson.
KNOXVILLE, September 25, 1792.
John Watts was a signer to the treaty of Holston; was in February with Governor Blount several days at Knoxville, received several very valuable presents from him, and expressed the strongest friendship for the United States, and his great personal attachment for the Governor. He again met the Governor at the Conference at Coyatee [not until May of 1792].... Thus, at parting with Watts at Coyatee, the Governor considered him as the great friend of the United States and himself, nor does the Governor yet doubt that was surely the fact. But there is great reason to believe that Watts received a runner at Coyatee, a few hours after the Governor left it, from Panton. It is beyond all doubt that Panton induced him to go to Pensacola.[57]

Apparently, Young Tassel and Governor Blount were apart from February to May. (The affair at Coyatee and Young Tassel's visit to Pensacola will be discussed later.)

More details of the circumstances surrounding Young Tassel's receipt of notification of Dragging Canoe's death is illustrated in a March 15, 1792, report from David Craig to William Blount:

> On the 29th of February, (during the stay of Mr. McKee and myself at the house of a friend near Look-out mountain), an Eagle-tail-dance was held, to which cause warriors from the Running Water, which was also danced with all the forms of a war-dance, exulting over the scalps, &c.... He [Path Killer] said the Turkey desired that the Hanging Maw and John Watts should send his talk to the governor ... he [Path Killer thought] it best that Watts should first go down to the Running Water, from whence he had been twice sent for since the death of the Dragging Canoe (which happened immediately after his return from the Chickasaws) ... Watts accordingly set out from Chota on the 13th Instant.[58]

Whether the two planned to meet at Chota or not, Young Tassel was there and Blount either was not or had not yet seen Watts. Likely, Young Tassel was preparing to deliver Little Turkey's message to Blount. Path Killer decided to courier the talk himself after Watts received the runners from Running Water Town advising of Dragging Canoe's death.

These events were a burden for Chief Young Tassel, as he desired peace with the settlers, but he also desired that his people would be successful in defending their way of life. He would not take that responsibility lightly, and it would change the relationship between him and Governor William Blount. Additionally, he needed to draw closer to his uncle, Chief Doublehead, who was unhappy that it was Young Tassel, and not he, chosen by the people to lead the Chickamauga. Doublehead was proud and haughty, with a bold, fearless spirit, and continued to be ready to wreak havoc on the settlements. Doublehead would continue to lead his own faction of the Lower Cherokee from Coldwater Town; however, he did often cooperate on expeditions with Young Tassel.[59]

Even so, the center of Chickamauga activity was in the Five Lower Towns of the lower Tennessee River. A good description of them was written as an attachment to David Craig's March 15, 1792, report to Governor Blount:

> Running Water lies on the south bank of the Tennessee, except five or six huts which are on the north side, three miles above Nickajack and twelve below the Suck [of the Tennessee River]; here some Shawanese are settled, containing one hundred huts in 1790, and is a common crossing place for the Creeks.
>
> Nickajack lies on the south bank of the Tennessee, five miles above the long Island village, and fifteen miles below the Suck, contained about forty huts in 1790; some Shawanese settled here in 1789 and 1790; here the Creeks and Northwards cross.
>
> Long Island Village, which comprehends an island called Long Island in the Tennessee, and a number of huts on the south side, is twenty miles below the Suck, and ten above Crowtown, contained ten or twelve huts in 1790; here the Creeks and Northwards cross.
>
> Crow Town lies on the north side of the Tennessee, half a mile from the river, up Crow creek; 30 miles below the Suck is the lowest town in the Cherokee nation, contained about 30 huts in 1790; the creeks [sic] and northward tribes cross here.
>
> Look-out Mountain town, on Look-out Mountain creek, lies between two mountains, 15 miles from the mouth of the creek, about 15 miles to the southward of the running water; contains 80 huts. A valley leads from the mouth of this creek, three or four miles wide, to this town.

> The warriors of these five towns are now computed at from two hundred and fifty to three hundred, and are, generally, that part of the Cherokees distinguished as the Chickamaugas.
>
> The Running Water, the upper of the four on the river, is about one hundred and fifty miles from this place [Knoxville], and the river may be passed in large canoes at all seasons.
>
> Chatanuga mountain, which lies to the southeast of these towns, can be passed at several places, either by cavalry or infantry, with but very little difficulty, if not opposed. The base of it is said not to exceed two miles, and the height not very great.
>
> It was in trying to pass this mountain that General Martin was repulsed in the year 1790.[60]

Even though the Chickamauga settlement was called the Five Lower Towns, there were several other adjacent villages. Young Tassel centered his life at Will's Town (Wiliyi), later referred to as Watt's Town, and the renowned Sequoya lived there when he created the Cherokee alphabet years later. (Will's Town was located just south of present-day Fort Payne, Alabama. It was named after its first headman, Chief Will Weber, a red-headed, mixed-blood Cherokee.)

Dragging Canoe's brother, Little Owl, operated a ferry at Nickajack and on March 15 became the headman of Running Water Town.

The leaders of the Lower Cherokee were Young Tassel, Bloody Fellow, Little Owl, Turtle at Home, Glass, Bench, and Doublehead, who still led his own faction. Though Doublehead did not live in the Chickamauga community, he was still loosely referred to as a Chickamauga chief because of the similarity of their actions.

Chief Doublehead's sect of the Chickamauga lived along the Muscle Shoals of the Tennessee River. This is about a 40-mile section of the river that stretches from near present-day Guntersville, Alabama, to the Mississippi border. He first established Oka Kapassa (Coldwater Town) near the mouth of Big Spring Creek (Coldwater Creek). (Coldwater Town was across the Tennessee River from present-day Florence, Alabama, near Tuscumbia. This was near the tail end of the Muscle Shoals. The Big Spring Creek location of Coldwater Creek is not to be confused with the Coldwater Creek that runs north to the Tennessee River east of State Highway 79 at Guntersville, Alabama.)

Doublehead relocated in the late 1770s to Doublehead's Town near the head end of the Muscle Shoals. He would live there until 1802. (Doublehead's Town was located 10 miles west of present-day Decatur, Alabama, at the Mallard-Fox Creek Wildlife Management Area, County Road 400 [Mallard Creek Road].) Bench (Robert Benge) reportedly took some 45 scalps during the late Cherokee wars in the 1790s; however, his notorious granduncle Doublehead may have taken twice that number.

Interestingly, Doublehead's two oldest daughters, Tuskiahooto and Salechiee were married to George Colbert, a Chickasaw chief. That was an interesting dynamic in that the Chickasaw had befriended the Cumberland settlers whom Doublehead despised. (Tuskiahooto died in 1837; however, Chief George Colbert and Salechiee were relocated to Indian Territory, Oklahoma, shortly thereafter.)

The action in the settlements began to pick up for the young warriors soon after Dragging Canoe's death. They had watched the older chiefs make their treaties for decades and then observed the settlers break them. The Chickamauga Cherokee went about their business of punishing the settlers for their years of harsh treatment of the Cherokee people and for their encroachment onto Cherokee land. Many of the young Chickamauga chiefs and warriors were mixed-blood descendants of white traders or soldiers, but they were 100 percent Cherokee in thought and spirit. Earlier chapters show that, as in the old Cherokee traditions, they believed war to be their profession, and these young warriors were ready to reclaim that distinction.

On March 5, 1792, 25 Chickamauga warriors attacked Brown's Station and killed four young boys. Then on March 12, they killed a Mr. McMurray at his plantation at the mouth of the Stones River (where it enters the Cumberland from the south at Nashville, across from present-day Peeler Park).

Shawnee Warrior led his band and some Creek braves to attack a group of boats on the Tennessee River in April. They killed two white men and captured a boy and two women.

On April 5, 1792, a war party killed a Mrs. Radcliffe and her three children near where McMurray had been killed one month earlier.

Yet in the spring of 1792, Bench paid a visit to the upper Holston. On the 6th of April, he attacked Harper Ratcliff's house in Stanley Valley about twelve miles from present-day Rogersville, Tennessee. The warriors killed Ratcliff's wife and three children, and then withdrew to the nearby mountains. Bench left three war clubs, a bow, and sheaf of arrows at the massacre site to proclaim war on the Holston settlements. Captain James Cooper led a company of militia from the Mero District to scout the vicinity of Stanley Valley to find and confront Bench, but they did not see him.

On April 8, 1792, Chickamauga warriors killed eight men, including Benjamin Williams, along the Cumberland; then they tomahawked a young girl to death near Nashville on May 13.

In the middle of May, it was time to prepare for the first distribution of the Cherokee's revised annual annuity. Governor William Blount would take care of this at Coyatee, at the juncture of the Little Tennessee and Tennessee Rivers, with many leaders of the Lower Cherokee to be present. (This is the session that is confused with the timing of Young Tassel's notification that Dragging Canoe had died [see earlier this chapter] and where some actions were accomplished involving Bloody Fellow that were attributed to his visit with the president and the secretary of war in Philadelphia [also see earlier this chapter].)

Young Tassel worked to make the conference a historic event. He prepared elaborate quarters for the reception of Governor Blount and hoisted the United States flag at its front. Chiefs Breath of Nickajack, Richard Justice of Lookout Mountain Town, Charley of Running Water Town, and several other chiefs and warriors arrived on Saturday, the 19th. They wore black paint sprinkled with flour that represented they had been at war but were ready for peace.

The chiefs paraded to the flagpole led by Bloody Fellow, Young Tassel, and Captain John Chisholm. Warriors fired volleys from their rifles to salute the flag.

Governor Blount was to arrive on Sunday, the 20th. Young Tassel and Bloody Fellow had requested that Blount notify them when he neared, and a young warrior met him while yet one-half of a mile away. The warrior, very well dressed and on horseback, held him at that location until they were notified that the chiefs were ready to receive him. Shortly thereafter, a messenger invited them to proceed. There were two thousand Cherokee chiefs and warriors arranged in two 300-yard-long lines. They fired salutes to the governor as he entered the alley between the lines, and they kept firing as he proceeded to the end where he was received by Young Tassel and Bloody Fellow.

After a few days of preliminaries, the meeting was opened by Governor Blount on Wednesday, May 23, 1792:

BROTHERS, CHIEFS, AND WARRIORS, OF THE CHEROKEES:
It is now near a year since I had first the pleasure to meet you in council, and to form a treaty with you on the part of the United States, the object of which was the benefit of both parties.

Since that event, your nation, in a grand council, held at the beloved town of Estanaula, appointed deputies, namely: the Bloody Fellow, Nontuaka, the Old Prince, the Jobber's Son, Captain George, and other good men, to wait on the President, himself, and to ask him whether he has authorized me to form a treaty with you, and, if he had, to solicit him, on your part, to give you one thousand five hundred dollars per annum, the same as the Creeks receive for their lands, instead of one thousand, as stipulated by the treaty.

The President answered you, that he had authorized me to make a treaty with you; that he had approved and ratified it; that he had instructed me not to stipulate for the payment of more than one thousand dollars per annum; but that he himself would give you one thousand five hundred dollars per annum for your lands, for which sum you are in future to receive....

Here, brothers, I think it proper to inform you, that the President has been pleased to direct that the Bloody Fellow shall, in future, be known and distinguished by the more honorable name of General Eskaqua [Clear Sky]....

I shall now speak about the objects of the present meeting: it is to divide the goods of the first annual payment for your lands, to talk about the proceedings at Philadelphia ... and about what has happened since the treaty.

The division of the goods is with yourselves; I have nothing to do with it; but I am glad to hear that you have determined, that the four Lower Towns shall have a large share of them, and that so many of the people of the Lower Towns are here ready to receive them. If they had as generally attended the treaty, they would have had a full share of the goods they paid the nation. That they did not get a full share, the fault was their own.

Thanks and credit are due to the Badger for his talk, respecting the division of those goods....

What has happened since the treaty has appeared in a very bad light to the white people. With difficulty I have restrained those whose relations have been killed and scalped, or made prisoners, and those whose horses have been stolen, from falling on the Indians, without regard to age or sex, and taking, instantly, what they termed satisfaction.

Since the treaty have been killed, wounded, or made prisoners, the persons described as follows.... [Governor Blount then details several attacks of those that had been made throughout the settlements.]

I did not say, Brothers, your people have done all these murders, and stole all these horses, because I do not positively know. But, from a variety of circumstances, suspiscion [sic] falls on the people of your Lower towns, and the Creeks. I write General McGillivray, and make the same complaints....

My brothers, you must exert yourselves to restrain your young people, as well as all others, from such acts. Attend to what General Eskaqua, and his associate deputies, shall tell you: they will tell you how much the President loves you, and how earnestly he wishes you to do well and be happy....

Now, my Brothers, I have to inform you, that, to secure the white people of the frontiers against the further depredations of your bad people, I have been forced to order out a part of the militia upon the frontiers, from Holston to Clynch, and up Clynch, and upon the frontiers of Cumberland....

[Several chiefs, including Young Tassel, Hanging Maw, and Breath rose and spoke briefly pledging their support.]

Finding the nation, in general, so apparently disposed for peace, and Eskaqua, and the other chiefs, soliciting me very earnestly to give a part of the goods in my possession, in addition to those they had received at Philadelphia, I agreed to it, believing they could never be disposed of more advantage to the United States.[61]

(It should be noted that the annuity was spoken of in terms of goods. This was always the request of the chiefs. They were well aware that there was no common currency for the United States [and there would not be until the time of President Abraham Lincoln]. The individual states offered their own scrips for a few years, and then it was issued by individual private banking institutions, thus there was no consistency for several decades. It would have been entirely possible that, had the Cherokee taken the annuity in scrip, whenever they tried to redeem it, the trader might have easily cheated them claiming a particular bank's scrip was not as valuable as indicated. The deliverance of the annuity in goods also benefitted the United States government since it was up to the chiefs to distribute the goods as they saw fit.)

At that point, as mentioned earlier in this chapter, governor Blount believed Young Tassel had received a request to meet with the Spanish in Pensacola. The Governor quickly reverted from his extreme optimism to almost total dejection. His words exhibit that he did not fully appreciate what was at stake for the Cherokee.

It was quite obnoxious of the United States to give a name to a Cherokee chief and warrior, and seemingly set him above the others, and ask the Cherokee Nation to heed his words. Additionally, when Blount spoke of restraining the whites whose kin had been killed, scalped, or captured, he provoked a quandary for Cherokee warriors. Culture and tradition led them to expect the kin would want retribution, such as a Cherokee clan member would, and they were prepared to deal with that. As in olden times, the Cherokee warriors realized that was a part of war, and a part of defending ancestral lands, and they were not fearful of vengeful whites. A Cherokee chief would never have been allowed to restrain a clansman from retribution. Likely, the Cherokee warriors believed this to be another sign of weakness among the whites. Regardless, many of those present at the conference would yet make expeditions into the settlements and wreak havoc on the inhabitants.

Governor Blount prepared to leave Coyatee for his home, and Chief Young Tassel reassured him he would meet him in ten nights at Knoxville. The chief was to spend several days there, and then escort the governor through the wilderness to Nashville. Blount had invited Young Tassel to be present at a conference that would involve the Chickasaw and Choctaw Nations on August 7, 1792. However, the governor was only a few hours out of Coyatee when Young Tassel was approached by a runner.

(Scotsman William Panton had immigrated to Charleston before the American Revolution. He had acquired large estates in South Carolina and Georgia that were confiscated at an early period of the war. He then established himself as a merchant and trader in Pensacola when the Spanish captured it in 1781. He soon formed a commercial treaty with Spain. It not only enriched him, but it also strengthened the relationship between Pensacola's Spanish governor Arthur O'Neill and the southern Indian tribes. Panton introduced Creek chief Alexander McGillivray to Governor O'Neill, and Panton continued to be a friend and confident of both and a great intermediary for their trade.)

Panton had written Young Tassel on March 2, 1792, from John McDonald's home in the Lower Towns. That letter is what Young Tassel received from the runner at Coyatee. Panton invited Young Tassel and Bloody Fellow, in the name of Governor O'Neill, to go to Pensacola with ten pack horses. There the Spanish would provide them with ample ammunition and arms, and Panton would himself supply many other trade goods at the expense of the Spanish.

The Spanish then were offering to help the Cherokee reclaim their lands; however, the offer of assistance would have to be covert, so as not to become an international embarrassment.

When Young Tassel received the letter, he left Coyatee and went to John McDonald's house at Turkey Town. McDonald wrote letters of commendation for Young Tassel and the young chief's nephew, Nettle Carrier (Tahlonteskee), to present to Governor O'Neill. McDonald and Panton were aware that both chiefs were nephews of Old Tassel, and that would carry much weight with the Spaniards.

Bloody Fellow, Young Tassel, Nettle Carrier, and Young Dragging Canoe (Dragging Canoe's son) set out on the long trek. Bloody Fellow really desired to go; however, he kept thinking about the prestige he had gained with the president, the secretary of war, and Governor Blount. The honors and gifts he had received were too much to ignore; subsequently, he rode as far as the Coosa River, changed his mind, and returned to the Lower Towns.

The Spanish wined and dined the chiefs for nearly three months and put on a convincing display of their assistance. Spanish West Florida governor Francisco Luis Héctor de Carondelet likely assisted O'Neill with the persuasion. It was a difficult position for Young Tassel. He was very close to establishing peace with the white people; however, he knew that treaties had never lasted long in the past, and he desired to do what was in the best interest of his people. Governor O'Neill treated the chief with the greatest respect, presented him many gifts, and conferred on him the title of colonel. At that point, Young Tassel was committed to receive the proffered Spanish support and to aggressively approach the Cherokee problem of encroachment. Nettle Carrier, also won over, immediately painted himself black, raised a tomahawk, gave a war whoop, and declared himself for battle against the United States. (A detailed account of some of these affairs is recorded in the American State Papers, Indian Affairs, Vol. 1, pages 288–291. The Spanish even promised troops to Cherokee leader Richard Finnelson; however, they could not realistically afford such open support for a Cherokee rebellion.)

In the meantime, Shawnee Warrior was irked at the Chickamauga. He did not like such cat and mouse politics and thought it a weakness. He was so irate that some of his warriors reportedly thrashed Chief Fool Charles of Running Water Town who had accompanied Watts to Coyatee. (Sometimes this warrior is reported as Captain Charley, and could be Celarley of Running Water Town who did attend the talks at Coyatee. Captain Charley is the name of a warrior killed later, on June 12, 1793, by Captain John Beard.)[62]

On the morning of May 24, 1792, General James Robertson and his son, Jonathan, were astride their horses at the spring near their house. Warriors fired shots from the nearby brush and canebrake and each was wounded: the general with a shot that entered his arm at the wrist and exited near his elbow, and Jonathan with a shot that shattered his hip. The general's wound caused him to drop his rifle, and as he tried to recover it he fell from his horse. The ruckus startled the horse which ran toward the barn. Two warriors rushed the general with raised tomahawks, and Jonathan made a remarkable shot with his rifle. The ball passed through one warrior and hit the second. The two of them, however, were able to retreat to safety. Shortly thereafter, a boy was killed down the road from the Robertson residence, and a young girl was massacred near Bluff Fort.

Subsequent to the conference at Coyatee, Cherokee principal chief Little Turkey announced there would be a Grand Council session at Estanaula to be held on June 26, 1792. The time came for the session, and many chiefs were present; however, Young Tassel and Bloody Fellow did not attend. Young Tassel declared openly he would be in Pensacola tending to business of trade, and Bloody Fellow averred he had to tend to an ill relative. Hanging Maw attended as chief of the Northern Towns, and Badger (Ocunna), one of Dragging Canoe's brothers, represented the Lower Towns. The session lasted from Tuesday, June 26, to Saturday, June 30, 1792. Some excerpts:

> Present, the Little Turkey, great beloved man of the whole nation; the Badger, beloved man of the Southern division; the Hanging Maw, beloved man of the Northern division; the Boot, the Black Fox, the Cabin, Path Killer, &c. head-men of the Little Turkey's town; Kiatchiskie, and Sour Mush, of Hightower; Nontuaka of Cheestie; Tiakakiskie, of Hiwassee; Richard Justice, and The Glass, of the Look-out Mountain town; the Thigh, of Celicae, the Big Bear, and the Kingfisher, of Estanaula; Charley of Alljoy; Nanotey, of Kautokey; the Terrapin, of Kiukee; the Breath, and his nephew, of Nickajack; Chickasautehe, of Big Savannah, and warriors; Chinabee, from the Natchez, and the Creeks; Leonard D. Shaw, Esquire, agent, resident in the Cherokee nation, and James Carey, interpreter.
>
> THE KINGFISHER, or Jobber's Son, moved, that Captain Chisolm's [sic] papers should be brought forward, who sent immediately for them.
>
> THE BLACK FOX desired the audience to sit still; that Governor Blount's letters were to be read immediately; and to-morrow they would have nothing to do but make their answers. Captain Chisolm then presented to the Little Turkey a letter from Governor Blount....
>
> Captain Chisholm then, in the name of the United States, delivered a prisoner boy, named Abe, into the hand of the Little Turkey.
>
> THE BLACK FOX—The Dragging Canoe has left the world. He was a man of consequence in his country. He was a friend both to his own and the white people. But his brother is still in place; and I mention now in public, that I intend presenting him with his deceased brother's medal; for he promises fair to possess sentiments similar to those of his brother, both with regard to the red and the white. It is mentioned here publicly, that both whites and reds may know it, and pay attention to him. Another person I also nominate as a head-man, Taloteeskie, who is to be considered in the place of the Corn Tassel. Though some of the young fellows of the nation, and the white people together, occasioned the Tassel to fall under a flag of truce, his talks shall not be forgot. We have, therefore, appointed this man to support his talks and we hope that both whites and reds will attend to him....
>
> THE LITTLE NEPHEW then delivered the sentiments of the whole....
>
> I make not the least doubt but some of the whites are the cause of the President's wishing to purchase our land; this we are sensible of: for we have proven it. The whites settle on our land, and improve till he is obliged to purchase: for we are not of force to drive them off. We apprehend he is ignorant of the proceedings of the frontiers, who impose on us. We will stop till to-morrow, and consult. We will then meet again. Do not leave the ground, until we have finished what we have to say in answer to the President's speeches....
>
> [Little Turkey then proposed a change in the approved boundary line from the previous treaty in favor of more land for the Cherokee, in return for which the Cherokee would give up the Long Island of the Holston.]

THE BADGER.—I have heard my oldest brother Governor Blount's talks. He sent my flesh and blood to me by Captain Chisolm and now we undertake to send my nephew the Black Fox of Estanaula, with the Breath, to go and get the prisoner which one of my family has got. The Governor speaks so clever to us. I think it is for the benefit of our country to get the prisoners; as one of them is in my family, (the Paint) I consider it my duty to have her given up. The murders the Governor mentions, and requests information of the perpetrators of, I shall give every notice in my power. I tell you it is the Usauleys, a town in the Creeks; every person knows the loose Creeks frequently pass through our towns and do these mischiefs, and it is impossible for us to prevent them....

A letter per despatch from Governor Blount was read, containing a request of the Little Turkey ... to despatch some of his people to Tuskegee, there to meet certain boats and canoes on their way to Cumberland, with goods for the Chickasaws and Choctaws, and to escort them through the muscle shoals; they readily complied with the request.[63]

Some insight may be gleaned from this meeting. Badger, a brother of Dragging Canoe, is considered the headman of the Southern Villages, and Hanging Maw of the Northern Villages. Further, Black Fox is a headman of Turkey Town under Little Turkey.

(There has always been some confusion on just who Black Fox is: some have said a son of Attakullakulla; others, his son-in-law. However, Badger, a son of Attakullakulla, is clear that Black Fox is his nephew, therefore a grandson of Attakullakulla, likely by a daughter. Black Fox's father may also be called Black Fox, but that is unlikely. Kingfisher and Jobber's Son are two names for the same warrior.)

The chiefs were concerned that no effort had been made to remove the Virginia settlers. They had great expectations of President Washington, Secretary Knox, and Governor Blount. They also were averse to regular settler traffic on the Tennessee River, and to a settlement at Muscle Shoals.

Black Fox pronounced a favorable eulogy of Dragging Canoe. He also nominated Nettle Carrier, a brother to Bench, to be the overall principal chief of the Cherokee Nation in place of Old Tassel, excepting Little Turkey. By nominating one of their number, the younger chiefs indicated they desired more of a voice.

As Governor Blount prepared for a treaty session with the Chickasaw and the Choctaw to be held in Nashville, he sought help from Little Turkey to secure boats laden with goods for the tribes as they would pass the Chickamauga at Muscle Shoals. "The Breath of Nickajack ... met the boats with the goods for the Chickasaw and the Choctaw conference, at Tuskegee; went on board one of them with Mr. Allison, and proceeded down to Nickajack; giving undoubted and strong proofs of his friendship for the United States, declared, if the boats should be attacked as they passed the Running Water, which there was great reason to expect, by the Shawanese warrior and his party, that he would assist in the defense of them."[64]

The Creek had harried the Cumberland settlements constantly for over a year, and, in the summer of 1792, they were joined by a small band of Chickamauga from the Running Water Town led by Chief Little Owl, and a band of Shawnee under Shawnee Warrior. (Badger spoke of Little Owl during his eulogy for Dragging Canoe when he referred to giving the late chief's medal to his brother, who was like-minded.)

On the morning of June 26, 1792, the same day that Little Turkey's conference was opened at Estanaula, several hundred warriors were in the locale of Ziegler's Station. The advance party was loitering in the vicinity of the fort. The warriors shot and killed Michael

Shaffer (sometimes Shaver) while he was hoeing in a field that adjoined the station. As some of the fort's inhabitants tried to collect Shaffer's body, the Indians fired upon them from ambush. The shots wounded Joel Eccles, Thomas Keefe, and Gabriel Black. They abandoned the effort and fled into the fort. The Indians remained nearby for a while, firing sporadically to unnerve the settlers, but finally withdrew to carry intelligence to the main war party. The occupants of the fort brought Shaffer's remains inside at sundown.

The people in the area were alarmed, and 30 from smaller stations collected at Ziegler's. The inhabitants apparently retired early; however, they imprudently left no guards on duty.

About ten o'clock that night, Shawnee Warrior and Little Owl directed a furious attack against the fortification and set the buildings ablaze. The fire spread to the blockhouse where 21 settlers were taking cover. Mrs. Wilson begged her husband to take their 12-year-old son and flee. She believed that her life, and those of their five young daughters and one young son, would be spared. He did so, and although wounded, successfully escaped into the forest under the cover of darkness. His family was captured; young Zacheus was claimed by Little Owl.

Jacob Ziegler tried to seek safety in his loft and was burned to death. Archie Wilson fought hard, but was wounded. He had retreated for a ways, but eventually he was found and tomahawked to death. He was located the next morning 100 yards from the station.

Mrs. Ziegler escaped into the nearby forest with one child whom she quieted by jamming a handkerchief into his mouth. The Zieglers' three daughters, Mary, Elizabeth, and Hannah, were captured and claimed by Shawnee Warrior. The station was destroyed, and along with the Wilsons and the Zieglers, a Molly Jones and two unidentified black women were captured. One of the latter had been killed as the warriors retreated, apparently because she could not keep up the pace.

Mrs. Wilson's brother, Colonel James White of White's Station (present-day Knoxville), heard of her capture and that of the Wilson children. He was able to arrange a ransom for the freedom of those in the Lower Cherokee Towns. However, his niece, Sarah Wilson, was held by the Creek and remained captive for years. After she was finally returned, she maintained many of the Creek customs and cultural mores that she had developed during her captivity. The Zeigler girls were later ransomed from Shawnee Warrior for $58 each.

On June 27, General James Winchester (a brother-in-law to Gabriel Black who was wounded trying to rescue Shaffer's body) and Colonel Edward Douglass led a pursuit of the war party. Captain John Carr, John Harpool, and Peter Loony were sent ahead to scout. They followed the trail across the Cumberland River, and then they tailed the war party up Barton's Creek (about three miles downstream of present-day Lebanon). They found twenty-one packs of pillage from the station neatly tied up and hung from tree limbs. The bounty had been carefully protected from the weather with strips of peeled bark. The warriors were short of horses, and made the stash until a detachment could return to the settlements and steal a sufficient number of animals to transport their booty. In the meantime, the main war party hurried on with the prisoners.

The militia caught up with the scouts and sent a unit back with the captured goods. The small division was also to warn the settlers to watch for possible horse thieves. The main body continued to follow their prey's trail. The men stopped to rest and drink at a big spring (in present-day Lebanon). Later, they came to a small stream that crossed the path. They saw tracks of the barefoot captured children, and nearby they noticed the warm embers of a recent small fire at an apparent rest stop. Scraps of dressed deerskins were scattered around, indicating the Indians had made moccasins for the children. Farther down the trail, they found small moccasin footprints in some mud.

The militia camped that night at Martin's Spring. The next morning, they came to the place where the Indians had established a big camp for the first night. The warriors apparently had a one and one-half day's lead, so General Winchester advised they abandon the chase. He thought the Indians might kill the captives if they were pushed.

As they followed their back trail, they discovered hoof prints that signified the Indian detachment had returned for the stash.

When Mrs. Wilson returned from captivity, she related that the advance party of warriors halted with the captives at the Duck River to await the detachment they expected to have the plunder. An argument developed when that group arrived, and it grew into a fracas. Knives and tomahawks were drawn as the two parties threatened each other. Cooler heads prevailed, and the braves went home with their captives.[65]

Governor Blount arrived in Nashville in mid–July 1792 to preside at the Chickasaw and Choctaw conference. He had many plans for the meeting and directed some of his attention toward the safety of the Nashville settlements. He was made aware of all the recent activities, including those involving Shawnee Warrior and Little Owl.

Blount planned to utilize South Carolina brigadier general Andrew Pickens to assist in conveying the government's position to the Indians and also to explain the Indians' position to him. He wrote a letter to Secretary of War Henry Knox on July 4, 1792, prior to his visit, that explained what was on his mind:

> I have other information of parties of Creeks, and Cherokees too, having gone to Cumberland with declared intentions of hostility, particularly a fellow called the Pumpkin Boy, of the Look-out mountain, a brother of Doublehead, a rising popular character among the young warriors....
>
> These continued depredations, and the continued militia infantry turning out into actual service with great tardiness and reluctance, have induced me to order out a troop of cavalry for the protection of the frontiers, for a three months' tour, unless sooner discharged, which also serves as an escort to General Pickens and myself through the wilderness.
>
> I have not heard any thing lately which warrants an assurance that, the Chickasaws or Choctaws will turn out and join the arms of the United States, or the contrary; but I am informed that John Thompson, the late interpreter to the Cherokees, who will be at the Conference, is instructed by his great friend, the Little Turkey, to oppose it.[66]

Blount arrived at Nashville with 300 militiamen who comprised several companies under the command of Major Anthony Sharp to protect the frontiers. Sharp had been a major in the South Carolina State Militia that was assigned to the Continental Army during the war. The companies were positioned in the several small stations throughout the area.

Pickens was, at the time, a South Carolina state senator, and was still used by the United States government as a de facto Indian agent for special situations. He had developed a rapport with the southern nations, especially the Cherokee, Choctaw, and Chickasaw.

Late in the summer of 1792, Ensign William Snoddy led a 34-man scouting party near Horseshoe Bend of Caney Fork River where they had heard Shawnee Warrior was ranging with his band. They happened upon a large camp where the warriors had apparently left no sentries. However, while the militia was engaged with gathering the goods left behind,

Snoddy spotted an Indian meandering down the hill toward the camp with his rifle on his shoulder. He was apparently the only guard, and had been reconnoitering. The warrior, startled by the unexpected visitors, retreated to a nearby canebrake.

As it was late in the day, Snoddy led his force across the river and selected a hill on the south shore for a defensive campsite. The encampment was arranged in the form of a semi-circle with the ends against the bluff toward the Indians' camp, and it sufficiently enclosed the company's baggage and horses. Snoddy posted nighttime sentinels in the rain, and the men rested; however, they were not permitted to sleep due to their precarious position.

They could hear several groups of warriors returning to camp after dark, and, apparently alerted by their guard who had seen the whites, the Indians spent the night hooting like owls, barking like dogs and foxes, and screaming like panthers. The noise caused the militia's horses to become restless, and their whinnying gave away the position of Snoddy's force. The war party attacked at dawn following a ritualistic intimidation tactic. It began with a high-pitched yell, thought to have been emitted by Shawnee Warrior, followed by an eerie silence for several minutes. Then the unseen warriors united with a chorus of war whoops. Three of the militiamen became so frightened, they deserted through the brush. The attackers had crept to within 40 yards of the militia line before they were discovered. Their priming had become moist in the dampness, so most of their guns misfired on the first volley. Snoddy had ordered his men to protect their priming through the night, and they returned a devastating fire. The skirmish lasted for one hour. Once the warriors withdrew, Snoddy discovered that David Scoby and Nathan Latimer had been killed. Andrew Steel and Captain William Reid were badly wounded, and there was no sign of the deserters.

Many warriors had been killed or wounded, but no count was attempted. One of the dead was apparently a minor chief. As soon as James Madell had fired while behind a tree, he noticed that the chief was lying on the ground and loading his rifle. Madell loaded two balls into his own gun, and waited for the chief to rise for a shot. Both balls hit the chief when he raised his head to look for a target. (Horseshoe Bend of Caney Fork River is about four miles northwest of where the river crosses U.S. Highway 705, and about 60 miles east by southeast of Nashville. The militia was likely patrolling a large area in the vicinity south of present-day Center Hill Lake.)

Near Bledsoe's Station on August 31, 1792, John Berkley was working his peach orchard assisted by his son, John Berkley, Jr. Suddenly, a small war party emerged from some nearby brush, attacked, killed, and scalped the younger Berkley. John Berkley was wounded, but survived and managed to shoot and kill the warrior who slew his son.

Young Tassel returned from Pensacola in late August and immediately sent Little Owl to summon all headmen to a council at Will's Town. Young Tassel reportedly returned with seven packhorses, but it may have been ten since that is what he was invited to take with him.

Will's Town, the home of Young Tassel and Bloody Fellow, was about 30 miles from Running Water Town which had become the home of Dragging Canoe in his later years.

On the appointed day, September 2, Cherokees from all parts of the nation came to hear the chief's report, and to attend the coinciding Green Corn Dance. It was a Grand Council and was quite somber. Young warriors could hardly contain themselves with their enthusiasm. Young Tassel explicitly explained the courtesies of Governor O'Neill, who assured him the Spaniards never desired the Creek or Cherokee land. They preferred to reside along the coast rather than dwell inland. He continued that the governor declared the Americans first take your land, then make treaties, and give very little in the bargain. O'Neill explained to Young Tassel that the Spanish king had sent much powder, lead, and arms for the four southern nations, and that it was time for them to join quickly in war against the United States because it was busily engaged in war with the Indians to the north. He further stated that, if they did not act quickly, the United States would attack them after the whites had conquered the northern tribes.

Young Tassel then announced that since the young warriors always wanted war, it was time for them to try themselves. The chief believed there were plenty of Cherokee warriors, but he was happy the Creeks, Choctaws, Shawnee, and the Spaniards were with them.

Bloody Fellow risked much to be the first to rise and speak against war in this hawkish gathering. He avowed it was a bad step to go to war. He displayed the United States flag and asked the warriors to notice the stars. He explained those stars did not represent mere towns, but 13 small individual nations. He averred that the Americans were very strong, and were united as one man: "You had better take my talk, and stay at home, and mind your women and children."

Nettle Carrier rose next and stated that it was he who was asked to be made principal chief in the place of his uncle Old Tassel at Estanaula. (He was referring to the Grand Council in June—see earlier this chapter.) He then declared that he had been to Pensacola with Young Tassel and would hold fast to the talk of Governor O'Neill.

Bloody Fellow tried again. He held his silver medal in his hand, and displayed his coat with silver epaulets, and his scarlet match coat with broad silver lace. He asked: "When was the day that you went to your old brother [Stuart] and brought back the like of this?"

Thereupon Young Tassel removed his own medal and threw it on the ground. He stood and said he would send a runner to fetch in his Creek allies. The warriors painted their bodies black and did a war dance around Bloody Fellow's United States flag. They danced all night. At one point, some of them began to fire rifles at the flag, but Bloody Fellow threatened to kill any who continued.

The next day, Bloody Fellow tried once more to influence the decision: "I would wish none of you to go to war, but lay at peace, as I intend to do myself."

While Bloody Fellow was still standing, Little Owl interrupted and said: "My father was a man, and I am as good a man as he was. To war I will go, and spill blood in spite of what you say."

Whereupon Watts took him by the hand and said: "You are a man. I like your talk. To war we will go together."

Then, with Bloody Fellow still standing, Shawnee Warrior arose and addressed him: "With these hands I have taken the lives of three hundred men, and now the time has come when I shall take the lives of three hundred more; then I will be satisfied and sit down in peace. I will now drink my fill of blood."

Bloody Fellow sullenly responded: "If you will go to war you must go; I will not."[67]

On the third day, Young Tassel led all warriors to Lookout Mountain Town from where they were to begin an expedition into the Cumberland settlements the next morning. When they arrived, they heard that White Mankiller (Malachi Watts, Young Tassel's brother) had brought whiskey from Knoxville and was 15 miles away at the mouth of Lookout Mountain Creek. They sent a messenger to tell White Mankiller to bring the drink to Lookout Mountain Town. They got drunk and delayed their expedition for a few days. Half-blooded Cherokee Richard Finnelson and Frenchman Joseph De Raque, who were actually spies for Governor Blount, pretended that they were spies for the Spanish and declared that Governor O'Neill ordered them to spy out the Cumberland to tell Young Tassel the best way to organize the attacks. The war parties waited another ten days before they decided they were wasting their time. It was well into September before they began the campaign.

The Creek, and Chief Doublehead, had not let up on their attacks, but now the Chickamauga Cherokee would be rejoining them.[68]

At the Green Corn Festival in Chota on September 10, the Upper Village chiefs warned Southwest Territory governor William Blount of Young Tassel's new army, his Spanish suppliers, and that he was planning attacks in the settlements to be carried out yet that summer. He proceeded to warn the settlements, whereupon General James Robertson at Nashville declared he would gather a force and attack the Chickamauga as he had done before. Blount dispatched Captain Samuel Handly to lead a company of 42 to help defend the Cumberland settlements.

Young Tassel also heard Robertson's comments and quickly planned a strategy for the expedition. The Cherokee did not just blindly attack as they would have done had they been ignorant savages, as they were identified by the settlers, but they made intricate battle plans that rivaled those of the most intelligent white military commanders.

Young Tassel decided to throw the settlements off with a red herring before he continued with his plans for the attack. He convinced chiefs Bloody Fellow and Glass, who opposed the war, to write Governor Blount letters to throw him off guard. The chiefs avowed that they had heard of General Robertson's warning during the Chickasaws and Choctaws conference that, at the first sign of settlement blood caused from Chickamauga country, he would come and sweep it clean with their blood. Bloody Fellow and Glass averred that their young warriors resolved to attack Nashville, but Young Tassel cautioned them to end such talk. They said that Young Tassel instructed them to go home and hunt to feed their families.

Governor Blount received the letters of Bloody Fellow and Glass on September 13, 1792. He was completely deceived, and on the 14th, he again wrote General Robertson that his direct correspondence from Glass and Bloody Fellow indicated a desire for peace. He advised Robertson to exercise patience and leniency with the Indians. He ordered Robertson to relieve the militia from their active musters, and said: "I heartily congratulate you and the District of Mero upon the happy change of affairs."[69]

Young Tassel's strategy was to attack the Cumberland settlements first, then work east until his forces had taken the Watauga settlements. He, himself, would lead 300 Cherokee warriors, plus many Creek, who would be captained by Talotiskee of Broken Arrow (not to be confused with the Cherokee chief Nettle Carrier, see below). He would also have Shawnee Warrior as one of his captains along with his band, which included Tecumseh. Other leaders working under Young Tassel would include Little Owl, Pumpkin Boy (Doublehead's brother), and Black Fox (Little Owl's nephew). That large group would attack the Cumberland settlements.

Chief Doublehead liked his nephew's moxie and agreed to work with him. He, Young

10. The Final Onslaught

Tassel's nephew, Talotiskee (Nettle Carrier) would lead a band of 100 men and set up ambushes along the road from Nashville to Kentucky. Others have indicated that Bench assisted with that effort. (Bench was likely not there as he was reportedly on a raid in the Virginia settlements. See later this chapter.) Chief Middlestriker (Oonoyahka) of Will's Town would help to further isolate Nashville by setting up similar ambushes along the road from Nashville to Knoxville.

A few days after Blount had bridled Robertson, he received information, likely a messenger from Richard Finnelson, of an alarming consequence out of the Chickamauga towns. He immediately sent a courier to Nashville with the following message: "The danger is imminent, delay not an hour."[70]

Finnelson arrived at Nashville at the same time as the courier. Finnelson told General Robertson that Young Tassel was on his way and that the letter Blount received from Glass and Bloody Fellow was a fake. Finnelson sensed some doubt on Robertson's part, so he volunteered that, if the Chickamauga did not appear, he could be jailed and hanged. The courier's message from Blount did not alleviate Robertson's doubts because he knew the information therein likely originated with Finnelson. However, Blount ordered him to muster the militia, and he knew it was best to be safe. It would not be easy to inspire the militia again because the men had already wasted a lot of time on the previous muster only to learn it was a supposed false alarm.

The militia rallied and camped at Rains' Spring. Jacob and Abraham Castleman, along with other scouts, were sent out to reconnoiter. They patrolled as far as present-day Murfreesboro, Tennessee, where Chief Black Fox had maintained a hunting camp. The scouts returned and reported the camp was deserted with no sign of Indians between there and Nashville.

The disgruntled militia at Rains' Spring marched to Bluff Fort and disbanded. Another group of scouts consisting of John Rains, Abraham Kennedy, and two men named Clayton and Gee went over the same area previously covered by the Castlemans' party. They believed that Young Tassel would surely pass by Black Fox's known camp.

The scouts split up. Near present-day Lavergne, Tennessee, Clayton and Gee encountered Young Tassel who was dressed as a settler. Shortly behind him were a few warriors dressed in settler clothes. The charismatic chief, who could be very friendly and diplomatic, told the scouts he was the point for a militia company. He invited them to meet with the officers and discuss what they had encountered. The scouts were eager to do so, and they ran into seven hundred Chickamauga Cherokee, Creek, and Shawnee warriors. The scouts had no escape route and were easily killed. Rains and Kennedy saw no sign of Indians and returned with their report-no indications of danger. Finnelson was now getting nervous after his declaration.

Abraham Castleman was not convinced and molded a large supply of rifle balls. He filled his powder horn, cleaned his long rifle named "Betsey," picked his flint, and headed out. He pointedly stated that he was "going over to Buchanan's [Station] to see the enemy."[71]

After killing the two scouts, Young Tassel ordered his war party to conceal itself in the forest. He then sent his own outriders to perambulate the targeted area. While they rested, Shawnee Warrior told his followers that he had a vision that they would attack a fort. He stated that he would be shot in the forehead and averred it would be an honor to die in battle as his father had done.

The war party resumed its expedition at dawn September 30, 1792, and stopped one mile from Buchanan's Station. A few warriors were left in charge of the horses. At dusk, the Indians stealthily crept within sight of the fort. George Fields, a half-blood Cherokee, later declared that they saw the lanterns carried by the settlers as they moved around and could hear the horses and the cows. (Buchanan's Station, comprised of cabins and outbuildings surrounded by a picket stockade, was situated on a high hill overlooking the Cumberland River.)

As the warriors observed the station, a dispute ensued between Young Tassel and Shawnee Warrior (some report it was Tom Tunbridge, a white member of the war party, who had married a French woman, rather than the more likely Shawnee Warrior. Tom Tunbridge and his stepson, Kiachatalee, had taken young Joseph Brown into their home when the Brown family was attacked at Muscle Shoals. See Chapter 9).

Shawnee Warrior wanted to attack Buchanan's; however, Young Tassel insisted that doing so would cause an alert at Nashville. Tassel maintained they should bypass the station for the bigger prize at Bluff Fort. He stated they could always attack Buchanan's on the return. Shawnee Warrior was sure that, if they bypassed the station, the riflemen would come on their rear as they approached Nashville. However, they greatly outnumbered the garrison by 35 to 1, so that would likely not have been a danger.

The debate lasted for several hours until Young Tassel exasperatedly told Shawnee Warrior to go ahead and attack the fort with his own force, and threatened that he and the Chickamauga would not take part. Meanwhile, in the time leading up to the affair, Major John Buchanan had repaired the stockade and made other preparations. He had 20 well-armed men within the stockade: James Bryant, Thomas Wilcox, Jacob and Abraham Castelman, James O'Connor, James Mulherrin, Thomas McCrory, Morris Shane, William and Robin Kennedy, George Findleston, Samuel Blair, Charles Herd, Sampson Williams, Samuel McMurray, Robin Turnbull, Robin Hood, Thomas Latimer, Robin Thompson and Joe Durat—all renowned riflemen.

The moon shone brightly that night, and the sky was clear. Two sentinels discovered the warriors' approach at midnight and waited until the Indians were within range. They fired through some upper portholes and killed two warriors, one of which was Chief Shawnee Warrior who was shot in the forehead. The inhabitants were rudely alerted by the shots, and both sides opened fire. They battled furiously for one hour as the warriors attacked from all sides and repeatedly attempted to break the gate open.

A hole had been dug a few yards from the gate for the addition of a future outhouse. A few warriors took cover therein and sniped as they had occasion. Others used their bows to fire flaming arrows onto the roofs within the station. Meanwhile, the riflemen kept up a deadly barrage from the parapets. As the inhabitants had more portholes than they did riflemen, Mrs. Sallie Buchanan led other women to display hats sporadically from one opening to another to give the impression of a larger force.

Tom Tunbridge's stepson, Kiachatalee of Nickajack, a daring young chief whose talents and courage were much admired, quickly scaled to the roof of a cabin with a torch and was fatally shot. Before he died he unsuccessfully attempted to set the fort's palisades ablaze. His badly-burned body was found next morning. He was believed to have been the leader of a previous attack at Ziegler's Station (see earlier this chapter).

The Indians withdrew, having lost at least 14 warriors. Many dead and wounded had been carried away as exhibited by a bloody trail. Young Tassel had been severely wounded in both thighs, and Talotiskee of Broken Arrow was reportedly killed. Chief Little Owl was wounded by 11 rifle balls, but survived. The settlers found several swords, tomahawks, rifles, knives, and other items left by the withdrawing warriors. None of the whites had been killed or wounded.

It was a devastating defeat for Young Tassel regardless of who, Shawnee Warrior or Tom Tunbridge, caused the distraction of attacking Buchanan's Station. Chief Young Tassel might have exhibited a stronger position, gone ahead and moved the major portion of the war party to Nashville, and let those who wanted to do so stay and attack Buchanan's.

The next day General James Robertson and Captain John Rains led a company of 150 militiamen in pursuit of the attackers who, it was discovered, had separated into two parties. When the whites reached Stewart's Creek, they found that the war party was moving much faster, so they resigned the chase.

Doublehead had little activity while he monitored the Kentucky road, but he purportedly took two travelers' scalps then departed to assist Young Tassel at Nashville. On October 2, he participated in a skirmish with Captain William Snoddy's 34-man militia unit. Most of Doublehead's warriors were foraging away from camp. The next morning, Doublehead led most of his party to attack the militia encampment. Doublehead lost 13 warriors, while the militia suffered four killed. Reportedly, two messengers told Doublehead of Young Tassel's failure and had misinformed him that his nephew had been mortally wounded. Doublehead wept and declared vengeance for Young Tassel. Interpreter James Carey gave Governor Blount a long report of affairs that included:

> At Chota he met with three young fellows, just returned from the Cumberland ... Carey went then down to Coyatee, where he met with five other young warriors, with whom he entered into a confidential conversation, which lasted upwards of an hour; they informed him that they, with the three he had seen at Chota, and many others, had been out for war, with Talotiskee,* that they had waylaid the Kentucky road, until six travelers appeared, of whom they killed one ... they then turned off that road to the Cumberland road, and met with four fellows who had been with Watts in his repulse at Buchanan's Station, who gave them the particulars, upon which Talotiskee cried bitterly, then rose, and requested his men to divide into small parties to hunt ... deer....
>
> *The Talotiskee, who commanded the party on the Kentucky road, is a signer to the treaty of Holston, the same who was at Pensacola.[72]

(It is unimportant whether either Nettle Carrier or Doublehead received the messengers. They may each have done so separately as, with 100 warriors, they had often split into more than one group. Nettle Carrier was apparently not with Doublehead during the fighting with Captain Snoddy because the warriors that were with Nettle Carrier, and had talked later with interpreter Carey, made no mention of the battle in their detailed account. It is likely that each chief would have wept as Young Tassel was not only Doublehead's nephew, but also Nettle Carrier's uncle. Doublehead apparently had overall charge of the war party on the Kentucky Road, and Nettle Carrier acted as one of his captains. Thus, the footnote [*] on Carey's report is not in error, as Talotiskee was a captain on the Kentucky Road maneuver. Nettle Carrier was Doublehead's grandnephew and Bench's brother. It was Captain Snoddy, who a few weeks earlier, had a run-in with Shawnee Warrior on Horseshoe Bend of Caney Fork River—see earlier this chapter.)[73]

Breath and Charles (likely Captain Charley, but could be Celarley) also wrote a letter to Governor William Blount, and while it was dated September, 15, 1792, it was likely written on the 23rd. They diplomatically stated:

> We have heard your letter you sent to the Glass and the Bloody Fellow ... you mention that we ought to consider matters well, before beginning a war; it is very true; war is very bad, and I hope you nor us shall see no more of it, but live in peace.
>
> But we are sorry to inform you—you may think it is a lie, but we assure you it is the truth—that we are very sorry that ... there was a great number of Creeks passed by here for several days; it was out of our power to stop them; they said there was several hundreds crossed the river low down, and had with them 500 lbs. of powder and lead accordingly; they said they were going to Cumberlands ... young fellows, and indeed a great number of them boys.... We have told you of the Creeks always going, and we hope you will not let any of our people suffer for the bad doings of the Creeks....
>
> We heard that John Sevier says it will not be long before he sets out for war; that he is to come to this place, and that there is another warrior to come, with an army from Tugulo, in order to destroy the nation; such talks makes our young people very uneasy; we could wish that your warriors would not send such talks unless you intend to do so.[74]

Despite Breath's efforts to point the blame at the Creek, it was the Chickamauga Cherokee who were becoming very active. Prior to Young Tassel's expedition, on September 13, a young man named Cochran was returning to his father's house from Pistol Creek. A white man met him and engaged him in conversation during which time he was fired upon from ambush. Several rifle balls passed through his clothing without injuring him, and he escaped to the house. The family escaped out a back door and ran down the creek to alert neighbors.

On the 16th, Colonel George Gillespie and his two sons left Gillespie's Station to gather some corn. The same band of warriors attacked and killed Gillespie; then, they shot and killed the oldest son. They took the youngest son captive and a white man among them explained to him, in perfect English, they had to shoot his brother to make up for wasting powder and bullets a few days earlier when they missed a white boy.

Bench and his brothers, the Tail and Nettle Carrier, also became quite active at that time. In late September the Bench and the Tail passed through Hiwassee and declared they were going to kill John Sevier. On the 30th, Kenoteta (Rising Fawn) of Hiwassee penned a warning to Blount.[75]

On October 2, one and one-half hours after sundown, they attacked Black's Blockhouse on Crooked Creek where a small garrison from Captain Crawford's company was stationed. The warriors shot at some of the men who were sitting by a fire. George Moss and Robert Sharpe were instantly killed, and John Shankland was wounded. James Paul, who was in the blockhouse, was killed by a stray bullet. The warriors killed three horses and absconded with seven. They did not pursue the idea of killing John Sevier. (Black's Blockhouse was located at the head of Crooked Creek, a branch of Little River. Some have recorded that the attack took place one month earlier.)[76]

> On Monday, the 8th of October, William Stuart was killed about six miles from Nashville, on the north side of Cumberland. On the night of the same day, the Indians [typo corrected] burnt Stump's distillery, on White's Creek, on the north side of Cumberland; On the 9th of October, a party of Indians went to Sycamore Creek, eighteen miles from Nashville, and burnt the house of James Frazier, Mr. Riley and of Major Coffield, a large

10. The Final Onslaught

quantity of corn, and shot down a number of hogs. They then proceeded to Bushy Creek of Red River, where they burnt the house of Obadiah Roberts, and took off a number of horses; they were followed by a party of whites, who killed one of the Indians and regained the horses.[77]

Bloody Fellow discovered that his position was not very popular in the Lower Towns, and he had lost prestige with Governor Blount because of the letter he wrote to provide cover for Young Tassel. Late in October, Bloody Fellow, Glass, Breath, and their families went to Pensacola and returned with several packhorses laden with arms and ammunition for the Chickamauga. Bloody Fellow promised Spanish governor Miró that the Cherokee would attack the settlements. When he returned to Will's Town, he heard of Young Tassel's failed mission and the devastating loss of several leaders. However, Young Tassel was healing quickly. Strangely, he joked about the failed campaign and his wound.

On November 8, 1792, Governor Blount wrote a report to Secretary of War Knox that included: "On Monday night last, five Creeks, headed by young Lesley, the son of a Scotchman in the Creek nation ... came in upon the waters of Little river ... and stole and carried off eight horses; they were chased toward Chilhowie, the nearest Cherokee town. This gave reason to suspect the Chilhowie Indians of the theft: whereupon, as many as fifty-two ... assembled together in arms ... and actually did march; but General Sevier received information of their intentions, and despatched [sic] orders to them to disperse, and return home."[78]

(Lesley was the "white man" referred to in the attacks on the Cochran and Gillespie families in September.)

Middlestriker of Will's Town led an expedition of 60 Chickamauga, Creek, and Shawnee warriors to set up ambushes along Walton Road, in the neighborhood of Crab Orchard, in the Cumberlands. White Mankiller (Young Tassel's brother Malachi Watts) and Shawnee chief Tecumseh were with him. Tecumseh, mourning the loss of his brother, Shawnee Warrior, apparently wanted one last expedition before he left to assist his own people in their northern conflicts with the whites.

In the meantime Captain Samuel Handley led a 42-man company into the wilderness at Southwest Point and followed Walton Road to the west. Middlestriker's war party found his trail and fell in behind him. That night, while the militia was in camp, the Indians quietly passed it by and set an ambush at Spenser's Hill in Crab Orchard. On November 23, 1792 (some report the 25th), Handley approached, and his company received a devastating volley from the attackers. Three were killed, and the rest, except for Handley, escaped to Southwest Point.

Captain Handley desperately tried to rally his men, but they were on the run. In the confusion, the captain saw Trooper Leiper on foot and surrounded, so Handley attempted to rescue him. The warriors, however, shot Handley's horse from under him, and he was quickly surrounded by a crowd of Indians. He fought them hand to hand with his saber and eventually jumped behind a tree. Arthur Archibald "Archie" Coody, Jr., a half-blood Cherokee interpreter, was waiting for such a move: "Handley was immediately surrounded by Indians, furiously brandishing their uplifted tomahawks, the signal of death or submission. He jumped behind a tree, and was met by a warrior, who held over him a tomahawk, in the act of striking. He arrested the stroke, by seizing the weapon, with the cry 'Canawlla'—friendship. 'Canawlla' was responded by the Indian, who instantly began to seek his rescue."[79]

Tecumseh Saving Prisoners from Torture and Death in the North (Artist: John Reuben Chapin, Engraver: James Charles Armytage, 1860).

Handley surrendered to him. Coody accepted him as his prisoner, but then had to protect him from several eager warriors. Handley received numerous strokes from the flat of a tomahawk, was nearly gored by his own saber in the hands of a warrior, and was missed by a rifle shot. Eventually, Coody was able to hustle his captive to Chief Middlestriker.

Captain Handley was taken to Will's Town. The inhabitants required him to run the gauntlet, and he suffered other harsh treatment for about two weeks. A grand council was held on December 6, 1792, to determine his fate. On the third day, the chiefs decided to let him live and to discontinue his punitive treatment. The Indians, then, treated him more like a brother.

It is said that Shawnee chief Tecumseh spoke forcefully in his favor to bring about the final decision. Young Tassel had Captain Handley pen a "peace talk" for him addressed to Governor Blount. Handley was also allowed to write his brother-in-law:

> WILLS TOWN, Dec. 10, 1792.
> Dear Sir:—I am a captive in this town, in great distress, and the bearer hereof is a runner from the Upper Towns, from the Hanging Maw, and is now going up with a Talk from Col. John Watts, with the Governor, on terms of peace. These people are much for peace, and if Governor Blount sends a good answer back to the Talk they have sent up by the runner, I am confident their Talk is true and sincere; and, upon the whole, we are not ripe for war with these people, for they are properly fixed for war; but Watts is entirely for peace, at this time, and wishes for a good answer to their Talks. Dear Sir, I have been much abused, and am in great distress. I beg that you and John Cowan, and every good friend, would go to the Governor, and try all you can to get him to send a good answer, so that I

can get away—for if an army comes before, I am sure to die. Send word to my wife, and send me a horse down by the Hanging Maw's runner, for I am not able to come without. Dear friends, do what you can, for I am in a distressed way. No more, but—
SAMUEL HANDLEY.

N. B.—John Watts sends to the Hanging Maw to send Calaka, the Hanging Maw's nephew, and another young fellow, down with the Governor's Talk and the horse for me, for he is a safe fellow, and if they come I am sure to get home, but if not, I expect never to get home; and I once more beg you to do your possibles for me, and do them soon as you can.

To James Scott, Nine Mile, Henry's Station.[80]

Middlestriker, Archie Coody, and ten other warriors escorted the captain to Knoxville and, on January 24, 1793, released him without ransom.[81] (Running the gauntlet [or gantlet] is a form of physical punishment where a captive is to run [sometimes required to walk slowly] between two rows of warriors who repeatedly strike him with sticks.)

The Upper Cherokee and Creek warriors still attacked settlements; however, the Chickamauga confederation bore the brunt of the blame for the aggression. They often tried to convince Governor Blount of their peaceful intentions; however, they still had the incentive to protect Cherokee land and to avenge the mistreatment of their headmen, such as the murders of Old Tassel and others. Their overall goal was to still drive the encroachers out, and though they still held animosity for the Overmountain settlements, their primary focus was on the Cumberlands.

Chiefs Breath of Nickajack, Glass, Captain Charley of Running Water Town, and Dick Justice of Lookout Mountain Town, however, were strong advocates of peace with the whites. They could not control the young warriors. Towaka, Breath's nephew, and four or five other young fellows from Nickajack repeatedly attacked the Holston settlements. On December 22, 1792, they went to the house of a Mr. Richardson and waited in ambush atop a hill that overlooked his front door. Eventually, he left the house, and in half an hour they massacred Mrs. Richardson, Mrs. Foster, Miss Schull, and two children. They looted the house and left a war club as a warning of future attacks.[82]

> On the 7th of December, 1792, a party of cavalry, in service for the protection of the District of Mero, about eight miles from Nashville, was fired upon by about twenty Indians, who put them to flight, killed John Hankins, who was scalped and his body much mangled. The Indians stole horses in this district without intermission, through all the month of December, 1792.
>
> On the 29th of December, John Haggard was killed and scalped, about six miles from Nashville; twelve balls were shot into him. His wife was killed by the Indians in the summer.[83]

As bloody as 1792 was, 1793 would be worse. The focus had shifted: rather than staging large offensives, the Chickamauga were performing hit-and-run raids in small bands. This was an old-style Indian tactic very useful against enemies with large numbers. These bands would attack small groups (usually families) of settlers, take scalps, and run to look for another target. The settlers usually called this a cowardly and savage action; however, even the militias had often used this tactic in the American Revolution and later against the Indians. The Chickamauga disagreed with their older Upper Village chiefs, but they also respected them. The small war parties were manned by what the old chiefs called "their bad young men," whom they had no power to restrain. However, that too was ancient Cherokee tradition. Red (War) chiefs would often take charge of the war effort regardless of the position of the White (Peace) chief, and would lead however many warriors were willing to follow. Utilizing these small roving bands was the only avenue the Cherokee had to try and frighten the settlers into leaving Cherokee land. However, it is estimated that the coming year, 1793, yielded only 50 to 75 white slayings. Later, the first legislative assembly of the Southwest Territory would gather at Knoxville in February 1794 and declare that, since the Treaty of Holston in 1791, the Indians had killed more than two hundred citizens of the Territory and carried others into captivity and slavery.[84] Those numbers included both the Overmountain and the Cumberland settlements. The Cherokee could not win an all-out war by killing fewer than 100 of their avowed enemies, the whites, per year. Those statistics would not frighten any group of settlers enough to disband their settlements. The Chickamauga were losing the war of attrition; however, they had to keep trying—for now.

During the summer months, Cherokee parties crossed the Tennessee River almost daily with scalps and horses they had taken from the settlements. Early in January 1793, on White's Creek, they mortally wounded a man named Gower. He managed to escape to Hickman's Station before he died. On the same day, they stole some horses from Bledsoe's Station. The warriors dropped several guns and most of their loot as they hastily outran their pursuers.

On January 16, 1793, west of Clarksville on the Red River, Chickamauga warriors shot Hugh Tenin from ambush as he was building a fence around his cabin. They absconded with his horse.

Several individual war parties would range the Cumberland River where they usually attacked ascending boat convoys. The crews were busy rowing when they traveled against the current, and more susceptible to attack. Additionally, boats headed upriver were usually laden with goods for the settlements.

About January 1, 1793, Major Evan Shelby and others had gone to the Falls of the Ohio (present-day Louisville, Kentucky) for supplies. On January 18, while the settlers returned with their goods, a Creek war party fired on the boat from the riverbank (near present-day Dover, Tennessee). Major Shelby, James Harney, and a slave belonging to Moses Shelby were killed. The warriors looted the boat and set it ablaze. Some of them donned the dead men's clothing and armed themselves with the captured swords and rifles. This was considered a very successful raid on the part of the Indians, not just for the loot, but for the slaying of such a prestigious man as Major Shelby.

Creek warriors fired on several French traders that same week killing David Crow and Mr. Gaskins outright. Mr. Priest was mortally wounded, but Mr. Wells and Mr. Milliken survived the attack. Milliken became a novelty as he would not allow the rifle balls to be removed from his wounds.

> Acting under the orders of the Secretary of War, Gov. Blount gave orders, Nov. 29th [1792], that all the troops of Sevier's brigade, except two companies, should be marched to Knoxville, and mustered out of service. This was accordingly done early in January of 1793.
>
> On Tuesday, the 22d of January, the Indians killed and scalped John Pates, on Crooked Creek, about sixteen miles from Knoxville.
>
> On the 29th, the Cherokees stole three of William Davidson's horses from Gamble's Station, on Little River; and, on the 26th of February, they stole ten horses from Cozby's Creek. These aggressions prompted the spontaneous assemblage of the militia at Gamble's Station, for the purpose of marching to the nearest Indian towns, and retaliating upon them the injuries they were suffering.

The Governor immediately ordered Col. Kelly to go to the dissatisfied and incensed citizens on the frontier, and endeavour to restrain them from going with arms across the Tennessee River, or entering any of the Indian towns....

On the 9th of March, a party of Indians, led by Towakka, formed an ambuscade, near the house of Mr. Nelson, living on Little Pigeon, twenty-five miles from Knoxville. Two of his sons, James and Thomas, were killed and scalped.[85]

Also on January 22, Captain William Overall and a settler named Burnett were returning from Kentucky with nine packhorses loaded with goods, salt, and whiskey. Such a prize was more than any Chickamauga warrior could resist. A war party led by Doublehead, Pumpkin Boy, and Bench ambushed and killed the pair while they rested at Dripping Spring in southern Kentucky. Afterward, Doublehead scalped them and then stripped their flesh with his knife. He proposed an ancient Iroquois ritual of eating the enemy. Bench and the other warriors joined Doublehead as he roasted the flesh and ate. They also devoured the brains and hearts of the victims. (Overall had been a scout for years. Warriors and militiamen had been very familiar with their counterparts' personal features and traits for years, and the warriors may have been seeking vengeance against Overall; however, it is more likely that Doublehead wanted to use the ancient Iroquois rite as a dedication to the cause.) After the ritual, the Indians departed with the horses and plunder.

Doublehead returned to the Lower Towns where he exhibited the two scalps, told of the adventure, and recruited more warriors for raids into the Cumberlands. Bench, Tail, and one other joined with Doublehead for that last adventure. Bench had planned to raid in the Powell Mountain vicinity of Virginia. He decided his small band could assist Doublehead, and then they could proceed through Kentucky to Virginia without much delay.

Doublehead was ambitious and, on February 6, 1793, he attended a special conference at Henry's Station with Governor William Blount, Chickamauga principal chief Young Tassel, Northern Division principal chief Hanging Maw, and other important Cherokee chiefs. Excerpts from minutes of the conference:

Governor Blount.—I am happy, on this occasion, to speak to you on public business. What I have to say to you will be short, and will be concerning things that are yet to come, not about what is past. I have lately received a letter from the President, a part of which I will read to you. It is as follows: "The President of the United States is highly desirous that John Watts, the Little Turkey, and as many of the real chiefs of the Cherokees as you may judge proper to form a real representation of the tribes, should pay a visit to this place, where they shall not only be abundantly supplied with such articles as they may require for themselves, but also for their nation...."

I want to know your answer to this request of the President; if you are not prepared, withdraw, and consult each other. I will go with you any road you may wish to travel. The President supposes, if a full and complete representation should visit him, all matters of difference should be settled....

Hanging Maw—I am willing to go; but, there must be a consultation of the chiefs. You must not think the time long before we get ready, in case we conclude to go.

[Here, he, Watts, Doublehead, and Tuskegatahee (Long Fellow, Ghighau Nancy Ward's brother) withdrew; and returning, John Watts said:]

You are our father; you have told us you want us to go to Philadelphia. There are no head-men [meaning Principal Chiefs] here but the Hanging Maw and myself. I can speak but little, and can give no answer to the business you propose. I must first consult our chiefs, who are gone to the Creeks; perhaps, when we get back home, they may be returned. All the nation will assemble, in twenty-one nights, at the Running Water [Town];

then all things will be taken into consideration. You shall hear the result. The business of our chiefs, who are gone on to the Creeks, is to try to stop them from going to war. They are the Glass, the Turkey, Kittagiska, Dick Justice, Hovalta, Charley, the Water Hunter, the Breath, the Drunkard, Double-head, (not him of the same name that is present) the Person Striker, the Spider, Chulcoah, their linguister [sic]. My own nation is at war; the Creeks and the Chickasaws also. I want all these to be at peace, then I will take you by the hand and go to Philadelphia....

Governor—Have you heard from Mr. McGillivray? [Creek chief Alexander McGillivray.]

Watts—I have heard lately that he sickened and died at his own house.... [McGillivray died on February 17, 1793 at Pensacola, Florida.]

Governor—... Will it be agreeable that John McKee should accompany you? He can write and do business for you.

Watts—Your own sort of people like McKee as well as we do, but he must wait and go down with Hanging Maw.[86]

Governor Blount sent a dispatch to Philadelphia to report on his conference. On February 8, 1793, the secretary of war replied that the president was highly desirous that Young Tassel, the Little Turkey, and other important chiefs should visit Philadelphia, promising them abundant supplies of such articles as they might require, both for themselves and for their nation. The implication was that it would be held in May.[87]

Note that Governor Blount dispatched McKee to the Lower Towns, by way of other business, immediately following the Henry's Station conference. Hanging Maw did not travel with him as Young Tassel had desired. The escort, presumably, was to be for McKee's own safety.

McKee wrote a report to Blount dated March 28, 1792:

On the 8th of February last, I left Knoxville, accompanied by Mr. Thompson, under your instructions to proceed to the Lower towns of the Cherokee nation, for the purpose of using my best endeavors to restore peace between the United States and that part of the Cherokee nation which had declared for war. On the 10th, we arrived at Chota, where we were informed that the Hanging Maw was in Chilhowee ... where we found a large assembly of Indians ... and begged them to exert themselves in assisting me.... The next day we went to the Maw's, where we were detained two days by snow and rain ... I repeated to him the objects of my mission, to which he expressed his good wishes for my success, with his doubts, saying it was an useless and dangerous journey. He advised me to desist, and warned me, that if I perished, I went to the Lower towns at the great risk of my life ... we proceeded toward Hiwassee, where we arrived on the 14th ... we proceeded on to a small river called Amoe, ten miles below Hiwassee; here Mr. Thompson left me, and the next day, I was overtaken by Will. Elder and Unacata [Young Tassel's brother, White Mankiller], two Indians from Toquo ... were ordered by the Maw to attend and protect me. At this place I was detained six days by incessant rains, and high waters, at which time Nontuaka, who lived at Cheestowee ... visited me; he charged me ... to proceed no further ... I would probably never return ... through heavy rains and deep waters, in three days we arrived at Chatooga, a small village, about twenty miles from Will's town, the residence of John Watts ... I met Mr. Benge [the father of Bench, Nettle Carrier, and Tail].... He informed me, that Will. Webber, a half-breed trader, had been lately in Will's town ... interceding with Watts to have me put to death. I was advised to ... send some treaty person on to Watts, to inform him of my arrival ... Will. Elder returned ... on the 28th of February, with Watts ... met me with every appearance of his former personal friendship ... he talked jocularly of his trip to Cumberland, and of his wounds ... he assured me of safety whilst with him, but that I might on no consideration go any further, for he could not always be with me, and I might be killed by some bad young fellows.... He promised he would come in six or seven days ... I requested him to bring most of the principal chiefs....

March 8th—(the day I appointed to meet Watts) ... waited until the 16th without hearing anything from Watts.[88]

Arthur Coody wrote to McKee on the 10th, and explained why Young Tassel would not come: "John Watts is offended, by some of his people, is the reason he will not come."[89]

On the 19th, John Walker told McKee that Young Tassel did not come because his nephew, Talotiska (Nettle Carrier), was irked that the chief had visited McKee already at Chatooga. Talotiska averred that Young Tassel should not entertain any white man in the Lower Towns.[90]

On March 18, 1793, nine Upper Village warriors killed two unarmed young men named Clements as they left their father's house in search of cattle. These slayings avenged the deaths of Black Fish and Forked-Horn Buck, who had been killed November 12, 1792. Apparently, Black Fish of Chota and Forked-Horn Buck of Citico led a small party of warriors to attack Ebenezer Byron's Station in Grassy Valley near Knoxville. The Indians had surrounded the house before they were discovered, and they forced open a window. However, they picked the wrong house. As they pointed their rifles through the windows, two white men shot first and killed Black Fish and Forked-Horn Buck. The war party fled.[91]

After the ritual at Dripping Spring, Bench and his small band left his granduncle Doublehead and proceeded to Powell's Mountain, Virginia.

On March 31, 1793, Bench, his brother, Tail, and one other warrior were setting ambushes along various roads in the vicinity. While waiting during one such ambush atop Powell Mountain, 20 miles from Rogersville, Tennessee, they spotted three white men approaching with several laden packhorses. Bench recognized one of the men as being Moses Cockrell, a border ranger along the Holston settlements.

Cockrell was a large, handsome man with a macho personality, very active, and quite boastful. He often vocalized that he would like to come across the famous "Captain Benge." As the two approached the ambush spot, Cockrell happened to be loudly and sarcastically orating such diatribe.

Bench instructed the others to not kill Cockrell and let him capture the braggart. The other warriors fired, and Cockrell's two companions fell dead. Suddenly, Cockrell left his horse and dashed down the mountainside, with Bench waving a tomahawk hot in pursuit. It looked much like a cougar chasing a deer as they sprinted for two miles. Bench was steadily gaining on Cockrell, who was carrying $200 in gold. Cockrell jumped a rail fence at a cabin that sat on Wallen's Creek as Bench threw his tomahawk. The weapon buried its edge into the top rail of the fence, and Cockrell escaped safely into the cabin. Bench rejoined his companions and vowed he would meet Cockrell again.

Bench and his small band remained in the Overmountain settlements throughout the summer. They generally wreaked havoc wherever they could. Bench was especially fond of capturing slaves that he would later sell. July 17, 1793, he traversed twenty miles of the North Fork Holston River, fired on a man named Williams, and captured a black woman who was the property of Paul Livingston. She escaped after two days of captivity, and returned to Livingston's.[92]

Other warriors had been active in the meantime. In March, James and Thomas Nelson were killed and scalped on the Little Pigeon River, 25 miles of White's Fort. Then, on the 17th, Thomas Ross was killed while Joseph Brown and Colonel Caleb Friley were seriously wounded at the Little Laurel River en route from the Holston settlements to Nashville. On March 20, 1793, William Massey and Adam Greene were killed and scalped on Powell's Mountain Gap, near where Bench had ambushed Cockrell.

Young Creek warrior Lesley and a band burned James Gallaher's house on the Holston River in April. They then passed through the Upper Villages and asked Chief Hanging Maw for provisions, but he refused. Lesley shot the chief's dog and left. A company of mounted infantry pursued them to no avail. Upon the infantry's return, they found that the river level had risen sharply: John McCullough drowned as they crossed. A few days later Lieutenant Tedford led a company of rangers to continue pursuit of Lesley. As dusk enveloped them, they encountered two Indians on horseback. The rangers, assuming the Indians to be some of Lesley's, fired and killed one; however, he was Young Tassel's friend, Noonday, of Toquo.

Governor Blount wrote to chiefs Hanging Maw and Young Tassel on April 17, 1793:

> Noon-day was unfortunately killed by mistake for a Creek, as he was off the path, with a gun on his shoulder, by the people who were ranging to protect the frontiers. If they had known him to be a Cherokee, they would not have injured him. This, you may know, is true; because, since they have been ranging, they have often seen Cherokees, and some with guns, off the path, and did not injure them. There is another proof they did not mean to kill him, that is, when they found that they, by mistake, had killed a friendly Cherokee, they did not scalp him, as they would have done had he been a Creek.... Let us forgive and forget what has passed, and endeavor to make and keep peace for the future.... But, it may be that the Noon-day's friends will not be content without satisfaction; and if they will not, and will take it in goods, I will pay them, and send the goods for them immediately to the Maw's ... I beg you to explain everything fully to the chiefs.[93]

Young Tassel responded the next day with:

> I am going now to tell you the truth. I sent your people word of the Creeks being at the Hanging Maw's, and as they returned from the pursuit of them, one of the men got drowned. I suppose that was the reason of Noon-day's being killed, and, as I wish peace, let both go together—Noonday [sic] for the man that was drowned. Noon-day was my brother in our way of kindred. Noon-day was a good man, and they wanted to kill him. They knew very well it was not Creeks, for they took his gun, and belt, and knife, and garters. At the talk at Samuel Henry's, Major Craig wanted the bad people to come to his house; and Noon-day went to Craig's, and got killed. Noon-days own two brothers was very cross, and wanted to take satisfaction at once, but I went to them yesterday, and told them to stop; they promised me that they would. I hope they will listen to my talks. We all wish for peace. I hope the white people will do the same. Noon-day is dead, and it can't be helped. We must try to make peace, and make our peace talks fast.
>
> To-morrow I start for the Running Water to the talk, and the Hanging Maw. I wish Mr. McKee to come on as fast as possible. My good brother, you must send a talk to Craig, and his bad young men, to take care not do any more mischief. When the talk is over, I will come and let you know all our talks. The wife and children of Noon-day has no corn, and if you will find them some to live on till corn comes, I shall be glad.[94]

In the Cumberlands, on the morning of April 1, 1793, Colonel Isaac Bledsoe and several of his slaves were going from Bledsoe's Station to a nearby clearing to tend some brush pile burns. Some warriors were hidden in ambush along the path awaiting an opportunity. They opened a deadly volley at the group, and the colonel was mortally wounded. The Indians scalped him and departed. Captain Sam Hays was killed about the same time near the property of John Donelson, Jr. Nothing seems to have been recorded about the fate of the slaves.

A large, notable mountain man named Thomas Sharpe Spencer (who often lived in a large hollowed-out tree), Robert Jones, and Mrs. Nathaniel Parker, former wife of the late Anthony Bledsoe, were riding from Walnutfield Station to Greenfield Station and met a war party about two miles from present-day Gallatin, Tennessee (about 25 miles northeast of Nashville). The Indians opened fire, and Jones was killed with the first volley. They rushed the other two with raised tomahawks, but stopped when they recognized Spencer, of whom they were in awe. Spencer yelled for Mrs. Parker to turn her horse and run toward Gallatin while he covered her retreat. He dashed back and forth in front of the warriors pointing his gun as though likely to shoot. Once Mrs. Parker was at a safe distance, Spencer wheeled his own horse and escaped.

During the afternoon of April 26, 1793, three black men were plowing in a field near Bledsoe's Station. One of them was Abraham, the former body-servant to the late Colonel Anthony Bledsoe. An armed Irishman named Jarvis was acting as their sentry.

Two hours before sundown, Captain William Hall left the fort to inspect the work. While he talked with Abraham, the dogs resting near Jarvis suddenly became agitated and ran towards a nearby canebrake. Hall ordered the men to unhitch their horses, and they all returned to the station.

Mrs. Clendening and several other women began their chores early the next day. They were nearly overrun by a herd of wild cattle as they began to milk their own cows. Mrs. Clendening was sure the cattle had been spooked by a war party, so she warned Jarvis not to take his work party to the field. Jarvis told her he had to make up for lost time and that he believed the small stampede had nothing to do with Indians.

Mrs. Clendening returned to the station and then heard gunshots which awakened several sleeping men. Captain Hall saw a war party chasing Jarvis and his field hands toward the fort, so he rushed outside with his rifle. He was accompanied by William Wilson, but they no sooner exited when they were ambushed by 20 warriors. Neither of the two were hit, and Wilson rushed the Indians who suddenly withdrew leaving four of their detachment lying dead. Wilson and Hall killed four of the warriors.

William Neely and James Hays emerged from the fort to assist Hall and Wilson but were fired upon by another group of warriors. Hall and Wilson returned fire and killed one of the attackers.

The four men then began to lay cover for the field hands as they rushed toward the station. Jarvis was killed in the skirmish as was a workhand called Prince. A shot scraped Hall's head enough to shave off a lock of hair. Neely said the tress jumped one foot straight up. Hall had a four-inch long scar from the close call.

The Indians apparently withdrew, but Abraham (who had killed one warrior) was still darting for the fort with a huge brave hot on his trail. Hays fired a well-placed bullet and killed the warrior. The war party was estimated to number 250 men.

Major George Winchester had heard the battle and came with a company of 50 militiamen but arrived too late to assist. He held a council, and it was decided not to pursue recovery of the horses.

A few days later Abraham, a good marksman, was traveling from Bledsoe's Station to Greenfield at dusk. While walking a little-used path in the midst of a dense forest, he encountered chiefs Maddog and John Taylor, two well-known raiders. Abraham quickly fired and killed Maddog then retreated. John Taylor buried Maddog and withdrew from the Cumberlands. (Maddog is said to have been Creek, and John Taylor, Cherokee.)

On May 9, 1793, an attack was made near Isaac Johnson's Station near Nashville. One young boy was grabbed and scalped before he made his escape. Another lad was grabbed by his jacket, but he slipped out of it and safely returned to the fort. None of the three boys was killed.

Then on May 10, Nathaniel Teal, a letter carrier, was killed near General James Robertson's property five miles from Nashville. On the 12th, Captains John Rains and John Gordon led two companies of militia to pursue the war party. There were a total of 100 men in the chase. They found the Indian campsite on the 17th near the mouth of Elk River. A 20-man advance was detailed to divert attention from the main group of militiamen. Rains' company quietly maneuvered around the right flank while Gordon's crept to the left. The detail fired on the warriors; then, both companies attacked. Six warriors were killed, and a teenaged Cherokee captured, before the war party withdrew.

On the 25th, a war party killed Thomas Gillum and his son, James, in the Raccoon Valley near the Clinch River. Governor Blount ordered Major John Beard and his company of 125 men to pursue the assailants. Blount gave Beard some specific instructions in a message dated April 18, 1793: "You will have with you, for your guide, Richard Finnelson, a Cherokee ... on whose fidelity you may fully depend ... you are to consider all the Indians you come across ... Creeks and enemies, unless the contrary appears, and treat them as such. But should you come across Chickasaws, Choctaws, or Cherokees, and know them to be such, you are to consider them as friends, unless they give you proofs of their hostility."[95]

Beard, however, had other plans. He expected to set an example of any group of Indians to deter future attacks within the settlements. He had awaited just such an opportunity to disrupt the Cherokee community. To set that up, Major Beard swore that the trail of the attackers led to the town of Hanging Maw.

In the interim, while the Cherokee and the Chickasaw tried to arrange peace with the settlers, the Creek were a burr in the saddle. Chickasaw chief Piamingo wrote, apparently to General James Robertson, and said: "It was General Pickens' request to me, that, in case a war should arise in my nation, that I should personally acquaint him with it. Now, the Creeks have opened war with us, and, I am informed by a certain Creek half-breed, by the name of Alick Cornell, that General Pickens has treated with the Creek nation for peace.... Now this confirms a war with us and the Creeks. So we all unanimously desire and require your assistance."[96]

The council planned by Young Tassel for Running Water did not occur as he had stated it would in his letter to Governor Blount of April 17, 1793. On the 28th, Governor Blount wrote, apparently to General Robertson: "On the evening of Saturday (25th), Mr. Ore arrived here from the Maw's, who informed me that, on the 24th, Bob M. Clemore, a warrior of Watt's party, had arrived at the Maw's, as a runner, with a message from Watts, in the following words: 'That the council of Will's town, with the Shawanese ambassadors, had broke up, and that all was straight; that he himself (Watts) would be up in five nights ... and with him, Talotiske, the Bloody Fellow, and other chiefs.'"[97]

On June 3, 1793, United States Indian Agent John McKee informed Governor Blount that Chief Doublehead, Chief Otter Lifter, and several other chiefs from the Lower Villages were at Hanging Maw's in Coyatee, and that Chief Young Tassel was expected that day. They had come at the request of Governor Blount, and, under escort of McKee, were gathered for the long-awaited trip to Philadelphia to meet with President Washington.[98]

Governor Blount did not assemble with them as he felt reassured that it was going well, so on the 7th, he left for Philadelphia, expecting to meet them there. He left Secretary Daniel Smith in charge as acting governor of the Southwest Territory during his absence.

Hanging Maw was the principal chief of the Upper Villages and Little Turkey of the Lower Towns. Those in the north had generally accepted Hanging Maw as principal chief of the nation; however, a number of the Cherokee in Upper Villages and all residing in the south had recognized Little Turkey. The allegiance in the south was beginning to shift toward Hanging Maw.

The Chickamauga chiefs were gathering at Hanging Maw's house to prepare for the trip to Philadelphia. He had been a famous chief since Young Tassel was a child.

Hanging Maw had gotten to know George Washington during the French and Indian War, and each respected the other. In a letter that Hanging Maw wrote to the president on the 15th, he said: "I am writing to the President of the United States. It is a long time since I have seen him, when we were both young and warriors."[99]

Three United States officials were also there: Major Robert King, who was courting Hanging Maw's daughter, and James Ore and Daniel Carmichael, who helped prepare for the trip.

On June 12, Major Beard acted upon his story that the attackers of the Gillums were from Coyatee and were protected by Hanging Maw. Although Beard had been ordered not to cross the Tennessee River, he did so about daylight and attacked Coyatee. He killed chiefs Scantee, Captain Charley, William Rosebury, a white man who had an Indian wife and a small family, and Betty, the daughter of Kittagiska. Among the wounded were the Hanging Maw, his wife and daughter, and Betsy Martin (daughter of Ghighau Nancy Ward and wife of General Joseph Martin).

Major Robert King, who was in bed with Hanging Maw's daughter at the time of the attack, escaped by jumping out of a window. James Ore and Daniel Carmichael were shot at, but not injured.

The United States representatives begged Beard to spare the rest of Hanging Maw's family and to not burn the chief's house. It was, at first, incorrectly reported that both Doublehead and Hanging Maw's wife were killed.

Acting governor Daniel Smith believed Beard's action would mean war and wrote the next day to Secretary of War Henry Knox:

> It mortifies me much that the first communications I make you, after Governor Blount's departure, should be of so disagreeable a nature. The enclosed report ... will inform you of the perpetration of so inhuman an act as ever was committed—committed by Captain John Beard, who was ordered out by Governor Blount, before his [Blount's] departure, to inflict punishment on the murderers of the Gilhams, and positively restricting him from crossing the Tennessee. How detestable is this act to all good men!
>
> I shall direct Colonel White to call a court martial for the trial of Captain Beard ... that they may exert the force of law against him under the eleventh article of the Holston treaty.
>
> I had been, for some time past, suspicious that the rage of many of the inhabitants of

this district would burst out in some unjustifiable act. But this exceeds any thing that could have been supposed."[100]

On the same day, Smith wrote to chiefs Hanging Maw, Doublehead, and Young Tassel as follows: "The young inconsiderate men have taken advantage of his [Governor Blount's] absence to commit the atrocious act of yesterday morning ... of which I am ashamed, and despise the perpetrators: for their act was horrid and unmanly.... Be not rash and inconsiderate. Hear what your and our great father, the President, will say. Go and see him, as he requested. I assure you, in great truth, I believe he will give you satisfaction, if you will forebear to take it yourselves."[101]

Hanging Maw's letter of the 15th to the president included: "We thought very well of your talk of restoring peace, and our land being made safe to us; but the white people have spoiled the talk for us at present. The heads of our land thought very well of going to Philadelphia, but some of them now lie dead, and some of them wounded. You need not look for us to go there at this time."[102]

The chief wrote to Daniel Smith on the same day: "It is but a few days since you were left in the place of Governor Blount. While he was in place, nothing happened. Surely they are making their fun of you. I am just informed you will take satisfaction for me, and I shall reckon it just the same as if I had taken it myself. I reckon you are afraid of these thieves, when you talk of sending to Congress. If you are left in the place of Governor, you ought to take satisfaction yourself."[103]

Hanging Maw repeated several times that he believed Smith to be afraid of the men. Chief Doublehead wrote to Smith on the same day: "I am still among my people, living in gores of blood. When is the day that I shall get a full answer from you? Be strong, and don't be afraid, but get satisfaction for me. I am still waiting to get a satisfaction talk from you ... I can't think of going to the Lower towns until I get a fuller answer.... We have lost nine of our people, that we must have satisfaction for.... This is the third time that we have been served so when we were talking in peace, that they fell on us and killed us."[104]

First of all, Doublehead's point that the Overmountain leaders had acted as such in prior times is valid. The most memorable example is the attack that killed Chief Old Tassel and others. It is evident that those who owed allegiance to John Sevier were the perpetrators, and that is an indictment for his not exercising control of the hotheads under his purview. Sevier and Beard were known to be close friends.

It is also an indictment of Governor William Blount for having left when such a gathering of chiefs was taking place near a hostile area. He was aware that Major Beard was a hothead, yet he had left the major with an opportunity to run amok. It was a situation that invited disaster.

Acting governor Daniel Smith caused Major Beard to be arrested and tried before a court-martial; however, public sentiment among the Overmountain settlers was strong. Beard, unsurprisingly, was acquitted. Smith admitted that he could not punish Beard by law. Thus, Hanging Maw and Doublehead wrote their properly-demeaning letters.

The most telling response of all the primary headmen was that of Young Tassel: no response at all.[105]

The Chickamauga leaders eventually lost patience. They waited for over two months for the white authorities to take some significant action as had often been promised. Con-

10. The Final Onslaught

tinued sporadic attacks occurred throughout that time, especially in the Cumberlands. Full-scale Cherokee hostility broke out in late August, and the settlements were required to defend themselves once again. General John Sevier led 400 mounted infantry to garrison at Ish's Station near present-day Knoxville. Forty more were positioned at White's Station (the site of future Knoxville), and another regiment was located at Campbell's Station, 15 miles west.

On June 20, 1793, James Steele, his 17-year-old daughter, Betsy, his son, and his brother Robert, left Greenfield Station for Morgan's Station. Captain William Hall and eight militia cavalrymen were eating dinner, and the captain suggested that the party wait for them to complete their meal, so they could be escorted. Steele did not want to wait and stated they would be safe. The family group left, and shortly thereafter, the captain heard gunshots. He led his cavalry down the lane and found James Steele and Betsy had been killed and scalped. Young Steele was wounded and had escaped with his uncle. Betsy had put up a fight as evidenced by clumps of an Indian's hair in her hands.

Noted scout and hunter, Jacob Castleman, Jr., and his brothers, Joseph Castleman, and Hans Castleman, were killed during an attack at Hays' Station, near Nashville, on July 1, 1793. Abraham Castleman, another brother, was irate. He was fed up with the restrictions placed on militias by Southwest Territory governor William Blount and Secretary of War Henry Knox, who were trying hard to establish peace. General James Robertson, who reported directly to Blount, was sympathetic and allowed Castleman to muster a company to retaliate.

Castleman led a party of 15 in pursuit of the attackers who were racing to the southeast. They reached the Tennessee River, beyond which Secretary Knox had forbidden all militias to pass. Castleman later reported that, since they had killed no Indians "worth naming," he decided to go on. Ten others turned back and left him with Frederick Stull, Zackariah Maclin, Jack Camp, Eli Hammond, and Zeke Caruthers. The painted themselves, dressed as Indians, and crossed the river near Nickajack. Soon they spotted 50 Creek who were eating while seated on the ground. The Creek were painted black, which indicated they were a war party.

The well-disguised militiamen neared the band of Creek on foot. The Indians did not seem at all suspicious; then, suddenly the whites stopped, aimed their rifles, and fired. Each killed one man, except Castleman who had loaded his rifle with buckshot. He killed two. The surviving warriors quickly dispersed. Castleman and his company returned to Nashville.

On August 5, 1793, a Creek war party killed Samuel Miller near Joslin's Station. Captains Rains and Gordon pursued and caught the Creek warriors seven miles below the Duck River. They killed several Creek and captured a 12-year-old Indian boy. Then on August 30, two warriors slew Phillip Hunter's family while he was away. They scalped his wife, decapitated his daughter, and took her head for a trophy.

Young Tassel had been quiet since the attack at Hanging Maw's. He believed that the Cherokee were again betrayed by the whites. He and his uncle, Chief Doublehead, had been pleased with the Cumberland raids and with those by Bench in the Overmountain communities. They decided it was time to make an expedition into the middle settlements. They declared war in mid–September and called for warrior volunteers. They received many responses. Bench and his brothers (Tail and Nettle Carrier), one of Doublehead's brothers (Pumpkin Boy), James Vann, 300 Chickamauga warriors, and 700 of the Creek joined in. They crossed the Tennessee River the morning of September 24, 1793.

In early September, militia captain Michael Harrison left his post in Washington County, Virginia, and led 80 light dragoons to help John Sevier patrol the stations along the Pigeon River. He established his headquarters with that of Sevier's at Ish's Station. On the morning of the 24th, Captain Harrison detached several patrols along the roads leading to the various stations. They found things to be quiet, so they returned to Ish's.

The combined warrior force arrived in the vicinity late on the 24th and decided to await further action until dawn the next day. Once they began their movement on the 25th, they heard the regular morning cannon fire at Campbell's Station. However, the war party thought the cannon fire meant they had been discovered, so they eliminated Campbell's as their initial target. (Campbell's Station was a large, well-built fort with a habitation of 20 families, located at present-day Farragut, Tennessee.)

The decision to bypass Campbell's Station meant they would skirt Ish's and Cavett's stations on their way to the major fortification of White's Fort. The war party, though a joint effort, was composed of two factions. Chief Doublehead and his brother, Pumpkin Boy, led most of the Creek warriors as they had raided together for years. Chief Young Tassel, Bench, Nettle Carrier, and Joseph Vann led the Chickamauga and a few of the Creek. A dispute broke out between Young Tassel and his uncle Doublehead: Young Tassel and James Vann wanted to leave the smaller stations alone and directly attack White's Fort before the garrison had word of the war party's presence; Doublehead demanded to attack the smaller stations on the way.

Doublehead sent Pumpkin Boy to reconnoiter Ish's Station, and Young Tassel sent Nettle Carrier to accompany him. They crept near as stealthily as they could, but the sentries spotted and fired upon them. Pumpkin Boy was killed. Nettle Carrier carried him back to the main party. Doublehead was not only distraught, but furious. Another quarrel developed between the two primary chiefs. Doublehead avowed they would kill everyone in the stations. Young Tassel declared they should spare women and children. This disagreement delayed their movement long enough for a messenger from Ish's to ride to White's Fort and warn the settlers that the war party was on its way. Sevier had assumed that White's was the logical target. When Colonel James White received the message, he led his force to a ridge one and one-fourth miles west to set up a defense.

Doublehead absolutely refused to bypass Cavett's Station while Young Tassel knew that he had an insufficient force to attack White's Station without the Creek warriors. The Indians greatly outnumbered the whites at Alexander Cavett's small station. There were only Cavett and two unrelated riflemen to defend Cavett's family of 10 more members.

Young Tassel decided to destroy the station but spare the family. He sent his nephew, Bench, under a white flag to negotiate. Doublehead seethed during the deliberations. He wanted to taste blood for the death of Pumpkin Boy.

Bench offered that if the family should surrender the fort, the war party would take them as captives and later trade them for previously-captured warriors. Cavett realized their impossible situation and agreed. He believed it the only way his family would survive.

Once the family and the riflemen began to exit the fort, Doublehead and some of his Creek warriors made a sudden vicious tomahawk attack. It happened so abruptly that

10. The Final Onslaught

Young Tassel, Bench, and James Vann were stunned and could not counter. All of the inhabitants but one, young Alexander Cavett, Jr., were slain. Young Tassel had grabbed the boy in an attempt to save him. Meanwhile, Bench tried to compose his granduncle Doublehead to no avail. Doublehead not only killed the family members, but brutally mutilated them. As Young Tassel wanted to stop the slaughter, he handed the boy to some Creek warriors. He demanded they take him away from the vicinity and protect him. They took him away and killed him.

Bench reportedly wept because the warriors had gone back on his word to Cavett. James Vann had earlier lifted another child up to his saddle to protect him, but Doublehead rode up and tomahawked the child to death. Vann verbally assaulted Doublehead and called him a baby killer. Young Tassel and Bench were never close to their uncle Doublehead again. James Vann and Doublehead became bitter enemies. Vann would later participate in Doublehead's assassination.

There is a differing account that a skirmish ensued prior to the agreement. The three men reportedly defended the station, and Alexander Cavett was killed. He died with bullets in his mouth that he placed there to hold for reloading. Five warriors were shot, killed or wounded, which was the impetus for Young Tassel to send Bench under the flag.

(A marker labeled Cavett's Station is located in west Knoxville at the intersection of Kingston Pike [US Highway 11 & 70] and Gallaher View Road, one mile west of West Town Mall, which puts the station one-fourth of a mile north, which is north of I-40/75 near Ten Mile Creek. The marker is at 35° 55.389' N, 84° 3.515' W.)[106]

The Southwest Territory secretary, Daniel Smith, ordered General Sevier, who was garrisoned at Ish's Station, to pursue Young Tassel's war party. Interestingly, Smith took very little time to initiate the action although he had taken no action against the perpetrators of the attack on Hanging Maw's house.

Sevier left Ish's in early October with 400 men and was joined by 300 more as he traveled. On October 14, 1793, when he reached the town of Estanaula, he found the village abandoned, but it contained plentiful provisions. The general halted and rested his men. The Indians attacked his camp that night to no avail. The militia took some prisoners and learned that the main war party had passed a few days earlier. The captives volunteered that Young Tassel's destination was a small village at the mouth of the Etowah River. The troops reached the destination the evening of the 17th.

The Creek and Chickamauga were secured on the far bank of the river to defend against a crossing. James Carey and Richard Finnelson, Sevier's guides, mistakenly led Colonel Kelly's regiment to one-half of a mile below the ford where they immediately swam the river. The Indians discovered Kelly, abandoned their entrenchment, and dashed downriver to oppose Kelly. Captain Evans had discovered the blunder, turned his horse, and reentered the river. Chief King Fisher entered into a skirmish with Evans, and Hugh Lawson White killed the chief. The warriors withdrew. The whites lost three men in this engagement. Sevier then marched the militia down the Coosa River and burned several villages. (The battle at Etowah on the Coosa River was near present-day Rome, Georgia.)

This was the second major expedition that Young Tassel had led that ended in disaster. Each of the failures resulted because Young Tassel was unable to control another leader, the first instance being Shawnee Warrior at Buchanan's Station, then the event with Doublehead.

Also in early October, after W. H. Cunningham heard of the Cavett's Station massacre, he went to fetch his young son who was visiting with friends several miles away. He traveled back roads thinking to avoid trouble, but 30 miles later, he passed through an area that was heavily patrolled by some 30 warriors. This was about one-half of a mile from his destination of McGaughey's Station. Luckily, he noticed the Indians' presence and was able to creep past in the dark. Two weeks later, he was attacked and wounded by ten warriors outside the gate of McGaughey's Station; yet he was able to return to the fort. (McGaughey's Station was located at Boyd's Creek near present-day Sevierville, Tennessee.)

Later in October, a woman and a boy were killed 20 miles east of White's Fort. The warriors entirely removed the skin from their heads, stabbed them in their throats, and left them naked. W. H. Cunningham and Jacob Jenkins were riding in advance of the burial party when they were attacked by 50 warriors. Cunningham was clubbed to death and scalped; Jenkins was wounded, but escaped.

In the fall of 1793, Thomas Sharpe Spencer journeyed to Virginia to settle an estate. He completed his business the following spring and began his return trip. He carried $1,000 of gold currency in his saddlebags. His route took him by White's Fort where he picked up four traveling companions. On April 1, 1794, Spencer and fellow traveler, James Walker, were riding together in advance. When they reached the point where Doublehead had formed an ambuscade, they received a volley which killed Spencer, the famous mountain man, and wounded Walker. When Spencer fell, his saddlebags came loose and fell into the hands of Doublehead.

During these times, Governor Blount seemed confident with the councils and negotiations with the Cherokee. On April 15, 1794, he wrote General Robertson: "An attack on Cumberland by a large party of Indians, either Creeks or Cherokees, or both, is not to be apprehended this summer. Small parties, however, I fear will yet infest your frontier. I entreat and command you to let neither opportunity nor distant appearances of danger induce you to order out any party (of the militia) unnecessarily large. Economy is a republican virtue which from the injunction laid on me (by the Secretary of War) I feel myself bound to enjoin on you the observance of."[107]

However, the raids continued, albeit on a smaller scale because Young Tassel could not forcefully lead a large expedition. After Young Tassel's war party had dispersed, the Upper Village chiefs iterated that they desired peace.

Chief Doublehead recruited a party of 100 warriors, mostly Creek, and moved against the Cumberland settlements. His was the sole band that operated in that area during the spring of 1794. On the 12th of March, he ambushed 13 people, one of whom was the post rider, near Middleton's Station on the Kentucky road. Four men were killed; two of them, Baptist elders Haggard and Shelton. In the same month Doublehead killed the Wilson family, consisting of eight women and children, except one boy whom he took as his personal captive.

Governor Blount authorized General James Robertson to muster a 100-man militia force from Mero District to be divided between its counties.

On New Year's Day, 1794, John Drake left his home with three friends to hunt near Shackle Island. They hid near a salt lick to wait for game and skin the two deer they had already killed. A small band of Indians approached, fired a volley at the white men, and then rushed them with tomahawks waving. Surprisingly, none of the four was even wounded, and all escaped to Shackle Island. The warriors absconded with the deer and what weapons the men had dropped.

Miss Deliverance Gray left one of the Nashville stations en route to another and, at one point, was chased by warriors. They shot at her, and though slightly wounded, she made her escape. About the same time, John Helen was killed and scalped one-half of a mile from General Robertson's residence. He had run a long distance before the resolute warriors caught him.

At ten o'clock one morning the General's son, Jonathan Robertson, and three brothers named Cowan, who were from ten to fourteen years old, were hunting west of Robertson's property. They killed some game, loaded it on their shoulders, and walked single file through the forest. They soon became aware of some movement in the brush and saw the sun reflect off of a rifle barrel. One of the Cowans raised his gun to fire, but Jonathan stopped him and directed the boys to some nearby trees for cover. Two of the Cowan brothers each found a suitable tree, and Robertson hid behind a large tree with the other friend. A warrior fired a shot from cover and wounded the Cowan boy that was with Robertson. When Jonathan peered around the tree to look for a target, a rifle ball whizzed through his hat just over his left ear. The Indian who fired the shot was momentarily exposed, and Robertson accurately returned fire. The Indian dropped his gun, and, soon thereafter, another warrior was wounded. The band withdrew and took their injured with them. Robertson and the Cowans gathered up what weapons the attackers had dropped. A few days later the bodies of two dead warriors were found near the scene.

On March 20, 1794, Doublehead's warriors killed and scalped Charles Bratton near Bledsoe's Lick. The settlers had not yet fully become aware that, since the salt licks were great places for the hunters to ambush game, they were just as good for warriors to ambush white hunters.

Two young Bledsoe cousins, each named Anthony, each a son of Anthony or Isaac Bledsoe, had boarded during the winter at General Daniel Smith's home, Rock Castle. They attended a school on Drake's Creek near present-day Hendersonville, Tennessee. On the afternoon of March 21, 1794, after they left school, they were waylaid and killed at a rock quarry.

In the spring of 1794, Chief Bench (Robert Benge) made his last expedition to the frontiers of Virginia. On the morning of April 6, the Peter Livingston family was busily engaged on their property near present-day Mendota, Virginia. Peter's aged mother, Sarah, the widow of William Todd Livingston, was planting in the small garden. Peter and his brother, Henry, were at a distant barn, well away from and out of sight of the cabin. Henry's wife, Susanna, and two of Peter's children were working in an outhouse. Peter's wife, Elizabeth, was nursing their infant in the house with two children, aged two and ten, nearby. A black woman with a toddler and the Livingstons' eight-year-old black servant boy were engaged in some chores.

Elizabeth heard the dogs frantically barking. She glanced out the door and saw seven warriors, armed and painted black, approaching the house. She slammed and barred the door, and the Indians tried to burst it open. They fired a rifle ball through the door but nobody was hit. Mrs. Livingston took Peter's rifle from the wall and returned fire, also through the door.

The warriors next set fire to the house; the room filled with smoke. Elizabeth opened the door, and she and her three little children were taken captive. They had already captured her other two children, her sister-in-law, the black woman and her child, the eight-year-old servant, and a black servant that belonged to a neighbor, Edward Callahan. Another neighbor, Benjamin Sharpe, found Sarah Livingston's body.

Bench and his band retired to a secluded spot and divided the spoils. Two warriors were left in charge of the prisoners and were some distance behind the main party. Elizabeth discovered that their captors were not being mindful of the children, and she quietly told her ten-year-old daughter to take the baby and the other children and run to John Russell's house. The children were reluctant, but Elizabeth implored them to leave. The two warriors were obviously aware of their escape but paid no mind to it.

Once Peter and Henry Livingston saw the smoke rising above the nearby hills, they hurried home. They arrived to find the buildings in ruin. Besides their mother, a black child was dead. The Livingstons then sent word to the settlements for militia assistance.

Later, on April 15th, Elizabeth Livingston would make a deposition to explain details of the experience. It read in part:

> That evening the Indians crossed Clinch Mountain and went as far as Copper Creek, distant about eight miles.
>
> April 7. Set out early in the morning, crossed Clinch River at McClean's fish dam about 12 o'clock, then steered northwardly towards the head of Stoney Creek. Then the Indians camped carelessly, with no back spy nor kept sentries out. This day's journey was about twenty miles.
>
> April 8. Continued in camp until the sun was more than an hour high; then set out slowly and traveled five or six miles and camped near the foot of Powell's Mountain. This day Bench, the Indian Chief, became more pleasant and spoke freely to the prisoners. He told them that he was about to carry them to the Cherokee towns; that in his rout in the wilderness was his brother with two other Indians hunting, so that he might have provisions when he returned. That at his camp were several white prisoners taken from Kentucky, with horses and saddles to carry them to the towns. He made inquiry for several persons on Holstein, particularly old Gen. Shelby and said he would pay him a visit during the ensuing summer and take all his negroes. He frequently enquired who had negroes and threatened he would have them all off the North Holstein. He said all the Chicamogga towns were for war, and would soon be very troublesome to the white folks. This day two of the party was sent by Bench ahead to hunt.
>
> April 9. After travelling about 5 miles, which was over Powell's Mountain and near the foot of the Stone Mountain, a party of 13 men, under command of Lt. Vincent Hobbs of the militia of Lee County, met the enemy in front, attacked and killed Bench the first fire. I being at that time some distance off in the rear. The Indian who was my guard at first halted on hearing the firing. He then ordered me to run which I performed slowly. He then attempted to strike me in the head with the Tomahawk which I defended as well I could with my arm. By this time two of our people came into view, which encouraged me to struggle all I could. The Indian making an effort at this instant pushed me backward, and I fell over a log, at the same time aiming a violent blow at my head, which in part spent its force on me and laid me out for dead. The first thing I afterward remembered was my good friends around me giving me all the assistance in their power for my relief. They told me I was senseless for about an hour.[108]

In the meantime, news of the action at Livingston's property reached the settlements. Court was in session at the Lee County, Virginia, Courthouse when the news arrived. Court was immediately adjourned. Lieutenant Vincent Hobbs asked for volunteers to pursue Bench and try to retrieve the captives. Thirteen men offered to help. Hobbs was an expe-

10. The Final Onslaught 327

rienced backwoodsman as well as soldier, and he knew the mountain passes very well. He immediately led the militia to Stone's Gap where he was sure that Bench would cross Cumberland Mountain. When he reached the pass, he found that some Indians had apparently already crossed. Hobbs' party followed the trail, encountered two of Bench's hunters on the 8th, and killed them. Hobbs then became aware that the main party had not yet passed, so he hurried back to the gap where he immediately set up an ambush.

"Representation of Mrs. Casteel"—From *A Pictorial History of the New World*, Edited by John L Denison, published 1860.

Bench broke camp on the morning of the 9th, crossed Powell's Mountain, approached Stone's Gap, and the trap was sprung. Bench and three warriors were killed with the first volley. Lieutenant Vincent Hobbs scalped Bench. Virginia colonel Arthur Campbell sent the scalp to Virginia governor Henry "Light-horse Harry" Lee with the following note: "I send the scalp of Captain Benge … as requested by Lieutenant Hobbs, to your excellency … as a proof that he is no more, and of the activity and good conduct of Lieutenant Hobbs, in killing him and relieving the prisoners. Could it be spared from our treasury, I would beg leave to hint that a present of a neat rifle to Mr. Hobbs would be accepted, as a reward for his late services, and the executive may rest assured that it would serve as a stimulus for future exertions against the enemy."[109]

The Virginia legislature voted Lieutenant Hobbs a silver-mounted rifle, and Governor Lee sent the scalp to President Washington. It was later presented to the Smithsonian Institution.[110]

In April 1794, Thomas Bledsoe, son of the late Colonel Anthony Bledsoe, was mortally wounded at Bledsoe's Station (in present-day Greenfield, Tennessee). Trouble was also still brewing in the Holston area. On April 22, 1794, Anthony Ragan stopped at the Casteel home and found his friend, William Casteel, dead and scalped lying near the fireplace. Warriors had killed Mrs. Casteel with a butcher knife and left it distended from her side. She was also scalped, and one part of a hand was cut away. Her other arm was broken. The scene made it obvious that she had resisted with a tomahawk. One daughter and two sons were also found killed and scalped. A two-year-old was scalped and thrown into a corner of the fireplace. Ten-year-old Elizabeth was seriously wounded by tomahawk blows, and scalped, but she survived. She was in recovery for two years.

In June, William Scott, John Pettigrew, William Pettigrew, three other men, three women, four children, and 20 slaves were floating from White's Fort toward Natchez, Mississippi, on the Tennessee River. Warriors fired on their flatboat as they passed the Lower Villages. The white men returned the fire, and wounded two warriors. Young Tassel's brother, White Mankiller (Malachi Watts), rushed 150 Chickamauga downstream to Muscle Shoals and captured the boat. The whites were killed, the blacks were taken captive, and the Chickamauga warriors absconded with the trade goods. Three Cherokee were killed and one was wounded in the skirmish.

On June 26, 1794, Chief Doublehead traveled to Philadelphia to discuss the annual Cherokee annuity with Secretary of War Henry Knox. Lower Village chiefs Northward and Taken Out of the Water accompanied him. The delegation agreed that the Cherokee would pay for horses stolen by warriors in the settlements. They also obtained an increase in the annuity from $1,500 to $5,000 per year. Doublehead was grandly hosted, loaded with presents, and given the annuity in trade goods when he departed. The delegation returned by way of Charleston and arrived at the Lower Villages in late October. While they were en route, the Lower Villages had been severely attacked (see below).

Doublehead divided all of the trade goods among the Cherokee of the Lower Villages. The Upper Town chiefs had not been made aware of an annuity increase or that Doublehead had the goods. This is surprising considering Chief Hanging Maw of the Upper Towns was Chief Doublehead's brother.

On July 6, near Nashville, Isaac Mayfield was killed, then scalped and mutilated. One week later, Lieutenant McLelland led a detachment of 37 men from Captain Evan's company to Crab Orchard where 100 Creek warriors attacked them. The Creek chief and several warriors were killed. Paul Cunningham, William Flennigen, Daniel Hitchcock, and Stephen Renfroe were killed, and Abraham Byrd was wounded. The Creek drove McLelland from the field.

On the morning of July 9, 1794, Major George Winchester was killed and scalped near present-day Gallatin, Tennessee. He was a member of the county court and was on his way to a session. The next morning, Major George D. Blackmore led a company of 50 militiamen in pursuit of the war party. The Indians had too much of a lead and were not caught.

July 24, 1794, a Creek war party killed and scalped John Ish as he plowed his field. Hanging Maw sent his son, Williowee, John Oggs, and nine other Upper Town warriors to join Major King and Lieutenant Cunningham in the pursuit of the attackers. They picked up the trail on the road between Coyatee and Hiwassee, followed it through Hiwassee, and halted at Wococee. A runner from Hiwassee caught them and stated that Creek chief Obongpohego, of Toocaucaugee, was leading the war party and had rested two miles from Hiwassee. The pursuers turned around and found the house where Obongpohego had stopped. They agreed that Williowee and three other warriors would have the honor of capturing the Creek leader. They apprehended him, tied him securely, and, on July 28, delivered him to John McKee, United States Indian agent, at Tellico Blockhouse.

Governor Blount immediately had Obongpohego bound over for trial. Judge Joseph Anderson presided over a grand jury that filed an indictment against the chief. He surprisingly confessed and pleaded as a defense that his people had thrown away the peace talks of the United States and declared war. He later withdrew this plea and then pleaded not guilty. The trial jury found him guilty, and the judge asked if he had anything to say. Obongpohego replied in the negative. He was sentenced and then executed on August 4, 1794.

In August 1794, Captain Sampson Williams of the Cumberland settlements visited Colonel William Whitley of Kentucky to appeal for help. Williams proposed a plan of action. The colonel readily agreed to raise a force and cooperate in an invasion. Captain Williams organized a local volunteer militia when he returned to the Cumberlands.

Colonel John Montgomery raised a company near Clarksville; Colonel James Ford mustered troops in present-day Robertson County; and General James Robertson and Major George D. Blackmore called for volunteers near Nashville.

At the same time, Governor Blount had detached Major James Ore to lead 60 men and patrol along the Cumberland Mountains to prevent war parties from passing through the Mero District. However, Ore did not stop at the mountains, but continued westward. He rendezvoused with the Cumberland and Kentucky militias at Brown's Block House, two miles east of Buchanan's Station—a total force of 550 men.

They held a council of war, and it was agreed that, though he was outranked by the colonels, Major Ore should command the force because he was the only leader actually commissioned by a government official. Colonel Whitley retained individual command of the Kentucky troops, while Colonel Montgomery and Major Blackmore commanded the Cumberland volunteers. The primary targets were to be Nickajack and Running Water Town. These were located along the southeast bank of the Tennessee River just west of Lookout Mountain.

Before Major Ore initiated the expedition, he sent a small scouting party under the command of Colonel Isaac Roberts. His official orders were to scour the head waters of the

Elk River, but the real intent was to determine a route for the army to meet their objectives. This party of scouts included Joseph Brown, who had been a captive in the Lower Villages after his family's boat was attacked years before (see earlier this chapter).

General James Robertson accepted responsibility for redirecting Major Ore's orders. He wrote:

> Nashville, Sept 6, 1794
> MAJOR ORE: The object of your command is to defend the District of Mero against the Creeks and Cherokees of the lower towns, who I have received information are about to invade it, as also to punish such Indians as have committed recent depredations. For these objects, you will march, with the men under your command, from Brown's Block House on the 8th instant, and proceed along Taylor's Trace towards the Tennessee; and if you do not meet this party before you arrive at the Tennessee; you will pass it and destroy the lower Cherokee towns, which must serve as a check to the expected invaders; taking care to spare women and children, and to treat all prisoners who may fall into your hands with humanity, and thereby teach those savages to spare the citizens of the United States, under similar circumstances. Should you in your march discover the trails of Indians returning from commission of recent depredations on the frontiers, which can generally be distinguished by the horses stolen being shod, you are to give pursuit to such parties, even to the towns from whence they came, and punish them for their aggressions in an exemplary manner to the terror of others from the commission of similar offenses, provided this can be consistent with the main object of your command, as above expressed, the defense of the District of Mero against the expected party of Creeks and Cherokees.
> I have the utmost confidence in your patriotism and bravery, and with my warmest wishes for your success,
> I am, sir, your obedient servant,
> James ROBERTSON, B. G.[111]

The army embarked a day early on September 7, 1794, with Joseph Brown acting as its guide. They camped the first night at the site of present-day Murfreesboro, Tennessee. Then they crossed the Barren Fork of the Duck River near present-day Manchester. Next they crossed the Elk River and proceeded to the Tennessee River and, on the 12th, camped on the west bank (near present-day South Pittsburg, Tennessee) about two miles downriver (west by northwest) of Nickajack (near where present-day State Highway 156 crosses Nickajack Lake).

A few of the troops crossed over to the east bank that night to act as sentries while the main force made camp and rested. The next morning, they constructed rafts for their arms and ammunition. The sentries pulled the rafts to the east bank, and Brown led the force across. They quickly headed for Nickajack.

They moved in two columns: Colonel Whitley and the Kentucky troops to the right along the base of the mountain; Colonel Montgomery with the Tennessee portion of the force to the left along the river. Whitley was expected to pass the town and approach it from the northeast while Montgomery would march directly at it from the southwest.

Shortly after they began the march, the advance party came upon two lone cabins. The troops fired at the cabins, and the inhabitants returned fire. The shots alerted the warriors in Nickajack. When Montgomery's troops arrived they encountered several warriors who had run to the riverbank and tried an escape by canoe. The larger number fled toward Running Water Town (nearly six miles away as the crow flies, but about ten miles upriver following the route they had to take to circumvent the mountain. The route generally follows U.S. Highways 41/64/72). Nickajack normally housed about 250 warriors; however, less than 100 remained when the troops arrived.

Montgomery attacked the warriors on the river bank. Five or six large canoes were already loaded with Indians and were afloat. About 30 warriors were standing nearby preparing other canoes for departure. William Pillow opened fire, and the rest of the militia followed with a volley. Most of the standing warriors were killed except for a few good swimmers. The Indians already adrift in the large canoes took cover behind the goods. Colonel Whitley skirmished with a small band on the other end of town about 250 yards from Montgomery.

The warriors who headed for Running Water Town ran into others from there who met them head-on. The latter had heard the firing and were on the way to assist. So, they all joined together and headed for Nickajack.

The militia had already begun pursuit of the fleeing villagers and met the warriors at The Narrows along the Tennessee River. A battle ensued, and the Chickamauga warriors were devastated within a few minutes. Three whites were wounded and none killed. The militia destroyed both villages and had killed 70 warriors. One of those slain was Chief Breath who carried a letter from the Spanish. The letter was an apology that they could no longer supply the Chickamauga with arms and ammunition because they were required for their war with France.

The militia returned home with 20 prisoners, some of whom remembered Joseph Brown when he had been a captive there. Shortly after they returned, Governor Blount severely criticized General Robertson for authorizing such an expedition. His letter, along with the earlier one from Robertson to Ore, was likely intended for cover-up, so it would be hard for Secretary Knox to establish blame.

Though the impetus for Chickamauga attacks was broken, they did continue some sporadic raids on the settlements. However, there was no longer any chance of the chiefs and warriors mounting a sufficient offensive to remove the settlers from the ancestral lands. The Overmountain and Cumberland settlements were there to stay.

In the meantime, between September 12 and 16, four people were killed along the Red River, 40 miles northeast of Nashville. Chief Young Tassel then wrote General Robertson to initiate peace talks. The general replied that the chief needed to release their captive slaves and one white girl to prove their sincerity. In return Robertson declared he would release the captives from Nickajack. Robertson also averred that the militia would return soon if the Lower Villages did not seriously make overt movements toward peace.

Governor Blount was busy with requests from various Cherokee chiefs. Chief Doublehead wrote him on October 20, 1794, and asked if he could hunt in the Cumberlands now that peace was about to be established. He wanted to be sure that the Cherokee hunters would not be attacked by white militiamen. Doublehead blamed the recent outbreak of violence on the Creek. Hanging Maw complained bitterly to Governor Blount that the annuity was given to a renegade (Doublehead) and not to the Upper Villages. He reasoned that the Upper Towns had remained peaceful through all of the recent outbreaks, but Governor Blount knew that Secretary Knox wanted to appease the Lower Towns and establish peace.

On November 5, 1794, 50 warriors attacked the families of brothers Colonel Isaac Titsworth and John Titsworth. They killed seven whites whom they scalped, wounded a black woman, and took a white man, a black man, and three white children captive. The warriors soon realized they were being pursued by a militia and needed to travel faster than they could with prisoners, so they killed and scalped their captives.

The Creek demanded satisfaction from the Cherokee for the death of Obongpohego. The Creek blamed the Cherokee for his death because Hanging Maw's son and other warriors made the capture and turned him over to the whites. Their demand, however, was fruitless.

Governor Blount held a peace conference with Young Tassel, Hanging Maw, Glass, Little Turkey, and other chiefs (there is no mention that Chief Doublehead was present) at Tellico Blockhouse November 7 and 8, 1794. Governor Blount opened the conference by addressing Young Tassel: "Upon being informed by Mr. McKee that you were here, and wished to see me about the affairs of your nation, I hastened to meet you. I am happy in this interview, because your presence here is an evidence of the wish of the Lower towns for peace, whose principal chief I have ever considered you, and in Scolacutta [Hanging Maw] I behold the true head of your whole nation. Having opened the conference, I shall sit down, and first expect the talk of Colonel Watts."

Young Tassel responded:

> This meeting appears to me ordered by the Great Spirit, and affords me great pleasure. There is Scolacutta; he is old enough to be my father, and from my infancy he was a great man, and is now the great chief of the nation. In the spring of the year he sent a talk to the Lower towns, telling them he and the Upper towns had taken the United States by the hand, with a determination to hold them fast during life, and inviting the Lower towns to do the same. With tears in my eyes I have thought of this talk, and beheld the folly of the Lower towns, who at first refused to hear it. But, just before the destruction of the Running Water and Nickajack, by Major Ore, I went to them, as well as the Look-out Mountain town, and exerted myself for the restoration of peace, and I verily believe those towns had heard my talk, and were determined to be at peace with the United States. I do not say Running Water and Nickajack did not deserve the chastisement they received; nevertheless, it so exasperated those who escaped from the ruins, that, for a time, I was compelled to be silent myself; but the Glass went to the Running Water people, and they told the Glass that, notwithstanding the injury they had sustained, they had not forgot my good talks, but still held them fast, and desired me to take measures for the recovery of their prisoners ... I had my doubts, and could not act upon it; for they had told me so many lies, I was afraid to trust them ... I deliver you this (presenting a string of white beads) as a true talk ... Scolacutta, the head of the nation, is sitting by me; the Lower towns instructed me to request him not to throw them away, but to come with me to you, and present his talk in their behalf.

Chief Hanging Maw added:

> I too have a talk from the Lower towns; they were once my people, but not now; yet I cannot but think much about the talk I have now received by Watts. Before any thing happened to these towns, I had sent them many peace talks, which they would not hear; but now, since the attack made upon them by Major Ore, they send to me to make peace for them, in conjunction with Watts. I am the head-man of my nation, as Governor Blount is of the white people; it was not the fault of either that these towns were destroyed, but their own conduct brought destruction upon them; the trail of murderers and thieves was followed to these towns. Nevertheless, I cannot neglect the request they have made to me, to make peace for them; as I hope they have seen their folly ... I shall then hope to live much longer; for their bad conduct drew the white people on me, who injured me near unto death. This talk I deliver on the part of the Lower towns; and if they do not now desist

from war, and live at peace, I will give them up to the United States, to deal with as they shall see proper.

The next day, Governor Blount said in part:

The Lower towns have only to keep peace on their parts, and it will be peace.
I understand that they wish an exchange of prisoners; to this I agree, and propose that a general exchange shall take place at this post, on the 18th of December....
My letter to the chiefs of the Lower towns ... of the threatened invasion of those towns by General Logan, with a large party of men from Kentucky, unauthorized by Government ... in case Logan should carry his intended invasion of your country into execution ... it shall not prevent the meeting at this place on the 18th of December....
If you would secure a continuance of peace with the United States, it will be a duty you owe ... not to permit the Creeks to pass through your country; or, if any should slip through, and your people should discover them, on their return, with hair or horses, to seize them, and bring them to this place.

Young Tassel responded:

I wish the time proposed for the exchange of prisoners had been sooner; but, as I suppose you put it off to so distant a day to afford time to collect them, I agree to it. I fear the damage General Logan will do my people will be very great ... shall not prevent the proposed meeting and exchange of prisoners. What you say about ... the Creeks ... they are a great and powerful nation, and the Cherokees are but few, and cannot prevent their passing through their lands, when they please, to war; and on their passage they kill our hogs and cattle, and steal our horses, which we dare not resent.[112]

The dynamics of this meeting are interesting. Young Tassel (John Watts, Jr.) is a nephew of both Doublehead (Taltsuska) and Hanging Maw (Scolacutta) who are brothers. Apparently, once the Lower Villages (the Chickamauga) wanted peace, they were ready to accept Hanging Maw as the Cherokee Nation's principal chief over Little Turkey (Gundigaduhunyi); however, Little Turkey made no rebuttal regarding it.

Chief Hanging Maw was quite vocal regarding the Chickamauga warriors' acting on their own and not adhering to his policies of peace. However, he spoke for them anyway. He likely remembered the time when he had been one of them. He was last mentioned at war with the whites in February 1786 when he attacked the Peyton brothers' hunting and surveying party at Defeated Creek. He had ended his warring ways by August of that year when he stood beside Chief Old Tassel as John Sevier's henchmen, Colonels Alexander Outlaw and William Cocke, forced them into the Treaty of Coyatee (see Chapter 9).

Upper Village Chief, Hanging Maw, as Attakullakulla and Old Tassel had been, was considered a great friend of the United States. Friendship had never been a successful tactic for the Cherokee in the past and led to cession after cession of their lands to white settlers, both under the rule of Britain and the United States. However, it had become time. There was no other choice for the Cherokee. They were fighting a losing battle, and their survival depended on their accepting the fact that the ancestral land was lost. Hanging Maw would successfully establish a peaceful relationship where all previous principal chiefs had failed.

(Tellico Blockhouse was located across the Little Tennessee River from the site of Fort Loudoun. It was constructed by Governor Blount at the request of Hanging Maw for protection of the Cherokee from roving bands of settlers. The site is just southeast of where U.S. Highway 411 crosses Tellico Lake.)

Although Young Tassel pledged to end the warfare of the Chickamauga, Doublehead's faction would be active until June 1795. The Creek continued their attacks in the Cumberlands.

At 11:00 a.m. on November 11, 1794, a variously reported 15 to 40 warriors attacked Valentine Sevier's Station near Clarksville, Tennessee. Sevier successfully defended his cabin against the war party; however, the Indians killed his daughter, Betsy, her husband, Charles Snyder, and Valentine's son, Joseph Sevier, at a nearby cabin. Valentine's daughter, Rebecca, was scalped, but survived. Mrs. Ann King and her son James were also killed. Snyder's body had been severely mutilated. When the people in Clarksville heard the firing, several men hurried to assist. The warriors withdrew at the approach of the townsmen.[113]

Colonel Valentine Sevier wrote to his brother, General John Sevier:

CLARKESVILLE, Dec. 18, 1794.

Dear Brother:—The news from this place is desperate with me. On Tuesday, 11th of November last, about twelve o'clock, my station was attacked by about forty Indians. On so sudden a surprise, they were in almost every house before they were discovered. All the men belonging to the station were out, only Mr. Snider and myself. Mr. Snider, Betsy his wife, his son John and my son Joseph, were killed in Snider's house. I saved Snider, so the Indians did not get his scalp, but shot and tomahawked him in a barbarous manner. They also killed Ann King and her son James, and scalped my daughter Rebecca. I hope she will still recover. The Indians have killed whole families about here this fall. You may hear the cries of some persons for their friends daily.

The engagement, commenced by the Indians at my house, continued about an hour, as the neighbours say. Such a scene no man ever witnessed before. Nothing but screams and roaring of guns, and no man to assist me for some time. The Indians have robbed all the goods out of every house, and have destroyed all my stock. You will write our ancient father this horrid news; also my son Johnny. My health is much impaired. The remains of my family are in good health. I am so distressed in my mind, that I can scarcely write. Your affectional brother, till death.

VALENTINE SEVIER.[114]

Historian A. V. Goodpasture stated about Doublehead:

Doublehead ended his hostilities against the settlers in June 1795. The treaty of Tellico was held in October, 1805. Previously to that time Doublehead had declared himself as unalterably opposed to selling one foot of ground. But when the conference met two treaties were concluded, with his consent, one on the 25th, and the other on the 27th of October, 1805.

By the terms of the treaty of October 25th, there were reserved three square miles of land, ostensibly for the purpose of removing thereto the garrison at Southwest Point, and the United States factory at Tellico, but really for the benefit of Doublehead, his friend and adviser, John D. Chisholm, and John Riley, as the price of their influence in securing from the Cherokees the extensive cession of land granted by that treaty.

This was accomplished by means of a secret article attached to the treaty, but not submitted to the senate. This secret article also applied to a small tract at and below the mouth of Clinch River, likewise intended for the benefit of Doublehead; to one mile square at the foot of Cumberland Mountain; and to one mile square on the north bank of the Tennessee River, where Talotiskee [Nettle Carrier] lived.

The treaty of October 25th ceded all the Cherokee land north of Duck River, and also the Cumberland Mountain reservation known as the Wilderness. A large part of the nation bitterly resented this sale, but did not at once take any steps to punish Doublehead, who was chiefly responsible for it. Perhaps this was due to the fact that almost immediately after signing these treaties, Doublehead and a party of Cherokee chiefs accompanied Return J. Meigs and Daniel Smith, the commissioners who negotiated them, to Washington, and signed still another treaty with the United States, January 7, 1806, by which they ceded the Cherokee claim to what was really Chickasaw territory, lying between the Duck and Tennessee Rivers.[115]

In August 1807, the Cherokee were to receive their annuity from the government at Hiwassee Garrison near present-day Calhoun, Tennessee. A great ball play was scheduled in accordance with traditions. More than one thousand Indians were there to watch the game, along with the army officers from Hiwassee Fort, and a large number of white traders who wanted to sell their wares.

There are varying accounts of exactly what happened but the gist is as follows. A Georgia Indian trader, General Sam Dale of Mississippi, saw Doublehead and approached him. Doublehead said, "Sam, you are a mighty liar." When Dale took affront, Doublehead grinned and said, "You have never kept your promise to come and see me. You know you have lied." He flashed a bottle of whiskey and invited Dale and some nearby army officers to drink with him.

Once the bottle was empty, Dale offered to buy a new one. Doublehead said, "When I am in the white man's country, I will drink your liquor, but here you must drink with Doublehead."

Once the ball game was over, Chief Bone Polisher and a friend, both drunk, approached Doublehead and called him a traitor. Bone Polisher overtly accused him of selling Cherokee land. Doublehead sat stoically, and Bone Polisher became angrier. Then Doublehead quietly said, "Go away. You have said enough. Leave me, or I shall kill you." Bone Polisher rushed at him with his tomahawk, which Doublehead received with his left arm; his thumb was nearly severed.

Doublehead drew his pistol and shot Bone Polisher through the heart. (Some accounts say that Bone Polisher grabbed the reins of Doublehead's horse while his friend attacked with the tomahawk, after which Doublehead shot Bone Polisher in the head.)

After dark, Doublehead, who had continued to drink since the confrontation, ventured to Walker's Ferry on the Hiwassee River and entered McIntosh's Tavern.

(John Walker was a close friend of Chief James Vann, who had hated Doublehead since the massacre at Cavett's Station when Vann called him a baby killer [see earlier this chapter]. Vann despised Doublehead for other reasons including the common knowledge that Doublehead was using Cherokee land for personal gain. Additionally, Vann was married to a sister of Doublehead's second wife [no name known], which wife Doublehead supposedly had murdered for telling Vann about Doublehead's stealing from the nation.)

At the tavern, Doublehead encountered Chief Ridge, known commonly as Major Ridge, a mixed-blood called Alex

Chief Major Ridge.

Saunders, and an elderly white resident named John Rodgers (sometimes Rogers). Rodgers began to revile Doublehead as Bone Polisher had done. Doublehead rebuked Rodgers with, "You live by sufferance among us. I have never seen you in council nor on the warpath. You have no place among the chiefs. Be silent and interfere no more with me."

Rodgers persisted, and Doublehead attempted to shoot him; however, Doublehead had forgotten to reload after he shot Bone Polisher.

Someone extinguished the light, and at the same time another fired a pistol. When the light was fired up, Ridge, Saunders, and Rodgers had all disappeared, and Doublehead lay face down on the floor. The pistol ball had shattered his lower jaw and lodged in the nape of his neck.

Doublehead's friends showed up at the tavern and initially started out to take him to Hiwassee Garrison. However, they thought Doublehead's enemies would overtake them. They changed directions and hid the chief in the loft of Schoolmaster James Black's house. Two warriors from Bone Polisher's clan followed Doublehead's blood trail and found his hiding place. Ridge and Saunders arrived at the same time. They were sounding war whoops as they galloped in. Trader Sam Dale and Georgia colonel James Brown were shortly behind them.

The wounded chief was prone on the floor, his jaw and arm terribly lacerated. Ridge and Saunders each aimed a pistol, but misfired. Doublehead jumped up and rushed Ridge, but Saunders discharged his pistol and shot Doublehead through the hip. Saunders then rushed Doublehead with a tomahawk, but the chief wrenched it from him and, in turn, rushed Ridge with it. While they tussled, Saunders found another tomahawk and drove it deep into Doublehead's skull. Doublehead collapsed to the floor where another Indian crushed his head with a spade.[116]

Ridge, Vann, and Saunders were a part of a conspiracy to assassinate Doublehead because of his many sinister actions over the years, concluding with his Cherokee land schemes. The three had drawn the short straws and were assigned to slay the miscreant. Vann had ended up too drunk to follow through, so Ridge and Saunders completed the deed.

Doublehead's friends and family, aware that they were despised in the Cherokee community, generally began to leave about 1809, some 30 years prior to the Trail of Tears. They migrated to Arkansas and Oklahoma. Those Cherokee are now referred to as the Old Settlers, and are the reported progenitors of the present-day United Keetoowah Band of Cherokee Indians of Tahlequah, Oklahoma.

When the Cherokee were removed in 1838, many of those Old Settlers were eager for the arrival of Doublehead's old enemy, Major Ridge. Those on the Trail of Tears were generally the progenitors of the present-day Cherokee Nation (or the Cherokee Nation of Oklahoma), also headquartered in Tahlequah.

Major Ridge, his son John Ridge, and his nephew Elias Boudinot were all assassinated in Oklahoma on June 22, 1839. The reported killers were Doublehead's son, Bird Tail Doublehead, and others of a conspiracy numbering as many as 40 Cherokee. There still remain difficulties between the two western bands of Cherokee.

The Eastern Band of Cherokee is composed mostly of descendants of Cherokee who took refuge in the Appalachian Mountains to avoid the removal. The headquarters is in Cherokee, North Carolina. The Eastern Band of Cherokee and the Cherokee Nation of Oklahoma have held several joint councils and signed several joint resolutions. The two are generally cooperative.

Summary

The last years of Cherokee existence in the Upper and Lower Villages were wrought with difficulties. Those who lived in the Upper Villages and the Lower Towns rarely agreed on policy, politics, or principal chiefs.

It is important to ponder some important occurrences of those last years.

- What went wrong that culminated in their removal to the West?
- What might the Cherokee have done differently?
- How had the British defaulted on the trust of the Cherokee Nation?
- How did the Overmountain settlers exacerbate the destruction of the colonial Cherokee community?[1]

First, it is necessary to finalize the stories of some later Cherokee and their acquaintances.

John "The Tory" Pickens, first cousin of General Andrew Pickens, had long been a comrade of Dragging Canoe. He was so popular among the Chickamauga that Chief Bench named one of his sons Pickens Benge.

John had moved to Natchez, Mississippi, where he married a Chickasaw woman named Mary Adams. That was uncommon because the Chickasaw had become friendly with the Cumberland settlers and refused to rejoin the Chickamauga confederation. Pickens died January 18, 1789, just weeks before his son, Edmund Pickens, was born, and three years before the death of Dragging Canoe.

Mary moved with her son to Chickasaw country in Mississippi as she believed it a safer place to raise him. She married another white man, Bernard McLaughlin, sometime during the 1790s. Mary and Edmund eventually converted to Presbyterianism.

Edmund Pickens married Euth-li-ke, a Chickasaw woman, in 1826. The family was among those Chickasaw forced to remove to the Indian Territory in Oklahoma in 1837. They settled on the Red River near the present-day town of Enville.

Chickasaw chief Ishtehotopa died in 1847, and Edmund Pickens was the first elected principal chief (Chief Ok-chan-tubby) in 1848. He served eight years and died in 1868.

Young Tassel (John Watts, Jr.) reportedly died in Wills Town about 1808.

Chief Doublehead had been a primary instigator of troubles within the Cherokee community and caused it to divide into factions. The chief's good friend, John D. Chisholm, who had acted as Doublehead's attorney and agent, had also profited by Doublehead's schemes. (John Chisholm was the grandfather of Jesse Chisholm who founded the Old Chisholm Trail.) Chisholm had gone west in the early 1800s with the Old Settlers and died in Hot Springs, Arkansas, in 1818.

Chiefs Black Fox and Doublehead entered into several agreements with not only the United States, but with private white enterprises to financially benefit themselves. Often each tried to cover the action by entering into an agreement that only benefitted the other. On January 7, 1806, Doublehead signed the Cotton Gin Treaty which gave a lease to a white enterprise that netted Black Fox a $100 annual annuity for life.

Chief Hanging Maw had died about 1794 and was succeeded as principal chief by Chief Bloody Fellow; although Chief Little Turkey claimed the title as he had done when Hanging Maw was principal chief. Black Fox succeeded Little Turkey in his claim upon the chief's death in 1804. Southwest Territory governor William Blount, and the United States government, had always recognized the Hanging Maw-Bloody Fellow coalition over Little Turkey-Black Fox; however, many Cherokee backed the latter. The Lower Towns, headed by the Black Fox faction, had expressed an interest in migrating west in 1808; however, the Upper Town headmen led by Chief Bloody Fellow were not interested. Chief Black Fox was officially recognized as the Cherokee Nation's principal chief by the National Cherokee Council in September 1809. He died July 26, 1811, and was succeeded by Chief Path Killer. Shortly after Black Fox's confirmation as principal chief, the Old Settlers began their relocation (see Chapter 10).

Chiefs James Vann, Major Ridge, and Charles Hicks acted as a triumvirate of a head council in the east. The three agreed with Hanging Maw and Bloody Fellow that it was important to have a peaceful relationship with the whites, and they sustained Bloody Fellow's claim to be principal chief of the nation. They supported acculturation, so they implemented some European-American ways into the Cherokee lifestyle: white farming practices, white education, and even Christian teachings by the Moravians.

Charles Hicks married Nancy as his principal wife. Chief Broom, the headman of Broomtown, was Nancy's father. (Present-day Broomtown is located eight miles southeast of Fort Payne, Alabama, and one mile west of the Georgia border.)

The triumvirate established its operational headquarters at Broomtown. On September 11, 1808, the three held a council session called the Council of Broomtown. Doublehead's death (see Chapter 10) led the group to consider the viability of the Cherokee tradition of Blood Law or Clan Retribution. The triumvirate decided it would not be wise to continue such a tradition in light of the new relationship between the nation and the whites. That had often led to earlier problems as when Cherokee clansmen killed whites in retribution for slain kinsmen, regardless of whether the targeted whites were even from the same community as the original slayers. The whites could not understand the Cherokee thinking on such a matter, and usually war resulted. The triad abolished the practice with the Act of Oblivion.

On April 10, 1810, those headmen of the seven Cherokee clans who did not go west with the Old Settlers met at Oostanaula and confirmed the abolishment of blood vengeance. The Clans also relinquished individual council responsibilities in favor of the central Cherokee Nation Council. However, the Cherokee people did not always adhere to that decision. Chief Vann led with the formation of the Cherokee Lighthorse Guard. The guard operated as a police force; they monitored the roads in the nation, suppressed horse rustling, and generally punished those committing crimes within the nation. On February 19, 1809, five months after the initial Act of Oblivion, Chief James Vann was shot as he rode on patrol near Buffington's Tavern (in present-day Forsythe County, Georgia). The slaying was likely a retribution for the killing of Chief Doublehead. That was followed nearly 30 years later by the assassination of Major Ridge and some of his kin in Oklahoma (see Chapter 10). (Oostanaula was 10 miles southwest of present-day Calhoun, Georgia.)

Major Ridge's killing was primarily attributed to revenge for Doublehead's assassination as was that of James Vann. Many Cherokee, however, faulted Chief Ridge as the cause for the Trail of Tears, which added impetus for his assassination. It is estimated that 4,000 people died during the Cherokee removal. Chief Ridge had signed the Treaty of New Echota on December 29, 1835, which ceded all Cherokee lands east of the Mississippi River to the United States and agreed to Cherokee relocation to the Indian Territory in the west. Chief John Ross and the Cherokee Council of Chiefs rejected the treaty and appealed to the government that Chief Ridge had no right to establish such a treaty in the name of the Cherokee Nation. They were informed that it was too late to appeal because the United States Senate had already ratified the cession. Black Fox and the Old Settlers did not sign the Act of Oblivion, and they departed for the west prior to the Council of Oostanaula.

It is possible that the Cherokee Nation would have lost their prime territory in spite of all it could have done; however, there are certain things that might have been done differently to improve their chances of retaining their ancestral grounds.

The first consideration has to be the open-arms policy that Attakullakulla had established with the British colonists. He certainly had an affinity for the king and for the royal leaders within the settlements.

There is a line from *Lee Daniels' The Butler* when a mentor tells young Cecil Gaines: "We have two faces: ours, and the one we have to show the white folks!"

A similar statement was broadcast in a 1962 *Twilight Zone* episode, "A Piano in the House": "Of course, I've always believed that we have two faces. One that we wear, and the other that we keep hidden."[2]

I do not imply with those citations that Chief Attakullakulla was hiding the true nature of the Cherokee people; however, though they were courteous, they were steeped in tradition. The Cherokee people were very guarded and did not promote cohabitation with those of other groups. The Cherokee would get along with neighboring tribes, but they always established boundaries to protect each group's ancestral, or claimed, hunting grounds. That was the traditional face of the Cherokee people up until the white colonization. However, Attakullakulla presented a new face of the Cherokee, one that hinted the two cultures should live closely.

The primary result of such wide-open policy was the introduction of whites as permanent inhabitants of Cherokee villages. Traders from the settlements wanted to live where the trade existed, but Cherokee tradition was, that to do so, the traders had to marry into a Cherokee clan. Such closeness led to an extraordinary amount of trade between the two communities and the destruction of old Cherokee traditions. The people became too reliant upon the whites' trade goods. The Cherokee might have still prospered by trade on a lesser level had they kept the colonial settlements at arm's length, and not allowed white traders to remain in the villages. Such residence with the Cherokee was actually a precursor to settler encroachment. The Overmountain settlers, those along the Watauga, Holston, and Nolichucky rivers, had drifted in mainly from Virginia. Had this been decades earlier, and been encroachment from another tribe rather than white colonists, tradition would have demanded that the Cherokee go to war to secure their ancestral lands. The war would have established a boundary. However, Chief Attakullakulla countered the action by negotiating peace treaties with the colonies which always resulted with the Cherokee's ceding land. This allowed the encroaching settlers to gain a toehold and grow, which led to expansion, further encroachment, and more land cessions. Tradition would have forced the tribe to face the problem at the first sign of encroachment before the growth got out of hand and before there became more settlers than the Cherokee could evict.

Attakullakulla was guilty of two things. He personally got too close to the whites, and he was far ahead of his time. Years later, Chief Hanging Maw exhibited the same policies as Attakullakulla had done; however, the time had become right for those actions. The white community had gained control, and the only remedy left was to establish peace or the Cherokee would not survive as a people.

Another problem for the Cherokee was disunity. In 1775, Chief Dragging Canoe, Attakullakulla's son, promoted a return to Cherokee tradition. He tried to explain to the older chiefs that they were not just ceding land to the whites, but were relinquishing the future of the younger Cherokee people. Traditionally, there would have been such a presentation by competing chiefs; however, the leaders would not have implemented a major decision, such as divestiture of ancestral Cherokee lands, in the face of severe reluctance among the people. The result of that action forced the young warriors to withdraw from the community along with Chief Dragging Canoe, who had become the active voice to protect against encroachment.

The problem of white encroachment was not new, and it always seemed to be masked by the whites who convinced the Indians that giving up their land was in their best interest. The older dovish chiefs and the white negotiators of the treaties always seemed to place the Indians in a subservient role: younger brother or children of the whites. The words were flowery but mistakenly implied the Indian community was not intelligent enough to live without instructions.

In the mid 1700s, when the English and the French were jockeying for the influence of the northern tribes, and for new settlements on the ancestral lands, they often made it seem the Indians were blessed to have the Europeans' guidance.

In 1749, Christopher Gist represented the Ohio Company for the British and was at the forefront of the competition with the French. While actively surveying land, he was approached by an old Delaware chief who posed an interesting question for the explorer. Washington Irving wrote about the experience in his five-volume publication, *Life of George Washington*:

> An old Delaware sachem, meeting him [Gist] ... propounded a somewhat puzzling question. "The French," said he, "claim all the land on one side of the Ohio, the English claim all the land on the other side—now where does the Indians' land lie?"
> Poor savages! Between their "fathers," the French, and their "brothers," the English, they were in a fair way of being most lovingly shared out of the whole country.[3]

If the older chiefs had realized that the policy of innumerable peace treaties was only leading to numerous land cessions, they might have supported the younger chiefs' desires for a return to the tradition of defending against encroachment while there was still time. They did not. The result was catastrophic: the younger chiefs, who understood, fought encroachment while the older chiefs continued to accommodate the white settlers with peace treaties. Oddly, the older chiefs ignored the warnings of the northern tribes when the Shawnee and the Iroquois would visit the Cherokee to enlist them in a confederation against the whites.

There were spates when the British colonial leaders, the royal governors and the military, failed at reciprocity during their alliance with the Cherokee. The Cherokee had sent warriors to the aid of the British throughout the French and Indian War but were often met with derision and lack of respect from the British officers. Even Chief Attakullakulla had experienced some of that disrespect. However, the Cherokee continued to ally with the British throughout that war and again throughout the American Revolution.

The king had reached out to the Indian nations with his Proclamation of 1763 which established a firm boundary between whites and Indians and outlawed encroachment. However, the royal governors were more concerned with military use along the coast to alleviate the fears of plantation owners regarding possible slave revolts. The overall impetus for the use of the military was to protect the prized colonial exports of goods for the British Empire, and all profits that arose from those imports. They did not have enough manpower to even enforce criminal laws in the backcountry of Georgia and the Carolinas, let alone protect a remote boundary line for the benefit of the Cherokee.

After all the Cherokee had done for the British in the French and Indian War, the British turned on them and attacked the Cherokee community three years in a row. The Cherokee may have brought the first attack upon themselves in 1759, but Royal Governor William Henry Lyttleton certainly exacerbated the situation. After Cherokee warriors were attacked and killed while traveling through Virginia, the clansmen of the slain Indians enacted the tradition of blood vengeance. They did not just take it out on Virginians but also on some backcountry Carolinians. The tradition of clan vengeance specified that a victim's clan had the right to take satisfaction from the clan of the person who had initially wronged their clansmen. Had they treated Virginia Colony as a clan separate from the others, and left the Carolinas alone, they may not have been devastated with war over the next three years.

Three expeditions against the Cherokee resulted: late 1759 to early 1760 by South Carolina governor Lyttleton, mid–1760 by British colonel Archibald Montgomery, and, most devastating of all, by British lieutenant colonel James Grant in 1761. After all of these actions, the Cherokee leaders still honored their alliances with the British (see Chapter 4).

At the beginning of the American Revolution, the British prepared to attack Charles Town in July 1776. The British Indian agents were to have the Cherokee warriors attack the backcountry of the Carolinas on July 1, to provide a second front against the Americans. However, the British attacked Charles Town by sea early, in June. By the time the Cherokee attacked, the British had already been repelled, so the Cherokee were left in the lurch. That led to the Cherokee War of 1776. This was the most devastating of all. Huge militia forces attacked from the Carolinas, Georgia, and Virginia. The Cherokee had no chance (see Chapter 6).

The Cherokee had not learned from their past experiences that attacks in the Carolinas would lead to desolation in the Cherokee villages. Had the Cherokee directed their forces against the encroachers in the Overmountain settlements, and not been redirected to the Carolinas by the British, they might have had made some headway at clearing their land. Also, the South Carolina and North Carolina militias might not have attacked, as they would not have needed to apply any retribution.

The tribe missed opportunities for a forced resolution of encroachment because of mistakes by both the British and the Cherokee. The Battle of Kings Mountain arose because British major Patrick Ferguson had sent a warning letter to the Overmountain community. He had been assigned to guard General Cornwallis' left flank as he prepared to move into North Carolina. The Overmountain militias were the impetus for that assignment as Cornwallis feared the group would stage an attack.

Ferguson's methodology was to warn the militias to remain on their own side of the mountains. However, his warning proved to be an invitation for them to come over the mountains and attack him; thus, the battle occurred in October 1780. Ferguson and some of his soldiers were killed, and the rest were captured.

Ferguson could have taken a more proactive approach: gone over the mountain without any warning, coordinated attacks with Dragging Canoe's warriors, and possibly forced the encroaching settlers from the Cherokee lands. Ferguson, at worst, could have done enough damage to keep the Overmountain militia from attacking Cornwallis' army in North Carolina. That was the last chance for the British army to provide any reciprocity and assistance to their Cherokee allies with their white settler problem. The loss of Ferguson's force did not benefit the Cherokee, and it impeded Cornwallis, who had to withdraw back into South Carolina.

Then the Cherokee frittered away their last opportunity for major success against the settlements when they did not take advantage of the Overmountain militiamen's absence after they left to battle Ferguson at Kings Mountain. The militia had left Sycamore Shoals on September 26, 1780, and did not return until after October 15. There were three weeks for the Cherokee warriors to mount an offensive and do severe damage during the militia's absence. However, they had just begun such a movement when the militia returned and took up a proper defense of the settlements.

The final outcome of Cherokee removal may never have been avoided—even had these issues been handled in any other way. The Overmountain community certainly exacerbated the situation with goon tactics, such as the murder of Old Tassel and the other chiefs when it was obvious that the Upper Village chiefs had no control over the Lower Town warriors. The situation was ideal for the settlement leaders. When the Chickamauga attacked the settlements, some responsive action always occurred against the Upper Villages that resulted with more land cessions for the settlements. Attakullakulla and the other chiefs of his ilk had always trusted the settlements' leaders to be generous and treat the Cherokee fairly. That never happened in the Holston, Watauga, or Nolichucky white communities.

The methodology was obvious. Historian John Preston Arthur noted about the massacre of Old Tassel:

THE HORROR OF THE FRONTIERSMEN. Such was the indignation with which this deed was received by the better class of backwoodsmen that Sevier's forces melted away, and was obliged to abandon a march he had planned against the Chickamaugas. The Continental Congress passed resoliutions [sic] condemning such acts, and the justices of the court of Abbeville, S. C., with Andrew Pickens at their head "wrote to the people living on Nollechucky, French Broad and Holstein" denouncing in unmeasured terms the encroachments and outrages of which Sevier and his backwoodsmen had been guilty.[4]

Notwithstanding the Cherokee's loss of their ancestral land, the Trail of Tears removal, and the fact that the white men certainly did not provide the Cherokee with just compensation for such heinous actions, relationships between the three present-day Cherokee Bands and the white community did steadily improve over the years.

The Cherokee Nation (of Oklahoma), the United Keetoowah Band of Cherokee Indians, and the Eastern Band of Cherokee have all become very enterprising with their adaptation to living with the white community. There no longer is a necessity for boundaries to keep the two cultures apart. Indian reservations have mostly exhibited a horrific environment for Indian tribes across the United States. However, the Cherokee have often been noted as one of the leaders among Indian nations to have achieved success creating successful enterprises on their land. They have also adapted well to the new way of life that was forced upon them, while they maintained viability concerning their own heritage and traditions. Education of the white community regarding the history and plight of the Cherokee has led to a more cooperative existence between the two in today's culture than ever existed in colonial times.

One of the best examples of progress on the part of the white community occurred early, indeed, about the time of the removal. Many Cherokee hid out in the mountains of North Carolina and were never forced west.

Yonaguska (Drowning Bear), a chief of the Middle and Valley towns, was one of those who lingered in the east. He, as the only chief who remained, gathered others to form a civil community and generally watch over the welfare of all. They remained in hiding as long as they needed to; then, they established formal communities. They were not allowed, by law, to own property on the old eastern Cherokee lands.

William Holland Thomas was born in 1805. His father was Welsh and had fought at Kings Mountain with Colonel William Campbell. Young Thomas was an only child; his father had drowned shortly before William's birth. The lad was hired to tend an Indian trading store on Soco Creek when he was twelve years old. Chief Yonaguska admired William and adopted him as his own son. He was called Will-Usdi (Little Will). William Thomas had already learned to speak Cherokee, and Yonaguska taught him Cherokee traditions and the way of life. Thomas even learned how to write with the Sequoya syllabary. (Soco Creek is near the junction of U.S. Highways 19 and 441, near the present-day Indian Village of Oconaluftee in the Qualla Boundary.)

Thomas later became an attorney and represented the tribe in relations with the United States government. Chief Yonaguska, when he got old, selected Thomas to be his successor. William Holland Thomas served as the principal chief of the Eastern Band from 1839 to 1870, the only full-blooded white man to do so in any of the Cherokee bands.

Thomas knew that the Cherokee could not purchase land, but he, as a white man, could do so. He personally bought property and established a Cherokee reserve (or land in trust) for the tribe's use at what is presently called Qualla Boundary. Thomas bought a farm near present-day Whittier, North Carolina, and built a home which he called Stecoah for its namesake, an old Cherokee village that had once existed at the same site.

He owned five trading stores: in North Carolina at Quallatown, Murphy, Robbinsville, Webster, and in Charleston, Tennessee. As an agent for the Cherokee Nation, Thomas created five towns for them within the preserve: Bird Town, Paint Town, Wolf Town, Yellow Hill, and Big Cove. He drew up a legal, but simple, form of government for them which was effected by Chief Yonaguska and continued by Thomas. William Holland Thomas was elected to the North Carolina State Senate in 1848.

Thomas' health failed following the Civil War, and his affairs, intertwined with those of the Cherokee, were settled by arbitrators. It was found that Thomas had not personally profited by the property management; indeed, the Cherokee had prospered. Colonel William Holland Thomas died May 12, 1893.

EASTERN BAND INCORPORATED. "In order to acquire a more definite legal status, the Cherokee residing in North Carolina—being practically all those of the eastern band having genuine Indian interests—became a corporate body under the laws of the state in 1889. In 1894 the long-standing litigation between the East Cherokee and a number of creditors and claimants to Indian lands within and adjoining the Qualla boundary was finally settled by a compromise by which the several white tenants and claimants within the boundary agreed to execute a quitclaim and vacate on payment to them by the Indians of sums aggregating $24,552, while for another disputed adjoining tract of 33,000 acres the United States agreed to pay, for the Indians, at the rate of $1.25 per acre. The necessary government approval having been obtained, Congress appropriated a sufficient amount for carrying into effect the agreement, thus at last completing a perfect and unencumbered title to all the lands claimed by the Indians, with the exception of a few outlying tracts of comparative unimportance."[5]

Author's note: Although I cannot be considered for membership in any of the Cherokee bands, I am proud to be a descendent of the colonial Cherokee. I am as proud of that as I am of my heritage from the Pickens family. The Cherokee have proven to be exemplary as an intrepid and flexible people. They have survived deplorable treatment on the part of the white people; yet, have made the most of their situation, and they walk today with their heads held high.

Appendices

A. Author's Cherokee Genealogy

Regarding my own Cherokee pedigree, it is difficult to track Cherokee lineage since there is no official paper trail (i.e., birth certificates and marriage licenses). However, there are several Cherokee genealogists who have delved into the matter and have studied the word-of-mouth passage of their Cherokee origins. In developing the following information I found that the common rolls, and even Emmett Starr's great book of genealogical material, *History of the Cherokee Indians,* are incomplete. Luckily, many Cherokee genealogists have entered their information into the database of the Church of Jesus Christ of Latter-day Saints (Mormon). There are varying genealogies that are pertinent, and the accuracy of each depends on how the information was passed down. I combined the pedigrees that made the most sense and seemed to fit my data.

I had long ago determined that my third great-grandmother is Margaret Murphy of Arkansas who, in about 1845, married a man named McGee. She married my third great-grandfather, William R. Kelly, also in Arkansas, about 1858. She had three children by McGee, the youngest and only boy named William Acil McGee. He was deaf and mute and lived out his days with his mother. The Kelley family to this day refers to him as Uncle Asa.

Margaret Murphy had two sons by William Kelly, the youngest being my great-great-grandfather Elijah Richard M. Kelley. (The name was spelled Kelly for five generations before the "e" was added ahead of the "y." Prior to that time, the name was also spelled Kellie and Kellee.)

Family tradition is that Margaret was Cherokee and the daughter of Mary "Polly" Murphy. That is difficult to prove because she does not show up with the Murphy or Murphey family on the Henderson Roll (1835), or the Mary Murphy family on the Mullay Roll (1848), the Silar Roll (1851), the Chapman Roll (1852), or the Swetland Roll (1869). However, she was long gone from the Eastern Band of Cherokee, at least by after the Henderson Roll, because of her marriages in Arkansas.

Mary Murphy died in 1882, but the Murphy family continued to show up on the Eastern Cherokee rolls beyond that date. A Margaret Murphy shows up with the family on the Hester Roll (1883), the Churchill Roll (1908), the Guion Miller Roll (1909), but not the Baker Roll (1924). This Margaret Murphy was apparently younger than my Margaret Murphy because she is on the roll in 1909, and the Margaret in my family died in 1907. It does show, however, that Margaret was a family name, and the younger Margaret was likely named after the Margaret who moved west.

Margaret Murphy [Kelley] (left), third-great-grandmother of the author, second-great-granddaughter of Chief Doublehead. Acil Mcgee (right) was the son of Margaret Murphy by a previous marriage.

Margaret Murphy was born in Tennessee in October 1828 per United States census information. She likely went west during the Trail of Tears in 1838 when she was 10 years old, perhaps with the McGee family, since she was only about 17 when first married. The McGee surname does show up in the Henderson Roll (1835) which lists those to be removed to the west.

Mary Murphy is genealogically listed as born in Elbert County, Georgia, between 1795 and 1805. She is probably the great-granddaughter of Indian trader Daniel Murphy of the Augusta Company. He was reportedly killed in 1752 by a Middle Town Cherokee warrior named Chiotlohee (see Chapter 3). Daniel was married to a Cherokee woman (as were all traders who lived within Cherokee villages) and had a son who also married a Cherokee woman. That son, the grandfather of Mary Murphy, is likely the Tory Indian trader named Daniel Murphy who was killed by Whig militiamen at the Big Shoals of the Oconee River in Georgia in June 1782. (See Chapter 9.) Mary "Polly" Murphy was then probably seven-eighths Cherokee, though this is also hard to prove. No paper trail actually exists that tracks her prior to the 1848 rolls. Emmet Starr's book, *History of the Cherokee Indians,* is an excellent reference for Cherokee family studies as it lists the genealogy for several old families. Unfortunately, even though the Mary Murphy clan is listed on many rolls, Mr. Starr did not include the surname in his record.

Some genealogists (not Cherokee) have incorrectly listed another Mary "Polly" Murphey, the daughter of Caswell County, North Carolina, politician Archibald D. Murphey, as the same Mary Murphy. However, Archibald Murphey's Mary, having been born in Chatham, North Carolina, in 1794, is clearly older than my Mary Murphy. The older Mary married Daniel Robinett in Wilkes County, North Carolina, on March 25, 1819, and she died in Cherokee County, Georgia. Mary and Daniel Robinett are listed on the 1860 Federal census for Woodstock District, Cherokee County, Georgia.

The 1860 Federal census for Beaverdam District, Cherokee County, North Carolina, lists my Mary Murphy, so she is clearly not the daughter of Archibald Murphy. I can see the point of confusion since each of them lived in Cherokee County in 1860, but in different states.

Mary Murphy was born in Elberta, Georgia, in 1803. She clearly stated on the 1850 Federal census that she was born in Georgia, and there is no record of Archibald Murphey as having ever lived in Georgia. Additionally Mary's son, William R. Matoy, by James Matoy (one of her husbands) was born in 1819 in Murphy, North Carolina, when the other Mary was marrying Daniel Robinett.

Mary Murphy had several Cherokee relationships and husbands. Those known men are Tauhstaheesky whom she married about 1820, James (*Oowuhgah*) Matoy whom she married about 1825, and Whiplash (Cahstahyeestee, also known as Kunsteeneestah or Old Muskrat) who is the only one she is depicted with on the rolls where he took the white name Martin Murphy. (Interestingly, the 25th Congress, 3rd Session Senate: Report from the Secretary of War refers to "Name Whip Lash and Valuation 52[qm] as being on something called "The Trail of Tears Roll" which is explained to be created from two separate lists, each originated in 1835. One of them is undoubtedly the Henderson Roll; however, neither Whip Lash nor Martin Murphy is listed on it. A Muskrat is listed from North Carolina. If Whiplash [by whatever name he used] is on this Trail of Tears Roll, then he likely took his daughter, Margaret Murphy, on the trip.)

Whiplash's parents are genealogically credited as being Rachael (or Rachel) Riley and a minor (local) chief named Bell Rattle (sometimes Bell Ringer or Bell Ratler [sic]) of present-day Bell Town, Tennessee. The Rachel Riley identification is complicated. Rachel Riley is shown as a younger daughter of Indian trader Samuel Riley and Gulustiyu (one of two daughters of Chief Doublehead that Riley married and with whom he cohabitated). That is not indicated by Emmet Starr. He shows Rachael as being married to Daniel Milton and James McDaniel with no mention of Chief Bell Rattle, but it is common for historians to miss a connection because Cherokee family trees were mostly passed down by word of mouth (at least prior to the formal rolls). Multirelationships were common among the Colonial Cherokee women who dominated in the matrilineal Cherokee society. They had the right to end a relationship if they felt a different warrior would be better suited. The Silar and Chapman Roll lists a Rachael Murphy with the Mary Murphy family which indicates that Rachael was a family name, even if it was of Whip Lash's family.

The 1850 Federal Census implies a close relationship between Mary Murphy and Rachael Riley, her mother-in-law, because it shows Rachael as living next door to Mary. It also shows Mary Murphy's 17-year-old son, Jesse, living with 80-year-old Rachael Riley. Likely he was to help his grandmother in her old age. Additionally, Mary Murphy's son, William R. Matoy, is shown living two houses away. Some of Mary's children by Whip Lash are shown in her household on the census.

Rachael Riley was half-blood Cherokee while Bell Rattle was full-blood. Thus Whip Lash was three-quarters blood. Margaret Murphy, therefore, was also thirteen-sixteenths blood Cherokee. That reduces me to about 2.3 percent Cherokee when counting down the generations of full white blood that integrates into the line from Margaret Murphy. I certainly don't qualify (by the current criteria for membership) in any of the three present-day Cherokee Bands in the east or the west; however, that was not my original goal. While I would certainly consider registration an honor, my incentive is that pride in my Cherokee ancestry equates to that of my Pickens heritage.

Another way of looking at my ancestry is since Chief Doublehead is likely my 7th great-grandfather, the same number of generations back as Joseph Pickens, I have as much of Chief Doublehead's blood in my veins as I do Captain Pickens'.

Genealogy Chart Key

SMALL CAPS—Known active leader in Cherokee Chickamauga faction

Bold Italic—Known principal chief (first beloved man) or chieftess (beloved woman)

No.	Relationship to Author	Name
1	Self (Author)	William R. Reynolds, Jr.
2	Father	William R. Reynolds
3	Mother	Shirley Maxine Kelley
4	Grandfather	Lloyd Dorwin Kelley
5	Grandmother	Eula Ann Clevenhagen
6	Great-Grandfather	James William Jefferson Kelley
7	Great-Grandmother	Mary Louise "Molly" Roten
8	2-Great-Grandfather	Elijah Richard M. Kelley
9	2-Great-Grandmother	Syntha Melvina Carter
10	3-Great-Grandfather	William R. Kelly
11	3-Great-Grandmother	Margaret (Marguerite) Murphy (1st husband McGee)
12	4-Great-Grandfather	Cah-Stahyeestee (Kunsteeneestah) "Whiplash"
13	4-Great-Grandmother	Mary "Polly" Murphy
14	5-Great-Grandfather	Chief Bell Rattle (husband of #61, Rachel Riley)
15	5-Great-Grandaunt	Elizabeth Riley (sister of #61, Rachel Riley)
16	6-Great-Grandfather	Samuel Riley, Jr.
17	6-Great Grandmother	Gulustiyu
18	7-GREAT-GRANDFATHER	CHIEF DOUBLEHEAD (TALTSUSKA OR INCALATANGA)
19	7-Great-Grandmother	Create (or Creat) Priber
20	8-Great-Grandfather	Christian Gottlieb Priber
21	8-Great-Grandmother	Clogoitah
22	9-Great-Grandfather	Chief Savanah Tom Moytoy III Raven of Tellico
23	9-Great-Grandmother	Nancili "Nancy" Moytoy
24	10-Great-Grandfather	Chief Ahmahtoya Moytoy I "The Elder"
25	10-Great-Grandmother	Anigawi "QuedsSi" "Quatsie"
26	**10-Great-Grandfather**	***Chief Amadohiyi (Amaedohi) "The Emperor" "Trader Tom" Moytoy II***
27	10-Great-Grandmother	Chalekatha "Nancy" of the Wolf Clan
28	11-Great-Grandmother	Lokacholakatha "The Pride" (Shawnee)
29	11-Great-Grandfather	Thomas Pasmere Carpenter "Cornplanter"
30	11-Great-Grandmother	Locha "Cornstalk" (Shawnee)
31	12-Great-Grandfather	Chief Opechan "Stream" (Shawnee)
32	12-Great-Grandmother	Matachanna "Cleopatra" "the Shawano" (Powhatan)
33	13-Great-Grandfather	Chief Algonkian "Running Stream" (Shawnee)

Appendix A: Author's Cherokee Genealogy

No.	Relationship to Author	Name
34	13-Great-Grandmother	"Scented Flower" (Powhatan)
35	14-Great-Grandfather	"Murmuring Ripple" (Shawnee)
36	14-Great-Grandfather	Chief "Dashing Stream" (Powhatan)
37	**9-Great-Granduncle**	**Chief Connecorte "Old Hop" (Guhnagadoga, Kanagatoga)**
38	n/a	Sugi of the Wolf Clan
39	1st Cousin 10x removed	"Young Hop" Moytoy
40	9-Great-Granduncle	Raven of Hiwassee Carpenter of the Potato Clan
41	9-Great-Granduncle	White Owl Raven
42	**9-Great-Granduncle**	**Chief Oshasqua "Ammouskossittee" Moytoy V**
43	9-Great-Grandaunt	Aganunitsi "Quatsie" Moytoy of the Wolf Clan
44	n/a	Small Pox Conjuror of Settico, the Fox, Tsula or Cheulah
45	n/a	John Beamer
46	1st Cousin 10x removed	Chief Ostenaco "Ustanakwa" "Skiagusta" "Big Head" "Mankiller" "Outacite," also known as "Judd's Friend," then "Judge Friend"
47	1st Cousin 10x removed	Kittagusta "Prince Skalilosken"
48	**9-Great-Granduncle**	**Chief Oconostota "Aganstat" "Ground Hog Sausage" "Stalking Turkey"**
49	n/a	Unknown
50	8-Great-Grandaunt	Ollie of the Red Paint Clan
51	**8-Great-Granduncle**	**Chief Adagalkala "Atagulkalu" "Attakullakulla" "Little Carpenter" also "Okoonaka" "White Owl"**
52	1st Cousin 9x removed	Chief Tsiyagunsini "Dragging Canoe"
53	1st Cousin 9x removed	Chief Ooskiah "Oskuah" "Old Abram of Chilhowee"
54	1st Cousin 9x removed	Ocuma "The Badger"
55	2nd Cousin 8x removed	Chief Enola "Black Fox"
56	1st Cousin 9x removed	Turtle at Home
57	1st Cousin 9x removed	Chief Colonah "Savanooka" "The Raven of Chota"
58	1st Cousin 9x removed	Wyukah "Little Owl"
59	8-Great-Grandfather	Chief Willenawah (Tifftoya "Great Eagle of Tanassee")
60	6-Great-Grandaunt	Nigodigeyu (Like her sister, married to Samuel Riley, Jr.)
61	5-Great-Grandmother	Rachel Riley
62	n/a	Others
63	8-Great-Grandaunt	Wutehi of the Red Paint Clan
64	n/a	Nathan (Nathanial or Nathaneal) Gist
65	2nd Cousin 7x removed	Sequoya (George Gist)
66	2nd Cousin 7x removed	Tobacco Will Gist
67	8-Great-Grandaunt	Tame Doe Raven "Cati" "Catherine" of the Wolf Clan
68	1st Cousin 9x removed	Tuskeegeetee "Long Fellow" of the Wolf Clan
69	**1st Cousin 9x removed**	**GhiGau Nan-Ye-Hi "Nancy" "One Who goes About" of the Wolf Clan**
70	8-Great-Granduncle	Anakwanki "Skyagustuego"
71	2nd Cousin 8x removed	Ka-Ti "Catherine" King Fisher
72	2nd Cousin 8x removed	Hiskyteehee "Fivekiller" "Little Fellow" King Fisher
73	n/a	"King Fisher" of the Deer Clan
74	2nd Cousin 8x removed	Elizabeth "Betsy" Ward
75	n/a	Brigadier General Joseph L. Martin
76	n/a	Bryant (Bryan) Ward
77	8-Great-Grandmother	Woman of Aniwadi
78	**7-Great-Granduncle**	**Chief Corn Tassel "Old Tassel" (Kahnyatahhee)**
79	2nd Cousin 7x removed	John Jolly Carpenter
80	**7-Great-Granduncle**	**Chief Standing Turkey (Cunne-Shote)**
81	7-Great-Granduncle	Chief Uskwaliguta "Hanging Maw"
82	7-Great-Granduncle	Pumpkin Boy Carpenter
83	7-Great-Grandaunt	Wur-Teh "Ghi-Go-Ne-Li" "Gi-Yo-Sti-Ko-Yo-He" of the Bird Clan
84	n/a	John Watts
85	1st Cousin 8x removed	Kunokeski "Young Tassel" John Watts, Jr.

Appendix A: Author's Cherokee Genealogy

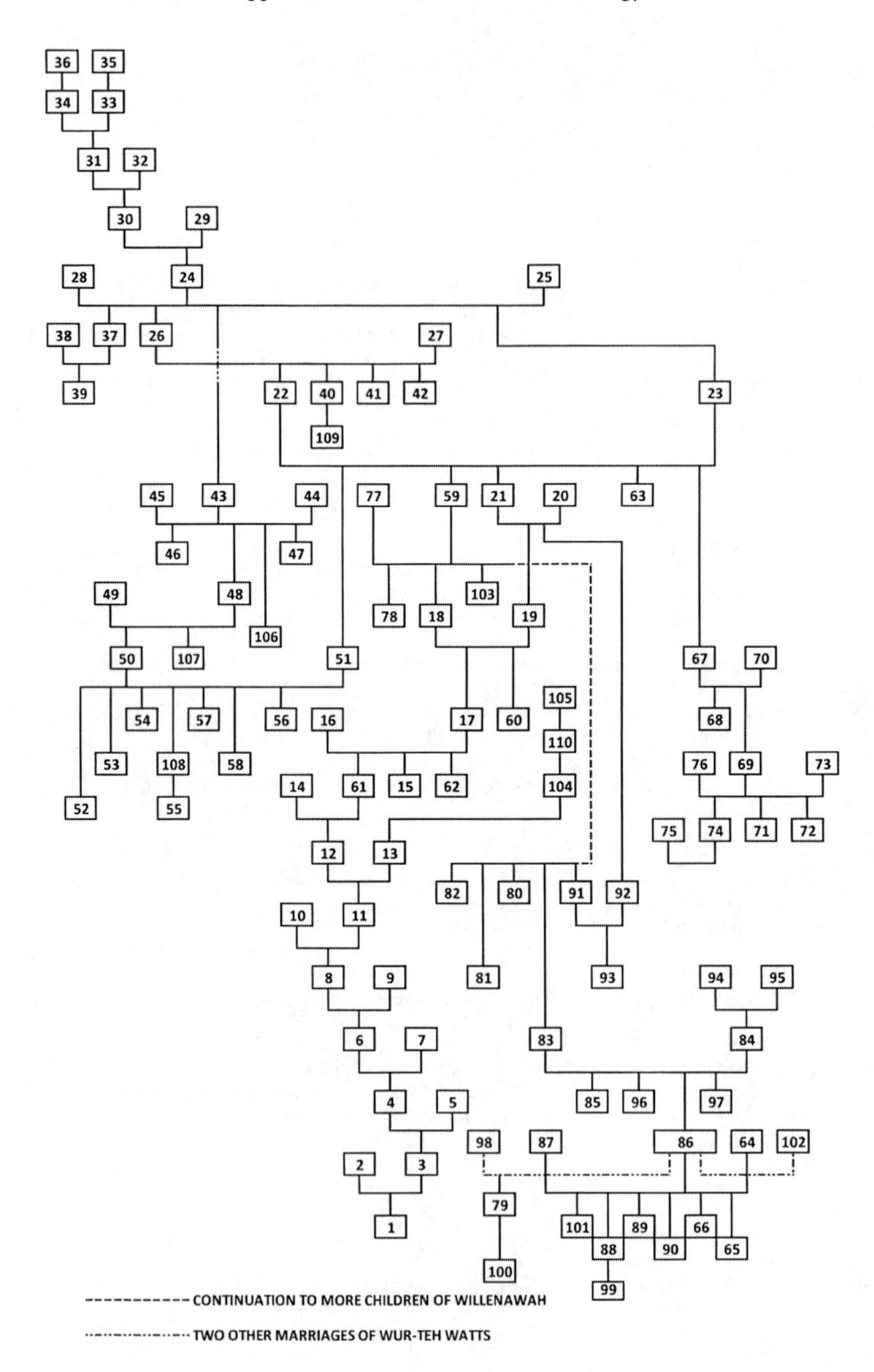

---------- CONTINUATION TO MORE CHILDREN OF WILLENAWAH
·—··—··— TWO OTHER MARRIAGES OF WUR-TEH WATTS

Pedigree Chart.

No.	Relationship to Author	Name
86	1st Cousin 8x removed	Wur-Teh Watts
87	n/a	John Benge
88	2ND COUSIN 7X REMOVED	ROBERT (BOB) BENGE (THE BENCH, CAPTAIN BENGE)
89	2ND COUSIN 7X REMOVED	MARTIN BENGE (THE TAIL)
90	2nd Cousin 7x removed	Lucy Benge
91	7-GREAT-GRANDUNCLE	RED BIRD CARPENTER (RED BIRD I, AARON BROCK, TSISQUAYA)
92	7-Great-Grandaunt	Susan Priber
93	1ST COUSIN 8X REMOVED	RED BIRD II (JOHN BROCK)
94	n/a	George Watts
95	n/a	Cherokee woman
96	1ST COUSIN 8X REMOVED	MALACHI WATTS (UNACATA, WHITE MAN KILLER)
97	1st Cousin 8x removed	Thomas Watts (Big Tom)
98	n/a	Robert Dew (Due)
99	3rd Cousin 6x removed	Pickens Benge
100	3rd Cousin 6x removed	Sam Houston of Texas fame (adopted)
101	7-GREAT-GRANDUNCLE	TAHLONTESKEE (ATA'LUNTI'SKI, NETTLE CARRIER)
102	N/A	NENETOOYAH (BLOODY FELLOW) & ISKAQUA (ESKAQUA, CLEAR SKY)
103	7th Great-Granduncle	Sequechee (Cheh Chuh, Big Half Breed)
104	5-Great-Grandfather	Murphy (1st name unknown)
105	7-Great-Grandfather	Daniel Murphy—Indian trader with The Augusta Company
106	1st Cousin 10x removed	Cherokee Billy (Will Scott)
107	1ST COUSIN 10X REMOVED	TUCKASEE (THE TERRAPIN)
108	1st Cousin 9x removed	Unknown daughter of Attakullakulla
109	1st Cousin 10x removed	Pouting Pigeon
110	6-Great-Grandfather	Daniel Murphy—Tory Trader—Hanged in June 1782 at Big Shoal of the Oconee in Georgia by the expedition of Andrew Pickens and Elijah Clarke

---

B. Short Biographies of Some Cherokee and Other Indians

(The following are cited from A. V. Goodpasture. Specific references are included in the Chapter Notes. Original spelling and grammar are maintained.)

Ostenaco

"Judge Friend was a picturesque character. The Indians called him Outacite, which means the 'Man-killer,' on account of his martial exploits, while his English name of Judge Friend (corrupted from Judd's Friend) was given him for saving a man named Judd from the fury of his countrymen. He fought with Washington against the French and Indians on the frontiers of Virginia; and on his return took a leading part in the war against the Carolinas. He was imprisoned and liberated with Oconostota by Governor Lyttleton, and with him received the surrender of the garrison of Fort Loudon.

"After the treaty with Colonel Stephen in November, 1761, Henry Timberlake was sent to the Overhill towns. On his arrival at Tomotley, he was received and entertained by Judge Friend, who gave him a general invitation to his house while he remained in their towns. The following March, Timberlake conducted him, and a large party of Indians, to Williamsburg. A few days before he was to return home, Mr. Harrocks invited him to sup with him at the college, where, among other curiosities, he showed him the picture of His Majesty King George. The chief viewed it long and attentively; then turning to Timberlake, said: 'Long have I wished to see the king my father; this is his resemblance, but I am determined to see himself; I am now near the sea, and never will depart from it till I have obtained my desire.' He made his wish known to the governor next day, who, though he at first refused, finally consented, and Judge Friend set off for England, accompanied by Timberlake and two Cherokee warriors."[1]

"Judge Friend was also known by Ostenaco, or Austenaco, the name his parents gave him. He acquired the name of Judd's Friend, corrupted into Judge Friend, from his humanity in saving a man of that name from the fury of his countrymen. On the other hand, he received his name of Outacite, meaning 'man-killer,' from his martial exploits.

"He was ambitious for distinction and power, and Henry Timberlake, who accompanied him to England, and whose coveted commission as lieutenant depended largely upon the impression he should make, was interested in magnifying his greatness and importance. Timberlake says he was the rival of the celebrated chief, Attakullakulla, between whom the Overhill towns were divided into two factions; and declares he was superior in influence to the warlike Oconostota. Attakullakulla, he says, had done little in war to commend him, but had often distinguished himself by his policy and negotiations at home, which, he considered, the greatest steps to power. Oconostota, though surnamed the "Great Warrior" was not his equal. Judge Friend reached his great power by uniting in his character both war and policy.

"But there was one point on which Judge Friend felt himself inferior to Attakullakulla and Oconostota—they had both been to England and met the great Father face to face. Timberlake does not point this out, but a writer in the Royal Magazine, July, 1762, does. He says:

"'Outacite (Judge Friend), who is now in England, is not the King of the Cherokees, but only one of their principal warriors.... There is at this time no King of the Cherokees; and for sometime their affairs have been principally under the direction of Attakullakulla, commonly called the Little Carpenter, who was over here in 1730, and has been ever since treated with particular respect by the court, and considered as the principal and most sagacious person of the Cherokees. A jealousy of this particular honor paid to Attakullakulla has prompted Outacite to come to England, imagining that the Little Carpenter owes all his power and influence to his having visited King George. Outacite, in order to conceal his project of coming to England from the Little Carpenter, did not come through Carolina, which was his nearest way, but traveled through Virginia, and there embarked.'

"The presence of Judge Friend and his two warriors in London produced the greatest excitement. Thousands of people thronged to see them; and the impecunious Timberlake could hardly resist the temptation to exhibit them for profit. Their visit was recorded in grave histories; Goldsmith utilized it in his Animated Nature; and an unknown artist drew him from life for the Royal Magazine, in which it appeared, with 'Some account of the Indians now in England,' July, 1762.

"Judge Friend and his companions are described as:

"'Men of a middling stature, seem to have no hair on their heads, and wear a kind of skullcap adorned with feathers; their faces and necks are besmeared with a coarse sort of paint, of a brick-dust color, which renders it impossible to know their complexion, they have a loose mantle of scarlet cloth thrown over their bodies, and wear a kind of loose coat. Their necks are streaked with blue paint, something resembling veins in a fine skin. There seems to be a mixture of majesty and moroseness in their countenances....

"The chief ... is called Outacite, or man-killer; and notwithstanding the ignorance in which he and the rest of that and other Indian nations are involved, shows a sense of pure honor, and great generosity of mind."[2]

Dragging Canoe

(NOTE: For an excellent treatise on Dragging Canoe, the reader should consult D. Ray Smith, *Dragging Canoe, Cherokee War Chief,* smithdray.tripod.com/dragging-canoe-index–9.html, and E. Raymond Evans, *Notable Persons in Cherokee History: Dragging Canoe,* Cherokee NC, *Journal of Cherokee Studies,* Vol. II No. 1, Museum of the Cherokee Indian, Winter 1977)

"Dragging Canoe (Cheucunsene), the stout-hearted young chief of Mialaquo, or Big Island town, who had commanded the most important division of the Indian forces in their late irruption, and had suffered defeat at the decisive battle of Long Island Flats, still declared he would hold fast to Cameron's talks, and refused to make any sort of terms with the Americans; and had already been fighting with Captain James Robertson, on the Watauga. He seceded from the Nation's councils; drew off a large number of the most daring and enterprising young warriors of the Overhill towns; was joined by some of the refugees who fled across the mountain before the merciless devastation of Rutherford and Williamson; moved down the Tennessee River to Chickamauga Creek, a few miles above Chattanooga, and founded the notorious band called Chickamaugas.

"More has been said of this remarkable chief, and less is known of his personal history, than of any other Indian of his time. One historian says he was killed in the beginning of his career, at the battle of Long Island Flats, in 1776; another thinks he was killed at the battle of Boyd's Creek, in 1780; while a third says he served with Jackson in the Creek War, and participated in the last great encounter at Horseshoe Bend. Even a contemporary, well informed on Indian affairs, thinks he died soon after his removal to Chickamauga.

"All are equally in error; he died in his own town, Running Water, in the spring of 1792. No doubt this want of information is due to the fact that he was always at war with the Americans, dealt with them at arm's length, and in the sixteen years following the first Cherokee invasion, never once met them on the treaty ground.

"At this time [his defection from the Upper Villages, not his death] he was about twenty-four years old; in person large and powerful, with coarse, irregular features. He was the implacable enemy, not of the white man, for he was the devoted and faithful friend of the English, but of the Americans, who were the despoilers of his country. Ambitious of great achievements, he had a mind capable of bold resolutions. He was brave, daring, and magnanimous. On one occasion he is said to have shot a warrior dead on the spot, for insulting a white woman, though she was the warrior's own prisoner.

"Dragging Canoe was the son of Ookoonekah, or White Owl, (Attakullakulla) a prominent Overliill chief, and a signer of the treaty of Holston. He [Dragging Canoe] first became conspicuous in the public affairs of his nation at the famous Transylvania treaty [sic] at Sycamore Shoals, on the Watauga River, in 1775, the only treaty with the Americans he is known to have attended. Haywood has given the outline of a great speech delivered by a Cherokee orator, 'said to have been Oconostota,' in opposition to this treaty; but, so far as I have been able to find, Dragging Canoe was the only chief who publicly opposed the cession in open conference. On the second day of the treaty, when Henderson named the boundaries of his proposed purchase, Dragging Canoe became indignant at his pretentions, and withdrew in a passion from the conference. He was immediately followed by the other Indians, and the meeting was broken up for the day.

"Afterwards he warned Henderson that it was 'bloody ground,' and would be 'dark' and difficult to settle. Some have thought this was the origin of the significant appellation 'dark and bloody ground.'

"After the great grant had been agreed to, Henderson asked the Indians to sell him the land between them and his purchase, for a path by which emigrants might reach Kentucky without passing over their hunting ground; hence known as the Path Deed. Dragging Canoe then arose, stamped his foot against the ground imperiously, waved his hand in the direction of Kentucky, and said, 'We give you all this.' Colonel Charles Robertson, who was present on behalf of the Watauga Association, was alarmed lest this description should be taken to include the lands his Association had leased. But it seems clear to me that Dragging Canoe meant only to express his contempt for Carter's Valley as compared to Kentucky; as if he had said: 'We give you our great hunting ground; there is no game between Watauga and Cumberland Gap; when you have that you have all.' He did not sign the deeds, though he suffered them to be executed by the old chiefs on behalf of the whole nation.

"The Chickamauga towns prospered. A general tribal movement to the west, made necessary by the encroachments of the white settlements east of the mountains, had already set in.

"Refugees from the Savannah towns were building new homes upon the Coosa. Many of those driven out from the headwaters of the Little Tennessee and Hiwassee joined themselves to the Chickamaugas. They held fast to the talks of the English and continued in open hostility to the Americans. Chickamauga became the rallying point for the British interest in the Southwest. Colonel Brown, the successor of Superintendent Stuart, and his deputy, John McDonald, were regularly quartered there. They had also gotten in communication with the British Governor, Henry Hamilton, at Detroit, and promised a contingent of warriors to assist him in the reduction of the northwestern frontiers. [**Author's note:** I disagree that Dragging Canoe was a great fan of the British. He was disdainful of the entire white community and only temporarily allied with the British because he thought they would be useful in expelling the encroaching Overmountain settlers. The British were his source of ammunition.]

"The passage of the Tennessee River through the Cumberland Mountain range at Chattanooga is one of the most unique achievements of nature. In its rapid descent it has cut deep through the solid stone, leaving towering cliffs and precipices on either shore, in some places scarcely leaving room for a path between them and the impetuous current of the river. The prospect from Lookout Mountain is almost incredible, reaching, it is said, the territory of seven states. The favorite view is called the Point, a projecting angle of the cliff, almost directly above the river, which affords a commanding 'Lookout' from which the mountain received its name. Confined within its narrow banks, the rapidly descending stream rushes with fretful turbulence over immense boulders and masses of rock, creating a succession of cataracts and vortices, making it extremely difficult of navigation. Along its wild and romantic shores are coves and gorges running back into the mountains, forming inaccessible retreats. At a point about thirty-six miles below Chattanooga, Nickajack Cave, an immense cavern, some thirty yards wide, with a maximum height of fifteen feet, opens its main entrance on the river.

"Among these impregnable fastnesses Dragging Canoe found an asylum for his people; here he built the five Lower towns of the Chickamaugas—Running Water, Nickajack, and Long Island towns, in Tennessee, and Crow and Lookout Mountain towns, in Alabama and Georgia, respectively. In addition to the security offered by their positions, it gave them the advantage of being near the Indian path, where the hunting and war parties of the Creeks of the south, and the Shawnees of the north, crossed the Tennessee River. Their strength was augmented from the Creeks, Shawnees, and white Tories, until they numbered a thousand warriors, and became the most formidable part of their nation. It has been said that they abandoned Chickamauga Creek on account of witches, but I agree with Colonel Arthur Campbell, that the real cause was the raids of the Watauga and Holstou militia."[3]

John Watts, Jr.

"The Young Tassel, who, as we shall see, afterwards made a noise in the world under the name of John Watts, was both a good-natured and a diplomatic young fellow, and, while he abandoned the old towns and moved further down the river, he did not then [at first] attach himself to the Chickamauga faction.

"John Watts (Kunoskeskie) was the son of a white man of the same name, who resided among the Cherokees, and sometimes acted as interpreter for the nation; notably at the treaty [sic] of Lochaber in 1770, in consequence of which the settlement of Tennessee was begun. His mother was a sister of the Tassel, who was the head of the nation at the time of his assassination. He [John Watts, Jr.] was himself sometimes called Corn Tassel [actually Young Tassel].... He did not, however, join himself to the implacable Chickamaugas [at first]; and was not for some years distinguished as a warrior.

"The first glimpse we have of him is in the capacity of a diplomat. When Campbell and Sevier invaded the Indian country in 1780, Watts, and a chief called Noonday [who was] afterwards killed by rangers near Craig's Station, met them at Tellico and proposed terms of peace. Ramsey says it was granted to Tellico and the adjacent villages, but Campbell, in his official report, expressly states that Tellico was burned. Campbell probably refers to Watts, however, when he speaks of a chief of Coyatee who seemed to him to be the only man of honor among the chiefs, and in whose favor he would willingly have discriminated had it been in his power. Two years later, when Sevier marched against the Chickamaugas, he held a conference with the friendly chiefs, at Citico, and engaged Watts to accompany the expedition for the purpose of effecting, by friendly negotiations, an arrangement for peace with the whole nation.

"In July, 1788, as we have seen, the Tassel [Old Tassel] was treacherously murdered under a flag of truce. The whole nation was shocked and maddened by that horrible crime. Their young warriors once more dug up the hatchet. Watts had a double incentive for putting himself at their head. In the first place he was deeply affected by his uncle's death; so much so, that when he spoke of it three years afterwards, at the treaty [sic] of Holston, he was so overcome that he could not proceed, and had to request the Bloody Fellow to finish the business. Moreover, the law of his nation imposed upon every member of a family the duty of taking satisfaction for an injury inflicted upon another member of it. But he was never content to put himself at the head of a small predatory band, like his nephew, the Bench. He had the capacity to lead large bodies of men, and in his wars we always find him at the head of a formidable army. At this crisis he invaded the border at the head of some two or three hundred warriors."[4]

The Bench

(For an excellent treatise on Bob Benge, the reader should consult E. Raymond Evans, "Notable Persons in Cherokee History: Bob Benge," *Journal of Cherokee Studies* **I, no. 2, Museum of the Cherokee Indian, Fall 1976)**

"The most daring and crafty of these Chickamauga bushwackers [sic] was Bob Benge, the son of an Indian trader named John Benge, who married a niece of the old Tassel, and spent his life in the nation. The Tassel complained to the commissioners at the treaty [sic] of Hopewell, in 1785, that, in passing through Georgia, Benge had been robbed of leather to the value of 150 sterling. John McKee saw him, and was befriended by him, near Chattanooga, as late as 1793. His Indian wife had two sons, Bob Benge and the Tail [Martin Benge] ... through the inaccuracy of the pioneer ear, that has been almost lost, as he appears generally in our Tennessee histories and public documents under the more dignified name of the Bench, by which I shall still call him, though he is celebrated in Virginia tradition as Captain Benge.

"The Bench was red-headed, a circumstance which cost him his scalp, which Colonel Campbell, at the request of Lieutenant Hobbs, sent to the Governor of Virginia, as a proof that he was no more; seeing that, with the exception of Red-Headed Will, the founder of Willstown, whose dust reposes on its ancient site, there was not probably another red-headed Indian in the whole nation. He was remarkable for his strength, activity, endurance, and fleetness, and was a man of courage as well as intelligence and cunning. More than once he traversed the white settlements with such celerity and stealth that he fell upon the pioneers without an intimation of his approach, and retired to his wigwam beyond the Lookout Mountain, without leaving a trace of the route he had traveled, though the rangers were constantly on the lookout for his trail.

"He does not appear in history until after the death of his great uncle, the Tassel, when he drifted down to Running Water, and attached himself to a band of about thirty Shawnees who lived there, under the leadership of the Shawnees Warrior, afterwards killed in the assault on Buchanan's Station. In accordance with the customs of their nation, he, Watts, Talotiskee, Unacata, and the Tail, each in his own way, dug up the hatchet to take satisfaction for the death of their kinsman. How much mischief the Bench committed can never be known, but after his death Governor Blount charged that he had killed at different times forty or fifty people.

"The favorite field of his exploits was in southwestern Virginia. He so terrorized the people of that section that he has received a prominent place in the traditions of their descendants. They have made a kind of hero of him, crediting him with wonderful feats of daring and cruelty. On account of his having lived with the Shawnees at Running Water they call him a Shawnee chief, which appellation has lead them erroneously to ascribe to him some of the most daring exploits of the Shawnees of the northwest; notably with the capture of Mrs. Nancy Scott, whose escape and extraordinary wanderings are famous."[5]

The Colbert Family
Chickasaw Leaders

"The Colbert family was for many years the most powerful family in the Chickasaw Nation, and, in common with the rest of the tribe, was uniformly friendly to the United States. It was founded by James Colbert, a Scotchman, who married a Chickasaw woman and adopted the Indian life. He was the same who bore the English commission and conducted the siege of Fort Jefferson. Then for some years he conducted extensive piratical operations against the Spanish on the Mississippi River, which gave them great annoyance, and caused much uneasiness on the Cumberland. June 3, 1783, the committee of Cumberland resolved to send two men to the Illinois, with letters to be transmitted to the Spanish Governor, denying any connection or sympathy with Colbert's proceedings. Suspicion was especially directed against Colonel John Montgomery, who had seen service in the Illinois, and the Governor of North Carolina issued a proclamation charging him with aiding and abetting Colbert. The county court of Davidson County, at its first session, in 1784, placed Colonel Montgomery under bond to appear at the next term of the court and answer said charges. But before the next term of the court the governor's proclamation had been withdrawn, and the proceedings were dismissed as of course. When Colonel Robertson, having located two negroes, one taken at Mattattock and the other on the Arkansas, offered to assist in their recovery if the owners could be found, Monsieur Cruzat replied that Colbert and his people, scattered in several bands, were carrying on war by robbery and pillage everywhere, and consisted of so large a number of persons that it was impossible to procure the necessary proofs.

"This James Colbert had four sons, William, George, Levi, and James. General William Colbert, who succeeded Piomingo as the principal chief of the Nation, distinguished himself as the friend of the United States. He served under General Wayne against the Indians of the Northwest, and in 1794 made war on the Creeks to avenge their depredations in the Cumberland settlements. When the Creek war broke out in 1813, he hastened to join the third regiment of United States infantry for service against the old enemies of the Chickasaws. He served five months in the regular infantry, when he returned to his Nation and raised an independent force, which he led against the hostile Creeks, whom he pursued from Pensacola almost to Apalachicola, killing many, and bringing eighty-five prisoners back to Montgomery. In June, 1816, he headed a Chickasaw delegation to Washington, and in the treaty that followed, he is styled Major General, and is granted an annuity of $100 during life. Later, he supported the emigration principle, and, to give to it the weight of his example, he went himself to Arkansas in 1836, and died there in November, 1839.

"Colonel George Colbert, who was hardly less prominent than his brother William, owned and lived at the celebrated ferry on the Tennessee River which still bears his name. He had two wives, both daughters of the bloody Cherokee chief, Doublehead. He possessed a strong mind and a dictatorial spirit. Levi Colbert, on the contrary, is said to have been mild, amiable, liberal, and generous. He lived on Bear Creek, in Colbert County, Alabama, which was so named to perpetuate the memory of himself and his brother George, and was the principal chief of the Nation at the time of their removal to the west. The youngest of the four brothers was Major James Colbert, at one time interpreter for the nation, who also lived in Alabama, some forty miles south of Levi and George. They were all constant and active friends of the United States.

"William Colbert was the friend and follower, as well as the successor, of Piomingo. The following incident will illustrate their relations. In the fall of 1792 Piomingo, with a company of Chickasaws, went to Philadelphia after goods for their tribe, who were to meet him at Mussel Shoals on his return. Being delayed beyond the appointed time, the Chickasaws feared that some accident had happened to him. Their foreboding was strengthened by a report circulated by the Creeks, that the Cherokees had killed him and all his party. This report so exasperated them that William and George Colbert collected a party of Chickasaws on either side of the Tennessee, for the purpose of cutting off six canoes of Cherokees, who were moving down the river, but Levi Colbert and some others prevailed on them to desist until their information could be confirmed. Shortly after these canoes went by another appeared, loaded with corn, and having on board one man, two women, and two children. William Colbert hailed them, and ordered them to come ashore. They disregarded his order and kept on their way, which he construed into a confession of guilt, and gave chase. The canoe paddled to the shore, the man landed and hid himself in the bushes, and the others continued down the river, but were soon overhauled and brought back. William Colbert found the man, tomahawked and scalped him."[6]

Piomingo

"Piomingo was the great war chief of the Chickasaws before William Colbert had won his spurs. He proposed peace to Kentucky and Cumberland in 1782; he fought with the Americans under St. Clair; Dragging Canoe spent the last effort of his life vainly trying to induce Piomingo to join the confederacy of southern Indians against the United States, while they were engaged in a momentous struggle with the Indians of the Northwest; when the Spaniards of Louisiana made large offers to the Chickasaws if they would forsake the Americans in 1793, Piomingo treated the offer with contempt. He was a true and good man, had great natural ability, and possessed in a high degree the fundamental elements of statesmanship. He merits a high place among the great chiefs of his Nation, and deserves to be remembered by the Americans for his unfaltering devotion to their cause, after the treaty of French Lick on the Cumberland, November 12, 1783."[7]

(Piomingo was, at times, confused with William Colbert by historians.)

Attakullakulla—See **James C. Kelly**, "Notable Persons in Cherokee History: Attakullakulla," *Journal of Cherokee Studies* 3, no. 1, Museum of the Cherokee Indian, Winter 1978.

Doublehead—See **Rickey Butch Walker,** Doublehead: Last Chickamauga Cherokee Chief, Killen, AL: Bluewater, 2012.

Shawnee Warrior and Tecumseh—See **John Sugden,** *Tecumseh: A Life,* New York: Holt, 1997.

C. Short Biographies of Some White Settlers

(The following are citations from Edward Albright, John Preston Arthur, and A. V. Goodpasture. Specific references are included in the Chapter Notes. Biographies are not included for those individuals for whom much is readily available, such as John Sevier, Daniel Boone, or James Robertson.)

The Blackmores

"Maj. George D. Blackmore, who was in command of a part of the troops on the Nickajack expedition, was a native of Hagerstown, Md., and served for three years in the war of the Revolution. At the close of this conflict he came to the Cumberland country, residing for a while at Bledsoe's Station. He was one of the gallant defenders of the latter in its assault by the Indians, as previously recorded. Later on he commanded what was called a horse company, and was also employed as Quartermaster in supplying provisions for the troops stationed at the various forts. He was a brave soldier and an honored citizen. He married Elizabeth, daughter of Alexander Neely, and reared a large and highly respected family. Among them were Dr. James Blackmore, and Gen. William Blackmore, a hero of the Mexican war. The latter was the father of Hon. James W. Blackmore, now a prominent citizen of Gallatin. At an early date Major Blackmore settled on the tract of land now owned by David Barry, Sr., in the Second Civil District of Sumner County. On the present site of Mr. Barry's residence he built a settler's log cabin in which he lived for many years. He died in 1830, and was buried in the family burying ground in sight of his former residence."[1]

John Peyton, John Hamilton, and Margaret Hamilton Peyton

"John Peyton was the son of Robert and Ann Guffey Peyton and was born in Amherst County, Virginia, in 1755. He was descended from a prominent family of Virginians whose family tree may be traced to the reign of William the Conqueror. At the age of nineteen, together with his twin brother, Ephraim, he joined the army of the Revolution under Gen. Andrew LEWIS. Both were in the battle of Point Pleasant, at the mouth of the Big Kanawah, in 1774. He came to Middle Tennessee in 1779, where he fought with distinction in the various Indian battles. John Peyton was in command of Rock Island Ford, on the Caney Fork River, in which battle he displayed great courage and presence of mind. His father, Robert Peyton, came to visit his son John some years later, at what is now known as 'Peytonia Farm,' in Sumner County, and was the last white man killed by the Indians.

This occurred at Bledsoe's Lick, where he had gone to look after some cattle. John Peyton, who was by occupation a surveyor, married Margaret Hamilton, daughter of Capt. John W. Hamilton, of the British army. The latter was of distinguished Scotch lineage and participated in the battle of Fort Duquesne under General Braddock. He resigned years afterward and became a citizen of Tennessee, where he, too, engaged in the Indian Wars. His son, John W. Hamilton, Jr., was an able lawyer and jurist and was a contemporary of Jackson, Grundy, Houston and other legal lights.

John and Margaret Hamilton Peyton reared a large family, among them being Bailie and Joseph Peyton, both of whom became members of Congress from the district of which Sumner County was a part. As previously related, Ephraim Peyton was one of the party that accompanied James Robertson across the mountains from Watauga to the Cumberland."[2]

James Winchester

"In the settlement of Middle Tennessee Gen. James Winchester, who was a native of Maryland, rendered most excellent service. A Captain in the revolutionary army, he shared for more than five years its struggles and privations. At the close of the war he came to the Cumberland country and settled on Bledsoe's Creek, in what is now the first Civil District of Sumner County. Here in what is now the First Civil District of Sumner County. Here in 1801–2 he built on a cliff overlooking Bledsoe's Creek his fine old residence, Cragfont, which still stands. It is now the property of Mr. W. H. B. Satterwhite, a prominent farmer and stockraiser of Sumner County. Cragfont was built of native sandstone by skillful workmen brought for that purpose from Baltimore. It is yet in good state of preservation.

"The military services of General Winchester were invaluable to the early settlers, directing the scouts and spies and frequently pursuing the Indians in person, showing himself at all times a true and prudent officer. He was a member of the advisory council during the session of the Territorial legislature in 1794 and later a member of the State Senate. In the war of 1812 between the United States and England he received a General's commission and was ordered to take command of one wing of the army of the northwest. At the unfortunate battle of the River Raisin he was taken prisoner by the British and carried to Quebec, where he remained in captivity during the following winter.

"At the close of the war of 1812, General Winchester returned to the quiet walks of private life, and in all his later dealings, as merchant and farmer, enjoyed the utmost respect and confidence of his fellow men. He reared a large and worthy family, one of whom, George W. Winchester, afterwards represented Sumner County in the State Legislature. He was father-in-law to the late Col. Alfred R. Wynne, whose daughters, the Misses Wynne, still reside in the house built by their father at Castalian Springs in the early part of the last century.

"General Winchester died and was buried at Cragfont in 1826. There his remains now rest in the family burying-ground."[3]

Dr. John Sappington, Edward Douglass, and Thomas Molloy

"During the year 1785 ... the first physician to the settlement arrived at Nashville in the person of Dr. John Sappington ... acquired much reputation as a practitioner throughout the colony.

"The first lawyers in the settlement came this year in the persons of Edward Douglass and Thomas Molloy, who announced that they would practice in all the courts of Davidson County. A historian of that period says that neither of these gentlemen had studied law as a science, but being of sound practical sense, and possessed of good business talents, and of the gift of speech, they soon had a large clientage. The only law books they possessed were the Acts of the North Carolina Legislature in pamphlet form."[4]

Rev. Thomas B. Craighead

"The year 1785 was marked by the advent of Rev. Thomas B. CRAIGHEAD, a Presbyterian minister, and the first of any denomination to make his home on the Cumberland. Craighead was a graduate of old Nassan Hall, now Princeton University, a man of sound learning, strong intellect and earnest piety. By the presbytery of Orange, in his native State, North Carolina, he was ordained to the ministry in 1780. A few years later he removed to Kentucky and for a time preached to the Stationers there, but again changed his residence, coming to Middle Tennessee. It is said that this was done at the solicitation of Colonel Robertson, with whom he had become acquainted in North Carolina. On arriving at the Cumberland settlement he at once began his work, preaching his first sermon with a stump for a pulpit, and with fallen trees as seats for his congregation. Fixing his residence at Haysborough, six miles northeast of Nashville, he taught school during the week and preached on Sunday. A stone building twenty-four by thirty feet in size was erected at Nashville, and in this for thirty years thereafter he taught and held religious service. The declining years of this pioneer preacher were saddened by a trial for heresy, the result of which was his suspension from the ministry. This order of suspension, however, was revoked before his death. He was a man of strong character, and while active in extending the knowledge of the gospel, he was opposed to the revival measures which led to the formation of the Cumberland Presbyterian Church. He died at Nashville in 1824. Throughout all this trials Gen. Andrew JACKSON was his staunch admirer and loyal friend."[5]

Daniel Smith

"Daniel Smith became Secretary of the territorial government [to Governor William Blount] and later succeeded Andrew Jackson as Senator from Tennessee in the Congress of the United States. He was born in Farquier County, Virginia, October 29, 1748; was a skilled civil engineer, and by actual survey made the first map of the State of Tennessee. Coming to Middle Tennessee at an early period in its history, he married a daughter of Col. John Donelson, and selected a fine body of land on Drake's Creek, near Hendersonville, in Sumner County. Here in 1784 he built 'Rock Castle,' his historic residence, which still stands. Under General Smith's own supervision it was built from stone taken from a quarry a few hundred yards away. The land on which it stands is now the property of his great-granddaughter, Mrs. Horatio Berry, of Hendersonville. General Smith died at Rock Castle, June 16, 1818, and was buried in the family cemetery nearby."[6]

Thomas Sharpe Spencer

Two citations are used, the first of Edward Albright followed by that of A. V. Goodpasture.

"Thomas Sharp Spencer came ... as an adventurer into the Cumberland Valley. Having heard from his neighbors, Mansker and Bledsoe, of the rich lands and abundance of big game throughout this region he came over from his home in Virginia in the spring of 1776. Besides other companions he brought with him a man named Holliday, and together they fixed a station at Bledsoe's Lick, probably having been directed hither by Isaac Bledsoe, who had discovered it several years before.

"During the summer following, Spencer and Holliday hunted over and explored the country for many miles around. In the bottom adjoining Bledsoe's Lick they cleared a few acres of land which they planted in corn. This they cultivated and gathered in autumn, thus being the first crop of grain raised in Middle Tennessee.

"Later on Holliday became dissatisfied and decided to return to Virginia. Spencer accompanied him to the Barrens of Kentucky, near where Glasgow now stands, and through which in those days there ran a trail leading back across the mountains. When they had bidden each other adieu and were about to separate, Holliday discovered that he had lost his hunting knife, whereupon Spencer broke his own knife in two and gave half of it to his departing comrade. The latter was never heard from thereafter and it is supposed he was killed by the Indians on his journey homeward.

"Spencer returned to Bledsoe's Lick and spent the winter alone in a hollow sycamore tree which stood in the bottom near the present site of the post office at Castalian Springs. This tree perished many years ago, but so long as it stood it was called by the settlers 'Spencer's House.' Some time after the events above mentioned Spencer went back to Virginia, his native state, but returned to the Cumberland country in 1780.

"During the time of his residence in the sycamore tree he explored the country side from Bledsoe's Lick to the mouth of Red river, near Clarksville, always keeping a sharp lookout for choice tracts of land to which, in the future, he might lay claim. Because of a false impression as to the provisions of the preemption law under which he was laboring, he supposed that by clearing a few acres and building a cabin on each section of 640 acres an individual would thus be able to possess himself of as much land as he might desire. In pursuance of this idea he selected for himself four fine tracts in Sumner County. Three of these were in the region around Castalian Springs, and the fourth was near Gallatin, it being the same as that subsequently owned by General Miller.

"In 1781 the state of North Carolina, to which the territory embracing Middle Tennessee at that time belonged, defined by enactment its pre-emption law, which allowed only one section to each head of a family, or single man who had reached the age of twenty-one. Spencer was thereby forced to make a choice of the four tracts previously staked off, and he accordingly selected the one near Gallatin. This splendid body of land has ever since been known as 'Spencer's Choice.' It bounds the corporate limits of the town on the south, and comprises the land now occupied by the heirs of the late Capt. J. B. Howison, together with the farm just south of it, the latter the property of Mrs. John H. Oldham, and a part of the farm owned by Mr. R. P. Hite.

"The description of this tract, when granted to Spencer, called for natural boundaries which were supposed to embrace a section, but when an actual survey was made many years later it was found to contain about eight hundred acres. The records on file in the Register's office of Sumner county show that on August 17, 1793, Thomas Spencer conveyed to Stephen Cantrell two hundred acres of the above tract, the consideration being 'two hundred hard dollars.' The remainder of the tract was inherited by William Spencer, brother of Thomas Spencer, at the latter's death.

"Spencer was a man of great physical strength, a giant in his day, well proportioned, broad shouldered, huge in body and limb, and weighing nearly four hundred pounds. His traditional feats of strength were numerous. On one occasion, shortly after the beginning of the settlement at Nashville, he was hunting with a fellow sportsman on Duck River in what is now Humphries County. As evening came on they sought a secluded spot where they might build a fire, cook a deer they had killed, and camp for the night. While they were preparing the meal a skulking party of Indians espied them, and creeping up to within range of the camp fired at them, killing Spencer's companion. Spencer, who was unharmed, gathered up the dead body and gun of his fellow hunter and with the added weight of his own arms and ammunition dashed into the thick cane and was soon beyond the reach of danger. The Indians, seeing his great strength and activity, and knowing that he had with him two loaded guns, followed at a respectful distance. He succeeded in carrying off and burying the remains of his comrade, after which he returned in safety of French Lick.

The veteran pioneer of Sumner County, John Carr who has written so entertainingly of the early period of our history, says that on one occasion he rode through a parcel of ground which Spencer had cleared. There were five or six acres in the field, around which was a rail fence. The timbers used therein, each of which was equal in size to ten or fifteen rails, Spencer had cut from the clearing and carried on his shoulder to where the fence was being built.

Another instance of his strength is related. He was sick and lying on a blanket by a fire near where two of the settlers were building a cabin. For a long time he watched them both struggle under the weight of a log trying in vain to put the end of it in place. Finally he arose from his blanket, walked to the cabin, took hold of the log and brushing the men aside threw it into position with apparent ease. Spencer had a large foot, huge even in proportion to his immense body. During his first winter at Bledsoe's Lick, Timothy Demonbreun … was conducting a trading station near Nashville, and had associated with him a party of hunters from Indiana and Illinois. One morning just at daybreak Spencer, who was himself a mighty hunter, and who happened to be in that neighborhood of these Frenchmen was sleeping. It had been raining and the ground was very soft. The sleeping hunter, aroused by the noise near the door, became frightened, swam the Cumberland river, and ran north through the wilderness until he reached the French settlement at Vincennes. There he related his experience and declared he would never return to a country that was inhabited by such giants.

Spencer was of a quiet and peaceable disposition, and being possessed of a good face and gentlemanly manners was held in high esteem by all the settlers. Like Daniel Boone and others in kind who blazed the way of civilization on its westward march, he loved the solitude of the forest and often in times of greatest danger would for weeks hunt through the woods alone, and seemingly without fear. In this way he supplied food to the settlers in times of great need. He was never married, and after the settlements began to be established in Sumner and Davidson Counties, he had no abode of his own. When not away on an expedition it was his custom to spend the night at any station most liable to be attacked by the Indians. In the fall of 1793 Spencer returned to Virginia for the purpose of winding up an estate and receiving therefrom a legacy which was his due. Returning with a party on horseback by way of Knoxville, they had reached an elevation which, because of this event has since been called Spencer's Hill, near the headwaters of Caney Fork River. True to his custom Spencer was riding alone some distance in advance of his party, when at a gap near the top of the hill he was fired upon and instantly killed by a band of Indians who were lying in wait. Thus ended a career than which in all the annals of early history there is no more shining example of undaunted courage and heroic self-sacrifice. His horse, which was a splendid animal took fright from the fall of his master, and dashing through the line of howling savages which had surrounded him, fled back to the party and thus escaped capture.

"Spencer's early advent into the region of Bledsoe's Lick proved to be a connecting link between the roving bands of hunters and adventurers who first came hither, and that hardier company whose annals we are about to consider, and who through toil and bloodshed, with trowel in one hands and sword in the other laid broad and deep the foundation of a mighty commonwealth."[7]

"At this point let us pause long enough to notice a few incidents in the career of the earliest and most picturesque pioneer of the Cumberland, Thomas Sharpe Spencer. He was a man of giant proportions and herculean strength. A hunter left by Timothy Demonbreun in charge of his camp on Cumberland, in the fall of 1777, discovered Spencer's tracks, and was so alarmed by their uncommon size, that he fled and did not rest until he had joined Demonbreun at Vincennes on the banks of the Wabash. A few years later, at a general muster two boys became involved in a fight. Old Bob Shaw, who considered himself a mighty man, insisted on letting them fight it out. Spencer, however, was of a different opinion, and parting the crowd right and left, he seized one of the belligerents in either hand, pulled them apart with scarcely an effort, and bid them clear themselves. This Shaw took as a fighting offense, and struck Spencer in the face with his fist. Spencer instantly caught him by the collar and waistband of his trousers, and running a few steps to a ten-rail fence, tossed him over it. This much is on the authority of General William Hall. There is a tradition that when Shaw arose and brushed the dust from his clothes, he called out: 'Mr. Spencer, if you will be kind enough to pitch my horse over, I will be riding.'

"But Spencer was not more distinguished by his colossal frame and his marvelous feats of strength, than by his heroic self-sacrifice and knightly bearing. He was a Virginian of cavalier stock, and came to Cumberland with a party of adventurers in 1776. All of them except Spencer and John Holliday soon afterwards returned. Two years later Holliday also determined to go back to the settlements, and insisted on Spencer going with him, but he steadfastly refused. When Holliday departed Spencer accompanied him to the barrens of Kentucky, and put him on the path he was to travel; and when Holliday complained that he had no knife, Spencer promptly broke his own, and gave him half of it. So the two friends parted company, Holliday to make the long and perilous journey to the east, and Spencer to return to his solitary home in a large sycamore tree near what is now Castalian Springs. R. E. W. Earle, the artist, measured the stump of this old sycamore, which was still visible at the surface of the ground, about the year 1823, and found it to be twelve feet in diameter, quite a commodious residence, even for a man of Spencer's proportions."[8]

William Blount

"The western counties of North Carolina had now become the Southwest Territory, with William Blount as its governor. Blount was of an old English family, being descended from the Le Blounts who came over to England with William the Conqueror. His father, Jacob Blount, of Blount Hall, Pitt County, North Carolina, owned a considerable estate, and took an active and somewhat prominent part in public affairs. William, the eldest of his thirteen children, was born in Bertie County, North Carolina, March 26, 1749, and was educated in a manner commensurate with the ample estate and high position of his family.

"At an early age he began to take an interest in public matters, and at once allied himself with the Western people. As a member of the North Carolina House of Commons in 1783, he won the warm friendship of James Robertson, the founder and representative of the new settlements on the Cumberland, by his lively interest in their welfare, and the valuable assistance his talents and experience in parliamentary bodies enabled him to render these representatives. The same session of the legislature opened the Indian lands to appropriation and settlement by right of conquest, but their action was ignored by the United States two years later in the treaty of Hopewell. At this time Blount first became officially connected with Indian affairs; he appeared at the treaty of Hopewell as the agent of North Carolina, and entered a formal protest against it, on the ground that it violated the rights of his state, inasmuch as it assigned to the Indians territory which had already been appropriated by the legislature of North Carolina to the discharge of the bounty land claims of the officers and soldiers who had served in the Continental line during the Revolution. He was a member of the Continental Congress when this treaty came up for consideration, and stoutly resisted its ratification. His championship of the frontiersmen made him many friends in the western district of North Carolina.

He was a member of the convention that framed the constitution of the United States, over which George Washington presided; and was a member of the convention of North Carolina that ratified that instrument. At the same time he continued to cultivate his western friends. In 1787 he assisted James Robertson and David Hays, representatives from Davidson County, in framing a memorial to the General Assembly, looking to the free navigation of the Mississippi River, and the cession of North Carolina's western lands to the United States. As a member of the State Senate he advocated and the Legislature passed the second act of cession in December, 1789, and the deed of cession was accepted by the United States, April 2, 1790.

The Southwest Territory was erected May 26, 1790, with the same privileges, benefits and advantages enjoyed by the people of the Northwest Territory, and with a similar government. There were a number of applicants for the position of Governor of the new Territory. The propriety of appointing a citizen of the State which had made the cession was obvious; and Blount's influence in causing the cession to be made, his popularity with the people of the Territory, and President Washington's personal knowledge of his patriotism, integrity and ability, were sufficient to turn the scales in his favor. He was appointed Governor of the Southwest Territory, June 8, 1790. In addition to his appointment as Governor, he was also made Superintendent of Indian Affairs for the Southern District.

"This latter office was both delicate and difficult, requiring much alertness, tact and diplomacy, qualities for which Blount was distinguished, as well as for his fine address, courtly manners and commanding presence. To his voluminous correspondence and able state papers we are indebted for most of our knowledge of Cherokee affairs during this period, and also for many keen observations on their character and customs, as well as some strong historical presentations of their relations with the whites.

"After organizing the Territorial government in the various counties and districts,

Governor Blount turned his attention to Indian affairs. The boundary line prescribed in the treaty of Hopewell had never given satisfaction either to the Indians or the whites. Its violation by the latter called forth the vigorous proclamation of Congress in 1788, already mentioned. When the United States took jurisdiction of the country, President Washington declared it his purpose to carry into faithful execution the treaty of Hopewell, 'unless it should be thought proper to attempt to arrange a new boundary with the Cherokees, embracing the settlements, and compensating the Cherokees for the cession they should make.' The senate authorized the new treaty, and instructions were issued to Governor Blount, August 11, 1790, for that purpose."[9]

James Hubbert

"Major James Hubbert was the most inveterate enemy of the Indians to be found on all the border. His parents and all their family are said to have been killed by the Shawnees in Virginia, and he had sworn vengeance against the whole Indian race. He killed more Cherokees than any other man in the back country, seeking every opportunity to slay them, as well in times of peace as in times of war.

"On one occasion he came near involving the settlement in a fresh Indian war. He and a companion were shooting at a mark with two Indians. During the shooting one of the Indians were [sic] killed; the other fled to the Nation. It was believed that Hubbert had killed the Indian designedly, and that his people would take satisfaction for his death. The settlers, therefore, assembled near the mouth of Dumplin Creek and, through a half-breed, sought a friendly conference with the Indians. In response to the invitation six or eight warriors came in. Hubbert and a band of associates waylaid them on the other side of the river but, having missed them, followed on to Gist's, where the conference was being held. Fearing more trouble from Hubbert, the settlers kept the Indians in their center. Presently Hubbert, desiring to stampede them, found an opportunity to whisper to one of them to run, that the white men intended to kill them. His ruse was detected and defeated by Captain James White, who told them to remain and he would protect them. Thus reassured, they remained and the difficulty was satisfactorily adjusted.

"Later, in 1784, he killed a noted half-breed Indian warrior named Butler, in a private encounter, of which we have only his own account. Ramsey says the Indian killed was the chief Untoola, or Gun Rod, of Citico; but it could not have been Untoola, as he was still alive in 1785, and signed the treaty of Hopewell. However, the affair created great excitement on the border. The Indians believed Hubbert had murdered Butler, and complained to the governor of North Carolina, who ordered his arrest and trial. But the governor of Franklin openly justified his conduct, and the people of his county expressed their confidence in him by electing him to represent them in the Franklin legislature. So the matter passed off without a legal investigation.

"In time of war he hunted the Indians down like a very sleuth. One instance is related where, smelling a trail, he took a scouting party of ten men with him and, following a small path, surprised a party of seven or eight Indians in a house. He killed five of them, took one little fellow prisoner, and rejoined his command.

"Such was the character of the implacable Indian fighter, who, attach[ed] himself to the waning fortunes of his old commander, Governor Sevier."[10]

The Calloways

"Among the Kentucky pioneers was Col. Richard Calloway. Two of his daughters, Betsy and Fanny, were captured with Jemima, Boone's second daughter, in a boat at Boonesborough, Ky., on the 17th of July, 1776. They were recovered unharmed soon afterwards; and in the following August Betsy was married to Samuel Henderson, one of the rescuing party. Jemima Boone afterwards married Flanders Calloway, a son of Colonel Calloway. It was this Colonel Calloway who accused Boone of having voluntarily surrendered 26 of his men at the Salt Licks; that when a prisoner at Detroit he had engaged with Gov. Hamilton to surrender Boonesborough, and that he had attempted to weaken the garrison at Boonesborough before its attack by the Indians by withdrawing men and officers, etc.; but Boone was not only honorably acquitted, but promoted from a captaincy to that of major. Related to this Colonel Calloway was Elijah Calloway, son of Thomas Calloway of Virginia, who 'did much for the good of society and was a soldier at Norfolk, Va., in the War of 1812.' John Calloway represented Ashe county in the House in 1800, and in the Senate in 1807, 1808,1809; and Elijah Calloway was in the House from 1813 to 1817, and in the Senate in 1818 and 1818, and 1819. One of these men is said to have walked to Raleigh, supporting himself on the way by shooting game, and in this way saved enough to build a brick house with glass windows, the first in Ashe, near what is now Obid. He was turned out of the Bear creek Baptist church because he had thus proven himself to be a rich man; and the Bible said no rich man could enter the kingdom of heaven. The church in which he was tried was of logs, but the accused sat defiantly during the trial in a splint-bottomed chair, which he gave to Mrs. Sarah Miller of that locality. This may have been Thomas Calloway, whose grave is at Obid, marked with a long, slender stone which had marked one of the camping places of Daniel Boone."[11]

Other Long Hunters

"Following Boone and Calloway came Henry Scraggins, who explored the lower Cumberland in 1765, and for a while had a station near the present site of Goodlettsville in Davidson County. Of him but little is known save that he was a representative of Henderson & Company, of North Carolina, who were large dealers in western lands.... The explorations of Scraggins were the most extensive yet undertaken west of the mountains. During the summer of 1766 Col. James Smith, accompanied by Joshua Horton, William Baker, and Uriah Stone came hither for the purpose of exploring along the Cumberland and Tennessee. Some of this party were from the north, Baker being from Carlisle, Pennsylvania. They entered the region they proposed to traverse by way of East Tennessee, having first explored the Holston Valley. They brought with them a mulatto slave, a boy about eighteen years old, the property of Horton, and the first slave ever seen in Middle Tennessee. Stones River, near Nashville, was explored, and named by this party, being so called in honor of Uriah Stone. They traversed a large portion of the section now included in Sumner and Davidson Counties, and then going west, followed the course of the Tennessee River to its mouth at Paducah, Kentucky. There they separated. Smith, with the slave for company and protection, returned to North Carolina. The other members of the party went north into Illinois. Uriah Stone returned the following year, and in partnership with a Frenchman, spent the season trapping on Stones River. One day late in the spring when they were loading their boat with furs preparatory for a journey to market, the Frenchman, in the absence of his partner, stole off with the boat and cargo. Stone having thus lost the fruits of several months of labor returned empty-handed to his home in Virginia.

"Next in order came Isaac Lindsay and four others from South Carolina. They crossed the Alleghanies westward and hunted along the Cumberland as far as French Lick. Here they met Michael Stoner and a companion named Harrod, both of whom lived in Pittsburg, having come by way of Illinois on their way to the hunting ground. These parties were hunting for pleasure, and met by accident. It is quite probable that each also had an eye on valuable tracts of land upon which, in the future, they hoped to obtain concessions. After remaining together for some time in the region about French Lick they separated and returned to their respective homes. Later on Lindsay was an important factor in the early settlement at Nashville.

"The year 1769 witnessed the coming of the largest party of white men yet seen in Middle Tennessee. They were organized in June for the purpose of hunting game and exploring in the country west of the mountains, and were afterwards called 'Long Hunters' because of the length of time they were away. Among them were Kasper Mansker, John Rains, Abraham Bledsoe, John Baker, Joseph Drake, James Knox, Obadiah Terrill, Henry Smith, Ned Cowan, Robert Crockett, Thomas Gordon, Cash Brook, and Humphrey Hogan. Some of these were from North Carolina, some from the neighborhood of Natural Bridge, and others from a small settlement near Inglis' Ferry, Virginia. The party was well equipped with guns, ammunition and all other supplies necessary for a protracted hunting and exploring expedition.

"After having met at the town of New River in southwestern Virginia, they proceeded to the head of Holston River, traversing the north fork of same. Traveling on from thence they crossed Clinch and Powell Rivers, and passing on by way of Cumberland Gap, journeyed through Kentucky to the headwaters of Cumberland River. Proceeding down this stream they camped at a place since called Price's Meadow in Wayne County, Kentucky, six or seven miles from the present site of Monticello. This camp they agreed to make a station or rendezvous, for the deposit of their game and peltries. The hunters then dispersed in many directions, a part of them crossing what is now Tennessee, and exploring the country as far south as Caney Fork River and along its tributaries in Putnam, White and DeKalb counties. Most of the hunting, however, was done on Roaring and Obey Rivers in Clay, Jackson, Overton and Pickett Counties. Obey River, as it is now called, was at that time given its name, the same being in honor of Obadiah Terrill, a member of the party.

"A sad event of this outing was the death of Robert Crockett which occurred on the headwaters of Roaring River in Overton County. While returning to camp at nightfall he was fired upon and killed by a band of six or eight Indians who were hid in ambush. This is the first recorded death suffered by the whites at the hands of the Indians in the territory now embraced in Middle Tennessee.

"The country at this time abounded in small game, and the expedition was very successful. The entire landscape was covered with high grass, tall trees and low undergrowth, the whole forming a boundless wilderness hitherto untrodden by the foot of civilization. Most of the game they got by what was called 'still hunting.' Some deer, however was killed after having been lured within gun shot by imitation the bleat of a fawn. Some also were fired upon with scaffolds when they came to the salt licks at night. In mid-winter the hunters donned snow-shoes and followed the practice of 'crusting' the game … running it down in the snow. Of this practice, however, many of the hunters did not approve.

"They continued in the region above mentioned until the spring of 1770, when some of them returned home. Others, led by James Knox, went further north into Kentucky country where they hunted for a season before recrossing the mountains. The remainder, consisting of Stone, Baker, Gordon, Brook, Hogan and three or four others, all under the leadership of Kasper Mansker, having built two flat-boats, and hollowed out of logs two pirogues, or dug-out canoes, began a river journey with the proceeds of the hunt to Natchez, Mississippi. On their way down the Cumberland they stopped at French Lick, the present site of Nashville. There they saw enormous herds of buffalo, elk and deer, and great quantities of other game. The country surrounding was crowded with wild animals, the bellowing of the buffalo resounding from the hills and forest. They had found but little big game in the upper country, so some of this they now killed, and of the hides made coverings for their boats. At this point also they met Timothy Demonbreun, who, as before related, had erected his trading station there ten years before. This visit by Mansker to French Lick marked his advent into a region in the subsequent settlement of which he was destined to play a conspicuous part.

"Rowing on down the river they came at length to the Ohio. There some of their boats were looted by a band of Indians, but Mansker and his party fell in with some French traders who were generously inclined, and in return for what they had lost, gave them a supply of flour, salt, tobacco, and taffa, the latter a drink which was especially prized.

"Proceeding down the Ohio and Mississippi they arrived in due season at Natchez, then an outpost of the Spanish headquarters at New Orleans. There they sold their cargo, consisting of hides, furs, oil and tallow, after which Mansker and Baker returned to their home at New River, Virginia. Others went around by ship to North Carolina, and the remnant of the party settled at Natchez. Those who returned to the colonies gave such glowing accounts of the abundance of game and fertility of the soil on the Cumberland that the desire for western exploration became very intense.

"At Natchez Uriah Stone found his boat which had been stolen from him by the Frenchman on Stones River several years before. The latter had descended to that place by water and then disposed of the boat and cargo, departing thence for parts unknown."[12]

D. Timberlake's List of Cherokee Villages

**From "A Draught of the
CHEROKEE COUNTRY
On the West Side of the Twenty four Mountains,
commonly called Over the Hills;
Taken by Henry Timberlake when he
was in that Country in March 1762.
Likewise the
Names of the Principal or Head men of each Town and
what Number of Fighting Men they send to War."**

Mialaquo, or the Great Island......24 under the Governor of Attakullakulla.
Toskegee.............................55 Attakullakulla Governor.
Tommotley...........................91 Ostenaco Commander in Chief.
Toqua...............................82 Willinewaw Governor.
Tennessee...........................21 under the Goverment [sic] of Kanagatuckco. *
Chote...............................175 Kanagatuckco King & Governor. *
Chilhowey...........................110 Yachtino Governor.
Settacoo............................204 Cheulah Governor. **
Tellassee...........................47 Governor dead & none elected since.
*Standing Turkey
** Tsula, The Fox, Small Pox Conjuror, father of Oconostota

E. Published Accounts of the Wallen's Creek Massacre

There are many available sources for these citations. One of the best is freepages.genealogy.rootsweb.ancestry.com/~drakerobinson/OtherPages/BooneMass.htm

The Pennsylvania Chronicle and Universal Advertiser 7, no. 46, Monday, November 29, 1773, to Monday, December 6, 1773:

"BALTIMORE, November 27. By a gentleman of credit, lately from New River, in Virginia, we have the following tragical account. That on the 20th of last month, a party of 10 men, two of whom were Negroes, proceeding on their way from Holton's [sic] River to the great Falls of the Ohio, two of the company went into the woods in quest of game; the rest continued their journey till they arrived at their camp, where, in the night, they were surprised and fired upon by about 25 Indians, supposed to be Cherokees, who killed five of the white men, the sixth escaping, and carried off the two Negroes, with two horses, the property of Captain William Russell. As the two men who parted from the company have not since been heard of, it is supposed they together with a few families then travelling towards the Falls, have fallen a prey to those savages.

"A son of Captain William Russell, [a son of] Mr. Daniel Boone, and the son of Mr. John Drake, all of Virginia, were of the slain."

The Virginia Gazette, Thursday, 23 December 1773:

"The following inhuman affair we are assured, from good authority, was transacted on the frontiers of Fincastle about the latter end of September last: Captain William Russell, with several families, and upward of thirty men, set out with an intention to reconnoitre the country, towards the Ohio, and settle in the limits of the expected new government. A few days after they set out, unluckily the party was separated into three detachments; the main body in the front, with the women and children, and their cattle and baggage; in the center, Captain Russell's son, with five white men and two Negroes; who, the fatal night before the murder, encamped a few miles short of the front. In the morning, about daybreak, while asleep in the camp, they were fired upon by a party of Indians, who killed young Mr. Russell, and four other white men, and one Negro. Captain Russell, shortly after bringing up the rear, unexpectedly came on the corps [sic] of his son, which was mangled in an inhuman manner; and there was left in him a dart arrow, and a war club was left beside him. After this unexpected assault, the party, upon getting intelligence, returned to the inhabitants. It appeared afterwards that the Indians had pursued young Russell's party some considerable distance the day before, and, upon overtaking them, took that defenseless opportunity to perpetuate their barbarity."

The Virginia Magazine of History and Biography 74, 1966, a publication of the Virginia Historical Society, article "The British Indian Department and Dunmore's War":

"In the fall of 1773, Colonel William Russell from the Holston settlements and Daniel Boone from the Yadkin Valley of North Carolina with their families undertook to lead the vanguard of the movement by land to Kentucky. A party of Indians attacked them in Powell's Valley, however, and drove them back to Virginia where they spent the winter. In the fight, Henry Russell, James Boone, Samuel Drake and three others lost their lives at the hands of this Indian party numbering fifteen Delaware from Darby's Town, a village lying on the Scioto River. The band, evidently returning north along the Virginia frontier from a mission to the Overhill Cherokee towns, included two Cherokee and two Shawnee interpreters. Such episodes were not too uncommon when whites and Indians met beyond the frontier, but this brush seemed particularly significant for some forty Virginia families settled on the Watauga River fifty miles into the Indian country."

F. Bartram's List of Cherokee Villages

Source: *The Travels of William Bartram,* **page 301**
List of the towns and villages in the Cherokee nation inhabited at this day, viz.

No.			
	1	Echoe	On the Tanase East of the Jore mountains.
	2	Nucasse	
	3	Whatoga	4 towns.
	4	Cowe	
	5	Ticoloosa	Inland on the branches of the tanase.
	6	Jore	
	7	Conisca	4 towns.
	8	Nowe	
	9	Tomothle	On the Tanase over the Jore mountains.
	10	Noewe	
	11	Tellico	8 towns.
	12	Clennuse	
	13	Occunnolufte	
	14	Chewe	
	15	Quanuse	
	16	Tellowe	
	17	Tellico	Inland towns on the branches of the Tanase
	18	Chatuga	and other waters over the Jore mountains.
	19	Hiwasse	
	20	Chewase	5 towns.
	21	Nuanha	
	22	Tallase	Overhill towns on the Tanase or Cherokee river.

23		Chelowe	
24		Sette	6 towns.
25		Chote great	
26		Joco	
27		Tahasse	
28		Tamahle	Overhill towns on the Tanase or Cherokee river.
29		Tuskege	
30——.	Big Island	5 towns.	
31		Nilaque	
32		Niowe	

			Lower towns East of the mountains, viz.
No.	1	Sinica	On the Savanna or Keowe river.
	2	Keowe	
	3	Kulsage	
	4	Tugilo	On Tugilo river.
	5	Estotowe	
	6	Qualatche	On Flint river.
	7	Chote	

Towns on the waters of other rivers.

Estatowe great. Allagae. Jore. Nae oche. In all forty-three towns."

G: Description of Ball Play at the Conference of Coyatee, May 1792

Source: Goodpasture, A. V., *Indian Wars and Warriors of the Old Southwest*, pages 185–187

"Monday [the 21st of May 1792] should have been devoted to business, but on that day there was a great ball play, which was the national sport of the Cherokees. The game is played with a small ball of dressed deerskin, stuffed with punk, hair, moss, or soft dry roots, and two rackets, similar to those used in tennis. Two goals are set up at a distance of several hundred yards from each other, and the object of the players is to drive the ball through the goal of their opponents by means of the rackets, without touching it with the hand.

"Each team consists of twelve players, and an equal number of substitutes, and has twelve referees, six at each goal. One of the most daring and expert of the players some athletic young fellow like Kiaehatalee is made captain of each team. The ball is placed in the center of the field, and the players, except the captains, take their places about twenty yards out in their opponent's ground. The two captains stop with the ball at the center of the field.

"One of the captains now lifts the ball with his racket, and tosses it up thirty or forty feet. When it descend each captain leaps high in the air, and their rackets strike furiously together, as each tries to reach the ball and throw it in the direction of his opponent's goal. If they are evenly matched they may contend until they are exhausted before they are able to move the ball; but sometimes one catches it in its descent, and hurls it with great velocity in the direction of the goal. It is rare, however, that one of his opponents in the field does not catch it with his racket and send it as far back towards the opposite goal. In this way it may be sent back and forth many times; or, if the interference is good, it may fly off at right angles to the goal line. Occasionally all the players will contend en masse for the ball, while the bewildered spectator wonders where it is.

"There is no time for breathing from the time the ball is pitched off until it is pushed through one of the goals, unless a recess is called by the referees, when the players who have not been doubled up, are fatigued to the point of exhaustion. While no player is allowed to strike, scatch, or bruise his opponent, he may double him up, which is done by lifting him by the feet and pressing his head and shoulders against the ground until he is so disabled in the back that he has to be carried off the field. The players enter the game dressed in a belt and flap, but they generally emerge from it with only the belt.

"The betting on this occasion ran high, even chiefs staking the clothes they wore, down to their flaps. The Bloody Fellow's side lost. In the evening he made the leading players of the opposition drunk, and while he, personally, shared their condition, he managed to keep his best players sober. As a result of this diplomacy, on Tuesday he recovered all his losses, and was ready to enter upon the public business Wednesday.

H. The Black Hole

Until recently, it had been taught that Brigadier General Griffith Rutherford had taken the main trail over Wayah Gap to reach the valley towns, and that Colonel Andrew Williamson either followed his trail a few days later or went straight north following the Little Tennessee River. However, latter-day historians have done serious research on period documents that change the thinking of not only the routes the two armies took, but exactly where the Battle of the Black Hole took place. This essay justifies the author's selection of the Black Hole location.

Note the reference citations at the end of the following description and the map at the end of this appendix. The book by John Drayton is particularly treasured because he wrote it based on the papers of his father, Justice William Henry Drayton. The justice was privy to Andrew Williamson's reports about the expedition. (Williamson used a scribe because he was illiterate.)

Authors Nadia Dean and Richard Blackmon relied heavily upon Arthur Fairies' and Captain Francis Ross' diaries; each first-hand accounts. Charles Baxley's website *Southern Campaigns of the American Revolution (SCAR)* contains a version of Fairies' Diary, transcribed by Will Graves, which is most valuable. Lamar Marshall relied on his own personal experiences with Cherokee archeology and studies of Indian trails, village locations, and other pertinent scientific studies of the period. All have written (some in part) that Rutherford took a trail other than over Wayah Gap, Williamson took the Wayah Gap trail rather than travel up the Little Tennessee River or follow Rutherford's line of travel, and the Black (or Dark) Hole is along present-day Wayah Road. My own research of these author's writings, and of the period references of Arthur Fairies' and Francis Ross' Diaries, and John Drayton's *Memoirs of the American Revolution...*, identifies the likely Black Hole location along Wayah Road. (My thanks to all mentioned in this paragraph for pointing me in the right direction.)

The chosen site is on present-day Wayah Road and located with the following parameters and associated map:
1. Black Hole is a narrow valley one and one-half miles long—from the bottom of the hairpin curves (two miles east of, and below, Wayah Gap) eastward one and one-half miles to a narrow pass (three and one-half miles east of Wayah Gap) which is between the north end of a mountain ridge on the south and a parallel ridge on the north.
2. Canucca is two and one-half miles west by southwest from Franklin, North Carolina, (Nikwasi/Nequasee). (Canucca was likely located in the vicinity of present-day Industrial Park Road, and on Cartoogechaye Creek where it runs parallel to the south side of Highway 64, 500 feet south of Old Murphy Road, before it intersects Wayah Road.)
3. Nikwasi site (Franklin) is 10 to 11 miles east of Wayah Gap, and eight miles east of the east end of the Black Hole (as the crow flies).
4. Canucca site is 10 miles eastward from Wayah Gap, and four miles eastward from the LBJ Job Corps Center by Wayah Road.
5. LBJ Job Corps center is six miles east of Wayah Gap by Wayah Road.
6. Canucca site is six and one-half miles east of the east end of the Black (Dark) Hole.
7. The LBJ Job Corps Center is two and one-half miles east of the east end of the Black Hole by road.

Wayah Road picks up Wayah Creek (Nowe, Noewee Creek) about one-half mile east of the LBJ Job Corps Center. The primary Indian trail westward out of Nikwasi apparently left present-day Franklin on West Palmer Street and generally followed the route of today's Old Murphy Road until it intersects the Wayah Road at its junction with U.S. Highway 64. This would have been across the highway from the site of Canucca (see above list).

The Indian trail apparently split at that point and the more northern trail headed west from there to Wayah Gap generally following present-day Wayah Road. The more southern trail generally followed U.S. Highway 64 (Murphy Road) west by southwest toward what is now Murphy, North Carolina.

Colonel Andrew Williamson and the South Carolina militia were supposed to have met North Carolina brigadier general Griffith Rutherford and his force at Nikwasi. Rutherford left Nikwasi on September 15, 1776, since Williamson had not yet arrived and the General had no word from him. Rutherford apparently took the southern trail straight to the Valley Towns around Hiwassee. He left a force under Colonel James Martin with the baggage at Canucca.

The Cherokee were apparently expecting Rutherford to take the normal route over Wayah Gap, as Lamar Marshall (see below) explains they had set an ambush one-half mile east of the present-day LBJ Job Corps Center to attack the expected combined force of Rutherford and Williamson. It is unknown if the general had taken the wrong trail (as reported by some) or followed the south trail on purpose.

Williamson's 2,000-man army left Fort Rutledge on September 12, and 300 were left to garrison the fort. Some recent historians have written that the Battle of the Black Hole took place about nine miles south of Franklin (near Echoe) on U.S. Highway 23/441, the site where Lieutenant Colonel James Grant's army was waylaid in 1761. However, Williamson,

Appendix H: The Black Hole 375

as Nadia Dean pointed out, had warned his troops about the possibility because he had been with Grant's expedition. Surprisingly, the Cherokee did not attack them there since the action against Grant 15 years earlier had been successful.

Williamson's army arrived at Canucca on September 18 (see several of the references below) and camped for the night.

Some writers record that he left Canucca as late as 11:00 on the morning of the 19th, but others (especially John Drayton) state that the army was engaged with the Cherokee at the Black Hole by that time.

Colonel Williamson apparently took the primary trail toward Wayah Gap. He would have followed the main trail along present-day Wayah Road rather than Cartoogechaye Creek. That creek winds considerably and Wayah Creek enters it about three and one-half miles west of Canucca and north of U.S. Highway 64. Williamson would have picked up Wayah Creek where it approaches Wayah Road, just east of the LBJ Job Corps Center, after a march of nearly four miles.

Nadia Dean (see below) states that Williamson's army followed Wayah Creek, which was also called Cowechee Branch of the Tennessee by some of the soldiers, and Nowe Creek by the British.

John Drayton (see below) reported that the army followed Noewee Creek (likely a variation of Nadia Dean's spelling of Nowe Creek).

Arthur Fairies, in his diary, called the adjoining stream Coweckey (Will Graves' best transcription of the almost illegible word), perhaps a variant of Cowechee. At that point, John Drayton expressed, the army followed Noewee Creek.

Richard Blackmon (see below) explained that the army marched up Waya Creek valley.

Captain Ross, per Nadia Dean, declared that the march to the Black Hole from Canucca was six miles. Arthur Fairies verified that distance in his diary.

There would have been much conjecture as to the name of the creek. The soldiers likely though it the same stream as the Cartoogechaye Creek where they camped at Canucca. They may have thought it of it as a branch of the Tennessee River, and would have been right. Williamson apparently knew from before that it was Nowe (or Noewee) Creek because he had been in the area with James Grant 15 years earlier. The British Grant would have used the name Nowe (or Noewee) Creek.

The descriptions of the Black Hole in all period sources avow that the valley was long and easily accessible only at the entrance. The west end of the Black Hole was an extremely steep egress to a pass through the mountains.

The length of the march, and the description and location of the Black Hole in the sources, supports the theory of the location as pinpointed by the list at the top of this appendix.

Specifically, the army left Canucca, marched up present-day Wayah Road, passed the site of today's LBJ Job Corps Center, and entered the Black Hole one and one-half miles east of where the trail becomes markedly steep at the foot of the rise to Wayah Gap. Thus, the Black Hole is a one and one-half mile long narrow valley, on Wayah Road, east of Wayah Gap before the road begins its precipitous climb to the gap. The entrance to the Black Hole is about two and one-half miles west of the LBJ Job Corps Center.

Williamson had summoned a close-order march at the entrance because his scouts had noticed signs of Indian activity, and because the entrance trail to the Black Hole was very narrow. The length of his army stretched nearly two miles considering the men rode two abreast (allowing an average of ten feet from the tip of one horse's nose to the tip of the nose of the horse behind it).

Fairies indicated that the attack began when Captain Ross was half-way through; however, both John Drayton and Richard Blackmon state that Ross was at the end of the valley and beginning his climb. The latter makes more sense as an appropriate time for an attack as the Cherokee would have desired as many of the soldiers in the trap as possible. It may be that Fairies was talking about halfway to the Wayah Gap itself. However, Fairies was not a leader, or a guide, and may have been well back in the column.

The warriors involved were estimated by various sources as anywhere from 500 to 1,200.

Blackmon refers to the fight having lasted for six hours, while Fairies and others record about one hour. Blackmon did caveat, however, that the last several hours consisted of sporadic firing (likely sniping by warriors who lagged behind the main withdrawal).

Carolana.com places the Black Hole directly north of Franklin along the Little Tennessee River, and the old road marker was even further north on the same river. It would have made no sense for Williamson to have backtracked to Nikwasi from Canucca, and then head north to retrace the trail that Rutherford had used to come to Nikwasi. Rutherford had already encountered the Indian villages along that route, so Williamson would have wasted his time. Additionally, had the most direct route to the valley towns meant Williamson had to go north from Nikwasi to follow the Little Tennessee River, then Rutherford would have had no reason to come south down that same river to Nikwasi to meet Williamson and backtrack his own trail.

The Wayah Gap route was a major Indian trail that led to the area Williamson was targeting. It would have cost him several days of travel to have gone straight north first and then west.

All of the facts, and sensibilities of Williamson's goals and the reports of the journals, and especially the writing of John Drayton, indicate that the Black Hole was short, just east, of Wayah Gap. It definitely could not have been due south of Franklin near Etchoe or north of along the Little Tennessee River.

Some additional useful details:
a. Wayah Road takes off about where Old Murphy Road hits U.S. Highway 64 at Patton Road exit—about three miles west of Franklin.
b. Cartoogechaye Creek crosses U.S. Highway 23/441 about one-half mile south of where 23 joins 441 from the east (south of Franklin). The creek empties into Little Tennessee River south of Franklin and about two-thirds of a mile past the east-west portion of 23 before it hits 441. The mouth of the creek is in the vicinity of Wide Horizon Drive.
c. Cartoogechaye Creek approaches U.S. Highway 64 from the south about two and one-half miles west of 441 (likely site of Canucca).
d. Cartoogechaye Creek crosses U.S. Highway 64 from south to north at Bill Dalrymple Road about one mile west of Patton Road exit (see #2. above) or about five miles west of U.S. Highway 441.
e. Wayah Creek enters Cartoogechaye Creek about six miles west of U.S. Highway 441 and north of U.S. Highway 64—Carl Slagle Road off of 64 to Valley Lane.

Appendix H: The Black Hole 377

REFERENCES

- **Nadia Dean, *A Demand of Blood***

Page 194, paragraph 3:

"At noon, Dells's baggage guard left Nikwasi and moved camp two miles southwest to Canucca on Cartoogechaye Creek. One hour later they were surprised by the arrival of the Light Horse from the South Army. Williamson and his 1,730 men passed through Canucca enroute to the valley towns."

Nadia Dean's references for above passage: *Revolutionary Diary of William Lenoir, The Journal of Southern History 6, no. 2.*

Pages 158 last paragraph–159, paragraph 3:

"Williamson's army crossed through Rabun's Gap on September 16. On September 17.... The men marched ... through The Narrows. Williamson ... warned his men of the potential dangers ahead, as Grant had been ambushed at the same place. To their surprise, the Cherokees did not attack [near Echoe]."

"September 18 ... they arrived at Nikwasi to learn that Rutherford had already left for the Valley towns. Williamson's army then marched two miles to Canucca and found Rutherford's baggage guard under the command of Colonel Martin. At 1:00 p.m. Williamson's Light Horse companies arrived in Canucca ...

At 11:00 a.m. on Thursday, September 19, Williamson's army began thier [sic] march toward the Valley towns. The troops trekked along a branch of the Tennessee River they called Cowechee (now known as Wayah Creek). [In note 195 page 397, she states "British called it Nowe Creek."] Six miles from their camp near Canucca, Ross reported they marched into 'a long valley ... surrounded by mountains on all sides.' They marched into a mountain hollow—a large glade between mountains dubbed the Black Hole—where the militia encountered hundreds of Cherokee warriors posted in the form of 'a half moon on two spurs of a mountain.'"

Nadia Dean's references for above passage: The diaries of Ross, Fairies, and Dells. (*Diary of William Dells, A Journal of the Motions of the Continental Army Commanded by the Honble. Griffith Rutherford Esqr. Brigadear Generall Against the Cherokee Indians* [sic], Filson Historical Society, Louisville Kentucky; *Diary attributed to Arthur Fairies* (more likely spelled Farris) South Carolina Department of Archives and History, Columbia, South Carolina; *Diary fragment in Henry Laurens Papers,* 37/45a/13, South Carolina Historical Society, Columbia, South Carolina.

- **Richard D. Blackmon, *Dark and Bloody Ground***

Pages 81 paragraph 2 through 83 paragraph 1:

"On September 19, Williamson started his army in pursuit of Rutherford's column. He led his militiamen west out of Nequassee up the Sugartown River. Williamson had several traders and guides and therefore knew the trails and locations of many towns. After about an hour, the column swung to the north, taking the main trail to the valley towns over the Nantahala Mountains. The trail led up Waya Creek valley called 'the Dark Hole,' directly to Waya Gap. Steep mountainsides covered with a dense forest formed the valley, limiting the amount of sunlight that came through. At about 10:30 a.m., Catawba scouts reported signs of Cherokee warriors.... The advance guard of one hundred men [Captain Ross] had just about reached the steepest part of the trail leading up to the gap when the valley [where the main body was] erupted with musket fire.

Williamson and his men did not realize that Oconostota led the Cherokee in person. The Great Warrior had positioned himself below Waya Gap and along the sides of the valley so that when the battle began they almost completely enveloped Williamson's column … the Cherokee poured a steady fire into the militiamen as the column recoiled under the galling fire…. The advance guard fell back to the rest of the column, which had halted in the floor of the valley, an open area of about forty or fifty acres…. The militiamen beat back the Cherokee assaults … Hammond managed to … with a body of fifty troops … flanked the Cherokees, who began to withdraw …

Around four o'clock in the afternoon, the flanking troops … gained and occupied Waya Gap … scattered firing continued throughout the last hours of light…. The Battle of the Dark Hole continued for approximately six hours …

Colonel Martin, back in Nequassee, heard the battle and sent about 150 men … to Williamson's aid … arrived as the Cherokees began their withdrawal."

Richard Blackmon's references: John Drayton, *Memoirs of the American Revolution*, vol. 2, 356–357; Draper MSS 1KK85–85(2), 3VV126(1)

- **Arthur Fairies Journal, found in Charles Baxley's *Southern Campaigns of the American Revolution (SCAR)* 2, no. 10.0, dated October 2005, southerncampaign.org, pages 20–34 *Arthur Fairies' Journal of Expedition Against the Cherokee Indians from July 18th, to October 11th, 1776,* Transcribed and Annotated by Will Graves**

This is a transcription of two previous transcriptions.

Pages 23–24:

"Wednesday the 18th [of September 1776]: … we started in pursuit of them [Rutherford] as far as called Canutee [this would likely be Canucca] where we found a party of the aforesaid Army, that is to say, a baggage guard …

Thursday the 19th September: … We marched along the waters of Tennessee first on branches of [Will Graves' note: largely illegible name that might be "Coweckey"]—we had gone about six miles from camp on the road, we marched into a valley, or rather a hollow, named Black Hole, surrounded by mountains on all sides only except the entrance. On our entering, our front guard, commanded by Capt. Ross, was about half through—the Indians were flanked all around us, and fired on our guard, and all our regiment was soon engaged, & the firing of the Indians was incessant. We continued our fight about one hour, desperate. But in getting possession of the mountain, we through mercy, defeated our enemies….

Friday the 20th: … We started & marched along the greatest of Narrows, where immense numbers of Indian camps. Our road continued up a vast mountain, or rather between two mountains, which led us to the most wildersomest part of the world, allowed by us. In this manner we march allowing to receive battle every moment, but through mercy we got safe to the top [likely still in the Nantahala Mountains west of Wayah Gap], allowing it little inferior to the mountain of Ararat. If here Noah's ark rested on the top of this, we camped—our days march about 5 miles, and this mountain was about 1 _ miles of them. We must mind that when the Indians fled, we found on the ground the luggage of about 200 Indians—that is to say, blankets, moccasins, boots, some guns, also powder, match-coats, deer-skins, &c, &tc."

Pages 30–31: Will Graves outlines differences between the two versions with regard to this portion of the expedition; however, it does not impact the important details covered above.

- **Smoky Mountain News—Waynesville, NC, Wednesday, 27 October 2010 20:45, *The 1776 campaign against the Cherokee*, www.smokymountainnews.com/index.php/component/k2/item/2173-the-1776-campaign-against-the-cherokee, by Lamar Marshall, Contributing Writer**

"The next ambush laid for Rutherford was to be on Wayah Creek, along modern Wayah Road, east of the Lyndon B. Johnson Job Corps Center in Franklin. This was to be the largest battle that Rutherford and Williamson's armies would engage. Unfortunately for Rutherford, he failed to take Indian scouts with him and got lost at Franklin. He crossed the mountains at the wrong place, basically following the route of modern U.S. 64, and burned the Cherokee towns along Shooting Creek, Hayesville and Peachtree....

"The South Carolina army arrived at Canucca Town very near Nikwasi at modern-day Franklin, and followed what is now the Wayah Road, where about 500 to 600 Cherokees attacked Williamson's troops. At least 13 American soldiers were killed before the Cherokees retreated. They were buried in a swampy place, with a causeway built over the graves to hide them. There is not so much as a historical marker to mark their graves or tell the story. The army then marched over the mountains to the site of modern-day Andrews, where they burned all the Valley Towns down to the Murphy area and soon met Gen. Rutherford."

- **John Drayton, *Memoirs of the American Revolution, From Its Commencement to the Year 1776***

Vol. 2, page 355

"In the meantime, General Rutherford ... had dispatched two men to inform Col. Williamson of his arrival ... not hearing from him, within the time agreed, he left Colonel Martin with a detachment at Canucca.... And with the rest of his army, he directed his course towards the Valley Settlements.... At this time, Colonel Williamson ... arrived at Col. Martins camp at Canucca on the 18th day of September; from whence, General Rutherford had departed three days before ... and, on the 19th of September, the army [Williamson's] proceeded on its march, with the intention of entering the mountainous pass at Noewee Creek....

The army now crossed Cannucca Creek [likely Cartoogechaye Creek], and was proceeding towards Noewee Creek, when tracks of the enemy's spies were discovered about half past ten o'clock A. M. It then proceeded on its left towards a narrow valley, bordering on Noewee Creek, and enclosed on each side by lofty mountains, terminated at the extremity by others equally difficult. These heights were occupied by twelve hundred Indian warriors; nor, were they discovered, until the advance guard [Captain Ross] of one hundred men began to mount the height, which terminated the valley. The army, having thus completely fallen into the ambuscade of the enemy ... compelling it to ... fall into confusion ... Lieutenant-Colonel Hammond caused detachments to file off, for the purpose of gaining the eminences above the Indians ... while, Lieutenant Hampton with twenty men, advanced upon the enemy, passing the main advance guard of one hundred men: who, being panic struck, were rapidly retreating. Hampton, however, clambered up the assent ... calling out, 'Loaded guns advance—empty guns, fall down and load': and being joined by thirty men, he charged desperately."

Appendix H: The Black Hole

- **Henry Lumpkin,** *From Savannah to Yorktown,* page 25, puts the Battle of Black Hole about nine miles south of present-day Franklin at the Narrows on present-day U.S. Highway 23/441 where the 1760–61 ambushes of Colonel Archibald Montgomery and Lieutenant Colonel James Grant occurred.

- **carolana.com**/NC/Revolution/revolution_coweecho_river.html shows the site to be on the Little Tennessee River, north of Franklin on State Highway 28 about halfway to the Macon/Swain County line.

- **In 1939, NC Office of Archives and History** placed a marker just north of the Swain-Macon County line on State Highway 28, but it was eventually stolen.

The author's map included herein indicates the Wayah Gap, Black Hole, Franklin, and Canucca area. The John Drayton map of Williamson's route in 1776, and a zoomed cropping showing the Franklin vicinity, are published in the Cherokee Nation section of author's website at therevolutionarywarauthor.com.

Note: The author's map included herein indicates the Wayah Gap, Black Hole, Franklin, and Canucca area. The John Drayton map of Williamson's route in 1776, and a zoomed cropping showing the Franklin vicinity, are published in the Cherokee Nation section of the author's website at therevolutionarywarauthor.com.

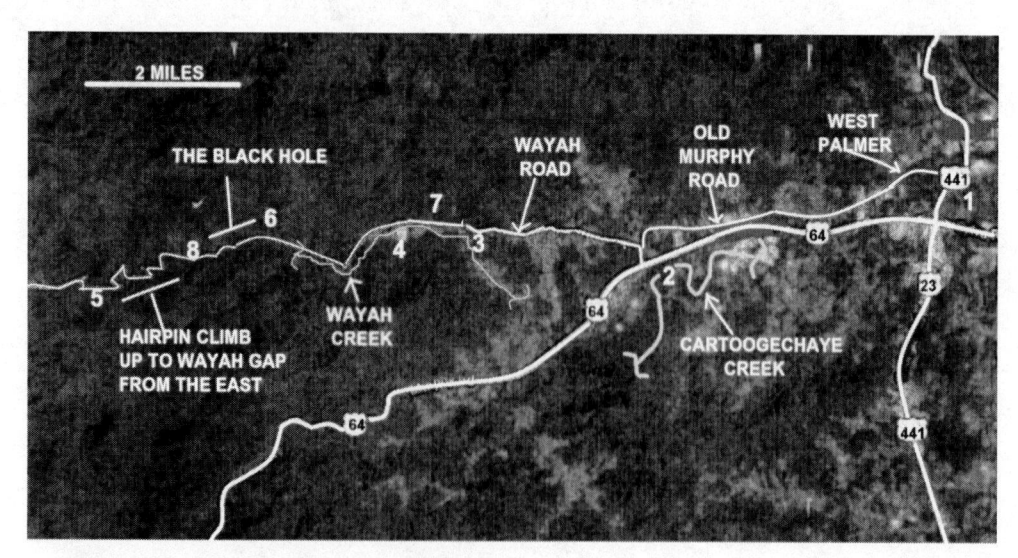

1. Nikwasi, Nequasee, present-day Franklin, North Carolina.
2. Canucca, Cannucca, Canutee.
3. Wayah Creek abuts Wayah Road from the south.
4. LBJ Job Corps Center.
5. Wayah Gap.
6. Ridge on south forms a narrow passage with mountain on north, likely beginning of the Black Hole (Dark Hole).
7. Location chosen by Lamar Marshall of the Cherokee waiting to ambush General Griffith Rutherford; however, Rutherford took the wrong split (the Indian trails split just North of Canucca, one following the trail to the vicinity of present-day Murphy and the other to Wayah Gap) and generally followed present-day US Highway 64 to Hiwassee.
8. Beginning of sharp climb to Wayah Gap.

BLACK HOLE MAP -- charted by William R. Reynolds, Jr. 9/21/2013

Chapter Notes

Preface

1. Mooney, *History, Myths*, p. 15, 182–183. Historian James Mooney wrote: "The proper name by which the Cherokee call themselves is Yun'wiya,' or Ani'-yun'wiya' in the third person." He continued with more direct interpretation of the word 'Cherokee': "This name occurs in fully fifty different spellings.... In the Eastern ... dialect, with which the English settlers first became familiar, the form is Tsa'ragi,' whence we get Cherokee. In the other dialects the form is Tsa'lagi.' ... In ... the Cherokee language the root form of the tribal name takes ... verbal prefixes ... and is ... conjugated, as follows: SINGULAR—first person, tsi–Tsa'lagi, I (am) a Cherokee; second person, hi–Tsa'lagi, thou art a Cherokee; third person, a-Tsa'lagi, he is a Cherokee. DUAL—first person, dtsi–Tsa'lagi, we two are Cherokee; second person, sti–Tsa'lagi, you two are Cherokee; third person, ani–Tsa'lagi, they two are Cherokee. PLURAL—first person, atsi–Tsa'lagi, we (several) are Cherokee; second person, hitsi–Tsa'lagi, you (several) are Cherokee; third person, ani–Tsa'lagi, they (several) are Cherokee."

Chapter 1

1. Adair, *Account*, p. 3, 5; Adair, *Adair's History*, p. 237–238, 240 (226–228) [The first set of page numbers is from Samuel Cole Williams' edition while the set in parentheses is from Adair's original history]; Conley, *The Cherokee Nation*, p. 6; Gilbert, *The Eastern Cherokees*, p. 178–179; Mooney, p. 14–15, 18–21; Woodward, *The Cherokees*, p. 6.
2. Adair, *Account*, p. 3; Adair, *History*, p. 237–238 (226–227); Conley, p. 6; Gilbert, p. 178, 186; Mooney, p. 14.
3. Gilbert, p. 316.
4. Alderman, *Nancy Ward/Dragging Canoe*, p. 3–4.
5. Alderman, p. 3–4; Conley, p. 5; Gilbert, p. 18; Hatley, *The Dividing Paths*, p. 6; Mooney, p. 15–17.
6. Alderman, p. 6–7; Conley, p. 7; Gilbert, p. 179, 198; Hatley, *Paths*, p. 8; Hoig, *The Cherokees and Their Chiefs*, p. 1; Mooney, p. 15; Woodward, p. 22.
7. Gilbert, p. 193–194, 316–317; Goodpasture, *Indian Wars and Warriors*, Chapter 1, p. 3; Hoig, p. 9.
8. Conley, p. 6–7, 11–14; Gilbert, p. 203, 208–209, 254, 323–324; Woodward, p. 33.
9. Hatley, *Paths*, p. 8 [This passage is recognizable as being from Anne Matthews' Memoirs, which is typescript in the South Caroliniana Library].
10. Hatley, *Paths*, p. 53.
11. Hatley, *Paths*, p. 53.
12. Hatley, *Paths*, p. 54.
13. Adair, *History*, p. 152–153 (144–145); Hatley, *Paths*, p. 54.
14. Adair, *History*, p. 152–153 (144–145); Hatley, *Paths*, p. 53–55, 58–63.
15. Alderman, p. 7; Timberlake, *Memoirs*, p. 36 (67–68) [The first set of page numbers is from Duane H. King's edition while the set in parentheses is from Timberlake's original record.]
16. Alderman, p. 7.
17. Alderman, p. 6–7; Conley, p. 7; Gilbert, p. 254, 256, 318, 340; Hatley, *Paths*, p. 8; Hoig, p. 8; Mooney, p. 15.
18. Alderman, p. 6–7; "Cherokee History," aaanativearts.com; Conley, p. 7, 11; Gilbert, p. 181, 187, 317; Goodpasture, Chapter 1, p. 3; Woodward, p. 31, 33, 51.
19. "Cherokee Myths and Legends," gypsywolf.weebly.com; "The Cherokee Story of the Origin of Diseases," suite101.com/article/animal-parliaments-a-cherokee-legend; Conley, p. 7; Mooney, p. 250–251.
20. Alderman, p. 6–7; Conley, p. 11; Gilbert, p. 187, 313, 316–317, 348–349; Hatley, *Paths*, p. 9, 15; Wells, *The Outline of History*, p. 10.
21. "The Cherokee Nation," cherokee.org/AboutTheNation/Culture/General/24404/Information.aspx; Gilbert, p. 325–326.
22. Adair, *History*, p. 431 (401).
23. Adair, *History*, p. 430–431 (401); Gilbert, p. 181, 318, 337–338; Woodward, p. 51–53.
24. Timberlake, p. 30 (55).
25. Timberlake, p. 36 (70).
26. Timberlake, p. 43–44 (87).
27. Timberlake, p. 36–37 (70–71).
28. Conley, p. 11; Gilbert, p. 318, 321–323; Goodpasture, Chapter 1, p. 4; Hatley, *Paths*, p. 10–14; Hoig, p. 9–15; Woodward, p. 51.
29. Albright, *Early History of Middle Tennessee*, Chapter 2; Sugden, *Blue Jacket*, p. 8–21.

Chapter 2

1. Adair, *Account*, p. 9; Adair, *History*, p. 244 (232), and Note 118.
2. Duffy, *Epidemics in Colonial America*, p. 82–83.
3. Duffy, p. 94–95.
4. Duffy, p. 75.
5. "Smallpox," Native American Heritage Programs, lenapeprograms.info/Wisdom/smallpox.htm.
6. Adair, *Account*, p. 9; Adair, p. 244 (232), and Note 118; Anderson, "The Cherokee World: Before and After Timberlake," p. 9; Duffy, p. 75–95; Gilbert, p. 198; "Smallpox," Native American; Reynolds, *Andrew Pickens*, p. 251.
7. Albright, Chapter 3; Conley, p. 18; Goodpasture, Chapter 1, p. 4; Hatley, *Paths*, p. 5; Hoig, p. 7–8; Mooney, p. 23–26; Woodward, p. 22–23.
8. Conley, p. 20; Hatley, *Paths*, p. 5; Hoig, p. 8; Mooney, p. 27–29; "Juan Pardo," northcarolinahistory.org.
9. Conley, p. 21.
10. Conley, p. 20–21; Mooney, p. 29–30.
11. Williams, *Early Travels*, p. 97–101, 122–127. [Early historian Samuel Cole Williams indicated that Chota did not become prominent until the 1740s when Conne-Corte (Old Hop) came into power (see Chapter 3). The prior "Mother Town" became Tellico in 1730 when Moytoy II (Trader Tom) was selected by Alexander Cuming to be emperor of the Cherokee. In the 1720s, the "capital" appears to have been Tanase because Tanase Warrior was the de facto headman of the collective villages. Tellico, Tanase, and Chota are generally in the same vicinity, and Chota may have been a part of Tanase in Abraham Wood's time. Tanase appeared on explorers' maps much earlier than Chota which indicates that Tanase was the earlier accepted destination of trade and exploration. Wood may have had a communication problem with his men, Needham and Arthur. He might have misunderstood their reports, they could have been confused as to just where they were (they were not adept with the Cherokee language), or they possibly did visit Chota as well as Tanase and combined their experiences in each community as one.]
12. Woodward, p. 28.
13. "Trade Guns," thefurtrapper.com; "Yamassee War," carolana.com/Carolina/Noteworthy_Events/yamasseewar.html.
14. Woodward, p. 29.
15. Woodward, p. 29.
16. Conley, p. 21–22, 26; Hatley, *Paths*, p. 17–18; Woodward, p. 27–30.
17. Mooney, p. 32.
18. Wells, *The Outline of History*, p. 890–891.
19. Gilbert, p. 187; Hatley, *Paths*, p. 17, 31–32; Mooney, p. 31–32; Woodward, p. 31.
20. Reed, *Beaufort County: Two Centuries of Its History*, p. 72.
21. Reynolds, p. 83.
22. Conley, p. 26; Hatley, *Paths*, p. 18; Mooney, p. 32; "North Carolina Historic Sites," nchistoricsites.org; "The Tuscarora War," en.wikipedia.org/wiki/Tuscarora_War; Woodward, p. 34, 57.
23. Mooney, p. 32.
24. Hatley, *Paths*, p. 24.
25. Alderman, p. 8; Conley, p. 26; Hatley, *Paths*, p. 3, 7–8, 19, 22–25, 34; Mooney, p. 33–34; "Yamassee War," carolana.com; "The Yamassee War," en.wikipedia.org.
26. Documents Relating to Indian Affairs [DRIA], Vol. 1, p. 149; Hatley, *Paths*, p. 35.
27. Lawson, *A New Voyage to Carolina*, Lawson's diary.
28. Conley, p. 26; Goodpasture, Chapter 1, p. 4; Hatley, *Paths*, p. 27–28, 35, 43–44; Mooney, p. 34–35.
29. Hatley, *Paths*, p. 50–51.
30. Adair, *Account*, p. 8–9; Adair, *History*, p. 237–238 (226–227); Conley, p. 27–28; Goodpasture, Chapter 1, p. 4; Hatley, *Paths*, p. 9–10, 18–19, 29–31, 45–46, 50–51, 54; Hoig, p. 1, 3–5; Mooney, p. 34; Morris, Michael, *The High Price of Trade*, p. 3; Woodward, p. 31–32, 59–60.

Chapter 3

1. Anderson, p. 8.
2. Anderson, p. 8; Hatley, *Paths*, p. 70; Mooney, p. 38.
3. "The South Sea Company," en.wikipedia.org/wiki/South_Sea_Company.
4. Samuel Gardner Drake, *Early History of Georgia*, p. 7.
5. Drake, Samuel, p. 7.
6. Rozema, *Cherokee Voices*, p. 13–14.
7. Woodward, p. 61.
8. Woodward, p. 61.
9. Goodpasture, Chapter 1.
10. Williams, *Early Travels*, p. 115–143; Woodward, p. 63.
11. Chalmers, *The General Biographical Dictionary*, Vol 11; Conley, p. 28; Drake, Samuel, p. 7–14; Goodpasture., Chapter 1; Hoig, p. 19–20; Mooney, p. 35–36; Rozema, p. 3–5, 13–14; Williams, *Early Travels*, p. 115–143; "The South Sea Company," en.wikipedia.org; Woodward, p. 61, 63.
12. Kelly, *Attakullakulla*, p. 3.
13. Williams, *Early Travels*, p. 115–143; Woodward, *The Cherokees*, p. 63–67.
14. "The Chickamauga Cherokee," chickamaugacherokee.org/friendship1730; Cherokee Documents in Foreign Archives [CDFI], Special Collections, Hunter Library, C054, 06442, Microfilm #197, p. 211–214; Autobiographies From Men of All Ranks [AFMAR], Sources from the British Library, London, Part 1: Autobiographies, c1760–1820, Reel, Sir Alexander Cuming, Autobiographical notes, Add. 39855; Rozema, p. 7–11.
15. "The Chickamauga Cherokee," chickamaugacherokee.org; CDFI, Microfilm #197, p. 215–216; AFMAR, Add. 39855; Rozema, p. 11–12.
16. Alderman, p. 7; Conley, p. 34–35.
17. Goodpasture, Chapter 1.

18. Goodpasture, Chapter 1.
19. Goodpasture, Chapter 1.
20. Alderman, p. 4; Anderson, p. 11; Chalmers, Vol. 11; Conley, p. 33–35; Drake, Samuel, p. 15–16; Goodpasture, Chapter 1; Hatley, *Paths,* p. 68; Hoig, p. 20; Kelly, p. 2–4; Mooney, p. 35–36; Rozema, p. 5, 7–14; Woodward, p. 64, 67.
21. Adair, *Account,* p. 9, 17–21; Adair, *History,* p. 252–257, (240–243), and Note 18; Alderman, p. 13; "Christian Gottlieb Priber," virtual.clemson.edu; Conley, p. 36; Drake, Samuel, p. 3; Hatley, *Paths,* p. 70–74; Hoig, p. 52; Kelly, p. 6; Mooney, p. 36–37; Walker, *Doublehead,* p. 39–46; Woodward, p. 68.
22. Adair, *Account,* p. 9; Adair, *History,* p. 244 (232).
23. Drake, Samuel, p. 3.
24. Maddox, p. 116; DRIA, Vol. 1, p. 261.
25. Woodward, p. 69.
26. Adair, *Account,* p. 9; Adair, *History,* p. 244 (232), and Note 18; Anderson, p. 9; Arthur, *Western North Carolina,* Chapter 26; Conley, p. 36, 39–41; Drake, Samuel, p. 3; Hoig, p. 22; Kelly, p. 7; Mooney, p. 36, 38–39; Rozema, p. 6; Woodward, p. 68- 69. (Side note: A potter named Andrew Duché had discovered magnificent white clay on Cherokee land. He carried an amount of it, with Cherokee permission, to his facility in Savannah where he made white china dishware for the first time in America. He sold clay and exported it to a London speculator who in turn opened porcelain factories that competed well with fine oriental products. "Andrew Duche," genealogy-georgiapioneers.blogspot.com.)
27. Kelly, p. 8.
28. Woodward, p. 70.
29. Dean, *A Demand of Blood,* p. 161, 163.
30. "George Washington," ushistory.org/valley forge/george1.html.
31. Irving, *The Life of George Washington,* Vol. 1, p. 158.
32. Kelly, p. 10.
33. Alderman, p. 2–4; Arthur, Chapter 26; "Cherokee Treaties," nanations.com; Hatley, *Paths,* p. 72–73, 75, 85–87; Hoig, p. 22–24, 28; Kelly, p. 7–11; King, *Long Island of the Holston,* p. 113–114; Mooney, p. 38–39; Reynolds, p. 18–19; Woodward, p. 71.
34. Hoig, p. 27.
35. Kelly, p. 11.
36. Hoig, p. 30.
37. Hoig, p. 31; Kelly, p. 14.
38. Hatley, *Paths,* p. 111; Hoig, p. 31; Kelly, p. 9–11, 14; DRIA, Vol. 2, p. 238, 263–264, 268, 270–271.
39. DRIA, Vol. 2, p. 138.
40. DRIA, Vol. 2, p. 249.
41. DRIA, Vol. 2, p. 224.
42. Adair, *History,* p. 444 (414).
43. Kelly, p. 16; DRIA, Vol. 2, p. 391–392.
44. Hoig, p. 36; DRIA, Vol. 2, p. 398.
45. Adair, *Account,* p. 21; Adair, *History,* p. 258 (244); Alderman, p. 15; Conley, p. 46–47; Drake, Samuel, p. 4–5; Goodpasture, Chapter 1, p. 6–9; Hatley, *Paths,* p. 69–70, 75–76, 93–99, 110; Hoig, p. 27–33; Kelly, p. 9–16; Mooney, p. 40; Morris, Michael, p. 4–10; Woodward, p. 71.

46. Kelly, p. 17.
47. Hoig, p. 35.
48. Adair, *Account,* p. 22–23; Adair, *History,* p. 259–260 (245).
49. Kelly, p. 18.
50. Alderman, p. 16; Drake, Samuel, p. 4; Hatley, *Paths,* p. 101–102; Kelly, p. 14, 17–19.

Chapter 4

1. Hatley, *Paths,* p. 105.
2. Hatley, *Paths,* p. 105
3. Hatley, *Paths,* p. 106. (Note: Presbyterian Covenanters seemingly believed that the church must not join hands with any political power that was obviously in rebellion to the "crown rights" of King Jesus. That is, they pledged the Covenanted Reformed Presbyterian Church to the support of lawful magistracy [i.e., magistracy that conformed itself to the precepts of God's Word] and declared themselves and their posterity against support of any power, in church or state, which lacked biblical authority. Covenanters of that era determined that the Church of Scotland [led by King William III of Orange], at the time of the Catholic Revolt [1690], was established on principles antithetical to the original Reformational moralities previously attained in Scotland by the Protestants. Since William was head of the Church of England, the Church of Scotland could not be said to adhere to biblical authority. (Basically, the Covenanters believed King William and the Church of Scotland, under his leadership, did not adhere to the Westminster Confession of Faith and Catechisms of 1647 as summarizing the historic Christian faith, and thus was not committed to Reformed theology commonly referred to as Calvinism.) The Battle of the Boyne fought in Ireland on July 1, 1690, O.S. (Old Style or Julian) between Catholic king James II of England and Ireland (James VII of Scotland) and Protestant king William III (King James' nephew and son-in-law being married to James daughter, Queen Mary II) who had deposed King James in 1688. The battle was won by William and was the straw that broke King James' attempts to regain the crown and reestablish Catholicism as the church of state in England, Scotland, and Ireland. That ensured the continuation of Protestant ascendancy in Ireland. The battle is celebrated in Ireland today on July 12, [Gregorian, though that correlates to July 2 O.S.] by the Protestant Orange Institution. The main Presbyterian bodies in the Colonial Carolinas were the Associate, Covenanter, Burgher, Anti-Burgher, and Seceders.)
4. DRIA, Vol. 2, p. 276.
5. Woodward, p. 72.
6. Adair, *Account,* p. 23–24; Adair, *History,* p. 261 (246–247).
7. Adair, *Account,* p. 23–24; Adair, *History,* p. 261 (246–247); Hatley, *Paths,* p. 105–107; Mooney, p. 41; Woodward, p. 72.
8. South Carolina Department of Archives and

History [SCDAH], *Letters of Governor William Henry Lyttleton.*
   9. Alderman, p. 16–17.
   10. Alderman, p. 17.
   11. Alderman, p. 16–17; Conley, p. 47; Hatley, *Paths,* p. 109; Judd, *The Overmountain Men,* p. 37; Mooney, p. 42.
   12. Hatley, *Paths,* p. 113–114; Judd, *Overmountain Men,* p. 37–38; Mooney, p. 42; Morris, Michael, p. 11.
   13. Conley, p. 47; Goodpasture, Chapter 1, p. 10–12; Hatley, *Paths,* p. 114; Hoig, p. 36; Mooney, p. 42; Morris, Michael, p. 11.
   14. Hoig, p. 36.
   15. SCDAH, *Journal of Council,* October 19, 1759.
   16. Goodpasture, Chapter 1, p. 10–12; Hoig, p. 36.
   17. Goodpasture, Chapter 1, p. 10–12; Hatley, *Paths,* p. 114, 121–122; Hoig, p. 36; Judd, *Overmountain Men,* p. 38; Mooney, p. 42; Morris, Michael, p. 11.
   18. Bass, *Ninety Six: The Struggles for the South Carolina Back Country,* p. 42–44; Reynolds, p. 20.
   19. Adair, *Account,* p. 28; Adair, *History,* p. 265 (250).
   20. Alderman, p. 18.
   21. Milligen-Johnston, *A Short Description of the Province of South Carolina, with an Account of the Air, Weather, and Diseases, at Charles-town, Written in the Year 1763,* p. 194–195.
   22. Alderman, p. 16–18; Conley, p. 47; Goodpasture, Chapter 1, p. 12; Hatley, *Paths,* p. 115, 120, 123–124; Hoig, p. 36–37; Judd, *Overmountain Men,* p. 38–39; Kelly, p. 19; Mooney, p. 42; Morris, Michael, p. 11; Rogers, *Archaeology at Cherokee Town Sites Visited by the Montgomery and Grant Expeditions,* p. 35.
   23. Salley, *The Calhoun Family of South Carolina,* p. 5.
   24. Salley, p. 5–6.
   25. Adair, *Account,* p. 32; Adair, *History,* p. 270 (254); Bass, *Ninety Six,* p. 38–39; Day, *Cousin Monroe's History of the Pickens Family,* Chapter 2, p. 30–31; Greene, *Ninety Six: A Historical Narrative,* p. 27–30; Hatley, *Paths,* p. 126–127; Hoig, p. 37; Reynolds, p. 17–18, 20–21.
   26. "South Carolina Genealogy Forum," virts.rootsweb.ancestry.com/~scroots/m_317.html, South Carolina Military Accounts for Thursday, April 24, 1760. (Note: Historical writings that chronicle the events at Fort Prince George do not usually provide the first names of Ensign Bell or Lieutenant Foster. The names are rarely found as they are inconspicuous. However, this reference provides them in account transactions numbers 142 & 143, "142. Thomas Foster for serving as Interpreter at Fort Prince George from March to November 1759 inclusive at £15 per Month, certified by Lieutenant Richard Coytmore … 143. John Elliott for Brass and Tin Kettles delivered Ensign John Bell for the use of the Carolina Regiment at Fort Prince George, amounting to £56; not being certified by the Officer, we disallow it.")

   27. Goodpasture, Chapter 1, p. 13.
   28. Goodpasture, Chapter 1, p. 13.
   29. Goodpasture, Chapter 1, p. 13.
   30. DRIA, Vol. 2, p. 503.
   31. Goodpasture, Chapter 1, p. 13.
   32. Milligen-Johnston, p. 196–197.
   33. Adair, *History,* p. 265 (250); Alderman, p. 16–19; Conley, p. 47–48; Goodpasture, Chapter 1, p. 12–13; Hatley, *Paths,* p. 125–126, 128; Hoig, p. 37–38; Judd, *Overmountain Men,* p. 39; Kelly, p. 19; Mooney, p. 42–43; Morris, Michael, p. 12; Rogers, *Archaeology,* p. 35; Rozema, p. 32.
   34. Hoig, p. 37–39; "Guide to Southern Campaigns of the American Revolution (SCAR)," lib.jrshelby.com/SCAR%20v7se.pdf; Mooney, p. 43; Morris, Michael, p. 12; Reynolds, p. 20–21; "Southern Campaigns of the American Revolution (SCAR)," Vol. 7, special edition, March 19, 2011, p. 2.
   35. Alderman, p. 19.
   36. Hoig, p. 40; Judd, *Overmountain Men,* p. 41; Kelly, p. 20.
   37. Alderman, p. 19; Arthur, Chapter 26; Goodpasture, Chapter 2, p. 13–14; Hatley, *Paths,* p. 148; Hoig, p. 38–40; Judd, *Overmountain Men,* p. 39–42; Kelly, p. 20; Mooney, p. 43; Morris, Michael, p. 12; Rogers, *Archaeology,* p. 34, 36.
   38. Woodward, p. 74.
   39. Goodpasture, Chapter 2, p. 14.
   40. Goodpasture, Chapter 2, p. 14.
   41. Goodpasture, Chapter 2, p. 14.
   42. Goodpasture, Chapter 2, p. 14; Woodward, p. 77.
   43. Goodpasture, Chapter 2, p. 14.
   44. Alderman, p. 19; Arthur, Chapter 26; Conley, p. 48–49; Goodpasture, Chapter 2, p. 13–15; Hatley, *Paths,* p. 129–133; Hoig, p. 39–40; Judd, *Overmountain Men,* p. 42; Kelly, p. 20; King, p. 113–127; Mooney, p. 43; Morris, Michael, p. 12; Rogers, *Archaeology,* p. 34, 36; Rozema, p. 32; Woodward, p. 74–75.
   45. Goodpasture, Chapter 2, p. 18.
   46. Conley, p. 52.
   47. Adair, *Account,* p. 32; Adair, *History,* p. 269 (254); Alderman, p. 20; Arthur, Chapter 26; Conley, p. 49, 52; Goodpasture, Chapter 2, p. 15–19; Hatley, *Paths,* p. 133; Hoig, p. 40–41; Judd, *Overmountain Men,* p. 47–56; Kelly, p. 20–21; Mooney, p. 41–44; Morris, Michael, p. 12; Rogers, *Archaeology,* p. 36; Rozema, p. 32; Woodward, p. 75.
   48. Horry & Weems, *Life of General Francis Marion,* Chapter 2.
   49. Alderman, p. 21; Kelly, p. 21.
   50. Kelly, p. 21.
   51. Alderman, p. 21.
   52. Hoig, p. 43.
   53. Adair, *Account,* p. 30; Adair, *History,* p. 267 (252).
   54. Alderman, p. 24; Goodpasture, Chapter 2, p. 21; Horry and Weems, Chapter 2, p. 19–20. (Note: In the 1875 *Cyclopaedia of American Literature,* by Evert A. Duycknick and George L. Duycknick, Vol. 1, p. 508, it is pointed out that the Horry-Weems

book was primarily created by Weems based on inputs from Horry, and that Weems embellished the work. That in itself is not an indictment; it just indicates that the book should be treated in the reference of a historical novel.)
55. Pickens, General Andrew, *Letter to General Henry Lee,* dated 28 August 1811.
56. Goodpasture, Chapter 2, p. 21.
57. Goodpasture, Chapter 2, p. 21–22.
58. Goodpasture, Chapter 2, p. 22.
59. Kelly, p. 20.
60. Kelly, p. 20.
61. Goodpasture, Chapter 2, p. 18.
62. Hatley, *Paths,* p. 157.
63. Drake, Samuel, p. 19.
64. Adair, *Account,* p. 6–8; Adair, *History,* p. 241–242 (230–231).
65. Adair, *Account,* p. 6–8, 21, 30; Adair, *History,* p. 241–242, 258, 267 (230–231, 244, 252); Alderman, p. 21, 24; Anderson, p. 8–9; Arthur, Chapter 3; Bass, *Ninety Six,* p. 50–53; Conley, p. 51–53; Goodpasture, Chapter 2, p. 18–22; Greene, p. 39–40; Hatley, *Paths,* p. 119, 134–148, 156–158, 172; Hoig, p. 42–44; Horry and Weems, Chapter 2, p. 17–20; Judd, *Overmountain Men,* p. 54, 192; Kelly, p. 20–21; Landrum, *Colonial and Revolutionary History of Upper South Carolina,* p. 35; Mooney, p. 44–45; Rogers, p. 34–37; Rozema, p. 32; Woodward, p. 77–79.

Chapter 5

1. Timberlake, p. 8 (9–10).
2. Timberlake, p. 36 (70).
3. Hoig, p. 45; Kelly, p. 22; Timberlake, p. 37 (72–73).
4. Alderman, p. 6; Timberlake, p. 38–39 (76–78).
5. Timberlake, p. 43–44 (87).
6. Alderman, p. 5–6, 25; Conley, p. 53; Goodpasture, Chapter 3, p. 25; Hatley, *Paths,* p. 167; Hoig, p. 15, 45–47; Kelly, p. 22; Mooney, p. 45; Rozema, p. 33; Timberlake, p. 8, 37, 43–54 (9–10, 72–73, 85–109).
7. Timberlake, p. 54 (107–109).
8. Chalkley, *Chronicles of the Scotch-Irish Settlement in Virginia: Extracted from the Original Court Records of Augusta County, 1745–1800,* Vol. 2, p. 510; Stalnaker, "Samuel Stalnaker," americanlineage.org/documents/Captain%20Samuel%20Stalnaker%20-%20Leo%20Stalnaker%20(1938).pdf, p. 3–5; Timberlake, p. 127, Note 147 (editorial note by Duane H. King) [The historic old Jacob Stalnaker, Jr., cabin has been moved from the hill overlooking Beverly, West Virginia, and is now located behind the Randolph County Museum in Beverly. Restoration is ongoing—see stalnakerfamilyassociation.org/history/cabin.html for more information. Jacob was a grandson of Samuel.]
9. Timberlake, p. 55 (111).
10. Timberlake, p. 55 (111).
11. Goodpasture, Chapter 3, p. 33–34.
12. Goodpasture, Chapter 3, p. 34; Timberlake, p. 55 (112).
13. Conley, p. 53; Hoig, p. 47; Woodward, p. 80.
14. Alderman, p. 26; Conley, p. 53; Goodpasture, Chapter 3, p. 33–35; Hatley, *Paths,* p. 143; Hoig, p. 45–48; Kelly, p. 22; Mooney, p. 45, 51; Rozema, p. 33; Timberlake, p. 55–58, 69–73 (110–114, 124–129); Woodward, p. 80–82.
15. Anderson, p. 4–7; Arthur, Chapters 3 and 26; Conley, p. 53–57; "The Treaty of Paris (1763)," emersonkent.com/historic_documents/treaty_of_paris_1763.htm; "The Treaty of Paris (1763)," en.wikipedia.org/wiki/Treaty_of_Paris_(1763); Goodpasture, Chapter 3, p. 24; Hatley, *Paths,* p. 159–168; Hoig, p. 48–49; Kelly, p. 23–24; Mooney, p. 43–46; "Proclamation of 1763," revolutionary-war-and-beyond.com/proclamation-of-1763.html; Woodward, p. 82–83.
16. Hatley, *Paths,* p. 159.
17. *The London Chronicle* 16, no. 1233, Thursday, November 15, 1764, p. 470.
18. Hatley, *Paths,* p. 207.
19. Hatley, *Paths,* p. 207.
20. Alderman, p. 27–32; Arthur, Chapter 3; Conley, p. 54; Hatley, *Paths,* p. 160–171; Hoig, p. 49–50; Kelly, p. 24; Mooney, p. 46; "The Treaty of Fort Stanwix (1768)," nps.gov/fost/historyculture/1768-boundary-line-treaty.htm; Reynolds, p. 26; Sugden, *Tecumseh: A Life,* p. 25–26; "The Treaty of Hard Labor," wvencyclopedia.org/articles/768.
21. Alderman, p. 27; Arthur, Chapter 3; Chalkley, p. 510; Goodpasture, Chapter 3, p. 24–25; Hoig, p. 49–51; Mooney, p. 46, 203; "The Treaty of Lochaber," theonefeather.com/2009/12/the-treaty-of-lochaber/; Woodward, p. 86.

Chapter 6

1. Conley, p. 54; Goodpasture, Chapter 3, p. 22; Hatley, *Paths,* p. 205–207; King, p. 117–118.
2. Alderman, p. 34.
3. Alderman, p. 34.
4. Alderman, p. 34.
5. Alderman, p. 34–36; Conley, p. 54.
6. Bartram, *The Travels of William Bartram,* p. 50–55.
7. "Augusta Indian Congress," ourgeorgiahistory.com/year/1773; Bartram, p. 50–55; Hatley, *Paths,* p. 209–210.
8. "Deposition of Thomas Sharp," whitesnet.org/13%20Worm-Wads/Flustered%20Pie.html; Drake, Donald, "The Boone Massacre," freepages.genealogy.rootsweb.ancestry.com/~drakerobinson/OtherPages/BooneMass.htm.
9. Arthur, Chapter 4; Bogan, "Dragging Canoe and the Chickamauga Cherokees," tngenweb.org/campbell/hist-bogan/massacre.html; Crabtree, "Crabtree Family History," freepages.genealogy.rootsweb.ancestry.com/~genbaby5/crab3.html; "Deposition of Thomas Sharp," whitesnet.org/13%20Worm-Wads/Flustered%20Pie.html; Dr. Charles Drake, "The Death of James Boone," web.infoave.net/~kfleming/drakanc.html, Second American Generation, Footnote 40; Drake, Donald, "The

Boone Massacre"; Draper, *Daniel Boone in Southwest Virginia,* edited by James William Hagy, vagenweb.org/wise/HSpubl51.htm; Fleenor, "James Boone Massacre," danielboonetrail.com/historicalsites.php?id=80; Flint, *The Life and Adventures of Daniel Boone, the First Settler of Kentucky,* The Arlington Edition, p. 78–81; Judd, *Overmountain Men,* p. 291–300; Jenny Tenlen, "McAfee Family," jtenlen.drizzlehosting.com/mcafee/life/life4.html; "William Russell," werelate.org/wiki/Person:William_Russell_%2886%29.

10. Alderman, p. 35–36; Faull, "Isaac Crabtree, My 'Infamous' Ancestor," dealerschoice1.com/pulaski/Bios/C/CrabtreeIsaac.htm; "Isaac Crabtree," wc.rootsweb.ancestry.com/cgi-bin/igm.cgi?op=GET&db=2007trickyriver&id=I6684; Judd, *Overmountain Men,* p. 321–332.

11. "The Battle of Point Pleasant," en.wikipedia.org/wiki/Battle_of_Point_Pleasant; Crump, "The Battle of Point Pleasant," wvgenweb.org/mason/firstbattle.html; Hatley, *Paths,* p. 186; Judd, *Overmountain Men,* p. 338; Kelly, p. 24; "The Treaty of Camp Charlotte," en.wikipedia.org/wiki/Treaty_of_Camp_Charlotte; "The Treaty of Camp Charlotte," wvencyclopedia.org/articles/766.

12. "Creek Indian History," ourgeorgiahistory.com/ogh/Creek_Indians; Hatley, *Paths,* p. 186; "Samuel Elbert," en.wikipedia.org/wiki/User:Mike33ekim/Sandbox; "Sir James Wright Paper," (1772–1784 three folders), Georgia Historical Society, MS 884; Zubly, *Collections of the Georgia Historical Society,* volume 19, p. 4 of 5, ebooksread.com/authors-eng/john-joachim-zubly. [The author has provided his own transcription of the original proclamation due to minor errors in those already available.]

13. Alderman, p. 37–38.

14. Alderman, p. 38–40; Hatley, *Paths,* p. 218; Judd, *Overmountain Men,* p. 351–352; Walker, p. 64.

15. Alderman, p. 40; Arthur, Chapter 4.

16. Arthur, Chapters 3–4.

17. Woodward, p. 90.

18. Alderman, p. 37–40; Arthur, Chapters 3–4; Conley, p. 57–58; Flint, p. 82–83; Hatley, *Paths,* p. 218–219; Hoig, p. 58; Judd, *Overmountain Men,* p. 337, 345–353; Kelly, p. 26; King, p. 118; Rozema, p. 34, 61; Walker, p. 62–65; Woodward, p. 87–90.

19. Dabney & Dargan, *William Henry Drayton & the American Revolution,* p. 104.

20. Hatley, *Paths,* p. 187–188.

21. Gibbes, *Documentary History of the American Revolution* [DHAR], Vol. 1, p. 194–195; Reynolds, p. 45.

22. Bass, *Ninety Six,* p. 103–108; Greene, *Ninety Six,* p. 64; Reynolds, p. 44–45.

23. Gibbes, DHAR, Vol. 1, p. 207–208; Reynolds, p. 47.

24. Gibbes, DHAR, Vol. 1, p. 247; Reynolds, p. 53–54.

25. Alderman, p. 40–41; Arthur, Chapter 3; Gibbes, DHAR, Vol. 1, p. 194–195, 207–208, 247; Hatley, *Paths,* p. 187–189; Reynolds, p. 45–54.

26. Alderman, p. 43–44; Woodward, p. 91.

27. Alderman, p. 42; Conley, p. 59; Judd, *Overmountain Men,* p. 367.

28. Alderman, p. 42; Conley, p. 59; Judd, *Overmountain Men,* p. 367.

29. Alderman, p. 42; Conley, p. 59; Judd, *Overmountain Men,* p. 367.

30. Alderman, p. 40–44; Arthur, Chapters 3–4; Conley, p. 57–59; Hatley, *Paths,* p. 186; Hoig, p. 59; Judd, *Overmountain Men,* p. 365–369, 392–396; Kelly, p. 26; Woodward, p. 90–93.

31. Bartram, p. 255.

32. Bartram, p. 255.

33. "Fort Moore, South Carolina," en.wikipedia.org/wiki/Savannah_Town,_South_Carolina. ["The site of Fort Moore–Savano Town (also called Old Savannah, even though it is nowhere near the Port of Savannah) was strategic in the relations between the government of the Colony of South Carolina and a number of powerful Indian groups located along and west of the Savannah River. Indian groups associated with the town and fort included the Savano, Creek, Yuchi, Cherokee and Chickasaw. The Savano Indians occupied the bluff prior to the arrival of traders, and remained until shortly after 1716, when the fort was constructed. The construction of Fort Moore at Savano Town along with construction of the Congaree Fort near the present city of Columbia was a step toward not only the control of the Indian groups in the interior, but toward the attempted monopoly of the southern skin trade. The fort served as a military deterrent even though some fighting took place. Its presence may have prevented intervention by French or Spanish controlled Indian groups. The settlement of Augusta on the west side of the Savannah River marked the end of Fort Moore as a controlling factor in the skin trade and the fort was abandoned in 1763. Little is known about the original appearance of the Fort Moore–Savano Indian town other than the limited view provided by the archaeologist from the soil, supplemented by a few oblique documentary references to construction or conditions present during the period of occupation. Listed in the National Register August 14, 1973."]

34. Bartram, p. 262–264; Davidson, *Early Records of Georgia,* Vol. 1, *Wilkes County.*

35. Bartram, p. 262–264.

36. Bartram, p. 264.

37. Bartram, p. 265–266.

38. Bartram, p. 265–266.

39. Bartram, p. 266–267.

40. Bartram, p. 268.

41. Bartram, p. 269.

42. Bartram, p. 269.

43. Bartram, p. 270.

44. Bartram, p. 271.

45. Bartram, p. 273, 276, 280.

46. Bartram, p. 284–286; Rogers, *Archaeology,* p. 38.

47. Bartram, p. 286, 296; Rogers, p. 38

48. Bartram, p. 296.

49. Bartram, p. 254–296; Judd, *Overmountain Men,* p. 369, 396; Kelly, p. 26; Rogers, *Archaeology,* p. 38.

50. Grasshopper cannons had barrels made of bronze rather than iron which rendered them light cannons. Bronze is less brittle than cast iron allowing the barrels to be thinner and lighter than on cast iron guns. They were easily maneuvered around a rocky or rutted battlefield because of their lightness and their large wheels. The grasshopper was a three-pounder, referring to the heaviest weight of ball it could successfully fire. Sometimes, when used at close range, the crew would fire three pounds of canister shot, rendering the cannon like a huge shotgun. The cannon jumped backwards in recoil when it was fired. That, plus its physical appearance, led to the nickname of Grasshopper.

51. Irving, Vol. 2, p. 291–292.
52. Gibbes, DHAR, Volume 3, p. 19–21.
53. Gibbes, DHAR, Volume 3, p. 22–23; Dr. A. L. Pickens, p. 18.
54. Gibbes, DHAR, Volume 3, p. 25–26.
55. Stephenson, *Patriot Battles*, p. 194.
56. Reynolds, p. 20.
57. Sharp, *Pickens Families of the South (incl. Excerpts from the Draper Papers)*, Appendices 2, 6–10.
58. Sharp, Appendices 2, 6–10.
59. Alderman, p. 40–42; Conley, p. 61; Goodpasture, Chapters 3–4, p. 22–28; Hatley, *Paths*, p. 191, 218; Hoig, p. 60; Judd, *Overmountain Men*, p. 397–400; Kelly, p. 26; Reynolds, p. 58–65; Sharp, p. 48, and Appendices 2, 6–10; Woodward, p. 93–96.
60. Woodward, p. 95.
61. Alderman, p. 46.
62. Alderman, p. 48; Judd, *Overmountain Men*, p. 441.
63. Adair, Account, p. 4; Adair, History, p. 239 (227); Alderman, p. 46–48; Conley, p. 61–65; Goodpasture, Chapter 4, p. 26–31; Hatley, *Paths*, p. 219; Hoig, p. 60–61; Judd, *Overmountain Men*, p. 410–411, 425–432, 440–441; Kelly, p. 25–26; King, p. 118–120; Mooney, p. 48; Woodward, p. 88, 93, 96.
64. Gibbes, DHAR, Volume 3, p. 24.
65. Gibbes, DHAR, Volume 3, p. 30–31.
66. Sharp, Appendix 2, paragraph 1.
67. Bass, *Ninety Six*, p. 135; Greene, *Ninety Six*, p. 78–79; Dr. A. L. Pickens, p. 18–19.
68. Gordon, *South Carolina and the American Revolution*, p. 48–49; Greene, *Ninety Six*, p. 78.
69. Gibbes, DHAR, Volume 3, p. 24–25.
70. Gibbes, DHAR, Volume 3, p. 26–27.
71. Gibbes, DHAR, Volume 3, p. 30–31.
72. Gibbes, DHAR, Volume 3, p. 28–29.
73. Pickens, Dr. A. L., p. 23.
74. Bass, *Ninety Six*, p. 136; Greene, *Ninety Six*, p. 78–79; Judd, *Overmountain Men*, p. 72; Pickens, Dr. A. L., p. 20–21.
75. Gibbes, DHAR, Vol. 1, p. 125–126.
76. Judd, *Overmountain Men*, p. 137–147; Pickens, Dr. A. L., p. 21–22.
77. Gibbes, DHAR, Vol. 1, p. 126.
78. Pickens, Dr. A. L., p. 21.
79. Bass, *Ninety Six*, p. 136–137; Gibbes, DHAR, Vol. 1, p. 126; Gordon, p. 50–51; Greene, *Ninety Six*, p. 78–79; Pickens, Dr. A. L., p. 21–22; Reynolds, p. 65–73.
80. Pickens, Dr. A. L., p. 24.
81. Bass, *Ninety Six*, p. 137; Gordon, p. 52–53; Pickens, Dr. A. L., p. 23–25.
82. Pickens, Dr. A. L., p. 24.
83. Bass, *Ninety Six*, p. 137–140; Gordon, p. 51–52; Greene, *Ninety Six*, p. 79; Pickens, Dr. A. L., p. 25–27.
84. Gibbes, DHAR, Volume 3, p. 32.
85. Goodpasture, Chapter 4, p. 31.
86. Blackmon, *Dark and Bloody Ground*, p. 81–83; Dean, p. 158–169, 190–200, 397 note 195; Drayton, *Memoirs of the American Revolution, From Its Commencement to the Year 1776, Volume 2*, p. 355; Graves, Transcription of *Arthur Fairies Journal of Expedition Against the Cherokee Indians from July 18th, to October 11th, 1776*, p. 20–34; Lumpkin, *From Savannah to Yorktown*, p. 24–25; Lamar Marshall, *The 1776 Campaign Against the Cherokee*. [The author, William R. Reynolds, Jr., has Cherokee ancestors from this region around Murphy, such as, 4th great grandfather CahStahYeesTee (KunSteeNeeStah), meaning Whiplash, born about 1796. He married Polly Murphy and took the name Martin Murphy; his father, Bell Ringer, the authors 5th great grandfather was born about 1775 and married Rachel Riley.]
87. Alderman, p. 51.
88. Alderman, p. 51.
89. Walker, p. 27.
90. Alderman, p. 51.
91. Alderman, p. 52.
92. Arthur, Chapter 26.
93. Arthur, Chapter 26.
94. Walker, p. 28–29.
95. Alderman, p. 49–54; Arthur, Chapter 26; Bass, *Ninety Six*, p. 135, 141–143; Conley, p. 61–65; "Fort Patrick Henry," tennesseeencyclopedia.net/entry.php?rec=493; Goodpasture, Chapter 4, p. 26–27, 31–32; Gordon, p. 54–55; Greene, *Ninety Six*, p. 79; Hatley, *Paths*, p. 191–197, 201, 218–219; Hoig, p. 57–61; Judd, *Overmountain Men*, p. 449–450; Kelly, p. 25–26; Landrum, p. 12, 90–95; Lumpkin, p. 26; Mooney, p. 48–52; Dr. A. L. Pickens, p. 18, 26–32; Reynolds, p. 73–80; "Smoky Mountain Historical Society Index," smhstn.org/cpage.php?pt=22; Templin, *John Denton: Patriot—Pioneer*; Walker, p. 27–29, 65–66; Woodward, p. 93–97.
96. Mooney, p. 48.
97. Mooney, p. 47.
98. Alderman, p. 53–54; Goodpasture, Chapter 4, p. 31; Hatley, *Paths*, p. 198–204; Hoig, p. 59; King, p. 118; Mooney, p. 47–51; Walker, p. 28–29.

Chapter 7

1. Kelly, p. 27.
2. Landrum, p. 12.
3. Alderman, p. 64; Haygood, *The Civil and Political History of the State of Tennessee*.
4. Alderman, p. 56; Hatley, *Paths*, p. 213; Hoig, p. 63; Williams, *William Tatum, Wataugan*. [The translation varies depending on the source. Samuel

Cole Williams is used as the primary source for this book; however, other sources were considered.]

5. Haygood, *The Civil and Political History of the State of Tennessee*.

6. Haygood *The Civil and Political History of the State of Tennessee*.

7. Arthur, Chapter 26; Haygood, *The Civil and Political History of the State of Tennessee*; "Cherokee Treaties," nanations.com/cherokee/tribe/treaty1721.htm.

8. Haygood, *The Civil and Political History of the State of Tennessee*.

9. "1777 Treaty of Long Island," bkoatohee.homestead.com/files/1777_TREATY_at_Long_Island.htm; Haygood, *The Civil and Political History of the State of Tennessee*.

10. Kelly, p. 27.

11. "1777 Treaty of Long Island," bkoatohee.homestead.com/files/1777_TREATY_at_Long_Island.htm; Alderman, p. 56; Arthur, Chapter 26; "Cherokee Treaties," nanations.com/cherokee/tribe/treaty1721.htm; Goodpasture, Chapter 4, p. 22–37; Hatley, *Paths*, p. 213–224; Hoig, p. 62–63; Judd, *Overmountain Men*, p. 451–452; Kelly, p. 27; King, p. 118–122; Mooney, p. 47–55; Reynolds, p. 79–80; Schleier, "Ann Calhoun Matthews," keeperoftherecords.blogspot.com/2010/11/my-portrayal-of-ann-calhoun-matthews.html; Woodward, p. 93–100.

Chapter 8

1. Mooney, p. 54.
2. Goodpasture, Chapter 4, p. 42.
3. Alderman, p. 54–57; "The Brainerd Mission," chattanooga.net/brainerdmission/stories/story_of_cher_indians.htm; "The Chickamauga Cherokee," chickamauga-cherokee.com/chickamaugahtown.html; Conley, p. 65–67; Goodpasture, Chapters 4–5, p. 37–45; Hatley, *Paths*, p. 225; Hoig, p. 64; Mooney, p. 54–55; Rozema, p. 34, 61–62; Walker, p. 28–29; Woodward, p. 98–100.
4. Alderman, p. 59.
5. Albright, Chapters 10–17; Alderman, p. 57; Goodpasture, Chapter 5, p. 41–44; Mooney, p. 54–56; Rozema, p. 62–63; Walker, p. 78–79. [John Donelson's journal is available at Rozema, p. 63–72 and Ramsey, p. 197.]
6. Albright, Chapter 18.
7. Kaler, *Hannah of Kentucky: A Story of the Wilderness Road*, p. 50.
8. Albright, Chapters 18–20; Alderman, p. 57; Goodpasture, Chapter 4, p. 37–38, Chapter 5, p. 45–49, Chapter 6, p. 112–116; Walker, p. 80–84; Woodward, p. 101.
9. Ferling, *Almost a Miracle*, p. 460.
10. Mooney, p. 57.
11. Bass, *Ninety Six*, p. 261; Draper, *King's Mountain and Its Heroes*, p. 211, 224; Landrum, p. 192; Reynolds, p. 175.
12. Lee, p. 200.
13. Landrum, p. 207.
14. Draper, *King's Mountain and Its Heroes*, p. 247.
15. Draper, *King's Mountain and Its Heroes*, p. 247; Lumpkin, p. 100.
16. Alderman, p. 59–63; Arthur, Chapter 11; Goodpasture, Chapter 3, p. 23, Chapter 4, p. 39; Mooney, p. 57–58; Reynolds, Chapter 8; Woodward, p. 101.
17. Alderman, p. 61–62, from *MS: Draper 11DD9*.
18. Albright, Chapter 22.
19. Albright, Chapters 21–23; Alderman, p. 62–64; Goodpasture, Chapter 6, p. 116–119; Mooney, p. 62–63; Walker, p. 84–85.
20. Alderman, p. 64.
21. Alderman, p. 65.
22. Alderman, p. 65.
23. Albright, Chapter 22; Alderman, p. 59–65; Arthur, Chapter 11; Goodpasture, Chapter 3, p. 23, Chapter 4, p. 39, Chapter 6, p. 120, Chapter 9, p. 137–138; Hoig, p. 67; Mooney, p. 59; Reynolds, p. 294–296; Walker, p. 86.

Chapter 9

1. Blackmon, p. 228.
2. Albright, Edward. *Early History of Middle Tennessee*, Chapter 23.
3. Pickens, General Andrew, *Letter*.
4. Pickens, Dr. A. L., p. 60; Reynolds, p. 298–300.
5. Pickens, General Andrew, *Letter*.
6. Albright, Chapter 23; Blackmon, p. 228–245; Goodpasture, Chapter 5, p. 106–109, Chapter 8, p. 139; Hatley, *Paths*, p. 201; Mooney, p. 54, 59–60; Reynolds, p. 296–300; Walker, p. 86.
7. Ramsey, p. 272–273.
8. Blackmon, p. 245–246; Ramsey, p. 271; Woodward, p. 109.
9. Alderman, p. 64.
10. Albright, Chapter 23; Alderman, p. 64; Blackmon, p. 246–248; Conley, p. 67; Mooney, p. 54, 60–61; Walker, p. 67; Woodward, p. 88, 99–100.
11. Adair, *History*, p. 398 (369), including footnotes 219 and 220.
12. A reader must be careful here. Historian Edward Albright, in his *Early History of Middle Tennessee*, writes that "late June" pertains to the actual treaty time rather than simply as the Cumberland settlement's agreement to hold the treaty later in 1783.
13. Albright, Chapter 24; Alderman, p. 65–66; Goodpasture, Chapter 5, p. 106–108, Chapter 7, p. 121–124; Mooney, p. 63; Walker, p. 86.
14. Albright, Chapter 24.
15. Brown, *Old Frontiers*, p. 246, Woodward, p. 102–103.
16. Brown, *Old Frontiers*, p. 222; "Chief Dragging Canoe," rootsweb.ancestry.com/~tnpolk2/DraggingCanoeBio.htm; Evans, *Notable Persons in Cherokee History: Dragging Canoe*, p. 185; Woodward, p. 102.

17. Historian John P. Brown had apparently initiated a reporting error by stating the conference between the Creek–Chickamauga alliance with the Spanish took place one year earlier than it really did. This error has been carried through by several other historians who cited Brown as the primary source of information. Creek chief Alexander McGillivray did not write Spanish governor Arthur O'Neill to recommend such a meeting until the first of January 1784. This error of citation likely extends to the oration made by the Spanish to the headmen. Miro may have been attributed to the speech because he had been referred to as the governor of West Florida rather than O'Neill; "Alexander McGillivray," britannica.com/EBchecked/topic/354434/Alexander-McGillivray; "Alexander McGillivray," georgiaencyclopedia.org/nge/Article.jsp?id=h-690; "Arthur O'Neill," floridairishheritagecenter.wordpress.com/2010/06/09/arthur-oneill-governor-of-spanish-east-florida-1781-to-1793/; Goodpasture, Chapter 8, p. 130; "The Treaty of Pensacola," pensapedia.com/wiki/Treaty_of_Pensacola.

18. Albright, Edward. *Early History of Middle Tennessee*, Chapter 25.

19. Albright, Chapters 24–25; Alderman, p. 65–66; Goodpasture, Chapter 5, p. 106–111, Chapter 7, p. 121–124, Chapter 8, p. 130–131; Mooney, p. 59; Walker, p. 87; Woodward, p. 102–103.

20. DRIA, Vol. 1, p. 42.

21. Albright, Chapter 26; Evans, "Notable Persons in Cherokee History: Bob Benge," p. 98–100; Goodpasture, Chapter 8, p. 139–140; Woodward, p. 103–104.

22. DRIA, Vol. 1, p. 40–41.
23. DRIA, Vol. 1, p. 41.
24. DRIA, Vol. 1, p. 41.
25. DRIA, Vol. 1, p. 42–43.
26. DRIA, Vol. 1, p. 42–43.
27. DRIA, Vol. 1, p. 43.
28. Mooney, p. 61–62.
29. Mooney, p. 61–62.
30. Mooney, p. 61–62.
31. Alderman, p. 69.
32. Albright, Chapter 27 [Albright cited this event as having occurred in 1786 rather than the actual year of 1785].
33. Albright, Chapter 26; Alderman, p. 65–69; Goodpasture, Chapter 8, p. 139–140; Hoig, p. 67–68; Mooney, p. 61–62; Reynolds, p. 302–303; Rozema, p. 73–74, 75–85; Walker, p. 87–88; Woodward, p. 104–108.
34. Albright, Chapter 27.
35. Morris, Ester, *The Story of Defeated Creek*.
36. Goodpasture, Chapter 8, p. 140–141.
37. Goodpasture, Chapter 8, p. 140–141.
38. Hoig, p. 68–70.
39. Goodpasture, Chapter 8, p. 140–141.
40. Alderman, p. 70.
41. Albright, Chapter 27; Alderman, p. 69–70; Goodpasture, Chapter 8, p. 140–142; Hoig, p. 68–70; Mooney, p. 60–65; Morris, Ester, *The Story of Defeated Creek*; Rozema, p. 74; Walker, p. 88; Woodward, p. 104–108.

42. Albright, Chapter 28; Goodpasture, Chapter 8, p. 121–124, 131–132; Mooney, p. 64; Walker, p. 90.

43. Albright, Chapter 28; Goodpasture, Chapter 8, p. 124–126; Mooney, p. 66; Walker, p. 69–74, 90–91.

44. Pickens, Dr. A. L., p. 132–133.

45. Goodpasture, Chapter 11, p. 172; Ramsey, p. 272.

46. "Alexander McGillivray to Robertson and Bledsoe, April 4, 1788," Goodpasture, Chapter 8, p. 128–129.

47. Goodpasture, Chapter 8, p. 128–129.

48. Albright, Chapters 28–30; Arthur, Chapter 5; Goodpasture, Chapter 8, p. 128–136, Chapter 10, p. 161–165, Chapter 11, p. 171–173; Hoig, p. 70–71; Mooney, p. 65; Reynolds, p. 302–303; Walker, p. 91–92.

49. DRIA, Vol. 1, p. 291, "letter from Governor William Blount dated September 26, 1792," and p. 277–278, "Note to #5, from John Sevier, dated 13th September, 1792." [In 1792, Chief Breath would escort boats laden with goods from Tuskegee to Nickajack as they headed for the Chickasaw and Choctaw treaty at Nashville. He declared that he would defend them if they should be attacked at Running Water Town by the Shawnee Warrior and his party, allies of the Chickamauga. Later, he would withdraw from Nickajack. Young Tassel invaded the Cumberland settlements as he was opposed to the war. That was an interesting dynamic for the chief of a Chickamauga village.]

50. Albright, Chapter 30; Goodpasture, Chapter 10, p. 161–167.

51. DRIA, Vol. 1, p. 48.

52. Goodpasture, Chapter 8, p. 142–143; Ramsey, p. 420.

53. Alderman, p. 70; Arthur, Chapter 6; Goodpasture, Chapter 8, p. 143–144, Chapter 10, p. 165–166; Hoig, p. 71; Mooney, p. 65; Ramsey, p. 420–421; Woodward, p. 92.

54. The original of this letter is archived at the South Carolina Department of Archives and History, Series: S165009, Message: 0462, Page: 00045, dated 6/25/1788. Much of it is illegible; however, the author is working on a transcription. The tragedy of the murders is evident in the tone of what is readable.

55. DRIA, Vol. 1, p. 56; Conley, p. 74.

56. Goodpasture, Chapter 8, p. 142–143; Hoig, p. 71; Ramsey, p. 421–422.

57. Arthur, Chapters 5–6; Hoig, p. 71; Williams, *History of the Lost State of Franklin*, p. 211.

58. Arthur, Chapter 6.

59. DRIA, Vol. 1, p. 28.

60. DRIA, Vol. 1, p. 48.

Chapter 10

1. Hoig, p. 71.
2. *The Maryland Gazette*, No. 2193, Thursday, January 22, 1789. [All excerpts from *The Maryland Gazette* used in this chapter are transcribed from

images of the actual issues by the author, William R. Reynolds, Jr. The format is altered from period English, i.e., the formal 's' is not used in the transcription.]
   3. *The Maryland Gazette,* No. 2194, Thursday, January 29, 1789.
   4. DRIA, Vol. 1, p. 204.
   5. DRIA, Vol. 1, p. 325—letter, Governor William Blount to Secretary of War Henry Knox, dated November 8, 1792.
   6. Albright, Edward, *Early History of Middle Tennessee,* Chapter 30.
   7. Albright, Chapter 30; Alderman, p. 70; DRIA, Vol. 1, p. 48; Goodpasture, Chapter 8, p. 134–136, Chapter 11, p. 171–174; Hoig, p. 71–73; Mooney, p. 65; Rozema, p. 49–51; Walker, p. 19–38, 94.
   8. *The Maryland Gazette,* No. 2194, Thursday, January 29, 1789.
   9. *The Maryland Gazette,* No. 2185, Thursday, November 27, 1788.
   10. Hoig, p. 73.
   11. DRIA, Vol. 1, p. 46–47.
   12. DRIA, Vol. 1, p. 46–47.
   13. Goodpasture, Chapter 10, p. 165–166.
   14. Albright, Chapter 30; Alderman, p. 71; E. Raymond Evans, "Notable Persons in Cherokee History: Bob Benge," p. 100; Goodpasture, Chapter 10, p. 161–166, Chapter 11, p. 173–174; Hoig, p. 73–74; Mooney, p. 66; Ramsey, p. 509; Woodward, p. 104–108.
   15. DRIA, Vol. 1, p. 47.
   16. Albright, Chapter 31.
   17. DRIA, Vol. 1, p. 57; Hoig, p. 74.
   18. Alderman, p. 71; DRIA, Vol. 1, p. 52–54; Woodward, p. 110.
   19. Alderman, p. 71.
   20. Albright, Chapter 31.
   21. DRIA, Vol. 1, p. 31.
   22. DRIA, Vol. 1, p. 35.
   23. DRIA, Vol. 1, p. 35–36.
   24. DRIA, Vol. 1, p. 37.
   25. DRIA, Vol. 1, p. 37.
   26. DRIA, Vol. 1, p. 65–68.
   27. DRIA, Vol. 1, p. 68.
   28. DRIA, Vol. 1, p. 68.
   29. DRIA, Vol. 1, p. 71.
   30. DRIA, Vol. 1, p. 72–73.
   31. DRIA, Vol. 1, p. 73–75.
   32. DRIA, Vol. 1, p. 76–79.
   33. DRIA, Vol. 1, p. 81–82.
   34. DRIA, Vol. 1, p. 83.
   35. Albright, Chapters 31–32; Alderman, p. 71; Arthur, Chapter 10; Goodpasture, Chapter 8, p. 133–136; Hoig, p. 74; Eric Miller, *George Washington and Indians,* Chapter 7; Walker, p. 94; Woodward, p. 109–110.
   36. Goodpasture, Chapter 10, p. 168–169, note 214, The Americana Society, *American Historical Magazine,* Vol. 4, p. 336, Letter, Pickens to Robertson [A. V. Goodpasture's reference to *American Historical Magazine* is incorrect. The reference is not anywhere in Volume 4. That is either a misprint or an error in his listing of the pertinent volume].

[The following, provided by Claudia Brumbalow, verifies that Andrew Pickens was involved and is found on archiver.rootsweb.ancestry.com/th/read/BROWN/2000-03/0952297858, "iv. James Brown, born Nov 25, 1763 married Nancy Burdine—(The 'orphans' as the fatherless children were called at that time of James Brown were forever grateful to their Uncle Joseph for taking care of them from the time they were delivered from their Indian captivity 26 Apr 1789 until the next fall when their mother arrived in Nov. A trader brought the children to their Uncle Joseph's home in SC. They went into the house and at first Joseph didn't recognized then. He was shown a letter from Gen. Andrew Pickens with whom they had stayed the night before, 30 miles away which explained the circumstances. The children's Uncle David also lived close by. The children's generous Uncle Joseph gave a good horse, a gun, and a sword to the trader for bringing back his nephew and two nieces.) from the Descendants of William & Margaret Brown, by Helen Rugeley."
   37. *The Maryland Gazette,* No. 2270, Thursday, July 15, 1790.
   38. DRIA, Vol. 1, p. 263–264.
   39. Albright, Chapter 32; Alderman, p. 72; Goodpasture, Chapter 8, p. 136, 145, Chapter 10, p. 165–169; Hoig, p. 74; Walker, p. 95–96; Woodward, p. 104–108.
   40. Albright, Chapter 33.
   41. Alderman, p. 72.
   42. Alderman, p. 72.
   43. DRIA, Vol. 1, p. 274–275.
   44. Albright, Chapter 32; Alderman, p. 72; Arthur, Chapter 26; "The Battle of Wabash," sinclair.quarterman.org/history/mod/battleofwabash.html; Evans, E. Raymond, "Notable Persons in Cherokee History: Bob Benge," p. 100–101; Goodpasture, Chapter 11, p. 175–176 Chapter 16, p. 256–258 Chapter 17, p. 264; Hoig, p. 74–75; Sugden, John, *Tecumseh: A Life,* p. 67–68; Walker, p. 97–99; Woodward, p. 113.
   45. DRIA, Vol. 1, p. 203.
   46. DRIA, Vol. 1, p. 203–205.
   47. DRIA, Vol. 1, p. 205.
   48. DRIA, Vol. 1, p. 205–206.
   49. DRIA, Vol. 1, p. 203.
   50. Albright, Chapter 34; Goodpasture, Chapter 11, p. 173–176, Chapter 12, p. 177–178, Chapter 17, p. 274–275; Hoig, p. 75; Walker, p. 100–102; Woodward, p. 114.
   51. DRIA, Vol. 1, p. 263.
   52. DRIA, Vol. 1, p. 269–270.
   53. DRIA, Vol. 1, p. 274.
   54. Goodpasture, Chapter 12, p. 180.
   55. DRIA, Vol. 1, p. 274.
   56. Alderman, p. 73; E. Raymond Evans, "Notable Persons in Cherokee History: Dragging Canoe"; D. Ray Smith, smithdray.tripod.com/draggingcanoe-index-9.html.
   57. DRIA, Vol. 1, p. 291.
   58. DRIA, Vol. 1, p. 264–265.
   59. Alderman, p. 73–74; Goodpasture, Chapter

12, p. 177–180, Chapter 13, p. 185–195, Chapter 17, p. 263–264; Hoig, p. 75; Walker, p. 69–77, 103–104; Woodward, p. 114.
60. DRIA, Vol. 1, p. 264.
61. DRIA, Vol. 1, p. 268–269.
62. "The Chickamauga Cherokee," chickamauga-cherokee.com/heartoftheeagle.html; E. Raymond Evans, "Notable Persons in Cherokee History: Bob Benge," p. 101; Goodpasture, Chapter 11, p. 175–176, Chapter 12, p. 177–180, Chapter 13, p. 185–195, Chapter 16, p. 258, Chapter 17, p. 265; Hoig, p. 75–80; John Sugden, *Tecumseh: A Life*, p. 67–68; Walker, p. 97–99; Woodward, p. 114.
63. DRIA, Vol. 1, p. 271–273.
64. DRIA, Vol. 1, p. 291.
65. Albright, Chapter 34; DRIA, Vol. 1, p. 276, 330; Goodpasture, Chapter 11, p. 173–174, Chapter 12, p. 181–183, Chapter 17, p. 265; Hoig, p. 80–81; John Sugden, *Tecumseh: A Life*, p. 68–70.
66. DRIA, Vol. 1, p. 270.
67. Goodpasture, Chapter 13, p. 190; John Sugden, *Tecumseh: A Life*, p. 71–72.
68. Albright, Chapter 35; DRIA, Vol. 1, p. 289–292, 327–329; Goodpasture, Chapter 12, p. 183–184, Chapter 13, p. 185–195; Hoig, p. 81–82; John Sugden, *Tecumseh: A Life*, p. 68–72.
69. Albright, Chapter 35.
70. Albright, Chapter 35.
71. Albright, Chapter 35.
72. DRIA, Vol. 1, p. 327–329.
73. Albright, Chapter 35; Goodpasture, Chapter 13, p. 185–195; Hoig, p. 82–83; John Sugden, *Tecumseh: A Life*, p. 73–74; Walker, p. 108–115.
74. DRIA, Vol. 1, p. 293.
75. DRIA, Vol. 1, p. 293.
76. DRIA, Vol. 1, p. 294.
77. Ramsey, Chapter 7, p. 598.
78. DRIA, Vol. 1, p. 326; Goodpasture, Chapter 16, p. 253–254.
79. Ramsey, Chapter 7, p. 571.
80. Ramsey, Chapter 7, p. 573.
81. DRIA, Vol. 1, p. 434.
82. Goodpasture, Chapter 13, p. 185–195, Chapter 15, p. 203–204, Chapter 16, p. 253–258; Hoig, p. 83–84; John Sugden, *Tecumseh: A Life*, p. 76; Walker, p. 108–117.
83. Ramsey, Chapter 7, p. 598.
84. Albright, Chapter 35; Goodpasture, Chapter 16, p. 252–253.
85. Ramsey, Chapter 7, p. 574–575.
86. DRIA, Vol. 1, p. 447.
87. DRIA, Vol. 1, p. 429.
88. DRIA, Vol. 1, p. 444–446.
89. DRIA, Vol. 1, p. 448.
90. DRIA, Vol. 1, p. 446.
91. DRIA, Vol. 1, p. 436–437, 440.
92. Albright, Chapter 36; E. Raymond Evans, "Notable Persons in Cherokee History: Bob Benge," p. 101–102; Goodpasture, Chapter 15, p. 203–206, Chapter 16, p. 252–253, 258–260, Chapter 17, p. 265; Hoig, p. 84–85; Walker, p. 117; Woodward, p. 115.
93. DRIA, Vol. 1, p. 450.

94. DRIA, Vol. 1, p. 450.
95. DRIA, Vol. 1, p. 453.
96. DRIA, Vol. 1, p. 456.
97. DRIA, Vol. 1, p. 455.
98. DRIA, Vol. 1, p. 457–459.
99. DRIA, Vol. 1, p. 459.
100. DRIA, Vol. 1, p. 459.
101. DRIA, Vol. 1, p. 459.
102. DRIA, Vol. 1, p. 459.
103. DRIA, Vol. 1, p. 459–460.
104. DRIA, Vol. 1, p. 460.
105. Albright, Chapter 36; E. Raymond Evans, "Notable Persons in Cherokee History: Bob Benge," p. 103; Goodpasture, Chapter 15, p. 203–207, Chapter 16, p. 254; Hoig, p. 85; Rozema, p. 86–100; Walker, p. 117–122, 142.
106. Albright, Chapter 36; E. Raymond Evans, "Notable Persons in Cherokee History: Bob Benge," p. 103–104; Goodpasture, Chapter 16, p. 208–209, Chapter 17, p. 260; Hoig, p. 85–86; Walker, p. 122–124.
107. Albright, Chapter 37.
108. Elizabeth Livingston's deposition is found in many places on the Internet, and most have a few verbiage differences between them. The following are two of the multitude of sources; Addington, *Chief Benge's Last Raid*, rootsweb.ancestry.com/~vahsswv/historicalsketches/bengechief.html; "Chief Bench Attack on the Livingston Home," hto-livingston.com/indianattack1794.html.
109. E. Raymond Evans, "Notable Persons in Cherokee History: Bob Benge," p. 103; Summers, *History of Southwest Virginia, 1746–1786, Washington County, 1777–1870*, p. 443; Walker, p. 141.
110. Addington, *Chief Benge's Last Raid*; Albright, Chapter 37; Goodpasture, Chapter 15, p. 209–210, Chapter 16, p. 260–262, Chapter 17, p. 266–269; Hoig, p. 86; "Chief Bench Attack on the Livingston Home," hto-livingston.com/indianattack1794.html; Walker, p. 124–129.
111. Albright, Chapter 38.
112. DRIA, Vol. 1, p. 537–538.
113. Albright, Chapters 37–38; Alderman, p. 73–74; Arthur, Chapters 2, 16; E. Raymond Evans, "Notable Persons in Cherokee History: Bob Benge," p. 104–105; Goodpasture, Chapter 15, p. 254–255, Chapter 17, p. 269–272; Hoig, p. 86–88; Rozema, p. 88; Walker, p. 68, 115, 133–141; Woodward, p. 115.
114. Ramsey, Chapter 7, p. 619.
115. Goodpasture, Chapter 17, p. 270–271.
116. Goodpasture, Chapter 17, p. 271–272; Walker, p. 220–234.

Summary

1. Arthur, Chapter 6; Hoig, p. 91, 98–99; Rozema, p. 88, 103; Walker, p. 155–156, 169, 220, 227.
2. Hamner, *A Piano in the House*.
3. Irving, (1st edition), Vol. 1, p. 63.

4. Arthur, Chapter 6.
5. Arthur, Chapter 6.

Appendix B

1. Goodpasture, Chapter 4, p. 33–34.
2. Goodpasture, Chapter 9, p. 155–156.
3. Goodpasture, Chapter 4, p. 33–41.
4. Goodpasture, Chapter 4, p. 33, Chapter 11, p. 171–173.
5. Goodpasture, Chapter 16, p. 256–258.
6. Goodpasture, Chapter 5, p. 108–110.
7. Goodpasture, Chapter 5, p. 110.

Appendix C

1. Albright, Chapter 38.
2. Albright, Chapter 27.
3. Albright, Chapter 31.
4. Albright, Chapter 26.
5. Albright, Chapter 26.
6. Albright, Chapter 23.
7. Albright, Chapter 9.
8. Goodpasture, Chapter 17, p. 267–269.
9. Goodpasture, Chapter 11, p. 175–176.
10. Goodpasture, Chapter 9, p. 142–143.
11. Arthur, Chapter 9.
12. Albright, Chapters 6–7.

Bibliography

Adair, James. *Account of the Cheerake Nation,* pamphlet. An excerpt from *Adair's History of the American Indians.* London: Printed for Edward and Charles Dilly, in the Poultry, 1775.

———. *Adair's History of the American Indians.* Ed. by Samuel Cole Williams. New York: Promontory Press, 1930.

Addington, Luther F. "Chief Benge's Last Raid." rootsweb.ancestry.com/~vahsswv/historical sketches/bengechief.html.

Albright, Edward. *Early History of Middle Tennessee.* Gallatin, TN: Brandon, 1909.

Alderman, Pat. *Nancy Ward: Cherokee Chieftainess/Dragging Canoe: Cherokee—Chickamauga War Chief.* Johnson City, TN: Overmountain Press, 1990.

"Alexander-McGillivray." britannica.com/EB checked/topic/354434.

"Alexander McGillivray." georgiaencyclopedia.org/nge/Article.jsp?id=h-690.

"American Archives, Documents of the American Revolution." lincoln.lib.niu.edu.

The American Revolution. theamericanrevolution.org.

"The Americana Society." *American Historical Magazine* 4. New York: 1909

"Sir Alexander Cuming, Autobiographical Notes." *Autobiographies from Men of All Ranks.* London: The British Library, Add. 39855, Part 1: Autobiographies, c1760–1820, Microfilm Reel 172.

Anderson, William L. "The Cherokee World: Before and After Timberlake." *Culture, Crisis & Conflict: Cherokee and British Relations 1756–1765.* Ed. by Anne F. Rogers & Barbara R. Duncan. Cherokee, NC: Museum of the Cherokee Indian Press, 2009.

"Andrew Duche." genealogy-georgiapioneers.blogspot.com/2009/10/andrew-duche-cherokee-clay-maker.html.

Arthur, John Preston. *Western North Carolina: A History From 1730 to 1913.* Raleigh, NC: Edwards & Broughton, 1914.

"Arthur O'Neill." floridairishheritagecenter.wordpress.com/2010/06/09/arthur-oneill-governor-of-spanish-east-florida-1781-to-1793/.

"Articles of Friendship and Commerce & Answers of the Indian Chiefs." Cherokee Documents in Foreign Archives, Special Collections. Hunter Library, C054, 06442, Microfilm Reel 197, pages 211–214, 215–216 respectively.

"Augusta Indian Congress." ourgeorgiahistory.com/year/1773.

Bartram, William. *The Travels of William Bartram.* Ed. by Mark Van Doren. New York: Dover, 1955.

Bass, Robert D. *Ninety Six: The Struggle for the South Carolina Back Country.* Lexington, SC: Sandlapper Store, 1978.

———. *Swamp Fox: The Life and Campaigns of General Francis Marion.* Lexington, SC: Sandlapper Store, 1974.

"The Battle of Defeated Creek." defeatedcreek marina.com/.

"The Battle of Point Pleasant." en.wikipedia.org/wiki/Battle_of_Point_Pleasant.

"The Battle of Wabash." sinclair.quarterman.org/history/mod/battleofwabash.html.

Baxley, Charles. *Southern Campaigns of the American Revolution (SCAR).* southerncampaign.org.

Belt, Thomas. "Timberlake's Journal: A Cherokee Perspective." *Culture, Crisis & Conflict: Cherokee and British Relations 1756–1765.* Ed. by Anne F. Rogers & Barbara R. Duncan. Cherokee, NC: Museum of the Cherokee Indian Press, 2009.

Blackmon, Richard D. *Dark and Bloody Ground.* Yardley, PA: Westholme, 2012.

Blankenship, Bob. *Cherokee Roots.* Vol. 1. Eastern *Cherokee Rolls*. Cherokee, NC: Blankenship, 1992.

_____. *Cherokee Roots*. Vol. 2. *Western Cherokee Rolls*. Cherokee, NC: Blankenship, 1992.

Bogan, Dallas. "Dragging Canoe & the Chickamauga Cherokees." tngenweb.org/Campbell/.

"The Brainerd Mission." chattanooga.net/brainerdmission/stories/story_of_cher_indians.htm.

Brown, John P. "Eastern Cherokee Chiefs." *Chronicles of Oklahoma* 16, no. 1 (1938).

_____. *Old Frontiers*. Kingsport: Southern, 1938.

Calloway, Colin G. *The American Revolution in Indian Country*. New York: Cambridge University Press, 1995.

Chalkley, Lyman. *Chronicles of the Scotch-Irish Settlement in Virginia: Extracted from the Original Court Records of Augusta County, 1745–1800*. 3 vols. Published by Mary S. Lockwood, 1912. Available at rootsweb.ancestry.com/~chalkley/volume_x/contents.htm. NOTE: Enter '1,' '2,' or '3' for 'x' for the appropriate volume.

Chalmers, Alexander. *The General Biographical Dictionary: Containing an Historical and Critical Account of the Lives and Writings of the Most Eminent Persons in Every Nation, Particularly the British and Irish*. Vol. 11. London: 1812. Available at search.ancestry.co.uk/search/db.aspx?dbid=7077.

"Cherokee History." AAA Native Arts. aaanativearts.com/Cherokee.

"Cherokee Myths and Legends—Story of the Origin of Diseases and Medicines (Council of Animals)." gypsywolf.weebly.com/cherokee-myths—legends.html.

"The Cherokee Nation." cherokee.org/AboutTheNation/Culture/General/24404/Information.aspx.

"The Cherokee Story of the Origin of Diseases and Medicines (Council of Animals)." suite101.com/article/animal-parliaments-a-cherokee-legend.

"Cherokee Treaties." nanations.com/cherokee/tribe/treaty1721.htm.

"The Chickamauga Cherokee." chickamaugacherokee.org.

"Chief Bench Attack on the Livingston Home." hto-livingston.com/indianattack1794.html.

"Chief Doublehead and Cannibalism." oldhuntsville.com/articles/Chief%20Doublehead,%20the%20Cherokee%20Cannibal.php.

"Chief Dragging Canoe." rootsweb.ancestry.com/~tnpolk2/DraggingCanoeBio.htm.

"Chief Robert Benge." rootsweb.ancestry.com/~vahsswv/historicalsketches/bengechief.html.

Christian, George. "The Battle of Lookout Mountain: An Eyewitness Account." Ed. by E. Raymond Evans. *Journal of Cherokee Studies* 3, no. 1 (Winter 1978).

"Christian Gottlieb Priber." virtual.clemson.edu/caah/languages/Riley/Priber%20Page/PriberMonth.html.

"Chronology of Public Health in South Carolina." scdhec.gov/administration/history/timeline.htm.

Clark, Chief Justice Walter. "The Colony of Transylvania." *The North Carolina Booklet* 3, no. 7, North Carolina Society of the Daughters of the Revolution. Ed. by Miss Mary Hilliard Hinton and Mrs. E. E. Moffitt. Raleigh: Uzzell, November 1903; collected as a portion of *The North Carolina Booklet: Great Events in North Carolina History* 3. Ed. by Mrs. E. E. Moffitt, North Carolina Society of the Daughters of the Revolution (undated). Reprinted by Nabu Public Domain Reprints, Preface by Mrs. D. H. Hill (undated).

Conley, Robert J. *The Cherokee Nation—A History*. Albuquerque: University of New Mexico Press, 2005.

The Connecticut Journal, No. 728. Thursday, October 11, 1781.

Crabtree, T. E. "Crabtree Family History." freepages.genealogy.rootsweb.ancestry.com/~genbaby5/crab3.html.

"Creek Indian History." ourgeorgiahistory.com/ogh/Creek_Indians.

Crews, Daniel C. *Faith and Tears: The Moravian Mission Among the Cherokee*. Winston-Salem, NC: Moravian Archives, 2000.

_____. *The Revolutionary War and the Moravians*. Winston-Salem, NC: Moravian Archives, 1996.

Crump, Suzie. "The Battle of Point Pleasant." wvgenweb.org/mason/firstbattle.html.

Cuming, Alexander. *Memoirs of the Life of Alexander Cuming*. Cherokee Documents in Foreign Archives, Special Collection, Hunter Library, Add. 39855, sch. no. 65528, Microfilm Reel 172, page 25.

Dabney, William M., and Marion Dargan. *William Henry Drayton and the American Revolution*. Albuquerque: University of New Mexico Press, 1962.

Davidson, Grace Gillam. *Early Records of Georgia*. Vol. 1. *Wilkes County*. Abstracted and compiled by Grace Gillam Davidson. Macon, GA: Burke, 1933.

Day, Kate Pickens. *Cousin Monroe's History of the Pickens Family*. Compiled by Thomas Mason Monroe Pickens. Revised by Kate Pickens Day. Greenville, SC: Hoitt Press, 1951.

Dean, Nadia. *A Demand of Blood*. Cherokee, NC: Valley River Press, 2012.

"Deposition of Thomas Sharp." whitesnet.org/13%20Worm-Wads/Flustered%20Pie.html.

"Documents Relating to Indian Affairs, Vol. 1 (1750–1754)." Edited by William McDowell. *Colonial Records of South Carolina*. Columbia, SC: South Carolina Department of Archives and History, 1958.

"Documents Relating to Indian Affairs, Vol. 2 (1754–1765)." Edited by William McDowell. *Colonial Records of South Carolina*. Columbia, SC: South Carolina Department of Archives and History, 1958.

Drake, Dr. Charles. "The Death of James Boone." web.infoave.net/~kfleming/drakanc.html.

Drake, Donald. "The Boone Massacre." freepages.genealogy.rootsweb.ancestry.com/~drakerobinson/OtherPages/BooneMass.htm.

Drake, Samuel Gardner. *Early History of Georgia, Embracing the Embassy of Sir Alexander Cuming to the Country of the Cherokees, in the year 1730, A Paper Read in Substance Before the New-England Historic, Genealogical Society, February, 1872*. Boston: Clapp & Son, 1872.

Draper, Lyman C. "Daniel Boone in Southwest Virginia." Ed. by James William Hagy, vagenweb.org/wise/HSpubl51.htm.

———. *King's Mountain and Its Heroes: History of the Battle of King's Mountain, October 7th, 1780, and the Events Which Led to It*. Cincinnati: Thomson, 1881.

Drayton, John, LLD. *Memoirs of the American Revolution, From Its Commencement to the Year 1776*. Vols. 1 and 2. Charleston, SC: Miller, 1821.

Duffy, John. *Epidemics in Colonial America*. Baton Rouge: Louisiana State University Press, 1953.

Early Records of Georgia. Vol. 1. *Wilkes County*. Abstracted and compiled by Grace Gillam Davidson. Macon GA: 1933. Submitted to GAGenWeb Project by Christina Palmer with transcription assistance by Donna Crawford, C. J. Crawford, and Jennifer Reddish, hiddenancestors.com/wilkesga/ceded_lands.htm.

"Eighteenth Century Manuscripts." Georgia Historical Society. archive.org/details/collectionsofgeo19geor.

Erdoes, Richard, and Alfonso Ortiz. *American Indian Myths and Legends*. New York: Pantheon Books, 1984.

Evans, E. Raymond. "Notable Persons in Cherokee History: Bob Benge." *Journal of Cherokee Studies* 1, no. 2 (Fall 1976).

———. "Notable Persons in Cherokee History: Dragging Canoe." *Journal of Cherokee Studies* 2, no. 1 (Winter 1977).

———, and Duane H. King. "Historical Documentation of the Grant Expedition Against the Cherokees, 1761." *Journal of Cherokee Studies* 2, no. 3 (Summer 1977).

Faull, LaVelda. "Isaac Crabtree, My 'Infamous' Ancestor." dealerschoice1.com/pulaski/Bios/C/CrabtreeIsaac.htm.

Ferling, John. *Almost a Miracle*. New York: Oxford University Press, 2007.

Fleenor, Lawrence J., Jr., "James Boone Massacre." danielboonetrail.com/historicalsites.php?id=80.

Flint, Timothy. *The Life and Adventures of Daniel Boone, the First Settler of Kentucky, Interspersed with Incidents of the Early Annals of the Country. New Edition, to Which is Added an Account of Captain Estill's Defeat*. New York: Hurst, 1868.

Force, Peter. *Marion, Francis. Peter Force Copies of Peter Horry's Transcripts of Francis Marion Letters, 1779–1782*. Microfilm reel P900013, 1846. Columbia, SC: South Carolina Department of Archives and History.

"Fort Moore, South Carolina." en.wikipedia.org/wiki/Savannah_Town,_South_Carolina.

"Fort Patrick Henry." tennesseeencyclopedia.net/entry.php?rec=493.

French, Captain Christopher. "Journal of an Expedition to South Carolina." *Journal of Cherokee Studies* 2, no. 3 (Summer 1977).

"George Washington: The Soldier Through the French and Indian War." ushistory.org/valleyforge/george1.html.

Gibbes, R. W. *Documentary History of the American Revolution*. Vols. 1 to 3. Spartanburg, SC: Reprint Co., 1972.

Gilbert, William Harlen, Jr. *The Eastern Cherokees, Anthropological Papers No. 23 from Bu-*

reau of Ethnology Bulletin 133, pp. 169–413. Washington: Smithsonian Institute, Bureau of American Ethnology, United States Government Printing Office, 1943.

Goodpasture, Albert V. "Indian Wars and Warriors of the Old Southwest." *Tennessee Historical Magazine* 4, Chapters 1–4 (March, June, September, December 1918).

Gordon, John W. *South Carolina and the American Revolution*. Columbia: University of South Carolina Press, 2003.

Graves, Will. "Transcription of Arthur Fairies Journal of Expedition Against the Cherokee Indians from July 18th, to October 11th, 1776." *Southern Campaigns of the American Revolution* 2, no. 10.1 (October 2005). southerncampaign.org.

Greene, Jerome A. *Ninety Six: A Historical Narrative*. National Park Service Brochure.

"Guide to Southern Campaigns of the American Revolution (SCAR)." lib.jrshelby.com/SCAR%20v7se.pdf.

Hamilton, Emory L. "Frontier Forts of Southwest Virginia." *Historical Sketches of Southwest Virginia*. Publication No. 4 (1968).

Hamner, Earl, Jr. "A Piano in the House," *The Twilight Zone*, season three, episode 87, broadcast February 16, 1962.

Hatley, Tom. *The Dividing Paths*. New York: Oxford University Press, 1995.

_____. "An Epitaph for Henry Timberlake and the First Cherokee and American 'Greatest' Generation." *Culture, Crisis & Conflict: Cherokee and British Relations 1756–1765*. Ed. by Anne F. Rogers and Barbara R. Duncan. Cherokee, NC: Museum of the Cherokee Indian Press, 2009.

Hawke, David Freeman. *Everyday Life in Early America*. New York: Harper and Row, 1988. Perennial Edition, HarperCollins Publishers, 2003.

Haygood, John. *The Civil and Political History of the State of Tennessee from its Earliest Settlement up to the Year 1796*. 1823. Reprinted, Charleston, NC: Nabu Press, 2011.

Henderson, Dr. Archibald. *The Conquest of the Old Southwest: The Romantic Story of the Early Pioneers Into Virginia, the Carolinas, Tennessee, and Kentucky, 1740–1790*. New York: Century, 1920.

Hoig, Stanley W. *The Cherokees and Their Chiefs*. Fayetteville: University of Arkansas Press, 1998.

Horry, Brigadier General Peter, and Parson Mason Locke Weems. *Life of General Francis Marion*. gutenberg.org/catalog/world/readfile?fk_files=1443764&pageno=1, March, 1997 [Etext #846]. Originally published Philadelphia: Carey, 1809. Copyrights 1824 by Joseph Allen, 1854 by J. P. Lippincott, Grambo. Reprinted Winston-Salem, NC: Introduction copyrighted by Blair, 2000.

"Indian Affairs." Vols. 1 (1789–1814) and 2 (1815–1827). American State Papers. Library of Congress. Washington, D.C.: Gales and Seaton, 1832.

Irving, Washington. *The Life of George Washington*. 1st ed. New York: Putnam, 1855.

"Isaac Crabtree." freepages.genealogy.rootsweb.ancestry.com/~genbaby5/crab3.html.

"Isaac Crabtree." wc.rootsweb.ancestry.com/cgi-bin/igm.cgi?op=GET&db=2007trickyriver&id=I6684.

"Juan Pardo." northcarolinahistory.org.

Judd, Cameron. *Boone*. New York: Bantam Books, 1995.

_____. *The Border Men*. Nashville: Cumberland House, 2000.

_____. *The Canebrake Men*. Nashville: Cumberland House, 2001.

_____. *Crockett of Tennessee*. New York: Bantam Books, 1994.

_____. *The Overmountain Men*. New York: Bantam Books, 1991.

Kaler, James Otis. *Hannah of Kentucky: A Story of the Wilderness Road*. New York: American Book, 1912. Heritage History, heritage-history.com/www/heritage-books.php?Dir=books&author=otis&book=kentucky&story=_front, copyright 2007–2012.

Kelly, James C. "Notable Persons in Cherokee History: Attakullakulla." *Journal of Cherokee Studies* 3, no. 1 (Winter 1978).

King, Duane H. "Long Island of the Holston: Sacred Cherokee Ground." *Journal of Cherokee Studies* 1, no. 2 (Fall 1976).

"King's Mountain." tennesseehistory.com/class/KingsMt.htm.

Landrum, Dr. J.B.O. *Colonial and Revolutionary History of Upper South Carolina*. Greenville, SC: self-published, 1897. Formatted for PDF on CD, Austin, TX: DMK Heritage, 2005.

Lawson, John. *A New Voyage to Carolina*. gutenberg.org/files/1838/1838-h/1838-h.htm.

Lee, Henry. *The Revolutionary War Memoirs of General Henry Lee*. Ed. by Robert E. Lee.

New introduction by Charles Royster. New York: Da Capo Press, 1998.

Letters of Governor William Henry Lyttleton. South Carolina Department of Archives and History (SCDAH).

Logan, John H. *A History of the Upper Country of South Carolina*. Charleston, SC: Courtenay; Columbia, SC: Glass, 1859. Available at openlibrary.org/books/OL6905207M/A_history_of_the_upper_country_of_South_Carolina.

The London Chronicle 16, no. 1233, Thursday, November 15, 1764.

The London Magazine or Gentlemen's Intelligencer 26, pages 281–283, 1757.

Lumpkin, Henry. *From Savannah to Yorktown*. Lincoln NE: toExcel Press, 2000.

Maddox, Jerry A. *The Legacy of Ludovic Grant*. Bloomington, IN: AuthorHouse, 2007.

Manly, Louise. *Southern Literature From 1579–1895*. Richmond, VA: Johnson, 1900.

Marion, Lieutenant Francis. "Sowing Tares of Hate." *Journal of Cherokee Studies* 2, no. 3 (Summer 1977).

Marshall, John. *The Life of George Washington*. Fredericksburg, VA: Citizens' Guild of Washington's Boyhood Home, 1926. Amazon.com Kindle Edition, Douglas Editions, 2009.

Marshall, Lamar. "The 1776 Campaign Against the Cherokee." *Smoky Mountain News*, Oct. 27, 2010. www.smokymountain news.com/index.php/component/k2/item/2173-the-1776-campaign-against-the-cherokee.

The Maryland Gazette. msa.maryland.gov/megafile/msa/speccol/sc4800/sc4872/001284/html/index.html.

McCall, Hugh. *The History of Georgia*. Atlanta: Cherokee, 1909.

McCandless, Peter. *Slavery, Disease, and Suffering in the Southern Lowcountry*. New York: Cambridge University Press, 2011.

Meriwether, Robert L. *The Expansion of South Carolina, 1729–1765*. PhD diss., Columbia University. Kingsport, TN: Southern Publishers, printed and bound by Kingsport Press, 1940.

Miller, Eric. *George Washington and Indians*. dreric.org/library/contents/shtml.

Milligen-Johnston, Dr. George. *A Short Description of the Province of South Carolina, with an Account of the Air, Weather, and Diseases, at Charles-town, Written in the Year 1763*. London: Hinton, 1770. Reprinted in *Colonial South Carolina: Two Contemporary Descriptions by Governor James Glen and Doctor George Milligen-Johnston*. Ed. by Chapman J. Milling. Columbia: University of South Carolina Press, 1951.

Moneypenny, Major Alexander. "Diary of Alexander Moneypenny, March 20-May 31, 1761." *Journal of Cherokee Studies* 2, no. 3 (Summer 1977).

Mooney, James. *History, Myths, and Sacred Formulas of the Cherokees, Including Myths of the Cherokee (1900) and The Sacred Formulas of the Cherokee (1890)*, with a biographical introduction by George Ellison. Reprint: Fairview, NC: Bright Mountain Books, 1992.

Morris, Ester. *The Story of Defeated Creek*. 1834. defeatedcreekmarina.com/storypage.html.

Morris, Michael. "The High Price of Trade: Anglo-Indian Trade Mistakes and the Fort Loudoun Disaster." *Journal of Cherokee Studies* 27 (1996).

New River Valley Historical Resources. newrivernotes.com/swva/swvahs.htm.

North Carolina Historical Sites. nchistoricsites.org

Parham, W. E. "(W. E. Parham Tells of) Interesting Old Places In (Blount) County." *Maryville* (TN) *Enterprise*, April 2, 9, 1930.

Patterson, Daniel W. "Backcountry Legends of a Minister's Death." In *The True Image: Gravestone Art and the Culture of Scotch Irish Settlers in the Pennsylvania and Carolina Backcountry* by Daniel W. Patterson. Chapel Hill: University of North Carolina Press, 2012. southernspaces.org/2012/backcountry-legends-ministers-death.

Pendexter, Hugh. *A Virginia Scout*. Indianapolis: Bobbs-Merrill, printed Brooklyn, NY: Braunworth, 1922. gutenberg.org/files/26631/26631-8.txt.

Pickens, Dr. A. L. *Skyagunsta: The Border Wizard Owl*. Greenville, SC: Observer, 1934. Reprinted Ann Arbor, MI: University Microfilms, 1966.

Pickens, General Andrew. *Letter to General Henry Lee*, 28 August 1811. Included in *The Sumter Papers*, vol. 1 of The Draper Manuscripts, Series VV, Sumter County Genealogical Society Research Center, Annex to Sumter County Museum, Sumter Carnegie Public Library, Sumter, SC.

"Proclamation of 1763." revolutionary-war-

and-beyond.com/proclamation-of-1763.html.

Ramsey, Dr. J. G. M. *The Annals of Tennessee to the End of the Eighteenth Century.* Charleston, SC: Walker & James, 1853. Reprinted Kingsport, TN: Kingsport Press, 1926. Electronic edition, Rockwood, TN: Eagle Ridge Technologies, 2007.

Reed, Colonel C. Wingate. *Beaufort County: Two Centuries of Its History.* Eastern North Carolina Digital Library, digital.lib.ecu.edu/historyfiction/fullview.aspx?id=reb.

"Revolutionary War in South Carolina." carolana.com/SC/Revolution.

"Revolutionary War in South Carolina." sciway3.net/proctor/marion/military/revwarsc.

Reynolds, William R., Jr. *Andrew Pickens: South Carolina Patriot in the Revolutionary War.* Jefferson, NC: McFarland, 2012.

Rogers, Anne Frazer. "Archaeology at Cherokee Town Sites Visited by the Montgomery and Grant Expeditions." *Culture, Crisis & Conflict: Cherokee and British Relations, 1756–1765.* Ed. by Anne F. Rogers and Barbara R. Duncan. Cherokee, NC: Museum of the Cherokee Indian Press, 2009.

Rogers, Anne F., and Barbara R. Duncan. *Culture, Crisis & Conflict: Cherokee British Relations, 1756–1765.* Cherokee, NC: Museum of the Cherokee Indian Press, 2009.

Rozema, Vicki. *Cherokee Voices: Early Accounts of Cherokee Life in the East.* Winston-Salem, NC: Blair, 2002.

Salley, A. S., Jr. *The Calhoun Family of South Carolina.* 1906.

_____. *Documents Relating to the History of South Carolina During the Revolutionary War.* Columbia: Printed for the Historical Commission of South Carolina by The State Company, 1908.

"Samuel Elbert." en.wikipedia.org/wiki/User:Mike33ekim/Sandbox.

Schleier, Joanne. "Ann Calhoun Matthews." keeperoftherecords.blogspot.com/2010/11/my-portrayal-of-ann-calhoun-matthews.html.

Scott, Brian, *Calhoun Burial Grounds Marker.* hmdb.org. *Military and Political,* July 15, 2009.

"1777 Treaty of Long Island." bkoatohee.homestead.com/files/1777_TREATY_at_Long_Island.htm.

Sharp, E.M. *Pickens Families of the South (incl. Excerpts from the Draper Papers).* Memphis, TN: Sharp, 1963; annotated 1995 by John Carr Pickens.

Sheriff, G. Anne. *Sketches of Cherokee Villages in South Carolina.* Forest Acres Elementary School, Easley, SC, Schoolwide Enrichment Program. //sciway3.net/scgenweb/pickenscounty/images/sheriff–01.pdf.

"Sir James Wright Paper." (1772–1784 three folders). Georgia Historical Society, MS 884.

"Smallpox." Native American Heritage Programs. lenapeprograms.info/health/smallpox/.

Smith, D. Ray. *Dragging Canoe, Cherokee War Chief.* smithdray.tripod.com/draggingcanoe-index-9.html.

"Smoky Mountain Historical Society Index." smhstn.org/cpage.php?pt=22.

"A Soldier's Story: Capt. Christopher French, 1761." trailofthetrail.blogspot.com/2011/05/soldiers-story-capt-christopher-french.html.

South Carolina Department of Archives and History, Columbia SC.

South Carolina Department of Health and Disease Control, Columbia SC.

The South Carolina Gazette, Charles Town, SC (several issues)

"South Carolina Genealogy Forum." virts.rootsweb.ancestry.com/~scroots/m_317.html.

"The South Sea Company." en.wikipedia.org/wiki/South_Sea_Company

Southern Campaigns of the American Revolution (SCAR). Southerncampaign.org,

Stalnaker, Leo. "Samuel Stalnaker." american-lineage.org/documents/Captain%20Samuel%20Stalnaker%20-%20Leo%20Stalnaker%20(1938).pdf.

Starr, Emmett. *History of the Cherokee Indians.* 1921. Reprinted Cherokee, NC: Cherokee, 2009.

Stephenson, Michael. *Patriot Battles: How the War of Independence Was Fought.* New York: HarperCollins, 2008.

Sugden, John. *Blue Jacket: Warrior of the Shawnees.* Lincoln: University of Nebraska Press, 2000.

_____. *Tecumseh: A Life.* New York: Holt, 1997.

Summers, L. P. *History of Southwest Virginia, 1746–1786, Washington County, 1777–1870.* Richmond, VA: Hill, 1903.

Templin, David W. "John Denton: Patriot—Pioneer." *Smoky Mountain Historical Society Journal and Newsletter* 3, no. 1. smhstn.org/cpage.php?pt=22.

Tenlen, Jenny. "McAfee Family." jtenlen.drizzlehosting.com/mcafee/life/life4.html.

Timberlake, Lt. Henry. *The Memoirs of Lt. Henry Timberlake*. Ed. by Duane H. King. Cherokee, NC: Museum of the Cherokee Indian Press, 2007.

"Trade Guns." Thefurtrapper.com.

"The Treaty of Camp Charlotte." en.wikipedia.org/wiki/Treaty_of_Camp_Charlotte.

"The Treaty of Camp Charlotte." wvencyclopedia.org/articles/766.

"The Treaty of Fort Stanwix (1768)." nps.gov/fost/historyculture/1768-boundary-line-treaty.htm.

"The Treaty of Hard Labor." wvencyclopedia.org/articles/768.

"The Treaty of Lochaber." theonefeather.com/2009/12/the-treaty-of-lochaber/.

"The Treaty of Paris (1763)." emersonkent.com/historic_documents/treaty_of_paris_1763.htm.

"The Treaty of Paris (1763)." en.wikipedia.org/wiki/Treaty_of_Paris_(1763).

"The Treaty of Pensacola." pensapedia.com/wiki/Treaty_of_Pensacola.

"The Tuscarora War." en.wikipedia.org/wiki/Tuscarora_War.

Walker, Rickey Butch. *Doublehead: Last Chickamauga Cherokee Chief*. Killen, AL: Bluewater, 2012.

Wells, H. G. *The Outline of History*. Garden City, NY: Garden City, 1920, 1931.

"William Russell." werelate.org/wiki/Person:William_Russell_%2886%29.

Williams, Samuel Cole, LLD. *Early Travels in the Tennessee Country: 1540–1800*. Johnson City, TN: Watauga Press, 1928.

_____. *History of the Lost State of Franklin*. Johnson City, TN: Watauga Press, 1924.

_____. "William Tatum, Wataugan." *Tennessee Historical Magazine* 7, no. 2. (July 1921).

Wilkins, Thurman. *Cherokee Tragedy*. 2nd ed. Norman: University of Oklahoma Press, 1986.

Woodward, Grace Steele. *The Cherokees*. Norman: University of Oklahoma Press, 1963.

"Yamassee War." carolana.com/Carolina/Noteworthy_Events/yamasseewar.html.

"The Yamassee War." en.wikipedia.org/wiki/Yamassee_War.

Zubly, John Joachim. *Collections of the Georgia Historical Society*. Vol. 19. ebooksread.com/authors-eng/john-joachim-zubly.

Index

Page numbers in ***bold italics*** indicate pages with illustrations.

Abbeville, South Carolina 80, 119
Abbeville County, South Carolina 180
Abbeville District, South Carolina 154; Court 259, 342
Abe (prisoner of the Cherokee) 298
Abel, Ezekial 290
Abingdon, Virginia 119, 125, 158, 284; *see also* Wolf's Hill, Virginia
Abraham (slave) 317–318
Abraham of Chilkowa *see* Old Abram of Chilhowee, Chief
Act of Oblivion 338
Ada-Gal'-Kala (Adagalkala) *see* Attakullakulla, Chief
Adair, James 4, 14–15, 19, 24, 51, 66, 69, 72, 76, 95, 99, ***128***, 227
Adam (slave) 125–126, 128
Adams, Mary 337
Adams, Mr. 270
Adamson, Lt. James 89
Adventure 196–197
Africa / Africans 17, 32, 110
Aganstat, Chief *see* Oconostota, Chief
Aganunitsi Moytoy of the Wolf Clan 349
Ahmahtoya, Chief 43, 348
Akonoluchta, Chief 239, 298
Alabama 7, 50, 174, 195, 232, 240, 246, 269, 355, 358
Albany, New York 85
Alexander, Sam 262
Algonkian, Chief 348
Algonquian (Indians) 7
Alijoy Village ***10***, 169, 372
Allagae Village *see* Alijoy Village
Allajoy *see* Alijoy
Allegheny Mountains 117, 252
Allegheny River 57
Allen, John 250
Allison, Mr. 299
Amadohiyi, Chief 13, 43–44, 46, 51, 67, 134, 348; death of 53
Amaedohi, Chief *see* Amadohiyi, Chief
American Enlightenment 123
American Independence 168
American Revolution 1, 58, 63, 65, 76, 97, 109, 141, 151, 178, 184, 208, 227, 231, 240, 252–253, 255, 291, 296, 311, 341
Amherst, Maj. Gen. Jeffery (also Jeffrey or Geoffrey) 24, 84–87, 92, 118–119
Amherst County, Virginia 359
Ammoah Village 270
Ammouskossittee, Chief 53–55, 67, 107, 349
Amogayunyi Village *see* Running Water Town
Amokontakona of Kutcloa 239
Amoya of the Valley Towns *see* Pouting Pigeon, Chief
Anakanoe, Chief 234
Anakwanki, Chief 349
Ancoo, Chief *see* Old Abram, Chief
Anderson, Judge Joseph 329
Anderson, Luke 245, 269
Anderson, Col. Robert F. 140; 1776 Cherokee War 161, 166; 1782 expedition against Tories and Chickamauga 218–219, 222
Anderson County, South Carolina 180
Angles 4, 23
Anglo-Saxon(s) 4–5
Anigawi 348
Ani-Keetoowahgi 3
Ani-Kitui-Hwagi *see* Ani-Keetoowahgi
Anikusatiyi *see* Nickajack Town
Ani-yunwi-ya 3, 12, 135
Annakehujah 186
Annecekah of Tuskega *see* Annakehujah
Anson, Capt. George Lord 45
Appalachian Mountains 7, 111, 130, 175, 233, 242, 336
Appalachian peas *see* black-eyed peas
Appalachian Plateau 8
Appalachians *see* Appalachian Mountains
Appomattox River Falls 28
Aquonatuste Village *see* Great Ecoche
Arkansas 135, 336, 345, 357
Arkansas River 357
Armytage, James Charles ***310***
Arne, Mr. 45

Arnold, Capt. Thomas 45
Arthur, Gabriel 28–30
Arthur, John Preston 137, 176, 359; regarding the murder of the Cherokee chiefs (1788) 259, 342; use of the word savages 199
Articles of Friendship and Commerce (1730) 46
Ashe, Col. John 149
Ashe, Virginia 367
Ashe County, Virginia 367
Asher's Station 202–203, 227, 252
Asheville, North Carolina 283
Ashley's Ferry, South Carolina 96
Aspey, Robert 202
Ata-cul-culla, Chief *see* Attakullakulla, Chief
Atagulkalu, Chief *see* Attakullakulla, Chief
Ata'Lunti'Ski, Chief *see* Nettle Carrier, Chief
Atkin, Ind. Agt. Edmond 85
Atlanta, Georgia 240
Atlantic Ocean 8, 110
Attakullakulla, Chief 4, 14, 21, 44, 49–57, 59–64, 66, 69–73, 75, 79, 81, 84–85, 92–93, 95–96, 102, 105–107, 111, 115–122, 129, 132–134, 142, 149, 159, 173–176, 179–182, 186–190, 215, 217, 224, 241, 266, 287, 299, 333, 339–342, 349, 352–353, 358, 370; Augusta trade conference (1763) 112; became Principal Chief 108; death of 214, 234, 238–239; England (1730) 44, ***45***, 46, 49, 108; Fort Assumption 67; Fort Duquesne 67–68; Fort Prince George (1759) 77–78; Fort Prince George (1761) 96; met William Bartram 148; Peace Treaty (1761) 97–98, 101; saved John Stuart 89–91; Sycamore Shoals 135–138
Attusah of the Mouth of Tellico River *see* Northward Warrior
Augusta, Georgia 26, 39, 52, 80, 123, 131, 145, 193, 215, 222; conference (1773) 123; Siege of (1781) 1, 26, 145; trade conference (1763) ***112***; *see also* Fort Augusta
Augusta Company 54, 346, 351

401

Index

Augusta County, Georgia 115
Aulola Village 54
Aurora Village *see* Aulola Village
Austenaco, Chief *see* Ostenaco, Chief
Avery, Col. Waightstill 181
A-wi (the deer) 17
Ayoree Village 93
Ayrate 7

backwater men (militia) *see* Overmountain militia
Badger, Chief 116, 134, 175, 224, 265, 269, 295, 298–299, 349
Baker, John 368–369
Baker, Mary 106
Baker, William 367
Baker Roll 345
Baker's Creek 162
Balestine, Jesse 202
ball game 11, 16, 19–20, 104, 335, 372
Ball Ground, Georgia 56–57
Balsam Mountains 9
Barker, Capt. Thomas 35
Barnett, Peter 242
Barnwell, Col. John 32–33
Baron of Stratton *see* Berkeley, John
Barren Fork of Duck River 330
Barren River 242
Barton, Col. Samuel 212
Barton's Creek 300
Bartram, William 119, 145, 147, 371; at Alexander Cameron's 146; meets Attakullakulla 148; at Augusta Conference (1773) 123; at George Galphin's 145
Basire, Isaac **45**
Bath, Carolina Colony 32–33
Battle at Bledsoe's Station (1788) 263–264
Battle at Cavett's Station (1793) 322–323
Battle at Clover Bottom (1780) 203–205
Battle at Little River (1776) *see* The Ring Fight
Battle at Ninety Six (with the Cherokee, 1760) 83
Battle at Tomassee (1776) 166
Battle Creek (Tennessee) 201
Battle of Black's Station (1792) 158
Battle of Bledsoe's Station (1793) 316–317
Battle of Boyd's Creek **128, 133**
Battle of Buchanan's Station (1792) 306–307
Battle of Cowpens (1781) 1, 124
Battle of Crow's Creek Pass (1760) 86, **170**
Battle of Echoe Pass (1760) *see* Battle of Crow's Creek Pass
Battle of Elk River (1793) 318
Battle of Etowah (1793) 323
Battle of Flint Creek (1789) **128,** 267–268
Battle of Fort Necessity (1754) 57
Battle of Franklin (1788) 251
Battle of Gillespie's Station (1788) 266–267
Battle of Great Cane Brake (1775) 140
Battle of Great Cane Break *see* Battle of Great Cane Brake
Battle of Hastings (1066) 24
Battle of Horseshoe Bend (1792) 301–302
Battle of Kanawha (1774) *see* Battle of Point Pleasant
Battle of Kings Mountain (1780) 3, 208, 342
Battle of (Long) Island Flats (1776) **128,** 156–157, 353
Battle of Nickajack (1794) 224, 329–331
Battle of Pine Island (1714) 34
Battle of Point Pleasant (1774) 129–130
Battle of Seneca (1776) 164–165
Battle of Stamford Bridge (1066) 24
Battle of Taliwa (1755) 56–57, 104
Battle of the Black Hole (1776) 57, **380**; *see also* The Black Hole
Battle of the Bluff (1781) 211–214
Battle of the Great Meadows *see* Battle of Fort Necessity
Battle of the Horses and Hounds (1781) *see* Battle of the Bluff
Battle of Ziegler's Station (1792) 299–300
Bays, J. 253
Beamer, John 349
Beamer, Mr. 56
Bean, John 122
Bean, Mrs. Lydia 158; saved by Ghighau Nancy Ward 159
Bean, William 119, 158
Bear Coming Out of the Tree 269
Bear Creek 285, 358, 367
Beard, John 246
Beard, Maj. John 265, 297, 318–320
Beaverdam District, Cherokee County, North Carolina 347
Belcourt, Gov. Louis 73
Bell, Ens. John 73–74, 82
Bell, Hugh F. 269
Bell Ratler *see* Bell Rattle, Chief
Bell Rattle, Chief 347–348
Bell Ringer *see* Bell Rattle, Chief
Bell Town, Tennessee 347
Belle Meade Plantation 212, 266
beloved woman 21–22, 104–105, 238, 348; *see also* ghigau
Beloved Woman *see* Nancy Ward
Bench, Chief 15, 116, 184, 188, 216–217, 224, 234, 262, 283–284, 293–294, 299, 305, 307–308, 314–316, 321–322, 337, 351, 356–357; assisted four white women near South West Point 284; ate enemies flesh 313; captured the Livingston Family (his last raid) 325–327; Cavett's Station 322–323; death of **128**, 326, 328; retrieved prisoner Jane Brown 268
Benge, Bob, or Robert *see* Bench, Chief
Benge, Captain *see* Bench, Chief
Benge, John 184, 234, 351, 356
Benge, Lucy 351
Benge, Martin *see* The Tail
Benge, Pickens 216, 234, 337, 351
Benton, Samuel 227
Berkeley, John 30
Berkeley, Sir William 30
Berkley, John 302
Berkley, John, Jr. 302
Bermuda 42
Bernard, Mr. 200
Bertie County, North Carolina 32–34, 365
Bethabara Settlement, North Carolina 84, 133
Betty (daughter of Kittagiska) 319
Big Bear of Estanaula, Chief 298
Big Bend of the Tennessee River 174
Big Bone Lick, Kentucky 124
Big Bullet 182
Big Camp Creek *see* Station Camp Creek
Big Cove Village 343
Big Foot, Chief 245, 269
Big Half Breed *see* Sequechee
Big Head, Chief (1714) *see* Uskwalena
Big Head, Chief *see* Ostenaco, Chief
Big Island of the French Broad River 45
Big Island Town of the Little Tennessee River **128, 133,** 134–135, 142, 155, 157, 173, 186, 353, 372
Big Jim 126
Big Lick *see* French Lick
Big Sagwa 157, 182
Big Shoals of the Oconee River **8–10,** 219, 223, 346
Big Spring Creek *see* Coldwater Creek
Big Tom 351
Billouart, Gov. Louis *see* Belcourt, Gov. Louis
Bird in Close *see* Chescoonwho of Tomotlug
Bird Tail Doublehead 336
Bird Town 343
Birmingham, England 29
Bishop, Mr. 160
Bishop, Mrs. 160
Black, Gabriel 300
Black, James 336
Black Dog of Notoly: letter to Andrew Pickens regarding the massacre of Old Chiefs 258
Black Drink 18, **104,** 155, 276
Black-eyed peas 17
Black Fish of Chota 315

Index

Black Fox, Chief 129, 134, 304–305, 338–339, 349; at Coyatee 298–299
The Black Hole 169, 373–379, **380**; see also Battle of the Black Hole
Black River 149
Blackmore, Maj. George D. 329, 359
Blackmore, Dr. James 359
Blackmore, Hon. James W. 359
Blackmore, Capt. John 195–197, 227
Blackmore, Mrs. Elizabeth see Neely, Elizabeth
Blackmore, Gen. William 359
Blackmore's Fort 196
Black's Blockhouse see Black's Station
Black's Station 158, 308
Blair, Council Pres. John 119
Blair, Samuel 306
Bledsoe, Abraham 368
Bledsoe, Anthony (son of Colonel Anthony Bledsoe): death of 325
Bledsoe, Anthony (son of Colonel Isaac Bledsoe): death of 325
Bledsoe, Col. Anthony 203, 227, 231, 247, 250, 263, 317; death of 264
Bledsoe, Col. Isaac 119, 203, 227–228, 362; death of 316
Bledsoe, Mrs. Anthony see Parker, Mrs. Nathaniel
Bledsoe, Mrs. Isaac 264
Bledsoe, Thomas (son of Colonel Anthony Bledsoe: death of 328
Bledsoe Academy Cemetery 264
Bledsoe Creek 242, 264, 283, 360
Bledsoe Creek State Park 283
Bledsoe Pioneer Memorial 264
Bledsoe's Fort see Bledsoe's Station
Bledsoe's Fort Historical Park 203
Bledsoe's Lick 278, 325, 360, 362–364
Bledsoe's Lick Historical Association 203
Bledsoe's Station **194**, 203, 220, 225, 227, 236, 242–243, 246, 249–250, 263, 283, 302, 312, 317, 328, 359; Doublehead attacked 263–264
Blood Law see Clan Vengeance or Retribution
Bloody Fellow, Chief 143, 184, 188, 224, 263, 265, 269, 290, 293, 297–298, 302, 304–305, 308, 318, 351, 356, 373; attacked Gillespie's Station (1788) 266–267; became Principal Chief 338; led a delegation to Congress (1791) 284–285, 294; receives new name, Clear Sky 295–296; signed Treaty of Holston (1791) 282; spoke for peace at Will's Town council (1792) 302–303
The Bloody Rangers (of the State of Franklin) 263, 267, 280

Blooming Grove Creek 242
Blount, Jacob 365
Blount, King Tom see Blunt, Chief Tom
Blount, Mary 32
Blount, Thomas 32
Blount, Gov. William 279–283, 285–286, 288–292, 294, 296–299, 301, 304–305, 307, 312, 316, 318–321, 324, 329, 331, 338, 356, 361, 364–366; Bloody Fellow renamed to Clear Sky 295; Coyatee Conference (1792) 294; Henry's Station conference (1793) 313–314; named Southwest Territory Governor 279; Tellico Blockhouse peace conference (1794) 332–333
Blount Family 32–33
Blount Hall, Pitt County, North Carolina 365
Blue Jacket, Chief 130
Blue Ridge (Mountains) 8, 112, 137, 168, 283
Blue Water Creek 247
The Bluff (Nashville) **8, 194**, 195–196, 200–205, 210–212, 214, 220, 227–229, 235, 250, 266, 298, 305–306
The Bluff Settlement see Nashborough Settlement
Bluff Station (Fort) see The Bluff
Blunt, Chief Tom 32–33
Bobby Brown State Park, Georgia 145–146
Bogges, Ens. John 89
Bone Polisher, Chief 336; killed by Doublehead 335
Boone, Daniel 58, 124–128, 132, 136, 138, 233, 359, 363, 367, 370–371
Boone, James 125, 127; death of 126, 128–129, 370–371
Boone, Jemima: captured at Boonesborough 367
Boone, Rebecca 127
Boone, Squire 127
Boone, Squire, Jr. 127
Boone, Gov. Thomas 84
Boone's Creek 119
Boonesborough, Kentucky 144, 367
Boot, Chief 298
Boston, Massachusetts 139
Boudinot, Elias: assassination of 336
bounty on scalps 60, 64, 69, 171, 176
Bouquet, Col. Henry 24
Bowles, Chief 286
Bowles, Gen. William Augustus (Creek Chief) 286–287, 289
Boyd, Mr. 287
Boyd's Creek 209, 231, 324, 353
Braddock, Gen. Edward 57–59, 360
Braddock's Defeat (1755) 57, **58**

Brainerd Mission see Chattanooga, Tennessee, Brainerd Mission
Brainerd Mission Cemetery 174
Brass Town **9–10**, 171
Bratton, Charles 325
Bray, Comm. William 34–35
Breath of Nickajack, Chief 254, 256, 294, 296, 299, 308–309, 311; at Council of Estanula (1792) 298–299; death of 331; at Henry's Station conference 314
Brennan, Mr. 166
Bridgeport, Alabama 224
Bristol 150
Bristol, Tennessee 119, 207
Britons 23
Broad River (Carolinas) **8–9**, 141
Broad River (Georgia) **8–10**, 145
Broadmouth River 161
Brock, Aaron see Red Bird I, Chief
Brock, John see Red Bird II
Brook, Cash 368–369
Broom, Chief 338
Broomtown (Cherokee Village) 338
Brown, Daniel 253
Brown, Elizabeth 253, 256; ransomed by Chief McGillivray 279; delivered to William Brown 279
Brown, George 253–254, 256; retrieved by Andrew Pickens 279
Brown, Hugh 162
Brown, Jacob 120–123, 138, 158
Brown, James 253
Brown, Col. James 253; death of 254
Brown, Col. James (of Georgia) 336
Brown, Jane (child) 253–254, 268; rescued by Chief Bench (1789) 268
Brown, John 253
Brown, Joseph (uncle of young Joseph Brown) 268, 279
Brown, Colonel Joseph 315; captured when young in Lower Towns (1788) 254–256, 268, 290, 306; guides expedition against Chickamauga (1794) 330–331; rescued (1789) 268
Brown, Mr. 54
Brown, Moses (#1) 229
Brown, Moses (#2) 235, 270
Brown, Mrs. James 253–254, 256; delivered to William Brown 279; ransomed by Chief McGillivray 279; see also Gillespie, Jane
Brown, Polly 253–254; rescued (1789) 268
Brown(e), Col. Thomas "Burn Foot" 1, 178; Indian Agent 193, 215
Brown, William 253, 269, 279
Brown Family Ambush 253–256

Browne Creek 141
Brownell, Henry Howard **58**
Brown's Blockhouse 329–330
Brown's Station 235, 270, 281, 294
Bryan, Rebecca *see* Boone, Rebecca
Bryan, William 124
Bryan Party 125–126
Bryant, James 306
Bryson City, North Carolina 12
Buchanan, Alex 196, 203; death of 212
Buchanan, Maj. John 196, 213, 227, 306
Buchanan, Mrs. Sallie 306
Buchanan, Samuel 229
Buchanan, Capt. William 156
Buchanan's Station *194*, 227, 229, 232, 235, 305–307, 323, 329, 356; *see also* Battle of Buchanan's Station (1792)
Buffalo White Calf *see* Unsuokanail of New Cussee
Buffington's Tavern 338
Bull, Col. Stephen 140
Bull, Lt. Gov. William II 75, 84–85, 87–88, 91–92, 95–97, 101, 110, 114
Bull Head *see* Uskwalena
Bullard, Maj. Joseph 265
Bullitt, Capt. Thomas 124
Bunning, Robert 38
Burlington, Earl of 46
Burnett, Mr.: killed and eaten by Doublehead 313
Burney, Simon 219
Burning Town *10*, 93, 171
Burroughs, Seymour 34–35
Bush, William 125
Bushy Creek of Red River 309
Bushyhead *see* Stuart, John
Bushyhead, Rev. Jesse 91
Butler (Cherokee warrior) 366
Butler, John 72
Butler, Nancy *see* Oninaa
Byrd, Abraham 329
Byrd, Col. William, III 11, 60–61, 66, 69, 87, 91–92, 97, 101, 106; refused to attack the Upper villages and resigned 95
Byron, Ebenezer 315
Byron's Station 315

Cabin, Chief *see* Akonoluchta, Chief
caciques 27
Caeser, Chief *see* Old Caeser, Chief
Caffey, Peter *see* Caffrey, Peter
Caffray, Mrs. *see* Caffrey, Mrs.
Caffrey, John 197, 199, 202
Caffrey, Mrs. 288–290
Caffrey, Peter 288
Cahstahyeestee *see* Whiplash
Cairo, Tennessee 283
Calaka 311
Calhoun, Anne *see* Matthews, Anne
Calhoun, Catherine: killed and scalped 80
Calhoun, Cathrine *see* Calhoun, Catherine
Calhoun, Ezekial 80
Calhoun, Georgia 261, 339
Calhoun, Mary: captured 80
Calhoun, Patk. *see* Calhoun, Capt. Patrick
Calhoun, Capt. Patrick 114; Deputy Surveyor 60, 79–80, 114; encroachment on Cherokee land 79–80, 114
Calhoun, Rebecca 80, 181
Calhoun, William 80
Calhoun, Tennessee 335
Calhoun Family 60, 79, 101, 181; massacre 80
Callahan, Edward 326
Callihan, Patrick *see* Galahan, Patrick
Callihorn, Patrick *see* Galahan, Patrick
Calloway, Betsy: captured with Jemima Boone (1776) 367
Calloway, Elijah 367
Calloway, Fanny: captured with Jemima Boone (1776) 367
Calloway, Flanders 367
Calloway, John 367
Calloway, Col. Richard 367
Calloway, Thomas 367
Calusa (Indians) 25
Calvitt, Frederick 191
Camden, South Carolina 140, 206
Cameron, Ind. Agt. Alexander 112–113, 115–117, 119, 134, 139–140, 144, 150–151, 153, 155, 162, 164–165, 172–176, 185, 191, 193, 208, 215, 225; attacks backcountry with the Cherokee 159–161, 181–182; Dragging Canoe relationship 187, 189, 353; Watauga settlers ordered off Cherokee land 121–122, 142; William Bartram visit 146
Camp, Jack 321
Camp Charlotte (Ohio) 130–131
Camp Creek 185, 240
Campbell (servant) 264
Campbell, Col. Arthur: Bench's scalp sent to Virginia governor 328, 356; Cherokee expedition (1780) 209, 211, 214, 251, 355; Chickamauga expedition (1782) 223, 355
Campbell, Judge David 245
Campbell, Capt. John 150, 156
Campbell, Gen. John 231
Campbell, Col. William 207; Kings Mountain (1780) 208, 343
Campbell, Gov. Lord William 139, 141, 149–150
Campbell's Station *128*, 321–322
Canada 85–86, 91–92
Cane Creek *9*, 88, 90, 169
Caney Branch, Tennessee 156
Caney Fork River 206, 301–302, 307, 359, 363, 368
Cannucca Creek *see* Cartoogechaye Creek
Canostee Village 171
Canucca Village *10*, 169, *170*, 374–379, ***380***
Canuga Village *see* Canucca Village
Canusee Village 171, 371
Canutee Village *see* Canucca Village
Canutry Village 54
Cape Fear, North Carolina 149–150
Captain Charley of All(i)joy, Chief 294, 297–298, 308, 311, 314; death of 319
Captain George, Chief 295
Captain Owean Nakan *see* Attakullakulla, Chief
Carey, James 284, 298, 307, 323
Caribbean 25
Carmichael, Daniel 319
Carolina Colony 28–33; Lords Proprietors 30–31, 33; Fundamental Constitution of 30; Grand Council 31
Carolina musket 29
Carpenter, John Jolly 349
Carpenter, Pumpkin Boy *see* Pumpkin Boy, Chief
Carpenter, Red Bird *see* Red Bird I, Chief
Carpenter, Chief Thomas Pasmere *see* Cornplanter, Chief
Carr, Capt. John 300, 363
Carr, Capt. Patrick 218
Carter, Charles 227
Carter, Col. John 119, 137–138, 143, 155–156, 158, 187
Carter, Syntha Melvina 348
Carteret, Sir George 30
Carter's Store 138
Carter's Valley 119, ***133***, 138, 156, 158, 177, 185, 210, 354
Carthage, Tennessee 243
Cartoogechaye Creek 169, *170*, 374–377, 379, ***380***
Cartwright, James 197
Cartwright, Robert 197, 204
Cartwright, William 204
Caruthers, Zeke 321
Carver, Mrs. 202
Carver, Ned 202
Carvin, Ned *see* Carver, Ned
Castalian Springs, Tennessee 203, 225, 264, 360, 362, 364
Casteel, Elizabeth 328
Casteel, Mrs. ***327***, 328
Casteel, William 328
Casteel Massacre 327–328
Castleman, Abraham 305, 321
Castleman, Hans: death of at Hay's Station (1793) 321
Castleman, Jacob 245, 269, 305
Castleman, Jacob, Jr.: death of at Hay's Station (1793) 321

Index

Castleman, Joseph: death of at Hay's Station (1793) 321
Castle's Woods Settlements 124–127, 130
Castlewood, Virginia 124
Caswell, Gov. Richard 149–150, 187, 247, 250
Caswell County, North Carolina 347
Catawba (Indians) 7–8, 17, 27, 30–31, 35, 53, 67, 92–93, 96–97, 112, 200, 206, 291, 377
Catawba, North Carolina 27
Catawba River 27, 59, 74, 168
Catawba Village 60
Catoogajoy Village 218
Catron, Phillip 202
Cavett, Alexander 322–323
Cavett, Alexander, Jr. 323
Cavett's Station *128*, *133*, 322–324, 335; see also Battle at Cavett's Station
Cavil, Jack 204; Nickajack relationship 225
Cayce, South Carolina 75
Cayuga (Indians) 11, 40, 117
Celarley, Chief 297, 308
Celtic (Celts) 23
Center Hill Lake 302
Centre, Alabama 261
Cessions: 1735 39; 1761 98; Attakullakulla's Ten-Year Lease (1775) 119, 122; see also Augusta trade conference (1763); Donelson Purchase; Treaties of Hard Labor and Fort Stanwix (1768); Treaty of Lochaber (1770); Treaty of Augusta (1773); Treaty of Saluda (1775); Treaty of Sycamore Shoals and the Path Deed (1775); Treaties of Dewitt's Corner (1777); Treaty of Holston (1777); Treaty of Dumplin Creek (1785); Chickasaw Treaty (1783); Treaty of Coyatee (1786); Blount's Treaty (1791); Treaty of Tellico (1805); Treaty of New Echota (1835)
Chalekatha 348
Chapin, John Reuben *310*
Chapman Roll 345, 347
Charitey Hagey, Chief see Hagey, Chief Charitey
Charles (slave) 125–126, 128
Charles II, King 30
Charles Town, South Carolina 24–25, 30–31, 34–35, 38–39, 42, 44–45, 47, 49, 53, 55, 60, 62–67, 70, 73–77, 79–80, 82, 84, 90–92, 96, 98, 108, 116, 140–141, 145–146, 148, 159, 173, 216; American siege of (1782) 218–219; British attack (1776) 149–150, 179, 341
Charleston, South Carolina 24, 146, 236, 284–285, 296, 328
Charleston, Tennessee 117, 343
Charley, Chief see Captain Charley of All(i)joy, Chief

Charlotte, North Carolina 206–207
Chatanuga Mountain see Lookout Mountain
Chatham, North Carolina 347
Chatooga River 8, *9–10*
Chatooga Village 64, 83, *128*, 167, 239, 314–315, 371
Chattahoochee River *8*, *10*, 167, *194*, 218, 221, 223
Chattanooga, Tennessee 135, 155–156, 174, 181, 190, 217, 253, 353–356; Audubon Acres 174; Brainerd Hills 174; Brainerd Mission 174
Chattanooga Village *194*, 264–265
Chatuga Village see Chatooga Village
Cheanoka of Kawetakac 239
Cheeseekau, Chief see Shawnee Warrior
Cheestowee Village 314
Cheh Chuh see Sequechee
Chehohee Village 167
Chelowe Village 372
Chenco see Chunk(e)y
Cheraw (Indians) 7–8
Cherokee, North Carolina 4, 336
Cherokee Bands (modern era) 5, 11, 20
Cherokee Billy 351; murder of 129
Cherokee Council of Chiefs 339
Cherokee County, Georgia 347
Cherokee County, North Carolina 347
Cherokee Lighthorse Guard 338
Cherokee Mountains 42, 46, 147
Cherokee Nation (of Oklahoma) 336, 343
Cherokee River see Tennessee River
Cherokee War (1776) 152, 155–169, *170*, 171–172
Chescoonwho of Tomotlug 239
Chesetoa of Tlacoa 239
Chesnut of Tellies 186, 269
Chestatee River see Chestatoe River
Chestatoe River *10*, 223
Chesterfield, Earl of 46
Cheucunsene, Chief see Dragging Canoe, Chief
Cheulah, Chief see Small Pox Conjuror of Settico
Chewe Village f 371
Chicamoga see Chickamauga Cherokee
Chicamogga see Chickamauga Cherokee
Chickamauga Cherokee 1–3, 15, 131, 134, 136, 155, 160–161, 165, 174, 178, 181, 184, 186, 188–193, 195–200, 203–206, 208–209, 211–221, 225–232, 234–235, 241–261, 264–265, 268–269, 271, 280–283, 287–288, 290–292, 294, 297, 299, 304–306, 308–

309, 311–313, 320, 322–323, 326, 328, 331, 333, 337, 342, 348, 353–355; Five Lower Towns of *194*, 224–225, 227, 253, 293, 305, 333, 355
Chickamauga Creek 174, 190–193, 198, 205, 223, 253, 353, 355
Chickamauga Settlement 174, 182, 190–192, *194*, 195, 198, 354
Chickamauga Town *8*, *128*, *133*, 165, 174, 193, *194*, 195, 197, 204, 209, 217, 354; destroyed (1779) 192–193, 211; destroyed (1782) 223–224
Chickasautehe of Big Savannah, Chief see Chickasaw Killer
Chickasaw (Indians) 7–8, 17, 35, 41, 96, 112, 144, 192–193, 195, 199–201, 205–206, 208, 210–211, 227, 232, 234, 238, 246, 252, 271, 281, 287, 292–293, 299, 314, 318, 335, 337, 357–358; inform settlers of Coldwater Town 246–248; Treaty of Hopewell (1786) 241
Chickasaw and Choctaw Conference (1792) 296, 299, 301, 304, 358
Chickasaw Bluffs 291
Chickasaw Killer 239, 298
Chickasaw Treaty (1783) 219–220, 228–230, 235, 251
Chicken, Col. George 35–36, 39
Chief of Settico see Small Pox Conjuror of Settico
Chilhowee Mountains 282
Chilhowee Village *128*, *133*, 143, 155, 158, 186, 257–258, 309, 314, 349, 370
Chilhowey Village see Chilhowee Village
Chilhowie, Virginia 106
Chilhowie Village see Chilhowee Village
Chimney-top Mountain see Chimney Top Mountain
Chimney Top Mountain 138, 172, 185, 237, 240
Chimney Tops Mountain 172
Chinabee from the Natchez, Chief 298
Chiotlohee: killed Daniel Murphy 54, 346
Chisholm, Jesse 282, 337
Chisholm, Capt. John D. 282, 294, 298–299, 334; death of (1818) 337
Chisholm Trail 282, 337
Chisolm, Capt. John D. see Chisholm, Capt. John D.
Chokasatahe of Tasonta see Chickasaw Killer
Chonosta of Cowe 239
Chota Council House 57, 63, 65, 70–71, 90, 122, 142, 270; war pole 74, 143

Chota Ford 144
Chota Village **8**, 11, 16, 20–21, 28, 30, 37, 43, 49, 53–55, 57–65, 67, 73, 75, 77, 91–92, 97, 102, 105–106, 116, **128**, **133**, 129, 132, 134, 136, 141, 144, 149, 155–158, 172, 175, 182, 185–186, 189–190, 192, **194**, 209–210, 214–215, 223–225, 231, 234, 238–239, 244–245, 258, 261, 267, 282, 291–292, 304, 307, 314; Council 21–22, 59, 66, 217; Creek and French visit Chota (1759) 73; Needham's description 29; Northern Indian Summit (1776) 142–144
Christian, Capt. George 265
Christian, Capt. Gilbert *see* Christian, Capt. George
Christian, Col. William 130, 181–182, 186, 189, 265; Cherokee Campaign (1776) 172–176, 180; death of 244; Long Island of Holston peace conference (1881) 214–215
Christie, Col. *see* Christian, Col. William
Chudkey John *see* John Sevier
Chulcoah, Chief 314
chungke *see* chunk(e)y
chunk(e)y 11, 19–20, 104–105
Churchill Roll 345
Chutlow, Chief *see* Jobber's Son, Chief (Kingfisher)
Cincinnati, Ohio 124
Citigo Town **194**, 244
Clans/Clansmen 11, 13–15, 18, 20–22, 36, 54, 70, 73, 78, 96, 98, 121, 129, 131, 173, 178, 339; Anigatogewi (Wild Potato) 13, 349; Anigilohi (Long Hair) 13, 73; Anikawi (Deer) 13, 73, 349; Anisahoni (Blue Holly, or Blue) 13; Anitsiskwa (Bird) 13, 349; Aniwahya (Wolf) 13, 73, 348–349; Aniwodi (Red Paint or Paint) 13, 349; vengeance or retribution 13–16, 61, 64, 70, 73, 78, 82, 84, 98–99, 115, 129, 182, 256, 263, 296, 336, 338, 341
Clark, Col. George Rogers 192, 195, 219–220
Clarke, Col. Elijah 24, 209, 218–219, 221–222; hanged Daniel Murphy (1782) 219, 351
Clarkesville, Georgia 218
Clarksville, Tennessee 201, 242, 283–284, 286–287, 312, 329, 334, 362
Clay Lick 220
Clayton, Mr. 305
Clayton, Georgia 169
Clear Sky, Chief *see* Bloody Fellow, Chief
Clements, Mssrs. 315
Clemore, Bob M. *see* McLamore, Bob
Clemson, South Carolina 42

Clemson University 164, 236
Clendening, James 264
Clendening, Mrs. 317
Clennuse Village 371
Cleopatra *see* Matachanna
Clevenhagen, Eula Ann 348
Clinch Mountain 138, 253, 284, 326
Clinch River **8**, 124–125, 127, **128**, **133**, **194**, 196–197, 245, 283, 295, 318, 326, 334, 368
Clinch River Settlements 157, 189
Clinton, Maj. Gen. Sir Henry 149–150, 179
Clogittah (male) *see* Clogoittah (male)
Clogoitah (female) 51, 348
Clogoittah (male) 44, **45**, 46
Cloud's Creek 138, 185, 197, 237, 240
Clover Bottom (near Nashborough) 200, 203, 220
Clover Bottom Mansion 203
Clynch River *see* Clinch River
Cochran, Mr. 308–309
Cocke, Col. William 156, 233, 244–245; Treat of Coyatee 244, 333
Cockrell, Moses: ambushed by Bench 315–316
Coffield, Maj. 308
Cofitachequi Village 25–26; *see also* Lady of Cofitachequi
Colbert, Chief George 293, 357–358
Colbert, Maj. James, Jr. 357–358
Colbert, Ind. Agt. James Logan 145, 227, 357
Colbert, Levi 357–358
Colbert, Chief William 357–358; sometimes confused with Chief Piomingo 358
Colbert County, Alabama 358
Colbert Family 357
Colbert's Landing 248
Cold Water Creek *see* Coldwater Creek
Cold Water Town *see* Coldwater Village
Coldwater Creek 227, 247, 293
Coldwater Village **194**, 227, 230–231, 246–247, 292–293; Expedition (1787) 248–249, 282
Collanah: 1730 trip to England 44, **45**
Colleton, Sir John 30
Colonah (general warrior) *see* Raven
Colonah, Chief *see* Raven of Chota
Columbia, South Carolina 39, 75, 377
Columbia, Tennessee 253, 269
Columbus, Christopher 25
Conasatche Village 85
Congaree River 75
Congaree Store 75–76, 84–85, 139, 141

Conisca Village 371
Conne-Corte, Chief *see* Old Hop, Chief
Contentnea Creek 33
Continental Army 24, 101, 176, 218; Southern Department 1, 141, 149, 151, 214, 218, 301, 365
Continental Congress 162, 168, 177, 233, 365; condemns massacre of Old Chiefs (1788) 259, 342
Conutory Village 93
Coody, Arthur Archibald "Archie," Jr. 197, 237, 309–311, 315
Cooper, Anthony Ashley 30
Cooper, James: killed 158
Cooper, Capt. James 294
Cooper, Joseph 39, 42
Cooper, William 42
Coosa River **8**, **10**, 37, 50, 73, **194**, 223, 240, 254, 261, 268, 297, 323, 354
Coosawatee River **10**, **194**
Coosawatee Village 268
Copper Creek 326
Corbett's Ferry 149
Core (Indians) 32
Corn Tassel, Chief *see* Old Tassel, Chief
Cornell, Alick 318
Cornplanter, Chief 348
Cornstalk, Chief 129–131, 142; delegation to Chota 142–143
Cornstalk, Locha 348
Corn-tassel *see* Old Tassel
Cornwallis, Lt. Gen. Charles Lord 1, 149–150, 193, 206, 208, 219, 342
Coste Village 34
Coteatoy, Chief 253–255, 286
Cothechney 32
Cotton, John 198
Council House 11, 19–20, 42–43, 63, 66, 70–71, 74, 77, 82, 84, 87, 90–91, 122, 129, 142–144, 155, 265, 270
Councils of Animals (legend) 16–17
Counie, Mathias 106
Cowan, John 310
Cowan, Ned 368
Cowan Brothers 325
Cowe Village *see* Cowee Village
Cowechee Branch (Creek) *see* Wayah Creek
Coweckey Creek *see* Wayah Creek
Cowee Divide 168
Cowee Mountains 9
Cowee Village **10**, 93, 147–148, 169, 239, 371
Coweechee Village 93
Coweta Village 41
Cowetan (Indians) 262
Cox, Thomas 269
Cox, Zachariah 280
Coyatee Village **128**, **133**, 226, 244,

292, 296–297, 307, 329, 355; Major Beard attacked Hanging Maw's 319–320; Conference of 291, 294–296, 298, 372; *see also* treaties of Coyatee
Coytmore, Lt. Richard 73, 75, 79, 81; killed by Oconostota 82, 99, 101
Cozby's Creek 312
Crab Orchard 309, 329
Crabtree, Isaac 125–126, 128; acquitted of killing Cherokee Billy 129
Crabtree, John 129
Crabtree, William 129
Crafts, William A. *27*
Cragfont Mansion 225, 360
Craig, David 292
Craig, Maj. 316
Craighead, Rev. Thomas B. 361
Craig's Station 251, 355
Crane 269
Craven, Gov. Charles 34–35
Craven, William Lord 30
Crawford, Capt. John 215–216, 308
Creek 7–8, 17, 21, 34–42, 50–57, 62–63, 70–73, 77, 81, 83, 109–110, 114–115, 123, 131, 144, 147, 156, 174–175, 186, 188, 193, 195–196, 198, 200, 205–206, 208, 215, 218–220, 227, 230–232, 247, 249, 251–254, 256, 261, 267–272, 279–280, 283, 286–290, 292, 294–295, 298–301, 303–305, 308–309, 311–314, 316, 318, 321–324, 329–334, 355, 357–358, Ochese 34
Creek Cession of 1773 123
Creek Treaty of 1790 272–278, 281
Cresswell, William 157–158
Crockett, David: killed by Dragging Canoe 191, 207
Crockett, Davy 156, 191, 207
Crockett, Elizabeth (Hawkins) 191
Crockett, Elizabeth (Hedge): killed by Dragging Canoe 191
Crockett, James: captured by Dragging Canoe 191
Crockett, John 191, 207
Crockett, Joseph: captured by Dragging Canoe 191
Crockett, Robert 368
Crockett Park 191
Croft, Luke 89
Crooked Creek 308, 312
Cross Creek, North Carolina 133, 149
Cross Plains, Tennessee 220
Crow, David 312
Crow Creek 292
Crow Town *194*, 224, 268, 292, 355
Crown of Tanasi 15, 43–44, 46, 48
Crow's Creek Pass: British Colonel Archibald Montgomery ambushed 86
Crutcher, William 242
Cruzat, Monsieur 357
Cuffytown Creek 117

Cullowhee, North Carolina 168
Cumberland, Duke of 46
Cumberland Gap 8, 144, 237, 240, 253, 354, 368
Cumberland Mountain(s) 237, 244, 287, 327, 329, 334, 354
Cumberland Presbyterian Church 361
Cumberland River **8**, 41, 54, 58, 134, 195–196, 201–205, 208, 211–213, 225–227, 230, 240, 242, 245–246, 248, 252–253, 256, 280, 283–284, 286–287, 294, 300, 306, 308, 312, 357–358, 361, 363–364, 367–369
Cumberland River Valley (region) 7, 35, 38, 124–125, 127, 132, 136–138, 192, 238, 252–253, 256, 266, 286, 295, 304, 307, 314, 318, 331, 359–360, 362, 364
Cumberland settlements (settlers) 189, 193, ***194***, 195, 199, 206, 208, 211, 214, 220, 223–230, 233, 235, 238, 242, 247, 252–253, 257, 263, 269, 279, 281–283, 286, 290–291, 293, 299, 301, 303–304, 308–309, 311–313, 316, 321, 324, 329, 331, 334, 337, 357–358, 361, 365
Cuming, Sir Alexander 20–21, 41, 44; death of 49; England with seven chiefs (1730) *45*, 46–49; Keowee Council House incident 42–43; Ostenaco's interpreter in England (1762) 108; *see also* Crown of Tanasi
Cuming, Alexander of Coulter 41–42
Cummings, Rev. Charles 157–158
Cuningham, Capt. Patrick *see* Cunningham, Capt. Patrick
Cuningham, Capt. William "Bloody Bill" 178, 215–216, 219
Cunne-Shote, Chief *see* Standing Turkey, Chief
Cunningham, Lt. Col. John 218–219
Cunningham, Lt. 329
Cunningham, Capt. Patrick 140–141
Cunningham, Paul 329
Cunningham, Capt. Robert 163
Cunningham, W. H. 324
Cunningham, Capt. William *see* Cuningham, Capt. William "Bloody Bill"
Cunningham brothers 161
Curtis, John 286
Cutbirth, Benjamin 124

Dale, Gen. Sam 335–336
Dan River 1, 214
Daniels, Lee 339
Darby's Town 371
The Dark Hole *see* The Black Hole
Dart River 145; *see also* Broad River (Georgia)

Dartmouth, Lord *see* Legge, William
Dartmouth, Georgia 145–146
Dashing Stream, Chief 349
Davidson, William 312
Davidson County, North Carolina 357, 361, 363, 365, 367
Davis' Station (Kentucky) 241
Davy Crockett Birthplace State Park 156
De Brahm, William 63
de Carondelet, Gov. Francisco Luis Héctor 297
Decatur, Alabama 293
Declaration of Independence 168
Defeated Creek 243, 249, 333
DeKalb County, Tennessee 368
de Kerkerec, Chevalier *see* Belcourt, Gov. Louis
de Lantagnac, Louis 73–74
de Las Casas, Marquis 32
Delaware (Indians) 7–8, 57, 116, 118, 124–125, 128, 130–131, 135, 202, 206, 340, 371; Delaware chief questions Christopher Gist (1749) 340; northern delegation to Chota 142; White Owl's son (Little Owl) north to ally with the Delaware (1791) 287
Dells, William 377
Dells' Diary 377
Demere, Capt. Paul 70, 72–75, 81, 84–85; death of; relieved his brother at Fort Loudoun (1757) 67; surrendered Fort Loudoun to the Cherokee (1760) 87–88; tortured and killed 88–89
Demere, Capt. Raymond 21, 61–67
Demonbreun, Timothy 363–364, 369
Denmark 23
Denton, Jonathan 248, 270
De Peyster, Capt. Abraham 208
De Raque, Joseph 304
Derezeoux, Mr. 274
Desha, Benjamin 281
Desha, Robert 281
Desha, Robert, Sr. 281
Desha Creek 281, 283
De Soto, Hernando, or Fernando 15, 25, 27, 34; death of (1542) 26, ***27***; Lady of Cofitachequi kidnapped 26
Devil's Fork Pass 267
Dew, Robert 180, 184, 351
Dewees Corner *see* DeWitt's Corner, South Carolina
Dewes Corner *see* DeWitt's Corner, South Carolina
Dewit's Corner *see* DeWitt's Corner, South Carolina
Dewitt's Corner, South Carolina *see* DeWitt's Corner, South Carolina
DeWitt's Corner, South Carolina **9**, 160, 162, 179–188, 238

Dickinson, James 283
Dickson's Lick 246
Dinwiddie, Lt. Gov. Robert 56–58, 60–61, 65–66, 68–69, 71–72
Discovering Country *see* Doctrine of Discovery
The Disturber *see* Teesteke
Dixon Springs 246
Doctrine of Discovery 110
Doherty, Col. George *see* Dougherty, Col. George
Donahoe, William 264
Donelson, Col. John 119, 200–204, 228, 229, 253, 361; to Cumberland 195–199; to Kentucky 220; death of 240–242, 244
Donelson, Capt. John, Jr. 197, 199, 204, 241, 317
Donelson Purchase 119
Donelson's Station 203
Double Springs 172
Double-head (not the notorious Doublehead) 314
Doublehead, Chief (a gladiator for the Cherokee) 1, 51–52, 79, 82, 116, 129, 134, 136–137, 143, 149, 156, 161, 178, 182, 184, 187–190, 193, 195, 206, 208, 215, 217, 224–227, 230, 233–234, 241, 247, 258, 261–262, 282–284, 292–293, 301, 304, 307, 315, 321–322, 325, 328–333, 337–339, **346**, 347–348, 358–359; assassination of 323, 335–336, 339; Battle of the Bluff attack (1781) 211–213; Campbell's and Cavett's Stations incidents (1793) 322–323; Coldwater Town destroyed 247–248; Coldwater Town established (circa 1770) 135, 174, 227; Coyatee attack (1793) 319–320; Donelson's flotilla attacked at Muscle Shoals (1780) 199; Dripping Spring, cannibalized slain enemies (1793) 313, 319–320; ended hostilities (1795) 334; Mark Robertson slain (1787) 247; Sycamore Shoals-opposed (1775) 134; Thomas Sharp(e) Spencer slain 324; Valentine Sevier's sons killed 286–287; vengeance declared for Chief Old Abram's murder 263–264
Doublehead's Town **194**, 293
Dougherty, Cornelius 31, 56
Dougherty, Col. George 264–265
Doughty, Maj. John 279
Douglass, Col. Edward 300, 360–361
Douglass, Elmore 227
Douglass Chapel 227
Dover, England 45
Dover, Tennessee 312
Downs, Maj. Jonathan 162, 166
Dragging Canoe, Chief (a gladiator for the Cherokee) 52, 116, 129, 134, **136**, 138, 141–144, 149, 155, 158–159, 161, 164, 172–173, 175–176, 178–182, 186–191, 193, 195–196, 205, 207–211, 215, 217, 223, 225–226, 230–234, 239, 241, 244, 246, 249, 258, 261–262, 265–266, 286–288, 290, 292, 294, 298–299, 302, 337, 340, 342, 349, 353–355, 358; death of 291; orations at Sycamore Shoals 135, 137; relocated to Chickamauga Creek 174; relocates to the Five Lower Towns 224; severely wounded at Island Flats 156–157; tribute by Black Fox 298; tribute by E. Raymond Evans 291
Drake, Benjamin 248
Drake, John 125, 324, 370
Drake, Joseph 368
Drake, Samuel 125–126, 371
Drake, Samuel Gardner 99
Drake's Creek 232, 252, 325, 361
Draper, Lyman C. 155, 161, 378
Draper's Meadow 68
Drayton, John 373, 375–376, 378–380
Drayton, William Henry 139–140, 152, 160–164, 167–168, 373
Dreadful Water *see* Ammouskossittee, Chief
Dripping Spring **194**, 313, 315
Drowning Bear, Chief *see* Yonaguska, Chief
Drumgole, Comm. 266
The Drunkard, Chief 314
Dry Fork Creek 242, 246
Duck River **194**, 203, 229–230, 239, 247–248, 250, 253, 269, 272, 321, 330, 334–335, 363
Duck River Ridge 230, 272
Due, Robert *see* Dew, Robert
Due West, South Carolina 162
Due's Corner *see* DeWitt's Corner, South Carolina
Duffy, John 24
Duke of Albemarle *see* Monck, George
Dumplin Creek 234, 241, 366
Dumplin Settlement(s) 241, 244, 267
Dungannon, Virginia 125
Dunham (two brothers) 200
Dunham, Daniel 212, 228, 266
Dunham, John 212, 266
Dunham, Joseph 228
Dunham, Miss 212
Dunham, Mrs. 212
Dunham, William 228
Dunham's Station 266
Dunkleberry, Abraham 69
Dunmore, 4th Earl of *see* Murray, Gov. John
Dunmore's War 129, 131, 371
Durant, Benjamin 279
Durant, Sophia 279
Durat, Joe 306
Dutch Creek 119
Dutch 32, 202

Eagle Tail Dance 44, 291
Earl of Clarendon *see* Hyde, Edward
Earl of Shaftesbury *see* Cooper, Anthony Ashley
Eastern Band of Cherokee Indians 4, 12, 336, 343, 345; incorporated 344
Eastern Dialect 12, 148
Eaton, Amos 196
Eaton's Station (Kingsport) **128**, **133**, 156–157, 182
Eaton's Station (Nashville) **194**, 201–202, 205, 211, 213, 220, 231–232, 248
Eccles, Joel 300
Echoe Pass 93
Echoe Village **10**, 86, 93, 147, 169, **170**, 371, 374, 376–377
Echoee Village *see* Echoe Village
Echota Village *see* Chota Village
Ecochee Village 171
Edisto River 39, 55
Edmonson, Robert 252
Edwards, John 280
Eighteen Mile Creek **8–9**, 164
Elbert, Gov. Samuel 131
Elbert County, Georgia 346
Elberta, Georgia 347
Elder, Will 314
The Elder *see* Ahmahtoya, Chief
Elizabethton, Tennessee 7, 132, 156–157
Elk River **194**, 230, 250, 318, 330
Elk Warrio(u)r 126–127
Eller's Gap 128
Elliot(t), John 56, 64–67, 77, 83
Ellis, William 203
Emory, Sussanah 91
Emperor Amadohiyi *see* Amadohiyi, Chief
Emperor Moytoy *see* Amadohiyi, Chief
The Englishman (a warrior) 269
Enola, Chief *see* Black Fox, Chief
Enville, Oklahoma 337
Epreuvre 107
Eskaqua, Chief *see* Bloody Fellow, Chief
Eskridge, John 248
Eskridge, Moses 248
Espie, George 232–233
Estanaula Village 323; 1792 Council Of 295, 298, 299, 303
Estatoe Old Fields 93
Estatoe Village **9**, 73–74, 77, 83, 85–86, 90, 107, 113–114, 167, 372
Estatowe Village *see* Estatoe Village
Estotowe Village *see* Estatoe Village
Etchoe Village *see* Echoe Village
Etowah River 8, **10**, 57, **194**, 223, 323
Etowah Village **194**, 323
Euro-Americans 4–5, 338
Europe / Europeans 2, 4–5, 7, 12–

Index

13, 16, 21, 23–26, 28, 30, 32, 36–37, 39–41, 52, 67, 81, 95, 98, 105, 108, 110, 113, 115, 153, 229, 280, 288, 338, 340
Eustash Village 167
Euth-li-ke 337
Evans, Capt. 323
Evans, E. Raymond 291, 353, 356
Evans, Maj. Nathaniel 245
Evans, Robert 250, 269
Everett, John 281
Ewing, Andrew 227
Experiment 151

Fain, Capt. John 264
Fair Forest Creek 206
Fairfield, South Carolina 140
Fairies, Arthur: diary 373, 375–378
Falling, William *see* Fawling, William
Falls of the Ohio River 312, 370
Fannon Spring 125
Farar, Lt. 165
Farquier County, Virginia 361
Farr, Samuel 280
Farragut, Tennessee 322
Farris, Arthur *see* Fairies, Arthur
Farris, Elisha 284
Farris, Mrs. 284
Farris, Nancy 284
Fauquier, Lt. Gov. Francis 69, 105, 107, 115, 117
Fawling, William 129, 144, 155
Fayetteville, North Carolina 133, 149, 266
Fayne, Capt. William 244
Federal Census (1850) 347
Federal Census (1860) 347
Fee, Thomas 131
Ferguson, Maj. Patrick 206–208, 226, 342
Ferguson's Hill 206
Ferguson's Ridge *see* Ferguson's Hill
Ferris, Elisha *see* Farris, Elisha
Festival(s) 19, 104; First New Moon 18, 19; Great (2nd) New Moon 18, 129; New Green Corn 18; Mature Green Corn 18, 302, 304; Propitiation and Cementation (Friends Made) 18–19; Winter 19
Fever bush 104
Fields, George 306
Filson Historical Society 377
Fincastle County, Virginia 126, 370
Fincastle Rangers 172
Findleston, George 306
Finnelson, Richard 291, 297, 304–305, 318, 323
(first) beloved man 2, 15, 20–21, 39, 50, 53, 55, 77, 79, 217, 298, 348; *see also* principle chief
1st Regiment of Foot 86
Fivekiller 159, 349
Fletchall, Col. Thomas 140

Fletcher, Thomas: killed 283
Fletcher, Sheriff Thomas 227; killed 250
Flint Creek 267–268
Flint River 262, 372
Flood, John 253
Florence, Alabama 174, 293
Florida 25–26, 30, 52, 109, 139, 141–142, 145, 155, 175, 187, 231, 252, 286, 314; East 110; Spanish West 110, 253, 297
Fogg High School 202
Fool Charles, Chief 297
Fool Charley *see* Captain Charley
Fool Warrior, (Creek) Chief 243, 258
Forbes, Brig. Gen. John 67–68, 70–71
Ford, Col. James 247, 329
Foreman, Nancy 91
Forked-Horn Buck of Citigo 315
Forsythe County, Georgia 338
Fort Attakullakulla (Virginia) 106, 117
Fort Augusta (Augusta, Georgia) 51, *113*
Fort Bluff (Tennessee) *see* The Bluff (Nashborough)
Fort Boone (South Carolina) 114
Fort Caswell (Tennessee) 155, 157–158
Fort Charlotte (Ohio) *see* Camp Charlotte
Fort Charlotte (South Carolina) **8–9**, 145, 153, 261
Fort Chiswell (Virginia) 144
Fort Congaree (South Carolina) 75
Fort Cumberland (Maryland) 58
Fort Defiance (Virginia) 57
Fort de l'Assomption (Assomption) (Tennessee) 67
Fort Detroit (Michigan) 266
Fort Dunmore *see* Fort Duquesne
Fort Duquesne (Pennsylvania) 57, 66–68, 130, 360
Fort Eaton (Tennessee) *see* Eaton's Station
Fort Frederica (Georgia) 51
Fort Frontenac (Ontario) 68
Fort Galphin (South Carolina) 26, 145
Fort Hancock (Tuscarora Indian fort in Carolina Colony) 33
Fort Henry (Virginia) 28–30
Fort Independence (Georgia) 154
Fort Independence (South Carolina) **8–9**, 154–155
Fort James (Georgia) 145–146
Fort James Dartmouth (Georgia) *see* Fort James (Georgia)
Fort Jefferson (Kentucky) 219–220; Siege of 192, 357
Fort Kaskaskia (Illinois) 192
Fort Lee (Tennessee) **128**, 156
Fort Lewis (Virginia) 106

Fort Lindley (South Carolina) *see* Lindley's Fort
Fort Loudoun (Tennessee) **8**, 21, 54, 63–64, 67, 72–74, 81, 91–92, 98, **128**, **133**, **194**, 333; Massacre of (1760) 88–90, 101; Siege of (1760) 83–87, 101, 106
Fort Mayo (Virginia) 68
Fort Moore (Old) (South Carolina) *see* Fort Galphin
Fort Narhantes (Tuscarora Indian fort in Carolina Colony) 32
Fort Nashborough (Tennessee) *see* The Bluff
Fort Necessity (Pennsylvania) 57
Fort Neoheroka (Tuscarora Indian fort in North Carolina) 33
Fort Ninety Six (Goudey's, South Carolina) 64, 76, 83, 87, 92, 98; *see also* Goudey's Trading Post; Ninety Six Trading Post
Fort Ninety Six (second, South Carolina) 140
Fort Patrick Henry (Tennessee) **128**, 172, 175–176, 184, 196
Fort Payne, Alabama 293, 338
Fort Pitt *see* Fort Duquesne
Fort Prince George (South Carolina) **8–9**, 59, 61–62, 74–77, 84–86, 88–89, 92–93, 96; Cherokee headmen imprisoned 79; Cherokee Headmen massacred 82–83, 90, 101; Cherokee women raped by garrison officers 72; Oconostota killed Lieutenant Coytmore 82, 99; Siege of 81; William Bartram visited 146–147
Fort Robinson (Tennessee) 87, 91, 95, 101, 105–106; same site as Fort Patrick Henry 172
Fort Rutledge (South Carolina) **8–9**, 167–169, 171, 374
Fort Sackville (Indiana) *see* Fort Vincennes (Indiana)
Fort San Juan (North Carolina) 27
Fort Stanwix (New York): treaty (1768) 117–118, 120–121
Fort Toulouse (Alabama) 37, 50–51, 63–64, 67, 72–73, 75, 91
Fort Vincennes (Indiana) 191–192
Fort Watauga *see* Fort Caswell
Fort Wayne, Indiana 287
Foster, John 269
Foster, Mrs. 311
Foster, Lt. Thomas 82
fountain of youth 25
Fox 45
The Fox *see* Small Pox Conjuror of Settico
Fox, Col. Joseph 51
Francis, Capt. James 83
Franklin, James 227
Franklin, Gov. Sir William 117
Franklin, North Carolina 12, 26, 43, 86–87, 93, 133, 168–169, **170**, 374, 376, 379, **380**

Franklin, State of 233–234, 245, 250–251, 366
Franklinite(s) 233–234, 240–241, 244–245, 251, 266
Frazier, Daniel 196
Frazier, James 308
Frazier, John 243
Frederica, Georgia 51
Freeland, George 193, 227
Freeland's Station *194*, 200–202, 205, 210–211, 213–214, 220, 228
French 2, 4, 11, 21, 23, 25, 36–38, 40, 42–43, 50–60, 62–73, 75, 77–79, 81, 83, 85–86, 91, 96, 98, 101–102, 108–109, 123, 177–178, 186, 218, 227, 231–232, 242, 246–248, 252, 271, 304, 312, 340, 363, 367–369
French and Indian War 1, 4, 25, 56, 87, 111, 114, 124, 153, 173, 186–187, 319, 341, 351
French Broad River *8*, 45, *128*, *133*, 172–173, 197, 209, 227, 231, 234, 238–241, 251, 259, 277, 283, 342
French John 21, 62–63, 70
French Lick *8*, 191, 193, 195–198, 228, 253, 358, 363, 368–369
Friley, Col. Caleb 315
Frog Town *10*, *194*, 223, 239
Frozen Head State Natural Area, Tennessee 138

Gadsden, Alabama 261
Gage, Maj. Gen. Thomas 139
Galahan, Patrick 147–148
Gallaher, James 316
Gallatin, Tennessee 203, 225, 227, 242, 245, 250, 252, 264, 280, 282–283, 317, 329, 359, 362
Galphin, George 145, 180, 273–274
Galphin's Fort *see* Fort Galphin
Gamble's Station 312
Gap Creek 158
Garland 45
Gaskins, Mr. 312
Gass, Capt. David 124–125, 127
Gatlinburg, Tennessee 127
Gee, Mr. 305
General Eskaqua, Chief *see* Bloody Fellow, Chief
Gentry, John 253
Gentry, Randal 250
Gentry, William 253
George II, King 42, 44–45, 49, 54–55, 67, 187
George III, King 3, 106, 110–111, 115, 187, 286; Proclamation (1763) 3, 111–112, 114–115, 117, 121–122, 130, 138, 177–178, 215, 226, 341
Georgetown, South Carolina 39
Georgia Gazette 110
Germanic Tribes 4, 23
Germans 32, 50, 63, 68–69, 141
GhigGooie *see* Gigui
Ghighau *see* Ward, Nancy

ghighau (general term) 21, 57
Ghi-Go-Ne-Li *see* Wurteh of the Bird Clan
Gibbs, Gov. Robert 32–33
Gibson, Capt. James 265
Gibson, John 283
Gibson, Jordan 246, 251
Gigui 91
Gilbert Town, North Carolina *8*, 206, 226
Gill, Peter 212
Gillespie, Col. George "Limestone" 279, 308–309
Gillespie, Jane *see* Brown, Mrs. James
Gillespie's Station *128*, *133*, 266–268
Gillespy's Fort *see* Gillespie's Station
Gillum, James 318–319
Gillum, Thomas 318–319
Girl of Tuskega *see* Annakehujah
Gist, Christopher 340
Gist, George *see* Sequoyah
Gist, Nathan *see* Gist, Nathaniel
Gist, Col. Nathaniel 56, 65, 69, 157, 172–173, 175–176, 184, 349, 366
Gist, Nathanael *see* Gist, Nathaniel
Gist, Tobacco Will 349
Gi-Yo-Sti-Ko-Yo-He *see* Wurteh of the Bird Clan
Glasgow, Kentucky 362
Glass, Chief 224, 265–267, 280, 291, 293, 298, 304–305, 308–309, 311, 314, 332
Glass, Roger 228
Glen, Gov. James 53–56, 59–62, 65, 80, 110
Glen, John 281
Goin, Mr. 201
Goldsmith, Oliver 108, 352
Goodlettsville, Tennessee 201, 231, 367
Goodpasture, Albert V. 44, 50, 87, 90, 97, 106, 251–252, 290, 334, 351, 359, 361, 372
Goodspeed's History of Tennessee 119
Goose Creek Ford 246
Gordon, Capt. John 318, 321
Gordon, Thomas 368–369
Gordon's Ferry 203
gorget 266
Goud(e)y, Robert 53, 64, 76, 83
Goudey's Trading Post 76; *see also* Fort Ninety Six; Ninety Six Trading Post
Gower, Capt. Abel 198, 204
Gower, Abel, Jr. 204
Gower, Mr. 312
Gower, Nancy 198
Gower, Russell 198
Graham, Col. Joseph 140
Grant, Esquire 243
Grant, Lt. Col. James 71, 85, 87, 96–97; expedition (1761) 92–93, *94*, 95, 101, 105, 163, 169, *170*, 186, 341, 374–375, 377, 380
Grant, Lt. 167
Grant, Ludovic 43, 54
Grasshopper Cannons 150, 267, 387 note 50
Grassy Valley 315
Graves, Will 373, 375, 378–379
Gray, Deliverance 325
Greasy Cove 267
Great Britain 32, 46–47, 109, 139, 236, 239, 252–253, 271, 275
Great Canaway River 118, 137; *see also* Kanawha River
Great Cane Brake(s) 140–141
Great Eagle of Tanasi *see* Willenawah, Chief
Great Eagle of Tanassee *see* Willenawah, Chief
Great Ecoche Village 171
Great Estatowe Village 372
Great Island *see* Long Island of Holston
Great Limestone Creek 185
Great Mortar, Chief 70, 73–74, 81, 83–84, 115, 118
Great Rocky Creek 154
Great Smokies *see* Great Smoky Mountains
Great Smoky Mountains 8, 27, 181
Great Smoky Mountains National Park 172
Great Taraqua Village 38
Great Tellico 67, *128*, *133*
Great Warrior *see* Oconostota, Chief
Green Corn Dance 302
Greenbrier Company 118
Greene, Adam 316
Greene, Maj. Gen. Nathanael 1, 214–215, 218–219
Greene County, North Carolina 266
Greeneville, Tennessee 156, 283
Greenfield, Tennessee 227, 263, 269, 281, 328
Greenfield Station 251, 317, 321
Greenville, South Carolina 59, 163
Greenwood, South Carolina 117
Griffin, Cyrus 275
Griffin, John 253
The Gritzs *see* Newotah of Chicamaga
Ground Hog Sausage *see* Oconostota, Chief
Ground Squirrel *see* Skyuka, Chief
Guasili Village 26, 36
Guatari Village 27
Guaxule Village *see* Guasili Village
Guffey (Peyton), Ann 359
Guhnagadoga, Chief *see* Old Hop, Chief
Guilford Courthouse, North Carolina 279

Index

Guinea-men 24, 52
Guion Miller Roll 345
Gulf of Mexico 8
Gulustiyu 347–348
Gun Rod, Chief *see* Untoola of Citigo, Chief
Gunagadoga, Chief *see* Standing Turkey, Chief
Gundigaduhunyi, Chief *see* Little Turkey, Chief
Gunshot *see* Shawnee Warrior, Chief
Guntersville, Alabama 34, 293

Hadrian, Emperor 23
Hadrian's Wall 23, 121
Hagerstown, Maryland 359
Hagey, Chief Charitey 36
Haggard, Eld. 224
Haggard, James 270
Haggard, John 311
Hale's Bar Dam 224
half-faced camp 200, 203
Hall, James: slain 246
Hall, Rev. James 168
Hall, John 249
Hall, Mrs. 236, 249
Hall, Prudence 249
Hall, Richard: slain 249
Hall, Capt. William *see* Hall, Gov. William, Jr.
Hall, Gen. William *see* Hall, Gov. William, Jr.
Hall, Maj. William 236, 242, 246; death of 249–251
Hall, Gov. William, Jr. 236, 246, 249, 317, 321
Hamilton, George 264
Hamilton, Gov. Henry 191–192, 354, 367
Hamilton, Capt. John W. 359–360
Hamilton, John W., Jr. 360
Hamilton (Peyton), Margaret 359–360
Hammond, Eli 321
Hammond, Capt. John 163
Hammond, Col. LeRoy 164–165, 180, 218
Hammond, Lt. Col. Samuel 377–379
Hampton, Col. Andrew 207
Hampton, Anthony 160
Hampton, Edward 160, 169
Hampton, Henry 160
Hampton, John 160
Hampton, Mrs. 160
Hampton, Preston 160
Hampton, Wade 160
Hancock, Chief 32–33
Handl(e)y, Capt. Samuel 304, 309–311
Hanging Man *see* Hanging Maw, Chief
Hanging Maw, Chief 116, 134, 233–234, 239, 241, 243, 249, 267, 269, 281–282, 286, 292, 296, 298–299, 310–311, 313–314, 316, 318, 323, 328–329, 331–333, 340, 349; Capt. Beard attacked chiefs at Coyatee (1793) 319; death of 338; letter to Andrew Pickens regarding massacre of headmen (1788) 258; letter to President Washington (1793) 319–320; letter to Sec. Smith regarding attack at Coyatee (1793) 320–321; Treaty of Coyatee 244
Hankins, John 311
Hanley, James 193
Hannon, Edwin 160
Hannon, John 160
Hannon, Mr. 160
Hannon, William 161
Hannon, Winnie 161
Hannon Family Massacre 160
Harald III, King 23–24
Hard Labor Creek 117
Harden, Capt. John 265
Hardrada, Harald *see* Harald III, King
Harlan, Ellis 172–173, 175, 209
Harney, James 312
Harold II Godwinsson, King 24
Harpeth River 203, 250
Harpool, John 278, 300
Harpool, Martin 278
Harrison, Gov. Benjamin V 217, 220, 228
Harrison, Capt. Michael 322
Harrison, Mr. 246
Harrocks, Rev. James *see* Horrocks, Rev. James
Harrocks, Mr. 352
Harrod, Mr. 368
Harrod's Station 195
Harrodsburg, Kentucky 195
Hart, Nathaniel 124, 132–133
Hartsville, Tennessee 203, 243
Hasecoll *see* Indian John
Havana, Cuba 25, 109, 187
Hawkins, Sen. Benjamin 236, 238, 278
Hawkins, Elizabeth *see* Crockett, Elizabeth
Hawkins County, Tennessee 138
Hay, Capt. David 247–248, 365
Hay, Joseph 200
Hay(s), Lt. Col. Robert 247
Hays, James 317
Hays, Capt. Sam 316
Hays' Station 321
Haysborough, Tennessee 361
Haywood, Judge John 109, 245, 354
Head Turkey, Chief *see* Mad Turkey, Chief
Heany, Frank 278
Heatonburg, Tennessee 228
Heaton's Station *see* Eaton's Station
Heckewelder, John 241
Hedge, Elizabeth *see* Crockett, Elizabeth
Helen, Georgia 218
Helen, John 325
Helin, John 269
Henderson, Richard 124, 132–138, 190, 195, 238, 354
Henderson, Col. Richard 200
Henderson, Samuel 367
Henderson, Maj. William 168
Henderson & Company 367
Henderson Roll 345–347
Hendersonville, Tennessee 325, 361
Hendrix, Joseph 210
Henley's Creek 140
Henry, Maj. Hugh 197, 234
Henry, Gov. Patrick 143, 172–173, 175–176, 180, 187, 189, 192
Henry, Samuel 316
Henry's Station **128**, **133**, 234, 311, 313–314
Herd, Charles 306
Hermitage Estate 203
Hessian Jäger(s) 67, 141
Hester Roll 345
Hickerson, John 278
Hickerson, Mr. 249
Hickman, Edmund 235
Hickman's Station 312
Hickory, North Carolina 60
Hicks, Chief Charles 338
Hicks, Mr. 281
Hicks, Nancy (daughter of Chief Broom) 338
High Rock *see* Chimney Top Mountain
Highlands, North Carolina 26
Hight, Col. 163
Hight, Mrs. 163; death of 167
Hightowa Village *see* Hightower Village
Hightower Village 239, 298
Highwassay Village *see* Hiwassee Village
Highwassee River *see* Hiwassee River
Highwassee Village *see* Hiwassee Village
Hillsborough, North Carolina 1
Hinds, Joseph 257
Hiskyteehee *see* Fivekiller
Hitchcock, Daniel 329
Hiwassee Garrison **128**, **133**, 335–336
Hiwassee River **8**, **10**, 11–12, **128**, **133**, 171, **194**, 209, 211, 223, 257, 264, 335, 354
Hiwassee Valley 171
Hiwassee Village **10**, 44, 96, 107, 171, 186, 209, 239, 270, 298, 308, 314, 329, 349, 374
Hoboi-Hili-Miko, Chief *see* McGillivray, Chief
Hocking River 131
Hogan, Edward 247
Hogan, Humphrey 368–369
Hogohege River 118; *see also* Tennessee River

Hogskin Creek 162
Holliday, John 362, 364
Hollingsworth's Mill 140–141
Holstein River *see* Holston River
Holston River **8**, 54, 65, 87, 91–92, 95, 98, 101–102, 105–106, 117–119, 121, ***128***, ***133***, 138, 147, 156–158, 161, 172, 175–176, 179, 181–183, 185–186, 189, 192, ***194***, 197, 206, 208, 211, 214, 225–226, 228, 234, 237–240, 244, 253, 257, 266–267, 277, 283, 294–295, 298, 316, 326, 339, 342, 368, 370; Middle Fork 106; North Fork **8**, ***128***, ***133***, 172, 196, 315, 326; South Fork **8**, 119, ***128***, ***133***, 137, 172, 207
Holston Settlement(s) 121, 130, 132, 136, 138, 155, 172, 177, 189, 192–193, 206–208, 211, 226, 236, 238, 240, 259, 277, 294, 311, 315–316, 328, 339, 342, 371
Homes, Mr. D. 147
Honored War-Woman (or Women) *see* Ghighau
Hood, David 210–211
Hood, Robin (legend) 5
Hood, Robin (real) 306
Hood, William 214
Horrocks, Rev. James 106
Horry, Col. Daniel 180
Horry, Col. Peter 92
Horse Creek 172
Horse Shoe Town 218–219
Horseshoe Bend of the Caney Fork River 301–302, 307
Horton, Joshua 367
Hoskins, Josiah: varied accounts of his death 220, 232
Hot Springs, Arkansas 337
Houston, Maj. James 257
Houston, Sam 351
Houston's Station 256–258, 267, 281
Hovalta, Chief 314
Howdyshall, Henry 280
Howe, Maj. Gen. Sir William 151
Hubbard, Maj. James 256–259, 280, 366
Hubbert, Maj. James *see* Hubbard, Maj. James
Hudson's Bay Company 110
Huger, Lt. Isaac 92
Hughes, Mr. 153–154
Hull Lake 243
Humphreys, David 275–276
Hunter, Capt. 264, 269
Hunter, Col. Harry 290
Hunter, Mr. 44
Hunter, Phillip 321
Hunter Family Massacre 321
Hunter's Ford of the Clinch River 125
Hunter's Valley 125
Huron (Indians) 57, 130
Hyde, Gov. Edward 30, 32–33
Hydon, Samuel 106

ilex verticillata 104
ilex vomitoria 104
Incalatanga, Chief *see* Doublehead, Chief
Indian John 29
Indian Territory, Oklahoma 293, 337, 339
Iroquois Confederacy 17, 40
Irving, Washington 340
(Isaac) Johnson's Station 296, 318
Ish, John 329
Ish's Station ***128***, ***133***, 321–323
Ishtehotopa, Chief: death of 334
Iskaqua, Chief *see* Bloody Fellow, Chief
Island Creek 134
Island Flats 156–157, 353
Itsati Village *see* Chota Village
Ivanhoe, North Carolina 149
Iyahuwagiatsutsa *see* Pumpkin Boy, Chief

Jack, Jeremiah 226
Jack, Col. Samuel 167
Jackson, Pres. Andrew 203, 272, 353, 360–361
Jackson County, Tennessee 368
Jacob the Conjurer 38, 43
James, Robert 252
James River: falls of 28
Jamestown Colony 27–28, 32
Jaora Village 27
Jarrett Creek 57, 171
Jarrett Creek Road 57, 171
Jarvis, Mr. 317
Jefferson, Pres. Thomas 32, 220
Jemmy (slave) 55
Jenkins, Jacob 324
Jennings, Edmund 125
Jennings, Jonathan 198, 202
Jennings, Mrs. 198
Jessamine County, Kentucky 124
Jim (servant, cook) 200
Jobber's Son, Chief (Kingfisher) 269, 284, 295, 298–299, 323
Jocassee Village 167
Jocelyn, Benjamin 270
Joco Village 372
John of Little Tallico 239
Johns family: massacre of 201
Johnson, Daniel 229
Johnson, Isaac 220
Johnson, John 251
Johnson, Mr. 232
Johnson, Supt. Sir William 97, 116–118
Johnson's Station *see* (Isaac) Johnson's Station
Johnston, Sen. Samuel 278
Johnston, William 203
Johnston City, Tennessee 156
Jones, Molly 300
Jones, Mrs. 201
Jones, Robert 317
Jonesborough, Tennessee **8**, ***128***, 138, 207, 233
Jore(e) Mountain(s) 148, 371

Jore(e) Village 148, 371, 372
Joselin, Benjamin *see* Jocelyn, Benjamin
Joslin's Station 321
journey cake 163
Judd's Creek 191
Judd's Friend, Chief *see* Ostenaco, Chief
Judge Friend, Chief *see* Ostenaco, Chief
Justice, Chief Richard 280, 294, 298, 311, 314
Jutes 23

Kahnyatah(h)ee, Chief *see* Old Tassel, Chief
Kanagatoga, Chief *see* Old Hop, Chief
Kanagatuckco, Chief *see* Standing Turkey, Chief
Kanawha River 7, 106, 117–118, 130, 137, 368–370; *see also* Great Canaway River
Kane's Gap 125
Kanuga Village 93; *see also* Canucca Village
Kaskaskia, Illinois 192, 195, 248
Kataquilla 186
Kaylor, Virginia 128
Keeakwee Village *see* Keowee Village
Keefe, Thomas 300
Keetoowah *see* Kituhwa
Kelley, Elijah Richard M. 345, 348
Kelley, Eula Ann *see* Clevenhagen, Eula Ann
Kelley, James William Jefferson 348
Kelley, Lloyd Dorwin 348
Kell(e)y, Margaret *see* Murphy, Margaret
Kelley, Shirley Maxine 348
Kelly, Col. 313, 323
Kelly, James 64
Kelly, James C. 358
Kelly, John 83
Kelly, William R. 345, 348
Kemp Family: massacre of 161
Kennedy, Abraham 305
Kennedy, Betsy 201
Kennedy, Col. Daniel 264–265
Kennedy, George 213
Kennedy, John (captured at Sulfur Spring Branch) 202
Kennedy, John (killed at Bluff Fort) 212
Kennedy, Mr. 201
Kennedy, Robin 306
Kennedy, William 306
Kenoteta of Hiwassee *see* Rising Fawn, Chief
Kent, Capt. 51
Kentucky 7, 16, 54, 118, 124–125, 128, 130–132, 134, 136, 138, 144, 192, 200, 205, 210–211, 219–221, 227–229, 241–242, 269, 283, 305, 313, 326, 329, 333, 354, 358, 361,

367–369, 371; Barrens of 362, 364; *see also* individual community names
Kentucky River 54
Kentucky Road (Path) 240, 256, 266, 307, 324
Keowe River *see* Keowee River
Keowe Village *see* Keowee Village
Keowee River **8**, 12, 146, 164, 238, 372
Keowee Village **8–9**, 42–44, 53, 59–61, 65, 73, 76–78, 81–83, 85, 87, 97–99, 101, 114, 140, 146–147, 167, 236, 372
Kesenger, John 213
Ketagusta, Chief *see* Kittagusta, Chief
Keukuck of Talcoa 239
Keywood, Mr. 200
Keywood Settlement, Tennessee 119
Kiachatalee of Nickajack, Chief 254–256; death of 306
Kialiages Village 289
Kiatchiskie of Hightower, Chief 298
Kilgore's Station 220
Killconnokea *see* Killianca
Killeannakea *see* Killianca
Killianca 78
Killugiskee 269
King, James 334
King, Mrs. Ann 334
King, Maj. Robert 319, 329
King, Maj. Tom 264
King Charles II *see* Charles II, King
King Fisher, Catherine *see* King Fisher, Kati
King Fisher, Kati 71
King Fisher of the Deer Clan, Chief (Nancy Ward's first husband) 57, 104, 349
King George II *see* George II, King
King George III *see* George III, King
King Harald III *see* Harald III, King
King Harold II Godwinsson *see* Harold II Godwinsson, King
King Tom Blount *see* Blunt, Chief Tom
King William I *see* William the Conqueror
Kingfisher *see* Jobber's Son, Chief
Kings Mountain 3, 207–209, 233
Kingsport, Tennessee 91, 144, 156–157, 172, 201, 240
Kingston, Tennessee 197, 284
Kinloch, Mr. 44
Kirk, John 257
Kirk, John, Jr. 257–258, 267; slaughtered peaceful Cherokee chiefs 258–259; wrote Young Tassel 263
Kirk, Mrs. 257

Kirk Family Massacre *see* Nine Mile Creek Massacre
Kirkendall, Benjamin 283
Kirkland, Moses 139–140
Kirkpatrick, Maj. 269
Kittagiska, Chief *see* Kittagusta, Chief (other than Prince Skalilosken)
Kittagista, Chief *see* Kittagusta, Chief (other than Prince Skalilosken)
Kittagusta, Chief *see* Skalilosken, Prince
Kittagusta, Chief (other than Prince Skalilosken) 239, 284, 314, 319
Kituhwa (ancient village) 4, 12
Kituhwa Dialect 12
Kituhwa Indian Mound 12
Kituhwa (middle) villages 8
Knights of the Garter 46
Knox, Sec. Henry 256, 259, 275–279, 285, 299, 301, 309, 319, 321, 328, 331
Knox, James 368–369
Knoxville, Tennessee 195, 197, 244, 257, 265, 267, 270–271, 275, 282–284, 291, 293, 296, 300, 304–305, 311–315, 321, 323, 363
Koatohee of Toquo, Chief *see* Old Tassel, Chief
Kodak, Tennessee 234
Kolakusta of Noth *see* Kuthegusta
Kollannah *see* Collanah
Konatota of Highwassay *see* Rising Fawn, Chief
Kostayeak of Wataga 239
Kowetatahee of Frog Town 239
Kulsagi Village 372
Kunokeski, Chief *see* Young Tassel, Chief
Kunsteeneestah *see* Whiplash
Kuthegusta, Chief *see* Kittagusta, Chief (other than Prince Skalilosken)

Lacrosse 19
Lacy, Capt. 166
Lady of Cofitachequi 25–26
Lake Keowee 59
Lake Pontchartrain 109
Lake Secession 154
Lanier, Congressman Robert 181
Larimer, D. 201
Larkin Sulphur Spring *see* Neely's Lick
Latimer, Nathan 302
Latimer, Thomas 306
Laurens, Lt. Col. Henry 92, 377
Lawson, John 14
Leach, Mr. 160
Leaning Stick *see* Attakullakulla, Chief
Leaning Wood *see* Attakullakulla, Chief
Leaper, Thomas 64
Lebanon, Tennessee 300

Lee, Maj. Gen. Charles 141
Lee, Gov. Henry "Light-horse Harry" 1, 26, 96, 145, 207, 221–222, 328
Lee County, Virginia 326
Leech Place *see* Tlanusi-yi Village
LeFeore, Isaac 202
Legge, William 2nd Lord Dartmouth 32
Leiper, Capt. James 203, 212
Leiper, Trooper 309
Le Jau, Francis 36–37
le Moyne, Jacques **104**
Lewis, Brig. Gen. Andrew 60–61, 63, 91, 95, 118–119, 130–131, 167
Lick Branch 200
Lick Creek 172, 209, 247
Liddell, Capt. Moses 216
Liles, Col. *see* Lyles, Col.
Lillington, Col. Alexander 149
Limestone, Tennessee 156
Lincoln, Pres. Abraham 3, 296
Lincoln, Benjamin 275–276
Lindley's Fort 162–163
Lindsay, Isaac 227, 368
Linville, North Carolina 27
Little Carpenter *see* Attakullakulla, Chief
Little Chota Village **10**, **194**, 218
Little Deer: legend of 17
Little Fellow *see* Fivekiller
Little Hickman Creek 124
Little Laurel River 316
Little Nephew (of Breath), Chief *see* Towak(k)a, Chief
Little Owl, Chief 116, 129, 134, 157, 174–175, 186, 224, 258, 266, 291, 299–304, 349; allied with the Cheyenne 287–288; battle at Buchanan's Station, severely wounded (1792) 307; battle at Lookout Mountain (1788) 265; Nashborough peace conference (1781) 231; Nashville peace conference (1787) 246; Running Water Town headman 293
Little Owl's Village 174
Little Pigeon River 313, 315
Little River (Tennessee) 68–69, 234, 237, 257, 266, 285, 308–309, 312
Little River (Virginia) 68–69
Little River, South Carolina **9**, 60, 165–166, 180; Bridge 180
Little Tallasee Village 262, 273, 279
Little Tallico Village *see* Little Tellico Village
Little Tellico Village **10**, 89, 171, 239
Little Tennessee River **8**, **10**, 11–12, 44, 54, 61, 63, 85–86, 93, 102, **128**, **133**, 134, 147–148, 169, **170**, 171–173, 175, **194**, 209, 214–215, 243–244, 257, 264, 294, 333, 354, 371–373, 376, 380
Little Turkey, Chief 261, 267–268,

Index

281–282, 292, 301, 313–314, 319, 333, 338; Estanaula Grand Council (1792) 298–299; at Holston (1791 Treaty) 282; at Tellico Blockhouse peace conference (1794) 332
Little Turtle, (Miami) Chief 287
Little Will *see* Thomas, Chief William Holland
Livingston, Elizabeth 325; deposition of 326
Livingston, Henry 325–326
Livingston, Mrs. 284
Livingston, Paul 315
Livingston, Peter 325–326
Livingston, Sarah 325
Livingston, Susanna 325
Livingston, William Todd 325
Lloyd, Maj. John 83
Locha *see* Cornstalk, Locha
Lochaber Estate *9*, 117, 119, 146, 355
Locke, John 30
Logan, Gen. Benjamin 333
Logan, Lt. Col. John 219–220
Lokacholakatha 43, 348
London 29, 44, *45*, 49–50, 59, *107*, 118, 352
London Chronicle 114
Long(e), Alexander 14
Long Canes, South Carolina *8–9*, 42, 60, 79–80, 110, 114, 153, 160
Long Canes Creek 59–60, 80
Long Canes Massacre 14, 80–81, 98, 114, 181
Long Fellow, Chief 159, 175, 239, 249, 313, 349
Long Island of the Holston River 65, 87, 91, 95, 97–98, 101, 105–106, 118–119, *128*, *133*, 137, 155–156, 172, 175–176, 179–189, 209, 214, 225, 228, 237, 239, 253, 298, 370
Long Island Town (Alabama) *194*, 224, 292, 355
Long Island Village *see* Long Island Town (Alabama)
Long Swamp Creek 57, 223
Long Swamp Town *10*, *194*, 221–223
Look Out Mountain *see* Lookout Mountain
Lookout Creek *see* Lookout Mountain Creek
Lookout Mountain 174, 193, 198, 223, 225, 239, 261, 264–265, 292–293, 301, 329, 354–356
Lookout Mountain Creek *194*, 224, 292, 304
Lookout Mountain Town *194*, 224, 234, 291–292, 294, 298, 303–304, 311, 332
Lookout Town *see* Lookout Mountain Town
Loony, Peter 300
Lord Commissioners for Trade and Plantations 46
Lords Proprietors 30–31
Lough-Abber Estate *see* Lochaber Estate
Louisiana 26, 231–232, 235, 278, 358
Louisville, Kentucky 312, 377
Love, Col. 264
Lower Dialect *see* Eastern Dialect
Lower Town(s) (original) 3, 7–8, *9*, 11–12, 30, 35–36, 42, 44, 53–54, 59, 73–74, 77, 81, 83, 101, 114–115, 139, 148, 153, 159, 163, 174, 181, 187–188, 190, 216, 223, 239, 257, 372; Grant destroyed (1761) 93; Montgomery destroyed (1760) 85–86; Williamson destroyed (1776) 165–173, 180
Lower Towns (Chickamauga) 224–227, 230–231, 249, 253, 268, 273, 290, 292–295, 297–298, 300, 309, 313–315, 319–320, 328, 330–333, 337–338, 342, 355
Lowndesville, South Carolina 119, 154
Loyalist(s) 76, 116, 139, 141, 143–144, 149–150, 178, 218–219, 221, 223; *see also* Tory
Lucas, Andrew 232–233
Lucas, Isaac 213
Lucas, Maj. Robert 138, 210
Lumsley, James 201
Luny, Adam 219
Lyahuwagiautsa, Chief *see* Pumpkin Boy, Chief
Lyin Fawghn 260
Lying Fish 185
Lyles, Col. James 140, 162
Lynn, Maj. James 246
Lyttleton, Gov. William Henry 61–67, 77–85, 92, 95, 99, 101, 110, 186, 341, 351; declared war on Cherokee (1779) 75; placed peaceful delegation of chiefs under guard (1779) 76; placed trade embargo on Cherokee (1779) 70, 74

MacDonald, Brig. Gen. Donald 149
MacLeod, Lt. Col. Donald 149–150
Maclin, Zackariah 321
Mad Turkey, Chief 131
Maddog, Chief 318
Madell, James 302
Madison, James 237
Madison, Capt. Thomas 156
Madison, Tennessee 205
Madisonville, Tennessee 282
Magna Carta of American Indians *see* Proclamation of 1763
Malaquo Village *see* Big Island Town
Mallard-Fox Creek Wildlife Management Area 293
Mallett, Polly 255
Manchester, Tennessee 330
Manifee, James *see* Menefee, James
Manifree, James *see* Menefee, James
Manila 187
Mankiller *see* Ostenaco, Chief
Mankiller of Hi(a)wassee *see* Pouting Pigeon, Chief
Mankiller of Ookunny 44
Mann, William 203
Mansker, Kasper 205, 212, 227, 362, 368–369
Mansker's Creek 227
Mansker's Lick 205
Mansker's Station *194*, 203–205, 225, 228, 241
Marion, Brig. Gen. Francis "Swamp Fox" 1, 92–93, 150; reference to the Grant Expedition 95–96
Marion, Virginia 207
Marrow, Sam 154
Martin, Gov. Alexander 223–224, 227, 231, 234
Martin, Andrew 270
Martin, Elizabeth "Betsy" *see* Ward, Elizabeth "Betsy"
Martin, Lt. Col. James 140, 374, 377–379
Martin, Gov. John 218–219, 227
Martin, Brig. Gen. Joseph *185*, 186, 191–192, 209–211, 214, 224–225, 228–229, 236, 238, 243, 245, 249, 251, 256, 259, 264, 267–268, 319, 349; failed expedition against the Chickamauga Lower Towns (1788) 264–266
Martin, Gov. Josiah 122, 149
Martin, Samuel 220, 252
Martin, William 225
Martin, Capt. William 250
Martin, Covenanter Rev. William 71
Martin's Spring 301
Maryland 57, 118, 286, 360
Maryland Gazette 266
Maryville, Tennessee 244, 281
Mason, Philip 231–232
Mason brothers 220
Mason County, West Virginia 118
Massacre at Cavett's Station (1793) 322–323
Massacre of Chiefs at Coyatee (1793) 319–320
Massacre of the Old Chiefs (1788) 258; Andrew Pickens denounces the massacre and continued encroachment 259
Massey, William 316
Matachanna 348
Matchepungo (Indians) 32
Mat(t)hews, Anne (Calhoun) 14; captured (1759) 14, 80; return negotiated by Andrew Pickens (1777) 98, 181
Mathews, George 272
Mat(t)hews, Isaac 181
Matoaka *see* Matachanna
Matoy, James 347

Matoy, William R. 347
Mattamuskeet 32
Matthews, Gov. John 218, 221
Maulding, James 227
Maulding's Station 228
Maxey, Jesse 252
Maxwell, John 202
Mayfield, George 270
Mayfield, Isaac 328
Mayfield, James 202
Mayfield, Southerland 270, 281
Mayfield, William 270
Mayfield's Station 270, 281
Mayson, Maj. James 140
McAfee, James 124
McAfee, Robert 124
McAfee party 124–125
McArdell, James *79*
McCain, James 227
McCall, Col. James 24, 152–153, 164
McCann, Capt. James 278
McCarter, Gen. 267
McClean's fish dam 326
McCormack, John 102, 182
McCrory, Thomas 306
McCullough, John 316
McCutcheon's Trace 272
McDaniel, James 347
McDonald, Dep. Ind. Agt. John 112–113, 115, 174, 225, 261, 290, 297, 354
McDonald's Trading Post and Commissary for the Chickamauga 174, 191, 193
McDowell, Col. Charles 206–208
McDowell, Maj. Joseph 208
McDowell, Mrs. 284
McDowell, William 284
McGaughey's Station 324
McGee, Mr. 345, 348
McGee, William Acil "Uncle Asa" 345, *346*
McGee Family 346
McGillivray, Chief Alexander 231–232, 252, 261–262, 267, 271–277, 281, 286–287, 289, 295–296; appointed honorary Brig. Gen. 275, 277; death of 314; rescued Mrs. Brown from captivity 279
McIntosh, Comm. Laughlin 236
McIntosh, William 219
McIntosh's Tavern 335
McKee, Ind. Agt. John 292, 314–316, 318–319, 329, 332, 356
McLamore, Bob 318
McLamore, Charles 105
McLaughlin, Bernard 337
McLauren, Capt. Evan 119, 140
McLean, Capt. Alexander 150
McLelland, Lt. 328–329
McMurray, Mr. 294
McMurray, Samuel 306
McMurry, William 225
McNamas Creek *see* Camp Creek
McNeil, Captain 105
Meckelrath, Joseph *see* Mucklerath, Joseph

Meigs, Return J. 334
Memphis, Tennessee 67, 247
Mendenhall, John 125–126, 128
Mendenhall, Richard 125–126, 128
Mendota, Virginia 325
Menefee, James 203, 212
Mermaid Tavern 45
Mero District 278, 281, 294, 304, 311, 324, 329–330
Mialoquo Village *see* Big Island Town
Miami (Indians) 57, 287
Miami River 236
Middle Dialect 12
Middle Fork Holston River *see* Holston River
Middle Town(s) 2–4, 7–9, *10*, 11–12, 35–36, 54, 74, 85–86, 101, 117, 148, 159, 173–174, 180–181, 187–190, 208, 215–216, 240, 282, 343, 346; Grant destroyed (1761) 95; Williamson destroyed (1776) 165, 168–172
Middle Tyger River 160
Middleboro, Kentucky 144
Middlestriker, Chief 305, 309–311
Middleton, Col. Thomas 92
Middleton's Station 324
Mill Creek 235, 270
Miller, Capt. 264
Miller, George 284
Miller, John Frederick 68
Miller, Mr. (Tyger area) 160
Miller, Mr. (Rolling Fork area) 283
Miller, Mrs. 283
Miller, Mrs. Sarah 367
Miller, Samuel 321
Milligen-Johnston, Dr. George 78, 82
Milliken (son of John) 200
Milliken, John 200
Milliken, Mr. 312
Mills, Joel 228
Milner, Ens. Alexander 82
Milton, Daniel 347
Mingo (Indians) 7, 57, 118, 130
Mingo Homaw, Chief 219
Miró y Sabater, Gov. Don Esteban Rodríquez 231–232, 235, 242, 278, 309
Mississippi 335, 337
Mississippi River 8, 26, 99, 109, 187, 192, 231, 235, 253, 275, 339, 357, 365, 369
Missouri 135, 192
Mobile, Alabama 109, 232
Moccasin Gap, Virginia 284
Mohawk (Indians) 8, 11, 40, 117, 142
Molloy, Thomas 227, 360–361
Monck, George 30
Monck's Corner, South Carolina 76
Monongahela River 57
Montgomery, Alabama 37
Montgomery, Col. Archibald 71, 84–85, 87, 92–93, *94*, 169; Expedition of 85–86, 101, 186, 341, 380
Montgomery, Col. John 192–193, 227, 329–331, 357
Montgomery, Sheriff John *see* Montgomery, Col. John
Montgomery, William 252
Montgomery County, Tennessee 201
Moody, Sec. Thomas 132
Moon, Chief 251, 278
Mooney, James 177–178, 207, 211, 240, 243
Moonshaw, Joseph 212
Moore, Alexander 157
Moore, Col. James 149
Moore, Gov. James 31
Moore, Gov. James II 31
Moore, Col. Maurice 33, 35–36
Moore, Mr. 165
Moore, Samuel: burned at the stake 158, 173
Moore's Bridge *see* Widow Moore's Bridge
Moore's Creek National Battlefield 149
Mooresburg, Tennessee 138
Moravians 16, 84, 115, 133, 225, 241, 338
Mordecai, Abram 290
Morgan, Charles 249, 251
Morgan, Brig. Gen. Daniel 58, 124, 242
Morgan, Capt. John 242, 249–250
Morgan, Squire John 250
Morgan County, Tennessee 138
Morgan's Station 242, 246, 249–250, 269, 278, 321
Morgantown, North Carolina 27
Morris, Ester 243
Morris, Col. Maurice 41
Morrison, Capt. 86
Moss, George 308
Moss Wright Park 201
Most Honored Woman *see* First Beloved Woman
Mother Town *see* Chota Village
Moultrie, Maj. John 92
Moultrie, Col. William 92, 150
Mouncey, Frederick 89
Mt. Carmel, South Carolina 145
Mount Vernon, Virginia 59
Moytoy I *see* Ahmahtoya, Chief
Moytoy II *see* Amadohiyi, Chief
Moytoy III *see* Savanah Tom, Chief
Moytoy V *see* Ammouskossittee, Chief
Moytoy of Telliko *see* Amadohiyi, Chief
Moytoy, Nancili "Nancy" 348
Moytoy, Young Hop *see* Young Hop Moytoy
Muckelrath, Joseph 278
Mulerrin Family 277; *see also* Mulherrin, James; Mulherrin, John

Mulherrin, James 196, 306
Mulherrin, John 196
Mulkey, Rev. Jonathan 158
Mullay Roll 345
Mullherin, William 229
Mungle, Daniel 203
Murfreesboro, Tennessee 305, 330
Murmuring Ripple 349
Murph(e)y, Archibald D. 347
Murph(e)y, Mary "Polly" (other) 346–347
Murphy, Daniel (author's 6th-great-grandfather) 346, 351; death of (1782) 219
Murphy, Daniel (author's 7th-great-grandfather) 346, 351; death of (1752) 54
Murphy, Jesse 347
Murphy, Margaret (author's 3rd-great-grandmother) 345, *346*, 348
Murphy, Margaret (other) 345
Murphy, Martin *see* Whiplash
Murphy, Mary "Polly" (author's 4th-great-grandmother) 54, 108, 219, 345–348
Murphy, Mr. (author's 5th-great-grandfather) 351
Murphy, Rachael 347
Murphy, North Carolina 12, 26, 36, 75, 169, 171, 343, 347, 374, 379
Murray, Dr. John 114
Murray, Gov. John 129–131, 134, 143
Murry, Capt. 269
Murry, Solomon 202
Muscle Shoals of the Tennessee River 17, 135, 174, *194*, 199, 206, 217, 225, 230, 247–248, 252, 254, 279–280, 285, 290, 293, 299, 306, 328, 358
Museum of the Cherokee Indian 4, 353, 356, 358
Muskogee *see* Creek
Muskohge *see* Creek
Mussel Shoals *see* Muscle Shoals

Nae oche Village 372
Nairne, Ind. Agt. Thomas 34–35
Nancy of the Wolf Clan *see* Chalekatha
Nanotey of Kautokey, Chief 298
Nantahala, Lake 57, 171
Nantahala Mountains 57, 171, 377–378
Nantahala River 8, *10*, 11
Nanyehi of the Wolf Clan *see* Ward, Nancy
Narrows of the Little Tennessee River 169, *170*, 377
Narrows of the Tennessee River 331
Nash, Gen. Francis 196
Nashborough Settlement 196, 199, 211, 215, 219–221, 226–229; Court of Pleas and Common Sessions 231; Court of Triers 227; name changed to Nashville (1784) 231
Nashville, Tennessee 157, 191, 195–196, 200–201, 203, 211–212, 230–232, 235, 240–242, 245–248, 253, 257, 266, 269–270, 272, 282–284, 286, 288–289, 294, 296, 299, 301–302, 304–308, 311, 316–318, 321, 325, 328–331, 360–361, 363, 367–369
Natchez (Indians) 8, 236, 298
Natchez, Mississippi 283, 328, 337, 369
Natchez Trace 283
National Cherokee Council 338
Necatee of Sawta 239
Needham, James 28–29
Neel, Capt. 166
Neely, Alexander 281
Neely, Charles 281
Neely, Elizabeth 359
Neely, James 281
Neely, Miss 205
Neely, Mrs. 205, 252
Neely, William 193, 205, 252
Neely, William, Jr. 317
Neely's Bend of the Cumberland 205
Neely's Lick 205
Neil, Col. Thomas 140, 167
Nelson, James 315
Nelson, Mr. 313
Nelson, Thomas 315
Nenetooyah, Chief *see* Bloody Fellow, Chief
Neowee Creek *see* Nowe Creek
Neowee Village *see* Nowe Village
Nequassee Village *see* Nikwasi Village
Nequisee Village *see* Nikwasi Village
nettecawaw *see* chunkey
Nettle Carrier, Chief 184, 217, 224, 297–299, 303–305, 307–308, 314–315, 318, 321–322, 334, 351, 356
Neuse River 32
New Acquisition Militia 140
New Bern, North Carolina 32–33, 149
New Bern Settlement, Carolina Colony 33
New Cussee Village 239
New Echota *194*
New England 32
New Jersey 117
New Orleans, Louisiana 38, 73, 109, 369
New Providence 286
New River *see* Kanawha River
New River, Virginia 193, 195
New York 33, 86, 116, 150–151, 205, 276, 279, 281
Newotah of Chicamaga 239
Nicholson, Gov. Francis 38, 43
Nickajack Cave 225, 355
Nickajack Creek 254–255
Nickajack Lake 225, 291, 330
Nickajack Town *194*, 224–225, 254–256, 268, 292, 294, 298–299, 306, 311, 321, 355; attacked (1794) 329–332, 359; Little Owl's ferry 293
Nigodigeyu 349
Nikwasi Village *10*, 12, 26, 42–43, 46, 86, 91, 93, 117, 147, 168–169, *170*, 171, 371, 374, 376–379, *380*
Nilaque Village 372
Nine Mile Creek 237, 311
Nine Mile Creek Massacre 257
Ninety Six, South Carolina *8–9*, 76, 114, 161, 215, 222; Articles of Secession (1775) 140; Jail 131, 162; Siege of (1775) 140
Ninety Six District, South Carolina 80, 83, 96; militia (Whig) 140, 152, 161, 163
Ninety Six Trading Post (Goudey's Fort) 53, 64, 76, 83, 92, 98; *see also* Fort ninety Six and Goudey's Trading Post
Niowe Village *see* Nowe Village
Noble, Col. James 165
Noewe Creek *see* Nowe Creek
Noewe Village *see* Nowe Village
Noewee Creek *see* Nowe Creek
Nolan, Joseph 229
Nolan, Thomas 229
Nolichuckey River *see* Nolichucky River
Nolichucky River 8, 120–123, *128*, *133*, 137–138, 156, 158, 185, 206–207, 223, 240, 259, 342
Nolichucky Settlement(s) 120, 132, *133*, 138, 142, 155, 161, 177, 189, 192–193, 206, 208, 224, 226, 339, 342; militia 176
Nollechucky River *see* Nolichucky River
Nollichucky Settlement(s) *see* Nolichucky Settlement(s)
Nonachuckeh River *see* Nolichucky River
Nontuaka of Cheestowee (Cheestie), Chief 186, 295, 298, 314
Noon-day *see* Noonday of Toquo
Noonday of Toquo 251, 355; death of 316
Normandy/Normans 5, 24
Norrington, Joshua 228
Norris, Miss 281
North Mayo River 68
North of the Holston Settlements 119
North Pacolet River 160
North River 54
Northward *see* Nontuaka
Northward Warrior *see* Nontuaka
Northwest Territory 191–192, 365
Norton, Virginia 124
Norwood, Capt. John 161
Notally Village *10*, *194*, 171

Nottely Village *see* Notally Village
Nowe Creek 374–375, 379; *see also* Wayah Creek
Nowe Village 10, 93, *170*, 371–372
Nowee Village *see* Nowe Village
Nowewee Village *see* Nowe Village
Nucasse Village *see* Nikwasi Village

Obey River 368
Obongpohego, Chief 329, 332
Occonne Mountain *see* Oconee Mountain
Occonne Village *see* Oconee Village
Occunnolufte Village *see* Oconaluftee Village
Oconaluftee River 8, *10*, 171
Oconaluftee Village 13, 343
Oconee County, South Carolina 181
Oconee Creek 164
Oconee Mountain(s) 147, 169, 240, 274
Oconee River *8–10*, 85, 219, 223, 273–275, 281, 346, 351
Oconee Village 43–44, 147, 165
Oconeechee (Indians) 28–29
Oconeeon Village *see* Oconee Village
O'Connor, James 306
Oconostota, Chief 44, 50–57, 60, 62, 66–67, 70, 75, 77–79, 81–85, 87–91, 93, 95, 97, 99, 102, 104, 107, 113, 116–119, 121, 129, 134, 136, 138, 142, 155, 159, 173–176, 179–180, 182, 186, 189–190, 206, 208–209, 214–215, 217, 222, 225, 238–239, 241, 282, 349, 351–352, 354, 370, 378; death of 234
Ocuma, Chief *see* Badger
Ogeechee River *8–10*, 112, 274, 281
Oggs, John 329
Oglethorpe, Gen. James Edward 51–52
Ohio Company 340
Ohio River 7–8, 16–17, 30, 57, 66, 69, 111, 117–119, 124, 130, 192–193, 195, 227, 253, 270, 275, 279, 340, 369; Falls of 312, 370
Ohio Territory 126, 130–131, 134, 235, 287
Oka Kapassa *see* Coldwater Village
Ok-chan-tubby, Chickasaw Principal Chief 337
Oklahoma 4, 12, 91, 135, 291, 336–337, 339, 343
Okoonaka, Chief *see* White Owl and Attakullakulla, Chief
Old Abram of Chilhowee, Chief 116, 134, 155–156, 158, 175, 234, 239, 262, 349; captured Lydia Bean at Watauga 158; killed in massacre 258; signed Treaty of Hopewell 239

Old Caeser of Hiwassee, Chief 35–37, 96
The Old Chisholm Trail *see* Chisholm Trail
Old Hop, Chief 20–21, 45, 53, 55, 59–68, 71–73, 75–78, 91, 349; death of 79
Old Muskrat *see* Whiplash
The Old Prince (of Noth) 239, 284, 295
Old Settlers 336–339
Old Tassel, Chief 20, 116, 182, 190, 215, 217, 226, 231, 233–234, 236, 239–241, 243, 245, 249–250, 256–257, 264, 267, 297–299, 303; death at massacre 258, 261, 282, 311, 320, 342, 349, 355; oration at Hopewell (1785) 237–239, 298, 355; oration at Long Island of the Holston (1777) 182–184; oration at Long Island of the Holston (1781) 214; 1782 letter to Governor Martin 224, 227; Treaty of Coyatee 244, 333
Ollie of the Red Paint Clan 349
Onanoota of Koosoate 239
Onatowe *see* Onatoy
Onatoy 89
One Who Goes About *see* Ward, Nancy
Oneida (Indians) 11, 40, 117–118
O'Neill, Gov. Arturo 231–232, 235, 242, 296–297, 303–304
Oninaa 72
Onondaga (Indians) 11, 40, 117
Onotony *see* Onatoy
Onwe-Hon-We 12
Ookoonekah or the White Owl of Natchey Creek *see* Little Owl, Chief
Ookoseta of Kooloque, Chief 239, 298
Ookunny Village *see* Oconee Village
Oo-no-dutu (Bushyhead) *see* Stuart, Ind. Agt. John
Oo-no-dutu (son of John Stuart) 91
Oonoyahka of Will's Town, Chief *see* Middlestriker, Chief
Ooskiah, Chief *see* Old Abram, Chief
Ooskuah, Chief *see* Old Abram, Chief
Ooskwha of Chilkowa *see* Old Abram, Chief
Oostanaula River 8, *10*, *194*
Oostanaula Village *194*, 338–339
Ootosseteh of Hi(a)wassee *see* Pouting Pigeon
Oowuhgah *see* Matoy, James
Opechan, Chief 348
Orangeburg District Militia 140
Ore, Maj. James 225, 289, 318–319, 329–332
Orr, Mr. 160
Osborn, Henry *see* Osborne, Henry

Osborne, Henry 273–274
Oshasqua, Chief *see* Ammouskossittee, Chief
Osioota of Chilhowie 143
Oskuah, Chief *see* Old Abram, Chief
Ostenaco, Chief 21, 56, 60, 62, 64–67, 74–75, 77, 87, *88*, 90–91, 96, 105–106, 115–116, 129, *180*, 182, 185, 189, 349, 351–352, 370; attacked Fort Loudoun garrison (1760) 88–89; at Augusta Trade Conference (1763) 112; death of 191; at DeWitt's Corner (1777) *180*, 181; hosts Lieutenant Henry Timberlake 102; at Siege of Fort Loudoun (1760) 84–85; at Sycamore Shoals (1775) 134–135; visits England (1762) *107*, 108
Otari 7, 132
Ottare *see* Otari
Ottawa (Indians) 52, 57, 130, 142
Otter Lifter, Chief 319
Oucounacou *see* White Owl and Attakullakulla, Chief
Oukaneka *see* White Owl and Attakullakulla, Chief
Ouka-Ulah, Chief 44, *45*, 46, 49
Oukayuda *see* Ouka-Ulah
Ounaconoa *see* Ounakannowie
Ounakannowie 44, *45*
Out Town(s) *see* Valley Town(s)
Outacite *see* Ostenaco, Chief
Outicite (general warrior) *see* Mankiller
Outlaw, Col. Alexander 244–245, 259, 333
Overall, Capt. William 193, 195, 229, 312–313
Overhill Cherokee Villages *see* Upper Towns
Overmountain Dialect *see* Upper Dialect
Overmountain militia 206–208, 215, 226, 241, 257–258, 269, 342
Overmountain Settlements 3, 11, 131, *133*, 155–156, 159, 161, 172–173, 176–178, 187, 192–193, 195, 199, 206–209, 214–215, 221, 223–224, 226–227, 233–234, 236, 238, 241–242, 263, 270–271, 311–312, 315, 320–321, 331, 337, 339, 341–342, 354
Overton County, Tennessee 368

Paint Town 343
Pamlico River 32, 34
Pamplico (Indians) 32
Pamplico River *see* Pamlico River
Pamunkey (Indians) 28
Panton, William 291, 296–297
Papal Bull of 1452 110
Parata (militiaman): derided by Andrew Pickens 222
Pardo, Juan 27
Parker, Cdre. Sir Peter 149–151
Parker, Messr. 119, 138

Parker, Mrs. Nathaniel 317
Parks, Reuben 250
Parsons, Francis *79*
Parson's Creek 201
Pates, John 312
Path Deed 138, 354
Path Killer, Chief 292, 298, 338
Patrick, James 283
Patrick County, Virginia 68
Patriot(s) 76, 97, 139–140, 144, 149–150, 157, 176, 184, 216, 222; *see also* Whig(s)
Pattonsville, Virginia 128
Paul, James 308
Payne, Mr. (killed at Asher's Station) 203
Payne, Mr. (killed near Chickamauga Town) 197
peace chief 13, 18, 22, 49–50, 57, 77, 282
Peace Council 13, 15
Peale, Rembrandt *185*
Pearis, Capt. Richard 60, 65, 119, 137, 139–140, 163, 178
Pearis, Mrs. 163
Peeler Park 294
Pendleton, Benjamin 284
Pendleton, Gov. Edmund 143
Pendleton, Frances 284
Pendleton, Mrs. 284
Pendleton, Reuben 284
Pendleton District, South Carolina 161
Pennington Gap, Virginia 125
Pennsylvania 117–118, 148, 367
Pensacola, Florida 231–232, 236, 291–292, 296–298, 302–303, 307, 309, 314, 357
Pepquannakek, Chief *see* Shawnee Warrior, Chief
Pereaugers *see* Pettiaugers
Periaguers *see* Pettiaugers
Person Striker, Chief 314
Pervine, John 250
Peters, Richard 117
Petersburg, Georgia 146
Petersburg, Virginia 28
pettiaugers 38
Pettigrew, John 328
Pettigrew, William 328
Peyton, Bailie 360
Peyton, Ephraim 220, 243, 360
Peyton, John 220, 243, 359–360
Peyton, Joseph 360
Peyton, Mrs. Ann *see* Guffey, Ann
Peyton, Mrs. Ephraim 198
Peyton, Mrs. Margaret *see* Hamilton, Margaret
Peyton, Robert 359
Peyton, Thomas 243
Peyton brothers 333
Peyton's Creek 220
Peytonia Farm 359
Phillips, Mr. 203
Phillips, Samuel 206–207
Phillips, Solomon 202

Pickaway Plains 131
Pickens, Brig. Gen. Andrew 1, 24, 26, 60, 80, 92, 95, 110, 140, 145, 154, 161, 215, 234, 236, 238, 241, 249, 279, 284–285, 351; assisted Gov. Blount with Chickasaw and Choctaw peace conference (1792) 301, 318; assisted with Creek Treaty (1789) 272–277, 279, 318; condemned the massacre of the Old Chiefs by letter to John Sevier (1788) 259, 342; First Expedition against Tories and Chickamauga (1782) 218–219; Grant Expedition reference (1762) 96; Hanging Maw and Young Tassel wrote Pickens for help following massacre of Old Chiefs (1788) 258; helped negotiate the release of Anne Calhoun from the Cherokee (1777) 181; interceded at prisoner exchange after Battle of Flint Creek (1789) 268; letter forwarded to Secretary of War by Richard Winn (1788) 259; Second Expedition against Tories and Chickamauga (1782) 221–223; Williamson expedition, Cherokee War (1776) 161–181
Pickens, Edmund *see* Ok-chantubby, Chickasaw Principal Chief
Pickens, John (brother of Andrew): capture, torture, and death of (1781) 216
Pickens, John "The Tory" 216, 234; death of 337
Pickens, John (uncle of Andrew) 154
Pickens, Capt. Joseph William 1, 110, 154, 161, 348
Pickens, Pvt. Robert Andrew 153–154, 155, 161, 257
Pickens, Pvt. William 155
Pickens, Pvt. William Gabriel 155
Pickens County, South Carolina 59
Pickett County, Tennessee 368
Picts 23
Piedmont 8
Pigeon of Natchey Creek *see* Pouting Pigeon, Chief
Pigeon River 227, 322
Pillow, William 245, 269, 331
Pinckney, Gov. Charles 284
Pine Island 34
Pine Log Village 239
Piney Creek 235
Piomingo, Chief 211, 219, 229–230, 232, 248, 281, 357–358; informed Colonel Robertson of Doublehead's Coldwater Town (1787) 247; refused to ally with Dragging Canoe (1792) 287, 291
Pistol Creek 308
Plummer, Capt. Daniel 140

Plymouth, England 107
Pocahontas 28
Pocotaligo Village 34
Point Pleasant, West Virginia 117–118, 130–131
Polk, Col. Thomas 140
Polson, Capt. 58
Ponce de León, Juan 25
Poor Valley 283
Porpoise *see* Tatliusta of Tilassi
Port Royal, South Carolina 26, 35
Porter, Mr. 202
Portugal 109–110
Pot Clay of Chilhowee *see* Kataquilla
Potomac River 117
Pouting Pigeon, Chief 106, 186, 351; voyage to England *107*
Powell Mountain 125, 128, 313, 315, 326, 328
Powell Mountain Gap 316
Powell River *8*, 125–127, *128*, *133*, 157, 368
Powell River Valley 124–125, 144, 371
Powell's Mountain *see* Powell Mountain
Powell's River *see* Powell River
Powhatan (Indians) 7–8, 12, 27, 348–349
Powhatan, Chief 28
Powhatan Confederacy 28
Poymace Tankaw, Chief 219
Presbyterianism / Presbyterians 71, 157, 337, 361
Preston, Col. William 181, 214
Priber, Christian Gottlieb 50–52, 348
Priber, Creat(e) 51, 348
Priber, Susan 51, 351
Price, Aaron 80
Price, John 285–287
Price, Mr. (Cherokee) 152
Price, Mr. (killed near Gallatin) 245
Price, Mrs. 245
Price, Comm. Thomas 132, 180
Price's Meadow 368
Pride of the Shawnee *see* Lokacholakatha
Priest, Mr. 312
Prince *see* Skalilosken, Prince
Prince (field hand) 317
Prince, Capt. 165
Prince, Mr. *see* Price, Mr.
Prince of Noth *see* Kuthegusta
Prince of Wales 46
Princeton University 361
Principal People *see* Ani-yunwi-ya
Proclamation of 1763 3, 111–112, 114–115, 117, 121–122, 130, 138, 177–178, 215, 341
Pruett, Capt. William 229
Pruett, Daniel 229
Pugh, Thomas 243
Pukeshenwa, Chief 130–131, 288

Pumpkin Boy, Chief 116, 134, 224, 263, 301, 304, 349; cannibalism at Dripping Spring 313; death of 322
Pumpkin Vine, Chief 269
Putnam, Col. 269
Putnam County, Tennessee 368

Quaker Meadows, North Carolina *8*, 206, 208
Qualatche Village *see* Qualhatchee Village
Qualatchee Village *see* Qualhatchee Village
Qualhatchee Village 85, 167, 372
Qualla Boundary 12, 343–344
Quallatown 343
Quanuse Village *see* Canusee Village
Quatsie *see* Anigawi
Quatsie of the Wolf Clan *see* Aganunitsi
Quawasee Village 218
Quebec 76, 110, 360
QuedsSi *see* Anigawi
Queeleekah of Hiwassee 186
Quigley, Patrick 201
Quinahaqui Village 27

R. B. Russell Dam 145–146
Rabbit *see* Chesetoa of Tlacoa
Rabun Gap *10*, 86, 169, 377
Raccoon Valley 318
Race to the Dan 214
Radcliffe, Mrs. 294
Ragan, Anthony 328
Rains, Capt. John 195–196, 202, 229, 247, 250, 272, 286, 305, 307, 318, 321, 368
Rains, John, Jr. 250
Rains, Patsy 229
Rains' Spring 305
Rains' Station 228, 270, 272, 286
Ramsey, Henry 201, 269, 281
Ramsey, J. G. M. 251, 258, 355, 366
Ramsey, William 281
Randolph, Gov. Edmund 249
Randolph, Comm. Peter 60–61
Rankon, William 226
Ratcliff, Harper 294
Ratcliff Massacre 294
Raven (general term) 18, 44, 134
Raven from the Mouth of Tellies River 186
Raven of Chota (Dragging Canoe's brother) 116, 129, 132, 134, 136, 143, 149, 155, 172–173, 175, 184, 186, 189–190, 215, 217, 258, 349; accepts Delaware headman's war belt (1776) 142; attacked Carter's Valley (1776) 156–158; met with Colonel William Christian (1776) 175; signed Treaty of Sycamore Shoals (1775) 136; Treaty of Holston (1777) 182–184, 214
Raven of Chota (general term) 22

Raven of Chota (other than Dragging Canoe's brother) *see* Amadohiyi, Chief
Raven of Estatoe *see* Young Warrior, Chief
Raven of Estatouih *see* Young Warrior, Chief
Raven of Hiwassee Carpenter of the Potato Clan 44, 107, 349
Raven of Nequasee 117
Raven of Tellico *see* Savanah Tom, Chief
Reason, Mrs. 287
Reason, Thomas 287
reciprocity, principle of: not extended toward the Cherokee by the British 2, 49, 60, 70, 100, 144, 177, 179, 341–342
Red Bird I, Chief 51, 116, 134, 351
Red Bird II 203, 351
Red Chief *see* War Chief
Red River (Louisiana) 26
Red River (Oklahoma) 337
Red River (Tennessee) 201, 283, 286, 309, 312, 331, 362
Reed, James 160
Reedy Creek 197
Reedy River *9*, 140–141
Reedy River Fight *see* Battle of Great Cane Brake
Reid, Maj. John 228
Reid, Capt. William 302
Renfroe, Benjamin 202
Renfroe, Joseph 201
Renfroe, Josiah 247–248
Renfroe, Moses 201
Renfroe, Peter 214
Renfroe, Stephen 329
Renfroe's Station 201, 203
Reyetaeh of Toquoa *see* Old Tassel, Chief
Reynolds, Sir Joshua *88*, *180*
Rheumatism (legend of the animals) 17
Richardson, Capt. 264–265
Richardson, Mr. 311
Richardson, Mrs. 311
Richardson, Capt. Richard 140
Richardson, Col. Richard 140–141, 162, 167
Richardson, Covenanter Rev. William 71–72
Richland, Tennessee 235
Richland Creek 200, 229, 247
Richmond, Kentucky 124
Richmond, Virginia 28, 228
Riddle, Cornelius 232
Ridge, Chief *see* Ridge, Chief Major
Ridge, Chief Major *335*, 338; assassination of 336, 339; conspired to assassinate Doublehead 336
Ridge, John: assassination of 336
Ridgecrest, North Carolina 168
Ridley, Beverly 250
Ridley, William 250
Riley, Elizabeth 15

Riley, John 289–290, 334
Riley, Mr. 308
Riley, Rach(a)el (author's 5th-great-grandmother) 347–349
Riley, Samuel, Jr. 347–349
Ring Fight 165–166
Rising Fawn, Chief 239, 308
River Dart *see* Broad River (Georgia)
Roanoke, Virginia 106
Roanoke River 32–33
Roaring River 368
Robbinsville, North Carolina 343
Roberts, Col. Isaac 400
Roberts, Mrs. 287
Roberts, Obadiah 309
Robertson, Col. Charles 138, 354
Robertson, Col. Elijah 272, 288–289
Robertson, Brig. Gen. James 122, 129, 155, 185, 191–192, 196, 205, 210, 221, 227–228, 231, 235, 245–247, 253, 257, 269, 272, 278, 282, 286, 297–298, 304–305, 307, 318, 321, 324–325, 329–331, 353, 357, 359–361, 365; alliance with the Chickasaw (1781) 211; at Battle of Point Pleasant (Kanawha, 1774) 130; Battle of the Bluff (1781) 212–214; the Coldwater expedition 247–248, 282; Colonel Christian's expedition (1776) 172; defended Fort Caswell against Chief Old Abram's attack (1776) 158; headed expedition to settle in the Cumberlands (1779) 193, 195; hosted Chickasaw Treaty Conference (1783) 230
Robertson, John Randolph 204
Robertson, Jonathan 286, 297–298, 325
Robertson, Mark 193; death of 247–248
Robertson, Peyton: death of 251
Robertson, William 272
Robertson County, Tennessee 329
Robertson's Station (eastern Tennessee) 192
Robertville, South Carolina 145
Robin Hood 5
Robinett, Daniel 347
Robinson, John 87
Robinson, Maj. Joseph 140
Rock Castle 325, 361
Rock Island Ford of the Caney Fork River 359
Rock Landing of the Oconee River 274–276, 279
Rockfish Creek 149
Rockford, Tennessee 267
Rocky Ford Gorge 267
Rocky River 154
Rodgers, John 336
Rogan, Hugh 204, 225, 247–250, 264
Rogana, Tennessee 242
Rogers, John *see* Rodgers, John

Rogersville, Tennessee 119, 191, 283, 294, 315
Rolfe, John 28
Rolfe, Rebecca *see* Pocahontas
Rolling Fork of the Cumberland 283
Rollowah, Chief *see* Raven of the Mouth of Tellies River
Romans 4, 23
Rome, Georgia 323
Rose Island *see* Big Island Town
Rosebury, William: death of 319
Ross, Captain Francis 373, 375–376, 378–379; diary 373, 375–377
Ross, Chief John 91, 113, 191, 339
Ross, Col. John 163, 167–168
Ross, Thomas 315
Roten, Mary Louise "Molly" 348
Round-O, Chief 75, 78, 89; death of 81
Roundsevell, David 227
running hard labor *see* Chunk(e)y
Running Stream, Chief *see* Algonkian, Chief
running the gauntlet 311
Running Water Town **8, 194,** 224–225, 234, 254–255, 268, 280, 283–284, 288, 291–294, 297, 299, 302, 311, 313, 316, 318, 329–332, 353, 355–357
Russell, Henry 125–128, 370–371
Russell, John 326
Russell, Col. William 124–127, 130, 172, 370–371; deposes on behalf of Nathaniel Gist 176
Russell Dam *see* R. B. Russell Dam
Russell Lake 146
Russell Party 127, 371
Rutherford, Brig. Gen. Griffith 140, 218; Cherokee Campaign (1776) 167–169, 171, 180, 353, 373–374, 376–379, **380**
Rutherfordton, North Carolina 206
Rutledge, Gov. John 168
Rye Cove 125

St. Augustine, Florida 51, 139, 141, 236
Saint Bartholomew's Parish, South Carolina 35
St. Clair, Gov. Arthur 287, 358
St. Clair's Camp: massacre at 287
St. George Chapel 46
Saint Helena, South Carolina *see* Santa Elena, South Carolina
St. James Park 45
St. Louis, Missouri 192
St. Simons Island, Georgia 51
Sale Creek 193
Salechiee 293
Salem, North Carolina 84
Salem, Virginia 106
Salisbury, North Carolina 27, 266
Salkehatchie River 35
Salkehatchie Village 35
Sally 116
Saloue, Chief *see* Young Warrior, Chief
Salt Catcher River *see* Salkehatchie River
Saluda, South Carolina 59
Saluda River **8–9,** 39, 60, 161–162
Salvador, Capt. Francis 114, 152, 160, 162–163; death of 164–165
Sand Bar Ferry 145
Santa Elena, South Carolina 26–27
Santee River 35, 38–39
Sapling Grove Settlement, Tennessee 119
Sappington, Dr. John 360
Saunders, Alex 335–336
Saunders, Col. James 283
Saunders' Station 283
Sautee Creek 218
Sautee Nacoochee, Georgia 218
Savage, John 140
Savage's Old Fields 140
Savanah Tom, Chief 43–44, 51–52, 65–67, 73, 96, 107, 134, 348
Savanna River *see* Savannah River
Savannah, Georgia 37, 123, 131–132, 193, 209, 218, 236, 275
Savannah River **8–10,** 11–12, 25, 34–35, 52, 59, 112, 131, 145–147, 153–155, 181, 215–216, 221, 354, 372
Savanuka(h) (generic warrior title): *see* Raven of Chota; Savanah Tom, Chief
Saxon(s) 4, 23
Scali Cosken, Ketagusta *see* Kittagusta, Chief
Scalping 4, 16, 18, 42–44, 46, 48, 64, 67–70, 77, 80, 89, 144, 156–158, 160, 164–165, 167, 191, 200–203, 210, 212–213, 216, 232–233, 235, 244, 246, 249, 251–252, 255, 257, 264, 269, 274, 278, 281, 283–284, 287–293, 295–296, 302, 307, 311–313, 315–316, 318, 321, 324–325, 328–329, 332, 334, 356, 358; bounties for (by whites) 60–61, 64, 68–69, 74, 82, 96, 153, 157, 166, 168, 171, 175–176, 220, 328; practice (in general) 81, 153; treatment for 211
Scantee, Chief: death of 319
Scayagusta Oukah *see* Ouka-Ulah
Scented Flower 349
Schenkingh, Benjamin 35
Schneider, Rev. Martin 16
Schofieldites 162
Scholauetta of Chota, Chief *see* Hanging Maw, Chief
Schull, Miss 311
Scioto River 371
Scoby, David 302
Scolacutta, Chief *see* Hanging Maw, Chief
Scopholites *see* Schofieldites
Scotland / Scottish 23, 41, 91, 150, 191, 296, 309, 357, 360
Scots-Irish 5, 12
Scott, Capt. 151
Scott, James 311
Scott, Nancy 357
Scott, Will *see* Cherokee Billy
Scott, William 328
Scott County, Virginia 125
Scraggins, Henry 367
Screamin' Boys *see* Overmountain militia
Seagrove, Ind. Agt. James 271, 279
Second Man *see* Sketaloska of Tilico
Sedam, Ens. 280
Seneca (Indians) 11, 40, 117
Seneca River **8,** 154
Seneca Village **8–9,** 146–147, 152, 154, 164–165, 167, 238, 372
Sequechee 116, 134, 351
Sequoya(h) 65, 157, 173, 184, 293, 343, 349
Seroweh, Chief *see* Young Warrior, Chief
Settacoo Village *see* Settico Village
Sette Village 372
Settico Village 59, 73–74, 88, **128, 133,** 264, 349, 370
Seven Mile Ferry of the Cumberland 287
Seven Mile Ford of Clinch River 157
Seven Years War *see* French & Indian War
77th Regiment of Foot 84, 86, 92
Sevier, Betsy *see* Snyder, Betsy
Sevier, Gov. John **128, 133,** 155, 158, 172, 207, 211, 214, 224, 226, 231, 239, 244, 251, 256–257, 261–267, 270–271, 278, 287, 308–309, 312, 320–323, 333, 355, 359, 366; Battle of Flint Creek (1789) 267–268; Cherokee expedition (1780–1781) 209–210; Cherokee expedition (1788) 251, 257–258; Chickamauga expedition (1782) 223; denounced by Andrew Pickens for encroachment and bullying tactics (1788) 259, 342; Franklinite movement (1784) 233–234, 244, 250–251; Kings Mountain expedition (1780) 207–208; saved Catherine Sherrill (Fort Caswell) (1776) 158
Sevier, Joseph: death of 334
Sevier, Mrs. 287
Sevier, Rebecca 334
Sevier, Robert: death of 286
Sevier, Col. Valentine 182, 286–287; at Battle of Point Pleasant (Kanawha) 130
Sevier, Valentine, Jr.: death of 286
Sevier, William: death of 286
Sevier's Island *see* Big Island of the French Broad River

Index

Sevier's Station *see* (Valentine) Sevier's Station
Sevierville, Tennessee 209, 231, 324
Shackle Island 252, 324–325
Shaffer, Michael 300
Shane, Morris 306
Shankland, John 308
Shannon, Capt. John 245, 250, 269
Sharp(e), Maj. Anthony 286, 301
Sharp, Thomas 126–127
Sharp Fellow *see* Kostayeak of Wataga
Sharpe, Benjamin 326
Sharpe, Robert 308
Sharpe, Congressman William 181
Shaver, Michael *see* Shaffer, Michael
Shaw, Bob 364
Shaw, Ind. Agt. Leonard D. 298
Shawanese *see* Shawnee
Shawano *see* Matachanna
Shawnee (Indians) 7–8, 17, 22, 30–31, 34–35, 38, 41, 53, 56–57, 60, 69, 106, 116–118, 124–132, 142–143, 156–157, 188, 195–196, 224, 231, 234, 251, 279, 287, 291–292, 299, 303, 305, 309, 318, 341, 348–349, 355–357, 366, 371
Shawnee Warrior Chief 130–131, 225; death of 306; joined Chickamauga 288, 294, 297, 299–305, 307, 309, 323, 359
Shelburne, Lord 118
Shelby, Col. Evan 130, 172, 176, 181, 192, 214; Chickamauga expedition (1779) 192–193, 211; death of 312
Shelby, Col. Isaac 206, 227–229, 247; Kings Mountain expedition (1780) 207–208
Shelby, Capt. James 156, 172
Shelby, Capt. Moses 247–248
Shelby's Fort **8, *128*,** 207
Shellmound, Tennessee 224
Shelton, Eld. 324
Sheriff of Nottingham 5
Sherrill, Catherine "Bonnie Kate" 158
Shine, Morris 229
Shoal Town 135
Shockley, John 202
Shonguttam, Chief *see* Round-O, Chief
Shooting Creek 379
Shorey, Anna 113
Shorey, William 91, 106–107, 113, 174; death of 107–108
Silar Roll 345, 347
Silver Bluff, South Carolina 25–26
Silver Bluff Plantation *see* Fort Galphin
Simpsonville, South Carolina 141
Sinica Village *see* Seneca Village
Sinking Creek 251
Six-and-Twenty Mile Creek 163
Skalilosken, Prince 44, 59, 77–78, 349; voyage to England **45**, 46

Skeahtukah of Citico 186
Skelelak 239
Sketaloska of Tilico 239
Skiagusta *see* Oconostota, Chief and Ostenaco, Chief
Skiuka, Chief *see* Skyuka, Chief
Skyagusta (generic for warrior) 18
Skyagustuego, Chief *see* Anakwanki, Chief
Skyuka, Chief 114, 153, 155, 159–162, 164–166, 172, 181, 208, 215, 223, 239, 257
slave ships 17, 24, 52
slaves: African 32, 35, 42, 47–49, 51, 54–55, 112, 125–126, 128, 146, 168, 204, 210, 251, 280, 289, 312, 315–317, 328, 341, 367; Indian 26, 30–34, 36, 40–41, 48, 63, 81, 92, 115, 168, 176
Slim Tom of Chilhowie 257, 263
Small Pox Conjuror of Settico, Chief 88, 129, 349, 370
smallpox 12, 24–25, 51–52, 77–79, 81, 83, 86, 89, 96, 198
Smith, Capt. Aaron 160, 164
Smith, D. Ray **136**, 353
Smith, Gen. Daniel *see* Smith, Sec. Daniel
Smith, Sec. Daniel 225, 319–320, 323, 325, 334, 361; death of 361
Smith, Henry 368
Smith, Col. James 367
Smith, Capt. John 160, 164
Smith, Mike **136**
Smith, Mrs. 160
Smith's Fork 278
Smoky Mountain News 379
Smoky Mountains *see* Great Smoky Mountains
Smyth, Frederick 117
Snider, John *see* Snyder, John
Snoddy, Ens. (Capt.) William 301–302, 307
Snoddy's Bridge 160
Snow Campaign 140–141
Snyder, Betsy: death of 334
Snyder, Charles: death of 334
Snyder, John: death of 334
Snyder, Mr. 286
Soco Creek 343
Somerset (slave) 204
Son of White Owl *see* Little Owl, Chief
Sour Mush, Chief *see* Ookoseta of Koolooque, Chief
South Carolina Gazette 51, 59, 74, 76–77, 79–80, 83–84, 87, 90, 97
South Pittsburg, Tennessee 330
South Sea Company 41
South West Point 284
Southwest Territory 279, 286, 304, 312, 319, 321, 323, 338, 364–365
Sower Mush, Chief *see* Ookoseta of Koolooque
Spain 41, 109, 187, 231, 235, 252, 271, 296

Spaniard(s) 25–27, 52, 199, 231, 252, 271, 274, 297, 303, 358
Spears, Jesse 219
Spencer, Thomas Sharp(e) 203, 232–233, 317, 324, 361–363; death of ***128***, 324, 364; lived in a sycamore tree 362
Spencer, William 363
Spencer's Hill 309, 363
Spenser's Hill *see* Spencer's Hill
Spider, Chief 314
Spring Branch of Henley's Creek 140
Springfield, Tennessee 220, 287
Springstone, Henry 209
Springstone, William *see* Springstone, Henry
Stalking Turkey, Chief *see* Oconostota, Chief
Stalnaker, Adam 106
Stalnaker, Mrs. 106
Stalnaker, Samuel 106, 117
Stalnaker Family 106
Stalnakre Family *see* Stalnaker Family
Standing Turkey, Chief 20–21, **79**, 81, 84–85, 87, 91, 97–98, 101–102, 105–106, 116, 258, 349, 370; deposed as principal chief (1762) 108; at Sycamore Shoals (1775) 134; voyage to England (1762) ***107***, 108
Stanley Valley 294
Stanwix, Gen. 69
Starr, Caleb 174
Starr, Emmet 15, 345–347
Station Camp Creek 227, 246
Staunton, Virginia 57
steatite 17
Stecoah 343
Stecoah Village 93, 147, 168
Stecoe Village *see* Stecoah Village
Stecooee Village *see* Stecoah Village
Stecoyee Village *see* Lookout Mountain Town
Steel, Andrew 302
Steel, David 242
Steele, Betsy 321
Steele, Col. 266
Steele, James 321
Steele, Robert 321
Stephen, Lt. Col. Adam 95, 97–98, 101–102, 106, 351
Stevens Creek 117
Stevenson, Alabama 224
Stewart, John *see* Stuart, John
Stewart's Creek 307
Stickleyville, Virginia 125, 128
Sticoe Village *see* Stecoah Village
Stone, Uriah 367–369
Stone Mountain 326
Stoner, Michael 124–125, 368
Stone's Gap 327–328
Stones River **194**, 203–204, 232, 367, 369
Stoney Creek 326

422 Index

Stono Rebellion (1739) 55
Stono River 55, 294
Stotoree Village 75
Stoval, Mr. 27
Stream, Chief *see* Opechan, Chief
Strom Thurmond Reservoir 146
Stuart, Dep. Ind. Agt. Henry 141–144, 146, 153, 155, 173, 182, 185, 187
Stuart, Ind. Agt. John 39, 63, 83, 87–92, 97, 101, 106, 111–112, 115–123, 139–142, 145–146, 148–149, 155, 159, 172, 174–175, 185, 187, 191, 303, 354; death of 193
Stuart, Thomas 198
Stuart, William 235, 308
Stuckley, John 201
Stull, Frederick 321
Stump, Edward *see* Stump, Frederick
Stump, Frederick 202
Stump, Jacob 202
Stump's Distillery 308
Suck Creek 198
Suck of the Tennessee River *see* Whirl of the Tennessee River
Sugar Town **9**, 152
Sugartown River 377
Sugi of the Wolf Clan 349
Sullivan County, North Carolina 251, 264
Sullivan's Island, South Carolina 150–151
Sulphur Spring (in Nashville) 195, 200, 202, 210, 212, 214
Sulphur Spring Branch 202
Sumner County, Tennessee 232, 246, 359–363, 367
Sumter, Brig. Gen. Thomas "Gamecock" 1, 102, 106–107, 140–141, 168, 219
Sunnewauh of Big Island Town 186
Surry County, North Carolina 172, 176
Swain County, North Carolina 380
Swan Creek 247
Swan Pond 209
Swannanoa Gap 168
Swanson, Edward 193, 195, 213
Swetland Roll 345
Sycamore Creek 201, 308
Sycamore Shoals of the Watauga River **8**, 121, **128**, 129, 132, **133**, 134, 137, 142, 157, 174, 190, 207–208, 210, 342; *see also* treaties
Sylva, North Carolina 168

Tahasse Village 372
Tahlequah, Oklahoma 336
Tahlonteskee, Chief *see* Nettle Carrier, Chief
Tail 116, 217, 234, 308, 313–315, 321, 351, 356
Taken Out of the Water, Chief 270, 328
Talcoa Village 239
Talipoosa River **8**, **10**, **194**, 254, 289
Tallapoosa River *see* Talipoosa River
Tallasee Village 371
Tallipoose Village 51
Taloteeskie, Chief *see* Nettle Carrier, Chief
Talotiska, Chief *see* Nettle Carrier, Chief
Talotiske, Chief *see* Nettle Carrier, Chief
Talotiskee of Broken Arrow 304; death of 307
Talotiskee, Chief *see* Nettle Carrier, Chief
TalTsuska, Chief *see* Doublehead, Chief
Tamahle Village 372
Tamassee *see* Tomassee
Tame Doe Raven of the Wolf Clan 349
tamemes 26
Tamotley *see* Tomotley
Tanase River *see* Little Tennessee River
Tanase Village *see* Tannassee Village
Tanasi Village *see* Tannassee Village
Tannassee Village 28, 39
Tarleton, Lt. Col. Banastre 124, 206
Tassetehee Village 43
Tassie Village 93
Tatham, William *see* Tatum, William
Tathtiowie, Chief 44, **45**, 46
Tathtowie, Chief *see* Tathtiowie, Chief
Tathum, William *see* Tatum, William
Tatliusta of Tilassi 239
Tatom, Absalom 227
Tatum, William 183
Tauhstaheesky 347
Tauqueto, Chief *see* Glass, Chief
Taylor, Chief John 318
Taylor's Trace 330
Teal, Nathaniel 318
Tecumseh, Chief 130–131, 225, **310**, 359; joined Doublehead 288, 304, 309–310
Tedford, Lt. 316
Teesteke, Chief 284
Tellassee Village 370
Tellico Blockhouse **128**, **133**, 291, 329, 332–333
Tellico Lake 135, 333
Tellico Plains, Tennessee 90
Tellico River **8**, **10**, 11, 44, 63, 78, 90, **128**, **133**, 134, 186, 223
Tellico Village 12, 20, 43–44, 49, 51–53, 55, 60, 63–65, 67, 72–73, 158, 234, 251, 270, 334, 348, 355, 371
Telliquo Village *see* Tellico Village
Tellowe Village 371
Ten Mile Creek 323
Tenase Warrior 138
Tenasee River *see* Tennessee River
Tenasee Village *see* Tannassee Village
Tenin, Hugh 312
Tennessee River 7, **8**, 17, 34, 118, **128**, **133**, 135, 174, 191–192, **194**, 195, 198–199, 209, 217, 224–225, 230, 234, 245–248, 264–265, 267, 269, 279, 283, 292–294, 299, 312–313, 319, 321–322, 328–331, 334–335, 353–355, 358, 367, 371–372, 375, 377
Tennessee Village *see* Tannassee Village
Terrapin of Chilestooch, Chief 186, 217, 222, 226, 239, 282, 298, 351
Terrill, Obadiah 368
Tessantee Village 93
Tethtowe *see* Tathtiowie
Thigh, Chief 269, 298
Thomas, Col. 140, 167
Thomas, Isaac 143–144, 155, 176, 209
Thomas, Joshua 229
Thomas, Chief William Holland 343; adopted by Chief Yonaguska 343; death of 344; personally purchased land to be held in trust for the Cherokee 343–344; selected as only full-blooded white Principal Chief 343
Thompson, Alex 203
Thompson, Alice 288–289; ransomed by John Riley 290
Thompson, James 288–289
Thompson, Capt. James 156–157
Thompson, John 283
Thompson, John 301
Thompson, Mr. 314
Thompson, Mrs. 288
Thompson, Robin 306
Thompson, Thomas 196
Thompson, Col. William *see* Thomson
Thompson and Caffrey massacre 288–289
Thomson, Col. William 141
Thornbury, Daniel 284
Three Pounders *see* Grasshopper Cannons
Three Sisters Ferry 145
Tiakakiskie of Hiwassee, Chief 298
Ticoloosa Village 371
Tifftoya, Chief *see* Willenawah, Chief
Tiftowe, Chief *see* Willenawah, Chief
Tilghman, Joseph 117
Tillehaweh *see* Chesnut of Tellies

Timberlake, Lt. Henry 11, 15–16, 20–21, 87, 98, 101–102, 104–108, 174, 351–352, 369–370; map *103*
Tipton, Sen. John 233, 251
Tipton, Jonathan 233
Titsworth, Col. Isaac 287, 331
Titsworth, John 287, 331
Titsworth, Miss 287
Titus, Ebenezer 227
Tlanusi-yi Village 12
tobacco 16–17, 19, 28, 40, 146, 235, 238, 248, 369
Toccoa Creek 155
Toccoa, Georgia 155
Toe River *see* Nolichucky River
Toka 246
Tom of Chatuga *see* Tulco of Chatooga
Tomassee Village (Lower Towns) *9–10*, 44, 166
Tomassee Village (Valley Towns) 171
Tomatly Village *see* Tomotley Village
Tommotley *see* Tomotley Village
Tomothle Village *see* Tomotley Village
Tomotley Village 85, 102, *128*, *133*, 239, 351, 370–371
Tomotlug Village *see* Tomotley Village
Toocaucaugee Village 329
Toogoloo Village *see* Tugaloo Village
Toostaka of Oostanawa 239
Toostooh of the Mouth of Tellies River 186
Top(p), John 248
Top(p), Roger 228
Toqua Village *see* Toque Village
Toque Village *128*, *133*, 158, 173, 186, 239, 256, 258, 314, 316, 370
Toquo(a) *see* Toque Village
Tories 3, 65, 115–116, 137, 139–143, 145, 150, 157, 159, 161–165, 167, 173, 176, 178, 180, 184, 187, 189, 206, 209, 215–216, 218–219, 221–223, 225–226, 234, 236, 337, 346, 351, 355; *see also* Loyaltists
Toskegee, Village *see* Tuskegee Village
Totopotomoy, Chief 28
Towak(k)a, Chief 311, 313
Tower of London 45
Town House *see* Council House
Toxaway Village *9*, 85, 167
trade gun(s) 29, 38, 108
Trader Tom, Chief *see* Amadohiyi, Chief
Trail of Tears 91, 336, 339, 342, 346
Trail of Tears Roll 347
Trammel, Nicholas 231–232
Transylvania Company 124, 132, 134, 137–138, 354
Travelers Rest Tavern 155
Treaties: of Augusta (1773) 123; of Augusta, Georgia, Council of Nations (1763) *112*; of Camp Charlotte (1774) 130–131; Cotton Gin (1806) 338; of Coyatee (1786) 244–245, 256, 333; of Dewitt's Corner (1777) 180–181; of Dumplin Creek (1785) 234; of Fort Stanwix (1768) 117–118; of Hard Labor (1768) 117; of Holston (1777) 179, 181–186; of Holston (1781) 214–215; of Holston (Blount's Treaty, 1791) 282; of Hopewell (1785) 236–241; Hopewell, Second (1786, Chickasaw) 241; Hopewell, Third (1786, Choctaw) 241; of Lochaber (1770) 118; of Long Swamp Creek (1782) 223, 226; of New Echota (1835) 339; of Paris (1763) 109–111; of Paris (1782) 252–253; peace with South Carolina (December 1761) 101; peace with Virigina (November 1761) 101; of Saluda (1755) 65; of Sycamore Shoals (1775) 134–138; of Tellico (1805) 334–335; of Tellico Blockhouse (1794) 332–333; Virginia trade alliance (1759) 69–70; *see also* Chickasaw Treaty of 1783
Trent River 32
Troy, South Carolina 80
Tsalagi 135; *see also* Cherokee
Tsisquaya, Chief *see* Red Bird I, Chief
Tsistunagiske *see* Ward, Nancy
Tsiyagunsini, Chief *see* Dragging Canoe, Chief
tso-la 16–17; *see also* tobacco
Tsula, Chief *see* Small Pox Conjuror of Settico, Chief
tuberculosis 12
Tuckasee of Allijoy *see* Young Terrapin
Tuckasee of Hightowa, Chief *see* Terrapin, Chief
Tuckaseegee River *8*, *10*, 11–12, 168, 171
Tuckaseegee Village *10*, 75, 93, 168
Tuckaseh of Chilestooch, Chief *see* Terrapin, Chief
Tucker, John 210
Tugalo Village *see* Tugaloo Village
Tugaloo River *8–10*, 12, 146, 155, 165, 167, 181, 238, 240, 372
Tugaloo Village *9*, 36, 41, 114, 153–155, 165, 308, 372
Tugilo River *see* Tugaloo River
Tugilo Village *see* Tugaloo Village
Tugulo Village *see* Tugaloo Village
Tulatiska of Chaway 239
Tulco of Chatooga 239
Tulluluh River 167
Tunbridge, Tom 254–256, 306–307
Turkey Town *194*, 261, 297, 299
Turnbull, Robin 306
Turnbull Creek 247
Turner, George 66
Turpin, Nathan 201
Turtle at Home 116, 134, 175, 186, 224, 258, 291, 293, 349
Tuscarora (Indians) 7–8; joined Iroquois Confederation 40, 117; Northern band 32–33; Southern band 32–34; war with Southern band (1711–1712) 32–33
Tuscumbia, Alabama 227, 248, 293
Tuskagee Village *see* Tuskegee Village
Tuskasah, Chief *see* Terrapin, Chief
Tuskeegee Village *see* Tuskegee Village
Tuskeegeetee of the Wolf Clan, Chief *see* Long Fellow, Chief
Tuskega Village *see* Tuskegee Village
Tuskegatahee, Chief *see* Long Fellow, Chief
Tuskegatahu of Chistohoe, Chief *see* Long Fellow, Chief
Tuskege Village *see* Tuskegee Village
Tuskegee Village (Alabama) *194*, 253, 255, 265, 299, 370, 372
Tuskegee Village (Tennessee) 54, 63, *128*, *133*, 158, 173, 186
Tuskiahooto 293
Tuskon Patapo, Chief 219
Twenty-three Mile Creek *8–9*
Twilight Zone 339
Tyger River *8*, 160; Middle 160; North 160
Tyger Settlement 160

Uchee (Indians) 8
Ukwaneequa, Chief *see* White Owl
Umatooetha of Choikamawga 239
Unakas (White people) 144, 156
Unaka(ye)s *see* Great Smoky Mountains
Unakata, Chief *see* White Man Killer, Chief
Unicoi County, Tennessee 267
Union, South Carolina 141
United Keetoowah Band of Cherokee Indians 4, 336, 343
Unlita, Chief *see* Breath, Chief
Unsuokanail of New Cussee 239
Untoola of Citigo, Chief 239, 366
Untoola of Seteco, Chief *see* Untoola of Citigo, Chief
Upper Dialect 11–12, 148
Upper Town(s) 2–3, 7–8, 11, 25, 35–36, 39, 44, 51, 54, 56, 60–63, 65, 67, 69, 71–75, 77–79, 83–85, 87–88, 92, 95, 98, 101–102, 105, 108, 110, 112, 116, 123, 126, *128*, 132, *133*, 134–135, 140–141, 143–144, 146–148, 155, 159, 161, 164–

165, 167, 172–176, 179–181, 185–191, 206, 209–211, 214–215, 223, 225–226, 231, 234, 240–244, 249–251, 256–258, 261, 280, 282, 304, 310–311, 315–316, 319, 324, 328–329, 331–333, 337–338, 342, 351–353, 371–372; *see also* Otari
Uskwalena 34
Us(k)waliguta, Chief *see* Hanging Maw, Chief
Ussinah Village 93
Ustanakwa, Chief *see* Oconostota, Chief
Ustanali Village: replaced Chota as Cherokee Capital 261
Uswaliguta *see* Hanging Maw, Chief

(Valentine) Sevier's Station 286–287; massacre at 334
Valley River 8, *10*, 11, 171
Valley Town(s) 2–3, 8, 11–12, 74–75, 89, 93, 107, 159, 165, 167, 169, 171–172, 180, 190, 211, 215–216, 244, 343, 374, 377, 379
Vann, Chief James 136, 322–323, 338; assassinated 338–339; Doublehead assassination conspirator 335–336
Vann, John 254
Vann, Joseph 182, 322
vigilantes 68, 115, 131
Vikings 25
Vincent, Capt. George 265
Virginian(s): slayings of Cherokee (1756) 61; slayings of Cherokee (1759) 73–74; slayings of Cherokee (1765) 115

Wabash (Indians) 244
Wabash River 227, 236, 287
Waddell, Col. Hugh 58
Wade, Capt. Robert 69
Waker *see* Toostaka of Ookanawa
Wales, Prince Frederick of 46
Walker, James 324
Walker, John 315, 335
Walker, Dr. Thomas 54, 106, 117–119
Walker's Ferry of the Hiwassee River 335
Wall, Lt. Robert 65
Wallen's Creek 315; massacre 125, 128–129, 370
Walnutfield Station 283, 317
War Drink *see* Black Drink
Ward, Bryan(t) 57, 84, 349
Ward, Elizabeth "Betsy" 57, 186, 225, 319, 349
Ward, Ghighau Nancy 15, 21, 56–57, 84, 142, 155, 159, 175, 186, 209–210, 225–226, 238, 249, 258, 313, 319, 349; oration at Treaty of Holston (1781) 214; oration at Hopewell 238; rescued Lydia Bean 159
Warner, Comm. Samuel 34–35

Warrior of Chota, Chief *see* Skiagusta, Chief
Warwoman Creek *9–10*, 169
Washington, Pres. George 56–57, *58*, 59, 86, 176, 270–272, 275–277, 279, 299, 319, 328, 340, 351, 365–366
Washington County, Virginia 207, 223, 322
Washington District of the Southwest Territory 278
Watauga Association 119, 122, 138, 354
Watauga River *8*, 119, *128*, *133*, 137–138, 156–158, 161, 193, 206, 226, 339, 353–354, 360, 371
Watauga Settlement(s) 7, 121–122, 129–130, 132, *133*, 134, 138, 141–144, 155, 157–159, 172, 177, 185, 189, 192–193, 195, 206, 208, 226, 236, 240, 279, 304, 339, 342
Watauga Village *10*, 93, 147, 169, *170*, 371
Water Conjuror of Tellico, Chief *see* Amadohiyi, Chief
Water Hunter *see* Umatooetha of Choikamawga
Wateree River 59
Waters, Mr. 264
Waters, Col. Thomas 221–222
Wattaga River *see* Watauga River
Watts, George 351
Watts, John 349, 355
Watts, John, Jr. *see* Young Tassel, Chief
Watts, Malachi *see* White Man Killer
Watts, Thomas *see* Big Tom
Watts, Wurteh 65, 184, 224, 234, 351
Wauhatchie Village 74
Waverly Place 228
Waxhaw Presbyterian Church 71
Wayah (Waya) Creek 169, 374–379, *380*
Wayah (Waya) Gap *10*, 57, 133, 169, *170*, 171, 373–378, *380*
Wayah (Waya) Road 57, 169, 171, 373–376, 379, *380*
Waylayer *see* Wooaluka of Chota
Wayne, Maj. Gen. Anthony 218, 357
Wayne County, Kentucky 368
Waynesville, North Carolina 379
Weakely, Robert 235
Wears Bend of the Little Tennessee River 134
Webb, Hugh 269
Web(b)er, Chief Will 293, 314
Webster, North Carolina 343
Weesock (Indians) 28, 30
weights and measures 37–39, 66, 101
Welch, John 153–154
Wells, H. G. 32
Wells, Heydon 227
Wells, Mr. 312

West Africa 110
West Florida (Spanish) 110, 253
West Indies 31–32, 41, 55, 63, 92, 115
West Virginia 7, 117–118, 129–131
Western Dialect *see* Upper Dialect
Western Territory (of North Carolina) 278; first cession 233, 278; second cession 278; Southwest Territory created 279
Whatoga Village *see* Watauga Village
wherry 29
Whigs 139–140, 143–144, 150, 155, 162–164, 179, 191, 206, 209, 346; *see also* Patriots
Whiplash 108, 347–348
Whirl of the Tennessee River 198, 224, 292
White, Hugh Lawson 323
White, Col. James 282–283, 319, 322, 366; ransomed the Wilson family captives taken at the Battle of Ziegler's Station 300
White, Thomas 287
White, Zachariah 193, 195, 213
White Bear, Old Chief (legend) 17
White County, Tennessee 368
White Hall Estate *9*, 152
White Man Killer 217, 303–304, 309, 314, 328, 351
White Owl 14, 44, *45*, 49, 186, 266, 353; *see also* Attakullakulla
White Owl of Natchey Creek *see* Little Owl, Chief
White Owl Raven 349
Whitefield, Mr. 262
White's Creek 202, 231, 253, 281, 308, 312
White's Fort (Gallatin) 282–283
White's Fort (Knoxville) *8*, *128*, *133*, *194*, 264–265, 282–283, 300, 315, 321–322, 324, 328
White's Station *see* White's Fort
Whitley, Col. William 329–331
Whittier, North Carolina 343
Wickcliffe, Kentucky 220
Widow Moore's Bridge 149
Wiggan, Aleazar *see* Wiggan, Alexander
Wiggan, Alexander 39, 44, 46, 49
Wilcox, Thomas 306
Wild Rose *see* Ward, Nancy
Wilderness Road 144, 215
Wiliyi Village *see* Will's Town
Wilkes County, North Carolina 347
Will of Akoha 239
Willanawas of Toquoa, Chief *see* Willenawah, Chief
Willenawah, Chief 51, 57, 61–62, 67, 84–85, 87, 116, 134, 138, 158, 182, 186, 329, 349, 370
Willett, Col. Marinus 272
William & Mary 106
William the Conqueror 5, 24, 359, 365

Williams, Benjamin 280, 294
Williams, Betsy 229
Williams, Col. 162–163
Williams, Curtis 250
Williams, Daniel 196, 202
Williams, Jarrett 144, 155
Williams, Col. Joseph 172, 176, 214
Williams, Mr. 315
Williams, Mrs. (prisoner of the Creek) 289
Williams, Mrs. Benjamin 280
Williams, Capt. Sampson 196, 272, 306, 329
Williams Island 197
Williamsburg, Virginia 54, 68, 87, 105–106, 180, 189, 236, 351–352
Williamson, Col. Andrew 114–115, 140, 152, 160, 181; 1776 Cherokee Campaign 57, 161–169, *170*, 171, 176, 180, 353, 373–379, *380*
Willinewaw, Chief *see* Willenawah, Chief
Williowee 329
Will's Creek 57
Will's Town *194*, 293, 302, 305, 309–310, 314, 318, 337, 356
Wills Town *see* Will's Twon
Willstown *see* Will's Town
Will-Usdi *see* Thomas, Chief William Holland
Wilmington, North Carolina 149
Wilson, Archie 300
Wilson, Capt. Joseph 283
Wilson, Mr. 290
Wilson, Mrs. 300–301
Wilson, Samuel 280
Wilson, Sarah 300
Wilson, William 317
Wilson, Zacheus 300
Wilson Family Massacre 324
Wilson's Spring Branch 212
Wilson's Stream Branch *see* Wilson's Spring Branch

Winchester, Maj. George 250, 317; death of 329
Winchester, George W. 360
Winchester, Gen. James 278, 300–301, 360
Winchester, Virginia 66, 69
Windsor, England 46
Windsor Castle 46
Winn, Gen. Richard 259, 272
Winston, Maj. Joseph 172, 181
Winston-Salem, North Carolina 133
winterberry 104
Wintle 89
Witcher, Capt. William 172
Wococee Village 329
Wolf, Chief 222
Wolf Town 343
Wolf's (Wolf) Hill(s), Virginia 119, 157–158, 171; *see also* Abingdon, Virginia
Woman of Aniwadi 349
Wooaluka of Chota 239
Wood, Abraham 28–30
Woodstock District, Cherokee County, Georgia 347
Woodward, Henry 30
Wright, Gov. James 123; Proclamation of 1774 131–132
Wright, Ind. Agt. John 34–35
Wrosetasatow, Chief 39, 43
Wurteh of the Bird Clan 116, 349
Wutehi of the Red Paint Clan 63
Wyuka of Lookout Mountain, Chief *see* Little Owl, Chief

Yachtino, Chief 370
Yadkin River 29, 59, 70, 74, 84
Yadkin Valley 68, 124, 371
Yahatatastenake, Chief *see* Great Mortar, Chief
Yamasee (Indians) 33–34, 37, 40; War of 1715 35–36, 41
Yamassee (Indians) *see* Yamasee

yaupin holly 104
Yellin' Boys *see* Overmountain militia
Yellow Bird 239
Yellow Bird of the Pine Log *see* Chesetoa of Tlacoa
yellow fever 31, 33, 206
Yellow Hill Village 343
Yemassee War *see* the Yamasee; War of 1715
Yonaguska, Chief 343
Young, Charles 157, 182
Young, Robert 182
Young Dragging Canoe 297
Young Hop Moytoy 68
Young Tassel, Chief 15, 116, 143, 182, 184, 186, 188, 217, 224, 234, 244, 251, 258, 262–264, 266–267, 282–283, 286, 291, 294–298, 302–306, 308–311, 313–316, 318–321, 324, 328, 331, 349, 354–356; death of (1808) 337; dispute with Doublehead at Campbell's Station (1793) 322–323; peace agreement at Tellico Blockhouse (1794) 332–333; severely wounded at Buchanan's Station (1792) 306–307; succeeded Dragging Canoe as Chickamauga Chief (1792) 291–292
Young Terrapin of Allajoy 235
Young Warrior, Chief 73–74, 77–78, 83–84, 86–87, 90, 107, 113–114
Yssa Village 27

Ziegler, Elizabeth 300
Ziegler, Hannah 300
Ziegler, Jacob 283; death of 300
Ziegler, Mary 300
Ziegler, Mrs. 300
Ziegler's Station *194*, 283, 299–300, 306